PSYCHOLOGICAL FOUNDATIONS OF SPORT

JOHN M. SILVA III, PhD

University of North Carolina-Chapel Hill

ROBERT S. WEINBERG, PhD

North Texas State University-Denton

EDITORS

HUMAN KINETICS PUBLISHERS, INC.

Champaign, Illinois

Production Director: Kathryn Gollin Marshak
Copy Editor: Peg Goyette
Typesetters: Yvonne Sergent and Sandra Meier
Text Layout: Lezli Harris and Denise Peters
Cover Design and Layout: Jack Davis

ISBN 0-931250-59-5
Library of Congress Catalog Card Number 83-083239

Printed in the United States of America

10 9 8 7 6 5 4 3 2

Human Kinetics Publishers, Inc.
Box 5076, Champaign, IL 61820

To the most positive of influences: my wife, Christine, and our families.

JMS

To my family and good friends for their constant support and encouragement.

RSW

About the
Contributing Authors

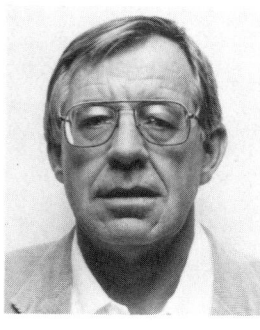

Richard B. Alderman, a professor in physical education at the University of Alberta, has been working as a psychological consultant to coaches and athletes since 1965. He has published extensively in the areas of sport, physical education, and psychology and is the author of several books, two of which focus on the psychology of sport and the psychological dynamics of coaching. His special interests deal with enhancing the performance of athletes and coaches through highly specific psychological skills training programs. Dr. Alderman has been a competitive athlete in football, hockey, basketball, and golf and has coached golf, soccer, hockey, and basketball.

Lawrence R. Brawley is a professor in the Department of Kinesiology at the University of Waterloo. His main interest is social psychology as it applies to human movement; his research focuses specifically on arousal and information processing, person perception, attribution, intrinsic motivation, group dynamics, and health-related problems. Dr. Brawley is currently the director of SIRLS, the international on-line bibliographic data base of research in the social science of sport and leisure. As a research advisor to the Canadian Amateur Diving Association, he has aided in the review of their application oriented research projects. Dr. Brawley also consults with fitness organizations about strategies for increasing motivation.

Brenda Jo Bredemeier, a native of Minnesota, received her master's degree at Smith College and her doctorate at Temple University prior to accepting a position at the University of California-Berkeley. She has recently initiated a research program which incorporates a structural developmental framework in the investigation of moral development and athletic aggression. Another major concern has been the development of a feminist perspective of gender roles. Special experiences include working as a clinician/consultant in Haiti, Jamaica, and Belgium. Among her favorite physical activities are running and racquetball.

Gary Warren Buffone received his master's degree from Appalachian State University and completed a doctorate at Florida State University in 1980. He has worked as a psychologist and consultant in schools, prisons, hospitals, and private corporations. His professional interests include the assessment and treatment of stress-related physical and mental disorders. He is currently a psychologist in independent practice and a consultant to the Center for Health Promotion at Riverside Hospital in Jacksonville. Concerning the area of sport psychology, Dr. Buffone is primarily interested in the application of physical exercise to the prevention and treatment of health-related problems. He himself is an avid runner and tennis player.

Albert V. Carron holds BPE and MA degrees from the University of Alberta and obtained an EdD in 1967 from the University of California at Berkeley, where he studied under Franklin M. Henry. Dr. Carron accepted a position at the University of Saskatchewan, where he taught and carried out research in motor learning, growth, and development. He also coached football. Since 1974, he has been on the Faculty of Physical Education at the University of Ontario and teaches sport psychology there. Dr. Carron has written numerous texts, monographs, and articles. He has worked with various sport associations and has served as a consultant to the Canadian Amateur Diving Association and the Federation of Canadian Archers.

P. Chelladurai is an associate professor with the Faculty of Physical Education at the University of Western Ontario. He holds the degrees of B.Com. and DPE from the University of Madras, India, a master's from the University of Western Ontario, and MASc and doctorate in management science from the University of Waterloo. A frequent contributor to the sport psychology literature, Dr. Chelladurai teaches sport management at the University of Western Ontario. He has been a teacher/coach of basketball and volleyball at the university, provincial, and national levels for the past 30 years, much of that time in India.

Rod K. Dishman earned his doctorate in sport psychology at the University of Wisconsin, Madison, and teaches at the University of California, Davis. His research interests concern exercise behavior, training and motivation, and the psychological effects of exercise including stress management and psychometrics. Dr. Dishman is a fellow of the American College of Sports Medicine and a member of the American Psychological Association. Besides doing editorial and review work for various scholarly journals, Dr. Dishman has published many papers and has made numerous presentations at national and international meetings. A former college baseball player, he now enjoys distance running, weight training, racquet sports, and water skiing.

Frederick H. Evans received a master's in guidance and counseling from Chicago State University in 1980. While a freshman undergraduate, he became the first black national swimming champion in the United States and went on to hold the NCAA Division II record for 4 years. As a graduate student Mr. Evans received an assistantship from the Department of Psychology, where he taught psychology and researched sport psychology. He later cofounded the Motivational Training Program with Frank O'Block. Mr. Evans was the head coach for both the varsity and age-group swimming program, helping to produce nationally listed swimmers. He has also conducted workshops and written numerous articles on the subject of motivation.

A. Craig Fisher is a professor and chairman of the graduate programs in physical education at Ithaca College. His research interests generally focus on personality as it relates to sport performance, with specific attention given to anxiety. His more recent research attention focuses on self-confidence, a personality parameter that he sees as being at the heart of maximal sport performance. Dr. Fisher has worked with high school and college athletes to improve their psychological outlook toward competitive sport, and has more recently worked with the Ithaca College swimming and diving teams. Dr. Fisher enjoys golf, camping, and other outdoor pursuits.

Diane Gill received her doctorate in sport psychology from the University of Illinois. Her research interests and scholarly activities center around cohesiveness, competitive anxiety, attributions, and achievement behavior in sport. Although closely involved with research, Dr. Gill has also developed and conducted psychological skills programs with intercollegiate women athletes. She has published a number of articles in the sport psychology literature and is also a frequent contributing author to sport psychology textbooks. Dr. Gill's current recreational activity is distance running, although she has coached and played a variety of sports.

Daniel Gould is an associate professor in the Department of Physical Education, Dance, and Leisure Studies at Kansas State University, where he teaches courses in sport psychology. He has researched coaching attitudes, psychological modeling, the psychological impact of sports on children, competitive stress, participation motivation, and the relationships between mental preparation techniques, expectations, and performance. Dr. Gould has also participated in numerous clinics for coaches and athletes, and consulted individually with athletes at all levels of competition. A former wrestler, and football and baseball player, Dr. Gould now enjoys running, swimming, and cross-country skiing.

Thelma Sternberg Horn is an assistant professor in the Department of Human Kinetics at the University of Wisconsin-Milwaukee. She received a doctorate in sport psychology from Michigan State University in 1982. Her main research interests center around the study of children's self-perceptions and anxiety in regard to their physical competence. Dr. Horn has had extensive coaching and teaching experience at both the secondary and collegiate levels, and continues to work with coaches and teachers in youth programs. She presently enjoys running, skiing, and tennis.

Burris F. Husman, professor emeritus at the University of Maryland, received his BS and MS degrees from the University of Illinois and his doctorate from the University of Maryland. He served on the faculty at Maryland for 32 years and chaired the Department of Physical Education for 9 years. During his academic tenure Dr. Husman published extensively on such topics as aggression, emotion, and personality variables affecting sport participation. He is considered one of the most influential sport researchers in the area of aggression, having conducted studies in it since the early 1950s. Dr. Husman has held offices in state, district, and national organizations and has also received distinguished honors at each level. He enjoys tennis and fishing.

Daniel S. Kirschenbaum, a clinical psychologist, received his doctorate at the University of Cincinnati in 1975 and has taught at the Universities of Cincinnati and Rochester. He is currently an assistant professor of psychology at the University of Wisconsin in Madison, where he conducts research in the broad area of self-regulation. This research has included studies of planning, affect, choice, and a variety of related topics with applications to obesity, study skills, classroom management, and sport performance. Dr. Kirschenbaum also practices what he studies: he has lost weight and maintained that weight loss for many years, and he participates actively in sports such as golf, squash, and tennis.

Robert M. Nideffer has taught at the California School of Professional Psychology and is president of Enhanced Performance Associates in San Diego. Dr. Nideffer has published extensively in the sport psychology literature, including the books *The Inner Athlete* and *The Ethics and Practice of Applied Sport Psychology*. He has chaired the NASPSPA ethics committee and is currently working with the U.S. Men's Olympic Track and Field Team. The *Test of Attentional and Interpersonal Style* developed out of his research relating attentional processes and arousal to athletic performance. Dr. Nideffer was a collegiate diver and holds a black belt in Aikido.

Frank R. O'Block received his doctorate from the University of Illinois in 1967 and has been on the faculty of psychology at Chicago State University for 12 years. He has worked with athletes on an individual and group basis for the past 15 years. He and Frederick Evans cofounded and operate the Motivational Training Program for Athletes, located in Chicago. Dr. O'Block, a state-licensed psychologist and certified school psychologist, has facilitated group motivation seminars for athletes around the country and is a national registered health service provider of psychology. He has conducted research and published several articles on motivation and the athlete. Dr. O'Block works out daily running and swimming.

Carole A. Oglesby is the coordinator of the Psycho-Social Interactions and Movement Laboratory at Temple University. Her primary research interests are gender identity development and psychological development through sport participation and intervention. Dr. Oglesby is active in many professional organizations, especially those concerning women in sport, and is a member of the House of Delegates for the United States Olympic Committee. Dr. Oglesby has written much about gender and sport participation, including her well known text, *Women and Sport: From Myth to Reality*. A former NASA championship participant, she has coached softball teams and also has begun marathon running.

Michael W. Passer is an assistant professor of kinesiology and adjunct assistant professor of psychology at the University of Washington. He completed his doctoral work in social psychology at UCLA. Dr. Passer's interests focus primarily on the psychological effects of competition on children, stress and anxiety, self-esteem, and cognitive factors that influence achievement behavior such as causal attributions and performance expectancies. He has conducted extensive research with young athletes and also has worked with intercollegiate and interscholastic athletes from a variety of sports. The latter research has included his examining the relationship between stress and injury among collegiate football players. Dr. Passer enjoys hiking, backpacking, skiing, white-water sports, and basketball.

Kenneth Ravizza is with the Department of HPER at California State University, Fullerton. Incorporating both philosophical and psychological orientations, his research has examined the nature of peak performance in human movement activities. More recently, he has functioned as a performance specialist for different sports teams and has developed sport-specific relaxation and concentration programs. Dr. Ravizza has conducted clinics at the U.S. Field Hockey Association and U.S. Gymnastics Congress. He has also developed and presented stress management programs for health care staffs, cancer patients, battered women, private business groups, prison inmates, and numerous public school staffs.

Glyn C. Roberts, a native of North Wales, graduated from Loughborough College and taught and coached in England for 4 years. He received his PhD from the University of Illinois in 1969 and taught at Kent State University until 1973, when he joined the Department of Physical Education at the University of Illinois. Two years later Dr. Roberts was appointed director of the Motor Behavior Laboratory in the Institute for Child Behavior and Development. Since 1982, Dr. Roberts has served as director of graduate studies of the department. He actively conducts research on motivation and achievement behavior and has published extensively on the topic. Dr. Roberts is a recent past president of NASPSPA.

Michael L. Sachs is a research project coordinator with the University of Maryland School of Medicine. He completed his master's in general-experimental psychology at Hollins College and his doctorate in sport psychology at Florida State University. Dr. Sachs was corecipient of the Outstanding Dissertation Award of the Sport Psychology Academy of NASPE/AAHPERD in 1980. He has published and spoken extensively on the psychology of running, particularly on addiction to running and cognitive strategies used during running. He is the associate editor of *Psychology of Running* and coeditor of *Running as Therapy: An Integrated Approach*. To keep fit, Dr. Sachs runs and swims regularly.

John H. Salmela is a professor in the Department of Physical Education, Université de Montréal. He is the author of *The World Sport Psychology Sourcebook* and *Competitive Behaviors of Olympic Gymnasts*. His research interests include decision making in sport, talent detection, and performance prediction. Dr. Salmela is a member of the Managing Council of the International Society of Sport Psychology and served as coorganizer of its 1981 Fifth World Sport Psychology Congress in Ottawa. He is chairperson of GRETSUM, the university's research group in sport talent. A former national-level gymnast and a 3:15 marathon runner, Dr. Salmela is now centering his applied research in the working-class area of English Montreal.

Tara K. Scanlan is an associate professor in the Department of Kinesiology at UCLA. She attended the University of Illinois, where she received a master's degree in motor learning and a doctorate in the social psychology of motor behavior and sport. Her research focuses on the social psychological effects of competition on athletes, with her major interests being competitive stress and motivation. Dr. Scanlan is a recent past president of the North American Society for the Psychology of Sport and Physical Activity. She is a member of the Medical Advisory Board for the athletic department at UCLA. Her own recreational pursuits include biking, hiking, and playing squash.

John M. Silva, an assistant professor at the University of North Carolina, completed his doctoral work in sport psychology at the University of Maryland. His research interests include intervention strategies, athlete/performance assessment, and the effect of social learning upon behavior in sports. Dr. Silva has coordinated research with the U.S. Olympic Wrestling Program since 1977 and has worked as a consultant with many athletes and teams. An active member of NASPSPA and the American Psychological Association, Dr. Silva has published and spoken extensively on sport psychology at the regional, national, and international level. He was recently the recipient of an Outstanding Young Men of America award. He enjoys playing squash, running, cross-country skiing, fishing, and canoeing.

Ronald E. Smith is a professor of psychology and the Director of Clinical Psychology Training at the University of Washington. He has published numerous scientific articles on personality and social behavior, stress and coping, and psychology and the law. Dr. Smith's research in sport psychology has focused on the dynamics of leadership behaviors and on methods for reducing athletic stress and enhancing performance. He is coauthor of *Psychology: The Frontiers of Behavior, Psychological Perspectives in Youth Sports,* and *KidSports: A Survival Guide for Parents.* Dr. Smith has served as a psychological consultant to youth sport, collegiate, and professional organizations.

Frank L. Smoll obtained his doctorate from the University of Wisconsin and is an associate professor of psychology at the University of Washington. Dr. Smoll's research focuses on psychosocial correlates of children's motor development and on educational programs for youth sport coaches and parents. He is a past officer of NASPSPA and is a fellow of the Research Consortium of AAHPERD. In collaboration with Ronald E. Smith, Dr. Smoll has developed and tested a psychologically oriented, nationally recognized training program for youth sport coaches, called Coach Effectiveness Training.

Robert Sonstroem, who teaches at the University of Rhode Island, served for nearly 3 years as the physical coordinator of the first national exercise-heart project conducted by the Laboratory of Physiological Hygiene. Dr. Sonstroem's research has centered on the measurement of attitudes and self-esteem. This has resulted in the development of the Physical Estimation and Attraction Scales (PEAS), and in his serving as a consultant in the selection of police and fire personnel. Dr. Sonstroem is also interested in personality trait theory and measurement, physical fitness, treatment compliance, and program adherence. His recreational interests include tennis, hiking, fishing, home gardening, and family activities.

Leonard Wankel received his doctorate from the University of Alberta, went on to teach at the University of Waterloo and McMaster University, and currently is on the faculty at the University of Alberta. His primary research interests include social factors that influence performance, motivation for involvement in youth sports, and program interventions for enhancing exercise adherence. He has served as a consultant to sport and recreation agencies and is a province master instructor for the National Coaching Certification Program of Canada. Dr. Wankel has published extensively in the professional literature and is a frequent speaker at sport psychology and recreation conventions.

Robert S. Weinberg received his doctorate in psychology from UCLA and, as a postdoctoral scholar, specialized in sport psychology. He is research coordinator for the Division of Physical Education and Dance at North Texas State University. His primary research interests focus on mental preparation strategies, the arousal-performance relationship, intrinsic motivation, and self-confidence. Dr. Weinberg has published widely in professional journals and has presented many papers at regional, national, and international conventions. He has also been involved in the applied aspects of sport psychology, working with athletes to help them develop psychological skills. A former tennis and basketball player, he remains active in these sports and also enjoys racquetball and cycling.

W. Neil Widmeyer, the associate dean of the Faculty of Human Kinetics and Leisure Studies at the University of Waterloo, holds a doctorate in sport psychology from the University of Illinois. His research interests include the relationship between group cohesion, group composition, and performance, as well as the aggression-performance relationship in sport. Dr. Widmeyer has published articles in various professional journals and speaks regularly at sport psychology conferences. He has also been involved with the National Hockey League in trying to determine the relationship between aggression and performance. His recreational pursuits include alpine skiing and tennis, and he also enjoys going to hockey, basketball, and football games.

David K. Wiggins is an assistant professor in the Department of Physical Education, Dance, and Leisure Studies at Kansas State University, where he teaches courses in the history of sport as well as the philosophy of sport and physical education. Trained in the area of sport history, Dr. Wiggins is interested in the development of sport in early 19th-century America, the involvement of black athletes in American sport, and regional differences in American sporting patterns. Dr. Wiggins is a former college football and baseball player who now enjoys racquetball, jogging, and spending the summers walking the beaches of his native California with his family.

David A. Wittrock recently completed a bachelor's degree at the University of Wisconsin-Madison. While majoring in psychology, he worked with Daniel Kirschenbaum on a variety of research projects pertaining to self-regulation. Most of that work has focused on studies of coaching feedback and methods of reducing the adverse impact of negativistic coaching. He has also conducted studies on depression and the impact of various planning strategies on academic study behaviors. Mr. Wittrock plans to attend a graduate program in clinical psychology beginning in the fall of 1984.

David P. Yukelson received his doctorate in sport psychology from North Texas State University. He teaches at the University of Houston and also is a clinical instructor in the Department of Pediatrics at the UT Medical School in Houston. Dr. Yukelson's research interests include group cohesion, individual and group motivation, psychosocial development of young athletes, and mental preparation. He is a consulting sport psychologist to the University of Houston tennis teams. Dr. Yukelson serves as administrative manager and sport psychologist at the Hermann Center for Sports Medicine, a multidisciplinary resource center in Houston specializing in the young athlete. He enjoys racquetball, baseball, basketball, golf, and jogging.

Contents

Contents

Contents

Preface

The last 25 years could well be labeled the age of the athlete. Organized athletics have experienced a steady increase in media visibility, technological and scientific advance, and commercialism. The advancement of sport in the academic community can be traced along three major thrusts: the physiological-medical, the biomechanical, and the psychomotoric. This text is designed to provide readers with a solid foundation in the third frontier—sport psychology.

Scholars from all over North America have contributed to this text, which exposes readers to the major research and professional issues confronting the field. Rather than cover a limited number of interest areas, or many areas superficially, this book is organized into eight major areas of sport psychology and addresses these topics clearly and in depth. It begins with a comprehensive overview of the evolution of sport psychology.

The authors in Part I analyze and discuss the origins, ethics, and future of sport psychology. In Parts II and III the focus narrows to relatively individualized concerns such as personality, performance, and anxiety—with some discussion about how intervention techniques can enhance performance by reducing anxiety. Part IV initiates a transition from relatively individualized concerns to more social-psychological issues by examining how individual motivation concerns are developed and maintained, eventually leading to group motivation. Parts V through VII clearly deal with social-psychological aspects of sport psychology such as aggression, group dynamics, leadership, and the socialization process itself. The authors in Part VIII relate important information on how sport and exercise can benefit participants by playing a role in the development and maintenance of their psychological well-being. In sum, *Psychological Foundations of Sport* examines and addresses individual, clinical, social, and applied research in the field of sport psychology from both historical and contemporary perspectives.

This text is targeted for the upper-level undergraduate and the beginning-level graduate student, and is envisioned to serve as a "swing text." In establishing a solid foundation the authors have appraised what is known, as well as what is unknown, in sport psychology. The issues are presented theoretically, factually, and occasionally with constructive criticism. Readers will not be confronted with an oversimplified or cookbook view of sport psychology. On the contrary, we anticipate that they will be stimulated and challenged by the problems and issues addressed herein. Students and professionals alike will recognize that the field of sport psychology is still in its adolescent stages. They must be prepared to nurture its growth, guide discovery, and refrain from excessive protectionism.

We hope the information presented, the questions raised, and the implications projected will stimulate today's reader in the same manner that the authors who contributed to this text were themselves stimulated by writings of the past.

John M. Silva III
Robert S. Weinberg

Acknowledgments

The quality of any text is judged by the papers it includes; whatever merit this anthology earns is a reflection of the careful and systematic work of its contributors. We are extremely pleased that some of the most distinguished members in the field of sport psychology have generously agreed to share their work in the creation of this text. So it is fitting that we first thank them for their suggestions and efforts.

In addition to the contributors I gratefully acknowledge the efforts of my wife, Christine, who generously offered assistance with all phases of this text and did so at any time of the day or night.

Several other individuals also supported the production of this text and are deserving of thanks. At the risk of omitting a few, it is far better to acknowledge the many. A special thank you goes to Kaye Buchanan for her tireless efforts in the preparation of this book. Kudos are also extended to Kelley Davis, Judy Flemming, Charlie Hardy, Mattie Hawkins, Chris Hunter, Debbie Lee, Delaine Marbry, Linda Prather, Beth Turner, Sharon Wagner, Janniffer Wang, Ellen Rosser, and Louann Yeattes for pitching in relief.

I am most grateful to John Billing, chairperson of the Physical Education Department at UNC-Chapel Hill for his support, Meg Dillon, administrative manager, for her efforts in coordinating the support services, and Rainer Martens for his personal interest and concern both for this text and the field of sport psychology.

JMS
Chapel Hill, North Carolina

Any endeavor as large as writing a textbook requires the contribution of many individuals, all working diligently toward the final goal — a quality product. Of course an edited book relies heavily on the quality of the contributors, and I am pleased that many of the top scholars in North America saw it fitting to make such a commitment. Their thoughtful and provocative contribution form the backbone of the text.

I would also like to express my sincere gratitude to John Silva, my co-editor. The book took us about 3 years from inception to publication and during that time John has been the epitome of professionalism and dedication. His tireless efforts and commitment to excellence were evident throughout the process.

There are also many other individuals who helped in the production of the text in terms of typing, proofing, and suggestions. Thus, a special thanks to Liz Durbin, Michele Murphy, and Malinda Pope, and to all the rest of you whose names elude me at this time.

RSW
North Texas State University-Denton

Introduction

During the past two decades sport psychology has emerged as a legitimate field of scientific inquiry. As with all scientific endeavors, sport psychology shares the same basic goals of science—the *observation* of events, the *description* of phenomena, the *explanation* of factors that influence events in a systematic manner, the *prediction* of events or outcomes based upon systematic and reliable explanations and, ultimately, the *control* of events or contingencies that result in expected outcomes. The accomplishment of each goal becomes progressively more difficult for scientists to achieve. Some sciences are based primarily upon observation and may never achieve predictive power or control over events. Astronomy increases our understanding of the universe, for example, but this field of study will never to able to accurately predict nor control the tremendous forces that are continually changing the universe around us.

Sport psychology in many ways is a fortunate scientific field of inquiry. Researchers are afforded ample opportunity to observe, describe, and explain the various psychological factors that influence diverse aspects of sport and physical activity. As naive scientists we have all observed the immense pressure placed upon an athlete poised for a crucial foul shot with little time remaining. Athletes and coaches have often described the crucial "psychological factors" that resulted in a momentum shift during a game, or explained an important loss on the road as a function of the influential forces of game location. While these "armchair" opportunities are often afforded to us, the fact that sport psychology is viewed as a science means that the processes of observation, description, and explanation must be conducted in a systematic, repeatable, and valid manner. Science allows us to go beyond speculation or opinion that is based upon subjective experiences. Through scientific methods we can test our hunches about how psychological factors influence sport performance or how sport participation may influence the athlete's psychological development.

You may have noticed that our discussion so far has been limited to the first three goals of science. Many would argue that the models and theories developed thus far in sport psychology have only allowed scientific progression to the point of explanation. That is, we are developing an ability to use models (also called paradigms) and theories to systematically explain the factors or forces that influence events in sport. One theory you will encounter throughout this book is called a social learning theory of behavior, developed almost 30 years ago by a psychologist named Julian Rotter. His work, initially published in 1954, was significantly influenced by the writings of two other psychologists, Tolman (1934) and Lewin (1951). All of these psychologists emphasized that human behavior is influenced to a great extent by learning, and furthermore that there is unity in the human personality. The person and the environment interact (an interactional model) and are interrelated in determining behavior in various social settings (Phares, 1976). Phares indicates that interactional models, which evolved from social learning theory, recognize that human behavior is changeable even though new experiences are significantly influenced by the accumulation of knowledge from past experiences. So when you read about personality and performance, anxiety, motivation, aggression, and other topics in this book, you will notice that many of the authors employ an interactional model to explain how behavior is developed, manifested, and potentially changed.

Change brings us to the concluding point of this introduction. The final two goals of a scientific field are prediction and control, two of the most difficult and controversial goals for many scientific disciplines. Before an athlete's behavior can be changed to enhance performance, we must be reasonably certain that if X occurs then Y will have a very high probability of occurring. This is true whether one is trying to change a mechanical defect in a hitter's swing or a nonadaptive stress response to high-level competition. If we can accurately predict "if X then Y," researchers can then experiment and expand upon this basic causal model.

Sport psychology usually has many "Xs" or predictor variables. In order to accurately predict Y (the event) we need an indication of the causal variables and how much each contributes toward predicting Y. As we gain this predictive ability, we increase the opportunity to change or control responses. For example, the athlete who is very nervous before major competition most likely has many "predictors" of his or her anxiety response. These predictors must be accurately identified before a sport psychologist can help the athlete control his/her anxiety. The athlete may be high on trait anxiety, may have had bad experiences at other high-level competitions, or may be focusing upon negative thoughts or bodily responses such as rapid breathing or muscular tightness. If we can identify the predictors of the undesirable anxiety responses that exist as a function of the interaction between the person and the competitive environment, and can effectively manipulate these predictor variables, we can expect change.

As sport psychology develops, it will be judged largely by its ability as a scientific field to predict and control behavioral responses and outcomes. Social learning theory and the interactional model have served the field well during the last 25 years. Many of the chapters in this text will provide you, the reader, with vivid examples of how social and individual psychological processes are influenced by this useful model. In our quest for knowledge, let us hope that sport psychology's predictive and controlling capacities will be used to enhance the health and well-being of all participants in sport and physical activity.

PART I

EVOLUTION
OF SPORT
PSYCHOLOGY

A major league baseball team is experiencing some player problems believed to be psychological in origin. Management hires a sport psychologist to help identify the problems and offer some solutions. After getting to know and understand the athletes better, the psychologist administers tests to assess personality and determine each athlete's individual psychological makeup. Although many of you may think this scenario represents a recent development, the sport psychologist referred to was Coleman Griffith — during the 1930s! In pursuing the study of sport psychology, Griffith conducted laboratory studies and interviewed such legends as Red Grange and Knute Rockne on the mental aspects of sport and competition. Unfortunately, the pioneering work of Coleman Griffith, considered by many the father of North American sport psychology, was not perpetuated by his students, so sport psychology as a formal area of study lay virtually dormant until the 1960s. Thus, what many see as a new area of inquiry is really the rebirth of a field whose seeds were sown over 50 years ago.

Definition of Sport Psychology

What does the term *sport psychology* mean? What do sport psychologists do and study? In reading through this text, you will come across sections dealing with the effects of anxiety on performance, aggressive behavior and sport, group dynamics, effects of physical activity on psychological well-being, motivation in sport, socialization into and through sports, personality and sport, and (in this section) the evolution of sport psychology. Although the topic areas are diverse, there is a common thread connecting the content of these chapters: All chapters deal with either the effect of psychological factors on behavior in sport (i.e., anxiety, persistence, morality) or the psychological effect that participation in sport or physical activity has on the performer. Thus, audience effects, anxiety, motivation, group dynamics, personality, confidence, and concentration are all psychological factors affecting the performer, whereas participation in physical activity can affect the performer in terms of anxiety reduction, personality development, aggressive behavior, and the enhancement of well-being.

History of Sport Psychology

In the first chapter, David Wiggins details the history of sport psychology in North America. Some of the earliest writings related to sport psychology occurred around the turn of the century. They attempted to explain why physical educators needed an understanding of psychology and pointed to psychological benefits that could be derived through physical activity. Wiggins also describes how related research in motor learning and social psychology in the early 1900s contributed to the development of sport psychology. After describing the contributions of Coleman Griffith and other noteworthy researchers, Wiggins discusses the formation of the North American Society for the Psychology of Sport and Physical Activity (NASPSPA) and the Canadian Society for Psychomotor Learning and Sport Psychology (CSPLSP), which together comprise the major research organizations in sport psychology. (In fact, after visiting countries around the world, John Salmela has termed NASPSPA the "single most influential academic professional society in the world focusing on the psychology of sport and physical activity.") Wiggins concludes his chapter by discussing the numerous sport psychology texts published in the last 10 years, and reflects on the vast amount of progress the field has made as an academic discipline.

Comparative Sport Psychology

Although Wiggins' chapter traces the history of sport psychology in North America, this does not mean that North America has a monopoly on sport psychology. In fact, it is found in over 40 countries around the world, although the relative interest and quality of activity varies depending on the academic, political, and economic conditions of each country. The lay person is usually not aware of the wide-based interest and international nature of the study of sport psychology—except when its visibility is increased by the Olympic Games. Such is the time when we hear about all the techniques, strategies, and mental approaches that different countries employ in preparing their athletes for maximum performance. However, it certainly would be erroneous to think that this alone constitutes sport psychology, since many other exciting discoveries are continually being made in this field.

John Salmela's comparative analysis of sport psychology in North America and Eastern Europe lends valuable insight into current developments in the East and West and describes the roles, research interests, and delivery capabilities of sport psychologists in various countries around the world. For example, differences between North America and Eastern Europe are examined in areas such as the degree of governmental control over research, the underlying purpose of this research, the scope and emphases of academic preparation, and the degree of professional involvement and priorities in sport psychology. Salmela concludes by discussing the strengths and weaknesses in both the Western and Eastern approaches to sport psychology and notes the positive effect each approach has had on the other. With the continued dissemination of such information across the world, sport psychology will grow and expand, helping to make sport a rewarding experience for all.

Applied Sport Psychology

As sport psychology evolves, it goes through many changes in terms of research interests and approaches to studying behavior in sport. One dramatic change, particularly in North America, has been the move from laboratory to field work. Unlike Eastern Europe, where the focus has been on using sport psychology to enhance performance (especially of elite athletes), researchers in North America have been primarily concerned with generating new knowledge in the field. In recent years, however, North American sport psychologists have begun to work with athletes in applied settings, the goal usually being to enhance performance. But the growth in this area has been so rapid that adequate guidelines have not been established to regulate sport psychologists' interactions with athletes or organized sport groups. We need to resolve questions such as the following: What qualifications must a sport psychologist have? What techniques should a sport psychologist be allowed to employ (e.g., hypnosis, relaxation, biofeedback, counseling)? What various roles can a sport psychologist play? How should athletes be tested psychologically? And, to whom is the sport psychologist responsible (i.e., owner, coach, athlete, organization)? In fact, the need for guidelines is so critical that NASPSPA has generated a code of ethics that serves as a guide for sport psychologists working in applied settings.

In the third chapter, Robert Nideffer discusses many of the issues in the ethical practice of applied sport psychology. Nideffer notes that as sport psychology organizations have begun to meet and work on the development of ethical standards, it became apparent that the existing standards of the American Psychological Association (APA) addressed most of the issues and concerns that were expressed. Therefore, sport psychology organizations have recommended that their membership adopt some modified sport-specific form of APA's ethical standards. Nideffer then turns his attention to the difficult question of who is qualified to practice sport psychology, and he discusses clearly both sides of the issue. Nideffer carefully examines a sport psychologist's potential roles — clinical, team building, crisis intervention, educational, and stress management. This chapter provides a good overview of what applied sport psychology has to offer and identifies problems that will confront the field during the next decade.

Future of Sport Psychology

The first three chapters of this section were designed to give the reader an understanding of the history and present status of sport psychology throughout the world, along with some of the current professional and academic concerns in the field. If it is difficult to categorize, organize, and integrate a field's past and present status, then certainly it is a monumental task to predict its future development and direction. Yet Rikk Alderman attempts to tackle this task in the final chapter. He is well qualified for this assignment, having spent 15 years as a sport psychology researcher, writer, and consultant. He is well aware of the limitations and prospects for sport psychology. Alderman acknowledges that the future of sport psychology is greatly affected by past and current practices, and thus he reviews the major problems, issues, and trends to consider when attempting to predict the future. Alderman argues that sport psychology's orientation in the 1980s will shift more toward an emphasis of community service, due in part to the pressure of public accountability and the saturated academic job market. In terms of orientation, he believes that a human development or educational model will be the dominant wave of the future, and he concludes with some carefully thought-out predictions concerning sport psychology and the challenges in store.

Whether one agrees with Alderman's predictions or not, this chapter should stimulate much thought and discussion. Ultimately, the evolution of sport psychology as a scientific field will be defined by its contributing members. We hope that some of the students who read this text will be stimulated to become contributing members of our field.

Chapter 1

The History of Sport Psychology in North America

David K. Wiggins
Kansas State University

It would be a misconception for scholars in the field to think that the study of sport psychology in North America is a new academic endeavor, devoid until recently of scholarly inquiry. To be sure, sport psychology did not attain the status of an academic discipline until the last three decades when it splintered from motor learning and emerged into its own field of study. But, as evidenced by theoretical and empirical studies that began appearing in the literature at the turn of the century in the United States, sport psychology has had a rather long if not uneven history in North America.

Beginning with a number of isolated research projects just prior to 1900, the field received its biggest impetus from the work of Coleman R. Griffith at the University of Illinois during the period 1925 to 1938. Unfortunately, a striking void exists in the number of sport psychology studies that were completed between Griffith's productive years at Illinois and the Second World War. When the conflict in Europe came to a close, however, motor learning courses were almost immediately implemented in various universities in the United States, and interested researchers were beginning to conduct an increasing number of studies in sport psychology. By the latter 1960s, sport psychology had advanced to the point where national and international societies were organized to promote, stimulate, and encourage study in the field. Sport psychology in North America has developed almost exclusively within departments of physical education, kinesiology, or leisure studies—but not within departments of psychology. Although some psychologists have made significant contributions to the field of sport psychology, most scholars within the parent field of psychology have not been particularly interested in examining sport and physical activity. It is apparent that the growth of sport psychology in both Canada and the United States has been the result of sustained efforts by physical educators. It was primarily through their writing and research that sport psychology has advanced so markedly over the last 80 years.

EARLY HISTORY: 1890-1920

Some of the earliest writings related to sport psychology were theoretical in nature and attempted to explain either why physical educators needed an understanding of psychology or what psychological benefits were derived from participating in physical education. What is immediately apparent from this investigation is that physical educators, and those who related closely to the profession, were never reluctant to espouse the psychological advantages a person could gain from a vigorous "physical training" program. For example, in 1895 the Reverend William Augustus Stearn, president of Amherst College and the man who placed Edward Hitchcock in a position of being the first physical educator with full academic status at an American university, wrote, "If a moderate amount of physical exercise could be secured to every student daily, I have a deep conviction . . . that not only would lives and health be preserved, but animation and cheerfulness, and a higher order of efficient study and intellectual life would be secured" (Leonard & Affleck, 1947, p. 275).

Similarly, Frances A. Kellor wrote an article in 1898 entitled "A Psychological Basis for Physical Culture," in which she advocated that women in American colleges should place less emphasis on formal gymnastics in their physical education classes and begin stressing participation in various sports and games. The switch should be made to these activities, she said, because in contrast to formal gymnastics, the playing of games directed the mind into new channels, brought entirely different faculties into play, and never failed to produce "enthusiasm, activity and energy" among the participants. By participating in games a person would be forced to reflect, reason, observe "and engage in the various other mental processes not associated with apparatus work" (Kellor, 1898, p. 104). Ten years later, G. Stanley Hall wrote that "physical education is for the sake of mental and moral culture and not an end in itself. It is to make the intellect, feelings, and will more vigorous, sane, supple, and resourceful" (Hall, 1908, pp. 1015-1016).

While many people were busy espousing the psychological benefits of physical education, another group of individuals in the United States was examining the social psychological aspects of sport from an essentially philosophical perspective. Most of the theories advanced in these studies were not experimentally based or supported with any empirical evidence but instead were based on personal opinion. The most prominent investigations among this group attempted to explain why humans play and how play affects their development. For example, G.T.W. Patrick's article which appeared in the 1903 volume of the *American Journal of Psychology* discussed the then current theories of play in an effort to explain the motives that attracted thousands of spectators to football games. Patrick wrote that the inhibition of emotional expression was characteristic of modern civilized man, and hypothesized that the game of football acted as "a sort of aristotelian catharsis for spectators, purging them of their pent-up feelings and enabling them to return more placidly to the slow upward toiling" (Patrick, 1903, p. 381).

In contrast to the above mentioned studies, a number of experimentally based motor learning projects were being conducted around the turn of the century that have had ramifications for the sport psychologist. One of the earliest studies in this category was George W. Fitz's investigation of reaction time which appeared in the *Psychological Review* in 1895. Fitz, head of the Department of Anatomy, Physiology, and Physical Training at Harvard's Lawrence Scientific School from 1891 to 1899 and the man responsible for establishing perhaps the first physical education research laboratory in North America, set up an apparatus to measure the speed and accuracy with which a person could touch an object suddenly presented in an unexpected position. It was noted that such measures were particularly applicable to sports requiring a quick perception of a stimulus and accurate, fast responses for successful performance. Data was collected on more than 200 subjects and an analysis was made by sex, speed of response, and average deviation error score (Fitz, 1895).

Shortly after Fitz completed his study on reaction time, two scholars from Yale reported their investigations on the question of cross-education or transfer of training. William G. Anderson, prominent physical educator and one of the men most responsible for the formation of the American Association for Health, Physical Education, Recreation and Dance, conducted a series of six experiments during the academic year of 1897-1898 on mental practice, the transfer of training, and the transfer of muscular strength (Anderson, 1899). The other researcher at the Ivy League school was Walter Wells Davis, who in 1897 received his bachelor's degree in hygiene and organic training from Stanford and eventually received his doctorate in psychology from Yale. Davis had conducted studies on the transfer of training and reported on them in the 1898 and 1900 volumes of *Studies From the Yale Psychology Laboratory*

(Kroll & Lewis, 1970). These particular investigations required subjects to lift 5-pound weights with just the right arm as many times as possible over a test period of from 2 to 4 weeks. To Davis' delight, the studies revealed not only that the right arm gained in strength but that the unexercised left arm also showed an increase in power.

Not long after the Anderson and Davis studies were reported, several other investigations in motor learning began to appear in the literature (Cummins, 1914; Murphy, 1916; Noble, 1922; Starch, 1911). The study by Robert A. Cummins (1914), an instructor in psychology at the University of Washington, is especially significant because it was one of the first direct experimental studies conducted on the value of sport and physical activity. Cummins' investigation, which appeared in the *Psychological Review*, attempted to determine the effect of basketball practice on motor reaction, attention, and suggestibility. "Much discussion has been published in recent years," wrote Cummins, "as to the probable value of athletics for college students, especially certain forms of exercise as that of football and basketball. In this connection it occurred to the writer that by singling out certain physical and mental traits it would thus be possible to reduce the problem to a measurable basis" (Cummins, 1914, p. 356).

While the vast majority of studies fall within the realm of motor learning, a few investigations that could more easily be classified as sport psychology research appeared in the literature prior to the mid-1920s. For example, just 2 years after Fitz's work on reaction time was reported, a psychologist from Indiana University named Norman Triplett conducted a study to determine the relationship between audience effects and motor performance. Drawing upon field observations and secondary data, Triplett analyzed the performance of cyclists under three conditions: (a) paced efforts against a clock; (b) paced efforts against a standard; and (c) paced efforts in actual competition against other cyclists. Triplett concluded that the presence of another competitor in a race served to "liberate latent energy in the cyclists not ordinarily available" (Triplett, 1897, p. 533).

Like Triplett's experiment on cyclists, E.W. Scripture's study on character development and sport which appeared in the 1899 issue of *Popular Science Monthly* can also be categorized within the area of sport psychology research. Scripture, director of the psychological laboratory at Yale University, felt that desirable character or personality traits could be fostered through participation in sport and that these traits would transfer to other areas of a person's life. To support his hypothesis, Scripture reported the results of a number of case studies which revealed that character could indeed be developed through active participation in sport. Although his methodological procedures were rather rudimentary, Scripture was one of the few investigators of the period who utilized scientific principles to support his contentions.

In spite of the above mentioned studies on the various aspects of sport psychology, the first person in North America to research the subject over an extended period of time was Coleman Roberts Griffith. Often referred to as the "Father of American Sport Psychology," Griffith helped establish what many people consider to be the first sport psychology laboratory in North America at the University of Illinois in 1925. The first sport psychology laboratory in the world was most likely established by either Carl Diem at the Deutsche Hochschule Fur Leibesubungen in Berlin in 1920 or A.Z. Puni at the Institute of Physical Culture in Leningrad early in 1925. According to Griffith, the idea for such a facility came from George Huff, the director of Physical Welfare for Men at Illinois, who was interested in establishing a research center devoted to the study of psychology and physiology of athletic activity.

After becoming acquainted with the series of informal studies that Griffith had been conducting since 1918 on various psychological factors in football and basketball, Huff formulated a plan to provide support for a facility that would conduct research along these lines of inquiry. The plan was approved by the Illinois Board of Trustees on September 15, 1925, with Griffith officially becoming director of the Athletic Research Laboratory shortly thereafter. Delighted with the new facility, Griffith later wrote that "few other psychological laboratories devoted to a single group of psychological problems are better equipped than this laboratory for research in athletics" (Kroll & Lewis, 1970, p. 1).

Griffith spent most of his career investigating three particular areas: psychomotor skills, learning, and personality variables. In order to gain information about these areas, he developed a number of psychological tests and pieces of special apparatus. For example, he designed a test of mental alertness for athletes; a test for measuring muscular sense; a test for reaction time to light, sound, and pressure; a test for steadiness, muscular coordination, and learning ability; a test for muscular tension and relaxation; a test of baseball ingenuity; and an apparatus for reaction time to muscular load (Kroll & Lewis, 1970).

While Griffith put more stock in those investigations that were conducted in a highly controlled experimental setting, he was not averse to collecting information from field observations and personal interviews. For example, he used an interview conducted with Red Grange during the 1925 Michigan-Illinois game to support his contention that superior athletes effectively performed skills autonomously. Similarly, through correspondence with Knute Rockne, Griffith gathered valuable information on the role of motivation in sport (Kroll & Lewis, 1970).

Recognizing the need to disseminate his research findings to practitioners in the field, Griffith published numerous studies dealing with the ways in which knowledge could be applied to teaching sports. Between 1919 and 1931 alone, he wrote some 25 articles dealing specifically with sport psychology. He also wrote two books that are classics in the area of sport psychology: *Psychology of Coaching* (1926) and *Psychology and Athletics* (1928). The former book is particularly noteworthy because it was essentially the outgrowth of a course entitled "Psychology and Athletics" that Griffith first taught at Illinois in 1923. He also began work on a book he never completed, tentatively entitled Psychology of Football (Kroll & Lewis, 1970).

Because of the withdrawal of financial support, Griffith chose to resign from his position as director of the Athletic Research Laboratory in 1932. But this did not end his career in sport psychology. In 1938 he embarked on one of his most extensive research projects—for the Chicago Cubs baseball club. Hired by Philip K. Wrigley to be the team's sport psychologist, Griffith was furnished with filming and laboratory equipment to conduct various tests on every player on the team from the beginning of spring training to the end of the season. He examined such things as leadership, training, personality, motor learning, ability, and various social psychological factors, all of which were summarized in an unpublished report. After finishing that project, Griffith devoted the next 6 years of his career to his duties as professor of educational psychology and director of the Bureau of Institutional Research. In 1944 he was named provost of the university, a position he held until his retirement in 1953 (Gould, 1976).

Griffith's contributions to the field were truly significant but, unfortunately, few academicians did any follow-up work or successfully claimed the legacy offered by the famous sport psychologist from Illinois. John Lawther, professor of physical education at Pennsylvania State, and Clarence Ragsdale, professor of education at the University of Wisconsin, did establish motor learning laboratories at their respective institutions in the 1930s (Vanek & Cratty, 1970). Ragsdale also published a book in 1930 entitled *The Psychology of Motor Learning.* Yet a striking void exists between Griffith's productive years and the work of more contemporary researchers in sport psychology. It was this unmistakable gap that caused Kroll and Lewis to describe Griffith as a "prophet without disciples" (1970, p. 4).

Most of the research in sport psychology that appeared during and immediately after Griffith's reign at Illinois were studies published by a single author and limited to a specific topic. Research involving several studies by one person or studies that built on each other were extremely rare. Two notable exceptions would be the line of personality research carried out by the well-known physical educator, C.H. McCloy, and a group of his students at Iowa, and the systematic studies on reaction time conducted by Walter Miles and a colleague at the Stanford Psychological Laboratories. The studies by McCloy's group are worth noting since their initial investigation appeared in the first issue of the *Research Quarterly,* a journal established in 1930 by the American Physical Education

Association to promote research within the field of physical education. The first study in this group of research projects was published by McCloy (1930) and entitled "Character Building Through Physical Education." Six years later the follow-up studies by B.E. Richardson, Jr. (1936) and F.W. O'Neal (1936) also appeared in the *Research Quarterly*. While this fledgling series of studies was a good start, McCloy and his students were very candid when they wrote that their findings suggested more problems than they solved: "There is apparently a need for further research in the field of character and personality studies" (Richardson, 1936, p. 66).

Unlike the studies by McCloy's group at Iowa, Miles' research at Stanford focused on measuring the reaction time of a football line charge (Miles, 1928, 1931; Miles & Graves, 1931). Utilizing a multiple chronoscope to simultaneously record the reaction of seven linemen to an auditory signal, Miles found that the measurement of reaction time was fairly specific to the task being performed. In other words, just because a man was quick in one area, such as moving the hand or finger, did not mean that he was necessarily quick in other motor performances. "In place of taking one motor test and enlarging on its interpretation," wrote Miles, "it is more informing and useful to arrange new reaction experiments to closely approximate the particular skill or motor task that we desire to study or train men for" (Miles, 1931, p. 12).

POST WORLD WAR II

The fact that physical educators were doing very little psychological research prior to the Second World War did not prevent them from writing texts that had chapters based on principles taken from the parent field of psychology. Physical educators were not opposed to applying the research findings from psychology to their own particular areas of interest. One of the best examples of this approach was the text written by Elwood C. Davis and John Lawther in 1941 entitled *Successful Teaching in Physical Education*. Several chapters in the book pertained to psychological factors in teaching, yet most of the authors' information came from the field of psychology rather than from the limited research published in the physical education literature.

Some research on better teaching methods began to appear in the physical education literature prior to the Second World War. However, it was after that global conflict had come to a close that courses in motor learning and motor development really began being taught at various universities in the United States. The most noteworthy classes were taught by Franklin M. Henry at the University of California at Berkeley, John Lawther at Pennsylvania State University, and Arthur Slater-

Hammel at Indiana University (Ryan, 1981; Vanek & Cratty, 1970). Henry, who initiated a course at Berkeley in 1935 entitled "Psychological Basis of Physical Activity," was a particularly strong influence because he trained a number of graduate students who have since become very influential in the fields of motor learning and sport psychology both in Canada and the United States. For example, he directed the graduate work of such prominent individuals as: Richard B. Alderman, University of Alberta; Albert Carron, University of Western Ontario; Ronald G. Marteniuk, University of Waterloo; Richard Schmidt, University of Southern California; George Stelmach, University of Wisconsin; and E. Dean Ryan, University of California at Davis.

While classes in motor learning were being implemented at various universities, systematic studies were being conducted by physical educators on various elements of stress and its effect on athletic performance. The initial study in this area was conducted by Warren R. Johnson and appeared in a 1949 issue of *Research Quarterly*. The purpose of this particular investigation was to compare pre-contest emotional reactions of participants in football with those in wrestling. Johnson concluded that "While strong pre-contest emotion of the nature of fear and anxiety does not seem to be a particularly prominent factor in football, there is strong indication that it is of serious importance in wrestling" (1949, p. 76).

Johnson's research is significant because it was the first of its kind to appear in the literature since C.O. Jackson's study entitled "An Experimental Study of the Effect of Fear on Muscular Coordination" was published in the 1933 issue of *Research Quarterly*. It was also a noteworthy investigation because it was the precursor of a number of systematic studies that Johnson and his collaborators conducted on personality and athletic competition. For instance, in 1952 John M. Harmon, educational researcher from Boston University, and Johnson, in the physical education department at the University of Maryland, explored the emotional reactions of college athletes (Harmon & Johnson, 1952). Two years later Johnson, along with Daniel H. Hutton of the University of Maryland and Granville B. Johnson from Emory University, studied the personality traits of a select group of superior athletes (Johnson, Hutton, & Johnson, 1954). Burris F. Husman, a graduate student of Johnson's at Maryland, made a significant contribution to the literature in 1955 when he published the results of his doctoral dissertation on aggression in boxers and wrestlers (Husman, 1955). In the same year, Johnson again collaborated with Daniel H. Hutton in an exploratory study to determine the effects of a combative sport upon personality dynamics (Johnson & Hutton, 1955).

At about the same time that Johnson's group was studying personality dynamics, two other contingents, led by Franklin M. Henry and Celeste Ulrich, were beginning to analyze the influence of stress on athletic performance (Carron, 1968; Hennis & Ulrich, 1958; Howell, 1953; Ryan, 1961; Ulrich, 1957; Ulrich & Burke, 1957). For instance, Maxwell L. Howell, Henry's first motor learning student, conducted a study as early as 1953 on the influence of emotional tension on the speed of reaction and movement. Howell, now an internationally known sport historian, was specifically interested in determining the relationship between "personal evaluations of emotional condition and the degree of emotional tension as exhibited by the physiological correlates of emotion, such as heart rate, blood pressure, breathing, and skin resistance" (Howell, 1953, p. 23).

In addition to being Henry's first doctoral student in motor learning, Howell was also one of the individuals responsible for the emergence of sport psychology in Canada. After graduating from Berkeley in 1954, Howell took a position at the University of British Columbia where he successfully established the first master's degree in physical education in Canada. There he began including bits and pieces of motor learning/ sport psychology material in a test and measurements course. Howell was forced to teach many of the principles of the subject in this manner because he met with resistance in trying to establish a course devoted exclusively to motor learning. Since no course focusing on motor learning existed in Canada at that time, Howell can be considered a pioneer of Canadian sport psychology and motor learning.

In 1961 Howell left the University of British Columbia to accept a position at the University of Alberta, where he was hired to begin the first doctoral program in physical education in Canada and was asked to develop labs and other research facilities. About 5 years later, at Howell's urging, Robert Morford of Berkeley was brought in to develop and teach perhaps the first motor learning/sport psychology classes in Canada. Morford left Alberta in 1968, but by that time the doctoral program established by Howell had become a reality and under the direction of Morford's replacements, Richard B. Alderman and Bob Wilberg, it has now become distinguished for training the largest number of graduates presently working in sport psychology/motor learning in Canada (Howell, personal communication).

At about the same time that sport psychology was beginning to make its presence known in Canada, Warren R. Johnson (1960) published a text entitled *Science and Medicine of Exercise and Sports*. This highly acclaimed text was a very significant step in the development of sport psychology because it successfully presented most of the current research available in the area. Four years later, Bryant J. Cratty of the University of California at Los Angeles wrote his very influential text, *Movement Behavior and Motor Learning* (1964), a book specifically designed for the graduate student. In 1966 Ogilvie and Tutko published a rather controversial text entitled *Problem Athletes and How to Handle Them*. This text focused upon the psychological assessment of athletes and was one of the earliest publications to use data obtained from studies of the superior athlete. Cratty again contributed to the literature in 1967 when he wrote a book entitled *Psychology and Physical Activity*, a text directed primarily toward coaches and physical education teachers.

The same year, two other texts intended for the physical education student were published. Robert N. Singer of Florida State University wrote *Motor Learning and Human Performance* (1967), and Joseph B. Oxendine from Temple University published *Psychology and Motor Learning* (1967). The latter 1960s witnessed the publication of some books dealing with the psychological aspect of sport from a somewhat different perspective than that taken by previous authors. For example, Arnold Beisser, a psychiatrist and former sports writer and competitive tennis player, wrote *The Madness in Sports* (1967), a book containing psychological case studies of outstanding athletes in various sports. A companion text to Beisser's book was one edited by R. Solvenko and J.A. Knight entitled *Motivations in Play, Games, and Sports* (1967). Psychiatrists had become interested in sport and the psychodynamics of athletes by the late 1960s, and this book contained approximately 50 essays describing the interaction between the human ego and an individual's sporting pursuits.

FORMATION OF NASPSPA AND CSPLSP

In addition to the numerous publications on the various aspects of sport psychology, the mid-1960s witnessed the first concerted attempts in North America to bring together groups of individuals interested in the subject. In 1965 a small group of individuals from various physical education departments in Canada and the United States met in Dallas during the National American Association of Health, Physical Education, and Recreation Convention to discuss the feasibility of establishing a society devoted to the study and promotion of sport psychology. The meeting, held primarily at the suggestion of Warren R. Johnson, included individuals who would be representatives at the First International Congress of Sport Psychology to be held later that year in Rome. This initial organizational meeting, and the positive dialogue between the American and Canadian contingents at the Rome Congress, engendered such enthusiasm that a subsequent meeting was planned. It was scheduled for Chicago one day prior to the 1966 National American Association of Health, Physical Education, and Recreation Convention to continue the discussion on the future of sport psychology in North America.

The gathering of various scholars in Chicago was significant because it was during that meeting that a steering committee was chosen to explore the possibility of establishing a North American Society for Sport Psychology. This initial committee consisted of Richard B. Alderman, University of Alberta; Donald A. Bailey, University of Saskatchewan; Roscoe C. Brown, Jr., New York University; Bryant J. Cratty, University of California at Los Angeles; Warren R. Johnson, University of Maryland; Gerald S. Kenyon, University of Wisconsin; Jack R. Leighton, Eastern Washington State College; Arthur T. Slater-Hammel, Indiana University; and Leon E. Smith, University of Iowa (Harris, 1977; Loy, 1974).

Just a few months after the meeting in Chicago two members of the steering committee, Warren R. Johnson and Arthur T. Slater-Hammel, attended a meeting of the managing council of the International Society of Sport Psychology in Barcelona. And on behalf of the yet-to-be founded North American Society for the Psychology of Sport and Physical Activity (NASPSPA), they agreed to host the Second International Congress of Sport Psychology in Washington, DC, in the fall of 1968. As a result of the action of these two men, the steering committee recognized NASPSPA's existence and began to officially organize and incorporate the society. The steering committee also elected the first officers of the organization: Arthur T. Slater-Hammel (president), Bryant J. Cratty (vice-president for national affairs), Warren R. Johnson (vice-president for international affairs), Roscoe C. Brown (secretary-treasurer), and Gerald S. Kenyon (publication director) (Harris, 1977; Loy, 1974).

The first annual meeting of NASPSPA was held just prior to the 1967 American Alliance for Health, Physical Education, and Recreation (AAHPER) Conference in Las Vegas. The program consisted of a morning business meeting of the executive council followed by an afternoon scientific session open to all interested persons. E. Dean Ryan of the University of California and David and Richard Nelson of Pennsylvania State University presented a paper on kinesthetic after-effects, while Richard Barthols of UCLA spoke on a psychologist's view of the science and mythology of sport, and Bruce Ogilvie and Thomas Tutko of San Jose State University spoke on the personality of the athlete. Shortly after this first meeting, NASPSPA was officially incorporated as a non-profit corporation under the state laws of Indiana (Harris, 1977; Loy, 1974). The initial professional activity of the newly formed society was the establishment of a *Sport Psychology Bulletin*, a semi-annual publication devoted to exchanging ideas and information about NASPSPA and sport psychology through book reviews, editorials, research abstracts, comments, short papers, and letters. A second major professional function of NASPSPA since its inception has been the sponsorship of annual meetings designed primarily to disseminate new knowledge in three major areas—motor learning and control, motor development, and sport psychology (Harris, 1977; Loy, 1974). Since its initiation NASPSPA has developed into the single most influential academic/professional society in the world that focuses on the psychology of sport and physical activity (Salmela, 1981).

NASPSPA's second annual meeting was held in St. Louis in 1968, again in conjunction with the AAHPER Conference. The organization's major activity that year, however, was cosponsoring with AAHPER the Second International Congress of Sport Psychology, held in Washington, DC. Boston was the site of NASPSPA's third annual meeting in 1969, Seattle was the site of the fourth annual meeting, and Detroit was the site of the 1971 conference (Harris, 1977; Loy, 1974).

NASPSPA's sixth annual meeting, held in Houston in 1972 during the AAHPER Conference, would prove to be one of the most influential in the organization's young history. The primary item of business was consideration of NASPSPA's reorganization to make it more responsive to the needs of the growing society. Group discussions were led by Rainer Martens of the University of Illinois, Richard Schmidt of the University of Michigan, and Leon Smith of the University of Iowa. A major outcome of these discussions was the decision to hold the meeting separate from any other organization so that NASPSPA members could discuss research ideas free from distractions from other conferees. Martens invited NASPSPA to meet at the University of Illinois and agreed to chair the first independent meeting of the organization (Harris, 1977; Loy, 1974). His invitation was accepted.

The 1973 conference, held at the University of Illinois' conference center at Allerton Park, marked a milestone in the development of NASPSPA. It contained many firsts: the meeting was held independently of AAHPER, it lasted over several days, it included several major addresses and, perhaps most important, members had the opportunity to engage in lengthy discussions with their colleagues before, during, and after each session. Moreover, in contrast to the six previous NASPSPA meetings, the entire conference proceedings were edited and published under the title *Psychology of Motor Behavior and Sport* (Harris, 1977; Loy, 1974).

From the Anaheim, California conference in 1974 to the East Lansing, Michigan conference in 1983, the society has consistently organized outstanding programs with prominent speakers from the numerous subfields of psychology.

As an organization, NASPSPA has not been concerned only with producing new knowledge and disseminating that knowledge through annual conferences. Rather, it has increasingly placed greater emphasis on the contributions it could make to society. This is evidenced by the studies done on youth sport and the recent emphasis in applied and field research. NASPSPA has also established guidelines to monitor professional activities, analyze marketing needs, and determine proper academic training for those interested in sport psychology. For example, the society has established an ethics committee that is examining the various controversial issues that will be discussed in the chapter by Robert Nideffer.

Concurrent with the rapid development of NASPSPA, another influential professional society devoted to the promotion of sport psychology and motor learning was originated in North America. During the Second International Conference of Sport Psychology in Washington, DC, in 1968, several Canadian scholars who had just completed their graduate studies in the United States became aware of their common interests in sport psychology. As a result, in the fall of 1969 Bob Wilberg of the University of Alberta founded the Canadian Society for Psychomotor Learning and Sport Psychology (CSPLSP). Originally under the auspices of the Canadian Association for Health, Physical Education and Recreation, this organization became an independent professional society in 1977. One of CSPLSP's main functions has been the organization of a 3-day symposium during the fall of each year.

Frequently meeting independently of other organizations, the symposiums have also been held in conjunction with larger meetings of the sport sciences. In 1974, for example, they met with the ISSP in Montreal; in 1976 the meetings were held in Quebec City prior to the Olympic Games; in 1978 they came together with NASPSPA and the International Federation of Physical Education in Trois-Rivieres; and in 1981 they assembled again with the ISSP in Ottawa. Like NASPSPA, the symposiums have featured speakers from the parent field of psychology and from the areas of motor control, motor learning, psychology of sport competition, and the social psychology of physical activity. The research presentations given at the annual CSPLSP symposiums have been published in edited proceedings and contain a wealth of information on the development of sport psychology in Canada (Salmela, 1981).

To say that the formation of NASPSPA and CSPLSP has had a significant influence on the development of sport psychology in North America would be an understatement. Since the genesis of these two organizations, there has been a proliferation of systematic research conducted in sport psychology. This research has appeared in the form of articles and sport psychology journals, conference proceedings, book chapters, and books. Sport psychologists from North America not only publish in such disciplinary journals as the *Canadian Journal of Applied Sport Sciences, Journal of Motor Behavior, Journal of Sport Psychology,* and *Journal of Sport Behavior,* but frequently contribute to leading psychology journals such as the *Journal of Experimental Psychology, Journal of Personality and Social Psychology,* and *Psychological Review.*

Since 1970 a number of outstanding books have been written by Canadian scholars in both the academic, applied, and subdisciplinary areas of sport psychology. Examples of those books include: Brent Rushall's *Psyching in Sports* (1979); Ron Marteniuk's *Information Processing and Motor Skill* (1976); Richard B. Alderman's *Psychological Behavior in Sport* (1974); Albert Carron's *Social Psychology of Sport* (1980); Peter Klavora and Juri V. Daniel's *Coach, Athlete, and the Sport Psychologist* (1979); Terry Orlick's *In Pursuit of Excellence* (1980); and John H. Salmela's *The World Sport Psychology Sourcebook* (1981).

Like their Canadian counterparts, sport psychologists in the United States have published numerous books during the last decade or so in various areas of the discipline. Examples are William P. Morgan's *Contemporary Readings in Sport Psychology* (1970); Robert N. Singer's *Coaching, Athletics and Psychology* (1972); Bryant J. Cratty's *Psychology in Contemporary Sport* (1973); Rainer Martens' *Social Psychology and Physical Activity* (1975a); A. Craig Fisher's *Psychology of Sport: Issues and Insights* (1976); William F. Straub's *Sport Psychology: An Analysis of Athlete Behavior* (1978); Frank L. Smoll's and Ronald E. Smith's *Psychological Perspectives in Youth Sports* (1978); Richard M. Suinn's *Psychology in Sports: Methods and Applications* (1980); and Robert M. Nideffer's *Ethics and Practice of Applied Sport Psychology* (1981).

The field of sport psychology has certainly come a long way since George W. Fitz conducted his study on reaction time in 1895! The highly sophisticated studies carried out by contemporary sport psychologists in North America are truly a testament to the evolution of the field since the turn of the century. Beginning with a few isolated studies, sport psychology in North America has evolved into an academic discipline characterized by professional societies devoted to the promotion and fostering of the field, systemic investigations employing elaborate research designs, and the creation of publishing outlets to disseminate new research findings. Whereas only a limited number of sport psychology classes were offered at the university level a few years ago, a student today can select this area as a major field of study and choose among several career options. Coleman R. Griffith might be justifiably delighted with the progress and status that the field of sport psychology currently enjoys within academic circles in North America.

Chapter 2

Comparative Sport Psychology

John H. Salmela
Université de Montréal

Sport psychology is an international phenomenon. Its activity can be found in over 40 countries, involving approximately 1,320 individuals from 6 continents which include the Americas, Africa, Asia, Europe, and Australia. In a recent international survey on the professional status of the field of sport psychology, about one half of that total population took the time to share their overall orientations, academic training procedures, and research methods with their colleagues (Salmela, 1981). If key words were selected to characterize the state of sport psychology from a global perspective, they might include: emerging, diversified, and enthusiastic.

The relatively small number of individuals involved in sport psychology around the world attests to the emerging nature of the discipline. While substantial pockets of them can be found in Canada, the United States, Australia, Germany, France, Italy, Japan, Poland, and the Soviet Union, countries as varied as Brazil, China, India, Iraq, South Africa, and Turkey also report some activity in sport psychology. As noted in the previous chapter by Wiggins, the roots of sport psychology can be traced back to the 1920s to pioneers such as Carl Diem in Germany, Coleman R. Griffith in the United States, and A.Z. Puni in the Soviet Union. But despite these fruitful initiatives in the field, there ensued a

Thanks are extended to Dr. Wayne R. Halliwell for his comments on an earlier draft of this chapter.

barren period created by two world wars and the Great Depression. Beginning in the late 1950s through the 1960s, however, traces of activity again sprang up within these countries as the result of the growth of sport science within educational and sport institutions. It was during the 1970s that sport psychology really began to flourish, both professionally and academically, as well as becoming more sophisticated in the majority of the other countries surveyed.

Economic, political, and philosophical differences between the 42 nations surveyed translate into a diversity of approaches to the study of sport psychology. For example, sophisticated technology in electronics and computer ware is only accessible to certain countries. Likewise, some governments support work in sport psychology — perhaps with strings attached to bring it in line with their prevailing policies. This multiplicity of viewpoints stems from the fact that people from different societies simply view the world, and sport psychology, differently.

In spite of the diversity, and perhaps because of the relative youth of the area of sport psychology, the enthusiasm shown by its members is remarkable. Workers in sport psychology, regardless of where they're from, are eager to find out more about what is happening in other countries. This curiosity is most pronounced and reciprocal between North Americans and Eastern Europeans, to the point that the approaches of the other group take on almost mystical proportions. In my recent travels throughout Eastern Europe, informal discussion was often directed toward North American sport psychology "secrets." Likewise, North American specialists have expressed interest in what goes on in sport psychology behind the Iron Curtain.

It is somewhat curious that more sharing has not gone on between the East and the West in sport psychology, given that one of the seminal books in the field, *Psychology and the Superior Athlete* (1970), was the result of a collaboration between a Czechoslovakian, Miroslav Vanek, and an American, Bryant J. Cratty. This book outlined certain similarities and differences in sport psychology practices in the East and the West, but did not discuss underlying reasons for these variations. Thus, this chapter will highlight a variety of concerns in sport psychology in North America as compared to Eastern Europe in an attempt to demystify the perceptions of the two systems. Sport psychology's relation to the society in general, to education, and to sport will be considered by comparing academic training and various forms of professional involvement in both systems. Although a number of unique aspects of sport psychology can be found in Germany, France, Italy, and Japan, many of these fall somewhere in between what is occurring in North America and Eastern Europe. In short, their exclusion from the present discussion is in no way meant to diminish their importance.

SPORT PSYCHOLOGY
WITHIN A SOCIETAL CONTEXT

The scope of this discussion, while limited to Eastern Europeans and North Americans, still encompasses approximately 61% of all the individuals working in the field. Of the estimated 1,320 teachers, researchers, or clinicians in sport psychology, 27% are Eastern Europeans and 34% are North Americans. Thus, a considerable proportion of the world sport psychology map is in fact contained within this sampled group.

The systems that spawned these two groups in sport psychology, however, have created very different profiles of the typical worker within each system. Each society's values and attitudes toward sport and psychology have significantly shaped the respective structures and functions with sport psychology to conform to these societal contexts. Three areas which have seen the most dramatic effects of this are the degree of control, the underlying purpose, and the direction of government intervention in sport psychology. Depending upon the vantage point of the observer, the outcomes of these emphases have either positive or negative aspects.

Degree of Control

Sport psychology in North America has been characterized by contemporary researchers, in often colorful language, as being free spirited, spontaneous, and perhaps disheveled. Consider the following descriptions in the *World Sport Psychology Sourcebook* (Salmela, 1981) "an undisciplined subdiscipline" (Martens, p. 1); "like tips of tentacles severed from the arms of various octupii" (Wilberg, p. 1); "fragmented and poorly organized" (Nideffer, p. 115); and "scattered and has a shotgun look" (Tutko, p. 115). Because no central body dictates the direction in which sport psychology must go, the discipline is interestingly diverse. However, editors of the most prestigious journals of the field exercise a certain degree of control in sport psychology through their selection or rejection of various articles. The rapid development of sport psychology has made it particularly susceptible to current fashion trends from mainstream psychology, which often determines what is appropriate for the current season. However, this control by journal editors appears not to be so authoritarian as to stifle new advances when someone treads into previously untouched areas.

The Eastern European situation differs somewhat in terms of the degree of external control put upon sport psychology pursuits. All Eastern European countries are characterized by Soviet-style centrally controlled governments. Thus, sport psychology there is characterized by conversion rather than diversion. The focus of research topics is much more limited in scope because they are determined within 5-year research plans by the State. However, there is significant input in how these guidelines are respected and followed, depending upon the particular interests and skills of the researchers. As Miroslav Vanek points out, "All of our sport psychology projects in Czechoslovakia are related and preplanned — but they are not dictated" (Salmela, 1981). Although the degree of control in sport psychology is much greater within these Socialist countries than in the West, it would be erroneous to assume that each country is a carbon copy of the Soviet model. Rather, the particular levels of liberalization, as well as the indigenous characteristics of the native people, result in a surprisingly varied mosaic for what is often believed to be a monolithic system.

There are advantages to having some formal degree of control over sport psychology: A unified approach to a particular problem by a large number of people can result in rapid and significant progress within a given field of knowledge. Central control provides a means of streamlining research efforts with the advantages of common methods, long-term planning, and interrelated projects. However, there are also risks such as stifling individual initiatives and preventing the freedom to explore seemingly peripheral areas that may potentially yield unexpected payoffs. Moreover, the attention may be focused on a trivial or even false problem, which could result in overemphasis to an inappropriate concern while more urgent matters are left untouched.

A positive example of this constrained focus of attention relates to stress management in sport. Without exception, the Eastern European countries I visited had implemented, with positive results, training in self-control of up to 30 hours of theory and practice for all elite athletes. These types of programs have recently been initiated in North America on a limited basis. But there are also certain drawbacks to an overly centralized approach to sport psychology in Eastern Europe. For example, a recent focal point of sport psychology research in at least two national 5-year plans in Eastern Europe has been to determine the personality of athletes, using standardized inventories. Taking one popular North American perspective on personality research and sport (see Morgan, 1979c), research using these tools within sport contexts may have serious limitations. Yet many Eastern European researchers are obliged to work within what might be called a sport psychology cul-de-sac until the next quintennial edict.

Underlying Purposes

Most sport psychology research in North America appears to be primarily motivated by the desire to generate new knowledge and thus contribute to the general body of knowledge in the field. Of course, the production of new knowledge is often driven by the publish or perish syndrome which significantly influences promotion or elimination from the academic ranks. Sometimes those in sport psychology are paid for their clinical services, consultations, or writing. But there is also evidence (Whiting, 1974) that individuals in sport psychology with backgrounds in physical education are primarily involved in the discipline because of an altruistic commitment to sport rather than personal gain.

Promotion within academic institutions in Eastern Europe is also somewhat dependent upon research and publication, but there are significant differences behind the approaches that motivate most sport psychology activity. Research in Eastern Europe is directed toward advancing the socialist state through sport rather than solely creating new knowledge for its own sake. This is ensured by employing control mechanisms such as the preselection of research along ideological rather than scientific lines, which produce guidelines for research that will be most advantageous for the promotion of the state.

Direction of Efforts

Activity in North American sport psychology is channeled to many target areas, due to the relative lack of central control mechanisms within Canada and the United States. Sport psychology research has been directed either to current themes arising from mainstream psychology or to specific problems pertaining to sport practice. For example, the topic of attributions for success and failure has emerged as a popular sport psychology focus after having received considerable attention from social psychologists during the early 1970s. In comparison, topics such as aggression or emotional self-control in sport arise from the need to improve sport performance using both educational and clinical interventions. This latter area of concern takes on much greater proportions in Eastern European sport psychology.

The primary focus of Eastern European sport psychology is utilitarian — directed toward improving sport performance. Success in sport is seen as a powerful propaganda tool for enhancing the socialist political profile, and much effort is directed toward this goal. The interest in this area is all-consuming, as evidenced by the Bulgarian sport chairman's request that the sport psychology program of development for the 1984 Olympic Games in Los Angeles begin 4 days after the end of the 1980 Olympic Games in Moscow (Salmela, 1981). Departing from the above overview, the following sections will deal more specifically with how North American and Eastern European sport psychology compare in academic preparation and professional involvement.

ACADEMIC PREPARATION
IN SPORT PSYCHOLOGY

The importance of the pursuit of sport excellence within Eastern Europe is evident from the academic profiles of those who work in sport psychology. The central focus of attention on sport achievement to demonstrate the benefits of their system translates into a very different perspective of the university level specialist in sport psychology than can be seen in North America. Compared to 69.8% of North Americans, 80% of Eastern Europeans surveyed said that the field of sport, rather than games, movement, or physical activity, was their primary focus of professional interest. This is particularly interesting since only 63% of the Eastern Europeans ever took part in sport on the local, regional, or national level as compared to 80% of the North American sample. The reason that many Eastern Europeans work in sport psychology without having had a background in sport is due to the assignment of psychology-trained individuals to the area of sport. North Americans, by contrast, are more often themselves sport participants who then choose to work in sport psychology.

Aside from the initial predisposition to study sport, a number of other academic training experiences differ for North Americans as compared to Eastern Europeans. North Americans generally have a greater focus on theoretical research (69.8% vs. 54.8%), more coursework (54.5% vs. 49.3%), and more counseling experiences (15.9% vs. 10.8%) than their Eastern European counterparts.

Further indications of the high degree of academization of North Americans in sport psychology can be seen when the various courses are grouped into specific indices reflecting biological, cognitive, social, differential, methodological, and professional concerns. In all cases, the North American academic indices are higher than the Eastern European ones, particularly the methodological index. This reflects the North American disposition toward the use of the scientific method with specific emphasis on statistics, computer science, and other forms of laboratory technology. Part of these differences between the two societies result from the degree of academic mobility permitted within the North American university system. Students in physical education can take courses across campus in the psychology department, and vice versa. Study in a number of different faculties is generally more constrained in the European university structure. There might also be a trace of academic over-compensation operating in North American sport psychology. This is especially strong within physical education departments that seek academic respectability by amassing coursework in other departments.

While there is no doubt that North Americans gain a much richer experience within the limits of offered coursework and related technological preparation, there is a serious lack within one area of their preparation compared to the Eastern Europeans. Only 37.3% of the North Americans indicated that they had any para-academic experiences working in applied settings as compared to 83.0% of Eastern Europeans. When further questioned about which aspect of their academic experience they would like to modify, both groups expressed a desire to have even more practical real world assignments. Obviously, the need is more pressing in North America.

The reason for the greater number of para-academic experiences in Eastern Europe is related to the manner in which sport psychology aspirants are selected and developed within the academic institutions. Promising students often receive posts within sport or research institutes that put them in direct contact with athletes *before* their program of graduate specialization in sport psychology has begun. Thus, research and counseling occurs within a secure applied setting, since the student is assured of a position in the field when he or she graduates. By contrast, the North American system of graduate study, in which students are prepared and then released upon the job market, does not lend itself to the sort of sport psychology apprenticeship found in Eastern Europe. Ongoing involvement with sport practice is more difficult in the North American situation because of high levels of graduate student mobility and turnover. Of course, the fact that the Eastern European countries have decided to give sport psychology a key role in a consistent and concerted attempt to achieve sport excellence permits the easy implementation of these procedures that connect sport practice to sport psychology.

PROFESSIONAL INVOLVEMENT
IN SPORT PSYCHOLOGY

In the previous section, it was evident that Eastern Europeans trained in sport psychology had done so in a pragmatic manner that allowed them a period of apprenticeship with on-the-job training in sport performance. Comparatively, the North American profile was one of high academic intensity in which many courses were taken in areas related to sport psychology, but involvement in field situations was minimal. Let us now see how these academic training experiences translate into further academic and professional activities within their respective working situations in sport psychology.

Intensity of Involvement

In order to make significant advances in any discipline, academic and professional involvement must be carried out on a full-time basis. In a number of Western European countries that do not have institutionalized positions in sport psychology, work in that field is considered a hobby. Medical doctors, general psychologists, or sport coaches work in some areas of discipline with neither governmental support nor specific academic training. Only 36% of the Western Europeans in sport psychology work in the field as their primary means of employment, spending only 47.4% of their professional time involved in these activities.

How does the intensity level of professional involvement compare within the present target populations? North America's level of involvement in sport psychology is somewhat higher than that of Western Europe but significantly lower than that of Eastern Europe. Over 78% of Eastern Europeans identified sport psychology as their primary means of employment, whereas only 55.5% of the North Americans reported the same. The proportion of total professional time North Americans spent working in sport psychology (54.6%) was considerably closer to that of the Eastern Europeans (59.6%), even though much of this time for North Americans was not carried out through full-time positions. One can perhaps better appreciate the relative youth of sport psychology in North America by considering the magnitude of these proportions if similar material were collected on medical doctors. Undoubtedly, they would reply that nearly 100% of their professional time is spent practicing medicine. In sport psychology, trained psychologists have been known to dabble in sport while physical educators have done the same in psychology. To a great extent, then, North American sport psychology is perhaps beyond the hobby status for most but still falls well short of the Eastern European degree of serious professional involvement.

Professional Priorities

One of the few systematic surveys on the degree to which the sport sciences interact with sport practice was carried out by the Coaching Association of Canada (Gowan, Botterill, & Blimkie, 1979). This survey, which consisted of technical directors of Canadian sport federations and Canadian sport scientists, found that the priorities of the two groups were almost reversed. The professional tasks that most needed the help of sport science, namely coach education, athlete preparation, and talent identification, were the very topics believed to be least important by Canadian sport scientists! The primary concerns of both the sport scientists and technical directors were identified as conducting new research and interpreting existing research. This same set of questions was added in the international survey of individuals working in sport psychology (Salmela, 1981), and the responses of the Canadian sport technical directors were compared to the responses of sport psychologists from North

TABLE 2-1
Perceived Importance of Professional Behaviors of Respondents
From Sport Practice and Sport Psychology[a]

Professional Behaviors	Canadian Sport Technical Directors		North American Sport Psychologists		Eastern European Sport Psychologists	
	Score	Rank	Score	Rank	Score	Rank
Coach education	1.9	1	2.1	2 (tie)	2.2	3
Athlete preparation	2.3	2	3.0	4	2.3	4
Talent identification	2.7	3	4.0	5	2.4	5
Interpretation of research	2.9	4	2.1	2 (tie)	2.1	2
Carrying out new research	3.0	5	1.9	1	1.6	1

[a]Scores are averaged Likert scale values of 1-7, with 1 denoting "very important" and 7 "very unimportant."

America and Eastern Europe. A summary of the respondents' answers appears in Table 2-1.

Again, it can be seen that both American and Eastern European sport psychologists priorized their professional activities in virtually the reverse order to that of the Canadian sport technical directors. For the two former groups, the tasks of carrying out new research and interpreting existing research had been the most important, whereas these functions were deemed to be the least important for the sport practitioner.

However, one very important dimension distinguishes the response patterns of North Americans from Eastern Europeans. While the order of the task priorities is almost identical, their importance is reversed: Eastern Europeans most value athlete preparation and talent identification whereas North Americans consider these the least important. Thus on an absolute scale, tasks which have high importance to technicians in sport practice are also given more attention by Eastern Europeans than by North Americans working in sport psychology.

This brings us to a tentative conclusion that North Americans, in spite of lacking para-academic experience, may be better trained academically than Eastern Europeans; but the latter spend more time responding to the needs of the sport practitioner. This viewpoint is further substantiated by the fact that 55.6% of the research in North America was reported to be theoretical in nature as compared to 48.2% of research from the socialist countries.

Treated Populations

Once again, the fundamental differences that were previously found between sport psychology in the East and the West were consistently shown in the types of target populations for research or applied assessment. The academically based North American researchers whose primary aim is to generate new research knowledge of a theoretical nature spend 52.6% of their time testing nonathletes. Presumably, the past athletic history of these individuals is not important since the aim of the research is to create and test new basic theory and conceptual models. Only 38.5% of the sport psychology research conducted in North America is directed toward the elite athlete.

In contrast, the Eastern Europeans show a reverse pattern with 54.6% of their efforts devoted to the study of elite athletes whereas only 27.5% of their time is spent conducting research on nonathletic populations. The concerted efforts to lend essential psychological services to elite athletes whose success will reflect well upon the socialist society is evidenced by these figures. These efforts are of course facilitated in Eastern European countries by having central control over all aspects of sport and sport science. In comparison, the North American approach, which is often defended as academic freedom, appears to lack direction and does not presently respond to various needs expressed by sport practitioners.

Structural Comparisons

It would be somewhat inappropriate to criticize the North American sport psychologists for not becoming more intimately involved in field research. A number of factors aside from ideological ones prevent them from applying their advanced methodological and theoretical skills to practice. One of these is the actual makeup of job descriptions in Eastern Europe as compared to North America. Countries in Eastern Europe have well defined hierarchies within sport psychology sections of a single sport institute, with specific tasks assigned to each level. Chairs or professors primarily teach and conduct research, while lower level faculty and instructors carry out more mundane administrative tasks which may involve assignment to specific teams on a long-term basis in applied sport psychology. Other technical support staffers undertake specific tasks that provide a great degree of differentiation of responsibilities throughout the sport psychology team. At a sport psychology unit meeting in the main sport institute in Bucharest, Romania, I met with a team of eight individuals including professors, a psychiatrist, clinicians, and assistants. A group of faculty this size in sport psychology is considered normal for this type of institute.

This contrasts sharply to the typical North American situation, in which a sport psychology professor often functions with some technical or secretarial help and perhaps some graduate students. The sport psychologist in North America may often work in conjunction with other faculty but usually is the only person specifically trained in sport psychology. This means the professor's functions are centralized and increased because there is less of a support system. The workload of the North American sport psychologist is characterized by having more undergraduate (16.8%) and graduate teaching (18.1%) than his or her Eastern European counterpart, and the North American also has the administrative load.

What is somewhat worrisome is the trend now seen in North America that places even more emphasis upon purely theoretical issues. This approach widens the gap between sport psychology and sport excellence. Such a situation is partially avoided in Eastern Europe by associating academies of science with sport institutes. The former institutions conduct purer forms of research while the latter deal with issues in sport practice.

In a recent article, Feltz (1981) painted a rather pessimistic employment picture for prospective graduates of sport psychology in North America. She pointed out that research oriented graduates are being caught in a career crunch because the job market requires people with clinical expertise. She suggested that graduate students also develop skills in grantsmanship, which could increase the attractiveness of a candidate for the few vacancies or postdoctoral positions.

COMPARATIVE PERSPECTIVES
IN SPORT PSYCHOLOGY

Due to an increase in sport psychology's information network, communication is occurring between countries that previously did not engage in much scientific dialogue. A great deal of North American information filters into Eastern Europe as the result of the publication boom during the 1970s and 1980s. In turn, the remarkable success of the Eastern European athletes, with the acknowledged help of their psychological support services, has attracted much attention in North American sport psychology circles.

One of the most fundamental strengths that the Eastern Europeans have is that of good sport organization, which implies concerted efforts in a common direction. They have decided that sport excellence is good for the political system, and that sport psychology is good for sport excellence. Within Eastern Europe, growth in sport psychology will continue more in terms of degree than in kind. They will stick to, and improve upon, the same basic system since it appears to succeed in attaining the desired goals. Put another way, the ideological inertia inherent within the system is somewhat cumbersome to redirect, and thus few drastic changes in this pragmatic approach appear forthcoming.

In contrast, the North American scene has been moved by extremely dynamic influences over its recent period of growth. Initial singular efforts in the mid-1960s and early 1970s have now borne fruit, resulting in an increasing number of professional and scientific meetings for all who are interested. Earlier research that was methodologically and theoretically weak or of little use has given way to better designed projects, which often have greater practical application. It may be that current needs from the sport environment, when coupled with methodological advances and a greater demand for accountability, will bring previously unexplored programs to both East and West. As the discipline of sport psychology matures, this type of expansion and positive growth can be optimistically expected.

Chapter 3

Current Concerns in Sport Psychology

Robert M. Nideffer
Enhanced Performance Associates, San Diego

Since the beginning of the 1970s, there has been a growing interest in the application of psychological theories and techniques to sport. The pressure of performing in sport has been accelerated by the athlete's pursuit of excellence, the use of sport as a powerful political tool, the high salaries and recognition offered to athletes in many sports, and the intense spectator interest shown in sport as a form of entertainment.

One major consequence of the increasing pressure placed upon the athlete has been the recognition of the importance of sport psychology. Interestingly, the need for sport psychology seems to be increasing in two contradictory ways. First, athletes and coaches, in search of the "winning edge," are looking to sport psychologists for a mental advantage. They are asking for techniques and procedures that will make the good athlete even better. As physical skills, training techniques, and work loads reach their maximal levels, the remaining frontier is the mind.

Another reason for the increased awareness of the potential significance of sport psychology is due to the increasing pressures in sport, pressures which often have negative consequences. Who will treat the casualties of the system? Should we place this kind of pressure on our athletes? How do we minimize or prevent emotional and physical trauma?

What is the sport psychologist's role? Do the different roles outlined above conflict with each other? Is the sport psychologist who is involved in the "pursuit of excellence" contributing to the exploitation and abuse of athletes? As for the psychologist who eschews competition and seeks to minimize pressure, is he or she denying reality and stunting the emotional and physical development of individuals?

Recent accounts in newspapers have chronicled the fact that medical and health care professionals have intentionally withheld from athletes information about injuries because they didn't want them to worry needlessly. Some of those athletes have taken legal action, believing their health and welfare were sacrificed for the sake of winning. Physicians and psychiatrists have been asked to prescribe medications ranging from amphetamines to tranquilizers to steriods in order to give athletes an edge. Sport psychologists have been asked to change the attitudes of some athletes in order to get them to take medications. For example, "I need you to convince this athlete that she should take steroids. She has some crazy block against it. She is afraid of the long-term effects on her femininity and on her ability to have children. Doesn't she realize she won't be competitive unless she takes them? Everyone else takes them!"

One reads in the newspaper that parents put their 8-month-old child on water skis. A popular television program shows an 8-year-old girl lifting a car. Young football players are doing exercises that their bodies aren't developmentally ready for. Parents are pushing 5-year-old children to be the youngest to run a marathon. Sport psychology practitioners are being asked to speak out both for and against these practices. In fact, it has become difficult to pick up a newspaper or to turn on the television without reading or hearing something about the application of psychology to sport. Self-appointed "sport psychologists" are using hypnosis, meditation, biofeedback, psychological tests, behavior modification, and other techniques to improve performance, treat anxiety, and increase endurance. At times they have even promised to draw on the athlete's "extra-sensory" or supernormal abilities to facilitate performance.

The growing interest in application—both within the North American Society for the Psychology of Sport and Physical Activity (NASPSPA) and the Canadian Society for Psychomotor Learning and Sport Psychology (CSPLSP)—as well as the increasing demand for service, began generating concern within these two organizations. Many members wanted to protect both the public and the profession from what they perceived as unethical and/or uneducated behavior. The problem lay in defining that behavior. Although there was general agreement within NASPSPA and CSPLSP that some type of control or statement regarding appropriate behavior was necessary, there was considerably less agreement on what that statement might be.

The present situation in North America is that individuals who have entered the field of sport psychology either bring a heavy emphasis in sport and a minor emphasis in psychology (and often no emphasis in clinical psychology), or they have been trained in clinical psychology and received little formal education in sport. Obviously, the different training these individuals have received contributes to their not always seeing eye to eye on problems. Although most of the members agree that a better training balance is needed, there is still disagreement regarding where to draw the line. In addition, individuals who have had years of experience in the field are not eager to admit that they are inadequately trained or currently unqualified to provide services. The controversy really centers on the question of who will control the profession.

At one extreme is a fear that psychologists will control the field, excluding anyone from providing services who is not a licensed psychologist. Associated with this is the fear that a clinical training model will be applied to sport and that sport psychologists will have to be trained to recognize and deal with psychopathology, thereby perpetuating the idea that sport psychologists are "shrinks" who deal with crazy athletes (Nideffer, 1981).

At the other extreme are individuals who are trained as clinicians, are sensitive to clinical issues, and who have seen serious clinical problems in sport and are concerned that an educational model or approach to sport psychology is not sufficient. They are concerned that individuals who use an educational framework (teaching athletes to develop psychological skills) will not be sensitive to underlying psychopathology. The failure to recognize serious problems will lead to the inappropriate application of techniques such as hypnosis, biofeedback, or testing, and precipitate a crisis that the clinically untrained individuals will not be able to handle.

Added to the conflict and mistrust that exists between educators and clinicians is a concern of the more academically oriented members of NASPSPA and CSPLSP. These people were not sure that sport psychology had reached the point where services should be offered! In addition, they didn't want applied issues to dominate the associations they had founded. In spite of all these difficulties, both groups established special committees to explore service related concerns.

Committees for both NASPSPA and CSPLSP worked for 3 years preparing a modification of the American Psychological Association's Ethical Standards. In 1982, both associations accepted the modified ethical codes as standards that should guide the behavior of members.

The ethical standards begin with a statement of the general philosophy that underlies the development of each of the nine principles that follow. That philosophical statement is presented here, in its entirety:

> Sport psychology consultants respect the dignity and worth of the individual and honor the preservation and protection of fundamental human rights. They are committed to increasing the knowledge of human behavior and of people's understand-

ing of themselves and others in sports environments. The utilization of knowledge gained should be for the promotion of human welfare.

Sport psychology consultants require an atmosphere of free inquiry and communication without misinterpretation of their knowledge and methods by others. Further, they have the obligation to prevent misuse of psychological techniques in sport through their personal influence, public statements, and professional sanction. Sport psychology consultants also have an obligation to make the results of their research available to other colleagues, to related scientists, and to others in allied professions.

The essence of the underlying philosophy is that the providers of service respect the dignity and worth of the individual and promise to protect the individual's welfare. To this end, they expose their methods and the results of their work to the scrutiny of others. Few people would argue with the basic premise. As may be seen, however, the interpretation of both the philosophy and principles in relation to specific events is subject to widely divergent opinions.

In addition to their charge of developing a set of ethical guidelines, both committees considered establishing role definitions in sport psychology and recommended criteria for the provision of a given role. That is, what training, background, and experience should a practitioner have before offering service? Finally, the committees were concerned with whether there should be an attempt to certify individuals as meeting some set of minimal standards. Due to the sensitivities of committee members and of the membership at large, progress in these areas was painfully slow, and eventually it ceased.

In the meantime, national sport governing bodies in both the United States and Canada were becoming increasingly interested in sport psychology. The Coaching Association of Canada (CAC) had been incorporating information from psychology into its coach's certification programs for some time. Concern was expressed about the pressures being placed on youth in sport. The CAC wanted to educate coaches about the services that sport psychologists had to offer. They wanted to sensitize coaches to communication issues, to individual differences, to physical, emotional, and developmental issues, to the need to protect the individual athlete, and to the fact that intrinsic rewards should be considered as important as extrinsic ones. As a consequence, the CAC began asking psychologists to write portions of their training manuals; in effect, they began to define and describe some of the areas of psychological application to the field without waiting for some professional consensus.

In a similar way, elite sport governing bodies began to get involved. In Canada, it was Sport Canada that was interested in finding out what the sport psychologist could contribute to the athlete's total training and preparation. They were asking questions like: "Where does the psychologist fit in with the biomechanist, nutritionist, trainer, coach, exercise physiologist, and team physician?" Having funded CSPLSP's ethics committee, Sport Canada felt that the committee was obliged to help them provide information to coaches by answering questions such as: What is a sport psychologist? What do they do? How can I find a sport psychologist? When do I need one? How much psychological training can I provide for myself? Responding to this request, the CSPLSP committee drafted a document written specifically for the consumer. A question and answer format was used. Copies of that document can be obtained from the Coaching Association of Canada, 333 River Rd., Ottawa, Ontario.

Sport psychology in the United States was following nearly similar paths. Up to the time of this writing, the American Psychological Association as a body had shown very little interest in the area of sport. For many members, sport psychology represented at best a diversion from the real issues of pain and human suffering that a psychologist faces. So it might be viewed as a hobby, a time-out from more important clinical issues. Others saw sport psychology as a total waste of time and as demeaning to the profession. Their view was that clinicians were trained to help reduce the pain in the world, to help the oppressed, not to indulge the elite. Slowly, these attitudes are beginning to break down. They are changing because of consumer demand for service. They are changing because professionals within the field are being educated. And they are changing because of economic necessity; there is not enough "traditional work" to go around.

As more and more psychologists learn about the relationships between attentional processes, physiological tension and performance, and as they see the relevance and need for their services, they will move into sport. Because of the changes taking place, it will not be long before both the American and Canadian Psychological Associations begin to take an active interest in the issue of who calls him/herself a sport psychologist. In the meantime, much like its Canadian counterpart, the U.S. Olympic Committee's Sports Medicine Committee has taken matters into its own hands.

In 1981, the USOC Sports Medicine Committee funded an elite athlete development project designed to provide special services to five targeted sports (track and field, cycling, volleyball, fencing, and weightlifting). One of the services to be offered was sport psychology, with a sport psychologist available for each of these sports. Athletes and coaches responded enthusiastically and other sport governing bodies became interested in integrating psychological factors into their training programs. Dr. Kenneth Clarke, director of sports medicine at Colorado Springs, was besieged by individuals who called themselves sport psychologists and wanted to offer psychological services. He also found sports governing bodies requesting those services. Concerned that his own knowledge in this area was lacking and that he was unable to accurately evaluate either the need for service or the qualifications of service providers, Clarke sought professional assistance.

A psychology advisory committee was formed with the help of several recognized experts in the field, and the committee's first meeting was held in August of 1982. At that meeting the committee was charged with the following:

1. Define the services that psychologists could offer to the USOC that would facilitate its mission.
2. Define the minimum credentials of persons who would provide the identified services.
3. Clarify the relationship of sport psychology services to the entire USOC organization.
4. Define the professional relationships of sport psychologists at competitions.
5. Develop a registry of individuals who meet the minimum established criteria for providing services.
6. Suggest methods that ensure communication between sports regarding sport psychology issues.

The psychology advisory committee was expected to respond to all of these statements within a day and a half—in spite of the fact that the committee had been selected to represent both educational and clinical positions, and that its participants came from different philosophical and training backgrounds. The USOC committee did respond to most of the suggestions. However, the agreements reached by this committee really reflect upon the abilities of these particular individuals to work together. They do not represent a professional consensus nor the position of very powerful organizations such as the American and Canadian psychological associations. A full description of the Psychology Advisory Committee's deliberations is found in the *Journal of Sport Psychology*, 1983 (Vol 5, pp. 4-8). The following is a summary of the session.

Roles of the Sport Psychologist

The USOC psychology advisory committee divided into three very broad areas the services that sport psychologists have to offer—clinical services, educational services, and research services.

Each service provision area contains a variety of subareas. For example, the clinical sport psychologist deals with all the traditional clinical issues that occur both in and out of sport. These would include assessing psychopathology, providing individual and group psychotherapy, providing crisis intervention, treating neurotic, psychotic, and personality disorders, and dealing with drug dependency, psychosomatic problems, and eating disorders.

The educationally oriented sport psychologist provides information (e.g., group presentations or lectures on growth and development, effects of intrinsic vs. extrinsic motivation, learned helplessness, etc.), and training—based on an educational rather than a clinical approach. Working with healthy athletes, the educationally oriented sport psychologist teaches stress management, concentration skills, and performance enhancement. Assessment tools are used for educational purposes to facilitate the growth and development of already healthy individuals.

The researcher helps develop and evaluate services, and is expected to be not only an expert in his/her particular area of investigation but also to be sensitive to the special needs and issues of athletes, to the USOC's overall mission, and to relevant health, education, and welfare guidelines.

Minimum Educational and Experiential Requirements

Although the committee attempted to outline minimum requirements in each of the three areas mentioned above, it is important to remember that these requirements are for leadership positions. A leader would function as a resource person to a national sports governing body. That individual would have to be capable of evaluating service providers, providing services, recognizing his/her own limitations and those of others, and recognizing the limitations of psychology within a sport context. Thus, a fairly broad training background and depth of experience is required.

In addition to these leadership positions, the USOC is interested in identifying individuals with highly specialized knowledge in biofeedback, assessment, stress management, team building, and other such areas. Presumably these specialists would be quite differently trained and qualified, and many of the requirements for a leadership position would not apply.

Clinical Sport Psychologist.   Requirements for a clinical sport psychologist include (a) a degree in clinical or counseling psychology or psychiatry from an APA or LCME accredited university; (b) full membership in the American Psychological or American Psychiatric Association and some professional preparation in sports sciences; (c) a current license to practice psychology or psychiatry; (d) at least 3 years' experience as an athlete, coach, or practitioner in the application of psychological principles to sport; and (e) a personal interview with a review board if eligibility cannot be determined on the basis of the preceding four requirements.

Educational Sport Psychologist.   An educational sport psychologist would need the following: (a) a doctorate in psychology, psychiatry, or a related field such as physical education, with a background in psychology that would meet the requirements for APA membership; (b) at least 3 years' experience as an athlete, coach, or practitioner in the application of psychological principles to sport; (c) reference letters from recognized institutions, organizations, and/or individuals attesting to the applicant's teaching skills within a sport psychology perspective; and (d) a personal interview with a review board if eligibility cannot be determined from the preceding three requirements.

Research Sport Psychologist.   To be a research sport psychologist, one would need (a) a doctorate in psychology, psychiatry, or a related field that would meet the standards required for full APA membership; (b) evidence of scholarly research contributions to the field of psychology with applicability to athletes; (c) reference letters from recognized institutions, organizations, and/or individuals related to the applicant's research contributions; and (d) a personal interview with a review board if eligibility cannot be determined otherwise.

Certification

At the time of this writing, the USOC has begun to use application forms for certification in *one or more* of the areas listed. Copies of the forms are available from Dr. Kenneth Clarke, Director Sports Medicine, USOC Training Center, Colorado Springs, CO. Interested applicants are expected to fill out the forms, include a resume, and arrange for letters of recommendation to be sent to the Psychology Advisory Committee. The first applications were reviewed in the fall of 1983. Individuals meeting the minimum requirements have had their names placed in a registry that is available to the national sports governing bodies and other interested groups and/or individuals.

Although tremendous progress has been made in the past 10 years in applied sport psychology, the field still needs to mature. Presently, organizations such as the USOC are not only taking it upon themselves to certify individuals in the area of sport psychology, but they are doing it before we have any formal training programs developed. The next 10 years will be even more critical to the field than were the past 10 years.

Although interest in sport psychology has been slow to develop within the mainstream of psychology, the same is not true for the field of health psychology. In recent years we have seen widespread interest in studying the relationship between physiological and psychological functioning as they relate to general emotional and physical health. Psychologists have become concerned about stress and its effects on health. As a result, they have become interested in the role of nutrition and exercise in the prevention and treatment of psychological problems. This growing field shares many of the concerns that the sport psychologist finds him/herself dealing with. We may well see some more formal relationships established between these two fields.

The USOC and Sport Canada began to define the field for themselves because they are faced with practical, very real problems that they want addressed. These organizations could not wait for the profession to completely pull itself together. Their actions have increased the pressure upon professional organizations to get things moving. Training programs must be developed that will provide an adequate base both in psychology and sport science. To this end, individuals will have to get together and give up their partisan politics. We cannot expect students to earn doctorate degrees in two or three major programs. We must begin to separate sport psychology from general psychology and clinical psychology, physical education from biomechanics and kinesiology. A core of courses must be identified and some sacrifices will have to be made. We cannot possibly retain all of the coursework and experience in search of the "ideal" sport psychologist.

Training within the field of sport psychology could actually take several directions. Ideally, we would develop a curriculum that would bridge psychology and sport science. Training in both of these areas would directly relate to and focus on the application of psychological principles and theory to sport. Upon completing such a curriculum, individuals would have the skills to recognize clinical problems when they occur and would know how to make appropriate referrals. They would be trained to provide the educational and research functions that have been generally described by the USOC, but they would not be clinicians and would not deal with clinical problems. These research-practitioners would actually intern by working with coaches and athletes in carefully supervised settings.

For the clinical sport psychologist, some form of postdoctoral training program would seem to make the most sense. It would be very difficult to significantly reduce the current course work and practicum demands placed on graduate students in clinical psychology. Instead, special postdoctoral training programs need to be developed within university and/or hospital settings. One of the major goals of the postdoctoral program would be to teach the clinician when not to treat "underlying issues." That is, the individual would have to learn when it is not in the best interests of the athlete to pursue underlying problems.

The individual who wishes to pursue a career within the field of sport psychology today faces some very difficult decisions. The field has yet to be well defined, and today's training programs may be obsolete tomorrow. As it now stands, the future sport psychologist must assume a major responsibility for his/her own education and will likely enroll in either a program of physical education or a program in psychology. The responsibility for balancing the training between sport science and psychology will be determined by one's advisor and the constrictions of the graduate program. Yet even if the graduate student manages to gain the "optimal" education, this does not guarantee that his or her experience will ultimately be recognized or accredited.

What is one to do? Should you wait for the profession to define itself? That would mean waiting at least 4 years before a recognized and accredited program can be established. Should you move ahead instead? The risk there is that your choice of training may not be acceptable, at least not completely. It would also mean taking course work that may be only tangentially relevant to your primary concerns.

Obviously, the choice will be based on individual circumstances. If I were forced to make such a choice today, I would choose a program that would prepare me for licensure as a psychologist—not because training in sport science is less important. Rather, my choice would be based on the fact that independent practice in psychology, and the accompanying right to call oneself a psychologist, is restricted by law to those with formal training in psychology.

It is indeed unfortunate that prospective students of this exciting area are forced to make such difficult choices simply because some of the most powerful organizations to which present sport psychologists belong have, so far, failed to adequately address the issues of training and certification.

Chapter 4

The Future
of Sport Psychology

Richard B. Alderman
University of Alberta

Regardless of what many people may think, sport psychology is still a *new* field of endeavor and, because of this, the field is involved with three major organizational issues: (a) examining the legacy of its past; (b) attempting to cope with the problems of the present; and (c) trying to establish directions for its future. It is the purpose of this chapter to delve into the major problems and issues that now confront sport psychology and suggest what directions should be taken to solve them. The basic contention here is that the nature of sport psychology is, and always will be, determined by the orientation of the people working in it. The nature of sport psychology in the future will be determined by the research, writing, and applied practices of those now engaged in sport psychology. Whether they work in a laboratory with a computer or down on the pool deck with swimmers is immaterial because whatever they are doing they will be establishing the field of knowledge, its applied practices, and its philosophical orientation.

An analysis of where sport psychology is, and where it has been, is covered more extensively in the chapters by David Wiggins and John Salmela. Therefore, this chapter will avoid reiterating the past and present developments. Nevertheless, any prediction of the future rests naturally in the past and the present and thus necessitates some reemphasis of material.

PAST EVENTS INFLUENCING THE FUTURE

It is fairly obvious from the outset that the past dilemmas, problems, issues, and confrontations between the various disciples of different sub-disciplines within sport psychology will continue. The pure researchers will continue to say that more basic research is needed, the applied people will continue to emphasize the importance of training and internship, and those who support a human development approach will continue to press for a change in our approach to the athlete or young participant. The Iron Curtain countries will continue to engage in some practices that North Americans find distasteful, and it will still be difficult to persuade some coaches of the importance of the psychological dimensions in athletic performance. There will be more, not less, pressure on university sport psychologists to publish or perish; and there will be more, not less, competition for jobs in sport psychology regardless of their specific context.

This is not meant to be a cynical or pessimistic assessment, but rather a realistic comment on the vitality and energy of the people working in the field of sport psychology. In few other areas can one find people so enthusiastic and motivated about what they are doing! This enthusiasm is manifested by the acceleration of the knowledge and data base, the formation of societies and associations around the world, the solid attendance at conferences and symposia, and the increasing number of journals specific to sport psychology.

It is also evident that the field of sport psychology is maturing. In its current state, sport psychology has been with us only since the late sixties when the North American Society for the Psychology of Sport and Physical Activity (NASPSPA) and the Canadian Society of Psychomotor Learning and Sport Psychology (CSPLSP) were established to promote the exchange of research information and enhance discussion between people interested in the field. Out of these rather rudimentary beginnings has grown a dynamic, increasingly coherent field of knowledge that has both strong academic and professional aspirations. This aura of vitality creates dynamism in the field; let's look at the present state of knowledge.

Current Status of Sport Psychology

A contemporary analysis of the state of knowledge in the field has been done in the areas of sport sociology (McPherson, 1975), exercise physiology (Taylor, 1976), sport history (Redmond, 1980), and to a certain extent by Alderman (1980), Butt (1980), and Martens (1980a) in sport psychology. According to McPherson and Taylor (1980), these sub-disciplines of the physical activity sciences or sport sciences are still at the first or second stages of development as characterized by Selznick (1959). Selznick suggested that subspecialties within a discipline advance through basically three stages of development. The first involves people communicating a perspective and discussing common interests and experiences. The second revolves around attempts to conduct descriptive survey types of research on topics of common interest. And the third involves going beyond the point of mere interest into the analysis of basic phenomena and the establishing of guiding principles.

Low-level, often superficial, research characterizes the first two levels because research and statistical techniques are emphasized as the major contribution. As McPherson and Taylor (1980) observe, the concepts explored are usually those which are easiest rather than those of theoretical importance. One can speculate that sport psychology, as an academic subdiscipline, is generally located somewhere toward the latter end of stage two since a large amount of contemporary research can be seen as "technique stimulated" activity rather than theoretical.

Two aspects from the past have contributed to this state of affairs. First is the fact that we are just now entering the third generation of sport psychologists. The first generation earned their doctorates in related parent disciplines such as psychology and physical education. Their students, the second generation, gradually made the transition toward more specific knowledge in sport psychology but still felt a responsibility to physical education constructs and concepts. The current crop of graduate students and young staff members who make up the third generation are quite different in that their preparation and personal interests now revolve around a research-oriented approach to defining and analyzing highly specific sport psychology phenomena. In addition, their philosophy is one of scientific inquiry rather than one solely directed toward physical education. It is this generation of professionals who will take sport psychology out of its adolescent phase and into the third stage of development as described by Selznick (1959).

A second aspect in the rate of maturity attainable by the field concerns the lack of enough people in the field. Most individuals involved with sport psychology over the last 20 years have been isolated in small institutional pockets or have been working alone at institutions spread across the continent. Such isolation, accompanied by a previous lack of distinct identity, has slowed development and expansion. This situation is gradually improving but the field still has a long hard path ahead before it can attain some degree of stability and maturity. An expressed support of local and national associations by sport psychologists would seem an important step in coordinating interactional networks.

In a sense then, the current events influencing the future direction of sport psychology quite naturally are based on what has happened in the past. Sport psychology is still directly anchored in the university system program in North America and, because of this, the area will reflect events that influence the functioning of the North American university system. This was demonstrated with the sudden expansion of subject-matter areas in the 1960s when the universities themselves began to expand, and it will be true during the 1980s if the events to be described actually occur.

CURRENT EVENTS INFLUENCING THE FUTURE

A most obvious addition in the orientation of sport psychology in the 1980s will be a significant shift toward a role emphasizing service in the community. To a certain extent, this change is already occurring because of several developments in our thinking and because of the various pressures on sport psychology for more applied professional service. Thus, sport psychologists currently encounter and will continue to encounter similar challenges that other physical activity or sport science areas are confronting, such as exercise physiology, biomechanics, and sports administration. The challenges are naturally intertwined but they can be discussed independently.

The Pressure of Public Accountability

Most, if not all, universities in North America have been pressured to become more accountable to the public society within which they exist. This pressure is usually articulated as a demand for more service to the community and, in part, has resulted from the traditional criticism of universities as nonresponsible "ivory towers." This quasi-traditional antipathy between "town and gown" has been accentuated by the considerable restrictions and funding cutbacks instituted by various governmental agencies. Universities are being asked to get more involved with the problems of society, to provide more practical services, and to do it with less money!

Although this has been disastrous for some of the more traditional disciplines such as the classics or English literature, it has not been that much of a crisis for disciplines such as physical education, clinical psychology, or engineering, which were already highly oriented toward an applied and/or practical service focus. Nevertheless, this pressure has been felt, and both undergraduate and graduate programs are undergoing basic modifications to meet this public demand.

The training of young sport psychologists will reflect this pressure. Emphasis in academic programs will shift more toward the preparation of clinical practitioners, consultants, and counselors. For example, a master's degree program in clinical sport psychology has recently been proposed at San Diego State University. Each sport science area in academic programs will respond to this pressure by producing better trained graduates who are equipped to work in the community and conduct research in the community as well as university settings.

The Pressure of a Saturated Job Market

The job market at the university level in the 1960s and early 1970s was sufficient to cover those just graduating from sport science programs. This was particularly true for sport psychology from approximately 1963 to 1975 as new university programs in the area absorbed each other's graduates with academic staff positions. The preparation of sport psychologists was aimed almost exclusively toward careers in universities and colleges. However, this market has gradually become saturated since 1975 and is now extremely tight in both the United States and Canada. When coupled with the pressure for more public involvement, the preparation of sport psychologists must now diversify to include a broader range of career opportunities outside the university.

In a rather strange juxtaposition of pressures, a sport psychologist will be forced to become more of a generalist in order to become more involved in the broad recreational aspects of youth sport—and more of a specialist in order to provide a more direct service to the elite athletic groups. Coaches and athletes at all levels of competition seem to be more cognizant of, and more receptive to, psychological consultants than ever before. This recognition of the importance of psychology in training and preparing athletes is creating a third type of pressure on the area, which may be defined as a demand for more applied professional service.

The Demand for Professional Service

Since the early 1970s, there has been an ever increasing demand by both coaches and athletes for more professional service from sport scientists in the areas of exercise physiology, biomechanics, sport psychology, sports administration, and skill instruction. In Canada the demand has attained a degree of organization through the Coaching Association of Canada, which has provided for the inclusion of sport science expertise as part of the National Coaching Certification Plan (NCCP). That is, a concerted attempt is being made to certify all youth coaches in Canada through five levels of certification which are replete with knowledge from the sport sciences. Out of this involvement with the NCCP has come an increased demand for specific services to teams and/or athletes at all levels of competition. Most of the early requests were in the areas of fitness training and skill instruction, but the demand for psychological services is now predominating.

The same pressure is occurring in the United States, but because there exists no formal coordinating agency like the Coaching Association of Canada, the demand is less easy to identify, describe, and analyze. However, numerous sport psychologists across the country are already working with teams and at the request of specific sports organizations. Perhaps more professional psychological services are being provided for athletes and coaches in the United States today than one would think. The U.S. Olympic Committee's official and formal involvement with the training and preparation of Olympic athletes at Colorado Springs will create a more visible demand for psychological services in the United States.

Up until now most of the demand for service has been to help coaches coach more effectively. However, many of these coaches are beginning to recognize the value of having a psychological consultant work directly with their athletes. This type of service, though fraught with problems and issues that have yet to be settled, is a big step forward for the area of sport psychology. In a sense, sport psychologists are finally coming out of the closet; though they have been helping coaches and athletes improve their performance for years, they have rarely been officially or formally recognized as viable contributors. This increased demand for service fits in nicely with the recent change in our thinking as to the major role of the sport psychologist in sport, namely the move away from a therapy structure and toward a more educational or developmental framework.

The Promotion of a Human Development Model. There is little doubt that the dominant wave in sport psychology in both the near and distant future will revolve around a human development or educational model. Danish and Hale (1981) identify this framework as one that (a) incorporates statements about desirable goals of behavior; (b) focuses on sequential change; (c) emphasizes techniques of optimization (rather than remediation); (d) considers the individual as an integrated biopsycho-social unit and thus amenable to a multidisciplinary focus; and (e) views individuals (or systems) as developing in a changing biocultural context.

Whether or not such a model is new in sport psychology is open to discussion. As Wankel has aptly observed, "This has always been the dominant wave in sport psychology" (personal communication, Feb. 1982). From the beginning, sport psychology in North America has grown out of an educational physical education background, orientation, and philosophy. Though more individuals from the parent discipline of psychology (clinical, applied, etc.) are currently working in sport and recreation, the overwhelming majority in the area are essentially people with a perspective directed toward performance enhancement and overall human development. This perspective is consistent with the normal goals and attitudes of education in general. The "medical" or "therapeutic" model has been more representative of sport psychology in Europe and the Iron Curtain countries, and has never really been a prevalent force in North America. Thus, the "shrink" image of a sport psychologist has essentially been more a figment of the media's imagination than of our own.

Danish and Hale (1981), however, place the educational model into a better and more specific context. They suggest that this model: (a) views the crises and problems of athletes as being states of imbalance that precede growth and make growth possible—not as pathological states; (b) views psychological intervention in crises as attempting to help the individual enhance his/her ability to deal with these experiences—not simply as correcting the problem; (c) views athletes and coaches from a humanistic perspective, with an emphasis on long-term personal growth and development rather than on short-term "cures"; (d) views the goal of intervention as assisting athletes to control their own behavior and lives (rather than work under manipulative or dependency models)[1] (i.e., life management through planning); and (e) views the ability to set intelligent and realistic goals as central to the intervention process.

These authors view athletes as an ideal group to work with because the type of the situation that constantly confronts them requires a positive statement of what they want and expect to do. Athletes are also invariably high in motivation, with dedication and personal sacrifice being a common concomitant of their daily effort. Setting positive goals thus becomes the first step in optimizing development, with the second step being to identify and solve the problems in attaining these goals.

This direction is surely the one major development in sport psychology that is exciting and attractive to everyone. For some, who have been involved in the area for over 15 years, it is a rearticulation and reaffirmation of major objectives identified several years ago. For the young sport psychologist, it represents an opportunity to become involved in one of the major thrusts of the field. Psychological Skills Training Programs (PSTPs)[2] are appearing or are already operating at several North American universities. They are often directed toward elite intercollegiate athletes, yet their potential contribution to athletes of all ages and skill levels seems unlimited. Such programs are contributing to a ma-

---

[1]Author's emphasis.

[2]PSTPs can be described as programs that identify, analyze, instruct, and train the cognitive, mental, or psychological skills most directly related to athletic performance. They are based on the premise that cognitive skills are identical to physical skills in that they can be acquired or enhanced through instruction, training, and practice. The most obvious skills receiving attention now are those of stress management, concentration, and self-instructional imagery.

jor shift away from an image of team shrinks (i.e., a quasi-psychiatric person who deals only with "head cases" or problem athletes on the team) to one of counselor or consultant. The programs also give the sport psychologist an opportunity to work with the "normal," motivated, highly skilled athletes—not just athletes with emotional or social problems.

The Merging of the Human Performance and Sport Psychology Subareas

The image shift, to more service to the community, will increase the pressure on the more research-oriented and/or theoretical subarea of human performance (and its information processing emphasis) to become more applied. As this pressure increases, those working in the subareas of motor control, motor learning, and human performance may become involved in more sports-relevant research—a research emphasis that has been quite prevalent in the sport psychology subarea for several years. Such activity could draw these two subareas more closely together. These subareas (motoric area and sport psychology) began splitting apart in the late 1960s and early 1970s because of essentially different interests, objectives, and research techniques. One major difference has always been the division over the relative importance of theory building and testing versus the application of theory to practice.

Of course, this has not always been a clean distinction; individuals in each subarea have been involved in both theoretical or applied projects. There has been a subtle division along this line, however, and this demarcation could subside if professionals in the motoric area did more applied research and sport psychology professionals became more concerned about testing basic theory.[3]

Another major difference between both subareas has been the mutual "territorial" division of performance and behavior. Analysis of performance, particularly motor performance, has long been the territory of those people concerned with the motor learning, motor control, and information processing dimensions of human performance. (This is evident from scanning the papers published in the NASPSPA and CSPLSP proceedings during the 1970s.) A subtle division has occurred where one group became interested in the dependent variable of performance (motoric area) while the other group was concerned with the endless numbers of independent variables that influence performance (sport psychology).

[3]At the 1981 International Congress of Sport Psychology in Ottawa, there were over 30 papers dealing with information processing and "sport." In addition, at recent NASPSPA meetings sport psychology research has demonstrated more concern for theory testing and development.

This demarcation has now become obscured, due in part to the recent interest in "interactional analysis" and its emphasis on the complex interrelationships between personality, situations, and performance or behavior. Also, both groups are slowly realizing that they need each other to really explore problems and issues that are common to or intermixed within each of the two subareas. Cooperation, either willing or forced, could help merge both groups. The alternative to this greater merging, in contrast, would most likely result in the establishment of separate organizations for sport psychology and the motoric area.

PREDICTIONS FOR THE FUTURE

What, then, is the future for sport psychology? What will sport psychologists be doing 10 or 20 years from now? What will their major challenges be in the future? I am tempted to respond by saying "who knows?" After all, I am not a futurologist either by training or inclination! Proceeding carefully from what has happened and what is going on in the field today, however, the following predictions are offered:

1. The field will become much more applied over the next 20 years. Pressure from the community demands such a redirection, and this, coupled with the theoretical information and knowledge we now have, will enhance the willingness to apply this information to practical problems and issues.

2. Life as a sport psychologist at the university or college level will be tougher and more demanding. Government restrictions and cutbacks in funding for universities will continue well into the 1980s and this will put even more pressure on university personnel both to serve the public and to publish more and higher quality research.

3. Because of the paucity of university and college staff positions across North America today, more graduates will go into private business to utilize their training. Sport psychology consulting and counseling in the private sector will increase dramatically over the next few years, causing a significant change in the type of research done in the universities. First, the research will become more applied, clinical, and technique-oriented. Second, our general philosophical orientation toward sport will become more realistic and less idealistic. Third, the training of graduate and undergraduate students will have more of a vocational emphasis, involving internship and the possibility of certification/licensure.

4. There will be more pressure to certify sport psychology consultants working out in the field. There will also be considerable pressure to formulate an acceptable code of ethics to which everyone will be re-

quired to adhere. Standards of conduct and modes of behavior will be much more rigidly observed and, hopefully, enforced over the next few years. These issues will be of major importance to organizations such as CSPLSP and NASPSPA.

5. Sport psychology will show an obvious shift toward the human development or educational model. Academics and professionals in the field will be more concerned with the development of one's potential than with the therapeutic or remedial handling of an individual's social or emotional problems.

6. Though the latter approach will continue to exist, the emphasis will be on the former. Because of the current interest and demand by coaches, sport psychologists will become more formally involved with representative, national, and professional sports teams. Sports psychologists will become accepted as permanent experts working with teams on a daily basis.

7. We will see sport psychologists working more and more as consultants to the parents and families of young athletes, and people in the social psychology of sport will become more applied and aware of psycho-physiological advances. These adjuncts will help advise community sport agencies about how sport programs can and should be structured to ensure maximum benefits for all, regardless of the level of competition.

PART II

PERSONALITY
AND PERFORMANCE
IN SPORT

The study of personality and the role it may play in performance has interested sport psychologists for decades. Perhaps this is because contributions that enhance our understanding of personality have the potential to be more than passing academic interests. Consider that many individuals involved in the sport environment have written and spoken about "born winners" and "born losers." Such statements imply that in addition to physical talents there is a certain psychological mix—a chemistry—that successful athletes have and unsuccessful athletes do not.

Personality is Complex

Are there truly relatively enduring personality characteristics (traits) that can have powerful effects upon how athletes perceive situations and how they act in these situations? If there are such characteristics, can they be identified? Can they be measured by sport psychologists with the current instrumentation? Are these characteristics inborn and resistant to change? Or can sport psychologists intervene and modify the characteristics that may inhibit an athlete from performing up to his or her potential? These questions are central to understanding the relationships between personality and performance. By studying them, investigators have come to understand that in addition to traits, the situation itself is an important causative variable that influences behavior. Thus, the term *interactionism* has been used to describe the impact that the person's characteristics (traits) and the situational or environmental variables *both* have upon actual behavior.

How does this interactional model really work in sport? Let's consider a common problem an athlete might face. A tennis player (Jan) has been playing exceptionally well, yet is behind in the match and simply is not getting any breaks. Jan has been moving her opponent around the court with several very good shots. Her opponent has been constantly on the ropes, but has repeatedly hit shots that just clear the net and fall in for points at crucial times during the set. Could you predict Jan's response? To answer this question, we must realize that her personality characteristics will interact with the environment we have just described. If Jan is generally an anxious person with little frustration tolerance and poor emotional control in competitive situations, she will most likely be quite distracted and will play poorly. If we modify this situation slightly and hold the personality variables constant, we can alter the probability of the predicted response. For example, if the situation is a nonthreatening Sunday recreational match at the playground courts perhaps Jan would not get extremely upset. But if this were the final match for the conference championship, Jan's high anxiety, low frustration tolerance, and poor emotional control could become very evident in her behavior.

Multivariate Approaches

Someone's emotional response to a situation is often called his or her *affect*. Just as enduring characteristics or traits interact with the environment, affect also has a role in sport performance. A trait predisposes an individual to exhibit a state or affective response in given situations. An athlete with poor emotional control will exhibit anger, frustration, and upset in more situations than will a person with good emotional control. Once a person experiences (overtly or covertly) a particular affect this psychological state can influence subsequent performance. So as you can see, we have a complex circular relationship in that traits predispose a person to respond a certain way in various situations, the nature of the situation often influences the degree of manifestation and, third, when behavioral responses are exhibited they often influence one's psychological state, which in turn can help or inhibit subsequent performance. Because of the complexity involved in studying personality-performance questions, researchers have begun to use multivariate models of assessment. These models allow for the simultaneous evaluation of several variables. For example, researchers can combine variables and study how the interactions between them influence performance in sport settings. Traits and states can be evaluated concurrently as can traits, states, and situations. By looking at combinations of these variables, sport psychologists can approximate more closely the true nature of the competitive environment within which the athlete must perform.

Theory, Measurement, and Intervention

The following section on personality and performance will review some major problems and issues that researchers face in studying personality and sport performance. John Silva's chapter will focus on strategies employed in the past as well as contemporary models used to study personality. A brief review of various theoretical positions that have shaped research in this area will give the reader an indication of the inherent complexities. The chapter concludes by identifying the potential benefits of studying personality and performance through multivariate sport-specific models.

The second chapter, by Craig Fisher, provides many good examples of how complex questions about sport performance and personality can be studied using interactional methodologies and assessment instruments. How we measure the relationships between personality and performance is extremely important to understand, and future researchers in sport psychology will be challenged to develop more sensitive and accurate instruments. In his chapter, Fisher aptly demonstrates how questions about individual responses within the group or team situation can be divided out and systematically studied. Knowing how an individual responds in various competitive settings is often the foundation upon which intervention programs are built. Intervention means that a clinician or sport psychologist tries to modify particular psychological sets or thought processes that may be inhibiting an athlete's performance. Through various techniques such as biofeedback, cognitive behavior modification, anxiety management training, and attentional control training, an athlete can be taught to identify and modify undesirable psychological responses that may occur before and during competition. Through self-regulation techniques, athletes can also be taught to maintain the desirable responses.

Daniel Kirschenbaum's chapter on cognitive behavioral interventions in sport reviews some of the current techniques that sport psychologists practice in trying to help athletes modify their psychological approach and response to competition. Because intervention is very closely tied to personality, the clinician attempts to modify a behavioral response as well as the underlying cognitions that have habitually supported the undesirable action. As the response introduced in intervention becomes dominant, the athlete can reduce undesirable responses such as those that have caused poor or inconsistent performance in the past. Intervention is often directed toward controlling prematch anxiety, the "choker syndrome," overassertive play, and loss of confidence, as well as many other important habitual patterns of predisposition, affect, or behavioral response.

As you can see, it is extremely important that as sport psychologists we know what personality is, how we can best measure and understand its impact upon performance, and how we can best initiate change that will assist athletes in realizing their full potential. Personality and performance is an exciting area for students, athletes, coaches, and researchers to learn about. We hope this section will generate that type of interest and excitement in you!

Chapter 5

Personality and Sport Performance: Controversy and Challenge

John M. Silva III
University of North Carolina-Chapel Hill

One of the earliest areas of study to receive systematic attention in the field of sport psychology was the study of personality. To many researchers and coaches it seemed reasonable to assume that consistencies in behavior, or predispositions to behave in a particular manner (traits), could influence one's athletic ability. As with many reasonable assumptions, the simplicity of the assumption disguised the complex nature of the question. Understanding the relationship between personality and sport is indeed a complex and often confounding area of inquiry. Researchers have been investigating this area for over 25 years in their attempt to answer questions that could influence the very presentation of sport and physical activity to participants. Before we examine the general approaches of the past and prospects for the future, we should define personality and review some of the major questions in this area of sport psychology.

PERSONALITY DEFINED

What is personality? How can our personalities influence performance or the attractiveness of particular sports for us? The basic question is, what forces/factors influence how we behave? Personality consists of an individual's characteristic patterns of behavior that contribute to his or her uniqueness (Baron, Byrne, & Kantowitz, 1980). Personality can be studied along three distinct yet related dimensions: (a) the personality structure, (b) the dynamics of personality, and (c) the development and modification of personality dimensions.

Personality structure refers to the basic elements or traits of an individual and how they blend together to exhibit that individual's particular behavioral tendencies in certain situations. The study of personality traits, or relatively enduring characteristics possessed by individuals, has been an extremely popular area of inquiry in both psychology and sport psychology. Study of the dynamics of personality attempts to understand how an individual's various characteristics interact and operate to influence behavior. Many sport psychologists, for example, have been interested in how anxiety levels may influence athletic performance or how anxiety levels could interact with achievement motivation to influence performance. Personality development relates to the processes (genetic and environmental) that influence the likelihood that an individual will possess various characteristics. Additionally, this area studies how various modifications in behavior occur through experience or intervention. Obviously, sport psychologists working with athletes in the development of psychological skills are most interested in the processes that influence personality and behavioral change.

CONTROVERSY IN SPORT PERSONOLOGY

Sport psychologists studying personality have asked some very interesting questions relating to each of the three dimensions of personality reviewed above. For example, do athletes who play a particular sport possess similar personality characteristics? Do elite athletes from different sports possess homogeneous personalities? These questions clearly relate to the personality structure or behavioral tendencies of the athlete. When sport psychologists study how an athlete with a strong external locus of control is influenced by failure experiences in competition, or how highly aggressive athletes respond to frustration or delayed gratification, they are investigating questions that relate to the dynamic dimension of personality.

Questions in the third area (development) have significant impact, not only for the field of sport psychology but also for society as a whole. For example, does sport build character? Is competitive sport participation related to positive psychological development? These questions have ramifications that extend well beyond the boundaries of a football field or a basketball court.

Although the questions about personality and sport have been important and interesting, few conclusive answers have resulted from the hundreds of studies conducted. Researchers, coaches, and students have all been frustrated in trying to sort out the personality and sport jigsaw puzzle. Leaving fundamental questions unanswered has resulted in considerable controversy in the sport personality area. Morgan (1980a), for example, has argued that two "camps" have emerged from this confusion. The skeptical camp maintains that the study of personality structure is of little value and cannot help us understand the personality and performance relationships that may exist. A second camp, called the credulous perspective, is characterized by individuals who believe that the study of traits can predict various relationships between personality, participation patterns and, ultimately, performance.

Morgan's article quite effectively demonstrates two of the major reasons for the chaos that has existed, and to a considerable extent still exists, in the sport personology area. The first reason relates to the theoretical assumptions (or lack of them) made by many sport psychologists working in this area. Many "experts" unconditionally reject theoretical perspectives other than those they have selectively chosen to defend. Since several theoretical perspectives exist in the field of sport personology, some investigators have resorted to a brand of protectionism and censorship that attempts to constantly find the holes rather than the thread in the material of sport personality research. However, as we will discuss shortly, an interactional model could offer an accommodating theoretical perspective generating several testable hypotheses about the nature of personality and performance relationships.

The second major factor contributing to the chaos in the personology area relates to the methodological approaches taken in the past to study this area, and the problems that have plagued some of these approaches. The following section will review some of the more important paradigms used to explain personality that have been adopted by sport personologists. It will also review basic methodological approaches and the problems encountered when conducting studies in this area. The final section will examine some suggestions and current research that seems to be moving cautiously forward with the task at hand — understanding personality and sport performance relationships.

MAJOR PARADIGMS IN SPORT PERSONOLOGY

The term *paradigm* was popularized by T.S. Kuhn (1970) during the early 1970s. A paradigm is nothing more than a model adopted for an explanatory framework. The use of such a conceptual framework provides a procedure for observing and testing theoretical positions. Paradigms represent important advances that group together concepts in a cohesive, coherent, and testable form. Sport personologists have advocated various personality paradigms as "appropriate" facilitators to the understanding of sport selection, performance, and involvement or adherence. The model that a researcher adopts will strongly influence his or her general orientation to the study of sport personology questions. Although there are numerous personality paradigms, we will briefly review three models encompassing several major theoretical perspectives that are widely employed in sport personology research. These paradigms will be identified as (a) the deterministic perspective, (b) the trait perspective, and (c) the interactional perspective.

The Deterministic Perspective

Deterministic perspectives maintain that behavior is determined *for* an individual rather than *by* an individual. Generally, theories falling under this perspective were strongly influenced by 19th century deterministic-positivistic philosophy that viewed the human being as an energy system. Just as physical energy that produces physical output can be attributed to the interaction of various systems (circulation, respiration, etc.), psychic energy is produced by various systems of the subconscious (e.g., id, ego, superego) that interact to produce behavior. Each system is viewed as having its own principles and functions that influence and regulate behavior. Major theorists in this perspective include Freud (1900, 1901, 1917), Adler (1929), Fenichel (1954), Horney (1924), Jung (1926), and Klein (1950).

Common to most theories within the deterministic perspective was the idea that subconscious processes regulated behavior. It was also maintained that the basic dimensions of personality were being determined at a relatively early age through the resolution of unconscious psychic conflicts. The origins of these conflicts were said to reside in the individual's past and in the development of his or her sexual identity, competence strivings, and moral development (Gleitman, 1981). Additionally, some deterministic theories such as Freud's (1900) held that the basic psychic conflicts are biologically rather than culturally based. Thus, it has been argued that these conflictual determinants of behavior will be found in essentially the same form in all men and women.

Unfortunately, the deterministic perspective has not really helped answer the important sport personology questions raised earlier in this chapter. Specific and testable hypotheses relevant to sport have not been generated or investigated. While several sport psychologists may adhere to deterministic perspectives for clinical purposes (e.g., Freud's psychoanalytic theory) little useful data has been accumulated based upon this model. Since such a heavy emphasis is placed on subconscious processes, it is difficult to measure the cause-effect relationships between these psychic processes and overt behavior. Kubie (1952) over 30 years ago pointed to the great difficulty in predicting behavior from this paradigm. The major difficulty is that a given set of relational rules do not exist in many deterministic perspectives. The inability to predict behavior under certain psychic events has led some psychologists to maintain that deterministic models can explain all but predict nothing (a post hoc theory).

In spite of the limitations cited above, it should be noted that the deterministic paradigm has had some impact upon the theoretical approach taken by some to study sport personology. Kroll (1970) and Morgan (1972) have suggested that one explanation of the relationship between personality and sport participation may relate to a "gravitational model." This orientation would assume that individuals with a particular personality tend to participate in a certain sport. Deterministic perspectives note the early development of personality and the enduring aspect of personality characteristics. If certain personality characteristics are more desirable for a particular sport, those who possess these characteristics will have a better chance of succeeding in their chosen sport.

Since many participants get involved in sports at a very early age, some might question whether it is the child's personality that *draws* him or her to play in a sport. For example, the social environment (parents, significant others) has been shown to strongly influence young children's sport participation in research by Snyder and Spreitzer (1973). And the homogeneity of personality characteristics of specific sport groups from entry through higher competitive levels has yet to be documented through longitudinal research (e.g., Hardman, 1968, 1973; Whiting & Hendry, 1969).

In conclusion, the deterministic perspective has stimulated some thinking and writing among sport psychologists, and various consultants have used this orientation to intervene psychologically with athletes. Thus the heuristic value of the deterministic orientation should not be underestimated. However, this model has had limited value in contributing to our understanding of personality and sport. Psychologists and sport psychologists have looked to more testable concepts of personality that afford the opportunity to measure and predict subsequent behavior.

The Trait Perspective

The trait perspective gave psychologists a legitimate alternative to the relatively nonquantifiable tenets of deterministic models. The trait model's key assumption is that traits, as relatively enduring characteristics, predict an individual's behavior in a variety of situations. In other words, it is believed that personality traits are generalizable and allow one to predict behavior even in normal situations (Allport, 1937). Carron (1975) has suggested that sport psychology researchers searching for personality profiles in athletes or athletic groups implicitly or explicitly adopt the trait perspective. Generally what has happened in the past could be described as follows: A researcher gains access to a sample of high school, college, or Olympic athletes, finds an available trait test, measures the athletes, and then describes the sample. The results of this study are then compared and contrasted with other trait assessments made with a similar athletic group.

Simplistic attempts of comparing psychological profiles derived from different trait inventories with athletes from various competitive levels created contradiction and confusion in the personality area. While some sport psychologists (viz., Ogilvie & Tutko, 1972) proposed that a coherent personality picture had emerged and that this profile was most consistent at elite levels of competition, others argued differently. A more conservative estimation of the relationship between personality traits and athletic performance has been advanced by Fisher (1977) and also by Singer, Harris, Kroll, Martens, and Sechrest (1977). These authors have emphasized the need to modify the rationale for test selection and they also suggest revising the manner in which personality data are analyzed and reported. The trait approach, for example, is seen as an exercise in futility or a searching for the "ideal profile" that may not truly exist at any competitive level.

Other sport psychologists recommend, however, that the trait perspective not be abandoned but instead that it be used properly (Carron, 1980; Morgan, 1980a). That is, the basic assumption of sport psychology, which maintains that an individual's various characteristics can influence behavior in various situations, may not be totally invalid. Rather, the manner in which sport psychologists have employed trait measures to compare various athletes and athletic groups has been unsystematic, nonlongitudinal, and pseudoscientific.

To dismiss the trait perspective because of the improper use of trait measures may be premature. When researchers measure and describe an athletic group and then isolate its members from past members of the group as well as future members, it is not surprising that the results often conflict. Martens (1975b) and many others have documented the methodological problems that have plagued sport personality research utilizing the trait approach. Five of the major methodological limitations are outlined in the following paragraphs.

First, there is a reliance on univariate statistical analyses even though the study of personality in sport is clearly multivariate. Univariate techniques compare two or more groups on one variable at a time and cannot accommodate the interactions that may occur between various psychological or physiological variables. The researcher is left with several "snapshots" of what is being studied but never has the full picture in a realistic context.

Second, questionable sampling techniques are sometimes employed. A major limitation here is exemplified by researchers who study small, intact groups of athletes (teams) that are characterized by considerable heterogeneity of skill level and commitment. The evaluation of such groups makes it extremely difficult to generalize to other athletic groups.

Third, the use of the "average personality profile" is often inappropriate. When psychological measures are averaged across individuals, a mean or average personality is often reported. Yet this profile may not really represent any athlete in the sample because the mean is often affected by extreme scores. However, the reporting of the average personality is appropriate when the standard deviation within a group is small, in which case the average personality profile is actually quite representative and provides some evidence for the strength or importance of the dimension measured.

Fourth, there is a lack of systematic examination of sport forms from early competitive levels through higher competitive levels. Personologists should try to understand the consistencies and variations that exist *within a sport* at various competitive levels. After such an understanding concerning a particular level, researchers can then try to determine if any personality characteristics tend to generalize across sports at particular competitive levels.

Fifth, there is a general lack of specificity in the operationalization of the variables under study and the tests selected. Researchers must carefully define terms such as athlete and nonathlete, elite and nonelite, and college athlete versus college participant. One plausible reason for inconsistency in the findings of many personality studies may be that there has been considerable heterogeneity of athletic groups being compared with one another. The psychological test chosen should also be selected according to its ability to measure specific psychological characteristics deemed to be of value or interest.

In the following chapter, Craig Fisher will review some alternative methodologies that vary from the trait approach in that they employ the basic tenets of social learning theory by utilizing an interactional model. This model attempts to integrate information both from the individual's traits and the situation within which he or she is interacting. While the interaction approach is viewed by many as an improvement over the trait approach, it is important to note that the methodological problems reviewed above are generic to personality research. Although these methodological shortcomings have often been ascribed to trait research, they are not exclusive to that approach. Researchers studying personality from *any* model must be aware of methodological problems that can retard our understanding of personality and performance. In attempting to resolve these dilemmas, many sport psychologists have begun to seriously examine the interactional paradigm as a viable alternative perspective.

The Interactional Perspective

The interactional paradigm encompasses many social learning theories that integrate the influence of both the situation and the person upon overt behavior. The model emerged from various social learning perspectives such as Rotter's (1954) influential social learning theory and the work of Bandura (1962) and Mischel (1973). In examining the interactional paradigm some important concepts become evident. Perhaps this perspective's most distinguishing characteristic is its emphasis upon situational specificity; individuals regulate their behavior according to the situation (Rotter, Chance, & Phares, 1972). As characteristics of the situation change, behavioral expectancies are modified. Additionally, the individual's uniqueness is emphasized through the concepts of reinforcement histories and reinforcement value (Rotter, 1954; Rotter et al., 1972).

Reinforcement histories refer to the idea that behavior does not occur in a vacuum, and individuals are aware of the reward and punishment contingencies related to particular actions. This awareness comes from previous experiences, be they direct (Tolman, 1949) or vicarious (Bandura, 1962). Rotter (1954) has defined these learning histories as generalized expectancies. As such, they epitomize interactionism because they acknowledge that the individual's previous experiences interact with the stimuli of the present situation. The concept of reinforcement value operates similarly because it recognizes individual tendencies and situational specificity. For example, not all rewards hold the same value for an individual, and individuals often value the same reward differently. Thus, some diversity in behavior is implicitly built into this model.

Various sport psychologists have applied interactional principles to their research approaches in sport personology. Martens (1975b) was an early advocate of this perspective and has subsequently developed sport-specific measures such as the Sport Competition Anxiety Test (SCAT) in an attempt to detect situational variables in competition that may be anxiety provoking. By measuring anxiety through questions that relate directly to sports contexts, Martens' instrument can indicate a respondent's general expectancies to feel anxious in competitive situations as opposed to nonsport situations.

Morgan (1980a) has advanced what is essentially an interactional position by advocating the combination of state and trait testing when conducting personality research in sport. By measuring states, the researcher is examining the psychological responses a subject exhibits in a specific situation (usually the precompetitive period). The measurement of traits indicates one's dispositional tendencies to behave in a certain manner in various situations. Thus, by using this information "in concert," a researcher will not only enhance the understanding of how personality variables influence performance (e.g., Deshaies, Pargman, & Thiffault, 1979; Morgan, 1973a; Silva, Shultz, Haslam, & Murray, 1981) but will also get an indication of whether an athlete is responding to competition in a manner consistent with his or her trait profile or, instead, a manner that would indicate situational constraints (for example, a low trait-anxious individual experiencing extremely high state anxiety).

Interactional paradigms suggest not only specificity (e.g., Martens' SCAT) but also a multivariate approach in understanding the variables that may influence sport performance. In and of themselves, sport activities are different situations since they often place specific psychological, physiological, and motoric demands upon participants. If the interactional paradigm aids our understanding of personality and sport, it would seem that sport-specific multivariate models provide the most effective use of interactionism. Offered in the following section will be a sport-specific model for understanding personality and sport performance, along with a brief overview of some research examples that have employed both an interactional model and multivariate analyses.

INTERACTIONISM
AND SPORT-SPECIFIC MODELS

In the previous section we noted that various sports place specific demands upon the athlete. We also discussed how interactional models emphasize an individual's social learning in particular situations providing for behavioral diversity in the interactional model. If these premises are correct, a sport-specific model that would allow for some diversification as well as some homogeneity in personality characteristics would seem useful in testing for specific sports. This model is illustrated in Figure 5-1.

Shown in the pyramid are several important factors that should be discussed. First, the pyramid is related to what Kroll (1970) identified as the modification and attrition model, one of the five models he offered as possible explanations for the personality and performance relationship. In the Kroll model no common personality characteristics existed initially, but through modification (learning) and attrition athletes with adaptable or suitable characteristics persist in the sport. Thus, novice players would appear to be dissimilar whereas veteran players would be similar.

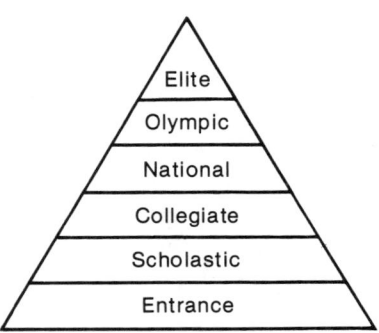

FIGURE 5-1   The personality-performance pyramid.

The pyramid offers a comparable view of the personality and performance relationship. The pyramid is broadest at entrance levels, allowing for the greatest amount of heterogeneity in personality characteristics. It would not be surprising to find inconsistencies among personality profiles of athletes *within the same sport* at this level. As athletes are exposed to the psychological, physiological, and other demands of their sport, however, some find that particular traits enhance their ability to perform while other traits may impede it. Therefore, in moving up the pyramid's competitive ladder we would expect more homogeneity in the personality of participants. Yet even at the elite level there is room for individual differences.

Another major point to remember is that the pyramid is a sport-specific model. Common characteristics of elite athletes in one sport may differ from those of elite athletes in another sport who are challenged by a different set of circumstances. While recognizing this situational specificity, the model does allow for investigators to determine if any factors are common components for success across various sports. For example, a variable such as emotional stability or low trait anxiety may be highly related to success regardless of the sport form being evaluated. Thus, specificity and diversity of characteristics can be evaluated as a function of competitive level and the nature of the sport form.

The final aspect of the pyramid is that it supports a multivariate approach to the study of sport performance. Researchers can develop a model measuring psychological, physiological, and motoric components that are unique or appropriate for a particular sport. For example, Deshaies et al. (1979) employed a multivariate model to evaluate national-level hockey players; the model differed considerably from the multivariate model Silva et al. (1981) employed for national-level wrestlers. Both models shared some common factors but each was unique enough to measure the specific demands required of participants in each sport.

Other researchers such as Landers and his colleagues (Landers, Christina, Hatfield, Daniels, & Doyle, 1980) have employed multivariate techniques that have recognized the interactional nature of competitive sports. In studying rifle shooters, Landers et al. (1980) found that psychophysiological processes such as heart rate, breath hold, and the degree of psychophysiological synchrony relate very highly with shooting performance.

Multivariate approaches such as those mentioned above were advocated by Morgan (1973a) over a decade ago. While several researchers have employed this technique (e.g., Deshaies et al., 1979; Nagle, Morgan, Hellickson, Serfass, & Alexander, 1975; Williams, 1978a) the refinement and development of sport-specific models has not been pursued until recently (e.g., Landers et al., 1980; Silva et al., 1981; Silva, Shultz, Haslam, Martin, & Murray, 1983). By conducting longitudinal research with specific sport teams, a reliable and accurate sport-specific model may eventually be established at higher levels of competition where greater homogeneity or pattern of responses may be expected.

Training prescriptions based upon these findings could then be offered from a data base. This is essentially what Daniels and Landers (1981) did with the results of some of the breath hold/heart rate research conducted on shooters. By employing biofeedback techniques, shooters were able to coordinate individual autonomic responses with shooting responses and thus optimize shooting accuracy. Thus when systematically approached, personality research can aid our understanding of sport performance and can also provide the important information needed for effective intervention or behavior change programs. (For a more thorough discussion of intervention techniques, see Chapter 7 by Kirschenbaum and Wittrock.)

CONCLUSION

As with any paradigm, the interactional model will not solve problems on its own. Rather, this model should be viewed in its broad context as a tool designed to help us answer the basic questions left unanswered by our initial efforts in the personology area. Without a systematic plan or approach, the interactional model could fall prey to the same shotgun approach that smattered the trait research during the 1960s and 1970s. An accumulation of 100 research studies that employ an interactional model may not be any more enlightening than the accumulation of the trait research we now have. The personality/performance pyramid, and the flexible structure it provides, should be pursued by contemporary sport personality researchers as a viable framework within which to conduct research.

Chapter 6

New Directions
in Sport Personality Research

A. Craig Fisher
Ithaca College

As mentioned in the preceding chapter by John Silva, personality literature of the recent past has been characterized by debates, controversies, and arguments about the relative merits of various theoretical positions and methodologies (e.g., Endler & Magnusson, 1976; Magnusson & Endler, 1977). Sport personality literature of the late 1960s and the 1970s examined such concerns as the personality trait differences between athletes and nonathletes, successful and less successful athletes (e.g., Olympic gold medalists vs. other Olympic athletes), athletes playing one position versus another (e.g., hockey goaltenders vs. other hockey players), team and individual sport athletes (e.g., football players vs. wrestlers), and male and female athletes (e.g., track). Several sport researchers also considered the impact of sport participation on personality development and change.

Although well over 1,000 studies were conducted in this so-called heyday of sport personality research, the unfortunate conclusion is that limited knowledge was gained in the areas that concern both sport psychologists and coaches. This leaves two inescapable interpretations: Either personality characteristics are not very significant to the various group differences investigated and personality does not change with sport participation, or the methodology and the subsequent results are suspect. Which explanation is correct?

Let's describe the methodology of the typical sport personality investigations referred to and then highlight the underlying assumptions. A

70

personality inventory was selected from the popular list (Cattell Sixteen Personality Factor Questionnaire—16PF, California Psychological Inventory—CPI, Minnesota Multiphasic Personality Inventory—MMPI, and Edwards Personal Preference Schedule—EPPS) and administered to specific athletic groups. The individual personality characteristics in turn were each examined for group differences, and hypotheses were accepted or rejected. That may sound quite acceptable at this point, but one should suspend judgment until the assumptions underlying this typical study are considered.

First, and most important, the trait model of personality was implicitly adopted. In this perspective, personality traits are viewed as enduring and nonchanging characteristics which remain relatively consistent regardless of the situation. Differences in behavior are thus due to individual differences in personality traits. For example, if two athletes are administered an aggression inventory the athlete who reveals the higher score will be expected to display more aggression in most sport situations. Yet doesn't experience tell us that we behave differently in different situations? Should we expect an aggressive person to continually exhibit aggression even in the face of impending defeat? Is not discretion sometimes the better part of valor? As you apply these questions to your own behavior, you are perhaps left with the very strong feeling that you adapt your behavior to the particular demands of the situation. You are living evidence that personality traits alone are not adequate precursors of behavior.

Research by Endler and his co-workers (e.g., Endler & Hunt, 1966, 1968), among others, has certainly raised the issue of the validity of explaining behavior using the trait perspective. Typically, personality traits explain no more than 10% of the behavioral variability in any given situation. That leaves 90% behavioral variance unexplained. This important finding needs to be elaborated because it is very damaging to the trait model of behavior.

As most of us already know, people do vary their behavior across situations. If the range of the fluctuations of behavior is represented by 100% variance, or all the variability there is, then 10% explained variance is not particularly illuminating. Such findings provide little confidence that behavior can be understood solely from the assessment of personality traits. Kroll (1970) offered a metaphorical conclusion about the methodological limitations of the trait model; he said investigators were fishing for minnows with a net designed to catch whales. It is not surprising that much of the catch sifted through the openings in their nets!

As a sport personality investigator who faced the dilemma of collecting data within accepted conceptual and methodological constraints, I felt it necessary to verify the limitations of the trait model. Certainly the findings from nonsport settings substantiated the arguments of the trait critics; traits do not adequately describe, explain, or predict behavior. However, the possibility exists that traits might explain substantial behavioral variance with athletes in sport settings, and thus the sport personality literature might be somewhat insulated from the critics of trait psychology. That possibility could be entertained if athletes were more homogeneous than nonathletes (i.e., athletes within a sport group possessed some common characteristics) and if the situations in which behavior was to be understood were also more homogeneous than general life situations (i.e., the task demands of a sport context were not as variable as general situations).

My colleagues and I conducted a series of investigations to compare our sport results with the nonsport findings. Research on anxiety in basketball (Fisher, Horsfall, & Morris, 1977) and football (Czarnecki, 1977), hostility in contact sports (Burton, 1977), and behavioral rigidity in various sport situations (Fisher, Borowicz, & Morris, 1978) paralleled almost exactly the results obtained in general psychology research. Variance explained by our subjects' personality characteristics in question was as minimal in sport settings as was reported earlier in general settings. From my perspective, searching for the elusive behavioral variance with a methodology whose ceiling is 10% is not something I would relish. This is not to indicate that 10% variance due to personality is insignificant, but to embark on a research strategy knowing that one is so limited is foolhardy. It was also very apparent from the sport studies that situational demands contribute to behavioral variance and need to be considered.

After weighing the debates among psychologists and knowing the growing reservations that sport personality researchers harbored toward the trait model (and given the results of our own investigations), it became apparent that a more appropriate research methodology was needed. Strong evidence exists for interactionism, a model that simultaneously considers both person and situation variables.

INTERACTIONAL MODEL OF BEHAVIOR

The social learning theorist assigns a great deal of importance to the situations in which people find themselves in order to explain behavioral responses to those situations. Just as the trait theorist views traits as important behavioral predictors, social learning theorists stress the interaction of the person and the situation. Sport personality studies have been limited because they have failed to include any systematic analysis of the sport environments in which athletes are immersed. "To remedy this deficiency some attention must be focused on various means of classifying situations," notes Mischel (1977, pp. 250-251). One such attempt to classify sport environments has been presented in a comprehensive system offered by Billing (1975). It is important to realize, however, that the singular focus on situations will be no more effective than the singular focus on traits has been (Endler & Hunt, 1966, 1968). How can we avoid what might be the inevitable disconsolate abandoning of the personality area? Where do we look for some assistance to our apparent dilemmas? In their review of personality literature, Phares and Lamiell (1977) offer a starting point upon which to build appropriate methodologies. They state,

> We somehow need to harness the potent technologies of factor analysis, multidimensional scaling, and related methods in order to provide some beginnings in the classifications of situations. Of course some guiding theory is absolutely necessary here also to impart a sense of direction to our efforts. (p. 115)

But before we look to new methodologies to solve our problems, we must adopt a guiding theoretical perspective that will direct our efforts. The logical replacement of the once popular trait model for many psychologists and sport psychologists is interactionism — a model that simultaneously takes into account both person and situation variables.

To seriously begin understanding athletes' behavior, and to improve or predict performance outcomes, the reciprocal interaction between the athlete as a person and the specific sport environment must be considered (Bandura, 1978). Reciprocal interaction means that behavior, personality, and environment are interdependent. Personality influences behavior and behavior affects personality. For example, highly anxious athletes who worry about their performance often behave less competently. To make matters worse, the less competent outcomes increase the athlete's anxiety or worry about both past and future performance. Environmental demands also predispose certain behaviors, and these behaviors subsequently lead to particular perceptions of the environment. In sport, pressure situations such as the final seconds of a close game often lead to behaviors not normally exhibited (e.g., poor decisions), and because of poor performance those pressure situations connote failure.

It should be readily apparent that any methodology that intends to capture the essence of interactionism must be multidimensional and address the basic beliefs of the interactional model. Foremost, the methodology must be able to assess and/or describe both persons and situations simultaneously without over- or underestimating either. It is not sufficient to collect personality trait data in some general situations, nor is it adequate to record mood states in some general situations. Interactional methodologies must place specific sport situations in the forefront and obtain athletes' responses to these situations. For example, when the athlete is faced with a "be the hero or zero" circumstance, what degree of self-confidence does he or she exhibit? With this specificity both person and situation variance are built into the athlete's response. That is, from the range of self-confident behaviors that the athlete displays in sport, what response is associated with the win-or-lose situation?

Another necessary criterion is that data analysis must be *ipsative*, not *normative*. That is, individual data must be analyzable to keep the essence of individual differences alive. Although it is efficient and often necessary for data reporting to collapse athletes' personality data into mean scores, in doing so the idiosyncratic nature of a particular athlete's behavioral response may never be unearthed. Although the response variance across athletes is important for group analysis, the nature of the interactional model demands that primary attention be addressed to response variance within individuals (Bem & Funder, 1978).

At this point it may seem fruitless to look for answers to the questions both sport psychologists and coaches have about the relationship of personality characteristics to sport performance and participation. Is there enough behavioral consistency across sport situations to warrant an investigator's time and effort? Do athletes always exhibit different responses even in similar situations? This is a very important consideration because, without response consistency, there is no possibility of categorizing athletes' responses to certain classes of situations (e.g., anxiety-eliciting). Fortunately, the solution to this problem is addressed in the interactional model. Because each of us can make decisions and we generally behave in accord with our personal perceptions of situational demands, there is some definite rationale for our behavior. For example, an athlete tends to respond with heightened anxiety in situations that are personally threatening. This athlete responds congruently with the personal perception of the situation. As the interactional model postulates, adequate methodologies must take the psychological meaning of situations into account.

The last important criterion to constrain our search for adequate methodologies is that they must be able to handle a wide range of personality characteristics and situations. No matter what the personality characteristic (aggression, anxiety, attention, self-confidence) or the sport environment (open or closed skill, competitive or recreational) the chosen methodologies must provide quality data. It would be more efficient to have a restricted number of methodologies to conduct our investigations, rather than a different set of rules for every question we ask.

Are there data collection and statistical techniques that can satisfy the aforementioned interactional model requirements? First, let us take a look at Morgan's (1980b) choice of methodology. He argues that a state-trait model of personality would theoretically be the most effective in predicting athlete success. In one respect the combination of state and trait measures is an interactional model, although somewhat additive rather than multiplicative or reciprocal. By adding personality trait measures to various state or mood indices collected in a precompetitive sport setting, some person-in-context data are derived (e.g., Silva, Shultz, Haslam, & Murray, 1981). To the degree that the precompetitive setting contains the range of situational demands of the entire sport task, the responses of athletes just prior to competition could allow an investigator to describe, explain, and predict subsequent sport behavior.

Particular traits are salient if they induce certain affect in particular situations. For example, low self-esteem might lead one to expect failure in a difficult competitive task, and the negative expectations might induce excessive arousal and worry about performance outcomes. The physiological symptoms of anxiety such as muscle tension and the attention directed more toward internal feelings than preparation for competition would probably lead to poor performance. However, the key point is to assess the personality characteristics that have a logical link to sport performance through the affect that is created in particular sport settings. Just combining a number of trait and state measures in an additive sense, as in regression analysis, for instance, does not necessarily satisfy the demands of the interactional model. The trait measures must be logically meaningful, and the more specifically they are addressed to the particular sport demands, the more useful they will be to answer important sport personality questions.

Although meaningful information can be derived from athletes in the immediate context of competition, that is not always possible. Not all personality investigators have access to athletes just prior to competition, and it is not at all uncommon for coaches and athletes alike to disapprove of data collection just prior to competition. Recently, a discussion with a world-class athlete centered around his refusal to agree to a sport psychologist's request for his time and attention the night before competition. He had declined because he was more concerned with his own personal preparation. What is significant about this example is that the athlete himself was in the process of conducting a sport personality study. Although he had requested and received cooperation from athletes for his own data collection (not in precompetitive situations, however), he did not view his own lack of compliance in the competitive arena as unusual. Basically the message he conveyed was that he did not want to be bothered at that time. Unfortunately, this attitude is often encountered by sport psychologists who are interested in testing during the sensitive precompetitive period.

It would be tempting for sport investigators and coaches to throw their arms up in the air and abandon the search for personality and sport performance relationships. However, the belief that athletes' personality characteristics are related to sport participation and performance does not die easily. There are several reasons for this resistance: (a) some investigators (e.g., Morgan, 1980b) concluded their review of the sport personality literature with a sense that there were some consistent research findings (e.g., athletes' personalities differed from nonathletes'); (b) other investigators (e.g., Fisher & Zwart, 1982; Martens, 1977) foresaw some conceptual and methodological advances that addressed some of the major criticisms of the sport personality skeptics; and (c) still others could not deny their own personal sport experiences wherein certain personality characteristics made an impact on their own or others' sport performance.

Although Morgan (1980b) claimed that the state-trait model offered perhaps the most efficacious operationalization and assessment of personality, he suggested that other directions be investigated. He speculated that perceptual-cognitive models may prove to be equally or more effective than previous models. The personality model that most clearly emphasizes cognition and perception is the interactional model. One simply need look no further than two of the basic tenets of interactionism to see how central perception and cognition are to this model. Magnusson and Endler (1977) state:

> On the person side of the interaction, the cognitive factors are essential determinants of behavior, although emotional factors cannot be discounted.

> On the situation side of the interaction, the psychological meaning of the situation is the most determining factor. (p. 4)

TRUE INTERACTIONAL METHODOLOGIES

The S-R inventory approach, introduced by Endler, Hunt, and Rosenstein (1962), examined the effects of both different situations and people's personal means of responding to express a particular personality characteristic. Originally the S-R inventory was designed to study general anxiety, but in the last two decades this approach has been used to study dominance, hostility, interpersonal behavior, leisure activity, basketball and football anxiety, and contact sport hostility.

The task of sport personality researchers is to construct meaningful sport situations from the environments that interest them, such as basketball, and then get athletes to respond to these situations with a variety of personality indicants (e.g., for anxiety—heart beats faster). Of course, the situations must be representative of the sport environment in question, and the response modes must be congruent with the personality dimension under scrutiny. With this strategy, individual athletes can use whichever response modes seem most appropriate to capture their unique individuality. Inherent in such athletes-in-sport context data are the important individual differences so central to the comprehension of personality.

Let's examine the typical S-R data. In a recent study dealing with basketball anxiety, athletes rated the extent of their anxiety responses to various basketball situations (Fisher & Zwart, 1982). The situations dealt with pregame, game, and postgame circumstances, and were designed to elicit varying degrees of anxiety responses. Some of the basketball situations were as follows: (a) You have just committed a shooting foul with the score tied 70-70 and only 2 seconds remaining in the game. (b) The crowd is very loud and directing most of its comments toward you. (c) You have just made a bad play and your coach is criticizing you. (d) You are in the locker room after losing a game you really expected to lose. In each of the situations, athletes were asked to report the degree to which they exhibited such responses as the following: get an "uneasy" feeling; react overemotionally; want to avoid situation; get a "choking" feeling; enjoy the challenge.

You will recall that Morgan (1980b) speculated on the importance of a perceptual-cognitive model of behavior. The S-R data just described are colored by athletes' perceptions of the specific demands of each basketball situation, and the particular cognitive and emotional makeup of the athletes. When the data are collapsed across all situations for all athletes, composite responses to potentially anxiety-eliciting basketball situations are possible. However, what is needed is a data analysis technique through which some sense can be extracted from the data, not only maintaining the individual differences inherent in the data but also deciphering the personal patterns of athletes' responses. Let's briefly review two techniques that give a researcher this type of flexibility.

INDSCAL.   Individual differences scaling analysis (INDSCAL), from the family of multidimensional scaling analysis, allows the investigator to find meaning in a set of data without the subjects even being aware of the pattern of their responses. In effect, INDSCAL allows one to "see inside another's head" and understand that person's cognitive schema (the rules by which he or she makes decisions or responds in particular settings).

With the basketball anxiety data INDSCAL revealed three anxiety dimensions, namely ego threat, outcome certainty/uncertainty, and anticipation. Consistent with the individual differences flavor of the interactional model, INDSCAL also revealed the relative importance of each anxiety dimension for each athlete. A retrospective look at the S-R basketball data analyzed by INDSCAL leads to the inevitable conclusion that this personality assessment and analysis procedure meets the criteria of the interactional model extremely well. Persons and situations are treated interactively, individual differences are revealed and explained, and the methodology can deal with a wide variety of persons and environments.

   Contextual Template Matching. Contextual template matching (CTM) is another useful tool for exploring how the characteristics of persons and situations interact to determine behavior. This technique is an extension of the original template matching introduced by Bem and Funder (1978). Each behavioral pattern of interest, such as self-confidence, is characterized by a template that is nothing more than the personality description of the hypothetical ideal person (e.g., optimally self-confident person) most likely to exhibit that behavior in the situation of interest. Any individual's behavior is predicted by comparing his/her personality description with the ideal model.

   A specific sport example should clarify the template matching technique. If a sport personality investigator were interested in the self-confidence of athletes, perhaps three levels of the characteristic would come to mind: optimal self-confidence, low self-confidence or overcautiousness, and overconfidence. Three templates or ideal models could be created to represent the levels of self-confidence. Athletes' personality characteristics could then be correlated with each of the templates in turn to assess the magnitude of the relationships. If the match with overconfidence were highest, then it would be predicted that the athlete would display the bragging and arrogant behaviors characteristic of overconfident athletes.

   The California Q-set (CQ-set) (Block, 1978) is the instrument used by individuals to characterize their own personality. The CQ-set provides comprehensive coverage of the personality domain, which makes it applicable to a limitless number of personality characteristics and behaviors. The CQ-set consists of 100 descriptive personality statements (e.g., is uncomfortable with uncertainty and complexity; seeks reassurance from others; behaves in an assertive fashion), which are sorted by the respondent into nine categories ranging from least to most characteristic.

   But where does the context or situational specificity enter the methodology? Up to this point I have only offered a general personality assessment tool, which can deal with various personality characteristics. There are two ways to transfer the individual's self-sort from a global to a contextual perspective. The first is to request the athlete to sort the personality descriptors of the CQ-set according to how well each statement is characteristic and salient (both standards are important) of the self in the particular sport environment of interest. To the degree that the athlete can capture the essence of the sport demands in his/her mind while self-sorting, the data will represent person-situation interactions.

Of course, this remedy might logically be proposed to improve the traditional trait study. The problem, however, is that many of the trait inventories (e.g., Cattell 16 PF) will not accommodate such a contextual imposition.

A second approach is to specify the exact situational demands of the particular sport environment (e.g., wrestling—demands one to physically assert against another) and request athletes to self-sort the personality descriptions in the context of what task demands athletes must meet. This approach deals more systematically with personal characteristics and situational constraints, and results in athlete-in-sport context data. However, this task demands more time and effort from athletes, as well as the ability to tolerate some frustration due to the number of sorts that must be made.

The last step in template matching is to compare the athlete's contextual sort with the contextual template(s) created by a number of experts. For their part, the experts must have some experience (e.g., coaching) with the environment in question and they must know something about the personality characteristic under study. After a brief description of the personality characteristic is given to prospective experts, selection is based on whether they can recall past athletes who fit the prototype description. The chosen experts' ideal sorts are averaged to create the template.

CTM has proven to be a more effective method of describing, explaining, and predicting behavior than has the context-free template matching procedure. This is not surprising because the interactional model demands that the unit of analysis be the person-in-context. CTM opens many doors to sport personality investigators, and it does so in a way consistent with the most supportable theory of personality—interactionism. Every important feature of the interactional model (i.e., person-situation interaction, individual differences, cognitive-perceptual constraints) is addressed by CTM, and its wide applicability to diverse personality characteristics and environments make CTM a valuable personality methodology.

THE RE-EMERGENCE OF SPORT PERSONALITY

The initial part of this discussion painted a fairly bleak picture of the personality area, with researchers abandoning the ship in great numbers. Even a cursory review of the sport literature reveals that sport personality studies dwindled drastically in the late 1970s and early 1980s. However, the personality area is alive and well! Instead of disconsolately abandoning the area of study, I see five reasons for resurrecting it:

1. The current debates among advocates of trait theory and those supporting interactionism have actually revitalized the study of per-

sonality. Arguments, counter-arguments, and position papers have sparked renewed interest.

2. As investigators rushed to be part of the so-called cognitive revolution that swept psychology (i.e., renewed interest in the role that perceptions and thoughts play in behavior), they needed methodologies that satisfied beliefs. Fortunately, the interactional model of behavior offered a framework for their investigations. Current cognitive theories of personality view people as intentional actors in charge of their own behavior, seemingly a more logical and humanistic stance. And in a period of time when humanistic views are prevalent, methodologies that allow the "head and the heart" to influence actions are in step with the times.

3. New methodologies emerged that enable investigators to capture the important aspects of person-situation interactions. Individual differences scaling analysis of S-R data and contextual template matching were offered as two examples that are relevant to sport personality investigation.

4. Personality is far from being a perfect predictor of sport performance; that point has been recognized for years. Recently, however, sport investigators have begun to combine personality and physiological data in an attempt to explain more behavioral variance (e.g., Landers, Christina, Hatfield, Daniels, Wilkinson, Doyle, & Feltz, 1981; Morgan, 1973a; Silva et al., 1981). Their results point to the efficacy of a psychophysiological model of behavior.

5. The importance of asking the right kinds of questions or collecting data in appropriate sport settings is more in line with the importance given to situation variability in the interactional model. Construction of such sport personality inventories as the Sport Competition Anxiety Test (Martens, 1977) and the Competitive State Anxiety Inventory (Martens, Burton, Vealey, Smith, & Bump, 1982), as well as various other inventories (e.g., in the area of attention) have promoted a resurgence of personality research. As more valid and reliable sport-specific assessment tools become available, research interests in the sport personality area will be renewed.

All students and investigators of sport psychology are urged to continue the task that was begun in earnest well over a decade ago, that being to search for the important relationships between personality characteristics and sport participation and performance. The questions we asked were good questions. However, the answers we obtained suffered from inadequacies of our theoretical premises and methodologies. We should no longer shy away from the task at hand. The guiding theory is obvious, the methodologies await; all that remains is to ask the questions and become immersed in their solutions.

Chapter 7

Cognitive-Behavioral Interventions in Sport: A Self-Regulatory Perspective

Daniel S. Kirschenbaum and David A. Wittrock
University of Wisconsin-Madison

It is very apparent that good physical conditioning, proper technique, and the best equipment can enhance one's performance in sport. Yet in order to maximize performance, these procedures must be supplemented by attention to two other aspects of sport. First, participation in sports, especially at the level of the elite athlete, requires hundreds of hours of practice beyond one's actual participation in the sport. Time spent in routine practice or conditioning often exceeds by tenfold or more the time spent participating! Thus, participating in even the most elaborate team sport can be a very solitary, isolated experience. Each participant must somehow find the time and energy to work on skills in order to achieve his or her potential. This defines participation in all sports as a type of self-regulated (i.e., goal-directed) behavior performed in the relative absence of immediate external constraints (Kanfer & Karoly, 1972).

A second element of sport performance, easily differentiated from physical skills, concerns the cognitive and affective determinants of performance. Along these lines, certain aspects of stress, anxiety, and personality are examined in other chapters in this book. But the focus of this chapter is on which aspects of thinking and feeling can be modified to improve athletic performance. For example, can we direct athletes' attention to their successes rather than their errors to enhance performance? Also, which techniques can help athletes manage their arousal—increasing it when appropriate (e.g., "psyching-up" in weight lifting, Shelton &

Mahoney, 1978) or decreasing it when necessary (e.g., before putting in golf, Kirschenbaum & Bale, 1980)?

Most interventions in sport psychology evaluated thus far have focused on various aspects of the mental side of sports (i.e., cognitions and affect). They are termed cognitive-behavioral interventions, which simply implies that these interventions emphasize the interaction between cognitive activities, such as imagining, and overt actions or behavior (see Mahoney, 1974). We could describe these procedures by simply grouping them by type (e.g., imagery techniques, self-monitoring techniques) and then reviewing the extant research in each area for various sports. But we opted not to do that here because such an approach would not provide a conceptual framework from which all cognitive-behavioral interventions could be considered. Instead we will describe a model of the five primary phases of self-regulation before considering the relevant interventions intended to improve sport performance.

This conceptual presentation will be followed by a review of the major cognitive-behavioral interventions in sport as they pertain to the five phases of self-regulation. The final section will include suggestions for future research in this area by considering which phases of the self-regulation model presented in the first section have been relatively neglected thus far and how this problem could be remedied in the future.

A MODEL OF SELF-REGULATION

Regulating one's goal-directed behavior without immediate external control involves a variety of complex interactions between cognitions (e.g., planning, goal-setting), affect (emotional states), physiology (e.g., physical conditioning), and environmental constraints. Researchers and theorists have tried to organize these complex interactions by describing them as sequences of activities or phases (e.g., Kanfer & Karoly, 1972; Karoly, 1977; Silva, 1982b). We think the following five phases most appropriately summarize the process of self-regulation: problem identification, commitment, execution, environmental management, and generalization. Each is described below with special reference to how it pertains to performance in sport.

Problem Identification

Sometimes sport participants do not recognize that they have a problem in regulating their participation in sports. Like everyone else, these individuals often function in a semi-automatic fashion (Kimble & Perlmuter, 1970). For example, most people have set routines about waking up, eating, and going to work. This automatic style of behavior can also be manifested in one's approach to sport performance. Told how and when to train, the athlete follows these directions, more or less. The same point could be made about actual performance in competition. Thus, under normal circumstances many sport participants see their involvement in their sports as proceeding quite smoothly.

The self-regulatory problem that athletes sometimes ignore concerns how they can maximize their performance, beyond meeting the usual demands of their coaches, teammates, or themselves. In other words, how can each individual assume more responsibility for the quality of his/her participation in a sport? Accepting responsibility for performance can invigorate the search for ways to improve it. Essentially, this phase of self-regulation leads to the recognition that behavior can be changed.

Commitment

Having identified the problem and recognizing that change is possible, one must decide to seek that change and be committed to it (see Chapter 29 by Dishman). Many factors affect whether someone does make such a commitment, among the more important being whether he/she makes a plan to achieve the desired outcome (Seidner & Kirschenbaum, 1980) and whether the aversive aspects of the problem become salient when compared to the expected benefits of changing. Certain steps could be taken that could help sport participants make firm commitments to improve their performance. For example, the athlete could list all the negative aspects of sitting on the bench (instead of playing) to increase the aversiveness of mediocre performance.

Execution

With the self-regulatory problem identified and a commitment formed to modify it, the individual must begin to change in order to achieve the desired results. Self-regulation theorists have proposed that this rather complex process of change can be viewed as a cybernetic model in which a negative feedback loop serves as the basic unit of functioning (Carver & Scheier, 1981; Kanfer, 1971). A cybernetic model is an information processing unit or a means of organizing how people receive and use information. This unit is "negative" with regard to self-regulation because its purpose is to negate, or reduce, behaviors that deviate from goals.

From this perspective, self-regulation involves developing plans for pursuing a goal and then monitoring one's behavior to find out what happens to it during the process of change ("self-monitoring"). The individual can then compare the observed behaviors with the goal; if this

FIGURE 7-1 A simplified version of a closed-loop model of self-regulation. Originally proposed by F.H. Kanfer in "The maintenance of behavior by self-generated stimuli and reinforcement." In A. Jacobs & L.B. Sachs (Eds.), *The psychology of private events.* (New York: Academic, 1971.)

self-evaluation is favorable, he/she should continue in the same plan and emit the same behaviors. If the self-evaluation is unfavorable, however, the plan should be altered and the behaviors changed to reduce the discrepancy between the desired goal and the current level of performance. Some theorists also postulate that people should administer consequences to themselves according to their self-evaluations to ensure sustained efforts at self-regulation (e.g., Bandura, 1977a; Kanfer, 1971). These "self-consequations" are described as self-reward for favorable evaluations and self-punishment for unfavorable evaluations.

Figure 7-1 shows how these elements of the execution phase of self-regulation form a feedback loop. You can see that self-monitoring leads to self-evaluation, which then leads to self-consequation. The loop goes back to the origin of the self-monitoring phase by informing the person to change his or her behavior if the evaluation and consequation were unfavorable.

During the past decade numerous studies have examined this cybernetic model of self-regulation (see Carver & Scheier, 1981, 1982; Karoly & Kanfer, 1982). This analysis has helped establish how to facilitate self-regulated behavior change and has suggested why people often fail in their attempts to self-regulate. Four important principles have emerged from these investigations and, as discussed below, they apply directly to the self-regulation of participation in sports.

Principle 1: Self-Monitoring is Necessary for Self-Regulation. However, self-monitoring is not by itself sufficient to maintain effective self-regulation (Kirschenbaum, 1976; Kirschenbaum & Tomarken, 1982). Studies supporting these assertions show that self-regulated behavior change occurred when self-monitoring was present but not when it was absent. This occurred in research on the academic behavior of children (Broden, Hall, & Mitts, 1971), classroom participation by adolescents (Gottman & McFall, 1972), and classroom behavior by teachers (Hendricks, Thoresen, & Hubbard, 1974). Similar evidence appears in research on self-focused attention (Carver & Scheier, 1981; Kirschenbaum & Tomarken, 1982). For example, Diener and Wallbom (1976) found that when subjects increased their self-focused attention (a type of self-monitoring, Kirschenbaum & Tomarken, 1982) the proportion who cheated on an achievement test declined to 7%, compared to the 71% who cheated when self-focused attention was not increased. The literature on self-focused attention generally shows that increasing attention to oneself increases attempts to match behavior to plans, and it also brings about a more careful and complete introspection (Kirschenbaum & Tomarken, 1982).

Principle 2: Differences Between Individuals in Certain Salient Dispositional Styles Influence Self-Regulated Performance.   This principle refers to a simple caveat that is mandatory when stating any law or principle of human behavior. There can be little doubt that persons (or personality) and situations, and the interactions between them, determine most of our behavior (e.g., Mischel & Peake, 1982). Our model of self-regulation and the first four principles here are not exceptions to this rule. However, some personality characteristics are probably more relevant to self-regulation than others. For example, it seems likely that among the more important dispositional styles are degree of self-motivation (Dishman, Ickes, & Morgan, 1980), level of self-regulatory skills (Rosenbaum, 1980), and self-reinforcement style (Heiby, 1982; Rozensky & Bellack, 1976). Certainly our previous emphasis on degree of task mastery also suggests that familiarity with a task, and degree of mastery or skill in it, also has an important effect on self-regulation. The nature of the task itself (e.g., its novelty, the degree of cognitive involvement required), a situational variable, probably interacts quite substantially with some of these personality or dispositional styles to affect self-regulated performance (e.g., Kirschenbaum, Wittrock, Smith, & Monson, 1984; Weinberg, Gould, & Jackson, 1980).

Principle 3: Differential Expectancies and Self-Monitoring Interact With Task Mastery in Self-Regulation.   When tasks are difficult, self-regulation is facilitated by thinking about one's successes, rather than failures, and otherwise having positive expectations about the likelihood of achieving one's goals (Kirschenbaum & Tomarken, 1982). For example, research on various tasks has shown that attending to one's successful performance (positive self-monitoring) can improve self-regulated performance for tasks that are poorly mastered and difficult (e.g., Gottman & McFall, 1972; Kirschenbaum & Karoly, 1977; Masters & Santrock, 1976).

Conversely, research on self-focused attention clearly shows that negative expectancies and subsequent failures often debilitate self-regulation when the individual is attending to his or her behavior (e.g., Carver, Blaney, & Scheier, 1979a, 1979b). For example, Carver et al. (1979b) exposed subjects to a failure experience. Subjects then undertook a second task that ostensibly measured the same intellectual skills "assessed" in the first task. They were told either to expect to do quite well or quite poorly on the second task. As anticipated, negative expectancies plus self-focused attention reduced persistence on the second task (see Carver et al., 1979a; Duval & Friedan, 1979; Kuhl, 1981). Similarly, studies of differential self-montoring (positive vs. negative self-monitoring) have also shown that thinking about one's failures (negative self-monitoring) often interferes with performance of poorly mastered tasks (for a review, see Kirschenbaum & Tomarken, 1982).

In contrast to these effects on poorly mastered tasks, negative self-monitoring can facilitate self-regulated behavior change when tasks are very well mastered (Kirschenbaum & Karoly, 1977; Tomarken & Kirschenbaum, 1982; Wade, 1974). In the Tomarken and Kirschenbaum study, for example, students preparing for graduate school admission tests either self-monitored positively by keeping track of their successes, or self-monitored negatively by recording errors, or received comparable feedback as the self-monitoring groups without concurrently self-monitoring performance outcomes. The positive self-monitors performed much worse, paid less attention to the training task, and failed to return for as many training sessions compared to the other groups.

Principle 4: Emotional States Can Influence Self-Regulated Performance Somewhat Independently of Effects Attributable to Cognitive Factors, Such as Expectancies and Attentional Focus. A great deal of evidence indicates that affect (emotion expressed in language) can function quite independently of cognition in determining behavior (e.g., Lang, 1971; Leventhal, 1980; Zajonc, 1980b). Regarding self-regulated behavior, for example, it seems that affective states have a greater effect on the performance of poorly mastered tasks than on that of well mastered tasks (Wright & Mischel, 1982; Kirschenbaum, Tomarken, & Humphrey, in press). It also seems that one mechanism by which positive self-monitoring and favorable expectancies may facilitate self-regulation of poorly mastered tasks pertains to affect. That is, these cognitive states may direct attention away from the painful sensations associated with maximum performance of certain motor tasks. Such distractions appear vital to sustaining high levels of self-regulated performance (see Kuhl, 1981; Leventhal, Nerenz, & Strauss, 1980; Morgan, Horstman, Cymerman, & Stokes, 1983; Pennebaker, 1982).

In sum, these principles of self-regulation suggest, among other things, that sport participants must (a) learn how to observe their performances systematically and continually, (b) attend to favorable aspects of performance and otherwise develop positive expectancies when the tasks are difficult or new, (c) focus on errors or problems when tasks become highly routine, and (d) use cognitive distractors or other means to reduce negative affect when performing very difficult tasks. Several of the interventions we consider in later sections of this chapter have used one or more of these principles to improve sport performance.

Environmental Management

Although the term "self-regulation" implies solitary pursuit of goals, it is clear that behavior does not occur in a vacuum. We can vigorously pursue a goal, but its achievement often requires learning how to manage the limitations imposed on us by our physical and social environments (see Mahoney & Thoresen, 1974). For sport participants, such factors as the availability of good training facilities and equipment are obviously important. In addition, they must have the time and energy to practice and participate in spite of competing demands from their work and their social life. People who are significant to an athlete can help by going beyond merely tolerating the athlete's involvement in a sport (Colletti & Brownell, 1982). For instance, they can help the athlete regulate his or her performance by encouraging him or her to practice and to keep proper nutritional habits. Other environmental effects on sport performance include interactions with coaches and teammates, variables which are discussed elsewhere in this book. Later in this chapter we will also consider some methods by which coaches can help or hinder an athlete's regulation of his or her performance.

Generalization

Often the pursuit of goals results in some behavior change and sometimes even the achievement of those goals. However, most self-regulatory problems, including participation in sports at high levels, require that efforts be sustained over long periods of time. Such efforts are much easier to abandon than maintain. People often fail to maintain self-regulated behavior change over time or across situations (Kirschenbaum & Tomarken, 1982). This means that self-regulated behavior often fails to generalize, generalization being defined as "the occurrence of relevant behavior under different, nontraining conditions (i.e., across subjects, people, behaviors, and/or time) without the scheduling of the same events in these conditions as have been scheduled in the training conditions" (Stokes & Baer, 1977, p. 350).

In a recent paper, Kirschenbaum and Tomarken (1982) argued that the empirical evidence pertaining to the nature of "self-regulatory failure" (Kirschenbaum, 1976) indicates that "obsessive-compulsive self-regulation" seems warranted to reduce the likelihood of failing to generalize self-regulated behavior change. The argument presented was that there are so many ways to produce self-regulatory failure that, to circumvent this problem, one must vigilantly self-monitor and engage in other relevant habit changes to the point of developing a type of obsessive-compulsive style of self-regulating (cf. Pollak, 1979; Rachman & de Silva, 1978).

Research in sport psychology supports this conceptualization by showing that elite athletes often develop an obsessive-compulsive style of involvement in their sport. Studies with gymnasts (Mahoney & Avener, 1977), golfers (Kirschenbaum & Bale, 1980), wrestlers (Gould, Weiss, & Weinberg, 1981; Highlen & Bennett, 1983), and divers (Highlen & Bennett, 1983) indicate that a variety of ritualistic behaviors and thoughts are associated with favorable performance outcomes. For example, Mahoney and Avener found that for elite gymnasts the frequency of thoughts about their sport in everyday situations correlated significantly with their performance. Kirschenbaum and Bale established an even more direct connection in that better golf scores obtained by university-level golfers were positively correlated with the "obsessive" factor of Nideffer's (1976b) Test of Attentional and Interpersonal Style. In a larger and more recent study, Highlen and Bennett found that qualifiers for Canadian national wrestling and diving teams reported relatively high frequencies of compulsive behaviors. These included withdrawal from others, frequent self-talk, and generally living a highly structured lifestyle.

COGNITIVE-BEHAVIORAL INTERVENTIONS IN SPORT PSYCHOLOGY

Very few of the published accounts of interventions that have been evaluated in sport psychology pertain directly to the first two phases of our five-phase model of self-regulation. In contrast, a number of researchers have tried to facilitate self-regulated execution and create supportive environments. Efforts to maximize generalization have appeared much less frequently. Let's review these latter sets of studies.

Improving Execution

Training in mental imagery, self-monitoring, self-instructions, attentional focusing, biofeedback, and positive expectancies have all been used to improve the self-regulation of sport performance. Here we will examine the effects of several of these techniques, with an emphasis on some of the most thoroughly evaluated ones.

High jumper Dick Fosbury spent several minutes in the runway "jumping in his head" before making a jump (Mahoney, 1979). Skier Jean-Claude Killy reported that his only preparation for one important race was to ski it mentally; an injury had made it impossible for him to practice physically for that race. Killy claimed that the race turned out to be one of his best (Suinn, 1980). Researchers have been a bit more circumspect in their enthusiasm about the efficacy of mental rehearsal (e.g., Corbin, 1972; Mahoney, 1979). Certainly it is important to consider the evidence when evaluating a technique that has been formally applied to an enormous range of motor skills, from balancing on a stabilometer (Ryan & Simons, 1982) to dart throwing (Mendoza & Wickman, 1978) to skiing (Suinn, 1980).

To determine if prior mental practice aids performance, Feltz and Landers (1983) conducted a comprehensive review of the research using a meta-analytic approach. Glass (1977) defined meta-analysis as the combination of results of independent studies on a topic. The procedure produces a significance level giving the probability that a set of studies exhibiting the obtained results could have been generated if no relationship actually existed. Meta-analytic procedures help categorize findings and provide information about the magnitude of the effects of experimental manipulations (effect size).

Feltz and Landers examined 60 studies with a total of 146 effect sizes. The overall average effect size obtained was .48, indicating a moderate effect of imagery. This led the authors to suggest that mental practice of a motor skill is better than no practice at all (for example, see Hall & Erffmeyer, 1983; Weinberg, Seabourne, & Jackson, 1981). Thus, mental practice is effective, but we must now consider which circumstances enhance this effectiveness.

Degree of familiarity with the task can influence the effects of mental imagery. In general, some prior experience with the skill enhances the effect of mental practice (Mahoney, 1979; Noel, 1980). Timing is also an important variable. Imaginal rehearsal appears most effective when interspersed throughout skill acquisition (cf. Landers, 1975b). Three other dimensions that Mahoney considered potentially important were (a) orientation, (b) use of coping versus mastery imagery, and (c) vividness and controllability of the image.

Orientation of mental imagery refers to the extent to which the image is viewed from an external or third-person perspective (i.e., as if it were being seen on a videotape) versus an internal or phenomenological perspective (i.e., as if the imagined actions were being experienced in the here and now). According to some anecdotal reports (e.g., Mahoney, 1979), successful athletes may prefer internal imagery, and internal imagery training has produced some gains in performance (e.g., Ryan & Simons, 1982). However, few studies have directly compared the efficacy of internal to external imagery. The one investigation we know of that made such a comparison yielded equivocal results concerning improvements in dart throwing (Epstein, 1980).

A similar point could be made about the contribution of the other dimensions of imagery training that have been hypothesized as important active ingredients in determining its efficacy. For example, a model who gradually learned a skill (a "coping" model) was just as effective as a model who performed flawlessly (a "mastery" model) in a study of motor skill learning (Martens, Burwitz, & Zuckerman, 1976). The impact of vividness and controllability of mental images in sport contexts analogously requires further study.

Regarding the mechanisms by which mental imagery can facilitate performance, a self-regulatory analysis may also prove useful. Imagery training is usually seen as a means to reduce anxiety and enhance concentration (see Suinn, 1980). According to our self-regulation model, imagery training could enhance the initial execution of self-regulation in several more specific ways. For example, by seeing specific and positive images of oneself executing a play successfully, positive expectancies may emerge. These favorable images may also lead to positive self-monitoring. Both positive self-monitoring and positive expectancies could promote maintenance of self-monitoring, self-evaluation, and self-reinforcement when tasks are new, difficult, or perceived as difficult (recall Principles 3 & 4). Thus, imagery training, particularly favorable images as discussed in most published accounts, may be seen as a means to direct attention to aspects of the self and the performance that can facilitate sustained and effective self-regulation.

Of course, the calming quality of imagery training may also prove useful, particularly when tasks are very difficult or involve high levels of tension for other reasons (cf. Kirschenbaum, Tomarken, & Humphrey, in press). All of these postulated mechanisms, as well as the particular elements of imagery training that may produce these favorable effects (e.g., familiarity with task, orientation, coping vs. mastery, controllability/vividness), obviously merit further investigation. Such studies could help increase our understanding of how and why imagery can produce favorable effects in sport settings which, in turn, should enable us to devise more effective imagery training procedures.

In the preceding analysis, we suggested that imagery training may yield favorable results in part because it increases positive self-monitoring and positive expectations. Several studies have attempted to manipulate more directly these elements of self-regulation in sport contexts (Johnston-O'Connor & Kirschenbaum, in press; Kirschenbaum, Ordman, Tomarken, & Holtzbauer, 1982; Kirschenbaum, Wittrock, Smith, & Monson, 1984). For example, Kirschenbaum et al. (1982) divided the scores of women in bowling leagues at the median to form a group of relatively unskilled bowlers (n = 60; M baseline bowling average = 123.7) and a group of moderately skilled bowlers (n = 67; M average = 147.3). Subjects either received no treatment (control), basic instructions on the seven components of an effective bowling shot delivered by a professional bowler, basic instructions and positive self-monitoring instructions and materials, or basic instructions and negative self-monitoring instructions and materials.

As shown in Table 7-1, the self-monitoring manipulations required subjects to review the seven components of effective bowling after finishing each frame. In the positive self-monitoring condition, subjects then recorded a number if, and only if, they felt that they had executed a particular component well. Conversely, negative self-monitors recorded a number if, and only if, they had executed a particular component poorly. These self-monitors were also advised to use either positive or negative self-instructions (reminders about how to execute key components or which errors to avoid) prior to each shot.

Figure 7-2 shows that the relatively unskilled bowlers substantially improved their performance more than all other groups. No other differences between groups in either the low skill or moderate skill cohorts were significant. Recall that the subjects who positively self-monitored and improved their performance were relatively unskilled. Therefore, these results accord well with Principle 3 of our self-regulation model by demonstrating that positive self-monitoring can facilitate self-regulation of poorly mastered tasks.

The extant research on a variety of related cognitive-behavioral interventions also shows that many techniques can affect sport performance and that mechanisms responsible for change seem to accord well with the model of self-regulation we described earlier. These studies have examined techniques including: positive self-monitoring (Johnston-O'Connor & Kirschenbaum, in press; Kirschenbaum et al., 1984), self-instructions (Meyers, Schleser, Cooke, & Cuvillier, 1979; Silva, 1982b), positive expectancy enhancement (e.g., Nelson & Furst, 1972; Ness & Patton, 1979; Weinberg, Gould, Yukelson, & Jackson, 1981), biofeedback (Daniels & Landers, 1981), hypnosis (Morgan, Hirota, Balke, & Weitz, 1976; Morgan, Raven, Drinkwater, & Horvath, 1973), dissociation (Morgan, Horstman, Cymerman, & Stokes, 1983), and psyching-up (Shelton & Mahoney, 1978; Weinberg, Gould, & Jackson, 1980).

Some of these studies have revealed surprisingly powerful effects attributable to cognitive-behavioral techniques. For example, Nelson and Furst (1972) told relatively weak subjects that they were stronger than their relatively strong partners in arm strength. The objectively weaker subjects proceeded to win arm wrestling competitions with their objectively stronger partners 83% of the time! Similarly, Ness and Patton's (1979) weight lifters hoisted more weight when they believed the weight was less than its actual value. On the other hand, some less favorable results (e.g., Kirschenbaum et al., 1984; Meyers et al., 1979; Weinberg et al., 1980) clearly indicate that dispositional and situational

TABLE 7-1
An Example of Instructions and a Record-Keeping Form
for Positive Self-Monitoring in Bowling

Brain Power Bowling

Self-Monitoring Sheet _____ Mary the Bowler _____   4/25/80
                                         (name)   (date)

Instructions: After bowling each frame review the seven components of Brain Power Bowling. For those components that you executed well, put a number from 1 to 3 in the box corresponding to that component: 1 = good; 2 = very good; 3 = excellent. If you did not do a good job on a particular component leave the box blank.

Frame	Foot position: same starting point each time	Stance: shoulders squared, elbow tucked in to hip, knees relaxed	Grip: same grip for every shot, thumb and palm position correct	Spot: pick a spot and watch your ball roll over it	Approach: take 2-3 second delay, walk in a straight line	Push away: elbow tight and locked, straight pendulum type swing near body	Finish position: lead foot pointed toward spot, body balanced, square at the line
1	3	2	2	2	1		2
2	3	3	3	3	3	3	3
3	3	3	3	3	3	3	3
4	3	2	2	2	2		
5	3	3	2	2	3	3	3
6	3	2	3	2	1	2	
7	3	2				2	2
8	3	2	1	1			
9	3	3	3	3	2	3	3
10	3	3	3	3	3	3	3

Self-instructions: Before making your approach it is very important to remind yourself of the correct way to complete the final 3 components. Review in your head the following: (a) Walk in a straight line for the approach. (b) Keep your elbow tight and locked on the push away. Use a straight pendulum type swing which stays near your body. (c) At your finish position your lead foot should be pointing toward your spot and you should be balanced at the line.

149   GAME TOTAL

Reprinted with permission from Kirschenbaum, D.S., Ordman, A.M., Tomarken, A.J., & Holtzbauer, R. Effects of differential self-monitoring and level of mastery on sports performance: Brain power bowling. *Cognitive Therapy and Research*, 1982, **6**, 335-342 (New York: Plenum).

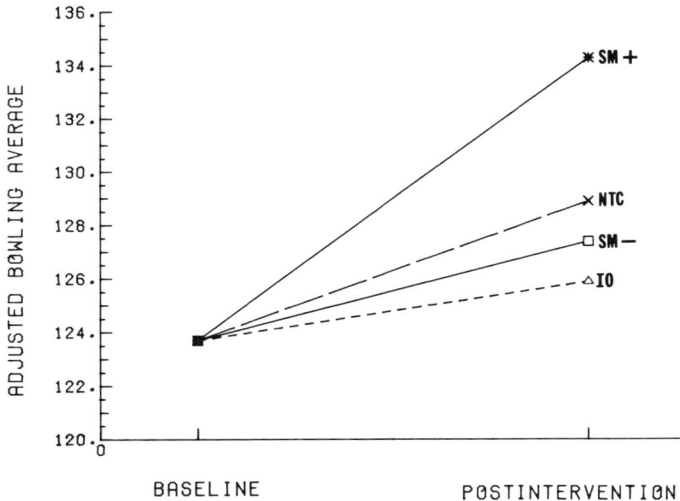

Figure 7-2   Baseline and adjusted postintervention bowling average for low skill bowlers. SM + : Positive self-monitoring; SM − : Negative self-monitoring; IO: Information only; NTC: No treatment control. Reprinted with permission from Kirschenbaum, D.S., Ordman, A.M., Tomarken, A.J., & Holtzbauer, R. Effects of differential self-monitoring and level of mastery on sports performance: Brain power bowling. *Cognitive Therapy and Research*, 1982, **6**, 335-342 (New York: Plenum).

parameters moderate the effects of these interventions. This latter point coincides with Principle 2 of our self-regulation model, just as the more favorable results are in accord with Principles 3 and 4.

Managing Sport Environments

One of the most important and manageable aspects of the sport environment is the manner in which coaches interact with their team members. The importance of this relationship has been discussed quite thoroughly in the literature, a review of which can be found in Chapter 26 by Smoll and Smith. Perhaps the clearest illustration of how coaches affect sport performance is the research showing the detrimental effects of negativistic coaching. That is, when coaches give mostly critical feedback, performance often declines, as do attitudes toward the game and sometimes attitudes toward the self. For example, Smith, Smoll, and Curtis (1979) rated the coaching behaviors of 51 Little League coaches and found that those who often made punitive remarks to their players had teams with less favorable attitudes toward baseball and, in some cases, less favorable attitudes toward themselves. In a related vein, Kirschenbaum and his associates found that excessive negative feedback, compared to no feedback, resulted in much lower basketball performance by college students and a decrease in favorable attitudes and sustained self-observation of performance (Kirschenbaum & Smith, 1983; Kirschenbaum et al., 1984).

To change negativistic coaching and other problematic aspects of the coach-player relationship, sport psychologists have begun developing an exciting, empirically based technology to improve the quality of feedback from coaches; it is sometimes called behavioral coaching (see Martin & Hrycaiko, 1984). In their chapter, Smith and Smoll describe their seminal work in this area. We can illustrate this approach for our purposes by describing the powerful results obtained by one other group of sport researchers (Allison & Ayllon, 1980).

Allison and Ayllon used behavioral coaching to improve performance in football, gymnastics, and tennis. Their version of behavioral coaching included breaking down plays or shots into specific operational elements, as well as having coaches use more specific instruction, modeling, and positive feedback. For a city league youth football team, for example, the psychologists helped the coach define an effective block as consisting of eight observable steps. These covered the stance before the snap to body position during contact, and maintaining contact until the referee's whistle concluded play. After the coach described these components, he modeled them and had the players imitate him. During practice the coach told all the players to "freeze" (stop moving) when they heard his whistle; he then observed individual players block. If the player executed properly, the coach blew his whistle and congratulated the player with "great," "right," "way to go," or some similar phrase. If the play was executed improperly, the coach "froze" the player upon noticing the error, then described the error in specific terms, modeled the correct action, and had the player imitate him.

Figure 7-3 shows that behavioral coaching dramatically improved the percent of blocks executed correctly in comparison to the standard coaching procedures used earlier. Overall, the baseline average of 5% correct plays improved to 51.39%. These researchers used similar behavioral coaching procedures to improve the performance of high school gymnasts on three moves: backward walkovers, front hand springs, and reverse kips. Similarly, university students enrolled in a tennis class improved their forehands, backhands, and serves.

These results and others (see Martin & Hrycaiko, 1984) clearly illustrate behavioral coaching's great potential in enhancing the self-regulation of sport performance. The process of operationally defining components of sport performance undoubtedly helps participants self-monitor their performance. The frequent use of highly specific, nonemotional feedback also facilitates accurate self-evaluation. Furthermore,

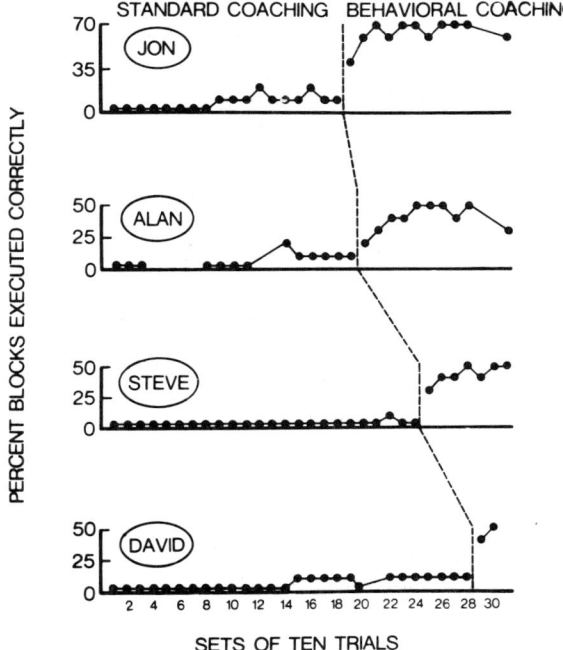

Figure 7-3 The percentage of trials in which football blocks were executed correctly as a function of standard coaching (i.e., coaching procedures used prior to the intervention) and behavioral coaching. Reprinted with permission from Allison, M.G., & Ayllon, T. Behavioral coaching in the development of skills in football, gymnastics, and tennis. *Journal of Applied Behavior Analysis*, 1980, **13**, 297-314 (published by the Society for the Experimental Analysis of Behavior, Inc., Lawrence, KS).

behavioral coaching promotes more task-specific and positive feedback. This emphasis should encourage the development of positive expectancies, the avoidance of negative expectancies, and task-focused attention. As indicated by Principle 3, all of these cognitions are vital to effective self-regulation of new and difficult tasks (Carver & Scheier, 1981; Kirschenbaum & Tomarken, 1982; Kuhl, 1981). From a self-regulatory perspective, then, behavioral coaching makes a great deal of sense. Therefore it should enhance performance of elite athletes just as it helped the more typical sport participants in the Allison and Ayllon study.

Generalization

Several elaborate case studies and exploratory experiments have tested the efficacy of multicomponent cognitive-behavioral interventions

(Gravel, Lemieux, & Ladouceur, 1980; Kirschenbaum & Bale, 1980; Meyers & Schleser, 1980; Silva, 1982b; Spinelli & Barrios, 1980; Suinn, 1977). In all of these reports, the purpose of the intervention was not only to improve the initial execution of the self-regulated performance but also to induce changes in the cognitive-behavioral skills of the participants that could promote generalization of those improvements (cf. Kanfer & Karoly, 1972; Mahoney & Thoresen, 1974). Unlike the previously reviewed set of interventions, the present set of studies focused on much more than an individual component of self-regulation (e.g., expectancy, positive self-monitoring) or on circumscribed sets of components (e.g., psyching-up strategies). Each intervention in the present set of studies attempted to improve several different but related self-regulatory skills to promote effective and long-lasting self-regulation (see Kirschenbaum & Tomarken, 1982).

The papers in this subsection focused on improving performance among various athletes, including skiers (Gravel et al., 1980), golfers (Kirschenbaum & Bale, 1980), a hockey player (Silva, 1982b), basketball players (Meyers & Schleser, 1980; Silva, 1982b), and sprinters (Spinelli & Barrios, 1980). For example, Gravel et al. developed a multicomponent cognitive-behavioral intervention for a university's cross-country ski team. The treatment included a version of Suinn's (1977) visuomotor behavioral rehearsal imagery training, deep muscle relaxation, thought-stopping (to reduce negative thoughts), and self-instructions. Subjects either received this intervention or a placebo consisting of a film and a few interesting "free association" exercises. The subjects did not differ in their ratings of the expected benefits of these two interventions. The results indicated, however, that the experimental group rated their intervention as significantly more beneficial (based on responses to interviews and a questionnaire) compared to the placebo group. Unfortunately, the limited sample sizes prevented any meaningful comparison of the groups on measures of performance that were available to the researchers.

The Gravel et al. research is quite representative of the studies in this grouping. All of them show promise but are largely exploratory at this point. Therefore, we do not yet know the extent to which these multicomponent interventions produce generalized improvements in sport performance and attitudes. Needed are studies that reliably assess performance over time and control for such variables as credibility of the interventions (cf. Kazdin & Wilcoxon, 1976), expectancies generated by them (with psychometrically sound assessments of same), and experimenter effects.

Other nonsport studies that have used such multicomponent interventions have shown some promise for achieving the difficult goal of improving generalization of behavior change (S.M. Hall, 1980). However, changing behaviors that involve many physiological demands, such as behaviors concerned with dieting, smoking, and sport performance, may require more radical interventions. It is for this reason that Kirschenbaum and Tomarken (1982) emphasized the necessity of inducing "obsessive compulsive self-regulation" to affect generalized behavior change for such target behaviors. The multicomponent interventions tested to date in sport psychology may not be intensive enough to achieve that kind of generalization.

CONCLUSION

This analysis and review demonstrates that a self-regulation model can help integrate the diverse cognitive-behavioral interventions that have been tested in sport psychology. The results obtained in these interventions generally accord well with our self-regulation model and several empirically derived principles of self-regulation. More specifically, several procedures have been shown to help coaches create an environment that enhances the ability of athletes to regulate their performances. Also, specific cognitive-behavioral interventions such as training in positive self-monitoring and expectancy enhancement can improve self-regulated performance. The efficacy of these interventions also depends on situational and dispositional variables including the nature of the task and the participant's degree of mastery of it.

While cognitive-behavioral interventions have clearly demonstrated their promise in sport psychology, it is equally apparent that many facets of the self-regulation model remain to be thoroughly explored in this context. With a few exceptions (cf. Dishman's chapter in this book), we know very little about how to improve athletes' abilities to recognize problems in regulating their sport performance and to make strong commitments to perform at peak levels. Several other issues requiring further study include the generalization of the effects of multicomponent interventions and the dispositional and situational parameters that moderate those effects.

As this knowledge accumulates, it will undoubtedly improve not only athletes' performance and satisfaction with their participation in sports, but it will give us a better understanding of the nature and nurture of self-regulation. Both of these purposes certainly seem to merit the attention of researchers, theorists, and practitioners in sport psychology.

PART III

ANXIETY, AROUSAL, AND PERFORMANCE

In the previous section, the relationship between personality and sport was examined. Although researchers have investigated the effects of many different types of personality factors on performance (e.g., extraversion-introversion, aggressiveness, independence, leadership, determination, etc.) one often studied personality factor among athletes is anxiety. Many athletes have reported that their performance has been adversely affected by being too anxious or aroused for an athletic competition. As a result, various strategies as described in this section have been developed to help athletes cope with high levels of anxiety or arousal.[1]

The relationship between arousal and motor performance is a critical one for the athlete and the coach who want to maximize performance. Indeed, most individuals involved in competitive sport have probably speculated about the relationship between arousal and athletic performance. In our own informal surveys, most people believe that a little arousal helps in preparing athletes for competition. Yet there also seems to be a consensus that too much arousal can be detrimental to performance. In essence, these observations are aligned with the inverted-U hypothesis which researchers have found best represents the relationship between arousal and motor performance. Specifically, the inverted-U

---

[1]Although often used interchangeably, arousal commonly refers to the entire continuum of a person's psychological activation whereas anxiety is restricted to high arousal states which produce feelings of discomfort.

hypothesis states that performance improves with increasing levels of arousal up to some optimal point, whereupon further increases in arousal will produce a decrement in performance. Thus, an athlete may perform poorly because he or she is either overaroused or underaroused. This means that a strong, emotional speech before the game will only enhance performance if it increases an athlete's arousal from a low level to a more moderate or optimal level. But if the athlete is already highly aroused, the speech may increase his or her arousal to the point of being detrimental to performance.

Specificity is Important

Consequently, coaches must try to help each athlete reach his or her optimal level of arousal to maximize performance. Yet researchers are unable to specify what this optimal level should be. However, the interactionalist model described in the introduction of this text provides some guidelines for coaches. This model states that behavior can best be understood in terms of an interaction between the individual's own makeup and his or her specific situation, a conceptualization that will help us determine potential factors mediating the anxiety-performance relationship. For example, one crucial situational variable is the type of task being performed. Researchers hypothesize that tasks requiring a great deal of precision coordination and control, such as golf, archery, free-throw shooting, and bowling, would probably best be performed at low levels of arousal. Conversely, tasks that require more speed or strength, such as weight lifting, tackling in football, or throwing a shot putt, would most likely be performed best at relatively high levels of arousal. Even for strength and speed tasks, however, too much arousal can still be detrimental to performance.

A second factor to consider in helping athletes reach their optimal level of arousal is the athlete's own personality makeup. For example, some athletes perform very well when highly aroused or under intense pressure whereas others tend to tighten up or "choke" under pressure. It takes a coach who is sensitive to athletes' reactions to the competitive arena to make the right decision. One coach has been known to separate his players in two rooms before the game, based on their reactions to competition. One group he would try to "psych up" whereas the other group he would try to calm down. He found that this maximized his chances of bringing all the athletes to their optimal levels of arousal.

Differentiating Anxiety From Arousal

Although we have used terms such as anxiety, arousal, and stress interchangeably, there are differences between these concepts. In this section's opening chapter, Robert Sonstroem defines the three terms and distinguishes between these important concepts. He presents an overview of the major theories that have attempted to explain the relationship between anxiety and motor performance, as well as the situational and personal variables affecting this relationship. In addition, he examines the relationship between anxiety and attention because this is crucial in determining performance. Of particular interest is how excess anxiety can cause an inappropriate focus of attention, causing an athlete to perform poorly under pressure.

The concept of anxiety itself also fits in well with the interactionalist model presented in the introduction. Specifically, anxiety has been conceptualized as having both a trait and state component, a distinction clearly delineated by Spielberger in 1966. State anxiety has been defined as an emotional state characterized by apprehension and tension—in essence a "right now" reaction that is transitory in nature. Trait anxiety refers to a predisposition to perceive certain situations as threatening and to respond to these situations with varying levels of anxiety. Thus, an athlete's anxiety before or during an event will be determined by an interaction of this general or usual level of anxiety (i.e., trait anxiety) and the specific situational constraints of the event (i.e., state anxiety). For example, both high and low trait-anxious individuals will probably exhibit higher levels of state anxiety when competing for the state championship than during a practice session, although the high trait-anxious person probably will feel more threatened by the championship game than the low anxious person and will react with higher levels of state anxiety.

Sources of Anxiety

Advances in the measurement of anxiety have led researchers to develop situationally specific trait-anxiety measures. Martens (1977) has developed the Sport Competition Anxiety Test (SCAT), which measures the anxiety an athlete generally feels when competing in sports. Since competitive trait anxiety is specific to sport, it is a better predictor of state anxiety than a more general measure of trait anxiety would be. This interaction between competitive trait anxiety and state anxiety is illustrated in both Tara Scanlan's and Michael Passer's chapters on competitive stress and young athletes. Scanlan surveys research from both laboratory and field studies that have attempted to delineate the sources of competitive stress for young athletes. Results support the interaction model, with personality variables such as competitive trait anxiety being the best predictors of state anxiety before the game whereas situational factors such as winning or losing are better predictors of state anxiety immediately after the game. Scanlan concludes her chapter with several suggestions for structuring the competitive situation to alleviate stress and maximize the many positive aspects of sport.

Passer's chapter discusses antecedents and consequences of competitive trait anxiety, as well as factors mediating the development of competitive trait anxiety such as interactions with significant others (e.g., coaches, parents, teammates) and history of success or failure. Competitive anxiety can have several adverse consequences: fear and worry about performance, susceptibility to illness, avoidance of competition, and disruption of normal sleeping patterns. However, Passer also notes that many athletes report that their worries about competition do not impair their performance. Some athletes even claim they perform better when anxious. Passer observes that competitive anxiety, in and of itself, does not positively or negatively affect performance outcomes. Rather, as the inverted-U hypothesis implies, sometimes an athlete has to raise his or her level of anxiety whereas at other times he or she has to lower it.

Being able to regulate an athlete's anxiety or arousal level throughout the competition is an extremely important skill for maintaining a high level of performance proficiency. This is no easy task; sports such as basketball, football, and tennis may require long periods of concentration, and thus maintaining one's optimal level of arousal in a changing environment is extremely difficult. For example, a basketball player may need to be pumped up to play defense and run a fast break offense, but then have to go to the foul line and relax to make a foul shot.

Arousal, Anxiety, and Performance

The idea that competitive anxiety can affect motor performance is at the heart of this section's final two chapters, by Robert Weinberg and Ronald Smith. Weinberg discusses mental preparation strategies such as imagery, self-statements, attentional focus, and preparatory arousal which athletes employ to gain or maintain an optimal level of arousal. In line with the interactionalist point of view, however, each coach and athlete must decide on the most appropriate technique based on the type of task to be performed, the athlete's skill level, and past experience history.

Following Weinberg's chapter, Smith discusses strategies for reducing or coping with high levels of anxiety. As the importance of winning continues to be stressed in competitive sports, the pressure and anxiety of performing well will also continue to increase. Thus, the problem with getting athletes ready for competition is often one of calming them down, not psyching them up. In several surveys of major college football teams, for example, more than 40% of the athletes have reported experiencing enough anxiety before and during competition to interfere with their performance. In essence, these athletes are already on the back side of the inverted-U hypothesis and need to lower their anxiety level rather than raise it.

Paralleling the increased pressure in competitive sport has been a rise in the level and intensity of anxiety that individuals experience in our fast-paced, highly competitive, and rapidly changing society. Several relaxation procedures have been developed to help people cope with elevated levels of anxiety. Smith reviews four of the major stress management models — extinction, counterconditioning, cognitive mediation, and coping skills — and discusses the treatment techniques they have inspired. He then points out how these techniques might be employed to reduce maladaptive responses in athletes. Arousal and anxiety will inevitably occur in athletic competition. The challenge is to help athletes recognize arousal and anxiety responses so that they are better able to cope with undesirable levels.

Chapter 8

An Overview
of Anxiety in Sport

Robert J. Sonstroem
University of Rhode Island

How do you feel 3 minutes before a final exam is to be given? Have you ever tried to speak to a distinguished visitor and found yourself stuttering and stammering? Have your knees ever trembled when you faced the class for your presentation or when you walked to the foul line with 5 seconds left and the score tied? Perhaps you know people who have trouble sleeping, who speak at a rapid pace, or who are distracted and "nervous." Anxiety in different forms permeates the lives of many, whether they are emotionally balanced or maladjusted. The reduction of anxiety is a contemporary cultural concern and forms the substance of many popular self-help books. And anxiety exists in sports. A poll of 458 wrestlers from 13-19 years of age, who were invovled in 1981 national championship competition, found that these elite competitors characterized themselves as being nervous or worried in 66% of their matches (Gould, Horn, & Spreeman, 1983b).

Anxiety often has been studied in sport and exercise in terms of its negative emotional effects. That is, its presence is believed to be injurious to optimal sport performance or to the individual personally. Today's exercise literature claims that physical activity reduces anxiety and leads to improved personal functioning. (See Chapters 30 and 31 by Sachs and Buffone.) A rapidly growing area of interest in sport psychology concerns the use of stress management procedures such as biofeedback and relaxation training to enhance athletic performance by reducing anxiety. This topic is reviewed in the chapters by Robert Weinberg and Ronald

Smith. Those interested may also wish to consult Nideffer (1976a), Nideffer and Sharpe (1978), or Suinn (1980).

An alternative conception of anxiety centers on its energizing properties rather than on its negative emotional aspects. Surprisingly, the wrestlers who experienced prematch anxiety in the Gould et al. (1983) study indicated that this nervousness sometimes helped their performance. Levels of physiological and psychological activity have been studied under the label *arousal* and may vary from very low (deep sleep) to very high (running or extreme excitement). Arousal often has been viewed as motivation, a term that immediately intrigues physical education instructors and coaches. Although used interchangeably, arousal actually refers to the entire continuum of an individual's psychological activation whereas anxiety is restricted to higher arousal states that produce feelings of discomfort or excessive concern.

The effects of arousal on motor performance will therefore be treated first in this chapter, followed by an overview of the study of anxiety in sport and exercise. In presenting this overview, certain information from the discipline of psychology will be discussed because this literature is believed to have immediate relevance for sport and exercise settings. This extensive topic cannot be treated in depth here, so models and measures often will be emphasized rather than inconsistent results. Those wishing further information will be directed to more extensive reviews of particular topics.

BASIC DEFINITIONS
AND MEASURES OF ANXIETY

Due to an abundance of diverse theoretical interpretations, a common formal definition of anxiety has never evolved. However, it has developed an equivalent meaning across centuries of studied interest: a state of depression or agitation accompanied by feelings of distress (Lazarus & Averill, 1972). It may be operationally defined by measurement of three response components: cognitive, overt behavioral, and physiological (Borkovec, 1976). However, it is important to distinguish between chronic and transitory anxiety. Spielberger defined *state anxiety* (A-State) "as a transitory emotional state . . . that varies in intensity and fluctuates over time." Trait anxiety (A-Trait) referred to "relatively stable individual differences in anxiety proneness, that is, differences in the disposition to perceive a wide range of stimulus situations as dangerous or threatening, and . . . to respond to such threats with A-State reactions" (Spielberger, 1972, p. 39). Predictions arising from his trait-state theory hold that high A-Trait persons experience a greater number of situations as threatening and that they respond to personal threats with A-State levels *disproportionately* higher than those of low A-Trait persons.

Anxiety and arousal have generally been measured by standardized paper and pencil questionnaires. One of the first was the Taylor Manifest Anxiety Scale (Taylor, 1951, 1953) assessing between-subject differences in chronic anxiety. Sample items of the TMAS with keyed responses are: "I am easily embarrassed" (T), "I have very few headaches" (F), "I worry quite a bit over possible troubles" (T). The 1970 development of the State-Trait Anxiety Inventory (STAI) gave researchers the opportunity to measure both A-Trait and A-State levels (Spielberger, Gorsuch, & Lushene, 1970). Most investigators gravitated from an early almost exclusive use of the TMAS to a reliance on the STAI during the 1970s.

While the direct measurement of physiological responses such as heart rate, skin conductance, blood pressure, and so forth would seem more valid than paper and pencil tests in studying anxiety and arousal, this has not proven true. A major reason is that there is no single physiological response to the anxiety state. For example, Elliot (1964) reports a peak coefficient of .16 between any standardly used physiological measures. One study from sport psychology literature found a correlation of .10 between pulse rate and palmar sweat measures collected 2 minutes before gymnastics competition in female varsity athletes (Basler, Fisher, & Mumford, 1976). Additionally, people respond to stress by activating only one or several body systems and tend to favor these systems across a variety of situations (Hassett, 1978; Schnore, 1959). It has also been found that favored systems vary between people. These problems, combined with individual differences in automatic reactivity (Schnore, 1959), have made for little success in identifying arousal, and particularly trait anxiety, via physiological values.

However, these limitations may be reduced if anxiety and arousal are not considered to be unidimensional and if individual response reactivity is accounted for. Subsets of similar psychophysiological responses have been identified (Lacey, 1959), and certain responses have been associated with attentional processes (Landers, Furst, & Daniels 1981). Finally, physiological responses have also been found to verify the presence of anxiety or arousal in experimental situations (Martens & Landers, 1970).

AROUSAL AND PERFORMANCE

The relationship between arousal and performance has been studied mainly under the rubrics of *drive theory* and the *inverted-U hypothesis*. The research testing these models will be reviewed in this section. Methods of treating task complexity, a mediating variable in the arousal-performance relationship, will also be discussed.

Drive Theory

Clarke Hull (1943) initially advanced a drive theory of behavior which was later modified by Spence (1956). Simplistically presented, this theory states that performance (P) is a multiplicative function of drive state (D) and habit strength (H). Thus,

$$P = D \times H$$

Drive, for Hull, was a global, nonspecific energizer of all behavior and has been equated in the literature with the construct of arousal. *Habit strength* refers to the dominance of correct and incorrect responses in a motor skill. Drive theory assumes that arousal increases the dominant response. If the dominant response is correct (i.e., in the latter stages of skill acquisition or when performing simple skills) then arousal increases will enhance performance in a linear fashion. However, when the dominant response is incorrect (early skill acquisition or when performing complex skills) then increases in arousal will be detrimental to performance. Early research inferred drive states by imposing aversive stimuli such as food deprivation on animals. But the use of human subjects necessitated less aversive measures of drive, and this resulted in the development of the TMAS. Experimental results have supported drive theory in relatively simple tasks involving paired-associate learning or the classical conditioning of an eyeblink to a puff of air (Spence, 1964).

Results of studies employing motor tasks have been much more equivocal. In examining the drive theory/motor performance relationship, Martens (1971) classified studies by whether the presence of an experimental stressor (e.g., shock) was or was not employed. The latter category examined the chronic hypotheses of drive, that high anxiety subjects respond with greater drive in all situations. The presence of a stressor examined the emotional reactivity or situational hypothesis reformulated by Spence and Spence (1966), which states that differences between high and low anxiety subjects would occur only when a stressor was present. However, only a few studies obtained positive results in both classifications, causing Martens to recommend abandoning the drive theory. Instead, the use of alternative measures assessing state as well as trait anxiety was advised.

The difficulty of accurately measuring habit strength is another major impediment to using drive theory in nonlaboratory settings. As an example, Martens (1971) poses the question of whether walking on a treadmill, a task in one study, should be considered a novel (dominant response incorrect) or well learned (dominant response correct) task. Because drive theory is best tested with simple, carefully monitored motor skills, it would seem inapplicable to studying the myriad of interesting motor behaviors found in sport and recreational settings

(Martens, 1974a). While not all have agreed with Martens' conclusions (Spence, 1971), there has been a tendency in psychology to forsake drive theory as the primary explanation of behavior in favor of models more accountable to the wide variety of human self-deterministic behaviors (Beck, 1978; Korman, 1974). The reader is directed to Martens (1974a, 1977) for more extensive reviews of drive theory and motor performance.

The Inverted-U Hypothesis

We have seen that the inconclusive results of drive theory predicted a linear increase in performance with increasing levels of anxiety. An alternative model for examining the arousal-performance relationship is the Inverted-U Hypothesis. This hypothesis predicts that performance effectiveness will increase as arousal increases — up to some optimal point — whereupon further increases in arousal will produce a decrement in performance. This theory has immediate face validity for sport practitioners, and especially for coaches concerned that their charges are not sufficiently "psyched" or that they are too "psyched-up." Unfortunately, Martens (1971) notes a large discrepancy between its universal acceptance in psychological literature and the very equivocal results of its experimental tests. Martens (1974a) suggests several reasons for these inconsistent results. First, many studies supporting the inverted-U relationship have done so indirectly by utilizing only two stress conditions, but at least three points along the arousal continuum are needed for a direct test. A related concern is that many studies failed to certify that distinct levels of state anxiety actually were present in the particular situation (e.g., by monitoring physiological responses). Martens and Landers (1970) satisfied the above constraints by assigning high, moderate, and low trait anxiety boys to a motor tracking task involving three levels of stress. The validity of these stress levels was supported by heart rate and palmar sweating responses and by questionnaire data. The inverted-U hypothesis was supported in that moderately stressed subjects performed significantly better than subjects in the high or low stress conditions. Additionally, boys with moderate A-Trait scores significantly outperformed low A-Trait and high A-Trait boys.

Recently, investigators have examined the external validity (generalizability) of the inverted-U hypothesis with research conducted in competitive athletic settings. These field experiments are capable of eliciting the high levels of anxiety needed to obtain three distinct points along the arousal continuum. For example, Klavora (1978) assessed 924 pregame state anxiety values from 95 boys throughout a Canadian interscholastic high school basketball season. Differences in playing ability were controlled by asking coaches (postgame) to evaluate each player's game performance in terms of the boy's customary ability. The distribution of five anxiety means across performance levels supported the inverted-U-curve hypothesis, clearly showing that best performances were associated with moderate pregame A-State and poorest performances were marked by either very low or very high A-State means.

Fenz and his colleagues (Fenz & Epstein, 1967; Fenz & Jones, 1972) have conducted a series of interesting field studies that indirectly support the inverted-U hypothesis. They measured the arousal level of sport parachutists by skin conductance, heart rate, and respiration rate several times from when they first arrived at the airport until they were about to jump out of the plane. All jumpers showed increased arousal as the time to jump drew closer. However, the novice jumpers tended to show increasing levels of arousal right up until the actual jump, whereas experienced jumpers began to reduce their arousal to a more moderate level prior to the jump. More importantly, better jumpers in both the novice and experienced groups displayed this pre-jump reduction of arousal to more moderate levels as compared to poorer performers (Fenz & Jones, 1972). These findings have been replicated and they support the idea that moderate levels of arousal are more beneficial to performance than are high levels. It should be noted that since parachute jumping is a "life or death" activity it was not hard to create high levels of arousal!

As the results of applied research have grown, most investigators tend to agree that the inverted-U hypothesis is a parsimonious and valid way of interpreting the arousal-performance relationship. If this is the case, then what implications does this have for the practitioner, the coach, or the teacher? One apparent application concerns the use of pep talks or other activities designed to get athletes psyched-up for an upcoming opponent or event. Many coaches in the past have felt that the more aroused an athlete was, the better he or she would perform. The inverted-U would argue against such a conception, cautioning that if an athlete becomes too aroused his or her performance will suffer. Thus, it is up to the coach and athlete to somehow get the athlete functioning at his or her optimal level of arousal. Although this might seem like a relatively easy task, two very important factors that mediate the arousal performance relationship must be considered: the characteristics of the task and the nature of the individual.

Task Complexity and Optimal Arousal

One of the difficulties in verifying the inverted-U curve lies in the mediating effects of task complexity. It is difficult to determine what arousal levels should be *optimal* for different tasks. Earlier, in examining Hullian drive theory, it was stated that high drive levels would impair performance at tasks that had not been well learned (i.e., dominant response is incorrect). A related maxim was established by the Yerkes-

Dodson Law (Yerkes & Dodson, 1980). Easily acquired habits not requiring difficult discrimination or complex associations can be readily learned under high arousal, whereas complex tasks can be acquired only under conditions of low arousal.

These principles were utilized by Oxendine (1970) in developing a hierarchical classification of sports based on complexity and the degree of fine muscle control and judgment involved. Sports requiring the highest levels of arousal for optimal functioning were gross motor activities such as weight lifting, sprinting, and football tackling and blocking. At the end of the continuum of five sport classes were activities requiring fine muscle control and judgment for best execution, such as bowling, field goal kicking, and figure skating. This type of activity is best performed with low levels of arousal. The results of Weinberg and Genuchi (1980) supported this hypothesis in that low levels of both competitive A-Trait and A-State were related to better scores across 3 days of tournament golf, which is considered a task requiring precision and fine muscle movements. Research conducted with gymnasts (Basler, Fisher, & Mumford, 1976) failed to support a similar hierarchy of motor tasks classified by degree of inhibition (steadiness) needed in the task (Gutin, 1973).

Task complexity may be controlled by repeated measures designs such as Klavora's (1978), which examine serial performance at the same task and negate the presence of order or degree of difficulty. Sonstroem and Bernardo (1982) did this by relating pregame A-State responses to performance of 30 female college varsity players across three games of a basketball tournament. They also controlled for individual differences in arousal reactivity. That is, an A-State score of 32 could represent a low score for one person but a peak score for another athlete. Therefore, in testing the U-curve, a player's *median* A-State value across the three games was identified as her optimal (moderate) level of anxiety and *within subject* analyses were conducted. As hypothesized, median anxiety values were significantly associated with best game performances. Results indicated that 18% of game performance variance was explained by a curvilinear relationship with pregame state anxiety.

On a more applied level, what does the idea of task complexity mean in reaching one's optimal level of arousal? For example, take the case of the football coach who is trying to get his athletes to the optimal level of arousal. Football includes a variety of positions, many of which have different task requirements. A quarterback has to be very precise in handing off the ball and throwing it accurately as far as 50 yards down the field. On the other hand, an offensive or defensive lineman might have to be predominantly strong and speedy, yet still be concerned about accuracy and precision. Thus, increasing the team's arousal level may benefit players in some positions but be detrimental for players in other positions. Coaches, teachers, and athletes must carefully assess the task requirements of their sport in attempting to reach optimal levels of arousal.

Individual Differences

In addition to the type of sport skill, an athlete's individual makeup is also an important factor in determining optimal arousal levels. Some athletes perform better under high pressure conditions whereas others perform poorly. Thus, when faced with a stressful situation like shooting 2 foul shots with 3 seconds left in the game and the team trailing by 1 point, one athlete may become aroused to the optimal level and perform well while another athlete may become overaroused and miss the shots. Therefore, the coach must know his/her athletes and recognize when to psych them up and when to reassure and relax them. Landers (1978, 1980) has suggested that the regulation of attentional processes may play a significant role in the relationship between arousal and performance.

ATTENTION AND PERFORMANCE

In delineating the role of attention in arousal-performance relationships, Landers has suggested that low arousal is associated with the uncritical acceptance of irrelevant cues. Moderate or optimal arousal increases perceptual selectivity, thus eliminating task-irrelevant cues. High arousal leads to a well documented deterioration in performance due to the elimination of relevant cues (Landers, 1978). This latter event can be related to perceptual narrowing which eliminates task-relevant cues (Easterbrook, 1959) or to distractibility (Wachtel, 1967). Thus, an athlete who is underaroused may pay attention to the crowd or be thinking about an opponent instead of concentrating on the game. Similarly, an athlete under high stress may be thinking about his or her own anxieties instead of concentrating on task-relevant cues like watching the ball.

A major contribution to the understanding of athletic performance comes from the extension of Wachtel's (1967) work by Robert Nideffer. Specifically, Nideffer (1976b) has described attention as consisting of two bipolar dimensions: width (broad-narrow) and direction (internal-external). As examples, free-throw shooting in basketball would require a narrow, external focus, and strategic coaching of a sport team most often would entail a broad, internal focus. Similarly, a point guard in basketball would require a broad external focus whereas a long-distance runner or swimmer would predominantly utilize an internal narrow attentional focus. His Test of Attentional and Interpersonal Style (TAIS) assesses trait measures of attention on these dimensions (Nideffer, 1979). Supposedly, these traits are modifiable, often via anxiety reduction, and have interested psychologists concerned with improving athletic performance. In support of the TAIS, Nideffer (1976b) found that inconsistent varsity swimmers tested as becoming overloaded with both internal and external stimuli and demonstrated an inability to effectively narrow attention. Conversely, swimmers rated by their coach as falling apart or choking under pressure tended to narrow their attention excessively.

Van Schoyck and Grasha (1981) modified the TAIS, applying it to situations specific to tennis. The Tennis-TAIS (T-TAIS) proved superior to the TAIS at distinguishing skill levels in 90 players. Data also questioned the existence of a directional (internal-external) dimension and a width (broad-narrow) dimension. Rather, the dimensions of both the TAIS and T-TAIS seem better represented by a multidimensional bandwidth incorporating at least the components of *scanning* and *focusing* as suggested by Wachtel (1967). Scanning refers to the perceived ability to attend to many aspects of the stimulus field, while focusing is the perception of ability to concentrate. For example, Landers, Furst, and Daniels (1981) found that trait anxiety related positively to a lack of focus in rifle, pistol, skeet, and trap shooters. While the recency of TAIS precludes conclusive evaluation, Landers et al. note that anxiety, attention, and performance relationships may be better examined by (a) developing multidimensional sport-specific scales, (b) using direct measures of behavior, or (c) modifying the TAIS to delete scale overlap.

Certainly Nideffer's contributions have served to accentuate the importance of attention and perceptual style in sports. Landers et al. (1981) present an impressive collection of research that examines theories of attention in terms of physiological responses and individual differences in shooters to perceive and control these responses while performing.

SITUATION-SPECIFIC TRAITS
AND INTERACTIONISM

The late 1960s and early 1970s witnessed the culmination of an historical battle waged between personality psychologists who emphasized the importance of traits in determining behavior and social psychologists who credited situations as the primary source of behavior (Magnusson & Endler, 1977; Mischel, 1968). The empirical efforts of Endler and Hunt (1966) and Endler, Hunt, and Rosenstein (1962) provided a particularly critical indictment of trait theory. Their S-R Inventory of Anxiousness contained 11 anxiety-eliciting situations and 14 modes of response varying from "heart beats faster" to "feel anxious." Each mode of reponse

was paired with each of the 11 situations to provide 154 inventory items
(14 $\times$ 11) which were reacted to on a 5-step scale. The responses of a
large number of subjects from three samples indicated that the individuals accounted for only 7% of the total score variance (Endler &
Hunt, 1966). However, approximately 27% of score variation was explained by the three single interactions: person $\times$ situations, person $\times$
response modes, and situations $\times$ response modes.

The effects of this novel instrument and analysis resulted in a ques-
tioning of global trait theory and reemphasized an interest in interactionism. That is, behavior is believed to be determined by the reciprocal
interaction of personal traits and the characteristics of different situations. When attempting to understand anxiety-performance relationships, it is necessary to consider both the trait anxiety of the athlete and
the constraints of the situation.

Competitive Trait Anxiety

A major consequence of this newer interactionist psychology was an emphasis on the development of situation-specific trait tests. By assessing
inter-individual responses to particular situations, the essential elements
of interactionism could be implemented (Endler & Okada, 1975).
Martens' (1977) construction of the Sport Competition Anxiety Test
(SCAT) has represented a notable standard of this principle by its
measurement of Competitive Trait Anxiety (CTA). This construct
assesses individual differences in perceiving competitive situations as
threatening and leads to corresponding differences in A-State responses.
The SCAT Manual (Martens, 1977) presents impressive data and information documenting theory, development, reliability, and validity of this
inventory. Essential validity was best demonstrated in that SCAT
predicted pregame A-State scores ($r = .64$) as compared to the STAI
A-Trait ($r = .30$) and coaches' ratings ($r = .12$) (Martens & Simon,
1976).

In its short history SCAT has uniquely advanced an understanding
of anxiety in motor learning and sport. Much of this research is presented in the subsequent chapters by Tara Scanlan and Michael Passer.
SCAT was also employed in the previously discussed studies of Weinberg
and Genuchi (1980) and Sonstroem and Bernardo (1982). Sonstroem and
Bernardo found the detrimental effects of high A-State in basketball performance to be particularly pronounced in high competitive trait anxiety
players. Martens has extended the concept of situation specificity to the
development of an A-State inventory specific to competitive settings
known as the Competitive State Anxiety Inventory (Martens, 1977;
Martens, Burton, Rivkin, & Simon, 1980).

Multidimensional Trait Anxiety

The importance of situations in evoking trait-influenced behavior has been advanced further by those investigators initially responsible for its empirical demonstration. Remarking that the STAI and TMAS focus almost exclusively on interpersonal and ego-threatening aspects of A-Trait, Endler and Okada (1975) developed the S-R Inventory of General Trait Anxiousness (SR-GTA). Four types of A-Trait are assessed in response to four classes of situations: *interpersonal, physical danger, ambiguous* (new or strange situations), and *innocuous* (general or daily routines). One of their validity experiments established a correlation of .64 (in females but not males) between physical danger A-Trait and A-State changes in response to threat of shock. The coefficient with interpersonal A-Trait was .003, supporting the theory that A-Trait must be congruent to the threatening situation to evoke A-State reactions (Endler & Okada, 1975).

Flood and Endler (1980) added a *social evaluation* scale to the inventory and identified premeet A-State elevations in 41 track athletes to be associated primarily with the threat of social evaluation. This same effect was observed in an academic examination setting (Phillips & Endler, 1982). Within the area of leisure, recreational participation has been related inversely to general trait anxiety (Bishop & Witt, 1970). Using the SR-GTA, Vitelli and Frisch (1982) have identified physical danger A-Trait as the major component of this association. Surprisingly, the above result was not replicated in a deepwater diving setting (Griffiths, Steel, & Vaccaro, 1982).

Kroll (1979) has suggested that scales such as the TMAS, STAI, and even the SCAT are capable of assessing the presence of anxiety but not the causes. While the SR-GTA assesses A-Trait in response to five general situations, these situations may or may not be construed by athletes to be present in all sport settings. Kroll (1979) has attempted to solve these limitations by asking large numbers of athletes what makes them anxious before competition. While final analyses are incomplete and yet to be reported, preliminary screening has identified 125 frequently voiced items forming five major clusters. These are somatic complaints, fear of failure, feelings of inadequacy, loss of control, and guilt. Fisher (1979) and Fisher and Zwart (1982) used an approach similar to Kroll (1979) and employed the model of Endler, Hunt, and Rosenstein (1962) with 13 anxiety-eliciting situations specific to basketball. Essentially, three dimensions of anxiety reflecting trait differences were revealed: ego threat, outcome uncertainty/certainty (threat of tie games or losses), and anticipation (anxiety fostered by pending situations). The two examples above demonstrate the advantage of studying stimulus content inherent in sport settings to develop knowledge of the anxiety processes present in sport. They also indicate the importance of understanding what makes an athlete anxious so that a coach or sport psychologist can effectively reduce precompetitive anxiety.

The Relevance of Somatic Anxiety

Although we have discussed the limited ability of physiological measures to accurately portray anxiety across people, these same limitations need not extend to perceptions of individual anxiety states. Mandler, Mandler, and Uviller (1958) demonstrated a relationship between perceptions of physiological responses and actual somatic responses under stress and between the former and TMAS scores. This concept has been advanced by those scientists studying anxiety reduction in therapy. Citing an impressive array of research, Davidson and Schwartz (1976) postulated that the perception of anxiety responses could be separated into *cognitive* and *somatic* components. The Cognitive-Somatic Anxiety Questionnaire (CSAQ) was developed to assess characteristically experienced anxiety responses in each mode (Schwartz, Davidson, & Goleman, 1978). This categorization has provided further tests of the anxiety system-treatment specificity principle advocated by Borkovec (1976). That is, cognitive anxiety reduction is more compatible with self-instruction and thought-stopping methods, for example, and somatic anxiety reduction is better accomplished with methods such as progressive relaxation, biofeedback, and exercise.

Schwartz et al. (1978) administered the CSAQ to subjects who were either consistent exercisers or meditators. As predicted, exercisers reported more cognitive anxiety and less somatic anxiety than meditators. No difference between cognitive and somatic anxiety levels were observed in the meditators. It is important to recognize, however, that these results fail to establish a causative effect of treatment on anxiety. Anxiety system-treatment specificity was better supported in a study by Lehrer, Schoicket, Carrington, and Woolfolk (1981), but it failed to control for baseline effects. Meditation produced a greater effect on cognitive anxiety, and progressive relaxation reduced somatic anxiety. Other studies have partially supported the model (Altmaier, Leary, Ross, & Thornbrough, 1982; Woolfolk, Lehrer, McCann, & Rooney, 1982). Although requiring replication and continued study, Heide and Borkovec (1983) found progressive relaxation (alternate flexing and relaxing body muscles) to be superior to meditation in reducing anxiety and in eliciting less treatment-induced anxiety. Recently, Lehrer and Woolfolk (1982) have used a scale to measure cognitive, somatic, *and* behavioral anxiety (social avoidance) responses.

All of the multidimensional measures presented in this chapter are in their developmental infancy. Yet their use seemingly would advance a discernment of *how* exercise reduces anxiety. The current literature indicates that only one study has employed the CSAQ as a state measure. In this study Heide and Borkovec (1983) found no cognitive or somatic A-State differences in response to progressive relaxation and meditation.

ANXIETY REDUCTION VIA EXERCISE

In addition to the area of anxiety and performance, the study of how anxiety may be reduced through physical activity and exercise programs has generated much attention. Research in this area has distinguished between acute (short-term) and chronic (ongoing) effects of exercise. Results have been quite consistent in documenting anxiety reductions 5-30 minutes post-exercise (acute effect) (deVries, 1968; deVries & Adams, 1972; Morgan, 1973b, 1979a). This effect appears to be particularly true for vigorous as opposed to light exercise (Mihevic, 1981; Morgan, 1979a) and may be especially pronounced in initially high-anxious subjects (Morgan, 1979a). However, comparisons with meditation or other anxiety-reduction modalities have failed to establish the superiority of exercise (Bahrke, 1979). In fact, Bahrke and Morgan (1978) failed to distinguish any anxiety-reduction differences between exercise, meditation, and a control group that had rested for 20 minutes in a recliner! The authors suggest and provide corroborative evidence that simply taking "time out" may be as effective as exercise or other techniques for reducing anxiety in the average person. Similarly, a group eating lunch and conversing with friends experienced A-State decrements comparable to exercise and running groups (Wilson, Berger, & Bird, 1981). Comparatively little systematic research has examined the chronic effect of exercise on anxiety. Briefly, the little available evidence indicates that chronic exercise does reduce anxiety states (deVries, 1968; Mihevic, 1981; Morgan, 1979a).

So far we are unable to postulate the manner in which exercise reduces anxiety. Our research designs sometimes have excluded control groups and have generally used the same pre-post designs that collect final A-State values 5-30 minutes after exercise. Longitudinal or repeated measures designs or those assessing A-State 2-4 hours after exercise are lacking. Additionally, one of the problems may be the almost exclusive use of global, unidimensional A-State measures such as the STAI. While paper and pencil measures are useful in this area of study, our greatest understanding of anxiety reduction via exercise may come from chemical-psychological studies yet to be done.

SUMMARY

Hopefully this brief review has oriented the reader to issues, directions, and methods involved in studying physical activity-anxiety relationships. The causes of human behavior are complex; alternative explanations can always be provided for results from simpler investigations. Enthusiastic investigators of sport are urged to avail themselves of psychological theory, multidimensional and/or situation-specific measures, replication, and varied, more complex designs. The preeminence of sport and exercise in contemporary America has brought the game into our ballpark.

Chapter 9

Competitive Stress and the Child Athlete

Tara K. Scanlan
University of California-Los Angeles

Of the millions of 6- to 16-year-old children participating in competitive youth sport activities, many do not experience competitive stress. But other athletes do. Some events that commonly occur in competition can create stress, and adults who are significant to the child play a role in the levels of stress exhibited by some youngsters. This chapter discusses the nature of competitive stress, examines the achievement characteristics of competitive sport that can induce stress, and reviews the research that identifies sources of competitive stress in children. Specifically, we will see what type of child experiences stress, what situational factors within competition can create stress, and what adult influences are associated with stress. Implications of these results are presented with an eye toward reducing stress and making competitive sport a positive experience for all children. Finally, some directions for future research are suggested.

THE NATURE OF COMPETITIVE STRESS

Competitive stress is the negative emotional reaction a child feels when his/her self-esteem is threatened. This personal threat occurs when the young athlete perceives an imbalance between the performance demands of the competition and his/her own ability to successfully meet those demands, under conditions where the consequences of such a failure are thought to be important (Martens, 1977). It must be emphasized that threat to self-esteem is based on the child's own appraisal of the competitive situation. It is his/her *perceptions* of inadequacy in successfully meeting the performance demands, and his/her *perceptions* of the consequences of failure, that create the threat to self-esteem which triggers the stress reaction.

The fact that stress is a function of the athlete's perceptions leads to two important considerations. First, the perceptions might not correspond to reality. For example, a very talented athlete could experience stress by overestimating the performance demands and exaggerating the importance of successfully meeting these demands. Second, stress can occur at any point during the competition that a child perceives the threatening discrepancy between demand and capability, such as *before* competition if he/she anticipates a poor performance, *during* competition if the child feels he/she is performing inadequately and may fail, and *after* competition if the child appraises the completed performance as inadequate (Scanlan & Passer, 1978b).

Researchers measure competitive stress by state anxiety responses. State anxiety involves the feelings of apprehension, tension, and activation that occur as an immediate, "right now" reaction to a situation that threatens one's self-esteem (Spielberger, 1966). State anxiety can be measured behaviorally, physiologically, and psychologically. Common behaviors associated with state anxiety include jitteriness, nervous laughter, appetite loss, and insomnia. Physiologically, increased activation of the autonomic nervous system can be measured by assessing heart rate, respiration, galvanic skin responses, and palmar sweating. Psychologically, state anxiety can be measured through inventories and questionnaires that more directly assess a child's feelings of stress. The two most commonly used psychological inventories in competitive stress research have been the State Anxiety Inventory for Children (SAIC) developed by Spielberger (1973), and the children's version of the Competitive State Anxiety Inventory (CSAI-C) developed by Martens and his colleagues (Martens, Burton, Rivkin, & Simon, 1980).

SOCIAL EVALUATION, COMPETITIVE SPORT, AND STRESS

Competitive sport can be stressful because it involves extensive social evaluation of athletic ability or competence (Scanlan, 1978a). Social evaluation is the appraisal information about ability that an individual receives from other people. Any achievement situation involving social evaluation of an ability, which the child considers important, can be threatening if he or she anticipates failing and getting negative appraisals from others. The typical child places great value on athletic competence and is particularly sensitive to the appraisals of others about this ability. Information about the child's athletic competence is transmitted through interactions with coaches, parents, other significant adults, teammates, and opponents — as well as by direct ability comparisons with peers. These ability comparisons are common in sport and can have significant consequences. Such comparisons often determine who starts and who warms the bench, for example, or who makes the all-star team and who gets cut from the regular team.

The importance of ability appraisals was demonstrated in a study by Pierce (1980), who found that many participants worry about poor performance, about making mistakes, and about the reactions of their peers and coaches. In fact, 26% of the athletes who expressed these concerns indicated that such worries might prevent them from participating in sports in the future. Worries about failure and negative social evaluation were also found by Orlick and Botterill (1975) to be the major reasons why some children drop out of sport.

When considering the social evaluation potential in sport, the specific sport context must be taken into account. Some sports are inherently more evaluative than others and therefore can be more stress inducing. For example, individual sports focus directly on personal performance. The responsibility for the outcome rests with the individual athlete and the performance process itself is highly visible, resulting in athletic brilliance or blunder being witnessed by all. In contrast, interactive team sports require that teammates share the responsibility for the outcome, and individual performance is typically less apparent by virtue of being only part of the general action of the group. According to field studies by Griffin (1972), Johnson (1949), and Simon and Martens (1979), athletes of individual sports exhibit greater precompetition state anxiety than athletes of team sports. Wrestling, in which an error can result in a sudden pin, was found to be a particularly stressful sport for boys (Simon & Martens, 1979) and college males (Johnson, 1949). Gymnastics, in which the individual performance process is closely scrutinized and each action's effect on eventual success or failure is magnified, was also found to be stressful for boys (Simon & Martens, 1979) and for girls (Griffin, 1972).

Interestingly, the study by Simon and Martens found that band solos caused higher pre-event state anxiety than did any sport that they examined. Again, and in another achievement domain, we see the potential stress effects of social evaluation when focused so directly on individual performance.

Within the interactive team sport context there are particular events that accent individual performance which can increase the social evaluation potential to levels perhaps more aligned with individual sports. For instance, the social evaluation can be quite intense for the star player of a team or for one who holds a key position such as the football quarterback. Specific events within a team sport that highlight individual performance include a corner shot in field hockey, a free throw in basketball, and batting in baseball. In such cases the action often stops abruptly and/or becomes highly focused, leaving the athlete to execute a skill—alone—under the watchful eyes of many. Coaches have long known that this sudden focus on individual performance can be stressful. Isn't it common for an opposing coach to call a time-out before a crucial free throw, just to give the player some time to think about it? Would you bet that "it" means social evaluation, important consequences, and inadequacy?

Hanson (1967), in an early study, demonstrated the impact that highlighting individual performance can have on the autonomic arousal levels of Little League players. When at bat, players' heart rates escalated dramatically to an average of 166 beats per minute (bpm), 56 bpm above their mean resting rate of 110. In fact, no other event during the game caused arousal increases that even closely approximated the levels experienced when batting.

A second study with Little League players (Lowe & McGrath, 1971) assessed their pulse and respiration rates before batting, under conditions where the consequences of their performance varied in importance. Players were tested throughout the entire season. The two important variables examined were the criticality of the game and the criticality of the situation. Game criticality involved the ranking of the two teams within the league, the difference in their win-loss percentages, and the number of games left in the season. Situation criticality included variables such as the inning and number of outs in the inning, the score, and the number and placement of the base runners. The findings indicated higher autonomic arousal levels under conditions of increased importance, with game criticality having an even greater effect than situation criticality.

These two ingenious field studies are evidence that autonomic arousal increases as personal performance becomes accentuated and as the importance of the performance increases. Yet arousal can be caused by many things besides stress, such as excitement, elation, and anger. Therefore, without also using psychological assessments to more directly assess threat, it cannot be conclusively determined that the boys were manifesting stress. It is quite likely that the arousal increases reflected stress reactions by some players, whereas for others they indicated more positive emotional states such as the excitement of facing a challenge.

As already noted, competitive sport can be stressful because it is an important achievement arena for many children, since athletic competence is demonstrated, tested, and evaluated in a very public manner. Whether a child actually experiences stress in this setting will depend on his or her perceptions of adequacy, which are based on the delicate balance between demands and capabilities.

Presented next is the evidence regarding the intrapersonal (individual difference), situational, and significant adult factors that tip this critical balance and create stress. In reviewing this literature on sources of competitive stress, we will begin in the laboratory setting and then move to the naturalistic contexts of team and individual sports.

SOURCES OF COMPETITIVE STRESS

Laboratory Research

Two laboratory experiments (Martens & Gill, 1976; Scanlan, 1975, 1977) were conducted in an effort to identify sources of competitive stress. These studies took place in the controlled environment of a van, which was driven to various schools where fifth and sixth graders competed individually on a complex motor maze task. The competition ostensibly occurred via a computer against a student in another school. Actually, there was no real opponent. All the feedback information the children received from the bogus computer was prearranged by the experimenter. To further simulate the individual sport context, the experimental procedures accentuated social evaluation.

In the Scanlan study (1975, 1977), the two potential sources of stress examined were the intrapersonal factor of competitive trait anxiety and the situational variable of win-loss. Competitive trait anxiety (CTA) is a stable personality disposition that reflects the tendency to perceive competitive situations as threatening to self-esteem (Martens, 1977). In contrast to the transitory nature of state anxiety, CTA represents a more chronic perception of competitive situations which probably evolves over time as the child accrues experiences in this setting. Boys who were extremely high and low in competitive trait anxiety, as measured by the Sport Competition Anxiety Test (Martens, 1977), were selected to participate in the study. Win-loss was manipulated by having the boys win 80% (W80), 50% (W50), or only 20% (W20) of 20 contests against their alleged opponent. Each contest involved one timed trial through the motor maze. Competitive stress was measured by the Spielberger SAIC (1973) and, to control for individual differences in state anxiety, a baseline measure was taken before the boys entered the van. Then, state anxiety was assessed immediately before and after the competition, as well as after a final debriefing session in which all boys in the W50 and W20 groups received success feedback.

The findings showed that CTA was a significant source of precompetition stress and that win-loss was the major cause of postcompetition stress. Just before competing, the high CTA boys exhibited greater state anxiety than the low CTA boys. After competing, the W20 group showed a significant increase in state anxiety from its precompetition level, the W50 group demonstrated no difference, and the W80 group indicated a significant decrease in pre- to postcompetition state anxiety. Comparing the postcompetition state anxiety means of the three groups, we can see that the W20 group (M = 39.73) evidenced significantly greater state anxiety than the W50 (M = 33.52) and W80 (M = 30.25) groups. The state anxiety differences between the W50 and W80 groups were also statistically reliable. A further indication of the importance of successful performance to these boys was shown by the dramatic drop in state anxiety that occurred after the W20 (M = 24.4) and W50 (M = 24.9) groups received success feedback in the debriefing.

The experiment by Martens and Gill (1976) involved similar procedures but extended the previous study in two significant ways. First, high and low CTA children of both sexes were tested. Second, state anxiety was assessed midway through the competition, after 10 of the 20 contests were completed. The findings replicated those of the Scanlan study and, importantly, showed that CTA and win-loss are common sources of stress to both boys and girls.

As this is one of the few studies examining sources of stress during competition, the midcompetition state anxiety results are particularly illuminating. With respect to CTA, the findings showed even greater state anxiety differences between high and low CTA children at midcompetition than at precompetition. Regarding the win-loss variable, the midcompetition state anxiety level of the already-winning W80 group still approximated its precompetition level, whereas the W20 and W50 groups already began to show significant increases. In fact, it was at midcompetition that the W50 group experienced its greatest stress, with the boys indicating even greater state anxiety than the girls.

In sum, the laboratory findings show that boys and girls who are high in CTA experience greater state anxiety before and during competition than do their low CTA counterparts. Win-loss, and even the degree of success achieved, are the primary determinants of postcompetition stress. The win-loss finding also has been demonstrated in two other laboratory experiments (Corbin & Nix, 1979; Gill & Martens, 1977).

Field Research

The Team Sport Context.   After identifying CTA and win-loss as sources of competitive stress through experiments in the laboratory, my colleagues and I conducted a series of field studies in the naturalistic environment of children's sports. We shifted the research methodology and setting for two reasons. First, we wanted to see if the results from the controlled confines of the laboratory would generalize to the more complex, real life arena of competitive youth sports. Second, we wanted to capitalize on the discovery potential of the natural setting to identify other factors associated with the experience of stress.

As a final methodological comment, the importance of replication (reproducing similar results in more than one study) should be emphasized. This replication process is critical to establishing confidence in the findings of both laboratory and field research. It is particularly crucial in field studies, where events occur naturally and the experimenter cannot impose the strict methodological control that is possible in the laboratory setting. With this in mind, the three field studies presented next were designed to replicate as well as to extend the findings of each other. Built into this replication process were some tests of the generalizability of the findings (called external validity) to various types of participants and sport contexts.

The first two field studies involved competitive soccer players participating with the American Youth Soccer Organization (AYSO). In the first study (Scanlan & Passer, 1978b) we tested 11- to 12-year-old boys. To see if the findings generalized to both genders, a year later we assessed girls from the same age group and geographic region (Scanlan & Passer, 1979a). Similar research procedures were used in both studies, and 16 teams were tested.

Several intrapersonal factors thought to be potentially related to stress were assessed at practice sessions prior to the start of the season. These included CTA, self-esteem, and, for control purposes, baseline state anxiety. Self-esteem, like CTA, is a stable personality disposition that reflects a child's overall opinion or evaluation of himself/herself and indicates how capable, successful, and worthy the child feels (Coopersmith, 1967). Competitive stress, measured by the Spielberger SAIC, was assessed before and immediately after each team's game on a set day. Also assessed before the game were players' expectancies about whether they thought their team would win or lose, and how well each player expected to perform individually.

The findings of these two studies were virtually identical, which demonstrated successful replication within the field setting and indicated the generalizability of the findings to both genders. Additionally, the previous laboratory results indicating CTA and win-loss as respective sources of pre- and postcompetition stress were replicated. This demonstrates the generalizability of these findings to the real-world setting of children's team sports.

The new intrapersonal factors found to be related to the precompetition stress experienced by boys and girls were self-esteem and team performance expectancies and, in the case of boys only, personal performance expectancies. Athletes with low self-esteem and low expectancies experienced greater precompetition state anxiety than did athletes who were high on these attributes. In contrast to these factors which all reflect *perceptions* of inadequacy, indicants of perhaps a more realistic demand/capability imbalance were not found to be associated with precompetition stress. These nonstress-related factors included the player's actual soccer ability, the team's overall win-loss record, and the score of the previous game against the same opponent.

Postcompetition stress was clearly influenced not only by win-loss but, again, by the level of success achieved. In the boys' study, players on teams that lost the game by only one goal indicated greater state anxiety than players on teams losing by two or more goals. In the girls' study, enough games ended in a tie to be able to examine this variable. We found that a tie game was not a neutral experience. Consistent with previous laboratory findings regarding the W50 group, the state anxiety levels of tying players fell in between those of winning and losing players, and differed significantly from both of the other groups. Extending the laboratory findings in which stress was shown to be related to personal performance outcomes, these field data indicate that players' personal stress levels are influenced by team outcomes.

One intrapersonal factor found to be associated with postcompetition stress was the amount of fun players experienced during the game. Players who had more fun experienced lower state anxiety levels than did players who had less fun. We could not determine a causal relationship from the data, so it is not clear whether more fun created less stress or less stress resulted in more fun. The important point is that fun and stress are inversely related, and that this relationship holds true for losing as well as winning players. It is possible, therefore, that fun may be an important factor that takes some of the edge off defeat.

The Individual Sport Context.   The most recent study (Scanlan & Lewthwaite, 1982) in this series tested 9- to 14-year-old wrestlers from all over the state who competed in the season's final tournament, sponsored by the California Age Group Wrestling Association. Although several issues were addressed in this study, only two are discussed here. First, we wanted to determine whether the variables associated with stress in the interactive team sport context would also be predictive of stress in the individual sport setting of competitive wrestling. Second, we wanted to examine the relationship between stress and various sport-related perceptions that wrestlers had about their parents and coaches. State anxiety was assessed in this study by the Martens et al. CSAI-C.

In accord with earlier results, CTA and personal performance expectancies were shown to be related to precompetition stress; win-loss and fun were again found to be reliably associated with postcompetition stress. These data demonstrate the context generalizability of previous findings in soccer, and show that these stress-related variables are common to the diverse contexts of both team and individual sports.

The role that significant adults play in the competitive stress experience has received popular notoriety but little research attention. Understanding this adult role is important because stress is based on a child's perceptions, and adults are critical in shaping these perceptions. To begin to achieve this understanding, we first administered a questionnaire in the wrestling study which was comprised of many items focusing on various adult influences that could be stress related. We then used a statistical technique, factor analysis, to determine if the specific questionnaire items would group together under more general, common themes. Two of these themes (factors) were found to be associated with precompetition stress.

The factor showing the strongest relationship to precompetition stress represented the general theme of "parental pressure to wrestle." Boys who felt they had to wrestle in order to please their parents experienced greater precompetition state anxiety than wrestlers who did not feel pressured to participate in the sport. The second stress-related factor depicted the theme of "worries about receiving negative performance evaluations from parents and coaches." Wrestlers who more frequently worried about this negative social evaluation before their matches experienced greater precompetition state anxiety than did boys who worried less about the appraisals of their parents and coaches.

POST-CHAPTER WRAP-UP

Competitive sport is an important achievement arena that involves extensive social evaluation of athletic competence through peer comparisons and appraisals given by adults. Competing can be a stressful experience to some athletes and under some conditions. Stress occurs if the athlete perceives that he/she is not capable of successfully meeting the demands of the competition and yet feels that it is important to do so. The negative consequences of this perceived demand/capability imbalance can include feelings of failure and/or the threat of incurring negative evaluations from significant people. The laboratory and field research reviewed here has identified some of the intrapersonal, situational, and significant adult factors that tip the critical demand/capability balance, heighten the importance and/or probability of negative consequences, and thereby cause stress. By knowing these factors, we are in a better position to achieve this balance.

Concerning intrapersonal factors, we have seen that children who manifest chronic perceptions of inadequacy (high CTA, low self-esteem), and perceptions of a more event-specific kind (low team and personal performance expectances), exhibit more stress when facing an upcoming competition than do children who feel more capable. Situational factors that intensify social evaluation and place great importance on successful performance (the individual nature of the sport, evaluative events within some team sports, game and situational criticality) can also intensify the stress that some athletes feel before and during competition. Finally, some recent data suggest that certain behaviors of significant adults (parental pressure to wrestle and worries about negative social evaluation), at least as seen through the child's eyes, are associated with precompetition stress.

The most potent situational source of postcompetition stress is defeat, with state anxiety levels even fluctuating with the degree of success or failure attained. It appears that many children interpret a win as the major standard for success. Unfortunately a loss, either by one athlete or by the whole team, becomes a personally threatening event. And finally, independent of victory or defeat, the amount of fun a child has while competing is inversely related to postcompetition stress.

Implications and Applications

By understanding the sources of competitive stress, we are in a better position to know how to structure the competitive experience to reduce stress. Implications and applications of the intrapersonal, sport context, and win-loss results will now be discussed with this end in mind. Additional applications of the findings reviewed in this chapter are presented in Scanlan (1982) and Scanlan and Passer (1981a).

Intrapersonal Factors.   The findings presented here clearly show that individual differences play a critical role in the experience of stress. Yet, some alarming results indicate that coaches vary greatly in their awareness of the precompetition stress levels characteristically manifested by their athletes and that, as a group, coaches' sensitivity in this regard is quite low (Martens & Simon, 1976; Martens, Rivkin, & Burton, 1980). In fact, players were found to be considerably more accurate in appraising the stress levels of their coaches than coaches were in assessing the amount of stress commonly felt by their athletes (Martens et al., 1980)!

The intrapersonal stress results illustrate the importance of being aware of individual differences, understanding the child's perceptions, and treating each young athlete as an individual. To do this one must be observant, communicative, and sensitive. Moreover, now that we are gaining a better understanding of the types of children who experience stress, and of their underlying perceptions of inadequacy, the processes of observation and communication can be enhanced. We now have a better idea of who to look for and what to be sensitive to when working with young athletes.

The Sport Context. The discussion and results pertaining to social evaluation suggest that the nature of the sport activity itself can be a source of stress. Certainly this does not mean that children shouldn't wrestle, participate in gymnastics, or play baseball! It does mean that greater attention should be given to matching the needs of the child to the demands and opportunities inherent in specific activities. A confident child who thrives on personal achievement might find individual sports to be very rewarding and team sports less motivating. On the other hand, a highly stressed athlete might benefit more from participating in team sports and positions that are highly interactive.

Win-Loss. The win-loss results point to the criticality of putting this seemingly paramount outcome into perspective for young athletes — and for adults working with them — to reduce this major source of stress. There is no question that victory and defeat are a natural part of competition, but how important should they be? As long as victory is the principle or only goal defining success, defeat must be defined as failure and will be stressful. Furthermore, because at least half of the competitors in any given contest incur defeat, the experience of failure will always be pervasive under this goal structure.

Important for reducing stress while fostering achievement is a challenging, success-oriented competitive environment as opposed to a threatening, failure-laden one. To create this atmosphere, realistic personal performance goals must replace winning as the principle criterion for success. These performance goals should focus on skill development and improvement. To be realistic, they must be specific and individually tailored for each athlete, and usually should be set slightly above the athlete's current performance level so that practice and effort can lead to success. Accordingly, the goals should be raised after consistent achievement or lowered in the face of setbacks. Finally, they need to be clearly measurable so that progress can be monitored and recognized (see Martens, Christina, Harvey, & Sharkey, 1981, and Chapter 14 by O'Block & Evans for a more detailed discussion of effective goal-setting techniques).

Positively striving to improve and perform one's best are obviously also important ingredients to winning. However, if a loss does occur under these conditions, because of a superior opponent or some other factor beyond the athlete's control, the child will not be robbed of the feelings of success that accompany the achievement of personal goals. We contend that it is not defeat itself that is so stress inducing. Instead, it is the complete failure that a loss represents when the only valued criterion for success is victory. By striving for and attaining performance goals, feelings of personal accomplishment and success can be achieved by all participants, regardless of outcome.

Future Research Directions

Competitive trait anxiety has now been clearly established to be an important source of competitive stress. However, very little is known about how this stable personality disposition actually develops. The reader interested in pursuing this topic is referred to the educational psychology literature on the somewhat analogous disposition of test anxiety and to Chapter 10 by Michael Passer.

A second finding that merits more refined examination is the inverse relationship between fun and stress. This result is interesting in that it consistently accounts for a large amount of the postcompetition stress variance and occurs independent of victory and defeat. Therefore, it is not simply indicating that winners have more fun than losers, a result that would be rather trivial and probably not worthy of further pursuit. To understand the relationship between fun and stress, one must establish the causal nature of the relationship, delineate children's definitions of fun, and determine why the two variables are related.

Finally, the results pertaining to significant adults open a whole new avenue for research on competitive stress. They provide the first empirical confirmation of earlier conceptualizations (Scanlan, 1978a) regarding the critical role that parents and coaches play in shaping children's perceptions of competition. Further, the results lend insight into some of the specific types of adult influences that are particularly salient to the stress that young athletes experience. So far, we have only scratched the surface in this area but the results clearly demonstrate that this is an important avenue for further research.

Chapter 10

Competitive Trait Anxiety in Children and Adolescents

Michael W. Passer
University of Washington

When people compete they are confronted with a variety of situational demands. These demands, which may pertain to performance evaluation, skill acquisition and improvement, and social interaction, represent "calls for action" (Sarason, 1980) to which the individual must respond. Many people view these demands primarily as sources of challenge and excitement. Although these individuals may sometimes experience anxiety or other negative affects while competing, they typically perceive competition as relatively nonthreatening and nonstressful. For some people, however, the challenge and excitement of competition often are accompanied or supplanted by anxiety or other stress responses. They frequently become tense and apprehensive prior to or during competition; instead of attending to the task at hand, they focus on their heightened emotional arousal or become preoccupied with worry. In short, certain individuals have a general tendency to perceive competitive situations as ego-threatening and stressful.

Competitive trait anxiety is a disposition conceptualized by Martens (1977) as representing these individual differences in the tendency to perceive competition as threatening. That is, high competitive-trait-anxious (high-CTA) people appraise competition as more threatening and respond with anxiety more frequently or intensely than low competitive-trait-anxious (low-CTA) people. This chapter will focus on competitive trait anxiety in children and adolescents. First, a model of competitive trait anxiety and the method used to assess this disposition are described. Second, age and gender differences in competitive trait anxiety are discussed. Next, aspects of the competitive setting that are perceived by youngsters as threatening, and cognitive variables that mediate this perception of threat, are examined. Potential developmental antecedents of competitive trait anxiety are then explored. Finally, consequences of competitive anxiety are addressed and several methods for helping youngsters reduce or cope with this anxiety are presented.

CONCEPTUAL MODEL AND MEASUREMENT OF COMPETITIVE ANXIETY

Martens' specification of competitive trait anxiety as a personality disposition was an outgrowth of two important distinctions made in the general anxiety literature. The first distinction is between the constructs of *state anxiety* and *trait anxiety*. According to Spielberger (1972), "state anxiety (A-State) may be conceptualized as a transitory emotional state or condition of the human organism that varies in intensity and fluctuates over time. This condition is characterized by subjective, consciously perceived feelings of tension and apprehension, and activation of the autonomic nervous system" (p. 39). In other words, state anxiety is an immediate or "right now" emotional response that can change from one moment or situation to the next. For example, a person's state anxiety might be low the night before an athletic contest or school exam, moderate the morning of the event, rise steadily as the contest or exam draws near, and return to a low or moderate level once the activity begins.

In contrast, trait anxiety is sometimes thought of as representing a person's characteristic overall level of anxiety (Mischel, 1971). Defined more formally, "trait anxiety (A-Trait), refers to relatively stable individual differences in anxiety proneness, that is, to differences in the disposition to perceive a wide range of stimulus situations as dangerous or threatening, and in the tendency to respond to such threats with A-State reactions" (Spielberger, 1972, p. 39). As Martens (1977) notes, high trait-anxious persons may perceive more situations as threatening than low trait-anxious persons, respond to threatening situations with higher state anxiety, or both.

The second major development upon which competitive trait anxiety is based is the distinction between *general trait anxiety* and *situation-specific trait anxiety*. The definition of trait anxiety given in the preceding paragraph is a definition of general trait anxiety. That is, there is an implicit assumption that people who chronically perceive one class of situations (e.g., academic) as threatening also perceive other classes of situations (e.g., athletic, social, occupational) as threatening. Although such a generalized response tendency may be characteristic of some people, it clearly is not characteristic of others. For example, some children or adolescents may habitually feel threatened and become anxious in academic test situations, but perceive athletic or social situations as completely nonthreatening. Other youngsters typically may feel calm and relaxed in examination situations, but have a disposition to become highly anxious when competing in sports. Thus, a major refinement in the anxiety literature has been the conceptualization and measurement of trait anxiety in situationally specific terms. Martens' model of competitive trait anxiety incorporates this situation-specific approach (test anxiety and social anxiety would be other situation-specific examples). According to Martens (1977), competitive trait anxiety "is a construct that describes individual differences in the tendency to perceive competitive situations as threatening and to respond to these situations with A-state reactions of varying intensity" (p. 36). Competitive trait anxiety represents a relatively stable intrapersonal factor that is hypothesized by Martens (1977) to be an important mediator of state anxiety responses to specific competitive situations (see Figure 10-1).

To assess competitive trait anxiety, Martens (1977) developed the Sport Competition Anxiety Test (SCAT). Test scoring is based on 10 questions that ask people how they *usually* feel when competing in sports and games (e.g., "Before I compete I feel uneasy," "I get nervous wanting to start the game"). Each item is answered on a 3-point scale ("often," "sometimes," "hardly-ever") and a summary score ranging from 10 (low competitive trait anxiety) to 30 (high competitive trait anxiety) is computed for each respondent. Research with children and adults in laboratory and field settings consistently has found a positive relationship between competitive trait anxiety and subsequent state anxiety reactions to competition (e.g., Gill & Martens, 1977; Scanlan & Passer, 1978b; 1979a; Weinberg & Genuchi, 1980), thereby supporting the predictive validity of the SCAT and Martens' conceptualization of competitive trait anxiety as a dispositional construct.

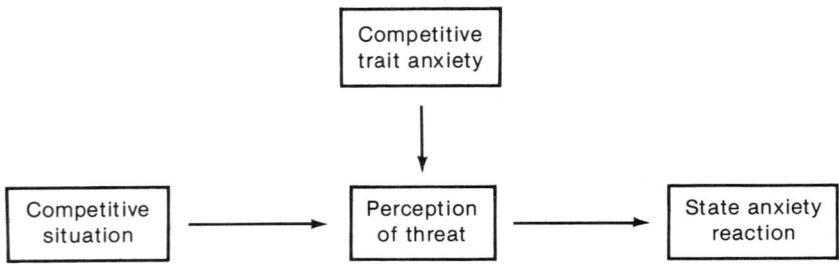

FIGURE 10-1 Competitive trait anxiety as a mediator between competitive stimulus and response. Adapted from Martens, 1977.

Congruent with the situation-specific approach, the SCAT has been found superior to general trait anxiety scales in predicting state anxiety reactions to competition (Martens & Simon, 1976; Simon & Martens, 1977). It should be noted that, in these studies, state anxiety typically has been assessed by self-report inventories. Physiological recordings and observational techniques represent other methods of measuring state anxiety.

AGE AND GENDER DIFFERENCES

Normative data compiled by Martens (1977) while developing the SCAT provide the most extensive information to date on age and gender differences in competitive trait anxiety. Summary statistics for each of his eight norm groups are shown in Table 10-1 and reveal two general trends. First, for the precollege samples, competitive trait anxiety increases slightly with age. Second, across all age groups, the mean for females is higher than the mean for males. Some studies have demonstrated age and gender differences even among children who choose to compete in sports. Passer (1983) found 14- and 15-year-old male soccer players to be more competitive trait anxious ($M = 19.70$) than 10- through 13-year-olds ($M = 17.08$). With regard to gender differences, Scanlan and Passer (1978b, 1979a) conducted two studies on youth soccer players from the same

TABLE 10-1
Summary of SCAT Test Statistics for Norm Samples

Sample	Number of Respondents	Mean	Standard Deviation
4th-6th grade			
Male	237	18.89	4.56
Female	241	19.71	4.40
7th-9th grade			
Male	841	19.32	4.64
Female	270	20.36	5.12
10th-12th grade			
Male	129	20.03	3.94
Female	113	22.22	4.40
College age adults			
Male	370	19.74	4.68
Female	158	22.60	4.87

Adapted from Martens, 1977.
Note. Scores on the SCAT can range from 10 (low competitive trait anxiety) to 30 (high competitive trait anxiety).

geographic area, one with 11- and 12-year-old boys and the other with 10- to 12-year-old girls. Consistent with Martens' results, the SCAT mean for girls ($M = 17.79$) was slightly higher than the mean for boys ($M = 16.67$).

Several cautions about these age and gender trends are suggested, however. It must be emphasized that the data on age differences are cross-sectional; that is, children from different age groups were compared. These studies did not examine whether competitive trait anxiety increased in the same sample of children as they grew older. Further, although females appear to be slightly more competitive trait anxious than males, the findings from laboratory and field studies suggest that there are few significant gender differences in children's *state anxiety* reactions prior to competing in sports or motor tasks (see Passer, 1982). This is surprising because, if females indicate higher competitive trait anxiety than males, this should be reflected in higher precompetitive state anxiety scores. Finally, it is interesting that some developmental research on another type of performance-evaluative anxiety, test anxiety, has yielded findings similar to those discussed here concerning competitive trait anxiety. The research on test anxiety has shown that it increases throughout the elementary and secondary school years, and that girls are more test anxious than boys (e.g., Hill & Sarason, 1966; Manley & Rosemier, 1972).

Test anxiety researchers, however, have questioned the interpretation of these findings, and their arguments may be relevant to the present findings concerning competitive trait anxiety. That is, older children and females appear to be less defensive about admitting to their anxiety than younger children and males. It is possible, therefore, that age and gender differences in anxiety reflect concomitant differences in defensive responses to anxiety questionnaires (Dusek, 1980). In sum, although age and gender differences in competitive trait anxiety have been found, the cause of these differences is not clear.

SOURCES OF ANXIETY
AND MEDIATING COGNITIONS

Potential sources of stress in competitive athletics are numerous and include spectators' behavior, uncertainty about getting a chance to start or play, conflict with coaches and teammates, and concern about injury (see Gould, Horn, & Spreemann, 1983b; Kroll, 1979; Passer, 1981). The major source of competitive anxiety for children and adolescents, however, is fear of failure (i.e., fear of inadequate performance), with fear of evaluation also representing a significant source of threat (Gould et al., 1983b; Pierce, 1980). Recent findings indicate that, as compared to their low-anxious counterparts, high-CTA youngsters worry more frequently about performance-related factors such as not playing well, making mistakes, losing, not playing up to their ability, and choking, and about evaluation-related factors such as what their coaches, teammates, and parents will think or say (Gould et al., 1983b; Passer, 1983). What thoughts or perceptions lead high-CTA children to respond with worry and become nervous when they compete? The data on this issue are limited but some insight into the mediating cognitions can be provided.

Perceived Ability.   It is tempting to assume that high-CTA youngsters' anxiety reactions to competition stem directly from perceived athletic or motor skill deficits. Current research, however, offers little support for this assumption or for the supposition that high-CTA is associated with actual deficits in athletic or motor skill. For example, Passer and Scanlan (1980) reported that male youth soccer players' preseason competitive trait anxiety was unrelated to four measures of their overall soccer ability: preseason ability as rated by a panel of five coaches, midseason ability as rated by teammates, midseason ability as rated by head coaches, and players' self-rated midseason ability. In a subsequent youth soccer study, Passer (1983) found no difference in high- versus low-CTA boys' preseason judgments of their sport-specific (i.e., soccer) ability, overall sports ability, and general physical competence. Competitive trait anxiety was also unrelated to head coaches' ratings of players' abilities. In a study examining sport participants and nonparticipants, Magill and Ash (1979) reported no association between competitive trait anxiety and the perceptual-motor ability of fourth- and fifth-grade children. In sum, existing findings indicate that the self-perceived and actual ability of high-CTA children participating in a team sport is just as great as that of low-CTA youngsters.

Expectancy of Success.   High-CTA children may worry more than low-CTA youngsters about their performance and about being evaluated because they have a lower expectancy of success. "Success" is used broadly to represent not only performance outcomes such as winning and losing, but also the quality of performance. It is important to emphasize that how well one expects to perform at a task is a function of many factors including perceived ability, intended effort, the perceived difficulty of the task, the degree to which one feels mentally and physically prepared, and one's own definition of success. Thus, even though it was concluded in the preceding paragraph that high- and low-CTA children have similar perceived and actual ability, their success expectancies could still differ. This was the case in a recent study of 10- to 15-year-old male soccer players (Passer, 1983); high-CTA players felt they had just as much ability in soccer and sports as low-CTA players, but reported a less positive expectancy of how well they typically would play in the upcoming season.

It appears, then, that higher competitive *trait* anxiety in youngsters is associated with a somewhat lower *generalized* expectancy of success (i.e., how well one generally expects to perform). An analogue to this finding is that, in specific game situations, children with higher precompetition *state* anxiety report lower expectancies of success *for that game* (Scanlan & Passer, 1979b, 1981b). Although all these findings are correlational, they are consistent with the hypothesis that lower expectancies of success may play an important role in mediating both a generalized and a game-specific tendency to perceive competition as threatening.

Expectancy of Negative Evaluation. Apprehension about performing and being evaluated by others should be heightened by the expectation that if one should fail or perform poorly, criticism or punishment may follow. Recent findings indicate that high-CTA youngsters do, in fact, have a greater expectancy of incurring negative evaluation in the event of poor performance than low-CTA youngsters (Passer, 1983). In particular, it appears that these two anxiety groups differ in their expectancy of criticism from adults (i.e., parents and coaches), but not from peers. This finding is consistent with current work on the mediators of test anxiety and general trait anxiety, which emphasizes the role of children's interactions with parents and other evaluative adults in achievement settings (Dusek, 1980; Krohne, 1980). Further, it must be pointed out that this finding does not imply that high-CTA youngsters expect to be criticized by adults every time they make mistakes or fail; to the contrary, they expect criticism or overt social disapproval for such performance only on occasion (Passer, 1983). This expectation is consistent with behavioral observation data that indicate punitive coaching responses to player mistakes are relatively infrequent (Smith, Smoll, & Curtis, 1978). Because parents and coaches represent "significant others" to the child, however, their criticism, especially when it is personally demeaning, can have an important influence even if given occasionally.

Expectancy of Negative Affect. Based on Atkinson's (1964) theory of achievement motivation, Passer (1983) hypothesized that high-CTA children may perceive competition as more threatening than low-CTA children because they expect failure to be more emotionally aversive. This hypothesis was supported by the findings of Passer's (1983) study with youth soccer players. That is, high- as opposed to low-CTA youngsters report that they would feel more ashamed and upset if they were making mistakes and playing poorly. Why might this be the case? One reason could be that high-CTA children have a relatively greater expectation of being criticized for such performance, which was noted in the preceding paragraph. The correlations between players' expectancies of negative evaluation and anticipated shame were significant but low, however, suggesting that there were more important determinants of anticipated negative affect.

Perhaps high-CTA children value success more than do low-CTA children, and therefore expect to feel more ashamed and upset if they do not achieve this goal. Another possibility is that the expectancy of negative affect represents, in effect, a classically conditioned response (Staats, 1967). That is, because past failures were associated with shame or emotional upset (due to external criticism or other factors), the thought of failure or performing poorly elicits an internalized (i.e., conditioned) anticipatory negative reaction. If this were true, or if high-CTA players place a higher value on success, they should anticipate more negative affect for failure than low-CTA children—even in situations in which they would know that no external evaluation would take place. This hypothesis could be tested in future research.

To summarize the findings from this section, high-CTA youngsters demonstrate a stronger fear of failure and fear of negative evaluation than do low-CTA youngsters. It is proposed that these fears are mediated, at least in part, by a lower generalized expectancy of doing well, an expectancy of receiving more frequent criticism or negative evaluation for poor performance, and an expectancy that such performance will produce intense negative affect. What factors might account for the development of these expectancies?

DEVELOPMENTAL ANTECEDENTS

According to Martens (1977), individual differences in competitive trait anxiety are largely determined by "the accumulated consequences of participation in the competitive process" (p. 32). Unfortunately, there is no theory and research specifying these consequences or other developmental antecedents of competitive trait anxiety, which may be due in part to the recency of Martens' (1977) conceptualization of competitive trait anxiety as a personality construct. Nevertheless, some propositions about the etiology of competitive trait anxiety can be formulated by examining the literature on the development of other anxiety dispositions, and by drawing upon relevant research in sport psychology.

Parent-Child Interactions.   Krohne (1980) proposes that four parental child-rearing behaviors play a central role in creating high trait anxiety: frequency of negative reinforcement, intensity of negative reinforcement, feedback consistency, and support versus restriction. Frequent and intense negative reinforcement may cause the child to develop corresponding negative expectancies concerning future parental interactions, and consequently to respond to a wide range of situations with a general perception of threat. Further, the child's ability to develop coping behaviors may be impaired by inconsistent parental feedback (e.g., at different times parents may punish, ignore, or reward the same behavior), which makes the child uncertain about how to behave in order to control the situation, and restrictive child-rearing practices, which limit the child's opportunity to experiment with various coping responses. Responses from high- and low-anxious boys and girls concerning the perceived child-rearing styles of their parents offered some support for these hypothesized relationships (Krohne, 1980).

The importance of punitive or unsupportive parental reactions is also noted in theories examining the development of test anxiety (Hill, 1972; Sarason, Davidson, Lighthall, Waite, & Ruebush, 1960), and behavioral observation data provide some information on these parental responses. A study of Dutch children by Hermans, ter Laak, & Maes (1972) illustrates this interesting approach. Subjects were 20 boys and 20 girls, 9 and 10 years of age, who were identified by a self-report inventory as either high- or low-anxious. Trained observers visited the home of each child and recorded parent-child interactions while the child engaged in four standard achievement tests (e.g., spelling anagrams, stacking blocks). Behaviors of the children were coded in 17 categories, which in turn were grouped under four headings: task independence, achievement standards, tension release and reactions to insecurity, and reinforcement. The latter two headings proved to be the primary discriminators of parents of high- and low-anxious children. Specifically, parents of high-anxious children (a) more frequently withheld reinforcement when their children displayed correct performance, (b) more frequently showed negative tension release (e.g., negative expressions of tension or signs of irritation), (c) less frequently showed positive tension release (e.g., signs of good mood and enthusiasm), and (d) less frequently responded to expressions of insecurity by their children.

In short, the findings suggested that the parents of high-anxious children provided a less emotionally supportive climate for achievement. The research method used by Hermans et al. (1972) is similar to that employed in several studies on the antecedents of achievement motivation (e.g., Rosen & d'Andrade, 1959), and could be adapted easily to the study of competitive trait anxiety. Other methods, including behavioral observations of parents in naturalistic competitive settings, interviews with parents and children, and laboratory experiments (e.g., assessing parental responses to the controlled success-failure outcomes of stimulus persons), can also offer insight on the relationship between parental behaviors and children's competitive trait anxiety.

Interactions With Other Adults and Peers. Negative reactions to a child's performance by adults other than the child's parents also are hypothesized as facilitating the development of dispositional anxiety (e.g., test anxiety) (Hill, 1972). Some findings indicate, for example, that children's anxiety in school is related to the type of class atmosphere set by the teacher (Zimmerman, 1970). Although corresponding anxiety research has not been conducted in athletic settings, behavioral observation studies of youth sport coaches have suggested that specific coaching behaviors (e.g., reinforcement for good performance, punitive vs. supportive responses to player mistakes) can indeed influence other psychological characteristics of children, such as their self-esteem and sport-related attitudes (Smith, Smoll, & Curtis, 1978, 1979). It is important to remember that because competitive trait anxiety is a situation-specific disposition, its development in children should be influenced more strongly by adult-child interactions in competitive as opposed to noncompetitive task situations or domains. For many children, the adults with whom they interact most frequently in competitive situations are not their parents but coaches, physical educators, recreation leaders, and so on.

Theory and research on the development of test anxiety has placed only minor emphasis on child-peer interactions (see Dusek, 1980; Phillips, Pitcher, Worsham, & Miller, 1980), but there are several reasons why peer behaviors may play a more important role in the etiology of competitive trait anxiety. First, youngsters often spend considerable time competing in games, contests, or sports without the presence of adults. Second, in contrast to the academic environment in which poor performance typically has negative consequences only for the individual child, competitive games and sports often involve considerable outcome interdependence among participants. Mistakes or poor play by one child can affect the success-failure outcomes of other children, thereby enhancing the tendency of peers to criticize or otherwise negatively react to the child's performance. Third, although coaches or other adult supervisors, if present, may well discourage such behavior, competitive game and sport settings provide youngsters with greater liberty to respond punitively to inadequate peer performance than does the teacher-controlled classroom environment. In sum, negative interactions with parents, other evaluative adults, and peers all may contribute to the fear of failure and fear of evaluation exhibited by high-CTA children. The fact that high- and low-CTA children differ primarily in the expectancy of negative evaluation from adults rather than peers (Passer, 1983), however, suggests that adult-child interactions play a greater developmental role.

History of Success-Failure. A child's history of success-failure in competitive situations can influence the development of competitive trait anxiety in at least two major ways. First, the more frequent the failure, the greater the *potential* for negative interactions with adults and peers. The word "potential" is emphasized because the frequency and intensity of these negative interactions are highly dependent upon the response style of the adults and peers involved. That is, one child may perform inadequately rather often but never be criticized or otherwise punished when he or she fails. Another child may succeed almost all the time but receive at least intermittent and possibly intense criticism when he or she fails. It is the latter child who will likely develop a greater expectancy of negative evaluation and who will thus associate failure with greater shame and negative affect.

Second, past success-failure outcomes are important determinants of current performance expectancies (e.g., Feather, 1966; Feather & Saville, 1967), and a higher incidence of failure at competitive activities may cause the child to perceive competition as threatening because of a lowered expectancy of success. Research consistently has revealed, however, that the causal factors to which success and failure are attributed play a significant role in mediating the effects of those outcomes on subsequent performance expectancies (e.g., Weiner, Nierenberg, & Goldstein, 1976). It has been found, for example, that the attribution of failure to stable factors such as task difficulty will result in lower expectancy of future success at that task than would attributions to relatively unstable factors such as bad luck or a momentary lack of effort. Importantly, people's attributions for their own performance outcomes can be modified by the attributional comments of other individuals (Dweck, 1975; Johnston, Cunningham, Passer, & Kanouse, 1974). Thus, teachers, parents, coaches, and even peers can lessen the negative effects of failure on a child's expectancy of success by emphasizing attributions to unstable and preferably controllable factors (e.g., effort, amount of practice).

In conclusion, there is little doubt that theory and research on the antecedents of competitive trait anxiety should explore the role of children's success-failure history in competitive and perhaps noncompetitive achievement domains. The need for such an analysis would also be suggested by the test anxiety literature, which indicates that high-anxious children have a greater history of failure in school and other evaluative situations than low-anxious children (see Dusek, 1980). The absolute frequency of failure may be a less critical variable in this analysis than the responses of parents, other adults, and peers; it is these responses that will accentuate or attenuate the potentially adverse effects of failure on the child's expectancies and subsequent tendency to perceive competition as threatening (see Figure 10-2).

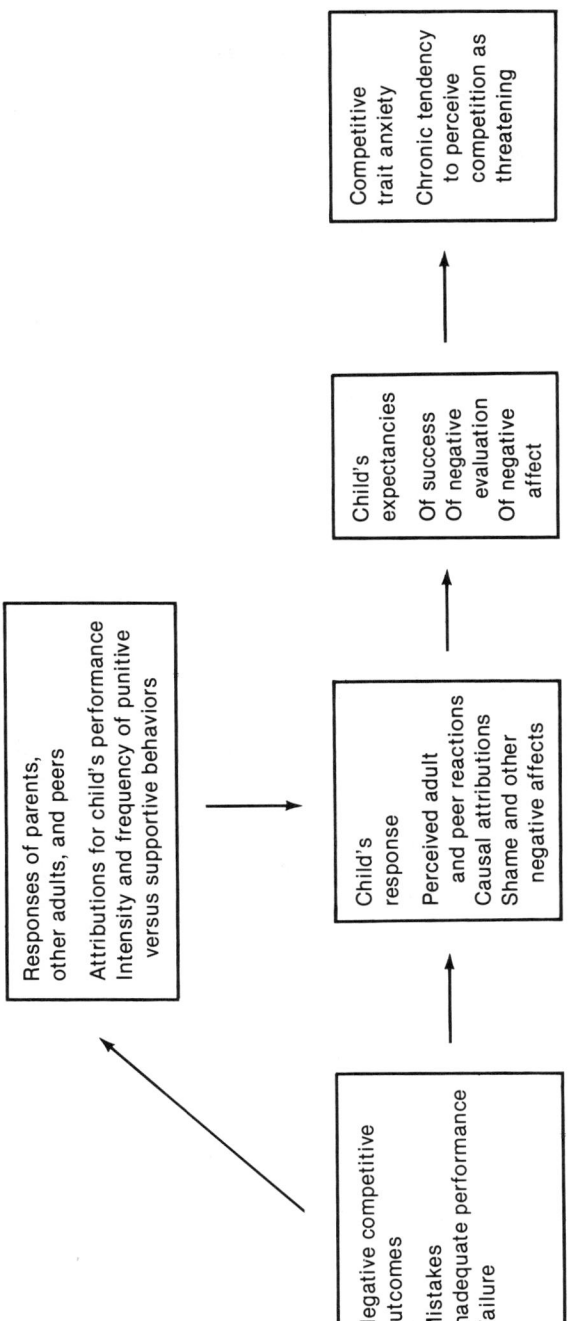

FIGURE 10-2   A framework for examining some antecedents of competitive trait anxiety.

CONSEQUENCES
AND INTERVENTION STRATEGIES

Competitive anxiety can have several adverse consequences for children and adolescents. Fear and worry about performance, evaluation, and other factors cause some youngsters to avoid competitive activities and may influence other youngsters to discontinue participation (Orlick & Botterill, 1975; Pierce, 1980). Laboratory, field, and clinical evidence demonstrates that athletic and motor skill performance can suffer if anxiety becomes too high (see Martens, 1974a; Smith, 1980a), and many youngsters report that various worries prevent them from playing their best when they compete (Gould, Horn, & Spreemann, 1983a; Pierce, 1980). Competitive anxiety can affect youngsters' health by disrupting normal sleeping patterns (State of Michigan, 1978) or creating skin and gastrointestinal problems (Smith & Smoll, 1982b). Further, stressful events may increase youngsters' susceptibility to illness and athletic injury (Boyce, Jensen, Cassell, Collier, Smith, & Raimey, 1977; Coddington & Troxell, 1980).

It must be emphasized that competitive anxiety often may have no short- or long-term consequences beyond the immediate feeling of mental or physical discomfort. For example, many youngsters report that their competition-related worries do not impair their performance (Pierce, 1980), and some young athletes even feel that they perform better when anxious (Gould et al., 1983a). Research findings on the arousal-performance relationship (viz., Martens, 1974) also indicate that increases in anxiety, at least up to a certain level, can positively affect athletic and motor skill execution. (These findings do not imply, of course, that anxiety *should* be induced to improve competitive performance.) The consequences of competitive anxiety for a child will likely depend upon the frequency, duration, and intensity of that anxiety, as well as other situational and intrapersonal factors such as the type of task, the child's coping skills, and social supports. The crucial point, however, is that some youngsters chronically feel threatened by competition, and the resulting anxiety can have deleterious psychological, behavioral, and health-related effects. (See Martens [1978] and Passer [1982] for further discussion on the consequences of competitive anxiety and stress.)

Cognitive Approaches to Anxiety Reduction. Stress management training represents one general approach to minimizing competitive anxiety. A common goal of such programs is to teach the person specific skills that will reduce or control anxiety in performance situations. Smith's (1980a) stress management program, which has been used with children, adolescents, and adults, incorporates techniques such as progressive muscle relaxation and deep breathing to reduce physiological arousal, and self-instructional statements to change the focus of attention from task-irrelevant to task-relevant cues. Another stress management strategy is to eliminate the negative expectations and self-statements that cause the individual to perceive the situation as threatening. Smith (1980a) employs a procedure called "cognitive restructuring" to help high-anxious people "realize that the beliefs that underlie their self-statements, though widely embraced in our culture, are often quite irrational" (p. 64). This strategy is more desirable because it can produce long-term change and prevent anxiety responses from occurring in the first place.

Unfortunately, it may be very difficult to change beliefs and expectancies that have developed from prior and perhaps ongoing negative competitive experiences. Limitations in youngsters' ability to introspect also can make it difficult to use cognitive restructuring (Smith, 1980a). Nevertheless, a variety of programs have been developed to provide training in stress-coping skills and these represent one option for the competitive-trait-anxious youngster. (For an elaboration of these techniques, see Chapter 12 by Smith.)

Environmental Approaches to Anxiety Reduction. Competitive anxiety can also be reduced by modifying the environment in which the child competes. For example, adults can lessen a child's fear of failure and fear of evaluation by consistently responding with support rather than punishment when the child makes mistakes, performs poorly, or loses. To this end, several training programs have been developed (Martens, 1981; Smith, Smoll, & Curtis, 1979), and an increasing number of publications have appeared (e.g., J.R. Thomas, 1977; Vandeweghe, 1979), to provide guidelines, techniques, and other information that will increase adults' supportive behavior and enhance their interactive skills with youngsters. There is more at issue here than simply recognizing that a supportive achievement climate is important to children. A variety of methods, including didactic instruction, modeling, role playing, group problem solving, behavioral feedback, and self-monitoring may be needed to produce behavior change in parents and other adults (Smoll & Smith, 1980).

Further, adults must understand that they should be especially careful in how they interact with high-anxious children. This is suggested by theoretical and empirical work on test anxiety, which indicates that high-anxious children express more signs of insecurity in achievement situations, are more dependent upon adults for direction, support, and evaluation of their performance, and are more sensitive to adults' social reinforcement than are low-anxious children (Dusek, 1980; Hermans et al., 1972; Hill, 1972; Phillips et al., 1980; Sarason et al., 1960). Thus, critical or punitive remarks that seem mild to a parent, teacher, or coach, and which are accepted by most youngsters as rather minor reproofs, may affect the high-anxious child rather strongly. Similarly, adults may feel that their level of supportive behavior (e.g., encouragement, praise, assistance) is quite adequate, and for most children it may be, but the high-anxious child may need even more frequent or intense support.

Finally, it should be stressed that modifying the competitive environment will reduce anxiety only when it alters the specific factors that cause the child to perceive competition as threatening. De-emphasizing the importance of winning or decreasing the frequency of punitive responses to player mistakes will likely have little effect in reducing a child's chronic fear of being injured. Some other intervention strategy would be called for in this case. Therefore, parents and other adults who work with youngsters must be able to determine not only if a child is anxious about competing, but also what the cause of that anxiety is. Neither task is easy. Drawing inferences from the child's behavior can be problematic, for example, if the child is highly anxious but shows no performance decrements or other immediate, observable consequences; additionally, the child may be reluctant to talk about his or her anxiety if it is perceived as a weakness or if adults are viewed as unable to help.

Obviously, the simplest solution is for adults to make it clear that they can and want to help; they should also establish a nonthreatening climate that makes these statements appear credible. Unfortunately, those adults who need to do this the most, such as parents whose punitive child-rearing style contributed to the development of their youngsters' competitive trait anxiety, may well be those who are least willing or able to change. This point underscores the importance of providing psychologically oriented programs and literature for adults who work with children in the competitive setting.

Chapter 11

Mental Preparation Strategies

Robert S. Weinberg
North Texas State University

There appears to be an optimal level of arousal that maximizes athletic performance, as pointed out by Robert Sonstroem in Chapter 8. Furthermore, research has demonstrated that this optimal level of arousal depends not only on the nature or complexity of the task but on the nature of the individual. For example, some football players like to get ready for a game by banging their lockers, whereas others prefer to be alone in a corner. In any case, most athletes report that they try to somehow get themselves emotionally ready prior to competition, which presumably means that they are trying to reach their optimal level of arousal. In addition to preparing for an athletic competition, athletes also stress that it is important to be able to maintain and regulate this optimal arousal level throughout the length of the competition. This is no easy task because many sports such as tennis, basketball, soccer, and golf require sustained concentration for several hours.

This chapter will discuss a number of mental preparation strategies that athletes employ, along with the empirical research supporting their effectiveness. However, before this can be done it is necessary to briefly discuss how our thoughts can influence our emotions and to show the importance of training or practice in the development of these mental preparation techniques.

THOUGHTS CAN INFLUENCE PERFORMANCE

Both coaches and athletes generally acknowledge the important role that thoughts play in achieving high levels of performance. More recently, researchers have provided experimental, correlational, and anecdotal evidence that patterns of thought can influence athletic performance (e.g., Corbin, 1972; Richardson, 1967a, 1967b; Shelton & Mahoney, 1978; Silva, 1982b; Suinn, 1976; Weinberg, Gould, & Jackson, 1979, 1980). For example, Mahoney and Avener (1977) found that gymnasts who reported experiencing occasional doubt about their own ability just prior to performance (e.g., "I hope I don't mess up") tended to perform more poorly than gymnasts exhibiting higher levels of confidence (e.g., "I can do it"). The idea that thoughts can influence behavior is also supported in the psychological literature. Specifically, cognitive behavior modification theory maintains as its basic premise that there is continuity between an individual's thoughts and his or her overt behavior. In essence, improper thoughts on a regular basis (e.g., "I can't beat that guy") can result in undesirable performance.

It should be noted that almost all athletes experience doubt, lack of confidence, or nervousness at some time or another during their athletic careers; this is normal and should be expected. However, it is the chronic self-doubt, lack of confidence, precompetition jitters, and other self-debilitating thoughts and emotions that keep athletes from reaching their full potential. Therefore, it seems imperative that both coaches and athletes be made aware of the mental preparation strategies for dealing with these psychological factors that can adversely affect performance.

MENTAL PREPARATION STRATEGIES

If one were to ask a coach what types of mental preparation strategies he or she employs to help get athletes "up" or ready for a tough opponent or an upcoming event, a likely answer might be, "I try to get my athletes 'psyched-up' before the game." This mental preparation strategy has apparently been espoused by coaches for a number of years. Coaches and physical educators make the implicit assumption that psyching-up will lead to maximum performance. This assumption has probably been based on many things including television shows and movies that show a coach delivering a dramatic, emotional speech to the team just before the big game. The team then goes out, plays great, and wins, of course. A popular example has the legendary Notre Dame football coach, Knute Rockne, making an emotional appeal to his players at halftime of a big game to "win one for the Gipper," referring to George Gipp, an All-American player for Notre Dame who lay dying in the hospital.

Although many coaches use some form of psyching-up procedures, very little research has been conducted about the effects of psyching-up on performance, as well as what specific psych-up techniques athletes themselves use in preparing for a performance. For example, if a coach tells an athlete to psych-up, what does that mean to the athlete? Do different individuals psych-up differently? Is one psych-up technique better than another? These are some of the important questions that need to be addressed before the psych-up performance relationship can be elucidated.

Psyching-Up Strategies

The first logical step toward answering these questions would be to determine what specific psych-up or mental preparation strategies athletes use to enhance performance. Along these lines, Shelton and Mahoney (1978) and Weinberg, Gould, and Jackson (1980) asked subjects to psych-up before performing a variety of motor tasks requiring strength, balance, and speed. Subjects were given 30 seconds to psych-up before performing and were told to psych-up in any manner that was best for them. After completing their performance trials, subjects were asked an open-ended question requiring them to describe what type of psych-up technique they used. The psyching-up strategies fell into five categories and were characterized by the following statements: (a) attentional focus, "I just tried to concentrate on the task and eliminate all irrelevant information"; (b) self-efficacy statements, "I told myself I could do it"; (c) relaxation, "I just tried to relax all of my muscles and think about something else"; (d) imagery, "I pictured myself in perfect balance"; and (e) preparatory arousal, "I tried to get mad, aroused, and psyched-up." Following is a discussion of these mental preparation strategies.

Attentional Focus.   Probably nothing is more important to athletic performance than the ability to focus one's attention on the proper cues in the environment (e.g., keeping your eye on the tennis ball, concentrating on the rim when shooting a basketball) and to maintain that concentration over the course of the game or event. Despite the importance of concentration and effective attentional focus in athletic performance, little research has been conducted in these areas. Nideffer (1976a, 1976b), however, has recently provided a theoretical framework which should help both researchers and coaches better understand the role of attention in athletic performance. Nideffer argues that to teach and coach effectively, the physical educator and the coach must be able to define the attentional demands of a particular athletic setting so that they can help athletes identify the proper attentional focus for their sport. Along these lines Nideffer defines attention across two dimensions:

width and direction. Width of attentional focus falls on a continuum from broad to narrow and can be conceptualized in terms of how much information an individual must attend to within a given period of time. Direction of attention can also be viewed on a continuum and refers to whether individuals are attending to their own thoughts and feelings (internal) or to things going on around them (external). Since an athlete's attention falls somewhere along the width and direction continuum, at a given point in time one may be described as having either a broad internal, broad external, narrow internal, or narrow external focus of attention.

Nideffer suggests that individuals have different attentional styles (as measured by the Test of Attention and Interpersonal Style, Nideffer, 1976b) and that specific sports require certain styles or a certain amount of flexibility (e.g., the ability to rapidly shift attentional focus). For example, a golfer might generally require a narrow external focus on the ball whereas a quarterback going back to pass might require a broad external focus to survey the defensive backfield and pick out primary and secondary receivers. Similarly, a weight lifter or a discus thrower might employ a narrow internal focus as they direct their thoughts toward successfully completing their skill.

Nideffer points out that mental mistakes often occur when an athlete focuses on inappropriate attentional cues in the sport environment. For example, a basketball player shooting free throws in "clutch" situations should be focusing his or her attention on the rim rather than attending to the noise and jeering from a hostile crowd. A tennis player should not worry that he or she got a "bad" line call last point but instead should refocus attention on the next point. Of course refocusing one's attention is easier said than done, but with practice one can stay focused on the appropriate cues. If a tennis player is distracted by bad line calls, he or she might first imagine himself/herself in a match and then picture the linesperson calling a close call in favor of the opponent. Instead of getting mad and continuously thinking about the call (inappropriate focus), the player should immediately say STOP, then take a couple of deep breaths, relax, and think, "I got a bad call but it's just part of the game and it won't do any good worrying about it." Then the athlete could focus back on the task, such as concentrating on a good ball toss and follow-through on the next serve. After practicing this routine, the athlete should try to employ it in practice matches and then in real competition.

Since many mental mistakes can be traced back to an inappropriate focus of attention, coaches and physical educators need to be sensitive both to the attentional demands of their sports and the attentional styles of their individual athletes. In addition, if coaches and physical educators can reduce the anxiety inherent in many learning and competitive situations this will help the athlete focus on the relevant cues in the environment. For example, when teaching a new skill, many times the learner is being watched by others. This can increase anxiety because the learner does not want to look like a klutz in front of his/her friends. So the learner worries about failing and this prevents him/her from attending to the relevant task demands. If the learner (especially an early learner) can instead be placed in a situation where social evaluation is minimal, he or she will have a better opportunity to focus on the task itself, rather than on the consequences of his/her behavior.

Self-Talk.   Another mental preparation strategy identified by subjects as useful was self-efficacy statements. In essence, individuals talk to themselves in an attempt to build up their confidence and convince themselves that they can succeed. Although both coaches and athletes have emphasized the important role that confidence plays in athletic performance, sport psychologists have only recently begun to systematically study the topic. This interest has been sparked by a theory developed by Bandura (1977b), which asserts that behavioral change is mediated by a common cognitive mechanism called self-efficacy. Self-efficacy is defined as the strength of one's conviction that he or she can successfully execute a behavior required to produce a certain outcome. Assuming that an individual is capable of a response and there are appropriate incentives for performance, then self-efficacy theory asserts that actual performance will be predicted by the individual's belief in personal competence.

Several studies and anecdotal reports in the sport literature reflect the important role that confidence plays in achieving optimal athletic performance. Nelson and Furst (1972), for example, investigated the effects of confidence and expectations on performance. They tested male subjects for arm strength and asked them to estimate their strength relative to their peers'. Subjects were then paired so that one was clearly stronger than the other, but both believed the stronger subject to be weaker. The results revealed that the objectively weaker subject won arm wrestling competition 83% of the time. It appears that if an individual *expects* to win, it is likely that he or she will perform at a higher level. The reverse also seems to be true for people who expect to lose! Ness and Patton (1979), for example, examined whether weight lifting was influenced by how much an individual thought he was lifting. Subjects were either unaware of the amount of weight they were asked to lift, believed the weight to be less than the actual value, or believed the weight to be of greater than the actual value. The results indicated that the subjects bench pressed more weight when they believed it to be less than its actual value. In essence, a subject's belief concerning his ability to lift a certain weight was an important determinant of his actual performance.

Weinberg, Gould, and Jackson (1979) conducted an early study investigating the relationship between self-efficacy and competitive motor performance. Subjects competed face-to-face on a leg endurance task against a confederate who was portrayed as either a varsity track athlete (low self-efficacy condition) or having a knee injury (high self-efficacy condition). Results supported self-efficacy predictions, with the high self-efficacy subjects extending their legs significantly longer than low self-efficacy subjects. Furthermore, after failing on the first trial, high self-efficacy subjects exhibited an increase in performance whereas low self-efficacy subjects displayed a decrement in performance.

In the previous investigations, efficacy expectations were manipulated by structuring the environment to create feelings of either high or low efficacy. Weinberg, Gould, Yukelson, and Jackson (1981) conducted a study examining the interaction of preexisting self-efficacy (i.e., subjects exhibiting an initial high or low level of efficacy) and manipulated self-efficacy (i.e., the environment is manipulated to create either high or low feelings of efficacy) in a competitive motor performance situation. Results again supported previous investigations indicating the importance of efficacy expectations as determinants of performance. More importantly, it was found that an individual's preexisting feelings of efficacy can be modified by his or her performance in specific situations. In essence, this implies that the coach or physical educator can alter an athlete's level of confidence by the kind of information that is provided or by structuring the environment to create positive expectations of success.

Although there is little empirical research in the sport literature that assesses the effectiveness of different intervention strategies, the following have been suggested by Mahoney (1979) for augmenting the self-efficacy expectations of athletes:

1. Response induction aids—devices that may reduce the perceived discrepancy between the athlete's current and desired performance;

2. Modeling—having the athlete observe another individual successfully executing the skill;

3. Self-efficacy statements—having an athlete practice saying positive statements to him/herself prior to performance;

4. Imagery—having the athlete imagine him/herself performing the desired response;

5. Verbal persuasion—reassuring and encouraging the athlete that he/she is capable of performing the desired response;

6. Performance accomplishments—structuring the environment to create successful experience. Avoid focusing solely on the out-

come of an event without considering the process or level of performance exhibited.

One important consideration for teachers and coaches who attempt
these strategies is the discrepancy between the athlete's present performance level and the desired performance level. In order to build confidence, the athlete should only be asked to make slight improvements or
set short-term, realistic goals since this will enhance the development of
confidence. A teacher's unrealistic expectations can destroy an athlete's
confidence and result in poor performance. However, it should be noted
that confidence is a mediator of performance only when the prerequisite
athletic skills are present; it should not be viewed as an alternative to skill
development. Consequently, the teacher must be sensitive to the athlete's
performance capabilities as well as helping the athlete build the belief in
his/her own capabilities. This is a major contribution that the teacher-
coach can make to an athlete's development.

Relaxation. A mental preparation strategy that has received
much attention in recent years and was used by subjects in our initial
psyching-up experiment is relaxation. Recently coaches have become increasingly aware of the stress created by competitive athletics. More importantly, they are realizing that increased levels of anxiety may undermine performance by causing increased muscular tension, nausea, inappropriate focus of attention, and decreased psychological flexibility.
Therefore, techniques designed to reduce anxiety and get athletes to
function at their optimal level of anxiety are increasingly being incorporated into regular training regimens. The many types of relaxation
techniques will not be detailed here but a brief description of some of the
more popular techniques will be offered.

Perhaps the best known of the relaxation techniques is Jacobson's
(1938) Progressive Relaxation. Jacobson proposed that muscular tension
and relaxation are incompatible physiological states and that in order to
relax, one must learn to distinguish between tension and relaxation.
Therefore, his technique teaches subjects to progressively tense and relax
all major muscle groups in the body, thereby sensitizing them to pro-
prioceptive feedback from these muscles.

Another technique that has become popular in recent years is biofeedback. This type of training involves receiving physiological feedback
(e.g., skin temperature, muscle tension, blood pressure) via a visual or
auditory signal that indicates the individual's present state of tension.
This helps the athlete recognize when he or she is tense, observe the cause
of tension, and develop techniques to reduce the tension. The major
drawback in biofeedback from a practical point of view is the cost and
availability of the instrumentation necessary to provide this kind of physiological feedback.

Benson (1975) has incorporated the work on transcendental meditation into a simple but effective relaxation technique. According to Benson, only four components are needed to achieve relaxation: (a) a quiet environment, (b) a passive attitude, (c) a mental device—this is similar to a "mantra" and involves the repetition of a one syllable word such as "one," and (d) a comfortable position. Benson states that this technique should be practiced twice a day for 20 minutes at a time. The aim of this technique is to achieve the relaxation response, which decreases the sympathetic nervous system activity and is characterized by lowering blood pressure, heart rate, respiration rate, oxygen consumption, and muscle tension. Although these relaxation techniques produce physiological changes, performance results have been equivocal, with some studies reporting positive performance changes (e.g., Bell, 1976; Bennett, 1978; Titley, 1976) and others reporting no performance effects (e.g., Bennett & Stothart, 1980; Williams, 1978b).

More research is needed to determine the effectiveness of these relaxation techniques in enhancing performance. In particular, future studies need to control for variables such as length of the training sessions, type of task (i.e., strength, speed, endurance, precision) and expectancy effects before more solid conclusions can be advanced. However, these relaxation techniques do appear to offer a mechanism for helping those athletes who exhibit a high level of precompetitive stress; they are discussed in more detail in the next chapter by Ronald Smith.

Imagery.   Many athletes have reported that just prior to performance, they try to mentally picture themselves going through the actual movement in their mind. For example, Jack Nicklaus has often said that he never hits a golf ball without visually seeing himself hitting the ball first in his mind. He further describes his shots as 10% swing, 40% setup and stance, and 50% mental picture (Nicklaus, 1974). In addition, high jumpers such as Dwight Stones and Dick Fosbury have reported that before they jump they visually see themselves running every step up to the bar and then clearing the bar. If they did not clear the bar in their mind they would continue to mentally rehearse the jump until they could visualize a successful jump. Numerous other anecdotes could be presented, but the point here is that many athletes and coaches feel that the way a player thinks is the way a player performs.

These ideas about the relationship between mental imagery and performance appear to have sound theoretical underpinnings in the psychological literature. Many researchers (e.g., Mahoney, 1974; Meichenbaum, 1977) have developed programs such as rational emotive therapy and stress inoculation training, which have as one of their basic premises that a person's thoughts and images exert a profound influence on his or her overt behavior. As indicated by Silva (1982b), virtually all cognitive behavior-modification perspectives emphasize that regular improper subjective conditioning can result in undesirable overt behavior. In essence, these researchers have argued that we can change our overt behavior by altering our covert behavior (i.e., thoughts and cognitions). Furthermore, research has indicated that when an individual imagines a movement, actual muscular activity is produced (Jacobson, 1930). In addition, Jacobson found that the muscular activity resulting from imagining a movement was of a greater intensity for individuals with movement experience. In a sense, then, mental imagery gets the musculature into action and can prepare an athlete for the actual physical competition. These mental preparations can be helpful to a wide range of sport activities, especially for elite athletes who seem to engage in a great deal of mental imagery before competition (Gould, Weiss, & Weinberg, 1981; Highlen & Bennett, 1979).

Although over 50 studies have investigated the effectiveness of imagery on physical performance, there is a lack of consistent results. A cautious interpretation of the literature is offered by Corbin, who states, "There seems to be little doubt that mental practice can positively affect skilled motor performance when practice conditions are optimal. It is equally clear, however, that mental practice is not always an aid to performance" (1972, p. 115). Consequently, it seems more fruitful to briefly discuss some of the important variables that may mediate the effectiveness of imagery in enhancing performance.

One variable that has received increased attention is the orientation of the imagery. A distinction has been made between what has been termed "internal" and "external" imagery. Internal imagery involves seeing or feeling something from the performer's own perspective and has also been termed kinesthetic imagery. An example of internal imagery comes from Olympic gymnast Karen Schuckman's statement during the 1976 qualifying rounds: "I see what I would see if I was actually doing it . . . therefore I have the memory of what it feels like." External imagery occurs when a person views him/herself from the perspective of an external observer, much like in a movie. For example, a tennis player may see his or her whole body, the ball, or the opponent as if watching the match from a spectator's point of view. Recently, studies by Epstein (1980), Shelton and Mahoney (1980), and Mahoney and Avener (1977) have attempted to assess if one type of imagery is more effective in enhancing performance than the other. Unfortunately, no firm conclusions can be stated at this time; it appears that both internal and external imagery can enhance performance and that their effectiveness depends on the athlete's skill level and the type of task being performed.

Another variable that appears important is the individual's ability to conceptualize the task. Specifically, early researchers have noted that the vividness and controllability of the image may be significant factors in determining the effectiveness of imagery. Controllability refers to whether the image changes according to an athlete's intention. For example, several athletes have reported having trouble with getting the image to do what they wanted. A high jumper reported that he hit the bar every time he visualized trying for a successful jump. A basketball player reported that every time he tried to visualize dribbling a basketball, the ball simply would not bounce! Vividness refers to the clarity of the image that is produced. There seems to be a great deal of variation in athletes' ability to get a clear image and it may be necessary to teach some athletes how to get a controllable, vivid image. Another factor that mediates the effectiveness of imagery in enhancing performance is the individual's skill level. Although some discrepancy exists in the literature, there seems to be a consensus that imagery will not enhance performance unless the individual has some prior practice at the task.

According to Corbin (1972), the extreme novelty of a task may make it difficult for individuals to visualize the task, thus minimizing the effectiveness of imaginal rehearsal. There is also some evidence (Corbin, 1967; Noel, 1980) that highly skilled athletes may benefit more from imagery than athletes of less skill, although more research is needed before firm conclusions can be drawn. It should be noted that a number of cognitive intervention techniques have been developed which employ some combination of imagery with relaxation. Three of the more popular programs used with athletes are Meichenbaum's (1977) stress inoculation training, Smith's (1980a) stress management, and Suinn's (1972b; 1976) visuo-motor behavior rehearsal. Although the effectiveness of these techniques in sport settings needs further documentation, some initial studies have been encouraging and these techniques may offer great potential for enhancing athletic performance. There is still much to learn in the area of imagery, but the following section provides some basic guidelines for using imagery as part of an athlete's training regimen:

1. Choose a place where there are no distractions so you can concentrate.
2. Try to use all sense modalities when imagining. If you imagine hitting a tennis serve, try to *see* yourself, *feel* the movement, and *hear* the ball hitting the racket.
3. Focus on performing the skill perfectly; although occasionally you might see yourself making an error, recover and cope with the failure.
4. Make sure imagery is included systematically into your workout regimen.
5. Use imagery to go over and learn different strategies that you might use throughout the game.

6. Before using imagery try to relax using one of the methods just described; this should put you in a state of relaxed concentration.

7. Practice controlling your image until you can get it to do what you want it to do.

8. Try to image as vividly as possible and practice getting a clear image.

Preparatory Arousal.   The final strategy identified by athletes is termed preparatory arousal. In essence, this involves getting mad, charged-up, excited, pumped-up and/or aroused just prior to performance. We often hear football coaches trying to psych-up their athletes by getting them fired-up and mad at the opposition. However, is this kind of mental preparation beneficial to performance?

To answer this question, it is necessary to refer back to Robert Sonstroem's discussion of optimal arousal, where it was noted that the type of task mediates the arousal-performance relationship. Specifically it has been hypothesized that tasks predominately requiring strength, speed, and endurance need high levels of arousal for optimal performance, whereas tasks requiring fine muscle coordination and precision are best performed at low levels of arousal. Since preparatory arousal by definition means raising one's level of arousal, this would be expected to benefit performance on tasks predominately requiring strength and endurance. This notion received empirical support in a series of investigations by Weinberg, Gould, and Jackson (1980) and Gould, Weinberg, and Jackson (1980). Subjects performed on an isokinetic leg-strength task using a number of different mental preparation strategies. Results consistently indicated that preparatory arousal produced superior performance to both control conditions as well as other mental preparation strategies. Thus it appears that for strength tasks, preparatory arousal is indeed effective in enhancing performance and might be appropriate for athletes such as weight lifters. When using this technique for a football team, however, it should be noted that not all football positions (e.g., quarterback, receivers) employ predominately strength moves. Thus, the use of preparatory arousal might not be advisable for athletes in the "skill" positions.

FUTURE DIRECTIONS FOR RESEARCH

The astute reader will have concluded from this discussion that many questions about mental preparation strategies are still unanswered. As we move through the 1980s and into the 1990s, mental preparation in sport will undoubtedly play an increasingly important part in athletes' training regimen if maximum performance is to be achieved. This challenges researchers to continue their pursuit of knowledge in this area of inquiry.

Along these lines, some questions for research might include: (a) Is there an optimal amount of time in which to mentally prepare? Some anecdotal work by Genov (1970) has indicated that weight lifters take more time as the lift becomes more difficult. (b) Are a combination of strategies better than one strategy? Which combinations would be best? Some initial work, for example, has indicated that relaxation combined with imagery appears to be effective. (c) Do different sports require different mental preparation strategies? Our initial laboratory work indicates task specificity but more field studies must be conducted with a variety of sports. (d) What are the physiological mechanisms underlying the effectiveness of certain mental preparation strategies? For example, are more motor units recruited to perform the task? Are the muscles used more efficiently in terms of agonists and antagonists?

If researchers can find the answers to these questions, athletes will come closer to realizing their full potential.

Chapter 12

Theoretical
and Treatment Approaches
to Anxiety Reduction

Ronald E. Smith
University of Washington

The determinants and effects of anxiety in the athletic setting have long interested sport psychologists and researchers. This interest has spawned a significant amount of research on aspects of the athletic environment that elicit anxiety (Gill & Martens, 1977; Passer, 1982; Scanlan & Passer, 1978a), individual differences in anxiety responses (Griffin, 1972; Martens, 1977; Scanlan & Passer, 1978a), and the effects of anxiety on performance (Landers, 1980; Lowe & McGrath, 1971). Evidence abounds that the competitive athletic setting is capable of eliciting high levels of anxiety in participants, some of whom are prone to experience anxiety that is sufficiently intense to create stress and disrupt their performance.

High levels of anxiety can be experienced at all age and competitive levels, from youth leagues to the professional ranks. Scanlan and Passer (1978a, 1979a) collected pregame state anxiety measures from youth soccer players and found that approximately 20% of the youngsters reported very high levels of tension and anxiety. Evidence also indicates that such anxiety can have at least subjective performance consequences. For example, Pierce (1980) found that 31% of a sample of youth sport participants and 50% of sport dropouts reported that various worries prevented them from playing up to their capabilities.

Performance pressures increase in intensity at the college level. According to several surveys of major college football teams, more than 40% of the athletes have reported experiencing high levels of anxiety before and during competition that they felt interfered with their performance (Smith, 1980a). The potentially disruptive effects of heightened anxiety on the performance of college athletes are more objectively demonstrated in data reported by Weinberg and Genuchi (1980). They found that collegiate golfers who were high in competitive anxiety performed significantly worse during tournament rounds than did low anxiety players of comparable ability. Finally, although the data are somewhat tentative at this point, there is evidence that the stress produced by life changes that require readjustment (e.g., academic, athletic, and personal relationship concerns and disruptions) is related to an increased susceptibility to sport-related injuries (Bramwell, Masuda, Wagner, & Holmes, 1975; Coddington & Troxell, 1980). Because of the potentially negative effects that anxiety can have on athletes' performance, physical health, and psychological well-being, much interest in reducing maladaptively high levels of anxiety has appeared in the recent sport psychology literature (e.g., Klavora & Daniel, 1979; Magill, Ash, & Smoll, 1982; Nideffer, 1981; Smith, 1980a).

FOUR MODELS OF ANXIETY REDUCTION

Four models of anxiety reduction have been generally recognized in the psychological literature. Two of them, *extinction* and *counterconditioning*, conceive of anxiety as an emotional response. Based on these models, two techniques employed to reduce anxiety are flooding and systematic desensitization. A third model of anxiety reduction, known as the *cognitive mediational* model, has particularly influenced the development of anxiety reduction techniques and is aimed at modifying affect-eliciting cognitions. A fourth and increasingly influential model of anxiety reduction is the *coping skills* model, which underlies several approaches (e.g., anxiety management training, stress inoculation training, and cognitive-affective stress management training) designed to increase the individual's own control of anxiety responses.

This chapter describes these conceptual models and the treatment techniques they have inspired, emphasizing how they might be employed to reduce maladaptive anxiety responses in athletes. Because there is no significant research literature on the use of these techniques with athletes, I will selectively review outcome studies performed on other client populations as well as animal and human research bearing on the processes that appear to mediate anxiety reduction.

The Extinction Model

Learning theories typically conceptualize anxiety as a conditioned emotional response. Anxiety responses are elicited by formerly neutral stimuli through a process of classical conditioning. By virtue of being paired with aversive or painful stimuli (unconditioned stimuli — UCS), the formerly neutral stimuli become conditioned stimuli (CS) capable of eliciting a conditioned anxiety response. An example of this process occurred when a professional jockey was thrown from his horse during a race and suffered painful fractures. He later found that riding a horse elicited intense anxiety, presumably because of the previous pairing of these stimuli with the primary aversive pain stimuli.

In many instances, people develop anxiety responses to particular situations when there is no history of their undergoing aversive classical conditioning themselves. It is possible for anxiety responses to develop through vicarious classical conditioning in which the CS-UCS pairing is observed to occur to someone else (Berger, 1962). For example, a gymnast began to experience intense anxiety that prevented him from attempting a difficult dismount after seeing one of his teammates fracture his back while attempting a similar routine.

Once a conditioned anxiety response is established through direct or vicarious classical conditioning, it becomes capable of motivating and reinforcing avoidance responses. That is, because anxiety is an aversive state, people (and animals) are motivated to reduce, escape, or avoid it. When successful avoidance responses occur, the resulting reduction in anxiety constitutes a negative reinforcement that serves to strengthen the avoidance responses (Rescorla & Solomon, 1967). This is one reason why the tendency to avoid anxiety-arousing stimuli often appears to become stronger over time even though no further CS-UCS pairings occur.

Extinction is the process whereby classically conditioned responses are eliminated by repeatedly presenting the CS in the absence of the UCS. Thus, one way of reducing a conditioned anxiety response is to expose the individual to the anxiety-arousing stimuli in the absence of the primary aversive stimuli with which they were originally paired. Undoubtedly, this process occurs in some people who are able to face up to their fears and remain in an anxiety-arousing situation until their anxiety is overcome. But a major factor that often prevents the natural process of extinction from occurring is the avoidance responses that remove the individual from the CS before extinction can occur. In animal studies, a technique of forced exposure to the CS while preventing the avoidance response from occurring (e.g., by restraining the animal) has been successfully employed in extinguishing anxiety responses (Baum, 1970; Mineka, 1979). The human therapeutic counterpart to this forced exposure procedure is known as flooding.

Flooding.   Flooding refers to the general technique of exposing the individual to anxiety-provoking stimuli while preventing the occurrence of avoidance responses (Boulougouris & Marks, 1969). Clinically, the technique usually involves the use of imagined scenes, although *in vivo* exposure to the actual feared stimuli or situations can also be used, either alone or as an adjunct to the imaginal exposure. It is assumed that prolonged exposure to the anxiety-arousing stimuli in the absence of an aversive UCS will extinguish the anxiety. Thus, the client is "flooded" with the CSs and the anxiety they elicit until the anxiety no longer occurs.

Since flooding is an aversive form of treatment, the client's informed consent should always be obtained before beginning the treatment. This can be accomplished by carefully explaining to the client the concepts discussed above: anxiety as a conditioned response, the concept of extinction, and the rationale and nature of the treatment that will be used. The client should be told that he or she will probably experience intense anxiety for a period of time before it diminishes. The client's informed commitment to the treatment technique is likely to enhance his or her willingness and ability to experience the aversive scenes and the anxiety they elicit.

A careful assessment should be made of the kinds of situations that are distressing to the client and the specific aspects of the situations that trigger the anxiety. In conjunction with the assessment phase, clients may be given imagery training in which they are asked to vividly experience events in the visual, auditory, kinesthetic, and olfactory-gustatory sensory modalities.

In my experience, the most common sources of anxiety in athletes are fears of failure and resulting social disapproval or rejection. To illustrate the use of flooding, let us consider how we might approach a highly anxious male basketball player who has a tendency to "choke" in pressure situations. After establishing through interview what the most fearful situations might be, we would ask the player to close his eyes and imagine a series of scenes involving his responding to pressure game situations with paralyzing fear, failing miserably in the clutch, and anticipating the disapproval and possible rejection of teammates, the coach, opponents, spectators, and significant others such as parents, relatives, and (former) friends. Each scene would be presented in vivid detail (with the player frequently being asked to provide additional details to enhance involvement) and would involve as many sensory modalities as possible.

For example, the player might be asked to imagine standing at the foul line waiting to shoot crucial free throws late in the game. He can vividly see every aspect of the scene—the crowd, with every eye focused on him, opponents smiling confidently at him, his teammates avoiding his eyes, his parents watching intently and looking very anxious. He can also hear the crowd screaming and one of his opponents muttering, "No way—you're going to choke." Kinesthetic cues (e.g., the trembling of his knees, his pounding heart, the weight of the ball in his slippery, sweaty hands) and olfactory-gustatory stimuli, such as the smell of sweaty bodies and the taste of sweat as he licks his lips with his dry, cotton-like tongue, would also be presented. The scene would be embellished and continued, depicting his missing the free throws badly and losing the game for his team; he would experience the booing and cries of "Choker!" from the crowd and sense rejection by his teammates, the coach, and perhaps even his parents.

Such scenes would be expected to elicit intense anxiety, and they would be prolonged until a visible and reported diminution of anxiety were observed. The extinction model emphasizes the importance of continuing stimulus presentation until extinction occurs; stimulus presentations that are too short will probably be ineffective and could even increase the fear response (Baum, 1970; McCutcheon & Adams, 1975; Staub, 1968). Flooding sessions typically last from 30 to 40 minutes.

Implosive Therapy.   Implosive therapy (Stampfl & Levis, 1967) is a flooding procedure that adds to the learning-based extinction model concepts derived from psychodynamic theories. The most important of these is the *avoidance serial cue hierarchy*, derived from the client's reports of fear-producing stimuli and the clinician's hypotheses concerning underlying psychodynamic conflicts of which the client is unaware. These underlying anxiety-arousing cues are typically related to themes of aggression and hostility, oral and anal scenes, sexual concerns, bodily injury, loss of impulse control, punishment, rejection, or guilt (Stampfl & Levis, 1967). The psychodynamic cues high in the avoidance serial cue hierarchy are strongly avoided and repressed because they are extremely anxiety arousing. Stampfl and Levis maintain that they are often the cues to which the anxiety was originally conditioned and that in such instances, the true elimination of anxiety requires exposure to them as well as to the external or symptom-contingent cues that can be identified by the client.

The effectiveness of flooding and implosion for anxiety reduction in athletes cannot be appraised due to a paucity of clinical reports and experimental outcome studies with this treatment population. However, much experimental evidence with animals indicates that prevention of avoidance responses and forced exposure to conditioned anxiety cues can be effective in reducing fear and avoidance (Baum, 1970; Mineka, 1979). Evidence also indicates that flooding can be an effective anxiety-reduction technique with human subjects (Boulougouris, Marks, & Marset, 1971; Girodo, 1974; Krawitz, Rimm, & Zimmerman, 1978; Yule, Sacks, & Hersov, 1974).

Implosive therapy is a somewhat controversial intervention technique. Many behavior therapists challenge its psychodynamic tenets and there is, in fact, no experimental evidence that the introduction of psychodynamic scenes facilitates therapy (Morganstern, 1973). However, this conclusion is tempered by clinical reports in which clients spontaneously recalled during flooding earlier psychodynamically toned experiences that seemed related to the development of their symptoms. These recollections and the re-experiencing of the anxiety connected with them was followed by rapid improvement (Boulougouris & Bassiakos, 1973). Thus, it is possible that in some cases exposure to psychodynamic cues may facilitate treatment.

My own experience in using flooding clinically is that it is more variable in its effectiveness from client to client than other techniques (e.g., Smith & Nye, 1973). When it is effective, improvement is often rapid and dramatic, as in one case in which a severe school phobia was eliminated in only two sessions (Smith & Sharpe, 1970). This pattern of greater variability but quicker improvement when effective has also been reported in an experimental outcome study by Barrett (1969). Flooding has occasionally proven to be highly effective after other anxiety-reduction methods have failed (Boulougouris et al., 1971; Kandel, Ayllon, & Rosenbaum, 1977). Because it is more aversive for clients than other techniques, many clinicians tend to use flooding or implosion only after other approaches have failed.

The Counterconditioning Model

An alternative to extinguishing a conditioned emotional response is to condition a response that is incompatible with anxiety to the anxiety-arousing cues. The general principle, according to Joseph Wolpe, the chief proponent of the counterconditioning approach, is as follows:

> If a response antagonistic to anxiety can be made to occur in the presence of anxiety-evoking stimuli so that it is accompanied by a complete or partial suppression of the anxiety responses, the bond between these stimuli and the anxiety responses will be lessened. (Wolpe, 1958, p. 71)

According to Wolpe, anxious people have learned through a process of classical conditioning to experience excessively high levels of sympathetic nervous system arousal in the presence of certain stimuli. The goal of treatment is to replace sympathetic activity with competing behaviors that have a predominance of parasympathetic innervation, a process Wolpe termed *reciprocal inhibition*.

Systematic Desensitization. Systematic desensitization, the treatment devised by Wolpe, is designed to permit the gradual counterconditioning of anxiety using relaxation as the incompatible response. Theoretically, other incompatible responses (among them Wolpe suggests assertion, sexual activity, and eating) could also be used, but not as easily or dependably. The process of systematic desensitization is carried out in such a way that the client should experience little if any anxiety, a feature that differentiates this approach from flooding.

The desensitization procedure requires a careful assessment of the situations that elicit anxiety and of the client's ability to relax and imagine scenes with appropriate levels of emotion. The client should not have many different phobias if this approach is to be used, since the treatment is directed at each fear separately.

The client is first trained in deep muscle relaxation, using a variant of Jacobson's (1938) progressive relaxation procedure. Relaxation is learned through a process of tensing and voluntarily relaxing the major muscle groups of the body. At the same time that relaxation is being mastered, the clinician begins to construct a stimulus hierarchy of scenes related to the client's anxiety. The hierarchy typically consists of 10-15 scenes which are arranged in terms of the intensity of anxiety they elicit. Hierarchies may be constructed along one or more of a variety of gradients, including time (gradually approaching a highly feared event), distance, seriousness, and so forth. Much care should be taken constructing the hierarchy in collaboration with the client so that the steps are gradual and roughly equivalent in the increments of anxiety they elicit.

Returning to the anxious basketball player discussed earlier in connection with flooding, sample items in his hierarchy (arranged from most to least anxiety arousing) might include scenes like the following:

- Preparing to shoot a free throw, with 1 second left in the championship game and your team trailing by 1 point (high anxiety scene);
- Sitting in the locker room before the game as your coach tells you how important this game is (moderately high anxiety scene);
- Walking toward the arena where the game will be played (moderate anxiety scene);
- Getting up from bed in the morning and thinking of the game that evening (moderately low anxiety scene);
- Thinking about the fact that the game will be played in 2 days (low anxiety scene).

A complete hierarchy would obviously have other scenes interspersed between the above scenes. Note that these scenes are basically arranged along an intensity dimension and a time dimension. When the client has mastered the relaxation skill and the hierarchy has been developed, treatment begins. The client is deeply relaxed and asked to imagine the lowest (least anxiety-arousing) in the hierarchy for perhaps 3 seconds. If any anxiety is experienced, the client is instructed to signal the clinician, who terminates the scene immediately and reinstates relax-ation. However, if the client is deeply relaxed, this should inhibit the low level of anxiety that would be aroused by a well chosen initial hierarchy item. If no anxiety is experienced, the scene is presented again for a slightly longer interval, perhaps 5 seconds. If again successful, the scene is presented for 10 seconds, then 15. Each time the client is able to imag-ine the scene without experiencing anxiety, some of the total anxiety is being deconditioned and the anxiety reduction is assumed to generalize to the other hierarchy items.

After the first item has been counterconditioned, the relaxation may well be sufficient to inhibit the reduced amount of anxiety now elicited by the second item. In this manner the clinician proceeds up the hierarchy. If the client cannot make the transition from a mastered item to the next highest item, the clinician may intersperse a new item to bridge the gap. Wolpe emphasizes that great care should be taken to pre-vent anxiety from occurring since this could partially undo the decondi-tioning that has already occurred. As in flooding, it is assumed that the reduction of anxiety that occurs to imagined stimuli generalizes to corre-sponding life situations.

Probably no behavior therapy technique has been as widely re-searched as systematic desensitization, and its efficacy as an anxiety-reduction technique is well established. More than 100 controlled studies have found desensitization to be superior to placebo or treatment com-ponent controls with a wide range of anxiety-based disorders (Kazdin & Wilcoxon, 1976; Rimm & Masters, 1979). The technique has proven very effective in the treatment of test anxiety, a form of performance anxiety analogous to that experienced by many athletes.

Positive changes have been observed on self-report test anxiety measures as well as on performance measures such as grade point average (Smith & Nye, 1973). Therefore, there is every reason to believe that the technique would be valuable for athletes, particularly if the anx-iety problem is a relatively circumscribed one; this qualifier applies to flooding as well. Because the extinction and counterconditioning models both focus on deconditioning responses to specific classes of stimuli, we should not expect a great deal of generalization of treatment gains to other areas of anxiety. And indeed, little generalizaton has been demonstrated with either flooding or desensitization (Goldfried, 1971; Rimm & Masters, 1979). Thus, other approaches are to be preferred for people who have multiple phobias or diffuse anxiety. Desensitization could prove to be a long and arduous process of working on hierarchy after hierarchy in dealing with the innumerable sources of anxiety in the lives of such people.

The generalization of treatment effects is a significant issue when considering the concepts of treatment efficacy and efficiency. Eliminating anxiety responses to specific situations may be a very worthwhile goal in and of itself for many clients, and the issue of generalization of treatment gains to other areas of the individual's life may be a moot one. However, some treatment approaches provide for the development of generalizable coping skills that are relevant not only to the specific anxiety-arousing situations that are the focus of treatment, but also to problem situations that may confront the individual in other circumstances or in the future. Now let us turn to the cognitive and coping skills approaches to anxiety reduction.

The Cognitive Mediational Model

The extinction and counterconditioning models are based on a concept of anxiety as a classically conditioned emotional response. Theorists such as Wolpe (1978) have eschewed the use of cognitive concepts in accounting for the development, maintenance, and reduction of anxiety responses. Other theorists, however, have given cognitive mediational processes a prominent role in their theories of emotion (e.g., Arnold, 1960; Beck, 1976; Ellis, 1962; A.A. Lazarus, 1971; R. Lazarus, 1966). These theorists assume that in most instances, emotional arousal is mediated by cognition rather than elicited directly by environmental cues. From this perspective, then, a powerful means of reducing maladaptive emotional responses, including anxiety, is to modify the cognitions that often elicit and reinforce emotionality.

According to Ellis (1962), irrational beliefs that are likely to generate anxiety include the following:

1. One must be thoroughly competent, adequate, and achieving in every way in order to be worthwhile.
2. It is necessary to be loved or approved of by virtually every other significant person.
3. It is catastrophic when things are not the way we would like.
4. Unhappiness and anxiety are externally caused and we have no control over our feelings.
5. If something is threatening or dangerous, one must keep thinking that it might happen.

Jones (1968) has developed an Irrational Beliefs Test to measure individual differences in endorsement of 10 of Ellis' irrational beliefs. Scores on specific belief scales have been shown to be related to daily mood ratings of anxiety, anger, and depression over a 6-month period (Rohsenow & Smith, 1982). In addition, Mahoney and Avener (1977) have reported similar beliefs in highly anxious elite athletes.

Cognitive Restructuring Approaches. Intervention directed toward the modification of affect-eliciting cognitions typically involves four related stages (Goldfried & Goldfried, 1980). The first step is to help the client recognize that his or her beliefs, assumptions, perceptions, or ideas (i.e., cognitions) mediate emotional arousal. These cognitions have typically become automatized—they are, after all, overlearned habitual ways of thinking and tend to occur without the client's awareness. Once the client accepts this tenet, the clinician helps him/her to identify some of the underlying ideas and to recognize their irrational and self-defeating nature. In the third phase, the client is helped to actively attack the irrational ideas and replace them with cognitions that prevent or reduce maladaptive anxiety. Finally, the client is helped to practice and rehearse the new modes of thinking and to apply them to the relevant life situations. For a more detailed description of various cognitive restructuring approaches, refer to Beck (1976), Ellis and Grieger (1977), and Goldfried and Davison (1976).

As stated earlier, the most common irrational beliefs that I have noted among highly anxious athletes are that one must be thoroughly competent to be worthwhile (a belief that leads to fears of failure) and that one must be loved and approved of by everyone who is a significant other (which leads to fears of social disapproval). Although I am unaware of any clinical outcome studies on the effectiveness of cognitive restructuring to reduce anxiety in athletes, the techniques have proven effective in reducing a related form of performance anxiety, test anxiety, which is typically mediated by similar beliefs (Goldfried, Linehan, & Smith, 1978).

Cognitive restructuring approaches are likely to be very useful in reducing anxiety in athletes. My own observations indicate that the techniques are likely to be most helpful to athletes who are fairly insightful and psychologically minded. As cognitive theorists have argued, the type of intervention likely to have the greatest impact in preventing maladaptive emotional arousal from occurring would be directed at modifying the cognitive mediators of emotionality (Beck, 1976; Ellis & Grieger, 1977). We should also expect that the modification of key irrational beliefs and self-statements will result in generalization across related anxiety-arousing situations.

The Coping Skills Model

Within the extinction and counterconditioning models, the client is viewed as the rather passive recipient of a deconditioning procedure carried out by the clinician. Basically, something is done *to* the client to undo past conditioning experiences. In the cognitive restructuring approach, however, the client plays a far more active role and assumes more personal responsibility for developing and applying new modes of thinking about problem situations.

The past decade has seen an emphasis on the development of active coping skills to deal with stressful life events, as well as several influential reconceptualizations of conditioning-based techniques. For example, Goldfried (1971) suggested that systematic desensitization could be more appropriately viewed as a procedure for learning and practicing relaxation as an active coping skill for the self-control of anxiety. At about the same time, Suinn and Richardson (1971) introduced an approach called anxiety management training, which was based on a similar conception of relaxation as an active coping skill. In this treatment, subjects practiced using relaxation to reduce anxiety elicited by the clinician.

Stress Inoculation Training. Meichenbaum's (1977) stress inoculation training provided a comprehensive treatment package that incorporated both cognitive and physiological coping skills. Meichenbaum conceives of the stress inoculation package as a kind of smorgasbord of coping skills that clients can master and apply as needed to deal with stressful situations. The coping skills are muscle relaxation and adaptive self-statements learned through a procedure termed self-instructional training. The latter involves teaching clients to give themselves adaptive instructions in dealing with stressors. Specific sets of self-statements are developed for preparing for a stressor (e.g., "Just think about what you can do about it. That's better than getting anxious"); confronting and handling a stressor ("Relax: You're in control. . . . Just think about what you have to do, not about fear"); coping with the feeling of being overwhelmed ("When fear comes, just pause"); and reinforcing self-statements for effective coping ("You did great!").

As the name suggests, the stress inoculation technique is aimed at allowing clients to practice using their coping skills to cope with low and manageable doses of anxiety. The rehearsal phase takes the form of asking clients to imagine anxiety-arousing situations and to imagine themselves using their coping skills in these situations. The notion is that practicing their coping skills to manage low levels of anxiety will help to "inoculate" clients against higher levels of anxiety in actual life situations. The stress inoculation procedure has been employed successfully to reduce anxiety and anger, as well as to increase pain tolerance (Meichenbaum, 1977; Novaco, 1975), and it would appear to be highly applicable to athletes. The self-instructional training could conceivably contain skill and strategy relevant self-statements as well as instructions relating to concentration and attentional processes.

Cognitive-Affective Stress Management Training. A coping skills approach that differs in several important respects from the stress inoculation treatment is cognitive-affective stress management training (Smith, 1980a, 1980b). Like Meichenbaum's approach, this program involves the acquisition and rehearsal of both cognitive and relaxation skills. The relaxation skills involve both somatic relaxation, learned through progressive muscle relaxation training, and cognitive relaxation, acquired through training in Benson's (1975) meditation technique. Cognitive coping skills are acquired through cognitive restructuring to approach and modify irrational ideas and/or self-instructional training to develop more adaptive cognitive control of attention and behavior.

A major difference between the stress inoculation and cognitive-affective approaches lies in the methods used to rehearse the coping skills once they have been acquired. Rather than rehearsing under low levels of anxiety, as in the inoculation model, a technique known as induced affect is employed to allow rehearsal of coping responses under high emotional arousal. The client is asked to imagine a stressful situation, then to focus on the feeling that the scene elicits. Suggestions that the feelings are growing more intense, and verbal reinforcement for signs of increased arousal, are used to shape a strong affective response (Smith & Ascough, 1984). When the client is highly aroused, he or she is instructed to "turn it off" with his or her coping responses. Initially, relaxation alone is used, then self-statements alone. Finally, the two classes of coping responses are combined into an "integrated coping response" that is tied into the breathing cycle. As the client inhales, a stress reducing or task relevant self-statement is emitted. Then, while slowly exhaling, the client gives the mental self-instruction to relax, thus inducing somatic relaxation.

In terms of rehearsal procedures, then, the cognitive-affective approach provides for rehearsal of coping skills to reduce levels of affective arousal that are as high or higher than those experienced in the actual situation. The level of affect intensity evoked during induced affect is likely to approximate that elicited by flooding, whereas the stress inoculation procedures elicit anxiety levels more closely approximating those observed in systematic desensitization. The assumption is that learning to master high levels of arousal ensures that lower levels can also be controlled, whereas the converse is not necessarily the case. One interesting finding here is that test-anxious subjects who were administered the cognitive-affective program expressed greater post-treatment confidence in their ability to cope in test situations than did subjects who rehearsed their coping skills with the stress inoculation procedures (Nye, 1979). However, both treatment approaches greatly reduced test anxiety scores.

Although few controlled outcome studies with athletes have been published, the cognitive-affective approach has been employed successfully with adult and preadolescent athletes in a variety of sports. This program has been administered in both an individual and a group format. To illustrate the use of the program to enhance self-control of maladaptive anxiety, the training of Ms. A, a 15-year-old competitive figure skater, will be described.

Although judged to have potential world-class talent, the disruptive effects of anxiety were evident in Ms. A's performance during the preceding year. She had failed to finish in the top five in her previous seven competitions, and her growing self-doubt and expectations of "choking" during her routines were interfering with her progress and increasing her anxiety. Her strong motivation to overcome her emotional block was evident when she began the stress management program, and she applied herself to the program with the same degree of dedication that she brought to her skating.

The training was presented to Ms. A as an educational program in self-control of emotion. It was explained that with time and practice, she could learn coping skills that many successful athletes employ to control anxiety and enhance performance. Practice was begun in progressive muscle relaxation, and Ms. A practiced her relaxation exercises faithfully several times a day. Like many athletes, she learned the relaxation skills quickly because of her good muscular control.

While relaxation training was proceeding, Ms. A was helped to monitor her thought processes during competition and to isolate the self-statements that elicited and accompanied her anxiety responses. These typically involved telling herself how awful it would be if she spoiled her routine and disgraced herself, her coach, and her parents, and that she was a worthless failure if she did not perform up to her potential. Cognitive restructuring was used to attack the irrational elements of her fear of failure and her perfectionistic demands, to show her how the ideas were self-defeating, and to substitute a set of self-statements designed to reduce or prevent her anxiety by focusing on effort rather than outcome. Her most effective thought was, "I can do no more than give 100%." Self-instructional training was also used to develop task-relevant thoughts such as, "Concentrate on what you have to do and nothing else," as well as imagery related to her routine.

During the rehearsal phase of the training program, Ms. A was asked to vividly imagine anxiety-arousing scenes such as skating onto the ice to begin her routine or falling down during the routine. The induced affect procedure was used to generate levels of arousal that she reported to be as high or higher than those experienced in the actual skating situations. She practiced reducing the arousal with relaxation, then with her self-statements and then with an integrated coping response involving a coping self-statement during the inhalation phase and the mental command to relax (accompanied by voluntary relaxation) during exhalation (e.g., "I can do no more than give my best . . . So . . . Relax").

Having learned her coping responses well and having practiced them to reduce high levels of anxiety during induced affect, Ms. A found that she could employ them very effectively within the actual skating situations. She used her training in meditation to control pre-event tension. She was surprised and pleased with her increased control over performance-disrupting anxiety, and her performance improved dramatically. Ms. A won a series of competitive meets and finished first in national competition in her age group. She attributed her improved performance to her ability to control anxiety and to focus her attention on the task at hand. Many coaches and meet officials commented on her more relaxed appearance and on the fact that as a result of mastering her anxiety, she appeared to be realizing her vast potential as a skater.

The coping skills approach to anxiety reduction in athletes offers two potential advantages over the extinction and counterconditioning approaches. First, the athlete assumes major responsibility for developing the coping skills needed to reduce anxiety and is more likely to attribute improvement to his or her efforts. This should enhance maintenance of treatment gains, since self-attributed changes appear to be better maintained than change attributed to external agents (Davison & Valins, 1969). Psychotherapy research has also shown that the more a specific treatment approach increases self-efficacy (confidence in one's own ability to cope) the more behavioral improvement is shown (Bandura, Adams, Hardy, & Howells, 1980). Nye's findings with test-anxious subjects indicate that demonstrated ability to control high levels of arousal during induced affect appears to result in high self-efficacy.

The second advantage of coping skills approaches over those based on conditioning models relates to the issue of generalization introduced earlier. As we noted, neither flooding nor traditional desensitization gains generalize readily to other areas of anxiety (Goldfried, 1971; Morganstern, 1973). To the extent that treatment is geared to the development of general and flexible coping skills that can be applied to a variety of situations, we should expect greater treatment generalization. Evidence to support this prediction comes from findings that subjects treated for test anxiety using a self-control variant of desensitization developed by Goldfried also showed a reduction in untreated speech anxiety, whereas subjects treated with traditional desensitization showed no speech anxiety reduction (Zemore, 1975). Thus, as applied to athletes, we should expect the results of coping skills programs to be useful over a wider range of both athletic and nonathletic situations.

The scientific study of intervention techniques designed to reduce anxiety in athletes is still in its infancy. Needed are controlled outcome studies with well defined and competently administered treatment procedures, dependent variable measures to tap behavioral, physiological, and self-report outcome indices, and appropriate control groups (including attention-placebo control conditions that are as credible as the treatment conditions). Clearly, the problem of anxiety is sufficiently widespread among athletes to justify the application and assessment of the many anxiety-reduction techniques that now exist and the development of more powerful and cost-effective ones in the future.

PART IV

MOTIVATION

In the previous section, the concept of anxiety was discussed and it was pointed out that, in excess, anxiety may be detrimental to performance. Thus one major task for a coach may be to keep anxiety within manageable limits for each athlete. Besides reducing anxiety levels in athletes, a coach must also be able to motivate athletes for short and long periods of time. We have probably all heard the saying that to be a good coach one has to be a good motivator. But "motivation" is a broad term and can encompass a wide array of behaviors; in fact, about one-third of all psychological literature is related to the topic of motivation. So before continuing, let's define what we mean by motivation.

Defining Motivation

Like many other psychological constructs, *motivation* has been defined in a variety of ways, but in general it refers to the intensity and direction of behavior. The direction of behavior indicates whether an individual approaches or avoids a particular situation, and the intensity of behavior relates to the degree of effort put forth to accomplish the behavior. Thus, motivation can affect the selection, intensity, and persistence of an individual's behavior, which in sport can obviously have a strong impact on the quality of an athlete's performance.

Although the definition of motivation is important, most coaches probably would be more interested in its determinants. Along these lines, Birch and Veroff (1966) have grouped the determinants of motivated or goal-directed behavior into four categories: availability, expectancy, incentive, and motive. Availability is the extent to which a particular situation makes available a certain kind of behavior. For example, if an athlete is interested in making friends and her softball coach does not provide any outlet for this need, she might leave the team and join another group. Expectancy is the anticipation that engaging in a particular action will lead to a particular goal. Thus, an athlete may practice 4 hours a day if he expects that this will enable him to reach his goal of winning the championship. Incentive is the specific consequence(s) attached to a particular course of action. For instance, a baseball player's contract may contain an "incentive clause" stipulating that he will receive an extra $1,000 for every home run he hits over 30. Motive is the strength of repulsion or attraction to a general class of consequences. A motive encompasses the reasons for a course of action and thus it answers the question "why?" It is important to understand that several of these determinants can exist for each person, and it is the interaction of these determinants that influences behavior.

The reader should note that these determinants of motivation could be broadly categorized as being influenced by either the person or the constraints of the situation the person is in. This is the essence of the interactional model, and motivation is perhaps best understood when considering the continuous interaction between the athlete and his or her specific situation.

Therefore, an athlete's motivational level is determined by the interaction of personal factors such as personality, needs, interest, or ability and specific situational factors such as the practice facilities, type of coach, or the team's win/loss record. This partially explains the fact that if you ask 10 coaches how to motivate athletes you will probably get 10 different responses! An appreciation for this principle will help coaches understand why two athletes may react differently to a game situation. Some athletes may be highly motivated by criticism and punishment whereas other athletes may become frustrated, angry, and depressed. Consequently it is incumbent upon coaches to understand these individual differences and motivate accordingly. Unfortunately, many coaches do not adhere to this principle but instead motivate according to how their former coaches motivated them, how "great" coaches in their sport motivate, or what motivates them personally. Although these bases for motivation have some merit, they neglect the fact that people and situations differ and that motivational strategies and techniques should be tailored to meet the specific needs of the coach and his or her athletes.

Types of Motivation

The first chapter in this section, by Robert Weinberg, provides a good example of the interactional model as it deals with the relationship of extrinsic rewards and intrinsic motivation. For years theorists and practitioners have felt that these two forms were additive, that is, the more the better. However, more recent research has indicated that under certain circumstances external rewards may undermine intrinsic motivation, especially if the activity initially was intrinsically motivating but the introduction of external reward turned play into work. This can have important consequences for physical educators and coaches since most children appear to enjoy physical activity at the outset, and such intrinsically motivated behavior can be undermined by the improper use of rewards. In discussing the research and theoretical underpinning of the relationship between external rewards and intrinsic motivation, Weinberg points out that rewards are not inherently good or bad, but rather it is the individual's interpretation of them that is crucial. Weinberg concludes by offering some suggestions on how to enhance intrinsic motivation in students and athletes in order to more effectively maintain desired behavior.

Setting Goals

Although many coaches rely on external rewards to motivate athletes, most coaches would probably agree that the key to long-term motivation is the athlete's own dedication and commitment to achieving excellence. One technique that both researchers and practitioners have found effective in eliciting the commitment, perseverance, dedication, and effort required for long-term motivation is goal setting. Certainly not a new idea, the use of goal setting in industrial and organizational settings goes back many years. Only more recently has the systematic use of goal-setting techniques been incorporated into the training regimen of athletes. In a subsequent chapter, Frank O'Block and Frederick Evans discuss the concept of goal setting as a motivational technique and provide both experimental and anecdotal evidence of its effectiveness in enhancing performance. They conclude by presenting the interval goal-setting technique they developed during a 2-year period of working with athletes, a technique that stresses the accomplishment of both short- and long-term goals. Athletes are encouraged to focus on their own performance accomplishments rather than that of their competitors. This is an important point since an athlete generally has more control over his/her own performance than over the outcome.

    A very influential theory in sport psychology for understanding motivation is achievement motivation theory, conceptualized by McClelland and Atkinson in the 1950s and 1960s. Its roots go back to the 1920s and 1930s with the work of Murray, Lewis, and Hull. The theory attempts to determine the direction, intensity, and persistence of behavior or performance in the limited context of achievement settings, which occur only when the person knows the performance will be evaluated according to some standard of excellence and that he or she will either succeed or fail. In looking at these criteria it becomes obvious that sport competition can usually be classified as an achievement setting. Thus the theory would be applicable and merits a brief description here.

Achievement Motivation

The theory postulates that achievement situations arouse an expectancy that an individual's performance could succeed or fail, which causes a conflict between two opposing tendencies — the tendency to approach success or the tendency to avoid failure. Both the motive to achieve success and the motive to avoid failure are relatively stable and result from the individual's previous experience (success and failure) in achievement situations. In addition to these motives, a second set of variables hypothesized as operating in any achievement situation are the probability of success (or failure) and incentive value of success (or failure). These are situational variables and thus may change according to each situation. Both sets of variables, stable and unstable, interact to determine an individual's preference, persistence, and performance at an achievement task. One of the theory's major predictions is that individuals who tend to achieve success (high achievers) choose tasks of intermediate difficulty (i.e., probability of success is .5) because these tasks are perceived as demanding and their outcome will depend on one's effort and persistence. Conversely, individuals who tend to avoid failure (low achievers) choose tasks that are very easy or very hard because, in this way, they can avoid the intense evaluation that characterizes tasks of intermediate difficulty. That is, because a very easy task has a high probability of success these individuals can avoid failure; and on a very difficult task they can always say they are not to blame because almost everyone fails.

Attributing Cause

While achievement motivation theory has generated a great deal of research in both the psychology and sport psychology literature in the 1960s and 1970s, its predictions for the intensity, direction, and persistence of behavior have recently been reinterpreted in terms of attribution theory. Attribution theory is the study of the perceived causes of an event, the manner in which these causal inferences are reached, and the consequences of these causal beliefs. For example, assume that you are at bat in a baseball game and the pitcher throws a ball close to your head and causes you to hit the dirt. You would like to know why this happened. The causal interpretation may be between an intentional bean ball or a pitch that just slipped and got away, and the causal decision reached in this case can have significant social consequences. An attribution of accident might lead to just getting set to hit again. However, an attribution of aggressive intent (bean ball) could lead to verbal or physical retaliation. Thus, one's attribution of the cause of an event can produce significantly different responses to the same behavior.

Attribution theory has grown out of an area of social psychology known as person perception or social perception. Its groundwork has often been credited to the pioneering work of Fritz Heider, who wanted to determine how the average person comes to know the causes of action. Heider felt that attribution theory had to do with ordinary people trying to understand their behavior and that of others. More recently, Weiner has conceptualized a model of attribution that can be applied in achievement related situations such as athletic competition. Weiner's original model denoted the four most important causal determinants of success and failure as: (a) ability (we are a good team), (b) effort (I trained hard and concentrated during the match), (c) task difficulty (the opposition was extremely tough), and (d) luck (we just happened to get the right bounces). However, more recent research in sport has demonstrated that athletes give other reasons for their successes and failures such as referee bias, injury, fatigue, illness, coaching, and the crowd.

Using these basic tenets of attribution theory, Weiner has conceptualized an attributional model of achievement motivation that provides more parsimonious explanation of direction, intensity, and persistence of high and low achievers in achievement situations. Recall, for instance, that high achievers persist longer than low achievers in the face of failure. Attribution theory explains this by stating that the high achievers' persistence is mediated by attributing failure to a lack of effort, which can be modified or reversed to yield future success. Conversely, low achievers quit in the face of failure because they attribute failure to a lack of ability, which presumably is unchangeable, and thus they expect failure to continue.

Two chapters in this section present some of the latest theoretical, empirical, and practical information about attribution theory and its implications for sport and competition. The chapter by Glyn Roberts and Larry Brawley gives an overview of the attributional process in sport and critiques the problems in sport attribution research. Concerning the conceptual and methodological problems of trying to apply attribution theory to competitive sport situations, the authors stress the need to consider an athlete's perception of his or her own success and failure, not just objective won-loss outcome. For example, if an amateur tennis player lost a set to Jimmy Conners, 6-3, he may see this as a personal success rather than failure since his opponent was one of the top players in the world! In the ensuing chapter, Roberts integrates attribution and achievement motivation theories to give a better understanding of the motivational processes in the competitive sport environment. He focuses upon a derivative of attribution theory and discusses the role of achievement goals in determining achievement behavior. It is argued that one's perception of ability forms the basis of a reconceptualization of motivation for sport achievement.

Group Motivation

The first four articles in this section focus on how to better understand motivation in the individual athlete. As we all know, however, coaching or teaching often involves motivating groups of individuals. Motivating a basketball or soccer team can be very different from motivating a tennis player. In an interacting sport such as basketball, athletes must understand that their own motivations, goals, and aspirations must fit within the goals of the team. For example, if an athlete's personal goal is to score 20 points a game but he or she is constantly double-teamed, he/she should sacrifice the personal goal for the team goal of winning and should pass the ball to an open teammate. However, getting the right chemistry of individual and team goals is a difficult and complex process. In a recent national survey investigating what coaches want to learn from the field of sport psychology, Silva found that the most frequent and critical factor mentioned was the issue of how to build and sustain group cohesion in sport teams.

Thus, in this section's final chapter David Yukelson provides the reader with some of the latest research on group motivation, along with specific recommendations on how to help build team harmony and motivation. Yukelson first explains the nature of groups and group involvement, giving special considerations to sport groups. Secondly, he discusses individual versus group motivation with particular emphasis on using goal setting to build confidence and to develop pride within the group. Yukelson then suggests several intervention strategies to develop group motivation and team harmony. This section, then, should help the reader understand not only what motivation is and how it operates, but also what can realistically be done to enhance an athlete's motivation toward excellence.

Chapter 13

The Relationship Between Extrinsic Rewards and Intrinsic Motivation in Sport

Robert S. Weinberg
North Texas State University

Anyone who has been associated with competitive athletics is well aware of the extensive use of extrinsic rewards. Most leagues have postseason banquets in which awards such as trophies, medals, ribbons, money, and jackets are given to athletes. Awards are given for accomplishments ranging from most valuable player to mere participation on a team. The advocates of external awards have held that giving awards will increase the athlete's motivation and desire to continue participating in that sport. This view went unquestioned until recently, when some critics have argued that giving rewards to athletes for activities in which they are already interested turns play into work and decreases their desire for future participation. Although it would be nice to have a simple answer for the question of whether rewards increase or decrease an athlete's motivation to participate, the research evidence indicates there is no simple answer. For example, in some situations external rewards have increased motivation whereas in other situations external rewards have decreased motivation. Therefore, it is the purpose of this chapter to provide information concerning the effects of external rewards on intrinsic motivation. To accomplish this, some background theoretical information from psychology will be presented, followed by the research evidence and, finally, implications and applications of this material for coaches and physical educators.

THEORY AND RESEARCH FINDINGS

Background

The most common definition of intrinsic motivation is that people are so motivated if they participate in an activity without receiving any external reward. That is, one is intrinsically motivated when he or she just plays for the pure fun and enjoyment of playing. Extrinsic motivation implies that performance or participation is controlled by external forces (money, trophies, grades) and that if these forces were not present, the individual would stop participating or would participate on a reduced level. Researchers and practitioners have generally held that a person's motivation for engaging in any activity is a function of both intrinsic and extrinsic motivation.

Although most early researchers and practitioners viewed extrinsic and intrinsic motivation as additive (i.e., the more the better), some individuals noted the potential undermining effect of external incentives. For example, Albert Einstein commented about exams, "This coercion had such a detering effect that, after I passed the final examination, I found the consideration of any scientific problems distasteful to me for an entire year" (Bernstein, 1973, p. 88). Some work by Harlow in the 1950s suggested an inverse relationship between extrinsic incentives and how primates learn complex problems. In addition, several noted researchers saw a distinction between extrinsic and intrinsic motivation and offered theories explaining the reasons behind the latter. For example, White (1959) has proposed that humans are active organisms who constantly interact with their environments and who strive to be effective in those interactions. He claimed that individuals gain satisfaction from mastering the environment and that this enhances feelings of competence. It is these mastery experiences and subsequent feelings of competence that provide the major source of motivation as opposed to the use of extrinsic incentives.

More recently, deCharms (1968) has proposed that whenever individuals see themselves as the cause of their behavior, they will consider themselves intrinsically motivated. Conversely, when individuals perceive the cause of their behavior to be external to themselves (i.e., I did it because of the money), they will consider themselves extrinsically motivated. The writings of White, deCharms, and others have led current researchers to reevaluate the common assumption that extrinsic rewards will increase one's intrinsic motivation.

Current Research

Although the previously mentioned theorists questioned the interaction of different forms of motivation, the specification of the exact nature of this interaction and its ramifications had to await the current round of research and interest in the topic (Condry, 1977). One of the first researchers who experimentally tested the relationship between extrinsic rewards and intrinsic motivation was Edward Deci. The typical research model employed by Deci and other researchers looks something like this: First, an individual's level of motivation for doing some task is measured and used as either a baseline measure or a determination of whether the task is intrinsically motivating. Next, some experimental intervention is attempted, usually involving different types of reward groups (e.g., expected, unexpected) along with a no-reward control group. Finally, a second attempt is made to assess an individual's intrinsic motivation toward the task either through questionnaires or a behavioral measure (e.g., how long he/she wants to work at the task without any rewards). Any change in the level of interest from the first to the second measure is taken as the primary dependent measure of the effect of reward on intrinsic motivation.

Deci's first studies (1971, 1972a, 1972b) used a game called SOMA (trademark Parker Brothers), composed of a number of blocks that may be arranged to form various patterns. Prior testing indicated that it was an intrinsically interesting task. Half the subjects were offered one dollar for each of the three puzzles they were able to solve in the alloted time, whereas the other half worked on the same puzzles with no mention of reward. After the subjects completed the three puzzles, the experimenter left the room and secretly observed through a one-way mirror the subjects' willingness to work on the puzzle even though they were not required to do so at this time. Thus the amount of time spent working on the puzzle during the free session was Deci's measure of intrinsic interest in the task. Results indicated that subjects receiving a reward spent significantly less free time (106 seconds) working on the puzzles than did subjects receiving no reward (206 seconds). In essence, the experience of being paid for working on an intrinsically interesting activity seems to have decreased the subjects' intrinsic motivation for the activity.

Since Deci's original studies, several researchers have conducted experiments designed to test the relationship between extrinsic rewards and intrinsic motivation. Some of the most interesting results have been uncovered in a series of studies conducted by Greene and Lepper (Greene & Lepper, 1974; Lepper & Greene, 1975; Lepper, Greene, & Nisbett, 1973), who extended Deci's laboratory findings to a field setting. Their field setting was a nursery school and they employed typical incentives for that situation. Children were selected who had a high intrinsic interest for a particular activity, picture drawing. In the expected award condition, the children agreed to draw a picture in order to receive a reward (called a "good player" award comprised of a certificate and a gold star). In the unexpected award condition, the same award was given to unsuspecting children after they completed the task. In the no-award group, the children neither anticipated nor received an award. One or two weeks later the children were unobtrusively observed for their interest in the same activity in a free-choice situation. The authors found that the unexpected reward and no-reward groups maintained significantly higher interest in drawing pictures than did the expected-reward group. This demonstrates the potential long-term effects of extrinsic rewards and also points to the importance of looking closely at how the reward is administered when attempting to determine its effects on intrinsic motivation.

Although numerous studies have demonstrated that extrinsic incentives can undermine intrinsic motivation, some research has found an increase in motivation due to rewards. For example, Deci, Casio, and Krusell (1975) conducted a study in which males and females were given positive, negative, or no verbal feedback concerning their performance on a puzzle task. Results indicated that positive feedback (reward) about performance increased intrinsic motivation of males but decreased intrinsic motivation of females. Negative feedback decreased intrinsic motivation of both males and females. How can we account for the fact that rewards sometimes undermine intrinsic motivation whereas other times they enhance motivation? Deci used a theoretical framework to address this issue.

Cognitive Evaluation Theory

To explain the differential effects of rewards on intrinsic motivation, Deci (1975) has suggested an approach that he terms cognitive evaluation theory. Cognitive evaluation theory assumes that intrinsically motivated behavior is motivated by a person's innate need to feel competent and self-determining in dealing with the environment. The theory then asserts that there are two processes by which extrinsic rewards can affect intrinsic motivation: controlling aspect and information aspect.

Controlling Aspect. First, in line with the work of Heider (1958) and deCharms (1968), Deci states that the experience of working for rewards can initiate a change in perceived locus of causality. When people are truly intrinsically motivated to perform an activity, the cause of their behavior resides within themselves (i.e., they perform because they enjoy the activity and want to feel competent). However, extrinsic rewards can decrease intrinsic motivation when the recipients of the reward perceive that the reason for their participation has shifted from their own control to factors external to themselves. Specifically, intrinsic motivation decreases when the external reward is perceived to be the primary reason one participates in an activity. When one only performs for rewards, his or her intrinsic interest is no longer sufficient to motivate the activity. A good example of rewards controlling behavior and producing a change in locus of causality from internal to external can be illustrated as follows: A child learns to play the piano because his parents promise him a new bicycle if he practices every day for the next 6 months. However, after 6 months the child receives the bicycle and thus has no more incentive to continue playing the piano. In terms of sport participation, I have heard many young athletes ask whether trophies would be awarded to the winner of the league, and then decide not to participate if the answer was no.

Information Aspect.   The other process by which extrinsic rewards can affect intrinsic motivation concerns one's feelings of competence and self-determination. Deci states that people are intrinsically motivated to perform activities that make them feel competent and self-determining. If a reward increases an individual's feelings of competence and self-worth, it will increase intrinsic motivation. If the reward makes an individual feel less competent and self-determining, this will decrease intrinsic motivation. For example, giving an athlete a most valuable player award would convey information about the recipient's athletic competence and probably increase his or her intrinsic motivation.

Informational Versus Controlling Aspect of Rewards.   It is important to note, however, that every reward potentially has controlling and informational aspects. Thus the effect of a reward will depend on which aspect is more salient in that particular situation. For example, on the surface it would seem a good idea to give an athlete a most improved player award, or give a team trophies for placing first since these provide information concerning the athletes' competence. As Halliwell (1978) notes, however, even though the informational aspect of the reward may provide information concerning an athlete's competence, the controlling aspect of these rewards may be more salient if the athlete perceives that his or her sports involvement is being controlled by the pursuit of trophies or other extrinsic rewards. Consequently, the reward may decrease intrinsic motivation because the athlete perceives his/her participation as a means toward an end, with the cause of behavior being external to him or her. This could easily occur, for example, when young athletes feel that they must excel to satisfy their parents. Since many parents derive vicarious satisfaction from their children's athletic accomplishments, they frequently exert pressure on their children to win at all costs. In this case, the controlling aspect of athletic awards would be more salient than the informational aspect because the young athletes would perceive that their behavior was controlled by the need to win trophies to satisfy their parents' vicarious needs. In summary, rewards can either increase or decrease an individual's intrinsic motivation. If the controlling aspect is more salient, rewards will decrease intrinsic motivation whereas if the informational aspect is the more salient aspect and provides positive information about one's competence, rewards can enhance intrinsic motivation.

INTRINSIC MOTIVATION
AND EXTERNAL REWARDS IN SPORT

Although psychologists have been investigating the potential undermining effects of external rewards on intrinsic motivation, physical educators and sport psychologists have only recently addressed this issue. From Little Leaguers receiving trophies and medals to professional athletes making huge sums of money, it is apparent that external rewards are an integral part of the sport experience. The question remains whether these rewards enhance or undermine subsequent intrinsic motivation. Quotes from two professional athletes are appropriate here. For example, Richard Todd, former quarterback at the University of Alabama who later became a quarterback in the NFL, said of the enthusiasm of his Alabama team, "It was fun for those fellows. They were not getting paid for it." Earvin (Magic) Johnson, star basketball player for the Los Angeles Lakers, was asked if he received any outrageous offers while being recruited by various colleges. He responded with, "I received my share of offers for cars and money. It immediately turned me off. It was like they were trying to buy me, and I didn't like anyone trying to buy me." Notice that what Magic Johnson was really referring to was the potential controlling aspect of rewards. He did not like anyone trying to control him through bribes and other extrinsic incentives. These anecdotes imply that rewards may undermine intrinsic motivation in sport. Let us now take a look at what researchers have discovered about this issue.

One of the first studies that attempted to assess the effects of extrinsic rewards in a sport setting was conducted by Ryan (1979), who began by looking at athletic scholarships. He administered a questionnaire to several different schools and several different sports. Specifically, male football and wrestling athletes were assessed, as were female athletes participating in six different sports. Ryan hypothesized that male athletes on scholarship would display less intrinsic motivation than those not on scholarship since the scholarship might act to control the athlete's behavior. However, he predicted that women athletes on scholarship would display more intrinsic motivation than those not on scholarship. Ryan reasoned that since athletic scholarships were relatively new and rare to women's athletics, the scholarship would serve as information about ability since only outstanding individuals receive them.

Results supported the hypothesis in that the football players on scholarship exhibited less intrinsic motivation than those not on scholarship, whereas women athletes on scholarship displayed more intrinsic motivation than those not on scholarship. Contrary to the hypothesis, however, male wrestlers on scholarship displayed more intrinsic motivation than those not on scholarship.

One reason for the differences between wrestlers and football players is the way a coach uses the scholarship: At most institutions, football is a high-pressure sport that emphasizes winning, so coaches might tend to use the scholarship as leverage to control the athlete's behavior. For example, Gary Shaw, a former football player at the University of Texas, stated that most of the players on the team felt that they had to perform well or lose their scholarship. In fact, he said when players were not performing up to the coaches' expectations, they were forced to participate in drills designed to make them miserable, in effect coercing them to give up their scholarship! Under these conditions the scholarship's controlling aspect was more salient than the informational, thus producing a decrease in intrinsic motivation for the football players. On the other hand, if wrestling coaches tell their athletes that they are special because of the reward and use other intrinsic measures to motivate the athletes, then the competence aspect would be salient and intrinsic motivation would increase.

In summary, it seems clear that the effect of scholarships on athletes' intrinsic motivation depends on whether the coach emphasized the salience of the informational or controlling aspect of the reward. As Ryan notes, "While not inevitable, it would seem quite possible for a coach in an effort to get improved performance to use the scholarship to force extra practice, longer hours, etc., and to turn sport into work, thereby killing most intrinsic motivation for that sport" (1979, p. 16).

Recently Deci, Betley, Kahle, and Abrams (1977) investigated the effects of competition on intrinsic motivation; they felt that competing appears similar in many ways to working for a reward. If this is so, then one can view competition as being both controlling and informational. In a sense an individual can be controlled by, or even obsessed with, the need to win, and winning replaces doing one's best or having fun as the primary goal. On the other hand, competing provides direct feedback from the environment concerning one's competence, that is, competition can provide positive or negative information concerning one's skill and/or competence in the sport. To investigate these notions Deci's group instructed subjects to compete on a puzzle task and then rewarded some but not others. Results indicated that males who competed for reward exhibited more intrinsic motivation than males who competed for no reward. Conversely, females who competed for rewards exhibited less intrinsic motivation than females who competed for no reward.

However, all subjects in Deci's study were allowed to win and therefore experience success. But in sport competition whenever someone wins and experiences success someone else loses and experiences failure. Previous research has demonstrated the potency of success and failure in providing information concerning competence (Scanlan, 1977). Thus, Weinberg conducted a series of studies (Weinberg, 1979; Weinberg & Jackson, 1979; Weinberg & Ragan, 1979) to investigate the effects of success and failure and external rewards on intrinsic motivation in competitive sport settings. The results of all three investigations were amazingly consistent in that subjects exhibited higher levels of intrinsic motivation after success than failure.

The potency of success and failure in terms of its effects on intrinsic motivation is not surprising when one considers the information it provides concerning one's competence. Besides giving the individual confidence in his or her ability, success may increase positive social evaluation and lead to favorable social recognition. Conversely, when an individual fails at a task, this failure indicates that he or she is not competent and does not possess adequate ability in the task. It is interesting to note that subjects in all three studies were rewarded for their performance, although these rewards did not undermine intrinsic motivation. It seems that in sport competition, the information contained in winning and losing is so potent that it overshadows the effects of the external rewards. This is not to say that external rewards cannot undermine intrinsic motivation in sport environments (especially since the subjects only received a small monetary reward of 2 dollars). However, it does show that coaches should be cognizant of the important influence that success and failure can play on an athlete's intrinsic motivation, particularly if the success or failure is consistent over a period of time.

Although success and failure appear to be mediators of subsequent intrinsic motivation in sport settings, we are still left with the question of whether competition *per se* can undermine the intrinsic motivation. Several researchers in psychology have indicated that competition can have negative effects although these studies have not dealt specifically with intrinsic motivation. Perhaps the most common outcome of these studies has been the finding that competition leads to disruptive emotional responding and impaired performance (Csikszentmihalyi, 1975; Deutsch & Krauss, 1962; Sherif & Sherif, 1969).

However, it should be noted that some research has found competition to have some positive effects (Scott & Cherrington, 1974; Weinberg & Ragan, 1979). Once again, the effects of competition on intrinsic motivation would appear to be tied to the two aspects of the competitive structure, namely, the controlling aspect and the informational aspect. If the competitive element leads people to view the activity as something they do in order to win (i.e., the goal is beating someone else and is thus extrinsic) rather than something they do because it is interesting, then the controlling aspect is more salient and should produce a decrease in intrinsic motivation. However, if competition is seen as exciting and just doing one's best with little concern for evaluation, then the informational aspect would be more salient.

IMPLICATIONS FOR COACHES
AND PHYSICAL EDUCATORS

Much of this chapter has shed light on the potential undermining effects of extrinsic rewards on intrinsic motivation. It has been argued that if an individual's reason for participation moves from the intrinsic value of the activity to an external motive, some serious consequences can result. Once the extrinsic rewards have ceased there may no longer be a sufficient reason to continue, and an individual may withdraw from the activity or participate to a much lesser extent. Coaches often establish a series of extrinsic goals and rewards to maintain motivation, but what happens when the extrinsic rewards are removed? As evidenced by Ryan's study on scholarship athletes, the dependence on external rewards may lead to lack of enjoyment since the athletes feel that they are controlled by the rewards. But here is the key point: *Rewards do not inherently undermine intrinsic motivation.* In fact, when initial intrinsic interest in an activity is lacking, rewards can improve motivation and stimulate interest in the activity. Furthermore, if the rewards provide positive information about the athlete's competence, as Deci notes, then intrinsic motivation will be enhanced.

This puts the coach or physical educator in a crucial position since they are the ones usually giving out the rewards. Adult leaders must therefore be very careful about the use of extrinsic rewards. According to the previously reviewed research, rewards should not be used to control or coerce athletes to participate in already enjoyable activities. Unfortunately, athletes, especially young athletes, often feel they must excel in order to satisfy their parents. Winning trophies and awards are tied to pleasing their parents and thus the athletes in effect are controlled by the rewards. Because parents and coaches play a vital role in determining how the athlete perceives the reward, they must put winning in perspective and stress the nontangible values of sport (fitness, fun, personal improvement) as opposed to participating solely for the rewards (Gould, 1980).

Enhancing Intrinsic Motivation

Although it is important to understand potential factors that may undermine intrinsic motivation, it is just as important to define strategies that will enhance intrinsic motivation. If a primary goal of physical education and coaching is to promote lifetime sport participation, then strategies must be developed that increase the satisfaction, fun, and enjoyment that can be derived from physical activity and competition. Incorporating the previously mentioned research as well as the work of other motivational theorists, the following six strategies are recommended to enhance intrinsic motivation in sport activities.

First, the work of Weinberg and his colleagues suggests that to increase intrinsic motivation, coaches and physical educators should make sure that athletes have a fair share of successful experiences in sport. The competitive environment should be structured so that athletes experience success, which increases personal feelings of competence. For example, many youth basketball leagues are played with the baskets set at a height of 10 feet; this makes it extremely difficult for young children to shoot well since many of them do not have the strength to do so. Lowering the baskets by 2 feet would allow for more success and probably make the game more fun.

Halliwell (1978) suggests that intrinsic motivation can be enhanced by allowing athletes to accept more personal responsibility for making decisions and rules. This would help increase the athlete's perception of control over his/her own behavior and would lend a feeling of personal accomplishment. Athletes could give input and suggestions concerning organization of practice sessions, making of team rules, establishing a dress code, or even decisions about game strategy. For example, athletes could be responsible for running one segment of practice and be encouraged to develop innovative drills. Likewise, more experienced players might be encouraged to have input in developing game plans for team sports.

A third way to increase intrinsic motivation is through praise, both verbal and nonverbal. This would be especially important to athletes who are second string and get little recognition. Some of the most powerful rewards are a pat on the back or a simple "nice job," and such rewards should be used frequently to acknowledge each athlete's contribution to the team or achievement of a personal goal. Emphasizing the importance of each player's role and its unique contribution to the success of the team will give each athlete a sense of self-worth.

Fourth, an athlete's sense of competence, and hence intrinsic motivation, can be enhanced by setting realistic goals. Not all athletes can be highly skilled and not all teams will finish in first place. However, the coach can help each athlete set realistic, attainable goals that can be reached with sufficient effort. Not all goals have to be centered around objective performance outcomes. For example, goals can be in terms of minutes played or improved personal skill. These goals should be periodically reevaluated and reset according to what the athlete has accomplished.

A fifth technique to enhance intrinsic motivation is to vary both the content and sequence of practice drills. This is important because people have an intrinsic need for exploration and stimulation. Along these lines, not only should drills differ in variety but their order of presentation should also vary. Another way to reduce boredom and increase interest with young participants is to give them a chance to play different positions. This should not only make practice more fun but also give players more awareness and appreciation of the demands of various positions on a team. Some Little League organizations have recently adopted the concept of requiring players to rotate positions after each inning. This is an encouraging development and could be implemented in other team sports such as football, soccer, and basketball.

A final comment on increasing intrinsic motivation stems directly from the innovative work of Csikszentmihalyi (1975). Although most researchers have tried to determine which factors undermine motivation, Csikszentmihalyi attempted to determine what makes a task intrinsically motivating. He examined activities such as rock climbing, dancing, and amateur athletics in which people participate with great intensity but not really for conventional rewards. Through interviews and questionnaires he was able to determine the common elements that make all of these activities intrinsically interesting: Each activity is characterized by the participant's complete involvement in it. The activity is constantly challenging and rarely boring. This holistic sensation that people feel when they are totally involved is termed *flow*. Csikszentmihalyi argues that individuals experience flow when they perceive opportunities for action as being evenly matched by their capabilities. By contrast, if skills are greater than the opportunities for using them, boredom will result. If the demands of the task are greater than the individual's capabilities, this will result in anxiety. Therefore, physical educators and coaches should design their activities, drills, and workouts so that they challenge the athletes.

The trick is to get students and athletes absorbed in the activity so that evaluation is minimized and attention is directed on a limited stimulus field. For example, a basketball player in flow had this to say: "The court — that is all that matters. . . . When I am playing well all that is on my mind is the game. I don't hear the crowd or other distractions." (Csikszentmihalyi, 1975, p. 41). If our competitive sports can be structured so that they are challenging, while at the same time provide the athlete with opportunities for problem solving and creativity, then the result might well be enriched experiences and long-term involvement in sport.

Chapter 14

Goal-Setting
as a Motivational Technique

Frank R. O'Block
Chicago State University

Frederick H. Evans
Olive-Harvey College

Top athletes of today are stronger, faster, and more efficient than athletes of years past. A great deal of the performance improvement can be directly attributed to better and more effective training techniques, innovative coaching approaches, nutritional programs, better designed equipment, and the recent attention to mental and motivational concerns. For many athletes, setting a new world or national record becomes a major goal during their careers. When goals are set too high or are too unrealistic, the athlete may experience severe frustration and anxiety, which in turn may produce burnout. However, coach/athlete goal-setting strategies, realistically employed, can help prevent burnout and increase the opportunity for success.

What type of goals should aspiring athletes set? Should they concentrate on specific short-range, general long-range, or open-ended goals? Should athletes set specific short-term increment goals, the accumulative effects of which when accomplished will equal the long-range goal? Should athletes set open-ended goals with no upper limitations, thus encouraging the athletes to try and achieve phenomenal feats? What are some important dimensions that a coach and athlete should consider in proper goal-setting, and how should team goals be set? This chapter will address some of these important issues and offer some guidelines for the coach and athlete.

GOAL-SETTING AND SPORT:
APPLIED APPROACHES

Zander (1975) said that athletes should set specific goals whether they participate in individual or team sports. When these specific goals are achieved, the athlete often experiences a sense of pride and should have increased positive expectancies about future performances. Group goals should also be specific rather than general. The goal of just winning is too general; specific goals should be identified—goals that can be achieved through individual and/or team efforts. In essence, athletes must ask themselves, "How good do I want to be?"

Swartz and Wayne (1979) have suggested that for marathon runners such as Jeff Wells and Tony Sandoval, to consistently run well requires predetermined specific goals. The process of setting these goals helps to modify and correct the athlete's mental expectancies, which in turn can help regulate actual performance. Swartz and Wayne recommend,

> Your goal must be realistic, specific and capable of being divided into manageable segments. Once your goals are set in this manner the stage is set for visualization. It is a process of intentionally programming an entire event into your subconscious mind to positively influence physical reality. (p. 90)

Swartz and Wayne concluded that setting goals prior to an event can mentally guide an athlete to train physically so that he or she can achieve goals.

McClements and Botterill (1979, 1980, 1981) have suggested that proper goal-setting and evaluation enhances the social value of sport competition. They suggest that a program for goal-setting should include a seasonal goal, which takes into account the athlete's long-term goal, commitment potential, opportunity, and present performance level. Furthermore, they divided goals into three categories: general subjective, general objective, and specific objective. Setting specific objective goals includes setting performance goals that should be specific (measurable), difficult yet achievable, verbally stated, recorded in writing, and checked. Good predictors are required in setting demanding yet reasonable specific goals. In order to have good predictors in timed and measured sports, McClements and Botterill (1980) developed a mathematical model for predicting performance, which can be used to help athletes establish long-term goals. However, they stress the importance of remembering that this form of goal-setting is only part of the process of goal achievement. Coaches and athletes interested in long-term goal-setting procedures should review the work of McClements and Botterill (1979).

Creel (1980) has offered another strategy for goal-setting: It recognizes the importance of long-range goals but maintains that long-range goals can only be attained if immediate short-range goals are established in some sequential order. Each player, besides accepting team goals, is encouraged to set his/her personal goals. Creel developed certain specific goals which, if met, would increase his football team's chances of winning. The goal objectives were divided into three aspects of the game: offense, defense, and kicking. Specific targeted goals for offense included: (a) maintain a 4-yard-per-play average, (b) average three touchdowns per game, (c) allow no interceptions, and (d) score on all goal line situations. Although accomplishing these goals did not guarantee success, achieving many of them would certainly increase the chances of winning. It was Creel's opinion that setting *concrete* process goals helped his team win more football games each season.

Hogue (1980) stated that one of the great motivators at the start of a new season was to set goals to reach by the end of the season.

> A goal may be to reach the quarter finals in the state tournament or to have a .500 season in league play. (A .500 season may not be great for some teams, but if you won two and lost eight the year before, winning five this year may be an outstanding accomplishment.) An individual goal may be to learn a new trick on the balance beam or to cut .5 off your 100 yard backstroke time. (p. 18)

As Hogue indicated, not all goal-setting is directed toward immediate success; rather, goals may be divided into subgoals which, when met over time, enhance the ultimate goal of success.

All of the suggestions discussed thus far have indicated that setting goals is tremendously useful because it provides an athlete with an objective to direct his/her efforts toward. Bell (1981), has noted, however, that if goals are too specific they can inadvertently limit one's performance. For example, if a swimmer limits what he/she thinks is possible (setting very specific, terminal goals) then that swimmer may perceive a limit to what he/she has to do in order to achieve the goal. Setting a specific, limited goal could in some instances inhibit extremely high levels of performance. Bell therefore recommended open-ended goals, which place no limits on performance.

Most of the suggestions for goal-setting strongly support the combination of long-range goals with seasonal specific short-range goal increments that are designed to eventually meet the long-term goal. It is reasonable to assume that there are some finite limits as to how fast, how high, and how far athletes can progress. However, it is most likely that many athletes have not reached their optimal level of performance. Several experts in the field of athletics and sport psychology support the idea of combining the setting of immediate short-range with long-range goals as one method to enhance performance. When a coach and athlete collaborate to determine goals, how is the athlete affected? The following section will discuss this issue and related questions.

GOAL-SETTING AS MOTIVATION

Botterill (1978) has strongly emphasized that goal-setting can be a motivating force in helping athletes perform. Goal-setting, particularly if realistic, may increase an athlete's commitment and confidence to achieve. In addition, Botterill has suggested that goal-setting can develop greater empathy and understanding, which itself often has a positive effect upon the athlete. Botterill (1979) noted it was very important that different, challenging, and realistic goals be set. Goal-setting helps athletes solve problems that arise when there is confusion, misunderstanding, or discrepancies regarding priorities and expectations the coach has for the athlete. However, McClements and Botterill suggest that the athlete should be involved in goal-setting and planning. This type of interaction with the coaching staff often helps motivate the athlete because of the personal interest shown toward the athlete as an individual. The collaboration between coach and athlete often provides incentive and can act as a powerful motivational tool for the athlete to train hard and excel. Such involvement also gives the athlete some practice in making decisions and assuming responsibility. Moreover, the athlete is afforded an opportunity to become more understanding and receptive to the coach's philosophy.

Jamieson and Wendelboe (1981) suggested that an athlete's goal be determined from previous best performances, projected improvement, and amount of training time completed up to that point. Achievement of each goal reinforces the athlete's training efforts, which in turn provides added incentive or motivation to pursue the new goal. The authors further state, "The net effect was that early small gains caused greater effort towards achieving later goals (thus increasing the likelihood of success there) and increased the confidence in the program."

Because it appears that goal-setting can have many positive effects upon an athlete or team, we have developed and implemented an interval goal-setting technique that is part of a motivational training program. A description of this program and some examples of how it can be implemented are discussed in the next section.

INTERVAL GOAL-SETTING

Interval goal-setting (IGS) was developed and tested over a 2-year period. After a great deal of applied testing and modification, a technique was established that can provide incentive for accomplishing both short- and long-term goals. The steps in the IGS process include (a) reengagement, (b) activation, (c) practice and training, and (d) trial and measurement. It has been our experience that when athletes incorporate the IGS model into their training programs, they are 90% effective in achieving the goals within the projected interval.

Procedure

The first step in implementing the IGS model is to examine with the athlete his/her long-range goals. These goals can and usually do cover a broader time span than short-term goals, particularly with the beginning competitor. We feel that coaches and athletes must have open and personal discussions to develop futuristic goals. This future oriented discussion is even more important if the athlete has ability, desire, and has already demonstrated some achievement. The use of the IGS model in developing long-term goals will be discussed later.

The second step in implementing the IGS model is to focus on the present, or more immediate goals. This is where the IGS model works best. At the beginning of the competitive season, after the athlete has competed twice in the same event, the IGS system can be used to compute and predict the interval goals for the third trial. After the athlete has competed five times in the same event, full computation and implementation of the IGS is more accurate.

Interval Goal-Setting Computation

The IGS model was developed out of a need to help coaches and athletes set more realistic and reachable goals. Through our experiences with athletes, we believe that in order to more accurately predict future performances, past performances must be considered. The IGS model incorporates an athlete's last five performances in predicting the next trial. The symbols used in computing the IGS model are given below (see Figure 14-1 for computation).

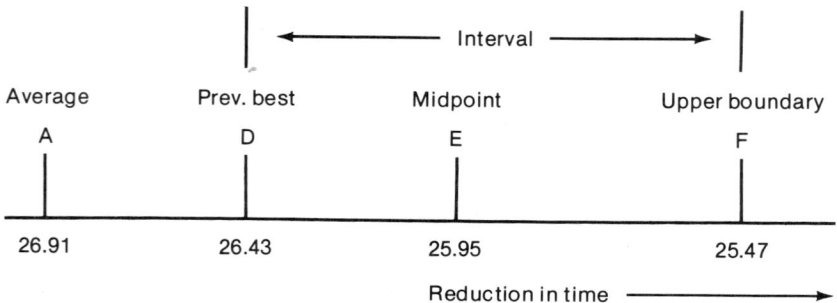

FIGURE 14-1   An example of IGS Model Computation.

A = Average over the last 5 performances

B = Best time within the last 5 performances

C = Difference between average and best performance (A − B)

D = Lower boundary of interval

E = Interval midpoint (D − C)

F = Upper interval boundary (E − C)

Example of the IGS Model.   Betty, age 12 years and 5 months, doing 50-yard freestyle.

Computation.   Times on last five performances: 26.48, 26.43, 27.12, 27.82, and 26.69. An example of IGS model computation is presented here in six steps.

1. Find A−average of 5 performances.
   A = 26.91

2. Find B−best time out of 5 performances.
   B = 26.43.

3. Find C−difference between average (A) and best time (B)
   C = A − B
   C = 26.91 − 26.43
   C = 0.48

4. Find D−lower boundary of interval or best time out of 5 performances
   D = B
   D = 26.43

5. Find E−interval midpoint
   E = D − C
   E = 26.43 − 0.48
   E = 25.95

6. Find F−upper interval boundary
   F = E − C
   F = 25.95 − 0.48
   F = 25.47

As can be seen in Figure 14-1, the interval midpoint (E) is realistically higher than the athlete's best performance (D). The upper limit (F) of the interval allows room at the top for an exceptional performance. Viewing the IGS with its lower, middle, and upper boundaries allows an athlete variability and a sense of expanded goals that are realistically possible, particularly if the athlete has demonstrated consistent gains throughout competition. Although the IGS model is not an open-ended goal strategy, neither is it a fixed target. It allows latitude in setting obtainable goals. This form of goal-setting encourages an athlete to perform within an interval of times. Any performance that falls within the boundaries of the interval can be considered successful regardless of the outcome of the event (win/loss). The higher the athlete's performance registers in the interval, the more significant the success and the more likely he/she will be motivated toward future performances.

After the sixth performance, a new IGS can be computed. In computing the seventh IGS increment, the former first time is dropped and the sixth time included. The seventh IGS increment is computed and the athlete proceeds as before. If an athlete's performance does not fall within the interval, this can be considered less than a desired performance. However, that performance time is still included in computing the next IGS increment.

With adaptation, the IGS model can be adjusted for use with events such as the long jump, pole vault, or shot put (where longer rather than faster is better performance). The adjustments occur with C, D, E, and F (C, the difference between the best and average, becomes $B - A$; E, the interval midpoint, becomes $D + C$; and F, the upper interval boundary, becomes $E + C$).

Although the IGS model is more applicable in developing short-term goals, it can be used to predict long-term goals. In the preceding discussion concerning short-term goal-setting, instead of using competitive times within a season, best season performances can be used to compute and predict long-term goals.

Athletes reported that one reason they incorporated the IGS model into their training was that they felt the model involved them in the process of their goal-setting. The projected goals, based on mathematical computation, invoked or solicited intrinsic interest and motivation.

When using the IGS, athletes actually use their own achievement performances in predicting their goal increments over a season. The computation is simple and straightforward. The IGS model, when computed, can provide intrinsic motivation for athletes to compete to their maximum. They are able to see the projected goal-interval incorporated into their training program, and this direction can help prepare them physically and mentally for improved performance.

Athletes who incorporate the IGS model in their training program often train for these process goals so that in their next competition their performance will fall within the interval. "I can see where I am and where I'm going," is a response they often give. The IGS technique can show an athlete where he/she can be after each competition. The increment phase of the IGS helps athletes maintain a sense of the "here and now" aspect of their competition, yet allows them to keep a record of their gradual improvements or declines. The model incorporates each performance into the computation and prediction for the next competition. When an athlete's performance is within the interval, he/she can gain a sense of accountability and knowledge of incremental growth, which helps maintain a continued drive for future success.

SUMMARY

The IGS strategy encompasses many of the significant goal-setting aspects suggested in the literature reviewed in the beginning of this chapter. The IGS model is not a fixed target, nor does it represent a pure, open-ended goal-setting approach. It is an interval (range) with lower, middle, and upper indicators of goal achievement. Under consistent environmental conditions, the IGS technique is effective and predictable.

Based upon more than 2 years of experimentation with the technique, several advantages of IGS have become obvious: (a) It is a practical demonstrable method for establishing realistic goals based on the athlete's previous performances. (b) The computation of a new interval for the next competition can strengthen the athlete's intrinsic involvement. Realization that his/her performance fell within the interval strengthens the athlete's desire to continue performing. (c) The method is based on an arithmetical model and is easily computed and remembered. (d) It is a tool to help the athlete determine realistic short-term process goals, which in turn enhance the accomplishment of long-range goals and, ultimately, outcome goals.

The IGS model alone is not the panacea for athletic success, but when incorporated into the total training program it has enhanced the performances of many athletes engaged in competitive sport.

McClements and Botterill (1981) developed a goal-setting model based on a negatively accelerating exponential curve to predict future performances. Both the IGS and the McClements and Botterill models incorporate the principle concepts found in the law of diminishing returns and various learning theories. The McClements-Botterill model helps athletes and coaches determine long-term goals for upcoming seasons, but does not compute realistic short-term goal increments needed to achieve the long-term goals. However, the IGS model, using in-season performances, can predict realistic goals for the next performance or short-term goal.

In summary, the establishment of short-term and long-term goals, regardless of the determining process, provides athletes with concrete objectives to work toward. Without question, the most effective means of determining an athlete's goals is through the collaboration of the coach and athlete. A programmed plan of goal setting should take into account the athlete's physical abilities, commitment, performance opportunity, and previous accomplishments. Setting and meeting realistic goals provides accurate feedback for standards of performance. By setting goals, athletes personally engage themselves in a systematic and regular target-setting and performance objective procedure. This procedure can become internalized and generate *self-directed* behaviors which athletes incorporate into pursuing their goals — whether in sport or life in general.

Chapter 15

Attributions in Sport: Research Foundations, Characteristics, and Limitations

Lawrence R. Brawley
University of Waterloo

Glyn C. Roberts
University of Illinois

INFERENCES ABOUT ACTIONS IN SPORT

One of the basic assumptions we make about individuals interacting with their social environment is that they attempt to understand why certain events occur. For example, people attempt to explain to themselves or others what caused a friend's out-of-character behavior or a teacher's strictness in class. The participants and observers of sport contests try to understand the cause of the outcome or the reasons behind particular strategies. More specifically, participants might ask questions such as: "Why did I lose that match? Why can't I please the coach? Why was the center the outstanding player in the game? Why did I get injured?" Alternatively, observers of athletes often ask questions such as: "Why didn't you try harder? What type of player is he? What kind of person coaches that team?"

The implication behind most of these action-type questions is that athletes and spectators are attempting to interpret and understand outcomes of competitions, coach-player interactions, or how the social environment of sport influences their perceptions. In trying to answer many of these questions, people go through the process of inference. That is, they infer the cause of some action in which they were involved; or they infer a disposition (e.g., aggression) to an athlete because of some

Both investigators contributed significantly to the development of this chapter and consider its authorship as joint. The authors' names appear in alphabetical order.

action they observed; or they infer that some person or environmental factor (e.g., the referee or the weather) caused the team to lose. After inferring, people also use these conclusions to help them predict future behaviors and outcomes (Shaver, 1975).

The general label that social psychology uses to categorize many inferences we make and the process by which we make them is attribution. We *attribute* cause and effect, capabilities and desires, emotions and personality traits. Understanding the sources leading to an attribution (antecedents), the attributions themselves (e.g., are they rational and logical or biased and self-serving?), and the results of making attributions (e.g., consequences such as changing one's mind, altering one's behavior, or developing expectancies for future athletic actions) may lead to some practical ends. For example, understanding attributions could result in a better understanding between coach and athlete concerning mutual expectancies. Certainly, Carron (1980) has pointed out the importance of comparable perceptions between athlete and coach for positive interaction.

Another example concerns changing some of the athlete's beliefs about his/her potential ability or effort within the sport. Different sources of information that invalidate a negative belief and lead to a positive attribution might help create self-confidence and positive expectancies (cf. Kruglanski & Jaffe, in press). These examples have yet to be tested in sport but are being examined and applied in other areas (e.g., cognitive therapy).

In the area of sport psychology, attribution research is still in its infancy. Much more research must be conducted before we truly understand the attributional process for people in sport; until then, we must be very careful about applying our findings to the real world. To achieve the ends of understanding and application, we must first understand what social scientists know about attributions in general. The first section of this chapter will review the foundations of attribution. The second section will briefly describe (a) a model used to consider attributions for winning and losing in sport and (b) some characteristics of the research paradigm that uses this model in the laboratory and field. The third section will examine the results of research about winning and losing. The final section will discuss the limitations of previous research and emphasize the need for a broader conceptual view if we are to understand how people express both logical and biased reasons for their actions in sport and physical activity.

PERSON-PERCEPTION:
THE FOUNDATION OF ATTRIBUTIONS

The study of attributions is associated with a broad conceptual domain of social psychology dealing with social perception. That is, just as the study of leadership or cohesion (teamwork) is examined under the larger context of group dynamics, the study of people's attributions is most closely related to social perception or *person perception*. Within the study of person perception, a chief concern has been considering the individual as an active perceiver of the social world. This person (athlete, coach, spectator, official, teacher) selects what he/she wishes to perceive by categorizing stimuli (Bruner, 1957) and then decides upon the response that seems appropriate to the social environment. The recognition here is that the person is an active, thinking/perceiving being and *not* just an individual passively responding to the environment. Social psychologists often say they are studying the individual's phenomenology in person perception.

In addition, person perception is governed by the same social rules and expectations of others that influence the social interaction of people. Thus, in person perception, we consider the individual's impressions of the environment in relation to the influence of that environment (Shaver, 1975). The social nature of person perception is that it is a two-way street of influence. Perceivers *interact* with the social environment.

Attribution as a Perceptual Process

The study of attributions, as an aspect of person perception, focuses on the contribution of the perceiver in his/her interaction with the social environment. In sport-specific terms, this would be the athlete's perceptions/interpretations of a competitive environment.

Sport investigators have studied attribution processes as a framework with which they can interpret people's self-judgments and self-evaluations of performance and behavior (e.g., the athlete's persistence in competition). More specifically, investigators have been interested in understanding achievement behavior in sport. First approaches to examining this behavior were primarily characterized by the study of individual differences (dispositions) in achievement motivation (cf. Atkinson, 1957, 1964; McClelland, 1951). However, as Roberts (1982) and Maehr and Nicholls (1980) have emphasized, this approach has trouble predicting achievement behavior because it fails to take into account the active interaction of the person's cognitions and many aspects of the social environment. Although an interaction is considered in earlier theoretical models of achievement motivation, it is very rigidly defined (mechanistic) rather than being dynamic. Thus researchers looked to attribution theory as a way to expand how they might explain or predict achievement behavior.

Cognitive Assessment of Achievement: The Attribution

The question one must ask is, "What does attribution theory offer that allows greater power to explain motivated behavior?" Attribution theory considers that the athlete actively processes information about an achievement event in an assumed logical fashion. Via this process, athletes construct what they believe has happened or caused the outcome of their athletic event (search for, assemble, and process relevant information). Based upon this cognitive process, the athlete decides upon present and future actions. Thus, attribution theory allowed sport researchers to conceptualize how achievement behavior may be influenced by cognitive and perceptual processes, as opposed to the notion of the person who is exclusively influenced by motive-states, inertial tendencies, or future orientations (cf. Atkinson & Feather, 1966; McClelland, 1951; Raynor, 1970). In the study of achievement behavior, the cognitive conceptualization suggests that the person acts as well as reacts, in contrast to the mechanistic approach which assumes the person merely reacts.

It should be noted, however, that attribution theory does not ignore the influence of needs and motives in the processing of information and making of ascriptions. In fact, there are two distinct approaches to examining attributions. They have been labeled cognitive and functionalist, or motivational (Tetlock & Levi, 1982). The former views the person as an information processor trying to obtain cognitive mastery and a rational view of the world. The latter approach examines the notion that attributions also serve psychological and social functions as motivated by learned or social needs (e.g., need to enhance self-esteem, need for social approval). In this view, the fulfillment of needs would motivate athletes to bias their view of the world.

THE ATHLETE'S INFERENCES
ABOUT ACHIEVEMENT OUTCOMES

Theoretical Models: Cognitive and Functional

A Cognitive Model.   One of two models adopted by sport investigators for studying achievement-oriented attributions is the two-dimensional taxonomy proposed by Weiner and his associates (Weiner, 1972, 1974). This cognitive model stems from an integration of Heider's (1958) work on the naive analysis of action with Rotter's (1966) theory of locus of control. According to the tenets of this model, athletes process information about outcomes according to whether they perceive the cause as within themselves or in the environment (i.e., internal vs. external locus) and whether the cause was perceived as stable (unchanging) or unstable (changing) over time.

Previous research by Weiner, mainly in educational settings, indicated that many of the specific causes people attributed to events fell into categories that could be described by four causal elements. These

Locus of causality

	Internal	External

		Internal	External
Stability	Stable	Ability	Task difficulty
	Unstable	Effort	Luck

FIGURE 15-1   Dimensions and elements of Weiner's two-dimensional taxonomy (1972).

elements were an individual's ability and effort (internal) and the environmental (situational or external) elements of task difficulty and luck. A schematic representation of the integration of dimensions and elements is shown in Figure 15-1.

As one can see, Weiner conceptualized a person's ability and the difficulty of the task as stable. The stability dimension is based upon the notion that unchanging factors will persuade a person to expect performances caused by those factors to be consistent and similar in the future. Thus, an athlete who lost because of low ability would expect to lose in the future because ability is not perceived to change. Obviously, this is an extreme example because the athlete would also take into account task difficulty, effort, and luck in making these judgments. Depending upon the strengths of these other elements for a given sport outcome, ability might be attributed as playing a greater or lesser causal role in determining the outcome of a contest.

By contrast, winning or losing that is attributed to the changeable elements of effort and luck (unstable) would indicate that athletes thought future outcomes could be different. For example, the athlete who loses might recognize that he/she could try harder next time and perhaps win, or the athlete who wins might recognize that luck could change and bring losses in the future.

This model suggests that individuals process information leading to the above inferences in a logical, rational manner. Therefore, predictions about the types of causal ascriptions made for success and failure are based upon the notion that individuals will follow the same search, analysis, and inference process for both outcomes. For example, athletes who have consistently failed or succeeded in the past because of ability will expect similar performance, and attribute similarly, in the future.

Weiner has modified this model in more recent years to incorporate other dimensions and to place greater emphasis on the relation of outcomes, attributions, and emotions (Weiner, 1979; Weiner, Russell, &

Lerman, 1979). However, the two-dimensional model has probably been the most influential in guiding sport research.

A Functional Model.   A second influential model falls under what is called the functionalist or motivational approach to studying attributions (Tetlock & Levi, 1982). Of the various motivations examined in attribution theory, the motivation stemming from the need to maintain or enhance self-esteem has been of primary interest in sport. Briefly explained, a person (athlete) needs to maintain or enhance that aspect of self-esteem concerned with achievement outcomes. When outcomes are perceived as positive, the athlete is motivated to enhance self-esteem by attributing the positive outcome to elements of personal control such as ability and effort. By contrast, when outcomes are perceived as negative, self-esteem may be threatened if the athlete takes personal responsibility for outcome. In order to protect self-esteem, the athlete is motivated to attribute the cause of the negative outcome to elements beyond his/her control (e.g., task difficulty, luck, or the referee).

This pattern of ascribing the causes of positive events to internal factors and negative events to external factors has been labeled the self-serving attributional bias (Miller, 1976; Roberts, 1982; Weary, 1980; Zuckerman, 1979). Athletes would not necessarily need to logically process information according to the self-serving bias model. Their immediate concern would be to maintain self-esteem for the present outcome (in contrast to Weiner's predictions). Keeping the brief sketch of these models in mind, let us examine what the research indicates about athletes' explanations for winning and losing.

Characteristics of Investigations

As in psychology, sport investigators sought to isolate variables that would determine the pattern of attributions and test either Weiner's model (cognitive perspective) or predictions about self-serving biases (functional or motivational perspective). Thus, researchers conducted a number of investigations in the laboratory before attempting field tests of the same models. Let us consider the characteristics of laboratory and field attribution investigations separately. Few individual investigations are cited specifically. One can examine these in greater detail in the sport-related reviews of Brawley (1980), Roberts, (1982), and Rejeski and Brawley (1983) as well as the social psychological reviews of Miller and Ross (1975), Zuckerman (1979), Kelley and Michela (1980), and Ross and Fletcher (in press).

Laboratory Research: Common Characteristics.   The typical characteristics of the laboratory experiments conducted between 1974 and 1980 are:

- Subjects in 69% of the studies were university students, whereas the remainder were children of various ages.
- The focus of attributions was the cause of personal outcome (self as opposed to other focus).
- The achievement tasks that subjects completed were generally novel, with motor maze and stabilometer being most common and imagined tasks being least common.
- The independent variables were typically outcome (win/loss) or outcome history (consistent history: wins/losses).
- The manipulations of independent variables were either false performance feedback (i.e., summed across performance trials to produce a history) or variable patterns of win/loss over trials (e.g., higher percent win/loss or ascending/descending patterns of success).
- Some attempts were made to manipulate the importance of the task to the individual (task ego-involvement) but the effectiveness of this manipulation was not always confirmed.
- Causes attributed were almost exclusively those imposed by investigators: ability, effort, task difficulty, and luck.

General Results and Interpretations.   From this sketch of typical laboratory experiments, what can be said about the effect of certain variables on the pattern of attributions evident in their results? How can these patterns be explained? Were cognitive or motivational explanations most accurate in explaining the results? Some of the answers to these questions can be summarized as follows:

- Attributions for success and failure were differentiated primarily by the internal elements of ability and effort.
- There appears to be support for a self-enhancing bias when subjects were successful, and some support for a self-protecting bias when subjects failed (e.g., Gill & Martens, 1977; Gill & Gross, 1979; Roberts, 1978; Investigation 2).
- Results of laboratory investigations were generally motivationally interpreted (e.g., Gill & Gross, 1979; Gill & Martens, 1977; Iso-Ahola, 1977b; Iso-Ahola & Roberts, 1977; Roberts, 1978; Investigation 2).
- The motivational interpretation behind the self-serving bias is that the need for self-esteem motivates subjects to bias their view of the world, interpreting it in a fashion that maintains or enhances personal worth (Tetlock & Levi, 1982; Zuckerman, 1979).

Regardless of criticisms that can be raised about these experiments, they indicate that the manipulation of success and failure can alter the pattern of attributions. In particular, people weigh ability and effort more heavily than external elements in their interpretation of these highly controlled outcomes. One major problem for many laboratory experiments in both psychology and sport is that a clear distinction cannot always be drawn between a cognitive and motivational interpretation of results. Although a motive could encourage one to perceive and bias causal interpretations of win/loss, so could certain cognitive processes such as selective encoding and retrieval of familiar information from memory. An additional problem has been that some investigations used Weiner's (1972) model to propose their study but never established conditions to properly test the model.

Lessons From the Laboratory Investigations. The student of attribution theory in sport may logically conclude that the laboratory research has offered little to the examination of athletes' causal inferences. However, such a conclusion would ignore the valuable lessons we have learned. Let us consider these with a view toward improving future research.

First, it is evident that manipulating outcome apart from other factors does change the elements that a subject perceives as causal. Second, laboratory experiments alone obviously failed to resolve cognitive versus motivational debates about the attribution process and its determinants. One main reason for their failure is that investigators could not safely assume the subject's ego-involvement in the novel task. It is apparent that when engaging in a task that is unimportant to self-esteem, a subject can be logical.

However, can the same conclusion be reached for a task that a subject is motivated to achieve? Miller (1976) conducted a laboratory experiment in which he actually manipulated ego-involvement. He found the self-serving attribution pattern for success and failure when ego-involvement was heightened as opposed to the more logical attributions made in non ego-involving conditions. Thus it was apparent to some researchers (Roberts, 1975) that field investigations about sports in which athletes were ego-involved might lend greater insight into the operation of real-world attributions.

Certainly, field investigations appear to offer a greater possibility for examining those situations in which attributions serve psychological functions (e.g., maintaining self-esteem). However, the authors are not suggesting that laboratory experiments be discarded. Rather, they should be encouraged as long as certain variables are controlled in order to test theory.

Field Research: Common Characteristics. The impetus to conduct a number of field studies concerning sport attributions may be credited to investigators such as Mann (1974), Iso-Ahola (1977a), and Roberts (1975). Of the investigations published, most have the following common characteristics:

- The age and gender of subjects vary, but most of them have been athletes.
- Several different sport types have been studied, but the majority are team sports (e.g., baseball, basketball, football, soccer).
- The studies have examined the effects of the independent variables of outcome of a competition or the team's competitive record.
- Most of this research has used designs in which subjects chose outcome (rather than outcome as controlled by the investigator) and the independent variables have not been manipulated. Thus they must be categorized as field studies, not experiments (i.e., true experiments allow the experimenter to vary the independent variable; see Kerlinger, 1973).
- Most of these studies have focused upon attributions about the cause of each athlete's outcome as well as team outcome.

General Results and Interpretations.   Theoreticians, applied researchers, and practitioners generally require investigations to support a theory. Such an approach is useful not only to advance science but also to help the practitioner predict and deal with the athletes' everyday attributions. Although many of these field studies have been developed on the basis of Weiner's (1972, 1974) earlier theoretical models, their designs do not accommodate a test of the model (i.e., motivational vs. cognitive model). Exceptions are a study by Roberts (1975) and a field experiment by Brawley (1980). Interpretations of results have generally been a motivational explanation of the self-serving bias. That is, winning players suggest that they or their team caused that outcome because of their ability and effort, whereas losing players causally attribute their loss to external factors (e.g., Iso-Ahola, 1977b; Mann, 1974; Scanlan & Passer, 1980).

Hindsight explanations of these attribution patterns are the rule rather than the exception because cause-effect designs have not been attempted in field studies. In other words, researchers had no control over the independent variables in the study, and therefore only an "after the fact" (post-hoc) explanation of the results can be made based on their pattern. Although this tells us something about the relationship between independent and dependent variables, it does not allow us to predict based upon theory. As most readers will probably recognize, prediction based upon a theoretical model is a powerful way of determining whether the model has any validity, particularly ecological validity for the real world of sport. To be fair to the field researcher, however, the control easily obtained in the laboratory is more difficult in the field. Thus, although these results should be viewed cautiously, some of the same outcome variables that altered the attribution of cause in the laboratory appear to be at work in the field.

What about a field test of Weiner's model? The only investigations that were actually designed to create field conditions so that this cognitive model could be tested were those by Roberts (1975: baseball) and Brawley (1980: hockey). Such conditions exist when players or teams experience a series of outcomes and thus can logically make inferences that result in ascriptions based upon previous experience. For example, a consistent series of losses must have been caused by my lack of ability (a stable cause) and I expect similar causation when I fail in the future. By contrast, I infer unstable causes when past experience and present or future outcomes are inconsistent. I logically deduce that the inconsistency is due to such elements as effort or luck (unstable causes). Under such conditions, the predictions of Weiner's model can be assessed by the degree to which attributions are determined by the interaction of prior and present outcome (as reflected in their consistency) or are determined by present outcome alone. Determination by the former would support Weiner's claims while determination by the latter would favor self-serving explanations.

Roberts (1975) concluded that attributions for teams were made in a rational, information-processing fashion by finding partial support for Weiner's predictions. On the other hand, when players attributed their own role in contributing to the same outcome, he found they were self-serving. One interpretation could be that when they were ascribing personally, players were motivated to protect and enhance their self-esteem. But when ascribing about the team they were more prone to logically and objectively process outcome information. This would seem to suggest that players can dissociate themselves from their team according to the way they perceive outcomes. Roberts' (1975) findings have some important practical implications if teams do operate as suggested in his study. However, there is evidence to the contrary. Certain social constraints and norms within a group situation have been suggested to alter attribution patterns so that the individuals do not divorce themselves from perceptions and inferences about team outcomes (e.g., Scanlan & Passer, 1980; Schlenker, 1976; Taylor & Doria, 1981). Players may be motivated as a group to present their team in a certain fashion to outsiders or to protect the group's self-esteem via their attributions.

A field experiment whose findings were contrary to Roberts (1975) was conducted by Brawley (1980). In an attempt to duplicate and extend Roberts' investigation, Brawley substantially increased the team sample size and manipulated variables that Schlenker (1976) and Bradley (1978) had shown would alter attributions. Although he reproduced the conditions that Roberts suggests are needed to test Weiner's model, they had no effect in determining causal ascriptions for either self or team. Instead, both self and team responses were described primarily by internal attributions and followed the same self-serving pattern (i.e., claims that ability and effort were important in causing a win but not important in causing a loss).

In addition, by manipulating conditions where egocentric ascriptions could be maximized or minimized, the experiment demonstrated that social variables interacting with present outcome can alter an athlete's attributional statements. One of these social variables was the influence of significant others. This influence was evident in two ways. First, athletes took more responsibility for losing when they made their attributions to someone who could evaluate the accuracy of their statements (i.e., a teammate). Failure to suggest that their lack of ability or effort was partly responsible would have been questioned by teammates. While normative effects of the group mediated these attributions, other investigations have shown that significant others outside the group can influence actors to make more or less egocentric public ascriptions (e.g., Schlenker & Miller, 1977; Weary, 1980).

Second, the motivation of groups to view themselves in a positive light was also evident in Brawley's experiment. Winning teams, in contrast to losing teams, described all causes for their outcomes in a positive fashion. Losing teams viewed the same causes as being of average to less than average importance. This result is in accord with a number of studies from the group dynamics literature which indicate the group's consistent tendency to evaluate their own products favorably (Austin & Worchel, 1979). Thus, these significant-other effects serve to emphasize the influence of the group in *motivating* both individual member and group ascriptions. Persons interested in applications of group motivation should consider this fact before hypothesizing about the influence of the group in motivating attributions.

Lessons From the Field Investigations. What does this seemingly contradictory research tell us? Three points should be emphasized. First, rather than throwing up our hands in dispair we should note that disparate support from two studies for either a cognitive or motivational model may be due to the influence of different social situation factors. Some social variables may produce unique perceptions of the situation, and therefore unique inferences. Such factors may also alter the psychological functions that attributions serve, and in turn could produce differences between investigations. Indirectly, this should suggest to sport researchers that a number of factors can influence ascriptions to function in either a cognitive fashion, a motivational fashion, or both. Tetlock and Levi (1982) have suggested such a mingling of theoretical perspectives, while the possibility of attributions serving simultaneous functions has been proposed by Forsyth (1980). The former article puts in perspective the debate between cognitive versus motivational theories. The latter emphasizes the interrelation between attribution functions while giving examples of how several could occur nearly simultaneously.

Thus, contrary research results may yield clues as to how athletes use attributions in different ways. These results also provoke additional questions about the social conditions that interact with the athletes' perceptions when they interpret their own outcomes in sport. To advance our theoretical and practical understanding of the role of attributions on behavior, these questions must be investigated.

Second, the field research suggests that task ego-involvement brings into play the needs that motivate the athlete to ascribe in a fashion (e.g., self-serving) that we assume fulfills those needs. Both Roberts (1978: Investigation 2, a two-person relay game) and Spink (1980: a racquetball contest) found that manipulations heightening ego-involvement resulted in self-serving ascriptions from subjects. These results seem to agree with Miller's (1976) contentions about conditions that promote a motivational bias. However, the reasons for this heightened ego-involvement may be due to many causes, one of which may be the athlete's own achievement goal. Roberts will discuss this in more detail in Chapter 16.

Third, the results of team attributions may be a reflection of interesting group effects. For example, highly cohesive teams may perceive causes for outcome identical to those for themselves. Alternatively, less cohesive teams may give different attributions for self and team. This suggestion derives easily from the field results. Those interested in a review of group effects on attributions to sport outcomes should refer to the discussion in a recent paper by Rejeski and Brawley (1983).

GENERAL PROBLEMS
OF THE SPORT ATTRIBUTION RESEARCH

As researchers have explored the various functions of attributions, they have discovered ways to improve their investigations by resolving conceptual problems and measurement errors. The research reported in this chapter thus far has not uniformly recognized such problems. But one should be aware of these issues when reading future sport studies about attributions. These problems include (a) the causes or attribution elements specified in studies, (b) the theoretical dimensions to which elements are assigned, (c) the meaning of achievement outcome to subjects, and (d) the measurement of attributions. In discussing these concerns, one should remember that the subject selectively perceives and remembers before offering an attribution. What is important in person perception and attribution is the subject's view of the world through his/her own rose-colored glasses.

Attribution Elements

The attributions typically seen in most investigations are those borrowed from Weiner's (1972) model (i.e., ability, effort, task difficulty, and luck). However, both psychology and sport (Falbo & Beck, 1979; Roberts & Pascuzzi, 1979) have recognized that these elements may not be the most appropriate (in terms of relevance to the athlete) to serve as an ascribed cause for personal outcome. The use of the four elements alone may restrict the response an athlete can make about their actions. In order for the athlete to become an active agent in the investigation, the mode of response must either conform to the sport situation and/or offer a greater number of causal alternatives. Roberts and Pascuzzi (1979) have demonstrated that athletes' explanations are descriptively richer than the four elements of ability, effort, task difficulty, and luck (e.g., teamwork, officials, practice, weather, injuries). Specific attribution elements may differ in importance and meaning from setting to setting.

Dimensions

Recall that the major dimensions of the attribution model (Weiner, 1972) adopted for sport were locus of causality and stability. Considering these dimensions respectively, they represent a theoretical division in the way people classify causes to the extent that causes reside within people or the situation (internal/external) and that the causes are either enduring or changing (stable/unstable).

While these dimensions have been convenient and theoretically logical divisions of ascriptions, are they the most meaningful and functional to the attributing individual? The psychological literature indicates that other conceptual dimensions may better reflect the actor's perceptions. Recognizing this, Weiner (1979) increased the number of dimensions in a more recent theoretical model (e.g., locus of causality, stability, controllability), Russell (1982) has involved the subject in actively categorizing attributions, and Kruglanski (1980) has suggested that people are able to classify causal problems in various ways that serve their functions at the time. Using Weiner's causal elements as an example, Kruglanski suggests that task ease may imply something other than the success of many people. It could mean a fast performance or success without preparation. Instead of trying, effort might suggest many hours of vigilance or post-task fatigue. What may well be important is that the *evidence* used to attribute must be relevant to the event, must stand out from other alternatives, and would depend on the ease with which it is recalled (availability in memory). Similarly, while stability and locus of causality may accomplish the actor's development of an inference in one set of circumstances, a different categorization might be more useful in other conditions. Kruglanski postulated that the lay person's problem might be to decide whether an act is an end in itself (endogenous attribution) or a means to future ends (exogenous attribution).

Meaning of Outcome

Most of the sport research has concentrated upon the causal attributions made to the win/loss outcomes of an organized sport. Investigators' unwritten assumptions may have been that win/loss could be considered synonymously with athletes' perceptions of their personal success and failure. However, according to more recent literature, this is not the case (e.g., Roberts, 1982; Ross, 1981). For example, although my team won the match, my perception of how I fared may have been one of personal failure. The team won in spite of my performance.

When interpreting results and studying achievement behavior, one must recognize that absolute and individual outcomes are not identical and may evoke different causal ascriptions. Attributions may be made about either type of outcome, but for the athlete they may be distinctively different (Spink & Roberts, 1980). Thus, the understanding of sport attributions for outcome is limited because of the concentration of research on winning and losing. From an applications viewpoint (i.e., restructuring attributional explanations or beliefs) the perceived outcome may be more important than absolute outcome in determining persistence, affecting emotions or expectations, and influencing coach-athlete interactions.

Measurement of Attributions

The reader will note that for each of the previously mentioned topics, failure to emphasize the subject's active role when interacting with the social situation has resulted in conceptual problems. As might be expected, measurement based upon such concepts often results in the measure acquiring these and similar problems. This has been the case in the assessment of some ascriptions in both psychology and sport.

Earlier it was emphasized that the subject's interpretation of and response to questions concerning the cause of outcome was the datum of interest. An investigator's arbitrary construction of a scale to assess the degree of causality assigned to a particular element (e.g., ability) may not correspond to the subject's view of a meaningful response. Elig and Frieze (1979) sensitized investigators to this concern by examining the various preferences of subjects for different types of scales. They noted that the different types of rating, open-ended, and scaled response systems not only varied in their values (i.e., they could not be equated) but also produced different data types. These discrepancies could lead to one data type supporting one theoretical model while another data type, assumed to represent a similar question, refutes the model. Their comments as well as those of Taylor and Fiske (1981) should be considered when planning measurement of attributions.

Conclusions About General Problems

The general problems just discussed emphasize that sport researchers are just beginning to recognize the importance of and difficulty in examining the athlete's view of the world. The common theme to the problems mentioned is that the subject has not been considered active in the research and social interaction process. Assessing this active subject is not as simple as just developing a quick questionnaire and collecting some fast data on attributions. There is a need for careful conceptualization and measurement, as in any other scientific endeavor.

This is not to say that results of sport investigations lack meaning. On the contrary, results are consistent within a limited range of conditions and assessment tools. Furthermore, learning from previous mistakes should speed up future research progress in sport. But even if the problems we have mentioned are rectified, one issue requires comment for any individual contemplating research on attributions in sport settings.

THE PROBLEM
OF A LIMITED CONCEPTUAL VIEWPOINT

Sport investigators have relied almost exclusively on Weiner's earlier models (1972, 1974) for conceptualizing their studies. They have also depended on the self-serving bias model to explain (post hoc, in many cases) results. Until 1981, the majority of published studies tended to follow these models for studying attributions. Little attention has been given to attributional tasks other than personal causal judgment of win/loss outcomes. Although Weiner's (1979) more recent conceptualizations offer interesting new questions to investigate, a single-minded devotion to this or any other model is analagous to fitting a person with blinders. The conceptual "view" is limited because only certain questions are examined. Research support from Weiner's model in particular comes predominantly from research in the educational setting. Surely there are other models and settings that can help us broaden our view of the attribution process.

Some Alternative Considerations

Fortunately, if one examines the breadth of attributional concepts, questions, and situations that have been previously examined in psychology, whole areas of research possibilities arise. For example, there are many other types of outcomes besides win/loss in physical activity, many other people who attribute than the athlete and his/her team, and many other variations of attributions. Using outcome as a specific example, ascriptions could also be made about outcomes concerning skill development, outcomes concerning the understanding of strategy, or outcomes of the rapport between player and coach, athlete, or family.

As to the issue of other people, rather than examining only the athletes' attributions, those of various observers should be studied. Most social interactions in sport involve at least two people interacting at times other than the competition. If attributions do influence psychological outcomes such as expectancies or future behavior, perhaps more can be learned about how this occurs if the ascriptions of actors *and* observers are examined.

Finally, attributions of responsibility, causality, and dispositional inferences are made in sport situations as in any other social situation. Unfortunately, we neither assess these variations in attributions nor recognize the differences between them. Regarding the latter point, some sport investigators have assumed that the ascribed cause of a seasonal outcome equates with the ascribed cause for a single game. The error in this assumption is not only conceptual, but it also ignores the athlete's perception while imposing that of the investigator (Rejeski & Brawley, 1983; Roberts, 1982; Shaver, 1975). If social as well as explanatory functions are served through various attributions, researchers would do well to understand their meaning and know when to use each one. The exclusive study of one type of attribution ignores the variety of inferences athletes make to give order and meaning to their world.

BROADENING THE CONCEPTUAL VIEW

This chapter has introduced and critically examined attribution research in sport. It is a relatively new area of investigation that has generated quite a number of studies in the short time devoted to its examination. The latest studies in the area do show signs of enlarging the investigative focus. Recent reviews by Rejeski and Brawley (1983) and Roberts (1982) have described some of these new research directions.

In Chapter 16, Glyn Roberts discusses in greater detail the achievement context of sport and physical activity, focusing upon a derivative of attribution theory in determining achievement behaviors.

Chapter 16

Toward a New Theory of Motivation in Sport: The Role of Perceived Ability

Glyn C. Roberts
University of Illinois

In the preceding chapter we stated that one of the assumptions about individuals in social contexts is that they infer cause and effect of everyday events. As authors, we dealt with this inference in some detail and were primarily concerned with illustrating the state of the art in this area of research. We demonstrated that individuals do use attributional processes to give order to their environment and that attributions serve both a cognitive and/or motivational goal—these goals biasing the view of athletes of their world. In this chapter, I explore this phenomenon in greater detail. The basic premise here is that holding various goals affects the perception of athletes of their environment and, further, systematically affects their achievement behavior in sport settings. In order to set the frame of reference for the rest of the chapter, we must first consider the achievement domain of sport.

The Domain of Sport

It is generally believed that sport plays an important role in the socialization of children in that they come into contact with social order and prevailing social values, and are given a structure within which to act and develop skills in the interest of developing the values held by the society (see Kleiber & Roberts, 1981; Roberts, in press). Thus, sports are viewed as anticipatory models of society. The evidence supporting such assertions is largely anecdotal and the impact of the sport experience upon such social attributes has yet to be effectively determined. But the possibility that involvement in sport can contribute to social and personality development has long been a coveted ideal of sport proponents.

Whether it is the influence of television, the increased mobility of individuals, or any number of other causes, organized sports for children have expanded dramatically in the last few decades. Children are increasingly likely to participate in childlike versions of recognized adult sporting activities in their recreational time (see Roberts, in press). Further, when observed participating in nonsport playful behavior, older children tend to qualify their play behavior with the word "just" as in, "just playing catch" (Eiferman, 1971). As children become older, they tend to increase their engagement in games that reflect sport activities. Estimates of the number of children participating in sport programs in the United States run upwards of 27 million and the numbers keep increasing. Add to this the investment in time and money of adults—parents, coaches, and administrators—and one can see that organized sports for children at all levels has a significant impact on the individuals involved and on the larger society of which it is a part.

As is readily apparent, the domain of sport is a classic achievement-oriented environment. It conforms to most definitions of an achievement-oriented context in the extant literature (e.g., Atkinson, 1957; Maehr, 1974). The individual or team strives to achieve a goal (usually beating an opponent) or standard of excellence and can thus be evaluated in terms of success and failure. The individual or team is in most cases responsible for the outcome and a sense of uncertainty prevails so that some level of challenge is perceived. The process is evaluative in that others present—teammates, opponents, coaches, parents, spectators—evaluate the performance as favorable or unfavorable in terms of reaching the goal or the standard of excellence.

Being competent in sport skills is very important to children, boys in particular (Roberts, 1978, 1980; Scanlan, 1978b). Indeed, Veroff (1969) suggested that comparing themselves in sporting activities may be *the* domain in which young boys utilize social comparison processes in order to determine their standing among their peers and thereby determine their self-worth. Recently, one of my students, Joan Duda, obtained some evidence to support this analysis.

Duda (1981) assessed the perceptions of high school boys and girls relative to their preferred domains of achievement. She looked at both classroom and playing field contexts and investigated four general categories—team versus individual contexts, and competitive versus noncompetitive contexts. Students were then asked to choose in which of these achievement contexts they would prefer to succeed, either the classroom or playing field. Across all four achievement categories, (team competitive, team noncompetitive, individual competitive, individual noncompetitive) boys preferred to succeed in sport rather than in classroom contexts. This confirms previous evidence of the importance of being competent in sport for boys (e.g., Coleman, 1961; Roberts, 1978, 1980; Scanlan, 1978b; Veroff, 1969). But, interestingly, with the exception of the individual competitive achievement context, girls also preferred to succeed in sport rather than in classroom contexts. The data for the individual competitive achievement context supports previous research which has found that girls prefer to avoid direct competitive conflict with other girls (see Kleiber & Hemmer, 1981). But it is revealing that girls do consider sport an entirely appropriate context in which to succeed against other girls.

The failure preferences were particularly revealing. Boys indicated that failure in academics was less aversive than failure in sports. For boys, failing in sport is very much an outcome to be avoided. Girls, on the other hand, reported that failure in sport was less aversive than academic failure. But the important point to establish here is that both boys and girls consider the achievement domain of sport an important context in which to engage.

But there is a paradox! According to the best available statistics, 80% of all children drop out of organized sport programs at all levels between the ages of 12 and 17 (Seefeldt, Blievernicht, Bruce, & Gilliam, 1978). One could argue that sport clearly does not meet the children's achievement goals and they probably drop out to seek other environments in which to succeed. Despite the topic's importance, research on dropouts in both educational and sport contexts is disappointing and inconclusive (see Ewing, 1981; Tinto, 1975). Clearly, some children do stay in sport but the vast majority do not. Why? It is to a potential resolution of this issue that we turn to next.

TOWARD A NEW THEORY OF MOTIVATION

When we consider the persistence of children or adults in any achievement context, we are in the realm of motivation. From a conceptual viewpoint, we are concerned with the motivational determinants of persistence in these contexts. We will limit our discussion to sport contexts, but it may be readily apparent to the reader that the concept can be expanded to other arenas (Maehr, 1983).

In the past, many approaches were taken to study persistence, or lack of it, when athletes drop out of sports. The first approach was to look for enduring characteristics of the person because it was assumed that those characteristics would explain why individuals persisted or dropped out. Typically, this research has looked at personality traits such as achievement motivation (G.C. Roberts, 1972), or locus of control characteristics (deCharms, 1976; Lefcourt, 1976), or it has looked at the stability of attributional characteristics (Roberts, 1975). The second approach focuses on the social context that exists for the person at that moment in the environment. Investigators usually focus on the social constraints impinging upon these individuals and upon the structure of the competitive environment (Devereux, 1976). The third approach is the logical combination of the first two, in which it is argued that individual differences and situational factors interact and affect the individual's tendency to behave a certain way. It is argued that the person's enduring characteristics interact with particular environments to affect behavior in systematic ways (Martens, 1977). But it may be argued that a fourth approach exists, and it is this new approach that provides the framework for the remainder of this chapter (see Maehr, 1983; Maehr & Nicholls, 1980).

The fourth approach argues that in order to understand the motivation and subsequent achievement behavior of individuals in any context, it is necessary to understand the *subjective meaning* of achievement to the achiever. It is assumed that whether a person demonstrates motivation in any competitive context depends upon the achievement goal of the athlete. And athletes may have many achievement goals, not just one, that operate in a given situation. Consequently, when members of athletic teams enter into sport settings with these different goals, their individual conceptions of success and failure will differ too. Some may be pleased with winning while others may be pleased with another outcome such as pleasing the coach. Understanding these goals and their criteria for success and failure becomes crucial to understanding the achievement behavior of athletes.

To fully understand the achievement goal of an athlete, we must first recognize that different goals will give rise to different perceptions of success and failure. Success for one athlete may not be success for another. Success and failure are best understood if regarded as psychological states that are based upon the athletes' interpretation of outcomes, based upon their own achievement goals (Maehr & Nicholls, 1980). Outcomes do not necessarily refer to the outcome of the game (see Roberts, Duda, & Devinatz, 1982; Spink & Roberts, 1980). Rather, based upon the athlete's goal, the experience is regarded as successful if the outcome reflects desirable qualities about the self; if the experience is seen to reflect undesirable qualities about the self, then the outcome is perceived as failure. The athlete's goal dictates the perception of success and failure, so the essential component of this conceptualization is clearly the achievement goal of the individual. Success and failure, and the athlete's behaviors to achieve success, can only be recognized if we know the behavioral goal of the athlete.

The Achievement Goals of Athletes

Maehr & Nicholls (1980) propose that at least three forms of achievement goals affect the behaviors of individuals in achievement contexts: (a) to demonstrate ability; (b) to be task-involved; and (c) to seek social approval. Let us consider each in turn with particular concern on how these goals interact within the achievement domain of sport.

Competitive Ability.   The first achievement goal to consider is one I term *competitive ability*. This goal is to maximize the subjective probability of attributing high ability to oneself and to minimize the probability of attributing low ability to oneself (Nicholls, 1980). The athlete's primary concern is with his/her own ability and how it relates to that of others. The focus of attention is on *social-comparison* processes, the athlete constantly evaluating his or her ability against the opponent's in order to judge whether ability has been demonstrated.

If one's ability is judged to be high, then one expects to demonstrate that ability — a desirable outcome. So the athlete is expected to try hard to demonstrate ability; one way is by beating other athletes. Thus, winning a game is an important criterion of success for the athlete who is motivated by the goal of competitive ability. But it is important to realize that losing is not always judged to mean low ability. For example, were I to win a tennis game in a set with my local tennis professional, I would be ecstatic despite losing the match. Winning one game from so able a performer would be success for me. Competitive ability assessments, then, are complex and need to be considered carefully.

In most sport contests, at least three assessments must be made by the athlete whose achievement goal is to demonstrate competitive ability. One is an assessment of the opponent's ability in relation to all other opponents. Is the opponent a weak or a strong team or player? The opponent's win/loss record is an important variable in judging relative strength. There is evidence that athletes, (Spink & Roberts, 1980), even child athletes (Roberts, 1975), can use the win/loss record of opponents in order to judge relative ability. Second, the athlete must also judge how his or her own ability compares to the opponent's. Social comparison processes become important here and one obvious criterion is whether the athlete won or lost the game.

In sport contexts, because of the social comparison processes involved, the outcome of the game is a very salient and unambiguous criterion. By contrast, in academic environments it is often difficult to judge how well one did: Is 8 out of 10 correct responses to a series of mathematical problems good or poor? If the child does not compare his/her number of correct responses to those of other children, then the child has ambiguous information. Also, because it is often difficult for the child to compare with all other children in the class, he/she may compare to friends who may or may not be representative of the class. In sports, however, there is only one relevant comparison—the opponent—and all participants and observers can readily observe who won and who lost. For competitive ability oriented athletes, therefore, the outcome is a very salient reference criterion.

The third assessment made by competitive ability oriented players is how much effort was applied by self and/or opponent; this assessment of effort is crucial. It is the one aspect coaches, spectators, and teammates constantly emphasize. It is a variable that coaches believe they can control somewhat and thus are always trying to encourage players to "hustle" more. But, for players, constantly applying effort does have other implications. For athletes who perceive themselves to be low in ability, applying effort that leads to failure clearly exposes one's lack of ability. Because of this, these players expect to demonstrate ability which is an undesirable outcome for them. Consequently, it would be logical for them to apply little effort. They would have two courses of action available, one being to drop out.

Some evidence does show that many who drop out have as their achievement goal the desire to demonstrate ability (Ewing, 1981). These children probably perceive that the sport experience does not allow them to demonstrate ability, so dropping out is a reasonable alternative for them. A second course of action is to play against other low ability players so that some success is possible. Such is possible in informal sport contests but this avenue is often unavailable to athletes in organized sport. Opponents are often scheduled many months in advance. Consequently, for these players, choosing own opponents of similar ability is not a viable option.

Repeated failure experiences for perceived low ability athletes leads them to conclude that they do indeed lack capacity. Because their achievement goal is to demonstrate ability, they avoid such achievement contexts in the future. If constrained by parents or peers to remain with the sport experience, these players often develop a bad attitude about trying. They will not try hard because they know they have very little chance of demonstrating their ability. Coaches may call them quitters, but the real reason they do not try hard is because of their perceived low ability.

For the perceived high ability players, failure violates their perception of ability and they exert immediate effort to correct this. Consequently, these players generally try hard. On the other hand, success may lead the athlete to exert less effort. These are the players that coaches often get most angry with because they clearly have ability but either "hot dog" it, begin to use risky strategies, or don't try very hard. They employ such strategies because not trying hard—and succeeding—is evidence of even higher ability.

Players with perceived high ability are expected to try harder and persist longer when confronted with athletes who are perceived to be as good or better in ability, or when the scoring remains close. These athletes may also show off during the game if they think they are winning or perceive that they are superior to their opponent. Low ability players are more likely to drop out or, if constrained to remain with the context, are likely to exert less effort. Thus, the achievement goal of competitive ability affects the achievement behaviors of athletes.

Sport Mastery.   Some athletes are not concerned with competitive ability. They are still ability oriented but tend to focus on performance, the goal of this behavior being to perform as well as possible regardless of the outcome. This type of achievement behavior is termed *sport mastery*. The demonstration of ability is not necessary in this form of achievement behavior; rather, the player tries to achieve mastery, improving or perfecting a skill rather than demonstrating higher capacity than others. In this sense, high versus low ability is judged in comparison to the individual's previous level of skill. This is similar to what Nicholls (1980) calls task-involved ability.

When individuals are striving to develop or demonstrate ability in the sport mastery sense, they are often described as being task involved or intrinsically motivated. With adults, extreme states of sport mastery are often characterized by a marked sense of personal control and an equally marked loss of ego. One becomes so totally absorbed in the task that all concept of time is lost and one is described as being in "flow" (Csikszentmihalyi, 1977). A sense of competitive ability is not salient; rather the individual is completely absorbed in the task for its own sake.

Sport mastery is less complex than competitive ability. The athlete does not have to assess competencies of others in order to reach judgments about probable success or failure. The sport mastery oriented player simply processes the information that the task or situation provides. The player does the task and processes his/her own level of mastery. Again, effort is important in this concept of achievement but, in this case, effort is seen to lead to greater learning, mastery, or eventual competence. Individuals who are sport mastery oriented cannot display low ability. If they work at an easy task, mastery may not be demonstrated but a lack of ability is not demonstrated either. The individual chooses a task and applies the degree of effort he/she perceives as necessary to complete it. Any ability cues in the task merely inform the athlete of his or her own level of mastery.

Social Approval.   A third form of achievement behavior proposed by Maehr & Nicholls (1980) is termed *social approval* behavior. It is argued that people sometimes perform well and are motivated because their achievement goal is to gain approval from significant others. The player's goal is to have significant others—coaches, parents, spectators, and teammates—attribute virtuous intent to him or her rather than focus on the goals of competitive ability or sport mastery. Typically, the player's goal is to have the coach signify approval.

This form of achievement goal also focuses upon effort. Usually, the approval of the coach is perceived to be dependent upon effort. Coaches often encourage this perception in that they constantly try to raise the effort of athletes. When they see athletes trying hard, coaches reinforce them for the display of effort. To the athlete, trying hard and obtaining coach approval becomes the criterion of success and failure. Rather than playing well or beating the opponent, this player believes that trying hard is the achievement goal, with success and failure being perceived when the coach either praises or criticizes them for their effort. To these players, winning and losing the game is relatively unimportant.

This form of achievement goal is particularly relevant to younger children, as some evidence shows that children under the age of 12 are unable to accurately assess their own relative competence (Nicholls, 1978). Consequently, children under 12 are particularly oriented toward effort and social approval. To the extent that they continue to gain the coach's approval, they perceive that they are successful. Doubtless we are all familiar with children who are clearly incompetent in the activity but who nevertheless continue to play and try hard. Coaches typically encourage such children even though their abilities are not high. However, children do become more perceptive as they grow older and begin to accurately assess their own relative competence in sports, an aspect to be discussed in more detail later.

If there are multiple goals, then this approach is a major departure from earlier ones that measure an individual's achievement motivation *before* investigating the meaning of the behavior. In the approach advocated here, we study achievement behavior of athletes and *infer* the goals from this behavior and the athlete's stated goals. By adopting this approach, we can investigate sport behavior such as persistence, dropping out, and/or performance intensity in relation to the stated goals. For example, an athlete may play tennis to beat other players (competitive ability goal) but play volleyball for the enjoyment of the activity (sport mastery goal). In both settings it is important to achieve and attain the goal, but the behavior to attain that goal may differ markedly. Thus, knowledge of the achievement goal of the player is crucial to understanding the achievement behavior of that player.

The Presence of Multiple Goals

But are there multiple goals? Two of my students have studied this question (Duda, 1981; Ewing, 1981) and so far have provided the only evidence in this direction. For example, using high school freshmen and sophomores, Ewing identified youths who had dropped out of sport, youths who had never joined, and youths who stayed in sports. Her major objective was to determine if multiple orientations existed and whether they interacted with the sport experience to affect persistence and participation. For example, if an athlete joined sports to demonstrate competitive ability and found himself/herself sitting on the bench, then the resulting conflict could cause the athlete to withdraw in search of other opportunities to exhibit competitive ability.

Ewing developed a questionnaire specifically to investigate the achievement goals of athletes and used factor analysis procedures to evaluate whether these multiple goals indeed existed. She found that multiple goals existed, and competitive ability and social approval goals in particular emerged as strong orientations of athletes. Sport mastery proved to be more elusive. But the important aspect is that both competitive ability and social approval emerged as strong goals and that sport mastery was present though in a weaker form. Importantly, the attributions underlying these goal orientations confirmed that ability was the major determinant of competitive ability, and that effort and its demonstration was the major determinant of social approval, but for boys only. Girls used the attribution "special skills" to explain social approval.

Ewing's major finding was that achievement behavior (dropping out in this case) was related to particular goal orientations and that the social approval goal-oriented players persisted longer in the competitive sport context. It may be argued that the competitive sport structure gives coaches, parents, and peers ample opportunity to socially support athletes, and thus social approval athletes find it relatively easy to meet their goal. Boys who were dropouts were more oriented toward competitive ability and had dropped out at a higher rate from competitive sports than had social approval players. Competitive ability oriented players see participation as exposing their limitations very quickly in unambiguous terms. But another reason may be that athletes drop out because they feel they don't get the playing time they deserve. Competitive ability oriented players want to demonstrate competitive ability, and sitting on the bench as all players do from time to time does not give them the opportunity to meet their goal. For the social approval players, sitting on the bench is perceived as being a loyal team member and thereby becomes a source of satisfaction.

Ewing's research, supported by Duda, is provocative. It shows that multiple goals exist and that they interact with the environment to affect achievement behaviors. This research was not designed to investigate whether the superstars were more competitive ability oriented (as one might hypothesize), and what activities such players turn to when they drop out of organized sports. We could speculate that they are the youths who initiate pick-up games in the neighborhood and meet their needs that way. Furthermore, sport mastery orientation's relatively weak showing perhaps says more about the nature of the sport experience than anything else. As we know, coaches tend to emphasize winning and have a pervasive belief that exerting players to hustle is a necessary part of coaching. Consequently, players who respond and demonstrate competitive ability and/or strong effort are typically reinforced within the competitive sport experience. The task-involved player, who plays for the sake of the task, may not be able to meet his or her goal in sport settings in the presently structured environment. This could well be the reason why Ewing failed to detect a strong sport mastery orientation with her subjects.

That dropping out was related to competitive ability was a persuasive finding and it is the first time such evidence has been documented in a systematic way. The emergence of competitive ability as an important variable to consider in sport contests is consistent with the following research concerning sport motivation.

ACHIEVEMENT BEHAVIOR
AND PERCEIVED ABILITY

Several investigators have argued that ability attributions, and the self-concept of ability, play a central role in mediating motivation (Bandura, 1977b; Harter, 1978; Kukla, 1978; Nicholls & Miller, in press), but the conceptualization most relevant to achievement motivation in sport is the one by Nicholls (Nicholls, 1980; Nicholls & Miller, in press; Roberts, in press). Derived from Nicholls (1979) and Maehr and Nicholls (1980), it is argued that individuals are intentional, goal-directed organisms who operate in a rational manner. Nicholls (1980) focuses upon the goals of achievement behavior and posits that the achievement goal of individuals is to demonstrate and/or develop high ability and to avoid demonstrating low ability. This is the central construct to the theory. Thus, the person's perception of ability is crucial to understanding achievement behavior.

In sport, a growing body of evidence supports the contention that the athlete's perception of ability is the essential mediating construct of achievement behaviors (Bukowski & Moore, 1980; Lau & Russell, 1980; Rejeski & Lowe, 1980; Roberts, 1975; Roberts, Kleiber, & Duda, 1981; Roberts & Pascuzzi, 1979; Spink & Roberts, 1980). For example, Roberts and Pascuzzi found that attributions to ability consisted of 57% of all attributions made by winners and 36% of attributions made by losers.

Further, Roberts, Kleiber, and Duda (1981) investigated the relationship of sport participation to perceived ability. Fourth- and fifth-grade children participating in organized sport were found to be higher in perceived ability and more persistent in sport contexts, with higher expectations of future success than nonparticipants. But contrary to Ewing's findings, perceived ability demonstrated little effect upon duration of involvement. Instead, the children who were higher in perceived ability seemed to be attracted to sport in the first place, rather than involvement in the sports affecting their perception of competitive ability.

Recently, Feltz, Gould, Horn, and Perlichkoff (1982) replicated and extended the Roberts et al. 1981 study. Using competitive swimmers and swimming dropouts between 8 and 19 years of age, Feltz and associates found that participants in competitive swimming were higher in perceived ability. More significantly, the dropouts indicated that having other things to do was the primary reason for dropping out. This may of course be a defensive response on the part of the athletes. For when they probed deeper, Feltz et al. found that 48% of dropouts considered "not having my skills improve" and 52% of dropouts considered "not being as good as I wanted to be" as important reasons for dropping out. Clearly, a large percentage of dropouts felt they did not have the ability to continue in sports. This finding is supported by Orlick and associates (Orlick, 1974; Orlick & Botterill, 1975) when one reanalyzes their data (see Roberts, in press).

Clearly, the athlete's perception of ability is an important mediator of motivation in the sport context. The developing new theory of motivation in sport advocated in this chapter has the perception of ability as its central construct (see Roberts, in press). I argue that the perception of ability mediates many achievement behaviors such as persistence, effort applied, concentration, attention, and sport selection as well as achievement cognitions such as attributions, confidence, and expectancies. The power of this developing theory remains to be determined, but it has already shed light on the dropout phenomenon so common to sport.

Dropping Out of Sport

Some data reveals that children under 12 do not drop out of competitive sports in great numbers (Seefeldt et al., 1978) and that self-perceptions of high ability actually attracts them to competitive sports (Roberts, Kleiber, & Duda, 1981). But when children enter their teens, they drop out of children's sport at dramatic rates (Orlick, 1974; Seefeldt et al., 1978; Roberts, in press). Why should age 12 be the watershed for this readily observed phenomenon? Research in developmental psychology on the perception of ability lends important insight here. This research illustrates that children go through several stages in their capacity to differentiate between effort and ability and recognize that success requires both (see Nicholls, 1978; Nicholls & Miller, in press; Roberts, in press).

Nicholls (1978) looked at the reasoning capacity of children from 5 through 13 years of age and was particularly concerned with reasoning about effort and ability. Four clearly identified stages in the perception of effort and ability became evident. Briefly, level 1 is typical of young children, ages 5 to 6, who believe effort or outcome (winning or losing) is ability. Children of this age do not distinguish between those two elements. Level 2 is typical of children 7 to 9 years of age, who perceive effort to be the cause of performance outcomes. For example, children believe that equal effort leads to equal outcomes at this level. Level 3, typical of children 7 to 11 years of age, is the first level at which ability and effort are partially differentiated. Children begin to recognize that when outcomes differ though effort is the same, this must be due to ability. It is only when children are 12 to 13 years of age that they achieve level 4 and can distinguish between ability and effort in the cause of outcomes and realize that ability is *capacity*.

In considering this data, it is easy to see why children after age 12 begin to drop out at such dramatic rates. Children younger than this fail to recognize whether their ability is sufficient to succeed at the activity; they believe effort is the most important determinant of success. But after age 12, children have the necessary developmental capacity to deduce whether their ability is too low and, if it is, they may drop out. Consequently, it is a reasonable hypothesis to suggest that the competitive ability oriented children who dropped out in the Ewing study were the ones who concluded they were low in ability and thus dropped out. As we can readily appreciate, only when children are able to differentiate the causes of outcomes are they able to judge their own ability at the task.

The very structure of sport involves competition and social comparison processes, which exacerbates competitive ability assessments. Evidence also shows that the achievement domain of sport is a very important achievement arena for children (Duda, 1981). Thus, the perception of low ability and its implication causes much concern to children (Orlick, 1974) and it is little wonder that many drop out of sports.

Implications of Competitive Ability Assessments

Because game outcome is emphasized in sports, children often use outcome to infer ability. Consequently, their perception of ability and their degree of effort should be closely related to their perceived *attainment* in sports. Children who perceive themselves as able should be more motivated than children who perceive themselves as unable. But because winners infer high ability and losers infer low ability (see Roberts, 1982), the degree of effort applied becomes dependent upon perceived attainment and the children's perception of ability.

This phenomenon is particularly unfortunate in children's sports, especially around the ages of 10 to 14. This is the age range of greatest variance in children's physiological maturity, and it is the physiologically mature who are the most likely to excel and win, thus making the most favorable ability assessments. These children perceive themselves high in ability, they expect to succeed, and they exert effort. Yet they are not necessarily the ones who will be the best athletes eventually.

If we believe that the sport experience is valuable for children and are committed to the fullest development of all children, then we must strive to hold the interest of all children — not just those who presently excel. That is why it makes sense to encourage all children who join to persist in competitive sports. We should not weed out certain children. But how are we to enhance the motivation of all children, given the competitive structure of sport, the emphasis upon winning, and the inevitable competitive ability assessments that children make? The next section deals with that question.

ENHANCING MOTIVATION

In competitive sports we must accept the fact that the outcome, winning or losing, is very salient and readily apparent to all observers. The very structure of competitive sports elevates the importance of the outcome as a criterion of success and failure. And as we have argued above, this focuses the participants' attention upon the achievement goal of competitive ability. To the extent that the coach also focuses on the outcomes, the importance of competitive ability assessments to athletes will be exacerbated. That coaches do become ego-involved is almost inevitable because of the pressure from parents and peers. But to the extent that they yield to these very real pressures, they lower their potential to motivate all athletes. No coach who is outcome oriented can meet the motivational needs of all athletes. This section offers suggestions for teachers and coaches who wish to enhance the motivation and maintain the participation of as many athletes as possible.

Emphasize Sport Mastery

A major contribution of the developing theory of motivation advocated here is that it erects a conceptual mechanism that suggests how a teacher or coach can enhance motivation and achievement striving. First, we must recognize two conceptions of ability (Nicholls, 1980). One is the ego-involving competitive ability, in which ability is judged in relation to others as I have argued above; it is this conception of ability that is most prevalent in competitive sport. The other conception of ability is evident as a personal goal when the athlete attempts to achieve mastery or improve his or her ability at the task rather than demonstrating a higher capacity than others. When individuals strive to demonstrate ability in this sense, they are described as being task-involved or sport-mastery oriented. It is this sport mastery goal that coaches should encourage in athletes.

Generally, this translates to de-emphasizing the outcome as a criterion of success and failure and emphasizing the athlete's *performance* within the activity. The athlete should be encouraged to move away from questions such as, Am I better than, equal to, or worse than my opponent? Can we win? Are we good enough? Instead, the athlete should ask questions such as, How do we improve? What do we have to do to win? What must we do to improve this skill? These latter questions are more sport-mastery oriented and focus the athlete's attention upon his/her sport capabilities. This general suggestion comes from the basic theory outlined above, but it is also consistent with the goal-setting literature (Locke, Saari, Shaw, & Latham, 1981).

In practical terms, coaches should focus upon realistic performance goals suitable to the athlete's age and experience. That is, rather than have athletes focus upon global ability assessments (I am good/no good at these sports), have them focus upon specific skills within the sport and set mastery goals for them. By focusing upon specific skills in this way and setting realistic performance or mastery goals, children are more likely to be sport-mastery goal oriented rather than competitive-ability oriented. When children's achievement goals are projected in a mastery manner, their assessments will be based on previous performance and not upon outcomes. In this way, children cannot display low ability. When their criteria is their own previous level of performance, the cues inform the athletes of their level of mastery. So their motivation, based as it is on perception of ability in the concept of motivation advocated here, is maintained at a higher level. The athlete may become absorbed in the activity to the extent that he or she is in a state of flow and not aware of the time (Csikszentmihalyi, 1977).

By emphasizing sport mastery goals, we de-emphasize the outcomes, or *product*, of achievement behaviors and emphasize the performance, or *process*, of achieving. In this way we maintain the athletes' perception of ability, which enhances their motivation to perform. At the very least, we reduce the likelihood that athletes will make ego-deflating competitive ability assessments.

To encourage athletes of all ages to stay in sports, we must be sensitive to the athlete who does not have the physiological maturity or experience to be effective at the present time. These athletes may be making inappropriate perceived ability assessments because of an overemphasis upon outcomes, and they are the ones who would especially benefit from a sport-mastery orientation. This is where an effective teacher or coach can help children remain persistent in the activity for the benefits and skills that they may bring to the game at a later date. We do have evidence with college students (Spink & Roberts, 1980) that people who participate in leisure activities stay motivated through sport-mastery oriented goals, and they evaluate success and failure by how well they did rather than by whether they won or lost. The game's outcome was not important in the assessment of success and failure of these athletes. We should attempt to imbue all athletes with a similar perception.

CONCLUSION

In this chapter I have outlined the basic framework of a new theory of motivation and particularly tried to make it a conceptual framework through which we can understand the perspective of athletes of all ages in the competitive sport experience. Furthermore, I have suggested that we need to be sensitive to children's developmental changes which affect their participation and motivation within sport. Twelve-year-olds are particularly sensitive to the competitive sport experience. I have suggested that an emphasis on sport mastery where possible and a focus on specific rather than general abilities will help defuse the negative impact of unfavorable assessments of ability. For children who would quit sports because ability assessments lead to self-perceived low ability, emphasizing sport mastery may increase motivation and achievement striving. If we can minimize children's concerns about how they compare with others, we can enhance the motivation of all athletes — not just those who are presently excelling.

This chapter implies that as sport psychologists we must attend to the needs of athletes by making coaches aware of the psychological processes inherent in the achievement domain of sport. By so doing, and considering the behavioral implications therein, we make the domain of sport more sensitive to the motivational needs of all athletes, not just those who currently excel. It is sound coaching practice to maintain the pool of available athletes at high levels for as long as possible.

Chapter 17

Group Motivation in Sport Teams

David P. Yukelson
University of Houston

In his book, *In Pursuit of Excellence,* Terry Orlick indicates that one of the most gratifying experiences a coach or athlete can have is to be a member of a team that gets along well and works together efficiently and cohesively (Orlick, 1980). However, in a recent national survey investigating what coaches want to learn from the field of sport psychology, the most frequent and critical factor mentioned was the issue of how to build and sustain group cohesion in sport teams (Silva, 1982a). Although many coaches seem to agree that cohesion or team harmony is an important construct related to successful sport performance, the question arises, "How does a coach go about creating this group-oriented desire or motivation among team members?" Therefore, the purpose of this chapter is to synthesize theory and research from the areas of sport, social, and organizational psychology in an attempt to provide athletes a better understanding of how group motivation and team morale can be enhanced. The chapter will be divided into three parts: (a) nature of groups and group involvement; (b) individual and group motivation; and (c) ways to develop group motivation and team harmony.

THE NATURE OF GROUPS AND GROUP INVOLVEMENT

Based on theoretical definitions that have appeared in the literature, Carron (1980) has advanced a variety of properties that distinguish a sport group from a random collection of individuals. According to Carron, sport groups possess "a sense of unity or collective identity, a sense of shared purpose or objectives, structured patterns of interaction, structured modes of communication, personal and/or task interdependence, and interpersonal attraction" (Carron, 1980, p. 177). This is consistent with the early work of Kurt Lewin (1948), who was interested in the dynamic forces associated with group involvement. Considered to be a forefather of group dynamic theory, Lewin introduced two classes of forces that influence group participation and group change. These forces can be labeled group cohesiveness and group locomotion. Although the two terms differ conceptually, they are highly interrelated. Cohesiveness represents activity pertaining to the development and maintenance of the group itself and implies "an adhesive property or force that binds group members together" (Carron, 1980, p. 234). Cohesion increases the significance of membership for those who belong to the group, it motivates members to contribute to the group's welfare, and it connotes a sense of loyalty, commitment, and a "we" feeling among group members (Carron, 1980; Cartwright, 1968; Fisher, 1976).

In contrast, locomotion is a motivational construct that represents the reason or purpose behind the group's existence and symbolizes activity of the group in relation to achieving task objectives. For locomotion to be efficient, Schein (1980) believes some integrative function from an authority figure is needed to ensure the coordination of group members. This direction enhances congruence in the efforts of group members and assists the development of roles that contribute to the goals the group is striving to achieve.

The Sport Group

The literature on group involvement indicates that individuals join groups because they feel it will satisfy some need or objective (Cartwright, 1951; Shaw, 1976). Common needs include the need for affiliation (friendship, companionship, belonging), esteem (pride, competence, personal worth) and/or achievement (recognition, approval, identity). When a group fulfills the needs of its members, individuals often consider the group desirable and membership in that group very valuable (Cartwright, 1951; Likert, 1961; Schaefer, 1977). Similarly, many athletes participate in competitive sport groups because they feel it affords them an opportunity to establish or maintain close personal relationships with people while at the same time providing them an opportunity to do something well. Along these lines, affiliation and excellence have been found to be two of the strongest incentives that motivate athletes to participate and persist in sport (Alderman & Wood, 1976). Although the Alderman and Wood study dealt with young athletes, the implications for older athletes are apparent. A coach should create an atmosphere that satisfies an athlete's needs for both excellence and affiliation. That is, in addition to working hard on mastering the fundamentals for athletic excellence, a coach should also provide opportunities for an athlete to socialize with teammates so they can develop interpersonal skills essential for the growth and development of psychological well-being. Coaches sometimes neglect this important factor.

Thus, sport groups may be thought of as a collection of interdependent individuals, coordinated and orchestrated into various task-efficient roles for the purpose of achieving some goal or objective that is deemed important for that particular team. Success in team sports is highly dependent upon teamwork and a sense of collective confidence in knowing that the group is well prepared and fundamentally sound (Wooden, 1972). A coach's major role is to integrate the group into a smooth working unit that performs efficiently with a sense of pride, excellence, and collective identity. To achieve these ends a coach should be firm but affectionate. He or she must think in terms of the philosophy, values, goals, and operating procedures set down for his or her team. Yet the coach must also be sensitive enough to let each athlete know that his or her role is valued and that efforts are appreciated (Ouchi, 1981). In essence, the coach must discipline athletes according to the norms that govern the team, yet be receptive to athletes' interpersonal needs for affiliation, belonging, recognition, and security.

Finally, a coach needs to realize that individual differences do exist among team members. Each athlete has unique abilities that can contribute constructively to the team's overall productivity. The coach is like a catalyst in a chemical mixture; the idea is to make the chemistry of the team gel. That is, enhance the potential of each athlete while at the same time getting the entire unit to gel in a synchronized, coordinated manner. What kind of techniques can be used to meet such a challenge? Several of them will be discussed in the remainder of this chapter.

MOTIVATION THROUGH GOAL SETTING

A major concern in sport is the concept of motivation. Contemporary motivational theories conceptualize an individual's behavior as varying along two dimensions: direction and intensity (Landers, 1978). Whereas direction specifies the goal a person is striving to achieve, intensity refers to how much effort that person exerts in trying to reach the intended goal. Consequently, motivation may be thought of as the drive a person has that serves to arouse, energize, and direct his or her goal-directed behavior (Carron, 1980; Landers, 1978).

Although motivation is primarily concerned with activation and persistence of behavior, an important cognitively based source of motivation operates through the intervening process of goal setting (Bandura, 1977b). Goals provide both direction and the evaluation of progress. Goals can represent a motivational factor that guides behavior and gives it purpose. Research indicates that goals should be challenging, yet realistic and attainable (Bandura, 1982; Bandura & Schunk, 1981; Botterill, 1980). In addition, certain properties of goals (specificity and proximity) help to provide clear standards of adequacy from which to evaluate ongoing performance (Bandura & Schunk, 1981; Latham & Yukl, 1975). A series of short-term proximal goals relating to long-term distal goals should be established with specific target dates for achievement. While long-range goals act as an incentive or guide for action, the attainment of previously set short-term goals gives the athlete a growing sense of pride, accomplishment, and self-satisfaction (Bandura, 1982; Locke, Cartledge, & Knerr, 1970). Consequently, if athletes can set short-term proximal goals just far enough ahead as to require continuous effort and improvement but not so far ahead as to be unreachable, then the corresponding success and satisfaction derived from attaining these short-term goals will build pride and confidence in one's capabilities as well as intrinsic interest in the activity itself.

In addition, goals are important because they provide self-evaluative standards from which to judge one's capabilities (Bandura, 1977b; 1982). People have an innate need to feel competent and self-determining concerning their environment (Halliwell, 1979; Harter, 1978; White, 1959). When people aim for and reach desired levels of performance, they experience a sense of self-satisfaction in knowing they have lived up to their own standards of reference. This is consistent with the philosophy of John Wooden, former basketball coach at UCLA, who defines success as "peace of mind which is a direct result of self-satisfaction in knowing you did your best to become that which you are capable of becoming" (Wooden, 1972, p. 87). The urge to do one's best, to excel, is part of a constant urge for self-improvement. Accordingly, goals provide us the standards to do our best, to find out what we are and what we are not capable of achieving. Chapter 14 by O'Block and Evans provides a formula that is relatively simple to use and that allows athletes to set reasonable, yet challenging goals for themselves.

Self-Confidence and Goal Setting

Personal excellence is largely a matter of believing in one's capabilities and performing with a sense of pride, perseverance and commitment to identified goals and objectives. However, a capability is only as good as its execution, and a factor that appears to be crucial in achieving personal excellence is an individual's level of self-efficacy or self-confidence. Self-efficacy is defined as the strength of one's conviction that he or she can successfully execute a behavior required to produce a certain outcome (Bandura, 1977b). Efficacy expectations determine how much effort people expend on a task and how long they will persist in the face of adversity or setbacks. Assuming that an individual is capable of a response and that appropriate incentives are available for optimal performance, Bandura (1977b) asserts that an individual's actual performance will be predicted by his or her feeling of competence or expectation of personal effectiveness. The feelings of satisfaction and competence derived from attaining previously set goals provide an important vehicle for the development of perceived levels of self-efficacy (Bandura, 1982; Bandura & Schunk, 1981).

The discussion so far has focused mainly on individual motivation and satisfaction associated with goal attainment. Recently, Bandura (1982) has elaborated his theory of self-efficacy to include what he calls collective efficacy (a group's confident expectation that it will successfully reach its intended goal). According to Bandura, collective efficacy requires a commitment on the part of factional interests within a group to specific shared purposes that are attainable through teamwork and concerted effort. Since success in team sport calls for sustained endeavors over a considerable amount of time, proximal short-term goals are once again needed to provide incentives and evidence of group progress along the way (Bandura, 1982).

Motivating Individuals Within a Group

Early traditional conceptions on how to increase the motivation and productivity of workers in industrial settings primarily stressed techniques that would mold or manipulate an *individual's* behavior. Believing that this orientation would foster negative consequences, Cartwright (1951) proposed that individual motivation and work group productivity could be greatly enhanced by making the group rather than the individual the target of change. That is, in order to change the behavior of individuals, it is necessary to change the standards of the group, its style of leadership, and its emotional atmosphere. Thus, you do not try to mold or manipulate an individual's behavior; rather, you change the way the system is being managed.

Along these lines, Murray and Johnson (1975) proposed that athletic organizations could greatly enhance the productivity of their teams if they too conformed to group dynamic principles. According to Murray and Johnson, an organizational system capable of changing and improving itself should possess clearly understood goals and objectives, a system of communication that enhances goal achievement, norms or shared expectations of appropriate behavior, and roles that are conducive to goal attainment. For a group to be effective, then, individuals must merge diverse self-interests to support shared purposes or common goals. Explicit shared purposes that are realistic challenges will facilitate concerted effort, collective efficacy, and pride in what the group is trying to accomplish (Bandura, 1982; Murray & Johnson, 1975; Ouchi, 1981).

Emerson (1966) tested the theory that individual motivation on a 90-day climbing expedition to the top of Mount Everest is a function of communication among team members, and of goals that are defined wherever uncertainty exists about their outcome. Based on motivational determinants of risk-taking behavior (Atkinson, 1957) and levels of aspiration of group goal striving (Zander & Meadow, 1965), Emerson predicted that the strength of motivation toward a task is greatest for tasks perceived to be of intermediate difficulty (that point at which evaluation and uncertainty about goal outcome is highest) and weakest for tasks perceived to be too easy or too difficult. Emerson made standard preplanned comments to his colleagues and, for data collection purposes, recorded their answers on a small tape recorder he carried with him through the snow. Results from the study indicated that motivation was maximized when Emerson emphasized to his colleagues that chances of making it to the top of the mountain were 50%. If Emerson made a discouraging comment, the tape recorder revealed that colleagues cheered him up. But if Emerson made an optimistic comment about reaching the top, then teammates would dampen his zeal or spirit. In either case, motivation was greatest when the outcome of the goal was made to appear uncertain to group members.

Based on these results, the following coaching implications become apparent. If my team were a decided underdog, I would provide information that we are not as bad as people claim, and that the opposing team has weaknesses and can be beat if we play to our potential. If our team were a decided favorite, I would want to place the probability of success at the intermediate range of difficulty in order to avoid complacency. I would focus on our opponent's strengths rather than our own strengths. Thus, I would provide proximal short-term goals for the team as an incentive or standard of excellence to shoot for.

Developing Pride Within the Group

The most comprehensive contribution to our current understanding of group motivation comes from the work of Alvin Zander (1971, 1978), who has developed a model of achievement motivation in groups that is similar to the model of individual achievement motivation proposed by Atkinson (1964). The theme of his model revolves around making pride in the group an important attribute, which in turn develops a desire for group success that can be a powerful motivating force among individuals within the group (Zander, 1978). According to Zander, the desire for group success is a group oriented motive from which members derive pride in performance and satisfaction with the group if it successfully accomplishes a challenging group task. In contrast, the desire to avoid group failure is a group member's disposition to experience shame or dissatisfaction with the group if it fails a challenging task.

Zander's pride-in-performance approach places a premium value on common goals, valued roles, teamwork, and group unity. According to Zander, groups that possess a strong desire for group success prefer realistic challenging goals and are not afraid to talk about how performance can be improved or what obstacles might prevent the fulfillment of these objectives. When group members establish a realistic but challenging goal for their unit, they simultaneously create a criterion from which to evaluate the group's performance. Upon achieving the specified goal, group members experience pride, satisfaction, and feelings of collective efficacy about expectations for future performance on similar tasks (Bandura, 1982; Zander, 1978). Thus, when the desire for group success is strong among team members, they have a heightened awareness of their mutual responsibility toward one another which enables them to coordinate their efforts with maximum efficiency.

A coach who was great in developing pride within his team was John Wooden, who coached UCLA during its National Collegiate Athletic Association (NCAA) dynasty. Wooden knew how to get the most out of his talent. He won NCAA championships with teams oriented around small forwards (1970-71), power forwards (1975), or tall dominant centers (1967-1969; 1972-1973). In addition, he won his first national championship in 1964 with no player taller than 6 ft. 5 in.

Wooden believed that every effort should be made toward maximum development of both the individual and the group. His famous "Pyramid of Success" offered a coherent philosophy from which to govern his players. According to Wooden, the success of his program was based on three principles: (a) mental, moral, and physical conditioning; (b) poise and confidence, which comes from hard work and careful planning in knowing that the team is well prepared and fundamentally sound; and (c) working together as a team, whereupon athletes acquire an understanding of their role within the system and show an eagerness to sacrifice personal glory for the welfare of the team.

Stressing the virtues of industriousness, enthusiasm, team spirit, and group loyalty, Wooden successfully developed a sense of pride, character, and responsibility within his athletes both on and off the basketball court. Although Coach Wooden certainly seemed to know what button to press in order to get his team's chemistry to gel in a synchronized, coordinated fashion, most coaches are unsure how to create this group-oriented desire for team success. Therefore, the final section will present various strategies that can enhance coach-athlete communication systems and facilitate the development of pride and team harmony within a sport group.

WAYS TO ENHANCE COACH-ATHLETE
COMMUNICATION SYSTEMS AND TEAM HARMONY

Open Communication Channels

The foundation for effective communication between coaches and athletes is trust and mutual respect for one another (Likert, 1961; Nesvig, 1980; Orlick, 1980; Ouchi, 1981). A coaching staff should create an atmosphere in which athletes have the freedom to express their ideas and feelings in a constructive, democratic way. Research indicates that athletes want to be involved in certain decisions that affect them directly (Carron & Chelladurai, 1978). Consequently, open communication channels between coaches and athletes will lend depth and rationality to both interpersonal and task-related situations. Orlick (1980) appropriately notes that communication is a two-way venture, and both the coach and athlete have a responsibility toward one another for making it work.

Develop Pride and A Sense of Collective Identity
Within the Group

Emphasize the importance of pride in the group, and its sources and consequences for the team (Zander, 1978). Pride is associated with feelings of efficacy and self-satisfaction that come with achieving the goals an individual or group is striving to achieve. The value of establishing realistic goals is that the athlete will have a criterion from which to evaluate performance. According to the work of Bandura (1982) and Halliwell (1979), it is this evaluation process that gives an individual pride in his or her accomplishments. In addition, a coach should think of creative ways to develop pride within subunits that exist within the group structure. He or she should give each unit goals and incentives to shoot for. This will enhance pride, determination, and consistency in effort. Dean Smith created this atmosphere very well at the University of North Carolina through the use of the Blue and White squads. Every player knew his role and expected to receive some playing time that could contribute to the team's outcome.

Common Expectations of Appropriate Behavior

Shared expectations of appropriate behavior refers to the norms or rules that govern a group. Norms should be conducive to the goals the group is striving to achieve (Murray & Johnson, 1975; Ouchi, 1981; Shaw, 1976). Groups unite behind common goals, so it is important to get athletes to think in terms of the philosophy, goals, and operating procedure the team is striving to accomplish. An organizational philosophy should specify not only the desired objectives the group is striving to achieve, but also the strategy, operating procedures, or means to reach these goals as well. By stating explicitly what is and what is not important, a philosophy offers efficiency in planning and coordination between people because it gives them a sense of values by which to work (Ouchi, 1981).

Thus, clearly understood goals and objectives will facilitate team productivity and intensity of performance, as well as help solidify the team. Furthermore, if goals and strategies are clear, individuals will coordinate their efforts more efficiently and they may begin to monitor their behavior and that of their teammates in a consistent and mutually agreed-upon manner.

Value Unique Personal Contributions

Each player's role on the team should be clearly defined and the importance of his or her potential contribution to the team should be emphasized at all times (Zander, 1978). Increasing the perceived significance of an athlete's contribution to a team can heighten one's sense of personal competence, importance, and self-worth.

A coach should in various ways underscore the fact that winning or losing is a product of team effort (Zander, 1978). Halliwell (1978) astutely points out that a coach should thoroughly analyze the tasks demanded of each player's position and give appropriate positive feedback concerning an individual's own personal accomplishments so that the athlete feels his/her efforts are indeed appreciated by the entire team. Similarly, the coach should emphasize the multifaceted contributions that non-starters make to help develop team solidarity (i.e., providing competition in practice to help the team improve, being supportive, filling important substitution roles, etc.). Along these lines, teammates must have mutual respect for each others' feelings, opinions, and capabilities. Since roles may change during the course of a season, players must have confidence in the ability of all members to make a positive contribution to the team when called upon.

Recognize Excellence

Recognize those individuals who excel within their designated roles and who contribute to group goals. After all, this is the goal you desire as a coach. You want your athletes to excel within their designated roles so that the team executes with a sense of collective confidence and mutual effort. Such recognition can serve to get your athletes ego-involved rather than just task-involved. Individuals come to a program with a variety of ideas, feelings, and solutions to draw upon. By utilizing a participative management style of leadership, a coach can get input from players in a responsible way so they can collectively turn their resources into meaningful action. Participation is defined as an individual's mental and emotional involvement in a group that encourages him or her to contribute to group goals and share responsibility in striving to achieve goals (Davis, 1963). Thus, it is my belief that morale and productivity will improve when individuals are given responsibility and a chance to express themselves creatively in group goal-setting and decision-making policies. By using the resources of group members to solve both task-relevant and interpersonal problems, a coach shows recognition and respect for player judgment. This acknowledgment can increase a player's trust, feelings of belonging, and attraction to the team.

Consensus and Commitment

Involving the entire group in goal-setting activities results in a form of psychological contracting, which instills in group members an increased commitment to team goals and a greater awareness of the degree of effort and discipline required to reach those goals (Botterill, 1980). Through a coach's guidance, teams should set both long-term distal goals and short-term proximal goals. Whereas long-term goals provide incentives, direction, and evaluation of progress along the way, the attainment of short-term goals reinforces intrinsic feelings of pride, confidence, and personal accomplishment.

According to Botterill (1980) the coach should initially think about the upcoming season and determine the goals, priorities, and expectations for the team. Group planning sessions could revolve around the following issues: What are we going to try and accomplish this upcoming season? What are our strengths and weaknesses or areas of concern on the team? What are some specific goals to strive for? What are some strategies that can be used to achieve these goals? (Botterill, 1980).

The biggest task confronting the coach is to make sure the goals and plans made through group consensus are realistic, attainable challenges. A coach should not be afraid to change goals that are deemed unrealistically difficult. Consequently, once goals have been set, consideration should be given toward what obstacles might prevent their fulfillment and how the team might overcome these obstacles (Zander, 1978).

Periodic Team Meetings to Resolve Conflict

During the season, it is important to conduct regular team meetings to allow both positive and negative feelings to be expressed in an open, honest, constructive manner (Nesvig, 1980). As Orlick has stated, "It is difficult to be responsive to other people's needs or feelings if you do not know what they are. It is difficult to respect another person's perspective if you do not understand what it is or why it is" (Orlick, 1980, p. 221). Consequently, a mature group can resolve its internal conflicts, mobilize its resources, and take intelligent action only if it has a means for consensually validating its own experience. Team talks could revolve around various topics such as developing realistic expectations, redefining goals that may have been set too high or low, or learning from mistakes or losses; or team talks could simply provide an outlet for the expression of positive or negative feelings. Thus, regular rap sessions that are genuine and constructively oriented can help improve team morale and overall productivity. However, it should be stressed that the person in charge of the regular rap sessions have some background in group dynamic principles in order to steer group members toward what he/she thinks the group needs most at that time. This will allow a coach and group to be more capable of dealing constructively with potentially disruptive issues.

Stay in Touch With Interpersonal Grapevines

Behind or within any formal organizational structure exists an informal interpersonal network that can greatly affect the functioning of the formal organizational system. A coach should not ignore those individuals who possess high interpersonal prestige and status within a team. Rather, those individuals with high interpersonal prestige and status (as measured through sociometric peer rating techniques) should be utilized as communication links between the coaching staff and the players so coaches can stay in contact with the prevailing attitudes and feelings of the group. Through this hierarchy of suggestibility, official avenues of communication could be provided for expressing ideas, opinions, or critiques of interpersonal and task-related relationships that exist within the group. Consequently, athletes will look to coaches with greater admiration and respect, knowing that their suggestions have been listened to and are valued. Recently, Yukelson, Weinberg, Richardson, and Jackson (1983) have utilized techniques designed to measure the nature of the interpersonal network in a team. These techniques may prove to be useful to the coach as he/she tries to more fully understand the interpersonal dynamics of the team.

Seek Grails Rather Than Slay Dragons

If you wish to inspire confidence in people, do not focus only on failure. Rather, reflect upon achievements gained, then point out how mistakes can be corrected. A few words of encouragement and a pat on the back will go a long way. Similarly, coaches and athletes must learn to keep competition in proper perspective. Winning means more than just beating one's opponent. It means personal improvement and striving to do one's best. The focus should be on long-term motivation — teaching athletes how to bounce back when things get tough.

CONCLUSION

Sport groups are made up of individuals who reciprocally affect one another in both interpersonal and task-related situations. Team harmony is facilitated when groups have common goals, compatible roles, a system of communication that enhances goal achievement, and respect for each others' opinions, capabilities, and feelings. We as coaches and educators need to instill pride, confidence, and a sense of personal identity within our athletes so they may become better people in the way they define themselves both on and off the field. The challenge is to motivate athletes to perform to their fullest capabilities and to help them realize their own needs and ambitions.

PART V

AGGRESSION AND SPORT

In the previous section, the importance of motivation was discussed along with specific techniques for motivating individuals and teams. Since motivation is a critical determinant of athletic success, most coaches and athletes strive for high levels of motivation to ensure maximum performance. However, motivation can sometimes become too strong, misdirected, or uncontrolled. When this occurs motivated behavior can easily turn into aggressive or violent behavior, which may result in injury to other players. For instance, many players and coaches refer to internal motivational factors such as pride, self-accomplishment, goal setting, and a sense of self-mastery as well as extrinsic factors such as winning, trophies, first place, and publicity.

At times, however, feelings about the opponent become a basis for motivation. In many sports, getting "psyched up" for an opponent means developing a rationale for why it is necessary to beat that opponent. If such motivational factors seem insufficient by themselves, coaches may define the opponents in a way that provides an extra reason for trying to defeat them. Some players and coaches have suggested that negative, even hostile, feelings about an opponent will lead to greater motivation for victory. In fact, many athletes in contact and collision sports have stated that in order to brutalize, intimidate, or injure an opponent they have to perceive the opponent as their enemy; as a result they build up an intense hatred for the opponent. Such a viewpoint is embodied by a quote from Vince Lombardi, who said, "to play this game you must have that fire in you and there is nothing that stokes fire like hate."

Unfortunately, the prevalence of violent behavior by players and spectators has escalated to become a major issue in competitive sports today. Examples of violence abound. South American soccer riots have led to the use of electric fences to keep the crowds from players, and moats have been built around some playing areas to keep violent fans from injuring officials and players. In Guatemala, soccer fans of a losing team recently attacked fans of the winning team with machetes, killing five people. The first criminal proceeding in the United States against a player for his conduct during competition took place in 1975. The player had struck the face of another player with his hockey stick, requiring 25 stitches and surgery to repair a fracture of the right eye socket. A basketball player named Kermit Washington hit Rudy Tomjanivich with a punch to the face that resulted in extensive surgery over a 2-year period. Jack Tatum's recent book, *They Call Me Assassin*, highlights the violence in football that includes deliberately trying to injure or intimidate the opposition. These examples demonstrate that sport has the potential to be violent and the present sanctions are evidently not strong enough to curtail the violence.

Aggression in Sport

The next question is, why does violent behavior continue in competitive sport? One explanation is that sport involvement and socialization presents a unique opportunity for young players to acquire behaviors that in most other social settings would be considered inappropriate. In addition to learning aggressive behaviors on the field, young athletes may be exposed to role models via television and other media which imply that violence in sport is legitimate and often pays off. This is consistent with the social learning theory approach, which emphasizes the importance of learning as a determinant of human behavior. Both anecdotal and experimental studies support this argument. For example, several years ago the Philadelphia Flyers ice hockey team won the Stanley Cup and admitted resorting to physical violence and intimidation to vanquish their opponents. The 1975 and 1976 Super Bowl championship Pittsburgh Steelers proudly attributed their success to their own ferocity in intimidating other teams into submission. Similarly, in a series of studies examining aggression and youth hockey, Michael Smith has found that aggression is learned by playing hockey and the more experience a child has in sport the greater the likelihood of learning aggressive tactics. Most respondents in his survey reported that viewing professional hockey taught them methods of illegal hitting, fighting, and "dirty tricks" along with the "enforcer" role in hockey. Smith contends that aggression is learned in hockey because it is socially sanctioned normative behavior, learned from observing professional players and reinforced by significant others in youth sport programs.

Violence in sport also gets considerable media attention: Witness the articles on enforcers and tough guys, cartoon characters shown striking one another with hockey sticks, full-length motion pictures such as Rollerball epitomizing the violence and brutality in sport, and Sport Illustrated's three-part series on brutality in sport. Thus, it is apparent that aggressive behavior in sport can be learned through the models that young athletes are exposed to, and this violence seems socially sanctioned or at the most is only passively punished.

Aggression in Society

This leads us to a second but related explanation of why violent behavior in sport is so pervasive, namely that sport simply reflects a society that fosters violent behavior. Sociologists and anthropologists have suggested that historically sport has been influenced by society's political and social events from the Roman times up through the present. The 20th century has seen world wars and sophisticated weapons that could annihilate humanity with the throw of a switch. On a national level there has been a general rise in homicide, rape, and other forms of brutality. The alarm about violence in society results not only from the activities of political extremists and professional criminals but also from violence among the general populace, particularly among the young. Many people are concerned because this violence seems to be without motive and has continued to escalate despite greater acquisition of material wealth in our society. Perhaps most frightening is the manner in which society appears to accept and adjust to it.

An interesting observational study by Richard Sipes provides some data on the relationship between sport violence and society. He found that 9 of 10 warlike societies had combative sports and only 2 of 10 peaceful societies had combative sports ("War, Sports, and Aggression: An Empirical Test of Two Rival Theories," in *The American Anthropologist*, Feb. 1973). Furthermore, in a follow-up study he found a positive relationship between military activity in the United States and the popularity of sports that involved combative and collision behavior. Although these data are purely correlational, they do suggest a relationship between violence in society and violence in sport.

Theories of Aggression

The preceding comments all suggest that violence and aggression are often perceived to be part of sport, particularly contact and collision sports. If this is so, what can be done to modify this incorrect perception? This question is critical especially for coaches of young athletes, since it is at an early age when their aggressive behaviors can be learned or the rules of fair play can be fostered. The answer to this question requires an understanding of the etiology of aggression as well as the conditions that tend to foster aggressive behavior.

The first chapter in this section, by Burris Husman and John Silva, sheds light on these issues by attempting to define aggressive behavior in sport and differentiating it from other forms of acceptable force. The problem of defining aggression has plagued sport research throughout the years; the variations in its usage and meaning have been extreme. Consider the following situation: An end in football cuts across the middle of the field to catch a pass and the moment he catches the ball a linebacker simultaneously crashes into him, causing him to drop the ball and injure his back. Some people might say the linebacker's play is clean and part of the game, whereas others might perceive it as a "cheap shot" and an act of violence. This disparity is due to the fact that although the overt behavior is the same, its intent remains unknown. Since intent is not easily discernable, it is difficult to determine if the linebacker wanted to injure the end or just have him drop the pass, or both.

Husman and Silva discuss how aggressive behavior in sport is often mislabeled and confused with appropriate assertive behavior. The authors distinguish between hostile aggression in which the primary reinforcement is to inflict injury, and instrumental aggression which also involves the intent to injure but the primary reinforcer is a reward such as money or victory. In turn, assertive behavior in sport is defined as involving the use of legitimate physical force with no intent to injure another person or to violate the formal rules of the sport. The authors review some of the major theories of aggressive behavior, ranging from instinctual to learning perspectives, and then discuss aggression and sport participation and spectating. They conclude by citing some problems that have plagued aggression research in the sports environment.

Acquiring and Maintaining
Aggressive Sport Behavior

From the discussion in the Husman and Silva chapter it is very obvious that aggressive behavior in sport can be learned. Additionally, various social-psychological factors help maintain this type of behavior. In the subsequent chapter, John Silva carefully reviews the learning process that legitimizes aggressive sport behavior. This process often begins at the youth sport level and is closely related to how various terms are used (or perhaps misused) by players and coaches to blur the distinction between appropriate force and inappropriate force in sport. Silva maintains that this legitimizing process helps lower the inhibitions against aggressive behavior in sport. Essentially, players learn to take as well as inflict aggressive behavior; they follow normative (unwritten) rules rather than the formal rules of their sport in trying to win. We have all seen the aggressive tactics of individuals or teams willing to take the penalty in order to gain a psychological advantage over their opponent. Unfortunately, many of these behaviors not only break the mutually agreed-upon rules of the sport but they often result in personal injury. Observers and administrators of organized sport publically deplore this type of behavior, yet it continues. Even professional athletes such as Bobby Hull, Kareem Abdul Jabbar, and Russ Francis have publicly denounced violent player behavior. Why, then, does it continue and jeopardize the careers of so many?

Silva's chapter continues with a detailed review of the vicarious and direct reinforcers that help maintain aggressive player responses. Concerning sports in which aggressive behavior is most common, it appears that the reinforcement-punishment structure actually makes it advantageous to break formal rules in order to gain strategic, tactical, or psychological advantages. The final section of the chapter offers suggestions that can make competitive sport less violent and more wholesome for players at all levels.

Aggression and Skilled Performance

Previously we mentioned that many coaches and athletes believe that aggression pays, but how does it affect athletic performance? This question forms the basis for the chapter by Neil Widmeyer. Anecdotal reports imply that coaches and athletes often feel that strong assertion is needed to achieve maximum performance. But what about aggression exhibited in sport? Does it facilitate success through intimidation and the other factors mentioned, or can players be so intent on being aggressive that they don't execute their plays with the precision and coordination necessary to be successful. Widmeyer's chapter systematically explores the complex aggression performance relationship by viewing aggression as both a trait and a state variable. Aggression has been measured as a trait by a number of psychological inventories and as a state by measures such as the number of penalty minutes accumulated over a hockey season. This analysis considers both the individual athlete and the team, and comes up with equivocal findings at both levels. Widmeyer concludes with a review of the problems concerning the study of aggression in sport, and makes some recommendations for future research in this area.

All the chapters in this section support the notion that learning plays a major role in sport aggression. This is indeed to our benefit because as coaches and administrators we always have the option to restructure the environment in a manner that can change what is learned and exhibited by participants.

Chapter 18

Aggression in Sport: Definitional and Theoretical Considerations[1]

Burris F. Husman
University of Maryland

John M. Silva III
University of North Carolina-Chapel Hill

Aggression is as old as the human race. Beginning with Cain's murder of Abel and extending throughout history, people have fought each other in tribal wars, ethnic and religious wars, and in worldwide conflicts. Today, man continues to exterminate large segments of humanity or prepares to do so.[2] It appears that the technical and cultural "advance" of man has led to more violent and destructive behavior.

What is aggression and why is it so commonly manifested by a supposedly higher form of intelligence such as man? In this chapter we will address some of these important issues as they relate to sport. We will begin by defining aggressive behavior and differentiating it from assertive behavior in sport contexts; then we will review some of the major theoretical positions that attempt to explain the origin and nature of aggressive behavior. Along these same lines, the following two chapters by John Silva and Neil Widmeyer should give the reader a comprehensive understanding of what aggression is, why it occurs in sport, and what can be done to reduce injurious behavior directed at opponents, officials, and spectators.

---

[1]This chapter is an extension of two previous presentations made by Burris Husman at the annual conference of NCPEAM (1973) and NASPSPA (1979), and an extension of a paper by John Silva published in 1980.

[2]Reference to "man" is used in a generic sense.

Definitional Problems

The word *aggression* comes from the Latin root *aggredi*, *ad* (to or toward) and *gradior* (walk). Literally, then, the word means to walk toward or approach, to "move against" or to "move with intent to hurt or harm" (May, 1972). The major problem when studying aggression in sport or any other environment is in finding an acceptable universal definition. Most psychologists describe aggression in terms of behavior (Johnson, 1972). Aggressive behavior has been associated with destructive acts, sexual attack, prejudice, speech, genital activity, drug and alcohol addiction, sport and exercise, crying, complaining, waging war, and so forth (Miller, 1979). There is, then, no simple behavior that may be described under the rubric "aggression." Obviously, the term aggression carries numerous connotations whether we are studying sport or nonsport behavior. Terms such as "acceptable aggression," "acceptable violence," "controlled violence," and "aggressiveness" are inaccurate uses of the term aggression when applied to a sport context. Unfortunately, the popularized uses of these terms often represent attempts to legitimize behaviors that are illegal and injurious to opponents.

The clear identification and labeling of aggressive behavior in sport settings has important ramifications both for participants and researchers. For example, the improper labeling of behavior as aggressive can often lead to retaliatory behavior that escalates aggressive exchanges between participants (e.g., an inside pitch in baseball being perceived as aggression). Additionally, moral responsibility and legitimate sanctions or punishments are assigned more accurately when acts of aggression can be identified and differentiated from nonaggressive behavior.

For the researcher, the indiscriminate use of the term aggression has resulted in a wide class of behaviors being conceptualized as aggressive. Many of these behaviors share little functional or motivational unity with each other. Thus, some researchers who have globally labeled all forceful sport behavior as aggressive have badly contaminated their data because appropriate forceful acts and inappropriate acts of force have been categorized together as if they were the same phenomena. In order to understand and further study aggression, we need some definitional consensus on what is aggressive behavior in sport and what is not.

Aggressive Behavior Defined

Aggressive behavior is an overt verbal or physical act that can psychologically or physically injure another person or oneself. Aggressive behavior against another person is called extropunitive behavior, whereas aggression against the self is often labeled intropunitive behavior. Aggressive behavior is nonaccidental; the aggressor intends an injury and the behavior selected for this is under his or her control. The aggressor has selected the behavior from various alternatives available in the situation, including nonaggressive responses.

Aggressive behavior is also classified according to the primary reinforcement sought via the act. The primary reinforcement in *hostile aggression* is seeing pain or injury inflicted on the target. The successful delivery of physical or psychological punishment is reinforcing itself. Hostile aggression is thus an end rather than a means. Berkowitz (1965) has called hostile aggression "angry aggression" because the aggressor is often perturbed with his or her victim.

A second type of aggressive behavior is *instrumental aggression*, which also involves an intent to injure. However, the primary reinforcement sought via instrumental aggression is a tangible reward such as money, victory, or praise. Instrumental aggression is thus a means to an end. The aggressor is willing to intentionally inflict pain or injury in order to receive a nonaggressive goal. Since both forms of aggression involve an intent to injure, neither should be encouraged in sport. The intent to injure an opponent violates the constitutive rule structure of all sports except those of direct pugilism such as boxing or full contact karate.

This definition of aggressive behavior considers the intent, behavior, effect, and social context of the act. It also restores a degree of social-ecological validity to the construct aggression. Tedeschi, Smith, and Brown (1974) have previously noted the restrictiveness of research that *requires* a subject to exhibit aggressive behavior and the inconsistency of research that evaluates supposed secondary indices of aggressive behavior (e.g., electric shocks). Tedeschi et al. (1974) have questioned the validity of several well known studies on the grounds that either actual harmful behaviors or the intent to do harm are not clearly established. Acts such as delivering electric shock at the request of the experimenter for "teaching purposes" (Baron, 1970), shock as compliance or obedience (Milgram, 1963, 1964, 1965), smashing a bobo doll (Bandura, Ross, & Ross, 1961), rating themes from Thematic Apperception Test pictures (Feshbach, 1955), or the recording of tardiness from school (Eron, Walder, & Lefkowitz, 1971) do not fit the criteria established as essential to an aggressive act. The most notable and frequent violations are in the lack of free choice (e.g., Baron, 1970; Milgram, 1963, 1964, 1965), or the absence of an actual aggressive behavior (e.g., Eron et al., 1971; Feshbach, 1955).

Assertive Behavior Defined

In many team sports where physical force and collisions are permitted, the term aggression has been used as an all-encompassing label. Yet, many forceful behaviors that are permitted by the rules may not necessarily involve the intent to injure. In several sports, assertive behavior has been unjustifiably equated with aggressive behavior. A clear definition of assertive behavior will facilitate the distinction between each concept in a sport setting.

Assertive behavior in sport is often exemplified by heightened physical behavior. This goal-directed behavior may, and often does, involve the use of legitimate verbal or physical force. Such behavior requires unusual energy and effort, which in most other social settings would appear to be aggressive behavior. These assertive behaviors must be exhibited with no intent to harm or injure another person, nor may they violate the constitutively agreed upon rules of the sport being played. Silva (1979b) has defined such behavior in sport as proactive assertion, a term which implies that the behavior is acceptable yet forceful or active. Proactive assertive behavior is exemplified by offensive or defensive behaviors. An offensive proactive assertive behavior is designed to acquire or gain a valued resource, as exemplified by a ball carrier thrusting ahead for extra yardage in a football game. Defensive proactive assertive behavior attempts to deprive another of a valued resource or expected gain. A defensive end tackling the advancing ball carrier by using legal body contact may demonstrate defensive proactive assertion. In each example, the behavior must be task oriented, constitutively acceptable, and involve no intent to injure.

Since institutionalized sport has a formal rule structure governing physical force and verbal exchange, the distinction between aggressive and assertive behavior, though often difficult, is certainly feasible. Unfortunately, few studies of aggression in sport and athletics have adopted a research strategy that attempts to distinguish these behaviors. Several studies have, however, restricted the free choice of a subject (e.g., Zillman, Johnson, & Day, 1974), or measured aggressive behavior through secondary indices (Eastwood, 1974; Lefkowitz, Walder, Eron, & Heusman, 1973). Future study of aggressive behavior in sport and athletic settings should focus on the clear identification and measurement of aggressive behavior. The development of well controlled field experiments and field studies is perhaps one of the sounder methods through which to attain this increase in precision.

Differentiating Aggressive From Assertive Sport Behavior

The definitions presented in this chapter attempt to show that not all forceful behavior exhibited in sport is aggressive. Tackling, blocking, checking, and other rule-sanctioned contact and collisions are not necessarily aggressive acts in sports in which they are constitutively legal. Such acts are an implicit task of playing these sports, just as hitting an overhead smash in tennis is implicit to that sport. There is often no clear evidence that such behavior is aggression. Behaviors such as spearing and clotheslining in football and slashing in hockey offer much clearer evidence of aggressive intent because they are not implict in playing these sports, are potentially injurious, and are seldom accidental.

Thus, the task that confronts research in collision and contact sports lies in determining a true index of aggressive behavior in an environment in which physical force, collision, and contact of a particular nature have been formally agreed to by both the participants and the governing body of the league. Yet any athlete who has played a contact or collision sport knows that a player can exhibit a legal behavior (e.g., a block or check) with the intent to injure. This is a major reason why many forceful behaviors in collision and contact sports have been mislabeled aggressive. However, as noted earlier, not all forceful behavior in these sports is necessarily aggressive. Attempting to determine whether a legal behavior, such as a check in ice hockey, was an aggressive act becomes somewhat of a subjective endeavor. The major source of supportive evidence for the act being aggressive rather than proactive assertion would come from the social environment. Circumstantial cues such as recent hostile interactions between the actor and the target, recent frustrations incurred by the actor from opponents, officials, or game developments, and recent verbal or nonverbal gestures all give information about the mood of the player exhibiting the behavior.

Ultimately, labeling a legal behavior as aggression will be a subjective conclusion. The intent of an actor can only be inferred by an observer, thus by necessity a subjective decision is made when legal behaviors are labeled as aggressive acts. Figure 18-1 illustrates the potential dilemma that confronts research on aggression in sport.

The lone circle in the upper portion of the figure illustrates how assertion and aggression are confounded when they are considered to be the same behavior. This creates a serious problem in interpreting research results. An overt act of assertion may be behaviorally similar to an overt act of aggression but the intent, motive structure, and desired effects of an aggressive behavior are very different from an assertive behavior. Research that fails to discriminate between these two behavioral forms studies neither assertion nor aggression. The interlocking circles in the lower portion of the figure highlight the independence that exists between assertion and aggression as well as an area of ambiguity or overlap. This illustration demonstrates that there are injurious, nonaccidental, rule-violating behaviors that are clearly aggressive acts. There are also forceful, rule-sanctioned behaviors that show no intent to injure and are clearly assertive behaviors. The shaded area represents the ambiguity that results when the intent of a legal behavior is in question due to its circumstances. The area of ambiguity varies in size according to the

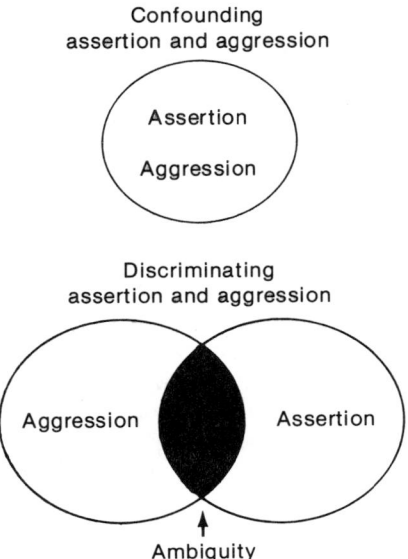

Confounding
assertion and aggression

Discriminating
assertion and aggression

FIGURE 18-1   Discriminating assertion and aggression in sport research.

sport being studied. In contact and collision sports, this area is often larger than it would be in noncontact sports. It is paramount that researchers studying assertion or aggression in any sport operationalize their definitions to reflect a sensitivity for forceful behavior that is constitutively sanctioned.

Now that we have a clearer understanding of what is aggressive behavior in sport, let's review some of the major theories of aggression. These theoretical positions are extremely important because they make some very basic assumptions about the origin of aggressive behavior and the prospects for changing it. Three major theoretical positions will be reviewed: (a) the instinctual theory, (b) the frustration-aggression hypothesis, and (c) the social learning theory. Following this theoretical review, we will examine how sport may encourage or decrease aggressive behavior.

THEORIES OF AGGRESSION

The Instinctive Theory of Aggression

The instinctive theory of aggression is usually attributed to the work of Sigmund Freud. It was Adler, however, who first emphasized that aggression built up in the id and required release either through reality or fantasy (May, 1972). Advocates of the Freudian school maintain that the two instinctual forces of sex and aggression had the most influence on human behavior. Since these two forces were instinctive and constantly operative, expression provided an outlet or a catharsis. Working, participating in or watching a violent sport, and/or violence on the stage or television was thought to reduce the inherent sex or aggression drive (Feshback & Singer, 1971; Lorenz, 1966; Menninger, Moyman, & Pruyser, 1963). Some followers of Freud believed if there were no outlets to express these drives, aggression would be turned toward the self and result in depression, masochism, or suicide.

A group of anthropologists and ethnologists (Ardrey, 1962; Lorenz, 1966; Morris, 1967) have supported this instinctual theory. Their research for the most part was conducted by studying the cultural background of humans and the ritualistic and aggressive behavior of animals. Lorenz's work showed that aggressive behavior was phylogenically transmitted and had the distinct function of preserving the species. Animals aggress to defend their territorial rights, to secure food, to mate, and to attain dominance (i.e., struggle for leadership that helps to protect the group from outside threats). Lorenz classified aggression into two categories: interspecific aggression (aggression between species) and intraspecific aggression (aggression within species). He also observed that animals such as lions and tigers (which by nature are armed with natural weapons to kill) have reliable inhibitions that prevent destruction of their own species. However, humans lack natural weapons to kill and are to a greater extent devoid of these inhibitions. According to Lorenz, animals fight but seldom kill each other; one animal usually withdraws. Humans, meanwhile, without natural inhibitions, have created artificial weapons such as the bow and arrow, gunpowder, and the atomic bomb, which are used to destroy each other. If Lorenz's concept is true, then humankind, devoid of any inhibition about killing its own species, is capable of destroying itself.

Proponents of the instinctive theory maintain that participation in vigorous contact sports or observing violent behavior reduces aggression (a catharsis). The catharsis concept is very old and can be easily found throughout the literature on aggression. Catharsis originated from the Greek, *katharsis* (cleanse or purify) and means to purge the body. While the concept of catharsis may be steeped in history, the 20th century research supporting the concept is meager. Researchers Weiss (1968) and Bramel (1969) reviewed the literature on catharsis and both noted that no conclusion was possible because the research evidence is highly equivocal. Berkowitz (1970) and other researchers, however, have not been so "equivocal" about the validity of the catharsis hypothesis. Berkowitz stated rather emphatically that no valid experimental findings support the contention that the need to aggress is lowered by observing others behave in an aggressive manner or by behaving aggressively oneself. Rather, the tendency to aggress may actually be enhanced by this type of activity. That is, rather than being drive reducing (a cathartic effect), the observation and exhibition of successful aggressive behavior may be drive enhancing.

Clearly, the instinctive theory emphasizing the drive reduction model of aggression has not been without its critics. It is known, however, that the mammalian brain seems to possess an inborn organization within the limbic system that provides every individual with the *potential* to engage in destructive attacks no matter what was previously learned or experienced. Physiological studies of aggressive behavior have shown that "there is no one center for aggression in the human brain, but that there are a number of widely separated portions of the brain that can elicit fighting and destructive attacks" (Johnson, 1972, p. 75).

While Freud viewed aggression as a destructive drive, Lorenz saw it more as an adaptive instinct related to survival and existant to some extent in all members of the species. Lorenz's work, however, has been criticized for extrapolating behavior from lower animals directly to humans. Gorney (1972) wrote, "He [Lorenz] knows very well that one cannot even judge the behavior of geese by observing closely related ducks. Yet, employing a method he would reject as unscientific within his own area, without considering studies of man himself in the process, he extrapolates directly from fish and birds to man" (p. 108). It appears, then, that current advocates of the instinctual theory have not considered the research completed on human aggression, especially laboratory research. In an attempt to make the study of aggression relate more directly to the human species, the frustration-aggression hypothesis was formulated. This position integrated some of the drive concepts of the instinctual perspective with various learning principles known to influence human behavior.

The Frustration-Aggression Hypothesis

In 1939, Dollard and a group of Yale psychologists utilized Freud's instinctual theory as the basis of the now famous frustration-aggression hypothesis. This hypothesis simply stated that aggression results from frustration. A cathartic effect was seen as operative in this model if the aggressive behavior successfully reduced the frustration. However, the model also acknowledged that fear of punishment or its actual occurrence could lead to more frustration and hence heighten the need to aggress. The frustration-aggression blocked-frustration-aggression pattern

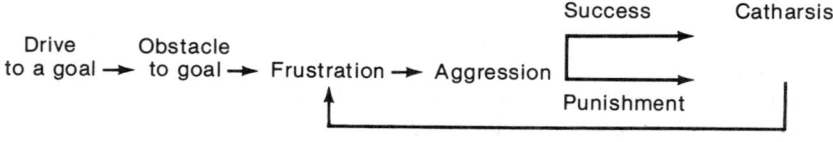

FIGURE 18-2   The frustration-aggression model.

became known as the circular effect because frustration and unsuccessful aggression usually led to more frustration and a heightened need to aggress. The Frustration-Aggression Model is illustrated in Figure 18-2.

Critics of the frustration-aggression hypothesis questioned whether all frustration caused aggression. Miller (1941), one of Dollard's associates, showed that not all frustration resulted in aggression, and that frustration was really an instigation or trigger cue to aggress and not necessarily the cause of aggression. He further noted that the relationship between frustration and aggression may not be instinctual as the early researchers believed but could be learned.

The major problem relating to the frustration-aggression hypothesis is one of definition. Is frustration interference with a goal response, task failure, lack of reinforcement, internal arousal, or continued failure resulting in low self-esteem? With the acceptance of learning as an intervening variable influencing the frustration-aggression relationship, frustration itself has become harder to define. Today the frustration-aggression hypothesis is of more interest as a historical document than a definitive statement about aggression. Yet, as a result of the research of Dollard, Doob, Miller, Mowrer, and Sears (1939), hundreds of studies have been completed that have enhanced the understanding of aggression; considerable contemporary theorizing on aggression is derived from this classical hypothesis.

It is also important to note that the frustration-aggression hypothesis and the instinctual perspective both have had an impact upon athletics. Many times we will hear people say that little can be done to change the violence in sport; "It's the nature of man" clearly reflects an instinctual view of aggressive behavior. Statements such as, "Let them get it out of their system" obviously show support for the idea of a catharsis being an outcome of aggressive behavior. Some league officials have gone to the extent of claiming that some violence is good if it is not allowed to build up and be manifested in an even more severe fashion. Others would argue, however, that fighting and slashing in ice hockey, spearing in football, and beanballs in baseball (common forms of violence) are severe enough! Adhering to theoretical propositions that have generated minimal experimental evidence supporting their position is all too common in contemporary sport. One paradigm recently developed that helps us best understand aggressive behavior is the social learning theory.

The Social Learning Theory

As described earlier in this chapter, the social learning theory evolved from the realization that the relationship between frustration and aggression was not necessarily an instinctual response but rather was influenced by learning.

Social learning theorists maintain that aggression is learned in social settings. Some support for this theory comes from the work of Bandura and his associates at Stanford University. Typically, these studies are based on children observing an adult exhibiting aggressive play with objects such as a bobo doll. The children are then given an opportunity to play with the toys themselves. Bandura and Huston (1961) showed that children "readily imitated aggressive behavior exhibited by a model in the presence of the model" (p. 316). Later, Bandura, Ross, and Ross (1961) found that children displayed aggressive behavior after being exposed to a film of a model's aggressive play and/or were allowed to play in a new setting with the model absent. These studies demonstrated that the children modeled the behavior they observed the adults being rewarded for exhibiting. Aggressive responses were being learned from simple observation. The parallel to sport is obvious; seeing aggressive behavior exhibited and rewarded in sport settings can lead to similar behavior being exhibited by the observer. In the chapter to follow, John Silva will extend this discussion of vicarious learning processes and how they operate in sport.

Another social learning theory is presented by Mosher (1965), who expanded Rotter's (1954) social learning theory. Mosher noted that aggressive behavior may lead to either positive reinforcements or to punishments, and the expectation that any particular reinforcing or punishing event will occur may vary depending on the individual's learning history. A modification of Mosher's Social Learning Model of Aggression is presented in the following:

$$\frac{SE_x\ Ra\ S_1\ +\ RVa\ +\ GE_{xa}}{SE_x\ Pá\ S_1\ +\ PVá\ +\ GE_{xá}}$$

This formulation is basically an approach-avoidance model with the variables above the equation facilitating aggression while those below the equation inhibit aggressive responses. Reading from left to right, the facilitators identify the situational expectancy (SE_x) that the aggressive behavior (x) will lead to positive reinforcement (Ra) in the present situation (S_1), plus the reinforcement value (RVa) of the positive reinforcement and the generalized expectancy (GE_{xa}) that aggressive behavior leads to rewards. These facilitators are weighed against the inhibitors identified on the bottom line of the equation. Reading from left to right, the inhibitors identify the situational expectancy (SE_x) that the aggressive behavior (x) will lead to punishment (Pá) in the present situation (S₁), plus the punishment value (PVá) of this punishment and the generalized expectancy (GE$_{x\acute{a}}$) that aggressive behavior leads to punishment or feelings of guilt. When the facilitators outweigh the inhibitors, aggressive behavior is most likely to occur.

Situational expectancies (SE$_x$) are educated guesses a person makes concerning the probability of a behavior leading to reinforcement or punishment. This probability is based on the peculiarities or uniqueness of the present situation.

Reinforcement/punishment value (RV$_a$/PV$_{\acute{a}}$) refers to the subjective importance attributed to the potential rewards and punishments one may receive as a function of exhibiting an aggressive act. These values are strongly influenced by what is deemed important by the group of which the aggressor is a member (the team, coach, management) and by significant others in the player's life (parents, peers, media).

Generalized expectancies (GE$_{xa}$/GE$_{x\acute{a}}$) are a reservoir of information built up over time. They refer to what has generally happened when one has exhibited aggressive behavior in a similar situation. As a function of sport socialization involving years of learning, generalized expectancies comprise a significant element that can function to either facilitate or inhibit aggressive behavior. There are two types of generalized expectancies, the first being that aggressive behavior is desirable, acceptable, and leads to positive reinforcement. This generalized expectancy obviously encourages aggressive behavior. The second generalized expectancy concerns external punishment or internal guilt over an aggressive behavior, and it serves to inhibit future aggressive behavior.

Generalized expectancies and reinforcement/punishment values are social-psychological factors that are taken into each situation as a function of past learning in similar situations. The situational expectancies, however, are processed repeatedly as social-environmental conditions modify. Apparently we learn early in life what behavior is acceptable and what is not acceptable by observing and modeling other children and adults. *Observation* and *experience* in various social settings gives us the "stop" and "go" signals that influence personal expectancies, the value of reinforcement, and the personal and social inhibitions (punishment, fear of punishment, or guilt) of the behavior.

Thus, each individual has a unique stop and go history based on his/her past experience in social environments including specific sport settings. Social learning theory would predict aggression to occur in sports where players' generalized expectancies for reward are high (e.g., praise from parents, coaches, peers) and where reward value outweighs punishment value (e.g., increased prestige, gaining a tactical or psychological advantage vs. a personal foul, a 15-yard penalty or a 5-minute penalty). Situational expectancies would indicate to the athlete whether this is a good time to exhibit the aggressive behavior. For example, aggressing against one of the physically larger and more notorious players in the league might not have a high situational expectancy for success! It is remarkable how extreme emotions such as aggressive outbursts can often come under cognitive control when the situational expectancy for punishment (especially physical punishment in the form of retaliation) is high. In the following section we will examine how the exhibition and observation of sport aggression influences the participant and the type of psychological responses to aggression that occur in the sport setting.

PARTICIPATION IN SPORT AND AGGRESSION

Sports offer an ideal area of life in which to study aggression. Psychologists, physical educators, and others have analyzed the aggressive behavior of athletes and sport spectators in order to better understand the effects of such activity upon participants. Some instinctive theorists believe that participation in sport provides a socially acceptable outlet for aggression without the accompanying feelings of guilt. If an athlete has a high drive to aggress, sport participation may lower that drive because the athlete is given the opportunity to aggress, especially in collision sports such as football and hockey and in pugilist sports such as boxing. Some have hypothesized that an athlete may escape the guilt feelings that result from violent expressions of aggression, providing that the athlete plays by the rules (Beisser, 1967; Husman, 1970). Does sport provide an opportunity for this kind of catharsis? Let's examine some research that has addressed this question.

Sport Aggression: Cathartic or Circular?

Martin (1976) administered the Rosenzweig Picture Frustration Study to 32 male basketball and wrestling athletes and found that following competition, the extrapunitive aggression of the athletes was significantly lower. His work supported similar research by Husman (1954), Johnson and Hutton (1955), Cory (1968), and Smolev (1976), whose findings also demonstrated a catharsis as a result of competition. The evidence for catharsis, however, has been contradicted by other research. The work of Stone (1950), Ryan (1970), Zillman, Katcher, and Milavsky (1972), and many laboratory studies show that the expression of successful aggression leads to an increase in aggression. This work would support the contention that aggression successfully exhibited in sport can lead to more aggression (a circular effect). This effect could explain the motivation to be aggressive at the level of or beyond the "stop" signal, since the reward for violent play is often higher than the penalty for such an act. Additionally, the coach, team owner, and/or spectators reward the athlete for rule violations and/or violent play in which the opposing player is "taken out," that is, injured and/or goaded to fight so as to be penalized.

Silva (1981) noted the existence of three important variables that influence the exhibition of rule violating behavior in sports: constitutive rules, normative rules, and reinforcement structures. "Constitutive rules are the formal rules of sport, normative rules are rules of consensus or behavior legitamized by peer decree" (Silva, 1981, pp. 11-12). Intentional violation of the rules to gain a tactical advantage, such as an intentional foul to prevent a lay-up in basketball or intentional flagrant play, becomes normative because the penalty for such behaviors is insufficient. Silva (1981) contends that a more severe penalty for rule violations (i.e., modifying the reinforcement/punishment structure) must be used to deter aggression in sport. Social learning theorists believe that reinforcement value and punishment value are major influences in selecting an aggressive behavior and that since many of the violent acts exhibited are considered part of the game (normative) players experience no guilt for such action. This hypothesis was supported in a field experiment by Silva (1979b) in which it was demonstrated that athletes could not distinguish assertive from aggressive behavior in a basketball sport setting. He concluded that aggression is potentially legitimized by an active socialization process. The role of socialization toward deviance is reviewed comprehensively by Silva in the following chapter.

Observing Violent Sports and Aggression

How does watching violent sports affect aggressive behavior? The research studies of Kingsmore (1968), Turner (1968), J. Roberts (1972), Goldstein and Arms (1971), and Arms, Russell, and Sandilands (1979) demonstrate conflicting results. The research of Kingsmore and Roberts, using projective tests, show a decrease (catharsis) in aggression as a result of watching basketball and wrestling. But Turner, also using projective protocols for football, basketball, and wrestling spectators, found an increase in aggression. Goldstein and Arms (1971) studied the effects of observing athletic contests on hostility. Spectators were interviewed before and after the Army-Navy football game in 1969 and the Army-Temple gymnastics meet (the control) which was held during the same month as the football game. The results indicated that the subjects at the football game had a significant increase in hostility as a result of watching the contest regardless of what team they supported, while the subjects' prehostility measures at the gymnastics meet did not differ significantly from their posthostility scores (Goldstein & Arms, 1971).

Arms, Russell, and Sandilands (1979) repeated the Goldstein and Arms study described above, except that they used the sports of ice hockey, professional wrestling, and swimming. Their results supported the findings of Goldstein and Arms (1971) in that there was a significant increase in expressed hostility as a result of observing the professional wrestling and ice hockey events, but no significant increase in hostility for the swimming spectators. Apparently the nature of the sport being observed has a significant influence upon the feelings of the observer. Collision and contact sports seem to increase hostile feelings in observers rather than create a cathartic effect. Competitive but noncontact/collision sports such as swimming and gymnastics do not appear to invoke hostility or a catharsis in the observer. The earlier studies that used projective techniques and found a cathartic effect could have possibly been plagued by the interpretation problems often inherent in the use of projective techniques.

CONCLUSIONS

The problems that have plagued aggression research are numerous but relate principally to (a) the definition of aggression and the determination of the intent to injure, and (b) the environment within which the research is conducted.

The term aggression has been defined too broadly to include concepts such as the "bold and energetic pursuit of one's goals." This has permitted some researchers to infer that the motivational drive to survive or excel is aggression. Since animals demonstrate survival behavior, researchers have studied the agonistic behavior of animals, comparing their behavior to that of human beings. Yet, it is commonly understood that there are major differences between humans and other animals. Many animals gain status by their size, strength, or their natural weapons, while human status is often determined by additional factors such as intelligence, wealth, education, and ability to manipulate or coerce others. Thus, sweeping generalizations from lower animal research to humans should be viewed with caution.

An additional problem clearly relates to how one determines the intent to aggress. Is a forceful tackle on a quarterback intended to injure or is it just hard, assertive play? Only the tackler knows. But researchers, for the most part, are determining the underlying intent of the subject when they classify all forceful behaviors as aggressive. When each investigator uses his/her own criteria for identifying aggressive behaviors, his/her own values are interjected into the research and little consistency is achieved from study to study. The definition of aggression will continue to plague researchers until the intent and value system of the subject can be accurately determined and the semantic confusion over assertive behavior and aggression is addressed by sport researchers.

Another area that has plagued aggression research relates to the environment in which the research is conducted. Field research is more difficult to control, but it provides more realistic situations for analyzing aggressive behavior. When research on aggression is conducted in the artificial environment of the laboratory, apparently something in that environment removes the inhibition to aggress or informs the subject that it is all right to exhibit aggression "for the purposes of this study." Most laboratory researchers, for example, tell the subject that it is all right to shock ("aggress"). The subjects are in effect instructed to shock! Few if any studies have given the subject the option not to shock, that is, not to aggress. Future laboratory research must create a more natural environment so that any inhibition to aggress that the subject has is not removed. Future field research must be theoretically structured and the variables controlled in such a manner that it becomes possible to repeat the research study and compare results.

The chapters that follow should provide an indication that progress can and is being made in this difficult yet intriguing area of study in the psychology of sport.

Chapter 19

Factors Related to the Acquisition and Exhibition of Aggressive Sport Behavior

John M. Silva III
University of North Carolina-Chapel Hill

In Chapter 18 it was pointed out that the term *aggression* is often misused to label various behaviors in competitive sport situations. Any spectator who views sporting events on television will hear sportscasters repeatedly use the terms "aggressive" and "aggression" when describing player behavior in activities as diverse as auto racing, football, basketball, tennis, and baseball. The common misuse and misunderstanding of the term aggression relates to a larger and significant problem in sport: the acquisition and exhibition of aggressive behavior by participants. This chapter will review three major factors that facilitate the acquisition and exhibition of aggressive behavior in sport. These factors include (a) the inaccurate use of the term aggression, which fails to distinguish between appropriate and inappropriate player behavior and thus contributes to a permissive atmosphere that views aggression as part of the game; (b) the socialization of sport participants toward exhibiting behaviors that are essentially sanctioned deviance; and (c) the reinforcement of aggression by social-psychological sources that sustain this behavior in sport activities.

LEGITIMIZING AGGRESSIVE SPORT BEHAVIOR

By labeling desirable competitive behaviors as aggression, various undesirable behaviors also labeled aggression receive a connotation of legitimacy. This problem is significant because the aggression that participants in various sports exhibit is not limited simply to other participants but is sometimes directed toward game officials, referees, umpires, spectators, and even police officers assigned to control conduct at the sporting event (Calabria, 1980; Falls & Surface, 1976; Soccer Referee Dead, 1978). This type of behavior often disrupts the sporting event, damages property, and causes serious injury. In addition, such behavior distorts the sport form to such a degree that the game's eventual outcome may be decided by rule-violating behavior (such as aggression) rather than by the exhibition of legitimate skills inherent in the sport.

How can such a state of affairs exist in sport? Sports are supposedly designed to ensure fair play and provide a healthy opportunity for competition between individuals or groups. What complex processes legitimize behavior that essentially involves the intent to injure? One powerful contributor to this legitimization process is language, which can be used to create an atmosphere of permissiveness regarding aggression in sport.

Linguistics and Legitimacy

Language can contribute to the disinhibition of aggression by blurring the distinction between acceptable and unacceptable sport behavior. For instance, players and coaches tell each other what behaviors are *expected* in various sport situations. Professional athletes in various sports (noncontact, contact, collision) often say they "have to be aggressive to win." The relationship between aggression and performance will be examined by Neil Widmeyer in Chapter 20, but the point here is that athletes often use this phrase to explain both performance outcome and the questionable behavior they exhibit to achieve the desired outcome. For example, aggression is often implied as being necessary to win (a desired outcome) while the lack of aggression is often related to losing. Furthermore, many players will justify rule-violating behaviors such as spearing and clotheslining in football and fighting in ice hockey as intimidating techniques available to them for facilitating team success.

A statement by Maurice Lucas, a professional basketball player, exemplifies this point well. Questioned about his aggressive play, Lucas responded:

> My fights come because I play so physical. Guys don't like it and become highly upset. But I play clean physical. Never hit anybody in the face. I keep my blows between the neck and the belly button. (Papanek, 1977, p. 44)

Clearly, Lucas was not apologizing for his aggressive rule-violating behavior! His statement that delivering blows between the neck and belly button in *basketball* is "clean physical" indicates how language can be effectively used to legitimize (to oneself and others) inappropriate behavior.

In Bandura's (1973) classic text on aggressive behavior, several forms of verbal self-reinforcement were identified as potent sources of justification for aggressive acts. The Lucas quote demonstrates two types of self-reward that tend to legitimize aggressive acts in sport,

The first form of self-reward is through a moral justification of the questionable behavior. "Clean physical" morally justifies the behavior to the player. Surely it is important to play clean and to play physical in basketball. Because the illegal blows are described as clean physical play, the behavior takes on a connotation of appropriateness. The association of acceptable behavior (clean physical play) with unacceptable behavior (blows between the neck and belly) effectively blurs the discrimination between legitimate versus illegitimate action. By labeling the acts as morally justifiable, the player removes the burden of guilt from the behavior. The second form of self-reinforcement in Lucas' statement is called misrepresentation of the behavior's consequences. The player implicitly assumes that hitting in the face is bad but hitting between the neck and the belly button is acceptable. Both behaviors are inappropriate in basketball; the degree of discomfort for the player receiving the blows should not be the criteria used to determine the appropriateness of the act! Defining the behavior as clean physical misrepresents the nature of the act within the context of basketball.

Bandura (1973) describes several other forms of verbal self-reinforcement that players often use in trying to convince themselves and others that their aggressive action is legitimate. Slighting comparisons (what I do is nowhere near as bad as what most players do), dehumanization of the victim, and attributing blame to the victim are common forms of verbal self-reinforcement that serve to legitimize unacceptable behavior in sport.

Removing Internal Constraints

The linguistic process is but one form of legitimization in the sport setting. Some players may feel guilty about exhibiting a group-sanctioned behavior, such as aggression, that violates their own personal value system. Bandura (1973) and Mosher (1965) both have emphasized that guilt, the expectancy for self-mediated punishment for acts deemed improper or wrong, can inhibit aggressive behavior. However, Fishbein and Ajzen (1973) have noted that guilt is a *learned* moral judgment influenced by the *environmental situation* as well as personal learning histories. As a potential inhibitor of aggressive behavior, then, guilt is characterized by being situation-specific. In addition, because guilt is a learned moral judgment it can be modified through subsequent learning experiences. Considering that a substantial amount of aggressive sport behavior is expected, the ability of a personal moral code to prevent an individual from exhibiting aggressive behavior in sport would seem to be limited.

Silva (1979b) tested the hypothesis that guilt over aggressive behavior in sport would be low and thus ineffective in inhibiting aggressive acts. This hypothesis was developed because situational and generalized expectancies for realistic punishment in response to aggressive behavior in sport tend to be low. Traditionally, players have not incurred significant negative sanctions for aggressive sport behavior. Incurring a personal foul or penalty time for a potentially dangerous and injurious act seldom outweighs the positive gains that can be achieved for a team. Removing a starting player, intimidating a highly skilled player, or taking a better player off the field, ice, or court can all result in a "net gain" for the aggressor. Such a permissive atmosphere toward sport aggression serves to either lower one's personal constraints against aggression or increase the perception of acceptability in sport settings. Both responses would weaken the ability of guilt to mediate aggressive behavior.

The results of the Silva (1979b) study found that basketball players who exhibited physical and/or verbal aggression against their opponent(s) experienced significantly less guilt than did subjects who exhibited similar aggressive acts in a competitive nonsport setting. Players in the sport situation indicated in a postexperimental manipulation check questionnaire that their aggressive behavior in the sport was not anything to be ashamed of and that it was actually "something you come to expect to take as well as give." Players in the nonsport competitive situation, however, did not demonstrate the same aura of legitimacy about their aggressive acts. Apparently, when engaging in a sport such as basketball, internal constraint against exhibiting aggressive behavior is to some degree nonexistent. Consistent with this notion, Brown and Davies (1978) have reported attitudinal data which indicated that members of male contact sport teams scored higher on an attitude toward violence scale than did male members of noncontact sports or male nonathletes. The attitude toward violence scale poses various questions about a subject's willingness to use aggressive behavior to solve situations that arise in sport competition.

In a follow-up study, Brown (1982) found a similar result in research on the legitimacy of aggressive sport behavior with male and female college students ($N > 1300$). Brown's work revealed that males scored significantly higher, indicating more willingness to use aggression, than did females on the questionnaire. However, both males and females who participated often in contact sports were more willing to use aggression in sports than were subjects who rarely participated in contact sports. Again, the internal constraints against aggressive behavior in sport appear to be low, and frequent participation in contact sports seems to maintain or even reduce any inhibitions against aggression in sport.

The use of linguistics to legitimize aggression in sport and the removal of internal prohibitions against it connote that a social learning process influences the acquisition of aggressive sport behavior both before and during sport involvement. The next section will examine how the sport socialization process contributes to the learning of aggressive and rule-violating behavior.

SOCIALIZATION TOWARD DEVIANCE

Aggressive behavior is but one form of social deviance that can be exhibited in sport. Another common form of deviance is violating the rules to gain an advantage. Some consider this to be good play while others consider it cheating or noncontesting behavior (Fraleigh, 1979). By carefully examining the social and psychological structure in which sport socialization occurs, we can begin to understand how various factors encourage aggressive behavior in sport.

Because each sport is a unique and complex social situation, its formal rules define and differentiate the behaviors that are acceptable or unacceptable in that particular event. The activities deemed appropriate in tennis vary considerably from those formally defined as acceptable in ice hockey. As mentioned in the previous chapter, a considerable amount of learning specific to sport involvement occurs through years of participation (direct experience) and structured observation (modeling). As part of this learning process, athletes learn two rule systems that influence their behavior in the sport setting.

The constitutive rule structure formally defines in advance the means allowed or prohibited for achieving various goals in a sport contest. Constitutive rules also control several other institutional functions of a sport form such as penalty systems and the means for evaluating the terminal outcome of an event. The major functions of sport rules have been reviewed in a previous article by Silva (1981). What is important to note here is that constitutive rules are the formal guidelines that contestants mutually agree to play by, and that without this mutual consent to abide by a constitutive rule structure no sport contest could occur. Learning to play by the rules is an important aspect of the sport socialization process and is essentially a prerequisite for participating in formal sport at any level.

While learning the formal rules of various sports, participants also learn the unwritten rules of a sport. This second major system of behavior guidance in sport is called the normative rule structure. These rules, which are group-sanctioned behaviors, often conflict directly with constitutive rules. They are called normative rules because they reflect the value system of individuals participating in the sport. Thus, it is expected that normative rules will be followed even if such behavior violates the written or constitutive rules. Normative rules exist because certain violations can result in an advantage that surpasses any disadvantage administered for breaking the constitutive rule system. The normative rule system is extremely influential in guiding player behavior.

McMurtry (1974) conducted a study sponsored by the Canadian government and found that individuals who repeatedly failed to comply to normative rules pertaining to aggression in ice hockey were often negatively labeled and sometimes ostracized from the team. An event during the 1981-1982 National Hockey League (NHL) ice hockey season demonstrates McMurtry's observations. A player on the Los Angeles team refused to go out on the ice and participate in a brawl. The coach objected to such nonnormative behavior and suspended the athlete. When the athlete objected, he was put on waivers. No other team in the entire NHL was interested in acquiring that player! It was a powerful demonstration of the sanctions a player can receive for not following normative rules.

This attitude of normative acceptance of aggression is clearly personified by the comments of John Ziegler, the current NHL president: "If we can talk about good violence versus bad violence, acceptable versus unacceptable, then we can have a meaningful discussion" (Mifflin, 1974). This attitude is actually quite prevalent and is by no means limited to professionals. Similar attitudes have also been found among youth participants. Vaz (1972) and M. Smith (1980) have noted that the socialization for aggressive behavior occurs at an early age. Vaz found that young hockey players did not determine the appropriateness of a behavior according to whether it violated formal rules. In their view, good penalties gained an advantage for the team while bad penalties resulted in an advantage for the opposition. Little consideration was given to the nature of the act. An aggressive behavior was good or bad based upon the consequences of the action rather than the nature of the act itself. Smith's (1980) article also supports the notion that socialization plays a major role in the *learning* of aggression at youth sport levels. Young participants in the Smith study indicated that they learned "how to trip properly," and how to "hit weak points with the stick, say the back of the legs." Moreover, 58% of the players at the *youngest* competitive level felt their teammates approved of fighting in ice hockey, and 63% of the players believed their teammates approved of fighting at the Midget level; the "approval" figure jumped to 84% at the Provincial Junior A level of competition. Obviously, players in the Smith study are internalizing a standard that accepts aggression, a rule-violating behavior, as an instrumental part of playing their sport.

Silva (1983) attempted to test the hypothesis that social psychological variables such as the competitive level of play influence the perceived legitimacy of rule-violating behavior. Male and female subjects were shown a series of eight slides; seven clearly depicted rule-violating sport behavior. Subjects were categorized according to (a) gender, (b) nature of sport participation (none, noncontact, contact, collision, combination), (c) highest level of organized sport participation (none, youth, high school, college), and (d) years of participation in organized sport (none, 1-5, 6-10, 11-above).

It was hypothesized that males would have significantly higher legitimacy scores than females and that the three remaining categorical variables would be positively related to increases in perceived legitimacy for both genders. Thus, if the socialization of males emphasized the legitimacy of rule-violating behavior to a greater extent than the socialization of females, the first hypothesis should be confirmed. Additionally, if playing sports longer, at higher levels (e.g., college), and playing contact and collision sports facilitate the perception of legitimacy for both males and females, the remaining hypotheses should be confirmed.

The results of this study found that, indeed, males scored significantly higher on perceived legitimacy than did females. Playing sports longer, at higher levels, and playing contact-collision sports all resulted in higher legitimacy scores for males. The results for females, however, were not best represented by these simple linear trends. The data for females clearly indicated that they did not approve of the rule-violating behavior displayed. Female nonparticipants and females who participated in a combination of contact-collision sports, however, had slightly elevated legitimacy scores. A similar result was found for females as a function of years participation and the highest level of competition. That is, female nonparticipants and those who had participated in organized sports for 11 years or more, or at the collegiate level, had slightly elevated perceived legitimacy scores. However, at no time did the scores of the female subjects indicate that they perceived the rule violating behaviors as legitimate. Thus, the legitimacy of unacceptable behavior in sport is socialized more strongly in male sport participants, with a similar trend occurring in female participants only at the higher levels of competition or in participants involved in a combination of contact-collision sports. As female sports continue to become more institutionalized, it will be interesting to observe if any concomitant increases occur in the perceived legitimacy of unacceptable sport behavior.

Chapter 20 by Widmeyer will suggest that male athletes appear to have considerable incentive to aggress because these behaviors are often taught as viable techniques that enhance the opportunity for success. The research reviewed in this section by Silva (1979b, 1981, 1983) Smith (1979, 1980) and Vaz (1972) strongly suggests that important agents of socialization such as coaches, parents, and peers are instrumental in determining the degree of legitimacy granted to aggressive and rule-violating behavior. Obviously, these same agents of socialization will provide models of behavior for future generations of sport participants. If the aggressive model is promoted and institutionalized, violence in sport may not only continue but could spread to expanding female sport programs.

This section has highlighted the importance of the social learning process in the athletes' acquisition of aggression. The socialization process was illustrated as a major means through which participants learn to exhibit aggressive and rule-violating behavior. Once these behaviors are learned, however, it takes an additional system to sustain the behaviors. That is, a reinforcement structure must directly or indirectly support the rule-violating behavior in order for it to be maintained. In the final section, both vicarious and direct reinforcers of rule-violating sport behavior will be reviewed and their impact upon the maintenance of sport aggression will be discussed.

REINFORCEMENT OF AGGRESSIVE BEHAVIOR

The previous two sections of this chapter focused upon how aggressive and rule-violating behavior is learned in sport. However, as Bandura (1965) demonstrated in his classic study on no-trial learning (also called vicarious learning or modeling) there are important distinctions between *learning* a behavior and *performing* a behavior. The present section will review the factors that serve to maintain the performance of aggressive responses in sport. Without a powerful reinforcement structure to facilitate aggressive sport behavior, there would be little chance for aggression to acquire the normative status it is often given in many sports.

The facilitation and maintenance of aggression in sport depends upon the conditions prior to the act as well as the consequences of the action to the performer. The two major forms of reinforcement that promote and maintain aggressive behavior in sport are vicarious reinforcement and direct external reinforcement.

Vicarious Reinforcement and Modeling

Vicarious reinforcement refers to the tendency to repeat behaviors that we observe others rewarded for performing. Vicarious punishment works in much the same way. That is, we are less likely to perform a behavior that we have seen another individual being punished for doing. Thus, vicarious learning serves a valuable informative function. Bandura

(1973) has noted that several factors influence the acquisition of behavior via vicarious processes. These include (a) the characteristics of the performer, (b) the value of the observed reward or the intensity of the observed punishment, (c) the similarity of the observed setting to the potential performance setting, and (d) the status of the model.

Generally, the more similarity between the model and the observer, the more likely that the observed behavior-outcome chain will have meaning for the observer. Observation of the behavior-outcome response chain of another child's actions may be more meaningful information to a younger observer (because of model similarity) than the observation of an adult's action. Furthermore, the more valuable the reward to the model, the more likely that the behavior will be repeated by the observer. The same principle holds for observed punishment. Intense punishment administered to the performer will lower the probability of the behavior being repeated by the observer. The third factor mentioned above relates to similarity of the environment or social setting. The observed behavior and its consequences will have higher transfer when there is similarity between the environment in which the behavior was observed and the environment in which the observer will eventually perform.

The status of the model is the final factor identified as influential in the vicarious learning process. Bandura (1973) cites several studies demonstrating that models with high social status elicit imitative behavior by observers. Many young athletes admire superstars that someday they want to emulate. The behaviors of those athletes held in high esteem are often imitated in very exacting detail by aspiring major leaguers. Modeling or vicarious learning is an extremely effective method by which sport participants learn behavior, including aggressive behavior.

In order for vicarious learning to occur, however, additional factors must function. For example, the observer must be able to recall in proper sequence the behaviors observed in order to perform them. Observing a complex gymnastics move that receives high scores and praise does not of itself mean that the observer can now perform the desired behavior correctly. All the component parts must be sequenced together correctly. *Recall proper* is extremely important for the correct exhibition of an observed behavior. Yet, even with recall proper the observer must have the ability to reproduce the behavior. Simply having a symbolic representation of the proper sequence of an observed action does not assure correct performance of the behavior. If the required ability is not developed in the observer, the correct performance of the observed action will be delayed.

When applying this information to the vicarious learning of aggressive behavior in sport, it becomes evident that observational learning is a powerful reinforcer. Many athletes observe peers, esteemed idols, and even professional coaches displaying rule-violating behavior that frequently includes aggressive outbursts. This behavior is often rewarded by peer approval (verbal and nonverbal), encouragement from the media and fans, or the gaining of a tactical advantage through transgression. According to Bandura (1973), observed reward has incentive-motivational effects. He states,

> Seeing others positively reinforced can serve as a motivator by arousing in observers expectations that they will be similarly rewarded for analogous performances. Given appropriate reinforcement systems, people can be as much inspired by observed social acclaim and tangible benefits to aggress as to excel in athletic, artistic or academic pursuits. (p. 206)

Thus, seeing role models display aggressive behavior for which they receive reward or minimal punishment can instill a desire in the observer to "play like that" or "be tough like him." Rewarding aggressive behavior, or failing to adequately deter it, not only maintains the behavior in the performer but can encourage the development and exhibition of similar behaviors by observers of the act. This may be especially unfortunate for young, impressionable athletes who carefully monitor and observe the actions of their favorite teams and players. Russell (1979), for example, conducted an extremely interesting study in this area and found that "hero selection" by young Canadian ice hockey players was influenced to a considerable degree by the model's degree of aggression. Russell found that aggressive players in the National Hockey League often received considerable media exposure and that player popularity was strongly related to the interaction between aggression and media exposure. Additionally, aggression appeared to be an important element that influenced the selection of a favorite NHL team by the youths studied. Thus, both individual "heroes" and favorite teams were selected partly through the observation of aggressive behavior which, as previously established, is considered normative in many sports.

Clearly, the action of others can influence the learning and reinforcement of aggressive behavior in sport. In addition to this powerful support system, we must consider the potential effects of direct external reward upon the maintenance of aggression in sport.

Direct External Reward

It is always possible that an athlete using aggression will incur physical punishment through retaliation by the victim. Inherent in the use of aggression is the desire to avoid or minimize aversive effects to oneself. In effect, then, one wishes to behave aggressively yet at the same time be aware of the risk involved. Thus, reinforcement of aggressive behavior regardless of whether the aggressor is injured often plays a pivotal role in sustaining behavior. In ice hockey, for example, a player may lose an altercation that he initiated with an opponent, yet be congratulated by his teammates and cheered by the home crowd as he skates to the penalty box. Even when an aggressor has been defeated, his/her aggressive efforts are often rewarded by meaningful figures such as teammates, coaches, or parents. The forms of external reward that Bandura (1973) identifies are functional in many sports including (a) tangible reward, (b) status rewards, (c) expression of injury, and (d) alleviation of aversive treatment.

Tangible Reward.   Aggressive behavior in sport often leads to tangible reward, which may take the form of gaining a tactical advantage for one's team or intimidating an opponent, an official, or even one's own teammates. In professional sport a further tangible reward is monetary gain. It is unlikely that aggressive behavior in sport is continually reinforced through tangible rewards. Rather, the reinforcement is most likely on an intermittent type of schedule that Walters and Brown (1963) have found best maintains aggressive behavior in young boys. The intermittent tangible rewards given in sport for aggressive behavior also appear to have functional value for the aggressor. Gaining an advantage, intimidation, and the other forms of tangible reward would certainly appear to have what Rotter has defined as reinforcement value (Rotter, Chance, & Phares, 1972). Combining the intermittent reward schedule with rewards that are both functional and meaningful to the aggressor appears to make the reception of tangible rewards a powerful reinforcer of aggressive sport behavior.

Status Rewards.   Previously we discussed the normative expectancy to exhibit aggression in particular sports. In order for players to gain or maintain status, they must often fulfill normative role expectancies. In some sports such as football, hockey, and even basketball, this often means establishing oneself in the league through various forms of aggressive behavior. A substantial body of research has demonstrated that verbal praise from significant others enhances status and serves to maintain aggressive behavior (e.g., Parke, Ewall, & Slaby, 1972). Reward for aggressive sport behavior by parents, teammates, and coaches has been well documented by Smith (1979) concerning ice hockey. Observations of several other contact and collision sports tend to indicate that status rewards function in these sports also. The acquisition of nicknames such as "The Assassin," "Enforcer," and "Policeman" often connote a special status awarded to a player because of his/her style of play.

Expression of Injury.   Injury infliction in some situations may inhibit further aggression while in other settings it may increase aggression due to a need to retaliate. Some psychologists have argued that pain expressions have reward value in that they often establish or restore self-esteem in the aggressor. In sport, aggression by one individual or team often results in retaliation by the offended team. Play gets more intense as a batter is hit by a pitch and subsequent brush back pitches are thrown by the opposition. However, little if any data exists concerning whether injury infliction reinforces aggressive sport behavior. Identifying the primary intent of an aggressive act may help future researchers separate instrumental components (injury infliction to gain an advantage) from hostile components (injury infliction that is personally oriented). Knowing the aggressor's motive structure can often assist in modifying the behavior. The instrumental aggressor may have an acceptable goal (to win or to gain an advantage) but selects inappropriate behavior (aggression) to achieve that goal. The hostile aggressor has an unacceptable goal (to hurt) and selects an inappropriate behavior (aggression). Because both instrumental and hostile aggression involve the intent to injure, neither is a desirable behavior to teach or exhibit in sport.

Alleviation of Aversive Treatment.   Aggressive behavior that results in the alleviation of aversive treatment is self-reinforced behavior. This type of "defensive aggression" not only stops the aversive treatment but may also reduce the occurrence of further aversive treatment. Failure to be aggressive or forceful can lead to loss of self-esteem, victimization, and loss of status in some sport settings. In many sports an athlete is expected to behave aggressively in order to stop aggression directed toward him/her. An eye for an eye, or counter-attack mentality, appears to be prevalent in many team sport settings. This type of a response not only alleviates aversive treatment but it may also gain an advantage for a team by establishing a style of play. While other response options are available to an athlete, teammates expect that the athlete will not back down. Thus, an aggressive counter-response is often elicited.

SUMMARY

The social learning process cannot be underestimated when assessing how aggression in sport is acquired, exhibited, or maintained. This chapter has described legitimization and socialization processes that elicit aggression in sport, as well as how this aggression becomes reinforced and maintained. Since the intent to inflict injury is not implicit in most sports, the athletes, coaches, and teachers must question whether this type of behavior can realistically be justified. It is interesting that while many athletes will resort to aggressive behavior in sport, few appreciate being aggressed against. Perhaps in the future our athletes, coaches, and teachers will be better able to distinguish intense, assertive play from aggression in sport. A critical examination of the reinforcement-punishment structures of some sports would indicate that they do not deter acts of violence even though they have formal rules against such behavior. If sports are to become less violent in the future, the administrators, coaches, and officials must remove the loopholes in rule structures that encourage sanctioned deviance. Some positive advances have been made in this area by collegiate ice hockey conferences. Other sports can surely follow their lead.

Chapter 20

Aggression-Performance Relationships in Sport

W. Neil Widmeyer
University of Waterloo

A well brought up boy in our society is taught that he must be aggressive in order to succeed in life. Whether his adult models are salesmen or statesmen, he learns that aggressiveness is a good thing and leads to success. (Scott, 1975, p. 99)

Introduction to Aggression-Performance Relationships

The idea that aggression and performance are thought to be positively related in sport settings is not surprising. The most frequently examined outcome of involvement in sport has been performance, referred to as effectiveness, success, or performance outcome. Also there has been increasing concern that incidents of behavior labeled as aggressive or violent are escalating in sport (Keefe, 1981; Thirer, 1981).

Although there is no universally accepted definition of aggression, most social scientists would agree that aggressive behavior is behavior designed to harm others. It can take physical and verbal forms and can be aimed at physically weakening (i.e., injuring) and/or psychologically harming (i.e., intimidating) another. In contact sports, certain high energy acts such as blocking in American football, tackling in soccer, and body checking in ice hockey appear to be aggressive but are not necessarily so if they do not involve the intent to harm. This chapter will not elaborate upon the distinctions of assertive and aggressive behavior because the previous chapter by Silva does this clearly. Rather, this chapter will focus on aggressive behavior, that is, physical and verbal acts designed to harm an opponent physically and/or psychologically, and its relationship to performance outcome in sport.

Determining how aggression and performance are related in sport involves answering two separate but related questions: Does aggression influence performance in sport? And does performance influence aggressive behavior in sport? Often those with a vested interest in the outcome of sport contests pose the first question, while those who are concerned about the quality of sport experiences raise the second question. Each question is associated with opinion, theory, and empirical research. The purpose of the following review of opinions, theories, and research is to find answers to these two basic questions.

AGGRESSION-PERFORMANCE RELATIONSHIPS: OPINIONS

The Influence of Aggression on Performance

Fans, coaches, and players all seem to believe that aggression has a positive influence on performance and outcome. Highlighted below are their viewpoints.

The fans' view has not been collected in any systematic fashion. However, the feelings of this group have often been portrayed on film, reported in the press, and related in popular literature. Regardless of the context, the urging to "kill da bum," and the excuse "we got pushed around" suggest that fans believe that aggression is *a* (if not *the*) way to succeed in a wide variety of sports.

The coaches' view seems to be that "You can't beat them on the ice if you can't beat them in the alley." The pervasiveness of this belief among the management community of the National Hockey League (NHL) is evidenced by each team's acquisition of "policemen" who "control what's going on out there." Enforcers are vital in basketball, according to former coach Pete Newell, who goes on to say that "They are a part of the game by whatever name you call them" (Papanek, 1977). Coaches in contact sports such as lacrosse, football, and ice hockey sometimes actually teach ways to hurt the opponents because they see intimidation by violence, or the threat of it, as an aid to winning (see Smith, 1975).

The players' view often appears to mirror those of the fans and coaches. For example, former football safety Jack Tatum, known as "the assassin," believed that he had to "punish" the man he was going after on every play if he and his team were to succeed. Former professional basketball player Kermit Washington said that getting "mean" helped him establish himself to keep from getting "pushed around," and therefore he was able to "survive" in his sport (Papanek, 1977). In a case study based on interviews with the 38 members of two American Hockey League teams, Faulkner (1974) discovered that players believed that when they instigated or reacted with aggression they received attention, "enhanced face," and the respect and trust of their teammates. Their responses indicate that they also believed that aggression can be a way to gain task success. For example, one player said that he "raps" opponents in the mouth with his elbow when they come in the corners so that they won't come into the corners so hard later in the game. Another player indicated how aggression can throw the opponent off his game. He said, "If you get a chance put them into the boards so that next time, they'll decide to shoot it instead of trying to go around you" (Faulkner, p. 298).

Among the 704 youths interviewed by Smith (1978), almost half of them said they felt that a player "who gets paid to beat up the other guys" probably does help his team to win. The fact that support for this "goon hockey" was more prevalent among the older and better players suggests that this belief was learned through hockey rather than brought to it. Pilz and LeFebvre (1981) cite an example of how players in yet another sport demonstrate their belief in the adage "aggression pays." They say, "During one of the first attacks in a handball game, an offensive player violently throws the ball towards the face of the defending goal keeper. The rationale behind this attack is an intimidation of the goal keeper in order to decrease the latter's self-confidence" (p. 246).

With fans, coaches, and players of the opinion that aggression leads to success, it is no wonder that aggressive behavior is encouraged, taught, and manifested in sport.

The Influence of Performance On Aggression

Very rarely have fans, coaches, or players expressed an opinion on the effect that performance has on aggression. No doubt their overriding concern with improving performance leaves them little time to worry about the development of aggression. Nevertheless, sometimes opinions about this relationship have been expressed through excuses such as "Our guys were so (bleep bleep) upset that we weren't beating them at basketball that we went out there to beat them with our elbows and fists."

AGGRESSION-PERFORMANCE RELATIONSHIPS: THEORIES

In a speculative analysis of aggression-performance relationships, Buss (1971) states,

> Whenever there is competition for rewards, and this is frequent, a variety of non-aggressive responses *might* achieve the rewards. Nevertheless, it is the most powerful aggressor who will surely achieve the rewards. (p. 11)

Unfortunately, Buss does not give evidence to demonstrate that aggression does pay, nor does he provide a theoretical explanation as to why aggression should pay. It will be instructive to look at some potential explanations for the hypothesized relationship between aggression and performance.

The Influence of Aggression on Performance: Theories

Why should aggression influence performance? A theory of performance outcome is one place to look for an answer. The performance outcome of an individual or a team in a competitive situation depends not only upon their own performance but also upon the performance of their opponent. Steiner (1972) states that group input (resources brought to the group, e.g., abilities and motives) and group process (what occurs within the group, e.g., leadership and cohesion) determine group performance, whereas individual performance depends only on individual input. Thus, a team's performance outcome could be altered by changing the team's input, the team's process, the opposing team's input, or the opposing team's process. Individual performance outcome could be changed by altering individual input or the input of the opponent. For example, aggression could have a positive influence on the performance outcome of an individual or team if the aggressive behavior harmed the opposition either physically (e.g., injuring their star quarterback) or psychologically (e.g., intimidating their batters with "bean balls"), thereby weakening their resources (i.e., input). Aggression could also improve a team's performance outcome by improving the process of that group.

Faulkner (1974) supports this notion when he states that violence can "strengthen existing bonds and establish new ones among players as they deal with their adversaries" (p. 302). Faulkner also suggests that a group's aggressive behavior can help its performance outcome by weakening the opposition's "unity bonds of collective strength" and reducing their "sense of control of the opposition" (p. 296).

Conversely, aggression could have a negative influence on the performance outcome of a team or an individual if their inputs were weakened because of penalties that they received. Likewise, group cohesion (a process variable) may be lowered on an aggressive team if some players are forced to work harder and have their chances for success decreased because their aggressive teammates have been penalized. Steiner's theory of performance outcome does not predict which influence (i.e., positive, negative, both, or neither) aggression will have on performance outcome. Instead it explains how aggression could bring about each of these influences.

The Influence of Performance on Aggression: Theories

The Frustration-Aggression Hypothesis. This frustration-aggression hypothesis explains how performance can influence aggression. The original formulation (Dollard, Doob, Miller, Mowrer, & Sears, 1939) stated that frustration always leads to aggression and that aggression is always caused by frustration. However, this formulation is generally viewed as being too inclusive (Bandura, 1973; Zillman, 1978). Nevertheless, most social scientists view frustration as an important determinant of aggression. Frustration occurs whenever a goal is being blocked. Buss (1961) lists failure as one of the major causes of frustration. In sport where the goal is victory, whenever it appears that this goal is unattainable the individual or team involved is usually frustrated and may be more apt to exhibit aggression. Thus, the frustration-aggression hypothesis would predict that aggression is prevalent in sport which is frustrational in the competitive context.

Social Learning Theory. Social learning theory has often been used to explain the occurrence of aggressive behavior. It is not proposed here as a theory to explain any relationship between performance and aggression. Granted, if an aggressive performance is successful, then the performer is likely to be more aggressive in similar situations. The initial aggressive behavior may have been taught directly or learned through what Bandura (1973) has called no-trial learning (modeling). Seeing other players use aggressive behavior or being taught that aggressive tactics increase the probability of success can influence an athlete to think that aggressive acts are appropriate in competitive sport situations.

AGGRESSION-PERFORMANCE RELATIONSHIPS: FINDINGS

Those who investigate sport may set out to determine the influence of aggression on performance, or the influence of performance on aggression. However, the design of their research, which is typically conducted in noncontrolled field settings, prohibits the establishment of any directional causality. Thus, even though opinions and theories exist for each potential influence, research must be viewed as dealing generally with aggression-performance relationships. This research can be divided into aggression-performance relationships at both the individual player level and the team level.

Relationships at the Player Level

At the individual level, aggression can be viewed as either a trait or a state phenomenon. The investigations conducted by Johnson, Hutton, and Johnson (1954), Ogilvie and Tutko (1965), Kane (1966), and Singer (1969) all suggest that the trait of aggressiveness is more prevalent in successful athletes than it is in less successful athletes. In two separate surveys Pilz (1979) found that highly successful athletes in soccer and European handball held more positive attitudes toward committing aggressive acts in these sports than did less successful athletes.

Investigations of individual aggression—individual performance relationships in which aggression has been treated as a behavioral state— have yielded more conflicting results. For example, Russell (1974) found that the total aggression ("challenge to authority" penalties and "physical aggression" penalties) of senior hockey players was positively related to the number of goals they scored and the number of assists they made, whereas physical aggression was positively related to assists made but not to goals scored. Russell (1974) explained the latter finding by noting, "The act of setting up a goal seemingly provides a somewhat greater likelihood of involvement in an altercation given that, unlike goals, assists are often made from the rink corners or along the boards where contact is closer and play, consequently rougher" (p. 833).

In two investigations of American collegiate hockey players, McCarthy and Kelly (1978a, 1978b) found that penalty minutes for physical and verbal actions directed toward another player were positively correlated with goals scored and assists made. Their research, which only involved players from the forward positions and which controlled for playing time, also showed that hostile aggression was positively related to the number of shots taken. This finding suggests that the greater success (goals scored and assists made) by the aggressive group was due to the fact that they were more energetic. However, the fact that aggressive individuals had a better scoring percentage suggests that this group was not only more active but also more efficient than the less aggressive group.

In a recent study, Widmeyer & Birch (1979) discovered a curvilinear relationship between individual aggression and individual success. Specifically, they found that highly successful (i.e., all-star) university ice hockey players were either extremely aggressive or extremely nonaggressive, whereas non all-stars were moderately aggressive. The fact that most of the highly aggressive all-star group were defensemen, while most of the very highly nonaggressive all-star group were forwards, implies that successful defensemen are more aggressive than less successful defensemen, and successful forwards are less aggressive than less successful forwards. Birch (1980) reported that regardless of position played, there were no differences in aggression among all-stars, all-star nominees, and non all-stars in the National Hockey League. However, his results do support Widmeyer and Birch's (1979) finding that defensemen were more aggressive than forwards.

Seeking better control, Silva (1979a) conducted a field experiment. He found that subjects who exhibited aggressive behavior and were thus behaviorally aroused showed poorer performance than did subjects who did not exhibit aggressive behavior. This effect was found for performance in a laboratory on a pegboard task and for performance in an actual game of "3 on 3" basketball. Silva also discovered that subjects who aggressed had lower concentration levels than did those not aggressing. His findings indicated that arousal, which generally accompanies aggressive behavior, can interfere with an individual's concentration which in turn can interfere with performance.

Relationships at the Team Level

Findings from examinations of aggression-performance relationships at the team level are as equivocal as those found in the studies conducted at the individual level. Andrews (1974), the National Hockey League's statistician, demonstrated a significant positive relationship ($r = .64$) between the number of penalties that teams accumulated and the order of finish in the NHL. Cullen and Cullen (1975) found that the mean number of penalties assessed to college hockey teams that were winning in a game was significantly higher than the mean number assessed to teams that were losing. A closer examination revealed that the winning teams were more aggressive either when the score was close or when it was extremely disparate. However, when the score differential was three or four goals, the losing teams were more aggressive. Albrecht (1979) showed that European handball teams that were winning committed more fouls than did losing teams. These three studies imply that aggression helps athletic teams succeed.

In contrast, Volkamer (1971), who examined soccer matches in Germany, found that teams that lost committed more fouls than did teams that won. LeFebvre and Passer (1974) demonstrated that during the course of 240 soccer games in the Belgium National League, teams that were behind in the contests received more yellow caution cards for their fouling behavior than did teams that were ahead in the game. Losing teams did not commit significantly more penalties (i.e., violations in front of their own goal to prevent an opponent from scoring) than did winning teams. Underwood and Whitwood's (1980) results showed no difference between the number of fouls committed by winning teams and the number committed by losing teams throughout two seasons of play in English First Division Soccer. As was the case in the hockey studies, they found that defending players committed more fouls than did attacking players.

In one of the few studies examining aggression-performance relationships among women, Sachs (1978b) found that the success of softball teams was not related to either the reactive aggression or instrumental aggression scores of team members. Similarly, Wankel (1973) showed that there was no difference between the aggressive penalties accumulated by winning and losing teams during one season of university ice hockey.

Recent studies have collected data for long time-intervals. For example, Widmeyer and Birch (1979) showed that there was a nonsignificant relationship between total penalty minutes and performance outcome across six seasons of university ice hockey. Birch (1980) identified 12 penalties as reflecting aggressive behavior and found that across five seasons there was no relationship between average aggressive penalty minutes per game and average points per game by teams in the National Hockey League. Widmeyer and Birch (1981) refined and revised Birch's (1980) procedures and found that across four seasons in the NHL, there was no significant relationship between team aggression and team performance outcome. However, subsequent analysis revealed that there was a significant relationship ($r = .48$) between aggression and performance outcome in the first period of hockey games and a negative relationship ($r = -.28$) between aggression and performance outcome in the third period.

The first finding was interpreted as evidence that aggression, when used early in a contest, can be an effective means to success. The second finding implied that aggression is also a behavioral response that is sometimes used as a reaction to failure and/or as retaliation to received aggression. This latter finding also suggested that successful teams effectively monitor their behavior and are less apt to incur penalties later in a contest when the penalty may disadvantage the team (e.g., playing short-handed late in a game).

AGGRESSION-PERFORMANCE RELATIONSHIPS: PROBLEMS

Problems associated with investigating aggression-performance relationships can be classified as conceptual, methodological, or interpretive.

Conceptual Problems

Theories to explain how aggression might influence performance and how performance might influence aggression have already been outlined. To date, none of these theories has been adequately tested in sport settings. Some investigators have given post hoc explanations for their results. However, these for the most part have been untested generalizations. Although Birch (1980) and Widmeyer and Birch (1979) outline Steiner's (1972) theory of performance outcome at the outset of their work, they do not test the theory. That is, they do not relate performance data to team input, opponents' input, team process, or opponents' pro-

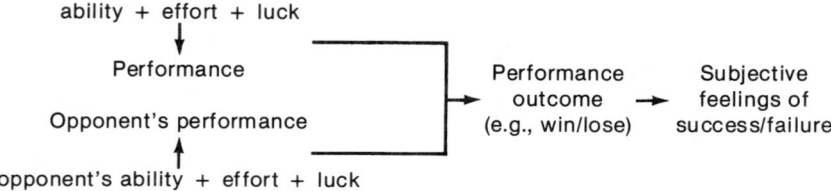

ability + effort + luck

Performance

Opponent's performance

opponent's ability + effort + luck

Performance outcome (e.g., win/lose)

Subjective feelings of success/failure

FIGURE 20-1   Relationship between performance, performance outcome, and success.

cess. Similarly, several researchers begin by citing frustration-aggression theory, yet they fail to verify if individuals or teams were frustrated.

Suggestions made elsewhere (Silva, 1978; Tedeschi, Gaes, & Rivera, 1977) for improving the conceptualization of aggression seem to have been ignored in examinations of aggression-performance relationships. In fact, only Silva (1980) differentiates between aggressive and assertive behavior, and so far no one has considered Tedeschi's concept of coercive power in this area of research.

Similarly, the lack of a precise conceptualization of performance has resulted in the interchangeable use of the terms success, performance, and performance outcome. Success is a subjective concept often based on such relative criteria as performing better than before. If investigators recognized this subjective aspect, then they might better understand why some teams are not frustrated by losses while others are frustrated even though they are winning. Likewise, there has been a failure to distinguish between performance and performance outcome. Performance refers to overt goal-directed behavior whereas performance outcome is the consequence of such behavior (Widmeyer, 1976). Performance is influenced by skill, effort, and luck. In any competitive situation, performance outcome is due to the performance of both competitors. Silva (1979a) showed that a performer's aggressive feelings interfere with his concentration, and in turn his performance. It must be recognized, however, that manifestations of these feelings can also have a great effect on the opponents' concentration. Aggressive outbursts by such tennis "bad boys" as Nastasse and McEnroe are reported to be detrimental to the concentration and performance of their opponents. The relationship between performance, performance outcome, and success is schematically represented in Figure 20-1.

Methodological Problems

The major methodological problems associated with this area of research revolve around the operationalizing of aggression and performance. The difficulty in operationalizing aggression stems from the fact that since intent to do harm is nonobservable, it must either be inferred from the athlete's behavior or directly ascertained by asking the individual the purpose of his/her action. So far only the first approach has been used. The most accepted indicator of aggression has been rule infractions observed by game officials.

Recognition that not all rule infractions are designed to harm the opponent (e.g., too many players, delay of game, etc.) has led to efforts to identify "aggressive penalties." Unfortunately, there is no consensus on what constitutes an aggressive penalty because, except for Birch (1980) and Widmeyer and Birch (1981), this identification has not been based upon any criterion other than the researcher's intuition. Even if soundly established, aggressive penalties are not perfect indicators of aggression because they fail to account for acts designed to hurt another that are not penalized — either because they are sanctioned (e.g., tackling in football, body checking in hockey), or because they go unnoticed by officials. In addition, as Underwood and Whitwood (1980) point out, behavior normally regarded as aggressive (e.g., charging in soccer) can sometimes occur because of inferior ability or improper playing conditions, even though there was no intent to do harm. Finally, it should be noted that many researchers forget that rule infractions are not penalized consistently from one official to another, or even by the same official at different times in a game (e.g., it is reputed that in order to incur a penalty during the overtime of a playoff game in professional ice hockey, a player must draw blood!).

Failure to understand the conceptual distinction between performance, performance outcome, and success has created problems in operationalizing these variables. Studies conducted at the team level have typically assessed winning percentage. This indicator and points-per-game are definitely objective measures of performance outcome, but they are not measures of performance or success.

Researchers examining the effect of performance on aggression have usually related the number of games won and lost to penalties. It might be more accurate to take note of who was winning or losing when the penalties occurred during the game. Likewise, goals and/or assists reflect individual performance outcome rather than performance or success. There has been a tendency to treat number of attempts on goal as a measure of performance. However, this indicator is also influenced by the performance of the opposition. Birch (1980) and Widmeyer and Birch (1979) criticize these measures of individual performance outcome because they do not account for defensive skills and leadership qualities. The indicator they use (i.e., all-star status) is not perfect either; it is susceptible to the halo effect and it does not discriminate finely among players, but instead it lumps individuals into two or three general categories.

In addition to the problems associated with operationalizing aggression and performance, the research fails to account for such mediating variables as the type and level of sport examined, and the gender of the athletes. Finally, one of the most prevalent and serious problems of interpretation in this area of research involves attaching causality to correlational data. Thus, the causative influences of one variable on another often cannot be determined.

AGGRESSION-PERFORMANCE RELATIONSHIPS: RECOMMENDATIONS

Based upon the research problems outlined here, the following suggestions are made for future research:

1. Future studies not only should be based upon a theoretical framework but also should test the theory or some aspect of it. Controlled field and laboratory experiments (e.g., Silva, 1979a) will be required to verify the findings of field studies.

2. Studies should distinguish between aggressive and assertive behavior as well as between instrumental and reactive aggression. If penalties are used to indicate aggression, those selected should have some empirical basis (e.g., Birch, 1980). Additionally, other means (e.g., asking the athlete) should be used for determining the intent to injure.

3. Studies should distinguish performance from performance outcome and success, and recognize the relationships among the three variables.

4. When studying how performance influences aggression, researchers should note the score at the time each aggressive act was committed rather than relating final outcome to total aggression.

5. Defensive as well as offensive skills should be assessed when evaluating individual performance. Since all-star categorization is not discriminating enough, players and coaches should rank the overall ability of each player.

6. Researchers should attempt to determine how the level and type of sport, as well as the gender, mediate aggression-performance relationships.

7. Conclusions about causality should not be drawn from correlational data. Instead, studies involving control groups should be conducted and/or cross-lagged panel and path analyses should be undertaken with data from field studies.

AGGRESSION-PERFORMANCE RELATIONSHIPS:
IMPLICATIONS

Although the findings are not definitive, and the causality not certain, past research strongly suggests that aggression in various contact-collision sports increases an individual's and a team's chances for a better performance *outcome*. Therefore, if performance outcome is the primary goal, aggression exhibited early in a contest is related to positive outcome. However, if one's concern is for the quality of sport and the participants rather than for the outcome of specific contests, then efforts should be made to see that aggression is minimized. Assuming that aggression contributes to winning and that reducing aggression is desirable, two approaches can be considered. First, aggression could be treated as it now is, and the importance attached to winning could be reduced. Second, the importance attached to winning could remain as it presently exists and the treatment of aggression be changed so that aggressive acts would lead to failure rather than to success.

The first approach was advocated by LeFebvre and Passer (1974) who suggested that the game structure be modified in order to minimize the need for aggressive behavior. Specifically, they suggested that cooperation be an objective of the game and that reinforcement be given for playing a strategically superior but nonaggressive game. Similarly, Vaz (1979) proposed an elaborate scheme "for reducing institutionalized rule violations," which involved awarding points to teams for not violating the rules. Both of these proposals are aimed at minimizing aggression by reducing the value attached to winning.

The second approach is presented by Silva (1981), who states, "When the reinforcement structure of a sport is modified so that rule violating behavior results in punishments that have greater punishment value than potential reinforcements, a reduction in the unwanted behavior should occur" (p. 14). Silva then explains how penalization could be altered to eliminate the intentional foul in basketball and fighting in ice hockey. His approach supports Brickman's (1977) idea that, "A harsher penalty (credibly enforced) is a stronger deterrent" (p. 141).

The research to date also suggests that losing creates aggression. Unless the nature of games changes and winning loses its importance, efforts should be made to minimize the aggression experienced when losing. LeFebvre and Passer (1974) suggest that this might occur if other, more desirable responses to frustration were rewarded (e.g., rewards for sportsmanship). They also advocate that players learn techniques that increase their tolerance for frustration and that make them less sensitive to the conditions evoking frustration and potentially retaliatory aggression. This represents a third approach to reducing aggression in sport.

In summary, the implications of aggression-performance research are:

- If your prime goal is to win, aggression exhibited early in a contest may be functional.
- If you are concerned about sport and its participants, make sure that aggression does not pay but that the aggressor does.

PART VI

GROUP DYNAMICS IN SPORT

Thus far we have been concentrating on the relationship between psychological variables and an individual's behavior in athletic situations. An individual's reactions in sport have been described as an interaction of personal factors and situational constraints. However, as every coach and athlete knows, we are not always dealing with just the individual athlete. In essence, a coach usually has to deal with a group of athletes who make up a team; somehow all these individuals have to mesh together for the common goals of the team. This does not mean that individual needs, interests, personalities, and abilities are not considered, but instead points out how difficult it can be to have diverse individuals working together in a group framework.

Anyone who has coached a team sport knows that the whole does not necessarily equal the sum of its parts! Specifically, the team with the most talent does not always win the championship, or conversely, teams win championships without having the best players. Examples of this can be seen in interscholastic, intercollegiate, and professional athletics. Basketball coaches say that in some cases they don't select the five most talented players to be in the starting lineup. Rather, they select a mix of players who play well together as a team and complement each other. Having five great shooters on the court at the same time usually means that a team needs five basketballs, one for each player! The Pittsburgh Pirates, who won the 1980 World Series, emphasized that they were "a family" both on and off the field and that effective communication and teamwork were the key to their success. This does not negate the fact that talent is extremely important in determining athletic success. However, it does point out that group dynamics plays an important role in the outcome of athletic competition. As stated earlier, responses to a national survey indicated that group dynamics is one of the coach's biggest concerns. Thus, from a practical sense as well as from a theoretical point of view, group dynamics and social interactions appear to be an important area of investigation.

This section will present the area of group dynamics in sport from four perspectives: (a) how spectators can affect performance; (b) the relationship of a group on individual performance; (c) the coach's effect on the group team; and (d) the interactions of people within a sport group, commonly known as group cohesion.

How Groups Affect Individuals

One area of interest to both practitioners and researchers is how the audience affects performance, particularly in sports typified by a supportive home crowd or an antagonistic away crowd. As a result, we often hear phrases such as "playing at home is worth 10 points" or "all we try to do is split on the road because we know we can win at home." This is called the home court advantage, and archival research has revealed that teams do win more at home than on the road. Although factors such as referee bias, travel, and condition of the field may account for this advantage, it is generally felt that the spectators themselves contribute greatly to this effect.

In a more scientific or experimental vein, researchers have been interested in the effects that observers or coactors (people doing the same thing at the same time) have on motor performance. This area of study has been termed social facilitation or the study of audience effects. One of the most influential lines of research in this area was published by Robert Zajonc, who argued that the nature of audience effects (positive or negative) depends on the complexity of the task and the performer's stage of learning. His work stimulated considerable research in this area in the late 1960s and 1970s.

In the first chapter of this section, Leonard Wankel reviews in depth the social facilitation effects starting with Triplett's work at the turn of the century through the latest developments in the area. Wankel reviews the applied research including several personal and situational factors that influence the effect an audience has on performance such as audience size and composition and its support or hostility. Wankel also discusses the more basic research on audience effects and identifies the underlying processes that mediate the audience-performance relationship. Some practical guidelines for coaches based on the research findings conclude this informative chapter.

Relationship of Individual and Group Performance

An important question in sport psychology is whether a group's product or output is as effective as it should be relative to the group's resources, which would include the collective talents, skills, and abilities of the individual group members. In essence, as the size of a group increases, problems can develop in coordinating the individual skills effectively. As the saying goes, "Too many cooks spoil the broth." Although superior resources may mean that large groups can be more productive than smaller groups, size also tends to complicate the procedures by which resources must be used to attain maximum efficiency.

Interactions become more complex as the number of individuals within a group increases, and this makes it difficult for coaches to work with teams. The task would be much easier if coaches could assess each athlete's ability level and then choose their team based on the highest scoring athletes. This could be partially accomplished in sports such as golf and singles tennis, perhaps, but not in team sports requiring the degree of interaction found in basketball, soccer, football, and volleyball. From a practical point of view, the more members of a team that are required to interact on the field, the greater chance that performance will suffer due to a loss in motivation or coordination. Motivation losses can occur when individuals tend to slacken off because they feel that other team members can carry the load and therefore their own contribution is not very important. Losses in coordination can occur when individual athletes fail to integrate, coordinate, and complement each other's skills, personalities, and abilities.

In her chapter, Diane Gill discusses how individual ability levels interact to influence group performance. Steiner's model of group productivity, which states that actual productivity equals potential productivity minus losses due to faulty group process is reviewed and related to athletics. Next Gill presents research on the relationship of individual and group performance with specific reference to the Ringelmann effect and the social loafing phenomenon, both of which empirically demonstrate that relative performance effectiveness decreases as the size of the group increases. The chapter concludes with some suggested directions for future research along with practical implications for coaches and physical educators.

How Individuals Affect Groups

Although Gill's chapter views group performance as an interaction of an athlete's ability and specific situational characteristics, one critical factor has been left out of the equation—namely the coach. The important effect that the coach has on developing teamwork, team unity, and group morale is widely recognized by the sporting establishment. The literature directly assessing the complex relationship between coaches, athletes, and the situations in which they interact is limited, but there is much anecdotal or experiential evidence that speaks to the issue. For example, people about to hire a coach are concerned that the coach must fit the particular needs of the organization or team. Leadership styles can vary, yet each can be effective given the right situation. Vince Lombardi was known as a hard-driving disciplinarian whereas Tom Landry's style is businesslike and nonemotional; yet both Lombardi and Landry have had great success in the same sport. In addition, coaches such as Billy Martin, John Wooden, George Allen, Earl Weaver, and Bobby Knight exhibit contrasting styles but they, too, are successful. It frequently happens that a coach who does poorly with one team and is fired then becomes extremely successful with another team—although his leadership style did not change. And of course there are teams that cannot seem to win until they get a new coach, and then begin winning even though they have not changed the composition of the team itself!

These anecdotal reports have some empirical support from the extensive research on leadership conducted in psychology and industry. Since the coach can be considered a leader this work has obvious implications for our field. Historically, the study of leadership examined the traits of successful leaders, an approach commonly known as the Great Man Theory of Leadership. After this line of research declined, the emphasis shifted to examining the behaviors of leaders and the situation within which they must lead. Foremost among these attempts were projects that are generally referred to as the Ohio State Studies and University of Michigan Studies. These studies concluded that the factors of consideration (friendship, mutual trust, respect, warmth) and initiating structure (organizing and defining relationships between leader and subordinates) accounted for most of what a leader actually did.

This approach was followed by a situation-trait interactional model which views leadership effectiveness as the product of the leader's style of interacting with subordinates and the favorableness of the situation. In Fiedler's Contingency Model, for example, style of interacting was classified as either task or interpersonal relations oriented, while situational favorableness comprised three factors: leader-member selections, the structure of the task, and the leader's power position. It is this kind of interactional model that seems most applicable to studying and understanding the relationship between coaches and teams. The chapter by P. Chelladurai discusses this model of leadership and relates it to the sport environment. Also presented and applied to sport is a multidimensional model of leadership developed by Chelladurai and Carron, which spans three dimensions in attempting to explain sports leadership behavior. The first dimension includes antecedents such as the characteristics, situation, leader, and members. The second dimension examines the leader's behavior from the perspectives of required, actual, and preferred behavior. The consequences of the interaction between these first two dimensions influence the final dimension, which is measured by member performance and satisfaction. Chelladurai reviews several studies conducted in the leadership area that have implications for sport organizations and participant-coach expectancies.

Interactions Within Groups

Although the coach's relationship and interaction with his or her team is an important variable in determining the team's success, the interaction between teammates is also crucial. According to Carron and Chelladurai, a group is distinguished from just a collection of individuals by the degree of attraction, commitment, and involvement the individuals have to the collective whole.

A traditional assumption in sport and physical activity has been that cohesiveness (togetherness, teamwork, chemistry, team unity) is directly linked with team success. Coaches constantly remind athletes that their individual goals must fit within the framework of the team's goals, or that they may even have to sacrifice their individual glory for the good of the team. In fact, many owners are building bonus clauses into athletes' salaries to provide extra money for team victories rather than individual accomplishments. Furthermore, athletes such as Doctor J, with long strings of individual accomplishments, may not be totally satisfied until they achieve the ultimate goal—a team championship.

But what is the relationship between group cohesion and sport performance? Bert Carron attempts to answer this by discussing the important role of the task in determining the cohesion-performance relationship. Although it is tempting to view group cohesion as a prerequisite for performance success, research findings do not entirely support such a broad generalization. There are many examples of teams that seemed to lack good interpersonal relations or cohesion, yet they still were successful. The Oakland Athletics in the mid-1970s and the New York Yankees in the late 1970s were both world champions despite numerous internal conflicts between players and between management and players. In addition, a study of German Olympic crews found that some crews won Olympic gold medals despite sharp subgroup and leadership conflicts. However, most coaches usually feel that conflict destroys athletic performance and that individuals who provoke conflicts and appear antagonistic to ideal group interactions must be eliminated if the team is to be successful. It is concluded that cohesion seems more important in interacting sport teams (e.g., basketball, soccer) than in coacting teams (e.g., riflery, tennis). Carron also addresses the circular nature of cohesiveness. Specifically, do teams with different levels of cohesion have different levels of success or does the team's success level directly influence the level of cohesion? In essence, does cohesion breed success or does success breed cohesion? Carron offers some interesting suggestions in this important area of sport psychology.

Chapter 21

Audience Effects
in Sport

Leonard Wankel
University of Alberta

Sport, by its very nature, is a social activity. Whether it be the first tennis lesson of a rank beginner, a neighborhood pick-up game of baseball, or a world championship figure skating event held before thousands of primary spectators (those present in the arena) and millions of secondary spectators (those watching on television), the athlete's performance is on display for others to see. The athletic event which is performed in social isolation is a rare exception. Even when spectators and other performers are not physically present, frequently some aspect of the individual's performance (his or her time, distance, etc.) will be subjected to the scrutiny of others. Further, as Cratty (1981) states, "Even a solitary workout may be accompanied by an unseen audience, a group of people residing psychologically and socially in the mind of the performer. This audience, the athlete knows, stands ready to judge his or her performance at some future time, harshly or with kindness and praise" (p. 191).

The investigation of how social factors influence sport performance has been a subject of inquiry for some time. In fact, an early study in this area by Triplett (1897) holds a prominent place in the history of social psychology as well as within sport research. This research, wherein observations from a sports setting (bicycle racing) led to the design of a controlled laboratory study to investigate alternate interpretations, holds the distinction of being the first experiment in social psychology (Allport, 1968).

Since the original study, research pertaining to the effects of coactors and observers upon performance has basically been of two types. On one hand, a number of researchers have attempted to describe the effects of different social conditions upon performance. This applied research has essentially attempted to relate different aspects of the immediate environment (e.g., audience size, supportive vs. denigrating audience, audience composition) to performance. On the other hand, researchers have conducted more basic research in an attempt to identify the underlying processes which mediate audience effects upon performance. This research has generally been of a hypothetical-deductive nature wherein strict controls and precise research designs are emphasized. Unfortunately, these two areas of research have remained relatively distinct without the close complementary association that would be most beneficial to understanding the effects of an audience upon sport performance.

A central aim of this chapter is to synthesize these two branches of study in order to more fully understand how the presence of others affects sport performance. In pursuing this end, social facilitation research will be examined as it contains the most systematic attempts to identify the psychological processes underlying how performance is affected by the presence of others. Social facilitation is defined as the behavioral effects due to the presence of others (Zajonc, 1965). It entails the two paradigms of audience and coaction. Audience refers to the presence of passive observers while coaction refers to the presence of others independently, but concurrently, doing the same or similar activity. This restricted definition of social facilitation specifically excludes effects due to modeling, social reinforcement, competitive instructions, cheering, and so forth. As these processes are an integral part of sport situations, however, a broader definition of audience and coaction effects will be utilized in the discussion of the more applied research and subjective observations on sport situations in the latter section of this chapter. First, the social facilitation research will be examined to identify the major theoretical issues pertaining to how the presence of others affects performance.

THEORETICAL ADVANCES IN UNDERSTANDING
AUDIENCE AND COACTOR EFFECTS
UPON PERFORMANCE[1]

Robert Zajonc's (1965) article entitled "Social Facilitation" constitutes a major turning point in the history of social facilitation research. Prior to that time the research had been largely atheoretical and the results viewed

[1]This portion of the chapter is largely drawn from Wankel's "Social Facilitation of Motor Performance: Perspective and Prospective." In C.H. Nadeau, W.R. Halliwell, K.M. Newell, & G.C. Roberts (Eds.), *Psychology of motor behavior and sport — 1979*. Champaign, IL: Human Kinetics, 1980.

as quite contradictory. By applying a new theoretical perspective to the field, Zajonc was able to interpret some consistencies in the previous results and, more importantly, he provided a stimulus for further research. Thus, it is appropriate to review social facilitation research in two historical periods—that research prior to Zajonc's article (pre-1965), and that after it (post-1965).

Pre-1965

In the early literature three individuals are particularly prominent: Norman Triplett, Floyd Allport, and J.F. Dashiell. In addition to having conducted the first experiment in social psychology, Triplett (1897) also provided the first attempt at developing a theoretical explanation for coaction effects. Allport (1924) and Dashiell (1935) were not only productive researchers in the social facilitation area, but both provided important reviews of the literature which made a number of observations that are still pertinent today (cf. Kushnir, 1978; Wankel, 1980).

Triplett's study grew out of a systematic analysis of the differences in official bicycling records set under the three different conditions: alone (unpaced), paced against time, and paced competitive races. It was observed that across different distances, performance consistently improved across the three successive conditions. After considering various mechanical (e.g., suction, shelter) and neurological (e.g., hypnotic suggestion, brain worry, autonomic action) explanations for these results, Triplett suggested his "dynamogenic theory" as being the most plausible for the facilitative effects. This "theory" identified two psychological bases for increased performance under the paced conditions. First, the presence of another performer was posited to arouse "the competitive instinct" which released latent energy not ordinarily available. Second, on the basis of ideomotor action, it was suggested that the sight of another's movements would suggest a higher rate of speed to the performer. Triplett designed a reel winding task to test these effects in a laboratory with school-age boys. He found that while most of the boys improved their performance under competitive-coaction conditions, others were unaffected, while still others performed more poorly.

Although Triplett's attempt to take the study of social facilitation out of the field into the more controlled laboratory context is noteworthy, his results were far from conclusive. Further, it is obvious that his laboratory study did not replicate the social conditions of the cycling track where the observations were first made. Whereas in the field setting competition against time was present in all situations and the differences were in terms of the coactor (i.e., no coaction vs. pacing, coaction vs. competing-coaction), in the laboratory study the two conditions were control (no coaction-no competition) and competition (coaction plus competition). Thus coaction was completely confounded with competition. Moreover, carry-over effects from one treatment to another, especially from the competition to the noncompetition condition, are especially problematic in such a within-subject research design.

Floyd Allport (1924) built upon Triplett's work and attempted to separate competition from coaction effects. Like Triplett, he referred to two distinct factors which accounted for performance increments due to competitive-coaction.

> The first of these is social facilitation — the movements made by others performing the same task as ourselves serve as contributory stimuli, and increase or hasten our own responses. . . . The second process is rivalry. Its occurrence is in direct proportion to the competitive setting of the group occupation, though a certain degree of rivalry seems natural to all co-activity. (Allport, 1924, pp. 284-285)

Although Allport should be credited with creating the label "social facilitation" for this field of study, it should be noted that his original usage of the term was more specific than that which is generally accepted today. Whereas Allport used social facilitation to refer to positive performance effects due to the movement stimuli provided by coactors, current practice has adopted Zajonc's broader definition of performance effects due to the presence of others.

Allport introduced further explanatory precision to the field by specifying limits to the beneficial effects of coactors. He was the first to clearly note the importance of task demands. He noted that coaction frequently enhanced *quantity* or speed of movement at the expense of *quality* or precision and that whereas muscular performance was improved, mental performance frequently suffered in the presence of coactors. Allport also clearly described the importance of individual differences for understanding coaction effects. He noted that facilitation was the greatest for slower and poorer performers and least for the more rapid and efficient. With respect to individual differences, he observed:

> Children are more susceptible to the facilitating influences than adults. But even among adults there are conspicuous differences. In the investigations described above certain individuals had a social decrement to their output, or failed to show the usual reaction to group stimulation in thought and conformity of judgment. Habit, customary work environment, nervousness, and distractability, as well as reclusiveness, negative suggestibility, attitudes of superiority, defect of sociality, and other traits are factors which may help to account for these typical reactions. (Allport, 1924, p. 278)

The next important review of the area was provided by J.F. Dashiell (1935), one of Allport's former students. Dashiell, in reviewing the progress of the field, noted that little significant advance had been made beyond Allport's earlier conclusions. He did, however, make a number of extensions and refinements to Allport's interpretations. He extended Allport's discussion of individual differences in reactions to social situations by discussing the inadequacies of conventional group statistics for dealing with the data.

> In many of the various studies of group effects upon the individual's work a handling of the data by combining all the individuals' scores and treating them in terms of means, differences of means, standard deviations, critical ratios, and whatnot of conventional statistical procedure, has brought precious little to light. Yet when the scores of the respective individuals are treated as such, to find how many of them show a difference in one direction or the other within his own results, certain strong, "populational" trends, heavy majorities of individuals, among these small differences may become marked. May it not be that a peculiar form of "group fallacy" is committed when the statistical technique for handling groups is applied with too great finality? (Dashiell, 1935, p. 1103)

Dashiell also added clarification to Allport's discussion of coaction effects by his observation that coaction effects are mediated by psychological processes and hence it is very difficult to obtain "pure alone" or "pure co-working" effects. Dashiell extended Allport's coaction review to include audience effects. After reviewing numerous studies he drew the following conclusion pertaining to the generality of the results.

> In the researches reviewed in this section the effects of audience-spectators have been observed on a dozen kinds of psychological function; and the readers who glance back over the pages will discover them to represent about as wide a range as could be imagined. To attempt to summarize and generalize the results, then, would be decidedly premature. All the more so as the variations in experimental procedure also differ, though hardly so enormously. (Dashiell, 1935, p. 1106)

Subsequent to this pessimistic conclusion, however, Dashiell (1935) did note the generalization paralleling Allport's earlier observation for coaction, that "The mere presence of others tends to speed up the individual's work but to make it less accurate" (p. 1106). This observation was an important precursor of the "mere presence theory of social facilitation" brought forward later by Robert Zajonc (1965).

In the years between 1935 and 1965 a number of studies investigated the effects of the presence of others, either as an audience or as coactors, upon performance. A number of disparate task and experimental situations were utilized but the results in total added little clarity to the area until Zajonc's attempt at integration in 1965. Some of the studies that have particular relevance to specific situational influences relevant to sport and/or motor performance will be referred to in the later section of this chapter. Prior to that, however, the contributions of Robert Zajonc and subsequent developments in theoretical understanding of social facilitation will be addressed.

Post-1965

A surge of interest in the study of social facilitation was triggered by Zajonc's (1965) now classic review of the field. In his article, Zajonc attempted to interpret what had previously appeared to be inconsistent and contradictory results. He noted an apparent generalization in the results of previous research and proposed a hypothesis to account for it. The noted generalization was that observers or coactors facilitated performance of simple or well learned tasks but deterred the acquisition of new responses. Zajonc's major contribution, beyond the earlier similar generalizations of Allport and Dashiell, was that he framed the generalization within the context of general behavior theory. This allowed the application of a well developed theoretical background to the field. Thus, rephrased in behavior theory terms, the generalization became "The presence of others, as spectators or coactors, enhances the emission of dominant responses" (Zajonc, 1965, p. 273). The hypothesis offered to explain this generalization was that the presence of coactors or spectators resulted in an increase in general drive or arousal level. According to the tenets of Hull-Spence behavior theory, such increased general drive would interact multiplicatively with habit strength in affecting performance. In other words, when the correct response was dominant (e.g., when a skill was mastered or was very simple) increased drive would benefit performance; on the other hand when the incorrect response tendencies were dominant (e.g., when a skill was complex and was not well learned) increased drive would hinder performance.

Although Zajonc's interpretation of the literature both in terms of his noted generalization and posited explanation for it were open to question (cf. Cottrell, 1972; Landers & McCullagh, 1976), there is no doubt about the tremendous influence that his position has had on the field (Geen & Gange, 1977; Wankel, 1980). Zajonc's article stimulated three major lines of inquiry. One area focused on testing the generalization that the presence of others, either as coactors or spectators, would augment dominant responses at the expense of subordinate responses. A second examined the hypothesis that the mechanism mediating social facilitation was an increase in arousal or general drive. The third investigated Zajonc's "mere presence" definition in an attempt to specify the minimal social conditions necessary for social facilitation.

The Augmentation of Dominant Responses.   Critical to the dominant response augmentation perspective is the ability to identify the relative strengths of correct and incorrect response tendencies within a given task. Essentially two distinct approaches have been taken to this problem. One approach involves the creation of habit strength hierarchies through a training procedure. The other utilizes information about existing response preferences or current levels of performance to make judgments as to existing response strengths. Two tasks, one employing each approach, have been predominant in the general social facilitation literature addressed to this question. Research with both the training procedure-based pseudo-word recognition task (Zajonc & Nieuwenhuyse, 1964) and the response preference-based word association test of Spence, Farber, and McFann (1956) has consistently supported drive theory predictions (Geen & Gange, 1977; Wankel, 1975a).

Attempts to extend this line of research to motor tasks, however, have been much less successful. In the clearest attempt to utilize the training procedure approach, Carron and Bennett (1976) were successful in establishing differential response strengths for the four stimulus alternatives of a discriminative reaction-time task. A competitive coaction treatment did not augment the speed of the dominant responses, however, thus contradicting predictions made from drive theory. A less straightforward application of a training procedure for developing habit strength involves the use of a "learning criterion." Pilot testing is utilized to establish a criterion performance level, at which point it is assumed that correct responses have become dominant. Although some success has been reported in using this approach with motor tasks (Haas & Roberts, 1975; Martens, 1969) its usefulness is limited by the necessarily imprecise manner in which the "learning criterion" must be set.

The clearest application of the existing response preference technique to motor tasks is research with the stylus maze (Hunt & Hillery, 1973). This task entails tracing through a maze with various decision points of set difficulty. On a simple maze there are two choices at each decision point, hence the probability of making a correct response is dominant (.5 probability of making correct response on basis of chance alone). On a complex maze there are four choices at each decision point, hence the correct responses are initially subordinate (.25 probability of making correct response on basis of chance). As learning occurs, the number of errors decreases and gradually the correct responses become dominant. The point at which this crossover takes place is readily quantifiable in terms of the number of errors (when number of errors drops below total number of decision points the correct responses are assumed to be dominant). In support of predictions based upon Zajonc's theory, Hunt and Hillery found that through practice the initially subordinate correct responses for the complex maze became dominant, resulting in a transition in coaction effects from impairment to facilitation.

Similar practice effects on how social factors influenced performance have been reported for a timing task (Martens, 1969) and for stabilometer balancing (Wankel, 1969). On the other hand, Paulus and associates (Paulus & Cornelius, 1974; Paulus, Shannon, Wilson, & Boone, 1972), in two of the few studies testing social facilitation theory in a sport context, reported contradictory results. They found that the presence of an audience had a greater detrimental effect on the gymnastic performance of experienced gymnasts than on that of novice gymnasts. In a more recent study in a sport context, Forgas, Brennan, Howe, Kane, and Sweet (1980) similarly found results contrary to what was predicted on the basis of social facilitation theory. They found that the presence of observers at a squash game (competitive-coaction) resulted in closer games than when no audience was present. This contradicts social facilitation theory if it is assumed that the winning competitor in a match has stronger correct responses, relative to incorrect responses, than does the losing competitor. Thus, increased arousal due to spectator presence should benefit his or her performance more than that of the less skilled opponent. The authors explained their results by suggesting that an audience led to an "automatic matching" effect on the part of the players as they attempted to keep the game going to maximize the pairs' game success in front of the viewers. Obviously there is a need for further research in this area. It would appear, however, that an alternate perspective to drive theory might better account for these results. More will be said about this later in the chapter when a more complex cognitive model for accounting for audience and coaction effects is suggested, and personal and situational factors influencing audience effects are discussed.

Some investigators have utilized preselected ability groups in an attempt to obtain groups with distinct habit hierarchies. In this approach it is hypothesized that subjects who performed well on a task pretest (high ability group) will benefit from increased drive while subjects who performed poorly on the pretest (low ability group) will be hindered by increased drive. Although Wankel (1969) found that initial ability significantly modified the effect of competitive-coaction upon stabilometer balancing, other research (Hrycaiko, 1978; Noble, Fuchs, Robel, & Chambers, 1958; Wankel, 1975c) has not found initial ability level to significantly influence social facilitation of motor performance.

The most common approach to operationalizing the social facilitation hypothesis with complex motor performance is a common sense assessment of whether correct or incorrect responses are dominant. When dealing with simple muscular activities such as single-leg extension (Martens & Landers, 1969), dynamometric or ergographic work (Berridge, 1935; Meuman, 1904 cited by Cottrell, 1972) walking (Kohfeld & Weitzel, 1969), or running (Obermeier, Landers, & Ester, 1977), the social facilitation effects might reasonably be attributed to dominant correct responses. In other more complex tasks, however, where considerable learning can take place, the situation is quite ambiguous.

Overall then, evidence concerning the utility of the generalized drive and competing response hypothesis for social facilitation is mixed. Whereas audience and coaction effects on simple tasks involving discrete competing-responses have generally been consistent with predictions, attempts to extend this interpretation to complex motor tasks have met with limited success. Although the generalization that an audience or coactors would impede initial learning and facilitate performance after the skill is mastered would still appear to be valid, in the case of complex motor skills it is virtually impossible to determine when the crossover from detrimental to positive effects will occur.

Arousal as the Underlying Basis for Social Facilitation.

Zajonc equated general drive with arousal, although in classical Hullian theory generalized drive was strictly a hypothetical construct with no inferred connection with neurophysiological structures. By using arousal rather than drive, Zajonc hoped to get independent evidence, distinct from performance effects, to indicate that the presence of others produces increases in arousal. He admitted, however, that at the time, the evidence in support of the hypothesis that the presence of others leads to increased arousal was quite tenuous. In the years since 1965, a number of researchers have taken arousal measures in their social facilitation studies, but the results of these studies have been far from consistent. Regardless of whether the particular arousal measure used was palmar sweating, palmar skin conductance, heart rate, state anxiety, or a self-report of activation, inconsistent results have been reported with increased arousal being indicated in some studies but not in others (Carron, 1980; Wankel, 1980).[2]

Although situational or task differences in the studies may account for some of the discrepancies, a more likely interpretation is that these results reflect basic conceptual and methodological problems pertaining to the nature and assessment of arousal. While Zajonc used the term arousal in the sense of the generalized activation level of the body (Duffy, 1962), more recent evidence suggests that arousal is multidimensional (Lacey, 1967). This creates a major problem as it is not clear how different measures of arousal might be expected to correlate. Evidence indicates that there is poor correspondence between different measures (Borden, 1980). Further, the correlation between measures over time does not remain stable (Martens, 1974a). An even more serious complication is the specificity of autonomic responses. The patterns of autonomic reactions to a given event (stimulus) reflect significant individual differences. For example, whereas one performer may react with increased heart rate and greater palmar sweating to an audience condition, another may experience an increase in heart rate but no change in palmar

---

[2]It should be noted that some reviewers of the social facilitation literature have drawn more favorable conclusions concerning the evidence supporting increased arousal as a result of the presence of others (cf. Geen & Gange, 1977; Landers & McCullagh, 1976).

sweating. Until significant advances are made in the theory and assessment of arousal it is unlikely that this concept will be very useful to social faciliation theory. This does not undermine a drive theory interpretation of social facilitation, however, for as was previously noted classical Hullian theory makes no reference to neurophysiological equivalents of drive and, hence, such arousal changes paralleling increased drive are not essential to (or indeed predicted by) the theory. It merely indicates that Zajonc's attempt to equate drive with arousal in order to get nonperformance measures of increased arousal or drive has not gained strong support.

Minimal Social Conditions Necessary for Social Facilitation. The third area of inquiry stimulated by Zajonc's (1965) review pertained to the minimal social conditions necessary for obtaining social facilitation effects. Zajonc proposed that the mere presence of another individual was a sufficient condition for triggering a biologically based innate source of drive. Although the extreme simplicity and easy operationalization of this perspective is very appealing, its validity was soon questioned and an alternate interpretation proposed. Cottrell (1968), while accepting Zajonc's drive theory of social facilitation, questioned the innate source of drive perspective and in its place suggested a learned source of drive interpretation. According to this perspective, the presence of others elicits drive only to the extent that there is potential for evaluation and the anticipation of positive or negative outcomes as a result of one's performance.

Since Cottrell's (1968) review, considerable evidence has accumulated in support of the view that evaluation apprehension is an important factor influencing how the presence of an audience affects performance. Evidence has come from studies utilizing direct manipulations of instructions pertaining to being evaluated by the observing viewers (Cohen, 1980; Cohen & Davis, 1973; Haas & Roberts, 1975; Paulus & Murdoch, 1971); from studies using the indirect approach of comparing the effects of an observing expert audience with those of a nonexpert audience (Gore & Taylor, 1973; Lombardo & Catalano, 1975; Sasfy & Okun, 1974); and from studies wherein situational factors were altered to control the observer's physical ability to observe the performance (Cottrell, Wack, Sekerak, & Rittle, 1968; Martens & Landers, 1972). Evidence for the importance of psychological presence as distinct from physical presence was provided by studies wherein performers were led to believe that they were being observed by an audience when in fact there was no audience (Criddle, 1971; Foot & Lee, 1970; Ganzer, 1968).

With respect to the coaction paradigm, evidence indicates that a similar underlying motivational basis is involved. Rather than anticipation of evaluation as in the audience paradigm, however, for coaction the motivational basis is probably a perception of competition or rivalry (Geen, 1980; Geen & Gange, 1977, Wankel, 1972). Evidence generally indicates that conditions which might be expected to increase competitiveness (e.g., competitive instructions, provision of own and other knowledge of results, the presence of observers) result in greater social facilitation (Geen & Gange, 1977; Wankel, 1980).

Across both the audience and coaction paradigms then, the potential for evaluation has been shown to be an important factor influencing social facilitation. This does not disprove Zajonc's "mere presence" hypothesis, however, as it is possible, as Zajonc (1980a) maintains, that the effects due to anticipated evaluation are in addition to those due to mere presence. Although Geen (1980) reports that "evidence has been mounting for the conclusion that the presence of others can be arousing without creating evaluation apprehension" (p. 70). . . . it is possible to conclusively settle this issue because we can never be certain how an individual has reacted psychologically to the situation. The problem was aptly phrased by Dashiell in his early review . . . "when working apparently in isolation an individual may actually be under social influences of representative character" (p. 1110).

What is apparent, however, is that from the practical viewpoint "mere presence" has little real importance. Studies that have removed most opportunities for evaluation have shown mere presence to have very little, if any, effect upon performance (Cohen, 1980; Cottrell et al., 1968). This becomes even clearer when it is recognized that frequently even the evaluative conditions in social facilitation laboratory studies have only minimal behavioral effects (Landers, Bauer, & Feltz, 1978).

Summary.   In summary, considerable research has been conducted since 1965 with respect to Zajonc's drive theory of social facilitation. Whereas there has been general support for the generalization that the presence of spectators or coactors will augment dominant responses and facilitate performance of well learned skills while reducing the frequency of subordinate responses and thus impeding the learning of new skills, evidence for the importance of arousal as an important underlying mechanism is quite ambiguous. Further, while some authors continue to advocate the use of multiple measures when assessing arousal in social facilitation research (e.g., Carron, 1980; Cohen, 1980) it would appear that little clear understanding will be achieved in this area until there is a clearer conceptualization of the specific nature of arousal and more reliable measurement instruments for assessing it. Zajonc's "mere presence" definition of the minimum conditions necessary for social facilitation has also been brought into question by subsequent research. Evaluative apprehension has been shown to mediate social facilitation effects.

In conclusion, drive theory has been the predominant theory underlying social facilitation research (Geen & Gange, 1977; Wankel, 1980). Further, drive theory's position as the most parsimonious explanation for social facilitation has been duly noted (Geen & Gange, 1977; Landers, Bauer, & Feltz, 1978). Despite these testimonials to drive theory's prominence in the social facilitation literature, the theory has not gone without criticism. This author (Wankel, 1975a, 1975b, 1980) has consistently emphasized that a mechanistic drive theory perspective has severe limitations for explaining complex human behavior. Recently, Landers (1980), who had previously been an advocate of drive theory (Landers, 1975a; Landers & McCullagh, 1976), questioned the continued preeminence of drive theory and in its place has advocated a cognitive arousal-attention model. Similarly, Geen and Gange (1977), in their major review of recent social facilitation research, while supporting the parsimony of drive theory as the best current explanation of social facilitation, have advocated further development of alternate perspectives. They state:

> Possibly in the next few years, work on social facilitation will be addressed more and more to cognitive processes that are involved in the phenomenon, and ultimately the inadequate cognitive explanations presented so far will be replaced by more sophisticated ones. Such formulations will augment our understanding of important mediating processes that to date have not been fully investigated. (p. 1294)

In other words, there has been increasing recognition that in the area of social facilitation as in other areas of complex human behavior (cf. Martens, 1974a; Weiner, 1972) drive theory has some major limitations and hence alternate perspectives should be more actively pursued.

ALTERNATIVES TO DRIVE THEORY

Although no current alternative to drive theory as an explanation for social facilitation has been fully developed, a number of alternate approaches have been suggested. Due to space limitations only brief reference will be made to a number of these perspectives prior to discussing in more detail a more complex cognitive model (Borden, 1980) which will be utilized as a framework for discussing how personal and situational factors mediate social effects upon performance.

Baron and Sanders and associates (e.g., Baron, Moore, & Sanders, 1978; Sanders, 1981; Sanders & Baron, 1975) have developed an attention-distraction interpretation of social facilitation. According to this perspective, social influences such as the presence of observers or coactors increase drive by serving as a source of attention distraction. Thus, although a different interpretation for the source of drive is presented, distraction rather than mere physical presence or anticipated evaluation, the performance changes due to the presence of others are still based on drive theory predictions. Hence this perspective is limited by the deficiencies of drive theory in dealing with the complexities of human behavior (cf. Weiner, 1972) even though considerable evidence has been reported to support the theory's predictions (Geen, 1980; Sanders, 1981).

Duval and Wicklund's (1972) theory of objective self-awareness has been used to interpret audience effects through the suggestion that the presence of observers leads to objective self-awareness which enhances task motivation (Duval & Wicklund, 1972; Wicklund, 1980). Although this theory overcomes some of the specific limitations of drive reduction theories, it too is a very simple mechanistic approach. The dichotomous perspective that an individual either focuses attention inward upon the self (objective self-awareness) or outward upon the environment (subjective self-awareness) would appear to be too simplistic to account for complex social behavior. It is possible, however, as Geen (1980) points out, that objective self-awareness might effectively be incorporated into an arousal interpretation of audience effects.

A number of authors have suggested some form of an arousal-cognitive information processing model for social facilitation (Geen & Gange, 1977; Landers; 1980, Wankel, 1975a). These suggestions essentially derive from Easterbrook's (1959) early research showing that increased arousal leads to a narrowing of attentional focus and cue utilization. Although such limited cognitive approaches move away from a pure mechanistic drive theory based on habit hierarchies to a consideration of how the individual reacts to input stimuli, they still emphasize the energizing rather than the informational effects of social factors. To this author, it would seem advisable to consider more complex models which place greater emphasis on cognition and how the individual interprets the information in the social situation. In this regard, the work of Robert Borden is particularly relevant.

Borden (1980) has developed a more dynamic model of audience effects wherein the performer is acknowledged to be a proactive individual in contrast to the reactive perspective employed in the previously discussed approaches. This means that the performer, through his or her perceptions and expectations, plays an active role in defining the social situation rather than being a more or less passive reactor to it. The performer actively interprets information from the situation and makes predictions about the audience's reactions and alters his or her behavior accordingly. Thus, cognition plays an important role as the individual attempts to understand the social situation in order to optimize the outcomes from it. Specific information about the makeup of the audience, particularly its value preferences pertinent to the performance situation, have important implications for the person's behavior. At the same time, Borden acknowledges the energizing or motivating role served by the presence of others and evaluation apprehension. Such a perspective wherein the subjective social situation, the performer's interpretation of the situation, is viewed as being more important than the objective social situation will be utilized in the following section which examines how personal and situational factors influence coaction and audience effects upon performance.

PERSONAL AND SITUATIONAL FACTORS INFLUENCING AUDIENCE OR COACTION EFFECTS UPON PERFORMANCE

Although a number of personal factors may be important in determining how an individual reacts to a given situation, researchers have essentially restricted their attention to anxiety. As Geen (1980) observed, this may occur because the construct is so close to evaluation apprehension which is a major intervening variable in many social settings.

When all anxiety measures are considered, the results of the research concerning how subject anxiety mediates audience effects upon performance are very inconsistent. Some consistency appears, however, when attention is paid to the particular anxiety measures utilized. General anxiety (as measured by such inventories as the Manifest Anxiety Scale or the IPAT Anxiety Inventory) has not been found to interact consistently with social factors. Test anxiety or anxiety measures specific to the type of performance situation (e.g., Audience Sensitivity Inventory), however, have been found to mediate audience effects upon performance (Geen, 1980; Wankel, 1975a, 1980). High anxiety-prone individuals tend to perform poorer in the presence of others than when alone whereas the reverse is true for low anxiety subjects.

With respect to other personality measures, Kohfeld and Weitzel (1969) found that individuals who performed better during a treadmill walking task when in the presence of an audience than when alone had different personality profiles than those who showed little performance changes. This finding, in the absence of subsequent replication, must be viewed with skepticism in view of the general contradictory results of studies pertaining to the personality traits of various athletic groups. Similarly, although Geen (1980) suggests that Atkinson's model of achievement motivation may be usefully applied to social facilitation, its utility can only be determined through future research.

A more task-specific individual difference measure is previous experience with similar tasks in similar social contexts. Lombardo and Catalano (1975) found that prior failure on a task in front of an audience led to poorer performance on another task in front of that audience. This is consistent with the view that the performer's expectations of positive or negative outcomes from the audience or coaction situation mediates social facilitation effects.

Along this same line of thought it is generally felt that experience with a stressful situation, such as an observing audience, can lead to reduced threat in the situation. A generally accepted coaching principle is that athletes or teams should be allowed to experience performing before a large, active audience prior to experiencing such a situation in the "big" game or meet. Model training programs that simulate such contest conditions in practices and preliminary games have become popular (Vanek & Cratty, 1970; Coaching Association of Canada, Level III Theory Manual, 1981). Although the importance of previous experience is broadly accepted and is reflected in such common statements as, "The champions have been here before (experienced the stressful and distracting situation of the championship event) and so have an advantage over the challengers," there is little specific research to support this view. Singer (1965) posited that athletes who were used to performing in front of audiences would perform better on a stabilometer balancing task in front of an audience than would nonathletes; however, the reverse was found. Nonathletes not only performed better than athletes during the practice trials (no audience) but their performance advantage was greater under the audience condition as well. These results may simply indicate that reactions to an audience are not general but depend upon the particular audience context, the task involved, and the performer's interpretation of the situation. As Borden (1980) notes: "The influence of an audience on the individual also depends on the specific performance requirements. The verbally facile public speaker may become noticeably shaken when called upon to dance or sing. The exhibitionistic rock star may appear ill at ease on a T.V. talk show, and so on (p. 99)."

Despite these obvious specific considerations it is also generally accepted that one's general previous experiences can influence coaction or audience effects. In this regard, age is viewed as an important factor when organizing a sport program. It is generally thought that young athletes should not be subjected to the same high pressure emphasis on winning and performing before large audiences as older athletes. Although obviously there are other important considerations relevant to this decision, the effect of large audiences upon the behavior of young athletes is one factor. Again there is scant objective information in this area. Missuiro (1964) found that the ability to translate the increased arousal due to the presence of an audience into enhanced performance improved with age in young children. Similarly, Crabbe (1971) found that second-grade children reacted better to learning a motor task in the presence of an audience than did younger preschool children. Conversely, Newman, Dickstein, & Gargan (1978) found that the presence of a peer observer inhibited the rate of learning for 11-year-olds, but not for 5- or 8-year-olds.

Like age, the participant's gender has received some attention as a variable influencing social influence effects. Although there is some evidence that females are generally more susceptible to social influence than males (Crowne & Marlowe, 1964), results in the social facilitation literature have been inconsistent (Carron, 1980; Wankel, 1975a). In a similar fashion, research investigating the effect upon performance of an audience of the same or opposite gender has been inconclusive. Again it would appear that more specific subject, task, and situational factors must be taken into consideration before any consistent relationships can be established. There is some evidence to indicate that given situations in which different behaviors are selectively encouraged (e.g., aggressive responses), values associated with a particular gender role (masculine vs. feminine role) may be selectively encouraged or discouraged by the presence of observers of a particular gender (Borden, 1980). As Sherif (1972) has noted with respect to competitive behavior, the particular context (task and environment) influences whether girls will be more or less competitive than boys. Similar findings might be expected for audience and coaction situations, as there are still certain tasks which are viewed as more appropriate for one gender than the other. As values change, however, and as girls and boys are increasingly provided with comparable performance experiences in sport and other areas, it is likely that the gender of the performer and of the observers will become less of an important factor.

In summary, a number of personal factors influence how an individual reacts to a given social situation and accordingly how that situation affects his or her performance. Such factors as previous experience, age, gender, and personality will influence the individual's subjective interpretation of the objective social situation. It is this subjective social situation that constitutes the reality to which the individual reacts. Again, as Borden (1980) emphasized, the individual is a proactive, not a simple reactive, agent in the social situation. The important interpretive role of the performer in any coaction or audience situation will be further emphasized in the following discussion of how characteristics of the others present affect social facilitation.

Audience Characteristics

As previously discussed the expertise of the audience and its ability to evaluate the individual's performance has been shown to be an important factor affecting social facilitation. Similarly, research has indicated that an audience of "liked peers" affects performance differently than an audience of "disliked" or neutral peers or strangers. The particular effect will depend upon the situation and the individual's competency on the task. If the task is novel and has a high potential for embarrassment, it appears that being observed by friends is more threatening than being observed by strangers or disliked peers. When skill is developed at the task, however, "liked" peer observers may enhance performance to a greater extent than other peer observers (Brown & Garland, 1971; Mathews, 1968 as cited in Landers & McCullagh, 1976).

Recent research also indicates that the performer's interpretation of the audience situation affects his or her behavior in more complex ways than by simply increasing evaluative apprehension which may increase dominant responses. This research indicates that the individuals use information that is available about what the audience may view favorably about their behavior and then act accordingly to increase the probability of getting favorable reactions. In other words, this interpretation holds that maximum performance is not encouraged by viewers under all conditions, and the performer takes this into consideration when altering his or her behavior. Essentially then, this explanation goes beyond the simple social facilitation paradigm and suggests that the presence of others provides informative cues as well as having motivational effects (increased drive or arousal) and that both these aspects influence behavior (Borden, 1980).

Grush (1978) found that the type of audience (pro-winning or pro-human relations) had a differential effect on performance of a Prisoner's Dilemma game. A pro-winning audience facilitated use of a dominant competitive response relative to a no-audience control condition, whereas a pro-human relations audience inhibited the dominant competitive response. Similarly, Borden (1975) found that the presence of supposedly different types of observers (purported members of a karate club vs. members of a pacifist organization) had different effects upon aggression displayed toward a partner. This indicates, as Geen (1980) notes, "Aggression in the company of an 'aggressive' observer may have been behavior that had been carefully adjusted to elicit a favourable impression from that person" (p. 90).

This phenomenon would appear to have considerable relevance to sport. The expectations of the fans for certain behavior, and the reinforcement of it, may have considerable effect upon an athlete's behavior. For example, the boisterous support of the home crowd encouraging the home team frequently results in the observation that some hockey players play more aggressively in home than away games. Not only may the expectations of observers influence the actual type of behavior exhibited but they may have less obvious effects upon performance. In fact, this may account for some of the previously reported inconsistencies in the social facilitation research conducted within a sport context.

In the Forgas et al. (1980) study of squash performance, contrary to expectations on the basis of social facilitation theory that the presence of observers would lead to greater score differences between competitors in a competitive game (competitive-coaction), it was found that there was a lessening effect. In other words, there was a "leveling effect" due to the presence of others, with poorer performing players improving more relative to better players. Similar results were reported in the two studies of audience effects upon gymnastic performance (Paulus et al., 1972; Paulus & Cornelius, 1974). These results can be interpreted in terms of the present "impression management" perspective of behavior in front of an audience. In both the squash game and the gymnastic performance situations, it is possible that the better performers did not wish to "run up the score" on the poorer performers. Forgas et al. (1980) have suggested such an interpretation for their results by referring to an "automatic matching" effect as the players attempted to present a successful pair image to the viewers. Although Paulus and his associates did not suggest such an interpretation for their results, it does seem plausible. It seems quite likely that performers who know each other would not like to "put each other down" in front of the spectators. This would be especially likely to occur in situations such as in the gymnastics studies in which the observers were peers.

It would be interesting to investigate whether similar results would be found with an audience comprised of judges in a competitive meet situation or evaluators for a course grade. In these situations, the view that performers act according to the information available in the situation to enhance positive outcomes could lead to the prediction that the presence of observers would lead to greater performance differences. Although this interpretation of these results is admittedly speculative, it would seem as plausible and as worthy of further investigation as the response-ceiling effect that Paulus and his associates invoked to interpret their findings in terms of drive theory.

An aspect of the objective audience situation that might influence audience effects is the size of the audience. Based upon a simple summative principle, it has been suggested that the drive due to the presence of different observers may have a cumulative effect upon performance (Weiss & Miller, 1971); however, little systematic evidence has been provided in support of this view. Research utilizing cognitive and motor tasks in controlled laboratory situations with relatively small audiences (Carron, 1980; Wankel, 1975a) as well as field studies of athletic performance in large audience situations (Kerr & Yukelson, 1977 cited in Borden, 1980; Paulus, Judd, & Bernstein, 1977) generally indicate that audience size has little systematic effect on performance.

Borden (1980), in reviewing other literature, noted that in some cases there is a systematic effect while in others there is not. He observed that, as in the case of other variables, the effect of audience size upon performance depends upon the individual's interpretation of the total situation. He suggested that audience size effects, when found, were due to an increased feeling of anticipated evaluation as the audience makeup was not initially clear to the performers. In other situations, where the audience composition was clear and anticipation of evaluation was established initially, adding more observers had no additional effect upon performance.

Applying this perspective to sport, the absolute number of spectators present is not that important; rather, it is the information conveyed to the performers by those present that has performance implications. There is nothing magical about a given number of spectators. For example, 100 spectators in a 100-seat auditorium is quite a different situation from 100 spectators in a 2,000-seat facility. Subjective references to difficulty in "getting up" for a game when playing in front of a half empty stadium are common. An evaluative message is conveyed to the participants by the empty seats—"We don't care about your performance even to the extent of not coming to the stadium to watch you"—which frequently can have a negative effect upon performance.

Beyond the actual and relative size of the audience are the reactions of the observers. In sport, references are frequently made to the quality of the fans as well as to the quantity. Enthusiastic fans are appreciated. The fact that large numbers of fans at an event is not all-important was illustrated by a controversy in 1982 regarding the home fans of the Edmonton Oilers of the National Hockey League. Although the more than 17,000 seats of the Edmonton Coliseum were sold out for every game and the team led the league in home attendance, some of the players together with the local media publicly chastised the fans for their passivity. The press urged the fans to help the team perform better by being more boisterous in their support. The fans of a neighboring team in the league, the Vancouver Canucks, provided a good example of "active fans" by their actions during the 1982 Stanley Cup play-offs. The fans, through their enthusiastic cheering and frenzied waving of white towels, gained appreciative recognition from the players; nevertheless, the team lost in the finals to a more talented New York Islander team. In the National Football League such demonstrative displays by fans have become commonplace. In some situations the fans may have a more direct effect on the game outcome than by just encouraging the home team. For example, wildly shouting Houston Oiler fans in the enclosed Astrodome have virtually been able to prevent the players of opposing teams from hearing their own quarterback's signals.

Although few athletes would question the value of an enthusiastic audience, objective evidence concerning the effects of reactive observers is very scarce. Laird (1923) in his early study did find that "razzing" by a group of peer observers disrupted performance of steadiness and coordination tasks. Evidence indicates that active audiences through their suggestions can influence the direction of a performer's behavior (Borden, 1980). This may have particular relevance to sport in encouraging a certain style of play. Spectators "screaming for blood" and encouraging aggressive behavior may significantly change the nature of the game. Evidence for such an effect occurring at college basketball games is provided in a recent study by Thirer & Rampey (1979).

As with audience size, the number of coactors has been shown to affect performance in some cases but not others (Carron, 1980, Wankel, 1975a). Again, as was discussed in the case of observers, the specific effects are probably influenced by the information provided to the performer by the particular situation. If it is assumed that coaction effects are largely mediated by evaluation apprehension or fear of failing at competition (cf. Geen, 1980), then adding additional coactors to a situation will affect performance only to the extent that they arouse these reactions in the performers. Hence, the number of coactors is probably not as significant a consideration as who the coactors are and the performers' feelings toward those coactors. If some of the additional coactors added to a situation lead to significantly increased rivalrous feelings on the part of a performer, then his or her subsequent performance will likely be affected.

In conclusion, a number of personal and situational factors have been shown to significantly influence how the presence of observers and coactors affects performance. Further, evidence is generally consistent with the view that how a given factor influences an individual's behavior is contingent upon the individual's subjective interpretation of that situation. It would, therefore, seem appropriate for future researchers to pay greater attention to how situational factors influence an individual's subjective interpretation of the social context (its nature and importance), the task requirements, his or her performance capabilities, and the potential outcomes and their perceived importance.

PRACTICAL APPLICATIONS

Although many areas pertaining to audience and coaction effects require further research before firm conclusions can be drawn, the current information does provide some guidelines for coaching practice. These guidelines will undoubtedly change as further insight is gained through future research; however, they seem warranted on the basis of information currently available.

The generalization that evaluative observers or coactors (e.g., competitors) can facilitate performance of well learned tasks but impede learning of new skills has ready application. The coach, especially the coach of young athletes who must learn many new complex skills, should eliminate evaluation apprehension as much as possible from the learning environment. Fear of failure can definitely inhibit trying and learning new skills. Later the coach can assist the athlete's preparation for performing under stressful conditions. The increasing evidence that the individual's subjective interpretation of the audience situation is pivotal to how the individual reacts makes it essential that the athlete be mentally prepared for dealing with stressful and distracting situations. By educating the athlete to the potential arousing and distracting effects of an audience and coactors, the coach can assist the athlete's mental preparation. Specifically in preparing for serious competition, the athlete must be prepared to deal with subtle distracting and harassing actions of other competitors and the negative reactions of fans. Model training programs, wherein aspects of the competitive environment are simulated in practices and preliminary games, together with attentional focusing and stress management techniques, would be useful.

The coach should be aware of his or her role in affecting the athlete's evaluation apprehension. In important competitions where the greatest danger is probably in being over-aroused to the point of losing concentration, the coach should serve as a calm model and provide the athlete with support and reassurance. Supportive teammates can also be invaluable in assisting the individual to cope with threatening situations. The importance of the athlete's performance and the competition must be kept in perspective. This is not the only meet, nor the only thing in the athlete's life. Another important consideration is that if the coach has done his or her job well prior to the major event, the athlete will have mastered the skills to the point that he or she is not intimidated by the situation, and the arousal stimulated by the audience may have facilitory rather than detrimental effects upon performance.

As in all areas of coaching, the coach must be aware of individual differences in reactions to audience and coaction situations. Although information on personality predispositions, especially anxiety proneness, may be useful it is probably more important to obtain more specific information on how the athlete reacts to different situations. Case study approaches to monitoring behavior and discussing an athlete's feelings prior to different situations can help provide useful individual information that the coach can use to assist the athlete in effectively preparing for optimal performance.

SUMMARY

This chapter has surveyed the broad literature pertaining to how the presence of others affects performance. A historical review of major theoretical contributions to understanding how the presence of coactors or passive observers affects performance was provided. The contributions of Triplett, Allport, Dashiell, and Zajonc were highlighted. Major emphasis was placed upon the drive theory of social facilitation, which has been the dominant theoretical model for much of the research in the field. It was observed that although drive theory accounts for many of the experimental findings, it has some major limitations when applied to complex human behavior. Further, it was noted that drive theory and Zajonc's (1965) restricted definition of social facilitation is not representative of most audience or coaction situations in sport. Accordingly, a more complex cognitive model proposed by Borden (1980) was suggested as being more useful for sport research. This model, which incorporates both drive-like motivational effects due to the presence of others and evaluation apprehension as well as information effects as to what performance behavior is most acceptable in the observers, was used as a framework for examining how personal and situational factors influence audience or coaction effects upon performance. Finally, some practical applications of the research were discussed.

Chapter 22

Individual and Group Performance in Sport

Diane L. Gill
University of Iowa

Most sport activities involve groups or teams; indeed, the psychological dynamics of sport groups are important components of sport psychology. Group performance is a particularly pressing practical issue as most coaches and others working with sport groups devote considerable effort to maximizing team performance. Unfortunately, most sport psychology work, especially the emerging applied sport psychology literature, focuses on individual performance and behavior and offers little guidance for those interested in group performance. Of course, all the variables that influence individual performance (e.g., evaluation, attributions, etc.) operate on individuals within groups; but when team performance is at issue a host of complex, interacting social psychological variables are introduced. The simple fact that a teammate is present creates a coaction situation that affects individual performance, as noted in Chapter 21 by Wankel.

By definition, group performance also adds the element of *interaction* among members. According to Shaw (1976, p. 11), "A group is defined as two or more persons who are interacting with one another in such a manner that each person influences and is influenced by each other person." An intramural basketball team, then, is a group, but a number of individuals who happen to be shooting baskets in the same gym do not constitute a group. The degree and form of interaction varies among sport teams; basketball teams, track teams, and children's play groups, for example, exhibit differing interaction patterns. Nevertheless, interaction is the key defining characteristic that sets a group apart from a collection of individuals, and one must consider the psychological factors and processes involved in group interaction to fully understand the performance of a team and its members.

RESEARCH ON PERFORMANCE
IN SPORT GROUPS

Steiner's Model of Group Productivity

To sort out the literature and shed some light on the individual-group performance relationship in sport, a conceptual framework is invaluable. Fortunately, Steiner (1972) has developed such a theoretical model, albeit a general one, of group productivity or performance. The essence of Steiner's model is: Actual productivity equals potential productivity minus losses due to faulty process.

Actual productivity or performance is what the group actually does. Potential productivity is the group's best possible performance given its resources and the task demands. The group's resources comprise all relevant knowledges and skills of individual members, including the overall level and distribution of such talents.

Individual ability, demonstrated by individual performance, is a resource—probably the most important resource for sport groups. Perhaps the most accepted maxim by both researchers and practitioners is that the best individuals make the best team. Undoubtedly coaches and researchers would agree that the rule is true in a general sense (five intercollegiate basketball players will defeat five intramural players consistently), but the relationship is not perfect. Most of us can recall incidents when teams with all the talent to win the championship did not do so, or when teams without individual stars performed exceptionally well as a group. Reviewers of the individual ability-group performance literature in social psychology (e.g., Haythorn, 1968; Heslin, 1964; McGrath & Altman, 1966) concur with those observations; individual member abilities are positively related to group performance, but the relationship is moderate at best and mediated by task and situational factors.

According to Steiner's model, greater resources increase potential productivity and, as in the general maxim, the best individuals make the best team. However, Steiner's model does go beyond the general maxim. Resources must be relevant to the task. Thus, height is a relevant resource for volleyball but not for a track relay team. Task demands, the rules and requirements imposed by the task, determine relevant resources. Steiner has developed an elaborate typology of group tasks and task demands to clarify the individual-group performance literature and encourage more precise predictions of group performance across a variety of tasks. Unfortunately, Steiner's typology is most applicable to problem-solving tasks, and although Landers (1974) applied Steiner's model and typology to group motor tasks, sport psychologists have not found Steiner's typology very helpful in advancing our understanding of sport group performance. Rather than applying Steiner's typology, sport psychologists often invoke a distinction based on the degree of interaction or cooperation required in the group task. Basketball, for example, requires considerable interaction whereas swimming and track require fewer cooperative efforts between team members. A classification or assessment system to differentiate sport group tasks in terms of interaction requirements could greatly advance the research on sport group performance. Even without a widely accepted, standard task typology, sport psychologists and other sport researchers should keep task characteristics in mind when interpreting the literature.

A group that effectively uses its available resources to meet task demands approaches its potential productivity. In Steiner's model, though, a group's actual performance falls short of its potential because of faulty process. Process, everything the group does while transforming its resources into a product or performance (putting it all together), is critical but somewhat mysterious in Steiner's model. Process is subdivided by Steiner into two general categories of coordination losses and motivation losses, but further elaboration is lacking. Process is the black box of group performance. The actions and interactions of group members are clearly essential variables in group performance (resources and task demands are relatively stable), and both research and practice should be directed toward group process if we are to understand and enhance group performance. Unfortunately, researchers have seldom delved into the black box of group process, and Steiner's model offers only limited guidance.

Research on individual and group motor performance, limited as it is, falls into two general categories. First, some research that evolved from the social psychology literature on group performance focuses on the relationship between individual abilities (resources) and group performance without considering intervening processes. A second line of research, stemming directly from Steiner's model, probes group process losses, particularly the "social loafing" phenomenon. The general individual-group performance literature will be reviewed first, followed by a more extensive discussion of the social loafing literature.

Individual and Group Motor Performance

Most social psychology research on individual and group performance involves problem-solving and decision-making tasks. Investigators have developed elaborate schemes to predict group performance (e.g., Davis & Restle, 1963; Lorge & Solomon, 1955), but such tasks are so far removed from sport and motor tasks that generalization to group motor performance is seldom warranted; only a few studies specifically have examined individual and group motor performance.

Napier (1968), in a study that paralleled group problem-solving research, investigated group performance on two motor tasks as well as a verbal task. Napier used individual performance data to create nominal group scores (statistical combinations of individual scores) to compare with actual group performance. When two group members each used a pursuit rotor task, the group time was defined as the time when *both* individuals were on target (a conjunctive task). Actual group scores were similar to nominal group scores formed with a conjunctive combination. Similarly, actual group performance on a maze task was similar to nominal group scores computed as averages of individual scores.

Wegner and Zeaman (1956) also used a pursuit rotor task, but created an interactive task by having groups of two or four, as well as individuals, use handles to manipulate a single stylus. Group performance was better and also more variable than individual performance. Wegner and Zeaman further noted that group performance was proportional to the performance of the poorer member's individual score in two-person groups, but proportional to the best member's score in four-person groups.

The most cited work on individual and group motor performance is that of Comrey and his colleagues (Comrey, 1953; Comrey & Deskin, 1954a, 1954b) and of Wiest, Porter, and Ghiselli (1961). Both Comrey, using the Purdue pegboard task, and Wiest et al., using puzzles, had subjects perform a series of individual trials followed by a series of group trials. In all cases the individual scores of both partners were positively correlated with group performance, and combining the two individual scores in a multiple correlation yielded a moderate, positive relationship with group performance. The overall findings further indicated that when partners were required to alternate performance on the pegboard task, group performance was more highly related to the score of the poorer partner, but with greater task flexibility on Comrey's cognitive task (Comrey & Staats, 1955) and the Wiest et al. puzzle task, group performance was more highly related to the better partner's individual score.

In a study directly involving sport teams, Jones (1974) investigated the relationship of team performance (rankings or final win/loss records) on available individual statistics (i.e., singles rankings in tennis, points for and against in football, RBIs and ERAs in baseball, and points, assists, and rebounds in basketball). Correlations ranging from .60 to .90 led Jones to conclude that group effectiveness was positively related to individual effectiveness in all cases. The relationship was weakest for basketball, with individual statistics accounting for about 35% of team performance variability. Jones noted that basketball was the only sport in which individual skills were balanced (in other sports the best individuals tended to be on the same teams) and suggested that the balance of individual abilities allowed other factors to operate such as cohesion, teamwork, and the ability to respond in clutch situations. It might also be noted that basketball involves the greatest interaction of the four sports examined, and that interaction requirement may reduce the individual ability-group performance relationship.

The studies cited suggest a positive individual-group motor performance relationship, but typically less than half of the group performance variability was explained by individual measures and the observed relationships were not really predictive. To predict group performance from individual ability, independent assessment of individual ability is needed and groups of varying ability combinations should be formed. Comrey and Wiest et al. did not control the ability composition of their groups, and in the Jones study individual measures were simultaneous with and actually components of the group measures.

In light of the limitations of the previous research, ability composition was manipulated in a controlled lab study (Gill, 1979) to examine the individual-group motor performance relationship. Two separate experiments were conducted within the study. In both, scores from an individual performance session with the motor maze task were used to form two-person groups representing a range of average ability levels and discrepancies between partners for a group performance session. In Experiment 1 two group tasks were used, one requiring maximum interaction or cooperative effort between partners and the other requiring minimum interaction. In Experiment 2 only the cooperative task was used, but groups performed under both competitive and noncompetitive conditions. Multiple regression analyses, using average ability and ability discrepancy as predictors, yielded a moderate, positive correlation with group performance in both Experiment 1 ($R = .54$) and Experiment 2 ($R = .64$). Average ability was the primary predictor, but ability discrepancy had a negative effect on cooperative performance, suggesting a conjunctive element.

In Experiment 2, a control group performed as individuals in the second session as well as the first, and the reliability of individual performance from session to session was .76. Thus, individual scores could predict only 58% of the variance of future individual performance as compared with the moderate prediction of group performance (41%). Individual performance was not especially reliable from session to session (and almost completely unreliable from trial to trial). Quite likely, sport performance, which is subject to numerous influences that could be controlled in the lab, is even less reliable or consistent. For example, a baseball batter may go 3 for 4 in one game and 1 for 4 in the next game. In light of the variability of both individual and group motor performance, one should not expect more than a moderate, positive prediction.

The Ringelmann Effect

Most of the previously cited research has assessed individual performance or ability and group performance with no attention given to the intervening group process. However, one line of research in the group performance literature has developed into a systematic investigation of group process. That research follows a limited experimental paradigm stemming from an obscure, unpublished study of individual and group performance on a rope-pulling task. Over 50 years ago a German psychologist named Ringelmann observed individuals and groups of two, three, and eight persons pulling on a rope (as described by Moede in 1927 and cited in many group performance studies, e.g., Dashiell, 1935; Ingham, Levinger, Graves, & Peckham, 1974; Latane, Williams, & Harkins, 1979). Groups in Ringelmann's study pulled with more force than individuals, but not with as much force as would be predicted from individual scores (an additive combination). Eight-person groups did not pull eight times as hard as individuals but rather only four times as hard. The average individual force for two-person groups was 93% of the average indvidual force, 85% for three-person groups, and 49% for eight-person groups. The decrease in average individual performance with increases in group size is known as the Ringelmann effect. (The work of unpublished authors does not always perish.)

The Ringelmann effect was mentioned frequently in discussions of group performance, but was not replicated or published with sufficient detail to allow interpretation until Ingham, Levinger, Graves, and Peckham (1974) resurrected the original Ringelmann paradigm with updated controls and modifications. Ingham et al.'s first step was to replicate the Ringelmann effect with a rope-pulling task in a controlled lab setting with individuals and groups of two, three, four, five, and six persons. Experiment 1 of Ingham et al.'s study partially replicated the reported Ringelmann findings. The average individual performance in two-person groups was 91% of the average individual performance, and average performance dropped to 82% in three-person groups. Groups of four, five, and six persons, however, did not evidence further decreases as the average performance in six-person groups was 78% of the average individual performance.

Ingham et al. not only demonstrated the Ringelmann effect, but extended their investigation within Steiner's theoretical framework. Steiner (1972) had interpreted the Ringelmann effect as coordination losses after noting that the observed drops in performance were a linear function of the number of coordination links (one in a two-person group, three in a three-person group, and 28 in an eight-person group). Ingham et al. examined possible motivation losses in group process by eliminating the coordination requirements of the group task. In Experiment 2 of the Ingham et al. study, only one real subject pulled on the rope. By using blindfolds and trained confederates who pretended to pull on the rope, subjects were led to believe they were performing in groups of one to six persons. The results were virtually identical to Experiment 1. Average performance dropped to 85% in three-person groups and no further drops were observed. Ingham et al. thus concluded that the decreases in average performance were due to motivational losses within groups.

In discussing the findings, Ingham et al. referred to sport groups that may be susceptible to motivation losses. Specifically, they cited the performance times of crews in the 1952 through 1964 Olympiads. Coxed fours were only 13% faster than pairs, and eights were only 23% faster than pairs. In 1972 the winning double scull was 4% faster than the winning single, and coxed eights were only 6% faster than fours. Of course, as Ingham et al. noted, differences in shell size, weight, and water displacement are alternative explanations for performance differences.

Social Loafing

More recently, Latane and his colleagues have undertaken a systematic investigation of group performance and process and, in light of Ingham et al.'s findings, dubbed the phenomenon "social loafing." Their series of experiments, systematically examining social loafing and delving into its causes and implications, merits extended discussion.

The first study of the series (Latane, Williams, & Harkins, 1979) included two experiments using clapping and shouting as group tasks. As in the Ingham et al. study, Experiment 1 attempted to replicate the Ringelmann effect with individuals and groups of two, four, and six persons. Again the Ringelmann effect was demonstrated as the average sound per person decreased from the alone condition to 71% in two-person groups, 51% in four-person groups, and 40% in six-person groups.

The main focus of the Latane et al. study was group process in the social loafing phenomenon. Although Ingham et al.'s findings implicated motivational losses and a diffusion of responsibility explanation, Latane et al. noted that in Ingham et al.'s study audience size increased as group size decreased (subjects observed when not performing in the six-person groups). Thus, the increased evaluation potential of the audience in the alone condition could explain the findings. To eliminate this alternate explanation, Latane et al. created pseudo-groups and actual groups in

Experiment 2. In the pseudo-groups, instructions and constant background noise played through earphones led subjects to believe they were clapping or shouting in groups when, in fact, they were performing alone.

Actual groups in Experiment 2 performed much like the groups in Experiment 1, as the average sounds in two- and six-person groups were 66% and 36% of the average sound in the alone condition. Pseudo-groups also demonstrated social loafing, with the average sound dropping to 82% in two-person groups and 74% in six-person groups. Because coordination losses (e.g., interfering sound waves) were eliminated in the pseudo-groups, Latane et al. concluded that this performance drop was due to motivation losses or social loafing. The greater performance drop for actual groups represented a combination of coordination and motivation losses. Thus, unlike Ingham et al., Latane et al. observed both coordination and motivation losses on their group tasks.

Social loafing, or motivation losses in groups, was the more intriguing issue for Latane and his colleagues. Observing the phenomenon was one step, but Latane and his colleagues pursued the issue in subsequent investigations probing the causes and explanations of social loafing. One possible explanation was that persons know or assume that others perform with less effort in groups and thus reduce their own efforts. However, when Latane, Harkins, and Williams (1980) asked individuals to predict the results of their earlier study, respondents estimated that the average subject would exert more effort and produce more sound in groups than alone, suggesting that preconceptions about individual and group performance do not account for social loafing.

Another plausible explanation was that when individuals know they must perform both alone and in groups, they allocate their efforts and save their best or maximum effort for the alone condition. In two separate experiments, Harkins, Latane, and Williams (1980) failed to support an allocational strategy in group performance; social loafing occurred even when persons performed only in groups.

A more likely explanation for social loafing relates to diffusion of responsibility. Williams, Harkins, and Latane (1981) proposed that *identifiability* of individual performance is critical and that when individual efforts are lost in the crowd, performance decreases. Williams et al. conducted two experiments to test the identifiability explanation. Experiment 1 included two stages; the first stage replicated the alone and pseudo-group conditions of the earlier study (Latane et al., 1979), and in a second stage the subjects were led to believe that their individual outputs were identifiable. Identifiability in the second stage eliminated social loafing. Experiment 2, using a between-subjects design, also indicated that identifiability led to consistently high individual performance, eliminating social loafing.

Introducing the identifiability factor reconciles the apparently conflicting coaction effects in social facilitation literature and the social loafing phenomenon in group performance literature. In typical coaction situations, evaluation potential *increases* with an increase in the number of coactors. In typical social loafing situations, evaluation potential *decreases* as group size increases. When identifiability remains high in group performance situations, evaluation potential does not decrease and Willams et al.'s findings indicate that performance does not decrease.

Williams et al. also noted that social loafing in groups shares some commonalities with the learned helplessness phenomenon described by Seligman (1975). When identifiability decreases in groups, the perceived contingency between individual efforts and outcomes lessens. As with learned helplessness, individuals perceive less control over outcomes, resulting in lessened motivation and effort.

The Williams et al. (1981) findings indicated that simply monitoring individual performance eliminated social loafing. If simple monitoring can eliminate social loafing, perhaps other factors can provide a social incentive and actually *increase* individual efforts in groups. Sport teams are natural examples of groups that seem to provide social incentives (e.g., cohesion, pressure from teammates, etc.). Latane and his colleagues noted that subjects in their studies believed people would do better in groups and specifically cited relays in track and swimming. Prompted by some of these suggestions, Latane, Harkins, and Williams (1980) tested the social loafing and identifiability phenomena in a sport setting.

Latane et al. (1980) first checked individual and relay times at the 1977 Big Ten intercollegiate swim meet. By comparing the times of swimmers who swam both individual and relay events in the same stroke and distance, Latane et al. observed no social loafing. Instead, times for relay events were faster than individual times. However, swimmers can get a faster start in relay events and this could account for the difference. Thus, Latane et al. designed a controlled experiment to test their swimming observations.

A competitive situation was set up with 16 members of an intercollegiate swim team divided into four teams of four swimmers each. All swimmers swam in two 100-meter individual freestyle events and one lap in each of two 400-meter freestyle relays. Starts were the same for both individual and relay events, and swimmers were told that starting techniques and timing procedures were being examined. Along with the individual and relay conditions, identifiability was manipulated either by announcing or not announcing individual lap times. Spectators were present at the experimental meet, and winners of individual and relay events received T-shirts. The investigators noted that good times, including at least one personal record, were recorded, suggesting high motivation and effort.

Latane et al. observed an identifiability by individual-relay interaction. Under low identifiability, individual times were faster (61.34) than relay times (61.66), suggesting social loafing. However, under high identifiability individual times were slower (60.95) than relay times (60.18). Announcing individual times not only eliminated social loafing, but under high identifiability the group situation seemed to provide a social incentive. The authors noted that although the time differences were small (1.43–0.39 sec.), that is often the difference between places in a competitive event. It is also notable that ceiling effects did not cancel out the interaction effect. Apparently the manipulation was sufficient to overcome other powerful factors (e.g., competition, spectators, high-level training).

Research Directions

Research on individual and group motor performance, limited as it is, suggests directions for sport psychology research on group performance and provides information of immediate practical value. Sport teams are especially vulnerable to social loafing or social incentive processes. Indeed, group performance researchers with no ties to sport or motor behavior fields have often invoked sport teams as examples. The research of Latane and his colleagues is especially applicable, but that research also leaves many questions unanswered. Latane et al. (1980) have outlined the following five directions for future research, and those directions seem applicable to research on sport group performance:

1. What psychological processes underlie social loafing? Does diffusion of responsibility, loss of control, lack of identifiability, or distraction operate in sport groups?

2. On what kind of tasks and in what kind of job settings does social loafing occur? How does the competitive situation affect social loafing?

3. How does social loafing relate to job satisfaction and the quality of work life? Do some people prefer social loafing situations, perhaps in recreational level sports?

4. Are the forces leading to social loafing moderated and/or modifiable by cultural backgrounds, philosophical or political ideology, or personal life history? Does gender, social class, or any other individual or social difference affect social loafing?

5. How can the effects of social loafing be neutralized or reversed? Does team cohesion or coaching style influence social loafing?

Although these and many other questions have yet to be answered, the existing literature does provide useful information. Perhaps the most basic finding is that research supports our common belief in the general individual ability-group performance relationship; the best individuals make the best team. No evidence suggests any reason for selecting any but the most skilled or capable individual performers.

However, the research does not offer any advice on the practical issue of identifying appropriate individual skills and abilities. Individual performance on a related task is not necessarily the most appropriate measure. A group task, especially a task with a high interaction component, may require skills not elicited in individual performance. For example, a track relay involves the skills of passing and receiving the baton as well as individual speed. Sports with considerable interaction impose many skill requirements not present in individual performance such as timing passes, coordinating double plays, and executing complex zone defenses.

IMPLICATIONS FOR SPORT GROUPS

Reducing Coordination and Motivation Losses

Identifying persons who possess individual interactive skills as well as individual performance skills could greatly reduce the coordination losses referred to in Steiner's model. In lieu of selection, or when selection is not possible, coaches and instructors might direct their efforts at developing interactive skills and reducing coordination losses. Indeed, most coaches direct a large portion of their efforts at reducing coordination losses. Drills in interactive skills, set plays, and formations all reduce uncertainty and variability in the group process and probably reduce coordination losses. Neither social psychologists nor sport psychologists can offer much additional information to coaches and instructors about reducing coordination losses. There is no research on the relative merits of different techniques and methods for teaching and practicing interactive skills or balancing the practice of interactive and noninteractive skills.

Psychologists have more to say about motivation, however. Zander (1971, 1975) is one of the few social psychologists to address the issue of group motivation at length and apply this work to sport teams. Using constructs analogous to the Atkinson model of achievement motivation, Zander proposes a desire for group success (Dgs) as a key element in group motivation. The Dgs is situation-specific, unlike the analogous motive to approach success (Ms) in Atkinson's model, but like Ms, Dgs spurs group members to set and strive for challenging goals. As with individuals, challenging but realistic goals with approximately a 50% chance of success elicit optimal achievement behavior. Emerson's (1966) unique participant observation study of a Mt. Everest climbing team indicated that team members directed their communication toward maintaining uncertainty (a 50% chance of success) to elicit maximum effort. With specific reference to sport, Zander advocates developing Dgs through a pride-in-team approach. One could interpret Zander as advocating emphasizing group goals and de-emphasizing individual goals (there is no I in team), but this is not necessarily true. Zander stresses the importance of making sure each member understands that his or her individual contribution is valued. Yukelson's chapter on group motivation provides a more extensive discussion of this and related group motivation issues.

Recognizing Individual Contributions

The research of Ingham, Latane, and their colleagues clearly points out the inadvisability of submerging individuals within the team. Group goals, like individual goals, must be specific and behavior oriented to effectively influence performance, but ultimately, the specific behaviors contributing to group goals are individual behaviors. Those desired behaviors may involve interactions with teammates in tasks or processes that are not as evident as individual and group performance outcomes (points, win/loss, etc.). Indeed, key interactive behaviors are often overlooked when we focus on performance outcomes in sport. The task for the coach, or anyone working with sport groups, is to identify individual behaviors that contribute to group performance and work to increase the identifiability and recognition of those behaviors.

After appropriate individual behaviors are specified, tactics to encourage and reinforce those behaviors are needed. Feedback is a relatively simple but effective tactic. Research (Zajonc, 1962; Zander & Wolfe, 1964) indicates that feedback to group members that includes individual scores as well as group scores elicits better performance than feedback of only group scores. Recently, Gross (1982) examined social loafing and the influence of group and individual feedback on a group motor task. Although four-person groups in the Gross study did not exhibit social loafing, possibly due to identifiability and evaluation potential in the group task, feedback effects were observed. Groups who received feedback of both individual and group times improved performance more than did groups who received only group feedback or no feedback.

Along with information feedback, encouragement and reinforcement for positive individual behaviors is logical. As research on individual motivation and rewards indicates, though, emphasis on extrinsic rewards can reduce intrinsic motivation (e.g., Weinberg's Chapter 13).

Thus, verbal encouragement and specific, informative evaluations of positive behaviors will likely be more effective and have fewer negative consequences than adding extensive extrinsic reward systems.

Currently attributional approaches to individual motivation are favored over behavioral approaches, and certainly attributional approaches may be appropriate for groups. Williams et al. (1981) identified lessened perceived contingency between individual behaviors and outcomes as a source of social loafing and referred to Seligman's work, which follows an attributional or cognitive approach. Logically, attributional approaches might be geared at heightening the contingency between individual efforts and desired group outcomes.

Effective coaches have developed methods of identifying and recognizing contributions to team performance. Latane et al. (1980) cited the example of football linemen at Ohio State. The individual contributions of linemen could easily be lost by focusing on the group outcome. Latane et al. noted that both Woody Hayes and Earle Bruce used several techniques to increase the identifiability and recognition of linemen's individual efforts, including filming and specifically grading each player on each play, "lineman of the week" honors, and decals to signify individual effort.

At the University of Iowa, basketball coach Lute Olson developed a "total performance chart" to rate each player in each game. Total performance included assists, steals, blocked shots, and forced turnovers as well as points and rebounds, and subtracted errors such as missed shots, fouls, and turnovers. Many of the components were not included in typical game reports, but the coach considered those behaviors essential for optimal group performance. At Iowa Olson touted his total performance concept to the extent that media reports often included this statistic and gave total performance statistics precedence over more typical point totals.

Many professional, college, high school, and even youth sport coaches use similar charts or other techniques to encourage and recognize individual efforts within teams. Current literature suggests that those coaches who explicitly recognize individual contributions may well have more effective teams than those coaches who follow more traditional strategies of rewarding only group performance outcomes and downplaying individual performance.

SUMMARY

Perhaps the most intriguing finding in the group performance literature is that not only may social loafing be reduced, but the group may provide social incentives to enhance individual efforts. At present, the research asks more questions about the incentive properties of groups than it answers, but the preliminary findings are encouraging. Identifiability of individual contributions, increased evaluation potential, feedback, behavioral and cognitive motivational techniques, and any number of intrapersonal and interpersonal psychological factors not yet examined, may enhance individual performance in teams. The investigation of precise influences and interactive effects of those and other variables within sport teams is a task for future research. In summary, then, the following suggestions are offered to those who work with sport groups:

- Identify the individual behaviors that contribute to desired group performance; be especially alert to interactive behaviors that are unique to your sport, yet are often overlooked.
- Make sure individual behaviors are recognized for the contribution they make to the overall performance and function of the group.

Chapter 23

Leadership in Sports

P. Chelladurai
University of Western Ontario

In no other field of endeavor except perhaps athletics will we find so
many young people voluntarily subjugating themselves to the authority
of one individual, the coach. Their reliance on the coach's expertise and
motivational techniques to achieve their personal goal is truly
remarkable. Despite this unique situation in athletics, research on the
phenomenon has unfortunately been sparse and sporadic (Loy, McPherson, & Kenyon, 1978). The study of leadership is critical to the
understanding of sport performance because leadership is instrumental
in enhancing the motivational state of the athlete and/or team (House,
1971).

LEADERSHIP DEFINED

The view that sport teams are formal organizations (Ball, 1975), and that
the coach is a manager (Sage, 1974), gives us an opportunity to differentiate leadership from the coach's many and varied managerial functions
such as planning, organizing, budgeting, scheduling, recruiting, and
public relations. Leadership, defined as "the behavioral process of influencing individuals and groups toward set goals" (Barrow, 1977,
p. 232), is interpersonal in nature, entails a high degree of direct interaction with the athletes, and bears directly on the motivation of the team
members. In contrast, the other managerial functions are performed

away from the actual coaching context, and can be carried on by other individuals in the organization. This emphasis on the effects of leadership on the motivational state of the *athlete* contrasts with earlier studies that have focused exclusively on the *coach* (e.g., Bird, 1977b; Lenk, 1977; Sage, 1975).

Insofar as leadership is aimed at enhancing the motivational state of the individual, it is useful to begin our discussion with a description of the individual's motivational process. Subsequent sections will elucidate the relationship between leadership, athlete motivation, and situational constraints and/or demands.

ATHLETES' MOTIVATIONAL PROCESS

Chelladurai (1981) modified Porter and Lawler's (1968) model of motivation for application in the athletic context. Briefly, the modified model (presented in Figure 23-1) is based on the assumption that the individual is motivated to participate in athletics because he/she values the rewards of such participation and has some beliefs about obtaining those rewards. This motivation (box 1) is translated into a degree of effort, (box 2) which in turn results in a certain level of performance (box 3). The performance achieved affects what rewards the individual receives (box 4). Receipt of those rewards leads to a certain level of satisfaction (box 5), which in a cyclic manner affects future motivation. Unfortunately, this simple paradigm is complicated by three personal factors that mediate the various linkages. The relationship between one's effort and resultant performance is contingent upon one's ability (box 6) and also on a clear perception of one's role (box 7). That is, not only should the athlete possess the ability required for a given performance level, but the athlete must also know how and where to expend his/her efforts. The next disturbance concerns the relationship between receipt of rewards

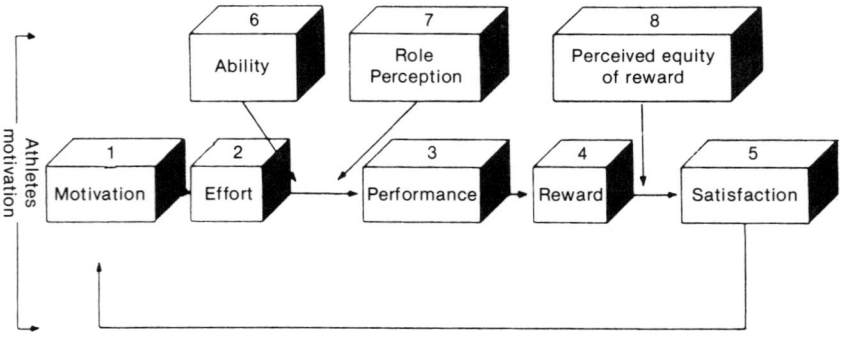

FIGURE 23-1 Model of motivation (from: Chelladurai, 1981).

and satisfaction and is caused by the athlete's perception of how equitable those rewards are (box 8). That is, the athlete compares the rewards he/she has just received to some internalized standard of how much should have been received. The internal standard could be based on the total cost in relation to total benefit, or it could be based on personal cost-benefit balance versus those of comparable others. The point is that if the athlete does not perceive the rewards to be equitable, his or her satisfaction would be reduced, which in turn could reduce future motivation.

LEADERSHIP-MOTIVATION INTERFACE

The motivational process depicted above is the basis of the more recent Path-Goal Theory of Leadership (House, 1971; House & Dessler, 1974). The theory suggests that the strategic function of the leader is "to provide . . . the coaching, guidance, support and rewards necessary for effective and satisfying performance that would otherwise be lacking in the environment" (House & Dessler, 1974, p. 31). More specifically, "The motivational function of the leader consists of increasing personal pay-offs to subordinates for work-goal attainment, and making the path to these pay-offs easier to travel by clarifying it, reducing road blocks and pitfalls, and increasing the opportunities for personal satisfaction en route" (p. 31).

In accordance with the above propositions, Chelladurai (1981) suggested some ways in which the coach can enhance an athlete's performance and satisfaction through his/her specific behaviors and reactions. In order to understand the intermingling of coaching behavior and athlete motivation, it would be useful to look at Chelladurai and Saleh's (1980) five-dimensional description of coaching behavior presented in Table 23-1. This table, the Leadership Scale for Sports, consists of 40 items representing five dimensions of leader behavior in sports.

Training and instruction behavior concerns the development and mastery of the skills, techniques, and tactics of the sport. These behaviors should increase the ability of the athlete (box 6), thereby strengthening the effort-performance relationship. Training and instruction also clarifies the role for the athlete (box 7) (i.e., the relationships between specific efforts and activities, and desired performance outcomes) and therefore would more strongly link effort with performance.

Coaching behavior can also affect the relationship between rewards and satisfaction. There are two types of rewards: intrinsic and extrinsic. Intrinsic rewards, such as sense of accomplishment and competence or the joy of mastering a skill or overcoming a challenge, are a function of certain performance standards internalized by the athlete.

TABLE 23-1
The Leadership Scale for Sports (LSS)*

Dimension	Description
Training and instruction behavior	Coaching behavior aimed at improving athletes' performance by emphasizing and facilitating hard and strenuous training; instructing them in the skills, techniques, and tactics of the sport; clarifying the relationship among the members; and by structuring and coordinating the members' activities.
Democratic behavior	Coaching behavior which allows greater participation by the athletes in decisions pertaining to group goals, practice methods, and game tactics and strategies.
Autocratic behavior	Coaching behavior which involves independent decision making and stresses personal authority.
Social support behavior	Coaching behavior characterized by a concern for the welfare of individual athletes, positive group atmosphere, and warm interpersonal relations with members.
Rewarding (positive feedback) behavior	Coaching behavior which reinforces an athlete by recognizing and rewarding good performance.

*The development of the LSS and its psychometric properties have been fully elaborated in Chelladurai, P., & Saleh, S.D. Dimensions of leader behavior in sports: Development of a leadership scale. *Journal of Sport Psychology*, 1980, **2**(1), 34-45.

That is, when these standards are reached, the intrinsic rewards accrue to the individual automatically and are not mediated by any external agent such as the coach. However, the coach's training and instruction can facilitate intrinsic rewards in two significant ways. First, in clarifying the effort-performance relationships, the coach can help the athlete set realistic standards and goals for personal performance. Second, the coach's training and instruction enhances the athlete's ability and thereby increases the probability of reaching the standard internalized by the athlete.

Extrinsic rewards such as status, prestige, and praise, which are administered by others, are not always equitable. This inequity can be somewhat offset by a coach's positive feedback, perhaps the most potent of all extrinsic rewards. By distributing his/her personal rewards equitably based upon the principle "equal rewards for equal performance," the coach can considerably strengthen the reward-satisfaction relationship. Robert Weinberg's Chapter 13 in this text expands the discussion of the relationship between instrinsic and extrinsic rewards.

Finally, leadership has a tremendous impact on the effort phase of the diagram in Figure 23-1 (box 2). In contrast to most work settings where effort and performance occur concurrently, athletics is character-ized by an inordinate proportion of time spent during the effort phase (practice sessions) relative to the performance setting (competition). Ob-viously, training and instruction is most effective in this stage. Addi-tionally, the coach's social support will often soften the impact of the strenuous and monotonous work required in practice by creating a warm and supportive social environment for the athletes to work in.

It must be noted that democratic behavior and autocratic behavior, not elaborated upon here, are also significant ingredients in the leader-ship mix. (For a discussion of these variables see Chelladurai & Haggerty [1978] and Chelladurai & Arnott [1983]).

INDIVIDUAL DIFFERENCES
AND PREFERRED LEADERSHIP

While the foregoing is a general description of specific leader behaviors affecting the motivational process, differences in personal characteristics would influence what kinds of coaching behaviors athletes prefer. For in-stance, gender has been found to be an important determinant of pre-ferred leadership (Chelladurai & Saleh, 1978; Erle, 1981). In their study of 160 physical education students, Chelladurai and Saleh found that males preferred their coaches to be more autocratic but yet more sup-portive than did the female respondents. Similarly, Erle's study of 335 male and female intramural and intercollegiate hockey players showed that the males preferred more training and instruction, more autocratic behavior, more social support, and less democratic behavior from their coaches than did their female counterparts.

Personality is also a significant determinant of preferred leader-ship. For instance, House (1971) and House and Dessler (1974) suggested that the leadership preferences of members high on social needs would differ from the preferences of those whose dominant needs are task-related. In the athletic context, Chelladurai and Carron (1982) reported that those high on cognitive structure (i.e., the need for more informa-tion and structure in one's environment) preferred more training and in-struction while athletes who were more impulsive preferred more social support. Erle (1981) reported that athletes' motivation for participation (affiliation, task or self) and instrinsic versus extrinsic motivation were correlated with preferred leader behavior. More specifically, the higher the task motivation, the higher the preference for training and instruc-tion; and the higher the affiliation and extrinsic motivation, the higher the preference for social support.

Ability of the individual was also hypothesized to be related to preferred leadership (Hersey & Blanchard, 1969, 1977; House, 1971). For example, the greater an athlete's ability, the less would be his/her preference for training and instruction. Unfortunately, the relationship between ability and preferred leadership has not been adequately tested. Both Chelladurai and Carron (1982) and Erle (1981) used experience as a surrogate measure of ability, and their results were not consistent with theoretical predictions. In Chelladurai and Carron's study, more experienced athletes preferred more social support, whereas in Erle's study competitive experience was positively related to preferences for training and instruction, and social support. One could argue that the higher the ability, the higher the costs of additional increments in ability. These costs would include more effort and energy in training, as well as sacrifices in social contact outside of athletics. Thus, it is not surprising to find athletes of higher ability indicating a high degree of preference for social support from the coach in each of the studies noted above.

Hersey and Blanchard's (1969, 1977) Situational Leadership Theory combines members' achievement motivation and their ability to derive the construct "maturity." According to the theory, as a member's maturity increases, the leader's task oriented behavior must progressively decrease (a linear and negative relationship); and the relation-oriented behavior must increase as maturity increases up to the middle ranges, and then progressively decrease with further increases in maturity (curvilinear relationship). Based on sports-related research, Chelladurai and Carron (1978) proposed as an alternative model that the relation-oriented behavior should progressively decrease with increasing maturity, and the task oriented behavior should take the curvilinear form. However, neither of these models have been supported by research (e.g., see Case, 1980; Chelladurai, 1984; Vos Strache, 1979).

SITUATIONAL FACTORS
AND PREFERRED LEADERSHIP

While individual characteristics are a group of variables that influence preferred leadership, situational differences also affect leadership preferences. These situational factors can be broken down into (a) the nature of the task, (b) the formal structure of the organization, (c) the primary work group, (d) the size of the unit, and (e) normative forces and organizational goals (Chelladurai & Carron, 1978).

As for task characteristics, House (1971) suggested that the greater the ambiguity surrounding the task, the greater the interdependence among tasks, and the greater the variability of the tasks, the greater the need for the leader to be directive, supportive, instructing, and coordinating. These propositions were supported by Chelladurai and Carron (1982), who found that athletes involved in interdependent tasks (team sports) preferred more training and instruction than did athletes in independent tasks (individual sports). Additionally, athletes in variable tasks (open sports such as basketball) preferred more training and instruction than athletes in nonvariable tasks (closed sports such as swimming). Also, athletes in open sports preferred more positive feedback than athletes in closed sports.

Erle's research (1981) was concerned with the effects of organizational goals on preferred leadership. His results showed that members of intercollegiate hockey teams (where pursuit of excellence is the goal) preferred more training and instruction, social support, and less positive feedback than members of intramural hockey teams (where pursuit of pleasure in physical activity is the goal). Clearly, the style of leadership selected must take into account these situational factors since the participants appear to expect different leadership behaviors in different settings.

CHARACTERISTICS OF THE COACH

The discussion thus far has focused on the individual athlete and his/her leadership needs as influenced by personal characteristics and situational differences. Now we will consider the coach and his/her leader behavior. The coach's behavior is a function of his/her own personal characteristics (personality, ability, experience, etc.) as well as the influences of the situation in which he/she operates.

Since both the athlete and the coach operate in the same environment, it can influence the coach as well as the athlete. A recent study by Fry, Kerr, and Lee (1983) reports the effects of task interdependence on perceived leader behavior of coaches. It was found that within interdependent sports (basketball, football, hockey, and volleyball), successful coaches were perceived to be higher on coordinating, exercising their leadership role, and emphasizing production than were the coaches of losing teams. Within the independent sports (swimming, track & field, golf, and wrestling), however, successful coaches were perceived to be more concerned with maintaining a closely knit group and resolving conflicts than were the unsuccessful coaches. Furthermore, successful coaches in interdependent sports, as compared to the successful coaches in independent sports, were perceived as displaying more role clarification, integrating group function, exercising the leadership role, and placing greater emphasis on production. These coaches also showed less tolerance for athletes' freedom and less concern for their comfort and well-being.

Regarding the personal characteristics of the coach, one approach has been "on providing a social psychological profile or description of coaches as a group of leaders" (Carron, 1980, p. 107). Although some researchers have found that coaches and physical education students possess certain personality characteristics (e.g., Hendry, 1974; Ogilvie & Tutko, 1966, 1970), the evidence is still meager and equivocal (Carron, 1980; Sage, 1975).

Another approach has been to apply and test Fiedler's Contingency Model of Leadership Effectiveness (Fiedler, 1967). Briefly, this model characterizes leaders as either task oriented and autocratic (the leader feels compelled to accomplish the task and therefore tends to be directive and assertive) or interpersonally oriented and democratic (the leader feels the need to establish rapport with subordinates and therefore tends to be affective). The model then describes the situation as either more or less favorable for enhancing the leader's influence. For example, the situation is favorable when leader/subordinate relations are warm and friendly, the task is simple and structured, and the leader has high authority. The theory's major proposition is that task oriented leaders will be more effective in both the least and most favorable situations, whereas the interpersonally oriented leaders will be more effective in moderately favorable situations. These contingent relationships are shown in Figure 23-2.

The few studies that have tested Fiedler's model in the athletic context have not supported the theory (e.g., Bird, 1977b; Danielson, 1978;

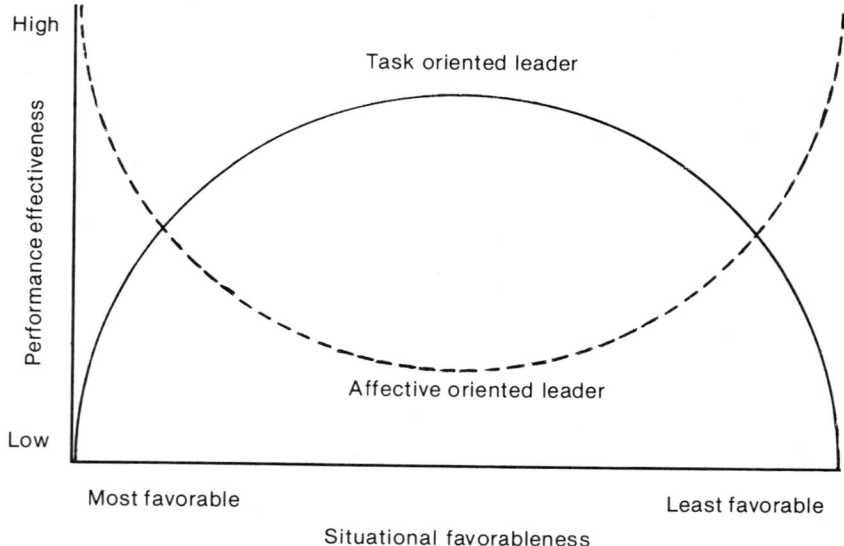

FIGURE 23-2 Fiedler's contingency model of leadership effectiveness (from: Chelladurai & Carron, 1978).

Gainter, 1976; Gilbert, 1977; Inciong, 1974; Lowry, 1972; Vander Velden, 1972). Although one can raise several issues concerning the operational measures used, the major criticism is that the teams in these studies were from the same league or organizational context and therefore could not have differed much in situational favorableness. "In the absence of differences in the situational parameters, Fiedler's model cannot be adequately tested" (Chelladurai & Carron, 1978, p. 29).

A useful approach to studying this area would be to analyze the role and task requirements of the coach and then try to determine if an individual possessed the needed personal characteristics. Katz's (1955) three-level classification of managerial competencies provides a framework for such an analysis. Technical competencies refer to a leader's knowledge and expertise in the specific group task and its processes. For a coach, this would mean a comprehensive knowledge and background in the skills, strategies, and tactics of the sport, as well as its rules and regulations. Conceptual competencies pertain to the leader's capacity to understand and react effectively to a problem in all its complexities. For example, the selection of a team and/or strategy depends upon the complex interrelationships among the players and their attributes, the performance requirements of the various playing positions in the chosen strategy and, of course, the athletes and strategies of the opposing team. As is readily apparent, competency in this domain is gained through a knowledge of the sport itself (technical competency) as well as through experience in handling the complex problems associated with coaching. But evidence suggests that conceptual competency is also a function of the trait called cognitive style or cognitive complexity (Foa, Mitchell, & Fiedler, 1971).

Cognitive style or complexity refers to the degree to which an individual is able to differentiate and integrate various bits of information and make judgments using a number of relevant factors. Finally, "human" competencies (i.e., a leader's power of persuasion and capacity to create and maintain harmony within the group) are most relevant to leadership. Since leadership is the process of influencing people toward greater effort and performance, the ability to persuade and influence people is critical to leadership. In this regard, an effective coach needs both the will and skill to exercise his/her influence. The "will" refers to one's willingness and eagerness to influence others and to exercise one's power. McClelland and Burnham (1976) reported that effective managers consistently scored higher on the need for power (i.e., the need to exert influence over others). The "skill" aspect of influencing members hinges upon the coach's ability to diagnose the needs and preferences of his/her athletes, and the group characteristics, and applying appropriate methods of influence. The methods of influence may be punishment or threat of it, reward or promise of it, persuasive arguments, legitimate authority, or manipulation (i.e., selective use of information) (Mowday, 1978).

THE MULTIDIMENSIONAL MODEL
OF LEADERSHIP

The three important elements in a leadership equation—the coach, the athlete, and the situation—have been described independently only for ease of presentation. However, it cannot be overemphasized that the congruency among the three elements is the most significant and necessary condition for team effectiveness. That is, what the athlete prefers and how the coach behaves or reacts must be consistent not only with each other's expectancies but also with the situational requirements or constraints (Chelladurai, 1978; Chelladurai & Carron, 1978). These contingent relationships are highlighted by the Multidimensional Model of Leadership as shown in Figure 23-3.

Briefly, the model envisages three states of leader behavior: actual leader behavior, leader behavior preferred by athletes, and required leader behavior. The antecedents of these three aspects of leadership consist of the characteristics of the leader, the athletes, and the situation. The model's major proposition is that the degree of congruence among the three states of leader behavior is positively related to performance and satisfaction.

Research testing this proposition is in the initial stages. For instance, Chelladurai (1984) reported that the discrepancy between ath-

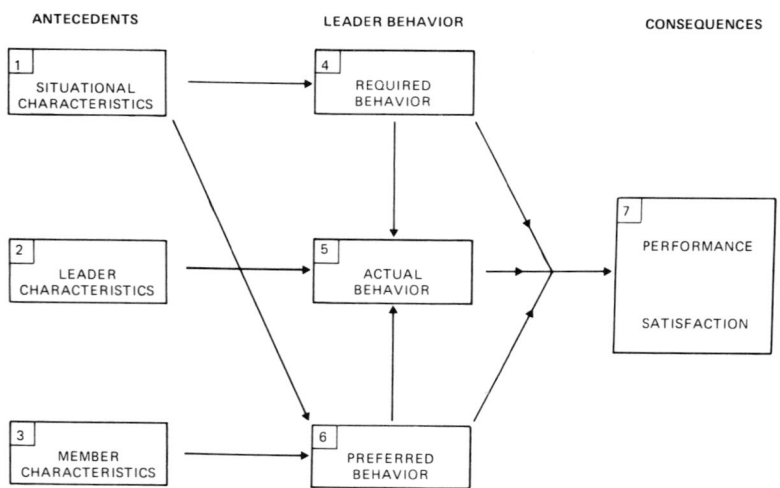

FIGURE 23-3 Mulitdimensional model of leadership (adapted from: Chelladurai, 1978).

letes' perception of coaching behaviors and their preferences for specific behaviors was significantly correlated with their satisfaction with leadership, team performance, and overall involvement. Although the pattern of relationships between the discrepancies in the five dimensions of leader behavior and the satisfaction measures varied in the three sport groups studied (basketball, wrestling, and track and field), the relationship between discrepancy in training and instruction and satisfaction with leadership was similar in all three groups. That athletes' satisfaction with leadership increased as the coach's perceived emphasis on this dimension also increased was considered to be consistent with the task-oriented nature of athletics. Another finding of their study highlights the effects of situational differences. Basketball players were satisfied even when the coach's positive feedback exceeded their preferences (linear relationship), while the wrestlers were dissatisfied with discrepancy in either direction (curvilinear relationship). Such discrepancy did not have any effect in the track and field group. Chelladurai argued that this pattern reflects the nature of the three sports:

> The availability of objective feedback from the task itself progressively increases from the interdependent-open task (basketball), through the independent-open task (wrestling), to the independent-closed task (track and field). (1984, p. 39)

In a study of female athletes and their coaches, Horne (1982) found that satisfaction with leadership was related to (a) discrepancy between perceived and preferred training and instruction, (b) discrepancy between coaches' self-reports of own positive feedback and athletes' perceptions of it, and (c) discrepancy between coaches' self-reports of democratic behavior and athletes' preferences for it. In all these instances, the results showed that the smaller the discrepancy, the greater the satisfaction with leadership.

The above two studies only partially support the model in that they deal only with member satisfaction and not with performance, which is also an important outcome variable. Although participation in athletics and satisfaction with such participation are of value in themselves, it is also important to relate the leadership variables and the satisfaction measures to some objective measures of performance.

In summary, this analysis of leadership has dealt with the three significant components of leadership (nature of the situation, characteristics of the leader, and participant expectancies) and their interrelationships. The results of some of the research studies have been cited here, but much of this discussion rests on the propositions and extrapolations from organizational psychology. Considerable research must be undertaken in our own field before a theory of leadership in sports can be authoritatively formulated.

Chapter 24

Cohesion in Sport Teams

Albert V. Carron
University of Western Ontario

Team unity is generally assumed to be one of the foundation blocks upon which effective team performance is built (Zander, 1974). Certainly, tuning in to a post game television broadcast from a championship team's locker room would only confirm this impression. Team members refer enthusiastically to "feelings of family," the "mutual affection and respect," and "the effectiveness of the team once it began to gel" at some critical point in the season. An outsider would likely conclude that the team has banded together in a single-minded successful pursuit of the championship.

Of course, sport teams are not the only groups that apparently experience such feelings of family and unity. Individuals who join together to campaign for the United Way, for instance, as well as members of religious orders, juvenile gangs, and even the participants in events such as the Jonestown tragedy and the Charles Manson orchestrated slayings also exhibited group unity, more commonly called *group cohesion*. But what is cohesion? How does it develop? What group properties is it related to? These issues are discussed in the sections that follow.

DEFINITION OF COHESION

The origin of the term *cohesion* is the Latin word *cohaesus*, which means to cleave or stick together. This concept of sticking together is contained

340

in the various definitions of cohesion. For example, Gross and Martin (1952) perceived cohesion as the resistance of the group to disruptive forces while Festinger, Schachter, and Back (1950) defined it as the total field of forces causing members to remain with the group. More recently, Carron (1982) advocated that in sport teams, cohesion should be viewed as a dynamic process that is reflected in the group's tendency to stick together while pursuing its goals and objectives.

This latter definition, with its emphasis on the existence of an underlying purpose within the group, serves to distinguish cohesion from adhesion. Adhesion also implies a sticking together but it does not contain the suggestions of communality of purposes, overall unity, and commitment to the whole. A metaphor that illustrates the distinction between adhesion and cohesion lies in the comparison of clay on a shoe versus clay molded into a sculpture. Clay may adhere to the shoe but it coheres in the sculpture (Hartman, 1981). Similarly, athletes on a sport team cohere because of a communality of purposes — achievement of personal and team success, satisfaction of affiliation needs, contribution to self-esteem, and so on.

DEVELOPMENT OF COHESIVENESS

In both the popular view expressed by laypersons and the media and the research paradigms adopted by investigators, cohesion is treated as a static, positive achievement — something that the group strives to reach. In short, there is assumed to be a critical target level which is either attained or not. We assume that its degree of attainment can be measured when the researcher administers a group cohesion test (e.g., at the end of the season). This is usually then correlated with some other important group outcome such as team performance, attitude and behavioral conformity, and satisfaction.

While there are advantages to this conceptual viewpoint, not the least of which is ease of measurement and interpretation, this viewpoint basically is not correct. Cohesion is never static, never fixed. Rather, it is a process — a dynamic process where dynamic means "simply seeing events as changing, breathing and evolving according to complex individual and social tensions and resolutions" (Budge, 1981, p. 13). There is now a large body of literature in the field of group dynamics that discusses how cohesion develops in a group. The literature centers around three conceptual issues, all of which imply that cohesion is dynamic in nature. First, does cohesion develop in a progressive, linear fashion once the group has been established? Or does the amount of cohesion oscillate in a pendular fashion throughout the group's existence? Or, finally, in the group's life cycle is there an increase in cohesion, then a leveling off, and then a decrease until the group dissolves?

In the various *linear models* (the first issue above), it is assumed that cohesion continually develops as the group moves through progressive developmental stages. Tuckman (1965), for example, referred to these stages as forming, storming, norming, and performing. Orientation problems predominate in the forming stage as the members become familiar with each other and the nature of the group task. The storming stage which follows is characterized by polarization, conflict, and rebellion. In the norming stage the group comes together, resistance is overcome, and cohesion and cooperative behavior are enhanced. Finally, the group directs its energy toward its goals and objectives in the performing stage.

The *pendular models*, which had their origin in psychotherapy and counseling groups, stress the extreme shifts that occur in interpersonal relationships during the development of group cohesion. Budge (1981), for example, proposed that as a group develops it oscillates from cohesion to differentiation to conflict to resolution (cohesion) to conflict to cohesion, and so on. This can be illustrated in a situation in which a group of athletes try out for a football team. In the initial period, prior to the start of practice, a feeling of unity (cohesion) is present which emanates from the experiences all athletes hold in common—the shared anxieties, aspirations, and unfamiliar task to be carried out such as drawing equipment, getting a locker, meeting new roommates, and coping with the playbook. When practice begins, differentiation occurs; the group physically and psychologically subdivides into smaller units under different coaches. Conflict then arises as individual athletes within different offensive and defensive units compete with each other to secure a position on the team. Cohesion of the team itself is now minimal. When the final cuts have been made the pendulum swings again and cohesion is renewed (there is "resolution," to use Budge's terminology) as the surviving members of the team draw together, develop a sense of team unity, and begin to prepare psychologically to face opponents. Throughout the season this pendular cycle of conflict to cohesion to conflict to cohesion continues.

The *life cycle models* also originated in psychotherapy and counseling groups, yet they have some relevance to sport teams. Many sport teams are time-limited; they exist for some fixed period such as the course of the season. In terms of cohesiveness, then, there is a life cycle for the group which proceeds from development to dissolution. Mills (1964) advocated a five-stage life cycle for cohesion which proceeds from (a) encounter to (b) testing of boundaries and the creation of roles to the (c) creation of a normative system to the (d) production phase to, finally, (e) separation and dissolution.

Whatever model is adopted to account for the development of cohesion—and some authors have advocated that a combination of the three is most plausible (Gibbard, Hartman, & Mann, 1974) — it must be assumed that cohesiveness is a dynamic process rather than a static entity. In sport, this implies that the absolute amount of cohesion will fluctuate over the course of a season. Ruder and Gill (1981) did provide some confirmation for this viewpoint with women's intramural volleyball teams. They found that postgame ratings were higher than pregame ratings, winners rated cohesion higher than losers did, and winners' ratings increased considerably from pre- to postgame while losers' ratings decreased slightly.

NATURE OF COHESION IN THE SPORT TEAM[1]

As indicated above, the reason underlying the development of cohesion becomes an integral part of its nature. In short, every group has its goals or objectives — its raison d'etre — and these are intimately interwoven into the development of the group. For example, social clubs, work groups, mutinous crews, delinquent gangs, counseling groups, and sports teams are all different. But they also are similar in the sense that their members stick together and remain united in the social unit because they ascribe to some underlying common purpose. An outsider unaware of those specific purposes would be unable to comprehend the basis for cohesiveness within those various groups. Similarly, an insider (group member) who was either unaware, unappreciative, or unaccepting of the basis for cohesiveness would soon leave or be forced to leave the group.

Traditionally, it has been assumed that individuals in task-performing groups such as sport teams cohere around two principal concerns: achieving the group's or organization's goals and objectives (productivity, work output, performance effectiveness, team success, etc.) and mediating the satisfaction of members' social emotional needs and motives (affiliation, friendship, morale, etc.). Thus, a number of writers have advocated that the definition and measurement of cohesion should also center around the two concerns.

For example, when Festinger et al. (1950) defined cohesion as the total field of forces causing members to remain in the group, they considered these forces to be of two types: attractiveness (the satisfactory relationships, interpersonal attractions, and friendships that exist within the group) and means control (the important goals and objectives that can be mediated through group membership). Similarly, Enoch and McLemore (1967) viewed cohesion as attraction to the group which, in turn, was assumed to comprise both intrinsic attraction and instrumental attraction. Also, Mikalachki (1969) advocated that cohesion should be

---

[1]The material in this section initially appeared in Carron (1982).

subdivided into social cohesion and task cohesion. And finally, a number of writers have stressed the importance of distinguishing between task and social cohesion within sport teams (Carron, 1982; Carron & Chelladurai, 1981a; Gill, 1977; Nixon, 1977).

In a study of individuals who rotated throughout the season to form different tennis dyads, Carron, Brawley, and Widmeyer (1982) found that performance outcomes such as win-loss percentage (an absolute measure of effectiveness) and achievement in comparison to preperformance expectations (a relative measure of effectiveness) were best predicted through estimates of team strength (task cohesion) made by participants prior to the season. Similarly, social psychological outcomes such as satisfaction with the social experience were best predicted through the participants' preseason ratings of friendship and social enjoyment (social cohesion). In a similar vein, Anderson (1975) found that interpersonal attraction (assessed through value similarity) was most closely related to cohesiveness in informal social groups while goal-path clarity (agreement on the task procedures to use) was most related to cohesiveness in task-oriented groups.

GROUP COHESION:
POSITIVE OR NEGATIVE?

Cohesion is essential for a group's existence. For as Donnelly, Carron, and Chelladurai (1978) observed, "There can be no such thing as a noncohesive group; it is a contradiction in terms. If a group exists it is to some extent cohesive" (p. 7). Because of this, it is commonly assumed that cohesion is a positive force within a group—something to be strived for. While this is generally the case, there are exceptions. As Kellerman (1981) pointed out, *"high cohesion—is not a universal cultural attribute that should be valued for its inherent goodness"* (p. 13). In a number of examples, both individual behavior and group performance are not as positive as they should be because of the impact of the group.

Insofar as individual behavior is concerned, the group, particularly the highly cohesive group, reduces individuality and increases conformity. History is replete with examples in which individual members of groups acted in ways that would have been unthinkable when acting alone. In essence the group serves to collectively diffuse the responsibility held by individual members. Festinger (1950) addressed this issue when he noted that the greater the group's cohesiveness, the more power it has in pushing its members toward conformity in attitudes and behaviors, as well as toward acceptance of the goals and assignments to tasks and roles.

Another potentially negative behavioral correlate of cohesiveness, which is also related to conformity, is the tendency toward self-deception (Bohm, 1981). To avoid upsetting the apple cart, individual group members may sometimes accept false ideas as true, overlooking negative aspects of the group or individual members and working to produce stability and avoid conflict at any price. Self-deception regarding ingroup properties and characteristics seems to be achieved at the expense of outgroup relationships. For example, Sherif (1970) found that a highly competitive situation resulted in intragroup harmony and solidarity but led to social distance and hostility between two groups of young campers. There was a breakdown in communication, increase in stereotyping, distorted perception of the group's strengths and the opposition's weaknesses, and reduced friendship choices of outgroup individuals but an increase for ingroup members.

As indicated above, cohesion also has the potential of being negative in relation to performance effectiveness. This may manifest itself in two related ways. First, social cohesiveness can serve to reduce intragroup competitiveness and detract from task cohesiveness. In Lenk's (1969) work with the German rowing crew, McGrath's (1962) research with rifle teams, and the Landers and Lueschen (1974) study with intramural bowling teams, lower interpersonal attraction (which is probably a component of social cohesiveness) was linked to performance success. An explanation advanced to account for these findings (Carron & Chelladurai, 1982; Fiedler, 1967; Landers & Lueschen, 1974) is that group situations in which the individual's task is either carried out independently (e.g., rifle shooting, bowling) or is under external control for initiation and overall coordination (e.g., rowing), group tension, rivalry, and intragroup competitiveness can serve to motivate the individual toward better performance. Thus, individual members who are distracted by social concerns or a desire to protect the feelings of fellow team members do not perform to their potential.

Second, a group that divides into smaller social units, which are often called cliques and therefore possibly are not a true manifestation of group cohesiveness, may strive to protect or enhance that clique at the expense of the total team. Both Klein and Christiansen (1969) and Fiedler (1967), for example, have reported that basketball players who were extremely close friends tended to pass to each other to the detriment of the total team effort. Fiedler (1967) proposed that "the team with overly close interpersonal ties among teammates tends to set up shots for team members on the basis of friendship rather than ability or advantage to the team, i.e., the particular boys who are 'set up' might not be the best players on the team . . . In close games this will, of course, be decisive" (p. 68).

STRUCTURAL ASPECTS OF COHESIVENESS

Advocates of sociobiology have argued that affiliation needs and group cohesion reflect inherent evolutionary biological strategies that enhance reproduction and the maintenance of the species (Plutchik, 1981). In turn, it is also assumed that the dynamics of group life and cohesiveness in animals has close parallels with humans. Some group characteristics from the social life of animals which affect sport teams include group size, physical proximity, permeability, role differentiation, compartmentalization, and information flow (Plutchik, 1981). These will now be briefly discussed.

The level of cohesiveness seems to be optimum in small groups. If the group is excessively large, cohesiveness begins to decrease and the group physically or psychologically restructures within smaller cohesive units. Thus, a football team might divide (in terms of highly cohesive units) into offensive, defensive, and special teams, as well as red-shirted athletes and so forth.

Physical proximity also seems to enhance cohesion. That is, individuals who are physically close to one another in playing position, locker location, and so forth, become more cohesive. This is usually due to the increased opportunities for task and/or social communication. There is an optimal level for physical proximity, however. Research on group density has revealed that crowding produces feelings of stress which, in turn, reduces cohesiveness.

Communication also plays a part in cohesiveness. For example, the degree to which the group communicates with other groups and with nongroup members is called permeability. The less permeable a group is, the greater its cohesiveness. Groups become socially isolated and draw upon their own membership to fulfill the important psychological needs of all the members. Similarly, information flow refers to the level of communication within the group itself; the greater that information flow, the greater the cohesiveness.

Groups with high role differentiation (which refers to the degree to which different members have specialized functions) have a better chance to develop a high level of cohesiveness. Thus, a volleyball team in which each member carries out equally the role of setter and spiker is less likely to be as cohesive as a team in which these two roles are differentiated and filled by different individuals.

In some teams subgroups operate as relatively independent units, such as offensive and defensive units in football and the scrum versus the backs in rugby. In times of stress, such as during competition, cohesiveness develops around these specialized subgroups to a greater extent than within the group as a whole.

CIRCULAR NATURE OF COHESIVENESS

In the earliest research on cohesion in sport, cohesiveness was treated either as an independent variable — Do teams with different levels of cohesion have different levels of success? Or as a dependent variable — Does the level of team success directly influence the level of cohesiveness? Subsequently, it has become apparent that cohesion is dynamic and that it interacts in a circular fashion with other group variables (Carron & Ball, 1977; Hacker & Williams, 1981; Ruder & Gill, 1981).

For example, on the basis of their study with women's field hockey teams, Hacker and Williams (1981) concluded that "a combination of the various cause-effect relationships among cohesion, performance and satisfaction suggested a circular relationship among these variables. That is, teams which are more cohesive are more successful and teams which are successful have greater satisfaction. Greater satisfaction, in turn, leads to higher levels of cohesiveness" (p. 99). The Hacker and Williams results are consistent with a proposal advanced by Martens and Peterson (1971).

If we accept that cohesion is a dynamic process rather than a static property, then it seems reasonable to assume that it will fluctuate and continuously interact with other group properties such as performance outcome, satisfaction, conformity, role acceptance, team stability, and so on. Consequently, while these variables are often treated experimentally as antecedent conditions or consequences of cohesion, it is probably more appropriate to view them as correlates. The following section discusses some of the predominant correlates of cohesiveness.

CORRELATES OF GROUP COHESION

One obvious correlate of importance insofar as sport teams are concerned is *performance success*. A number of field studies have examined the relationship of performance and cohesion. A predominant measure of cohesion has been the Sport Cohesiveness Questionnaire (Martens, Landers, & Loy, 1972). This questionnaire includes seven aspects of cohesiveness in sport: cohesiveness assessed as (a) friendship, (b) power among group members, (c) sense of belonging, (d) value of membership, (e) closeness, (f) enjoyment, and (g) teamwork.

Carron and Chelladurai (1981) have provided a summary of research carried out with the Sport Cohesiveness Questionnaire. Their summary along with some other recent research findings is presented in Table 24-1. It is apparent that the overall conclusion to be drawn is that cohesiveness and performance are highly related in interacting (team)

TABLE 24-1

An Overview of Studies Which Have Used the Sport Cohesiveness Questionnaire
(Adapted from Carron and Chelladurai, 1981a)

Authors	Athletic Group	General Findings	Cohesion Factors Which Discriminated
Arnold & Straub (1972)	Intercollegiate basketball	↑Cohesion = ↑performance	Teamwork, closeness
Ball & Carron (1976)	Intercollegiate hockey	↑Cohesion = ↑performance	Teamwork, closeness, enjoyment
Landers & Crum (1971)	Interscholastic baseball	↑Cohesion = ↓performance	Teamwork, closeness
Landers & Lueschen (1974)	Intramural bowling	↑Cohesion = ↓performance	Interpersonal attraction
Martens & Peterson (1971)	Intramural basketball	↑Cohesion = ↓performance	Teamwork, closeness, value of membership
Melnick & Chemers (1974)	Intramural basketball	Cohesion = unrelated to performance	
Widmeyer & Martens (1978)	3-on-3 basketball	↑Cohesion = ↑performance	Teamwork, closeness, value of membership, sense of belonging, enjoyment
Hacker & Williams (1981)[1]	Intercollegiate field hockey	↑Cohesion = ↑performance	Teamwork, closeness, value of membership, sense of belonging, power enjoyment, friendship
Gosset & Widmeyer (1981)[1]	Intercollegiate basketball Intercollegiate hockey	↑Cohesion = ↑performance	Teamwork, closeness, value of membership, sense of belonging, enjoyment
Ruder & Gill (1981)	Intercollegiate volleyball	Cohesion = unrelated to performance	
Carron & Chelladurai (1982)	Intramural volleyball High school basketball	↑Cohesion = ↑performance ↑Cohesion = ↑performance	Teamwork, sense of belonging, cohesion Sense of belonging, value of membership, enjoyment
	High school wrestling	↑Cohesion = ↑performance	Sense of belonging, value of membership, enjoyment

[1] A composite (average) score was used.

sports. And, as discussed earlier, this relationship is probably circular in nature; cohesion contributes to success, which in turn contributes to cohesion. The negative results observed by Landers and Lueschen (1974) are generally attributed to the nature of the task. This was, of course, discussed in an earlier section.

A second correlate examined in relation to cohesiveness in sport teams is *satisfaction*. The two are highly similar but, whereas cohesion is a group construct, satisfaction is an individual one. Numerous authors (Carron & Chelladurai, 1982; Hacker & Williams, 1981; Martens & Peterson, 1971) have reported a strong positive relationship between cohesion and satisfaction. In fact, it was also pointed out earlier that Hacker and Williams (1981) found a circular relationship between cohesion, performance, and satisfaction.

Conformity is yet another correlate of group cohesion. The more cohesive the group, the more influence the group has on its individual members (Festinger, 1950; Schachter, 1951). Consequently, greater pressure is brought to bear on the individual to demonstrate conformity in behavior and attitudes. At the same time, highly cohesive groups also demonstrate a greater conformity to the group's norm for productivity (Berkowitz, 1954, 1956; Mikalachki, 1969; Schachter, Ellertson, McBride, & Gregory, 1951; Seashore, 1954). It is important to emphasize that these norms might be for either high or low productivity. The result is the same; individual compliance is enhanced by the group's cohesiveness.

Factors associated with *role performance* are also interrelated to the group's cohesiveness. In task performing groups, different individuals have different responsibilities, assignments, and functions within the group. The group's effectiveness is determined by the extent to which group members understand their role and the responsibilities associated with it (role clarity), accept them (role acceptance), and carry them out (role performance). It has been demonstrated that the greater the cohesiveness, the greater the role clarity, role acceptance, and role performance (Bass, 1980; Grand & Carron, 1982; Stogdill, 1959, 1972).

Stability, which refers to the turnover rate for group membership as well as the length of time members have been together in the group, is also related to cohesiveness in a circular fashion (Festinger et al., 1950; Moment & Zaleznik, 1965). The longer the group has been together and the more opportunity that members have had to interact with each other, the more likely that cohesiveness will develop. Similarly, the more cohesive the group becomes, the less likely that its members will choose to leave (i.e., turnover rate decreases).

PRACTICAL IMPLICATIONS

Although research on cohesion in sport teams is still in its relative infancy, the findings to date do provide some basis for generalizations in terms of the conditions associated with high cohesiveness. The coach should attempt to:

1. Establish a high norm for productivity by setting up specific, quantitative, and challenging team goals. The positive impact of goal setting upon performance has been clearly established for both individual performance (Locke, Saari, Shaw, & Latham, 1981) and group performance (Zander, 1971). And, because cohesion is the tendency for a group to stick together and remain united in the pursuit of its goals and objectives, these must be clearly defined. Further, goal delineation should be carried out for both inseason and out-of-season programs.

2. Avoid an excessively difficult schedule early in the season, if possible, since lack of success reduces cohesion while success increases it.

3. Encourage intrateam competition and rivalry in individual sports such as wrestling, squash, badminton, and swimming. While social cohesion is important, care must be taken to see that it doesn't override the task cohesion dimension.

4. Clearly outline individual roles to team members and stress the importance of each role to the overall team success. Athletes must clearly understand, accept, and carry out their individual roles. The larger the number of team members who perceive their team roles as unimportant, the more apathetic the team (Bass, 1980).

5. Encourage task and social communication at all levels within the team: coach-athlete and athlete-athlete. The greater the intragroup communication, the greater the cohesiveness.

6. Encourage group identity. This may be done through team blazers, jackets, social functions, and so forth. Also encourage pride in subgroup performance—the defensive unit, offensive unit, special teams—but continually stress the importance of viewing the total team as a unit.

7. To the extent that it is compatible with eligibility requirements and group needs, avoid excessive personnel turnover. When new members join an intact group, specific steps should be taken by established players to integrate the newcomer socially and to outline the overall task expectations.

8. Avoid the development of social cliques by alternating roommates, thus encouraging socializing by the team as a whole.

It should be evident from the overall discussion in this chapter that cohesion is a critical aspect of group life for at least four reasons. First, groups cannot exist without it. Second, it is correlated with a number of important group processes such as communication, conformity, role performance, satisfaction, and performance. Third, according to Chelladurai, "As the athlete's involvement in the sport increases, the sources of satisfaction for social needs are more and more restricted to the team, and affiliation with outside groups is reduced" (1981, p. 3). Therefore, social cohesion is critical if the sport experience is to be an enjoyable and satisfying one for the athlete. Finally, a fundamental objective in sport is team success. Without task cohesion, it is unlikely that this will accrue. Consequently, the coach must be sensitive to the need to implement any procedures that would contribute to the development of cohesiveness, both social and task, within the team.

PART VII

ISSUES
IN SPORT
SOCIALIZATION

The authors in Part VI discussed the effect of group dynamics on sport performance. An important point made was that the social interactions within a group heavily influence the behavior and attitudes of people within that group. On a larger scale, the social interactions we experience exert a tremendous influence on our personality development. The socialization section will look more closely at how children are affected by social and cultural factors, with special emphasis on how these factors relate to young athletes' behavior in sport and competition. But first, we will briefly summarize some of the major issues concerning children and competitive sport.

Issues in Competitive Sport for Children

It has been estimated that over 20 million children between the ages of 6 and 16 participate in organized youth sports in the United States. With so many participating, we should be able to answer questions concerning the psychosocial effects of participating in youth sports: Do youth sports foster moral development (i.e., sportsmanship)? Do sports create stress for young athletes? Why do children participate? Why do they drop out? Are organized youth sports better than unorganized, sandlot games? Does youth sport participation help build character and confidence and enhance self-esteem? Should girls and boys compete against each other? The literature even as late as the mid-1970s failed to answer these questions because virtually no empirical research had been conducted in these areas. However, researchers have detected this void and have focused numerous field and experimental studies in this area.

But more research is needed to clear up the current controversy about the effects or desirability of youth sport programs. Proponents argue that youth sport programs enhance the development of desirable psychosocial attributes such as cooperation, assertiveness, persistence, and self-esteem. They also suggest that children learn to deal with the realities and competitiveness of real life. Critics counter by saying that youth sports place excessive stress and pressure on children by emphasizing competition and winning. They argue that youth sports are conducted primarily for the self-serving needs of parents and coaches and that children are robbed of their creativity and spontaneity. What is the answer?

Actually, both viewpoints have merit because youth sports are neither inherently good nor bad. Rather, it is the quality of the adult leadership that usually determines whether a young athlete has a good or bad competitive experience. No doubt we have all heard the horror stories depicting parents or coaches unmercifully chastising young athletes. We have heard of children being cut from Little League teams, cheating to win a game, crying for striking out in the last inning, or dropping out due to too much competitive stress and external pressure. Yet we have perhaps also seen young athletes develop close friendships, learn physical skills, develop confidence and self-worth, and learn responsibility, teamwork, and sportsmanship. Obviously, the specific outcome of the youth sport experience depends on the coaches, parents, and administrators; they must remember that organized youth sports are for children, not adults. Adults sometimes lose this perspective and treat children like miniature adults. Unrealistic expectations, a win-at-all-costs philosophy, long hours of practice, and constant punishment will eventually cause many children to drop out. A positive approach that emphasizes fun and develops skills, fitness, and friendship will go a long way to make sure that the youth sport experience is a positive one. Coaches and parents are in a unique position to structure the sporting experience in this way.

The Socialization Process

Since a child's experience in competitive sport is largely determined by the quality of interactions with coaches, parents, peers, and significant others, let's explore the social milieu in which the child competes. In essence this means understanding the socialization process. Socialization may be defined as the process by which individuals learn skills, attitudes, values, and behaviors that enable them to function within a particular culture. These patterns of behavior are learned primarily from significant socializing agencies such as the school, religion, and the media, and agents such as family, teachers, coaches, and peers. By being reinforced or punished for certain behaviors, a child learns and internalizes a variety of values, skills, and attitudes. Clearly, the behavior of significant others within the various social systems provides a child with values and norms that suggest *which* social roles to play, *who* to interact with, and *how* to interact.

In examining sport socialization two categories of study become apparent: socialization into sport and socialization via sport. Socialization into sport refers to the process through which individuals assume roles such as athlete, coach, or spectator. It is concerned with how significant others and social agencies affect an individual's decision to become involved in sport. Socialization via sport refers to the more general attitudes, values, skills, and dispositions such as sportsmanship, character, and citizenship — which may or may not be acquired while playing specific sport roles such as that of the Little League athlete.

Socialization Into Sport

As mentioned, children become socialized into sport roles but one of their primary decisions is whether or not to compete in organized athletic programs. This has recently led to research on the reasons children participate in competitive sport; although we are just beginning to understand the whys of participation, some consistent findings are emerging. For example, the most popular reasons children give for being in sports include making new friends or keeping the old ones, becoming skilled at something, having fun, becoming fit, and experiencing excitement. It should be noted that winning does not appear on this list. Obviously, perceptions of priority differ between young athletes and their adult coaches! These preliminary findings suggest that competition for children should provide opportunities for skill development, fitness development, and social interactions, in addition to being fun and exciting.

Paradoxically, children's growing interest for participating in competitive sports has been accompanied by increasing numbers of children dropping out. In their chapter, Daniel Gould and Thelma Horn discuss the issues concerning why children participate in competitive sport and why they quit. The authors review the latest major studies investigating these issues and promote some practical guidelines for motivating young athletes to participate. Although some are forced to leave when they are cut by a coach, an increasing number of children are deciding that organized sport is no longer enjoyable because of inadequate playing areas, lack of personal success, minimal activity or playtime, and the pressure to win. A recent survey noted that over 35% of the respondents indicated that they would not play again next season. Coaches and physical educators can do little to prevent children from dropping out due to their developing new interests, but if children drop out for the other reasons described above, then coaches can do something. Variables such as lack of success, overemphasis on winning, and lack of playing time are under the coach's control.

Socialization Through Sports

Youth sport coaches commonly believe that one of the primary objectives of competitive sport for children is socialization. They are not alone in this belief. Parents and administrators indicated in a recent study that they strongly agree with statements such as "participation prepares a child for adult life" and "participation develops sportsmanship." Although most of us would like to think that sport is a positive socializing agent there is observational data that competitive sport programs contribute little to the socialization process or may in fact be detrimental. The following quotes are typical of coaches and illustrate this contention: "I now confess that my coaching experience affords no evidence that any of these character-building virtues get into my players." "I personally felt the ugly emotion of hate, a surge of uncontrollable rage tempting me to lash out at my players and gloating rivals."

How can coaching behaviors affect young athletes' attitudes, thoughts, and affective responses? The chapter by Frank Smoll and Ron Smith summarizes the results of their extensive multi-year field study, which was one of the first to examine the relationship between the behaviors of volunteer Little League coaches and the players' reactions to those coaches. The authors begin by presenting a mediational model of coach-player interactions. In essence, the model argues that the effects of coaching behaviors are mediated by the players' perceptions of them. Unlike most research on coaches and other leaders, Smoll and Smith measure actual coaching behaviors in a naturalistic setting. Phase I of their study investigated the relationship between coaching behaviors and post-season player attitudes, self-esteem, and affective responses. With the findings generated from Phase I, Smoll and Smith derive behavioral guidelines for coaches and develop a psychologically oriented training program for coaches. Their research demonstrates that competitive sports can have positive effects on children—but only when coaches understand and are aware of the social context in which the child competes.

Gender and Sport

Another factor found to be an important determinant of sport role socialization is a child's gender. Research has demonstrated that almost from birth, boys and girls are treated differently by their parents. It is not uncommon to see a father buy his young son a football while his new daughter receives a doll. In addition, it has been discovered that from as early as 6 months, mothers handle and talk to their daughters more than their sons, and allow sons to exhibit more independent, vigorous, and exploratory behavior. As children get older, little boys learn that it is okay to get dirty, be assertive, and play sports while little girls learn that they should be neat and proper and not play sports.

It is not surprising, then, to find differences in attitudes and behavior in the realm of competitive sports based on gender. For example, some recent research has shown that most competitive sports are seen as appropriate for males but inappropriate for females, especially if the activity is physical in nature. It has further been suggested that differences in socialization and perceived sex-appropriateness of sports may help explain the large dropout rate by female athletes as compared to male athletes.

Although great strides have been made in this area in recent years, there is no denying that substantial differences still exist between how girls and boys are socialized into sport. The chapter by Carole Oglesby advances our understanding of the role that sport traditionally plays in socialization and gender identity development. In addition to defining the processes involved in gender identity development, Oglesby effectively shows how sport has been used to reinforce traditional sex-role stereotypes. By examining the results of current research in sex-role development, Oglesby concludes that there are viable socialization alternatives that would encourage both genders to engage in and appreciate sports.

Do Sports Build Character?

Of all the potential socializing effects of competitive sports, none has been as pervasive as the belief that sports develop character in American youth by instilling the moral ideals of our culture. This issue is addressed by Brenda Bredemeier in this section's final chapter. As has been presented earlier, this issue can once again find both proponents and opponents. Whether sport creates sinners or saints is a moot point since sport can facilitate either moral or immoral behavior, depending on the quality of the adult leadership. The important question is, what experiences in sport will enhance moral development? Bredemeier discusses the issue of moral development in sport with specific reference to how this might differ for males and females. The different theories underlying moral development are presented, with differences and similarities noted. Bredemeier then addresses the issue of gender differences within these developmental frameworks, and examines moral growth in sport with specific recommendations for how to structure competition and physical activity to promote the concepts of sportsmanship and fair play.

In sum, we find that the quality of an experience in organized sport is to a great extent defined by those who guide the participant. By being aware of the participant's social learning process, everyone involved with organized sport should be oriented toward maximizing positive socialization experiences and minimizing those that elicit undesirable behavior in the sport environment.

Chapter 25

Participation Motivation in Young Athletes

Daniel Gould
Kansas State University

Thelma Horn
University of Wisconsin-Milwaukee

Competitive athletic programs for children and youth involve a large and important segment of North American society. It has been estimated that 17 million American children between the ages of 6 and 16 are involved in over 50 nonschool-sponsored sports programs (Martens, 1978), while an additional 6 million children participate in a variety of school-sponsored sports (Shaffer, 1980).

Paradoxically, this growing interest among children for participating in competitive athletics has also been accompanied by an increase in the rate at which children leave sports. In an extensive investigation of children's sports in Michigan, it was found that approximately 35% of the participants planned to quit before the start of the next season (Sapp & Haubenstricker, 1978). This dropout rate seemed to be highest for children between the ages of 11 and 13. Further evidence of the alarmingly high attrition rate in youth sports was found in a study by Pooley (1981). Specifically, Pooley found that of 475 boys who had registered to participate in a nonschool youth soccer program, 22%, or 103 of them, had dropped out by the end of the season. Finally, recent evidence also reveals that the dropout rate in youth sports may be increasing, as Fry, McClements, and Sefton (1981) have reported that the attrition rate of first-year Saskatoon youth hockey players increased from 29 to 37% over a 4-year period. Thus, while there certainly does seem to be considerable interest among children to participate in competitive athletic programs, there is also substantial evidence to suggest that the attrition rate is correspondingly increasing.

Statistics like these, along with frequent personal testimonies and media accounts of young children becoming athletic burnouts, have caused more and more sport psychologists to become interested in studying participation motivation in children's sports. Questions of particular interest are: What motives do young athletes have for participating in sports? What motives do children have for quitting sports? Do children of differing ages, sex, and levels of experience have similar motives for participating and quitting? How do coaches and parents influence participation motivation? This chapter will review the existing sport psychology research in an effort to answer these questions. Specifically, the purposes of this review are threefold: (a) the research that has assessed young athletes' motives for sports participation will be examined; (b) the evidence focusing on motives for leaving youth sports will be reviewed; and (c) practical guidelines for maintaining and enhancing motivation in young athletes will be discussed.

MAJOR MOTIVES FOR PARTICIPATION

Understanding the major motives that young athletes have for sports participation is a topic of central importance for both the coach and the sport psychologist. It is unfortunate, then, that in the past most individuals interested in the area had to rely solely on conjecture and/or past experiences to explain why young athletes choose to participate. Recently, however, a number of investigators have begun to identify and examine the major objectives young athletes have for participating in competitive youth sports programs.

Skubic (1956) was one of the first to examine such participation motives in young athletes. She examined the attitudes of players, parents, and teachers toward youth baseball competition and found that getting acquainted with other boys, having fun, keeping out of mischief, developing sportsmanship, and improving playing skills were among the reasons given for participation. Similarly, in a survey of 289 youth league football players, Griffin (1978) found that players said they derived values from participation that included learning the game, conditioning, sportsmanship, having fun, teamwork, and forming friendships. Contrary to popular opinion, it was also found that more than 90% of the boys would rather be on a losing team and play than "sit the bench" on a winning team.

In a study of South Australian seventh-grade children, Robertson (1981) asked the respondents what they most liked about sports. Of the children's responses, 68% were categorized as some form of intrinsic reward (e.g., enjoyment, fun, excitement, getting fit) and 13.9% as achievement mastery responses (e.g., winning, playing well, beating opponents). Topics categorized as extrinsic rewards, social reciprocity, and aggression were rated as least important. In summary, these studies provide initial insight into the motivation of young athletes by identifying their major reasons for participation. Unfortunately, the assessment of participation motives was not the central theme of these investigations and, consequently, more detailed analyses of the data are not available.

A more extensive examination of participation motivation of young athletes was conducted by Sapp and Haubenstricker (1978). Assessed in this investigation were the participation objectives of 579 male and 471 female athletes, ranging in age from 11 to 18 years and participating in 11 different nonschool sports. The findings revealed that 90% of the children participated for fun, 80% to improve their skills, and 56% for fitness benefits. Among the motives rated least important were "I had nothing else to do" and "I wanted to feel important." Gender differences concerning participation motives were also found to exist. Specifically, 55% of the males as compared to 50% of the females participated because their friends did, while 44% of the females as opposed to 33% of the males became involved to make new friends. Finally, a comparison of the athletes participating in the various sports revealed few sport-specific motivation patterns.

Another extensive examination of young athletes' participation motives was conducted by Gill, Gross, and Huddleston (1981). In this study, participation motives were examined in 720 boys and 480 girls who attended the University of Iowa summer sports schools in either baseball, basketball, golf, gymnastics, football, wrestling, tennis, track, soccer and/or cheerleading. Boys listed the most important participation motives as "to improve my skills," "challenge," "competition," "fun," and "learning new skills," whereas girls rated "improve my skills," "fun," "learning new skills," "being fit," and "challenge" as most important. Factor analytic results revealed that success, team atmosphere, friendship, fitness, energy release, skill development, and fun are basic dimensions of participation motivation. Unfortunately, no separate comparisons were made for sport, age, or experience.

In a follow-up study to the work of Gill and her associates, Gould, Feltz, Weiss, and Petlichkoff (1982) examined the participation motives of 365 competitive youth swimmers ranging in age from 8 to 19 years. The results supported the Gill et al. study in that the swimmers rated fun, fitness, skill improvement, team atmosphere, and challenge as their main reasons for participating. However, a number of gender and age differences also emerged. Most notable was the finding that females, although equivalent to the males in emphasizing achievement-status, placed greater emphasis on friendship and fun than did their male peers. Important motives for younger swimmers, as compared to older swimmers, were achievement-status, travel, desire to please parents or friends, have something to do, fondness for the coach, and enjoyment of the facilities.

Fry, McClements, and Sefton (1981) examined participation motives of young athletes involved in ice hockey. Their results revealed that 98% of the boys expected to get a lot of fun from playing, while 87% expected to become good players, 68% expected to make new friends, 61% expected to win a trophy, and 54% expected to get exercise and travel. When asked what they liked best about playing hockey, 35% indicated enjoyment of the game itself, 20% indicated scoring goals, skating, or puck handling, 12% indicated winning, and 9% indicated meeting new people or being with friends. These findings are important because they are consistent with those of Wankel and Pabich (1982), who found that children involved in baseball, soccer, and hockey rated improvement of skills, a feeling of accomplishment, and enjoyment of a close game as major benefits of participation.

Other researchers such as Alderman and Wood (1976), Alderman (1978), and Petlichkoff (1982) have used a more theoretical orientation to examine objectives or incentives children have for athletic participation. In the Alderman and Wood (1976) study, for example, 425 ice hockey participants, ages 11 to 14, completed the Alberta Incentive Motivation Inventory which assessed the relevance of seven incentive systems in relation to children's athletic participation. These incentive systems included independence, power, affiliation, arousal, esteem, excellence, and aggression. Research findings revealed that affiliation, excellence, and arousal were found to be the most important incentives for participation, with independence and power incentives being least important. Similar results were found in a subsequent investigation of several thousand young athletes (Alderman, 1978), ranging in age from 11 to 18 years and representing a number of sports. Moreover, the young athletes were found to have similar incentives regardless of their age, sport, gender, or cultural background.

Later, Petlichkoff (1982) partially replicated and extended the findings of Alderman (1978) and Alderman and Wood (1976) by assessing incentives in 270 junior and senior high school athletes. As in the previous studies, excellence, affiliation, and arousal were found to be major incentives for both genders. Unlike the previous incentive motivation research, however, success was found to be a major incentive and a number of gender, age, and sport-incentive differences emerged. Although both genders rated excellence as the most important participation incentive, males also rated success, stress/arousal, aggression, power, and independence as more important than did females. In contrast, the females rated affiliation as significantly more important than did their male peers. Finally, athletes with 6 to 11 seasons of sport experience rated stress/arousal and aggression as more important incentives than those athletes with less than 5 seasons of experience.

Summary

A number of conclusions can be derived from the research on participation motives of young athletes. First, young athletes have diverse motives for participating in sports. They may want to have fun, seek affiliation, demonstrate power, improve skills, pursue excellence, exhibit aggression, have something to do, experience thrills or excitement, be independent, receive rewards, fulfill parental expectations, and win. Moreover, most young athletes have not one but several motives for participation. Second, of the various motives identified for participation, those consistently rated as most important are improving skills, having fun, being with friends, making new friends, experiencing thrills or excitement, achieving success or winning, and developing fitness. Third, gender differences have been found in participation motives of young athletes. Females, for example, rate fun and friendship as more important motives than males do, although no gender differences emerged on the achievement or excellence items. Fourth, a number of sport, experience, and age differences also showed up in participation motives but no consistent patterns emerged. Finally, while the results reveal that consistent patterns of participation motives are found across youngsters, substantial individual differences have also been found.

MAJOR MOTIVES
FOR DISCONTINUING PARTICIPATION

Losing repeatedly shattered my self-confidence, especially with my father always bawling me out in front of the other kids for every mistake . . . I would get so nervous before each meet, I would vomit. After a while the pressure got to me so I quit . . . I never got to play. I showed up at every practice, worked hard all the time and tried my best. Jimmy showed up at one practice and got to play in the next game. It just wasn't fair. (Martens, 1980b, pp. 382-383)

Failure, competitive stress, and not getting to play are only a few of the reasons young athletes give for quitting sports. Because of such reports, as well as the high attrition rates reported in many youth sports programs, there is increasing interest in understanding the youth sports dropout. In fact, according to a recent survey of sport psychologists and adult leaders in youth sports programs, understanding why children quit sports is the most important psychological issue requiring further study (Gould, 1982b). Fortunately, an increasing number of investigators have begun to examine this issue.

In his pioneering efforts to understand the athletic dropout, Orlick conducted extensive interviews with young athletes and former athletes (Orlick, 1973, 1974; Orlick & Botterill, 1975). In the first of these studies, 32 sport participants and nonparticipants ages 8 and 9 were studied. According to Orlick, "Children who dropped out of sports at an early age appeared to be merely reacting to negative stimuli, which were largely a function of the structure of the game and emphasis of the coaches" (1973, p. 12). The majority of children who quit, for example, did so because they were not given adequate playing time. Similarly, fear of failure, disapproval, and psychological stress seemed to make a number of children afraid to participate. Finally, the children indicated that they would like to see changes in sport that would increase playing and practice time, increase the chances of success (e.g., lower goals in basketball), and decrease boredom (e.g., less time spent in repetitious drills).

In a follow-up investigation (Orlick, 1974) interviews were conducted with 60 cross-country, ice hockey, soccer, baseball, and swimming dropouts, ranging from 7 to 19 years of age. Of the respondents, 67% were classified as discontinuing because of the competitive emphasis of the sport, 31% because of conflict of interests (general life conflicts, 21%; interest in other sports, 10%), and 2% because of injury. Of the 40 children who quit because of the competitive nature of the sport, 30 did so because of the emphasis of the program (e.g., seriousness, lack of enjoyment, and emphasis on winning) whereas the remaining 10 children said that the coach was the primary reason they dropped out (e.g., left people out of games, criticized players too often, pushed too hard). Of further interest was the finding that 60% of the high school dropouts quit because of conflicts of interest, while 40% of the elementary school children dropped out because they did not get to play and the remaining 60% did so because they were not successful. Thus, reasons for dropping out were found to be linked to age.

In an extensive investigation of young athletes sponsored by the State of Michigan, Sapp and Haubenstricker (1978) also examined children's motives for quitting sports. The subjects surveyed in this investigation were athletes from 11 to 18 years of age ($N = 1183$) and parents of athletes from 6 to 10 years of age ($N = 418$), representing a variety of youth sports. Over 35% of the older athletes and 24% of the parents of the younger athletes indicated that they or their children did not plan to participate again next season. Parents of the younger athletes who no longer planned to participate indicated that other activities (for over 65% of the respondents) and other interests (for 43% of the respondents) were the most important reasons for dropping out. Of the older athletes who said they would not participate again, 64% rated other activities and 44% rated working as important reasons for dropping out of sports. Less than 15% of these athletes rated motives such as lack of participation, dislike for the coach, injury, the expense, and dislike for teammates as important. Moreover, these findings were further supported by Petlichkoff (1982), who found that junior and senior high school athletic dropouts most often left sports because they had other things to do. Injury and lack of skill improvement, however, also emerged as important reasons for dropping out.

While many of the earlier studies attempted to assess motives for attrition in athletes who represented a number of different sports, several recent studies have assessed reasons for attrition in young athletes from specific sports, namely soccer (Pooley, 1981), swimming (Gould, Feltz, Horn, & Weiss, 1982) and ice hockey (Fry et al., 1981). Pooley, for example, conducted extensive interviews with 50 Canadian youth soccer dropouts, ages 10 to 15. When asked why they stopped playing soccer, approximately 33% of the respondents said it was because of an overemphasis on competition (e.g., "coach shouted when I missed a play"), while 54% cited conflicts of interest, and 10% cited poor communication. Age was also found to influence motives for discontinuing, with the 10- to 12-year-olds (as compared to 13- to 14-year-old dropouts) more often quitting because of an overemphasis on competition.

In another study, Gould, Feltz, Horn, & Weiss (1982) interviewed 50 swimming dropouts ranging in age from 10 to 18 years. Their findings supported those of Pooley (1981) and Sapp and Haubenstricker (1978) by demonstrating that having other things to do was the major reason cited for discontinuing swimming. Specifically, 84% of the dropouts rated "other things to do" as a somewhat or very important reason for dropping out. Moreover, 80% of the sample indicated that they planned to participate in another sport in the future. Other motives rated as important by 40% of the sample included such items as, "not as good as wanted to be," "not enough fun," "wanted to play another sport," "did not like the pressure," "boredom," "did not like the coach," "training was too hard" and "not exciting enough." Based on these findings, it was concluded that most young swimmers who quit are not doing so because of excessive pressure, dislike of the coach, constant failure, a lack of fun, or an overemphasis on winning. Rather, young swimmers who discontinue do so mainly because of interest in other activities.

It was recognized, however, that children sometimes drop out because of negative factors associated with the athletic environment. Those factors included lack of fun (28%), competitive pressure (16%), boredom (16%), and lack of excitement (10%). Thus, while the results show that the *majority* of former swimmers did not cite these more negative items as major reasons for dropping out, it is important to note that these motives are very important reasons for some youngsters. Finally, few gender and years-of-experience differences were found, although older swimmers generally rated a lack of teamwork, parents' and friends' opinions, lack of challenge, and injury as more important reasons for dropping out, whereas younger swimmers in turn rated having other things to do as more important reasons.

A similar pattern of findings emerged in a recent study of Cana-

dian youth ice hockey participants and dropouts, ages 8 to 16, conducted
by Fry et al. (1981). In this investigation, approximately 200 dropouts
were asked why they quit playing hockey. The findings revealed that conflict with other activities was the major reason, and 31% of the sample
cited this response. In addition, 15% of the sample indicated a lack of
skill, 14% disliked the coach, 10% blamed rough play, and 10% cited
organizational problems (e.g., inconvenient game times) as major
reasons for dropping out. Reasons for quitting were also related to age,
with lack of skill and fun (boredom) being more important considerations for those under 9 years of age. Finally, when active participants
were compared to those boys who had dropped out, the participants
demonstrated a higher achievement orientation.

Summary

Several conclusions can be drawn from this research examining children's
motives for dropping out of sports. First, young athletes drop out for
various reasons: interest in and conflicts with other activities, lack of
playing time, lack of success, little skill improvement, competitive stress,
lack of peer-parental support, lack of fun, dislike for the coach,
boredom, and injury. Second, when all the studies are considered, conflicts of interest appear to be most often cited as reasons for quitting.
However, some evidence shows that many other participants quit because of more negative factors associated with the athletic environment — factors that are under the control of coaches and adult leaders.
These include a lack of playing time, overemphasis on competition,
boredom, lack of fun, and dislike for the coach. Third, some preliminary
evidence shows that these more negative factors may be especially influential in affecting attrition patterns with athletes under the age of 9.

GUIDELINES FOR ENHANCING PARTICIPATION
MOTIVATION IN YOUNG ATHLETES

The findings generated from the review of the youth sports participation
motivation and reasons for attrition research literature can assist those
involved in children's sports in enhancing the young athlete's motivation.
Specifically, these findings have the greatest impact when interpreted
in light of the athlete-by-situation interaction model of motivation
(Alderman, 1978; Gould 1980). This model suggests that motivated
behavior results from the continuous interaction of both the athlete (e.g.,
personality, needs, incentives, motives) and athletic environmental factors (e.g., program emphasis on competition, skill development, affiliation). Thus, optimal athletic motivation occurs when an athlete's par-

ticipation motives are fulfilled by his or her athletic environment. For instance, if a young athlete's primary objective is to be with friends and make new friends, and the coach provides plenty of time for this affiliation, motivation will be enhanced. However, motivation may decline if the same athlete participates in a program that solely emphasizes high achievement and success.

This model implies, then, that the youth sports coach must understand his or her athletes' motives for participating. This understanding can come from careful observation, frequent discussions, and the development of open lines of communication. Additionally, the review of the participation motivation research revealed that young athletes have a number of motives for participating in sports, the most important of which are improving skills, having fun, being with friends, making new friends, experiencing thrills or excitement, achieving success or winning, and developing fitness. The attrition research also revealed that young athletes lose their motivation to participate when their objectives change (e.g., become interested in other activities) and when their motives are not fulfilled (e.g., no skill improvement, no fun, not with friends). Thus, it is imperative that every youth sports coach understand the young athlete's motives for involvement.

Once a young athlete's participation motives are recognized, the coach can enhance this motivation through one of two general strategies: If the young athlete has desirable motives (e.g., skill improvement, affiliation), the coach can structure the athletic environment to fulfill these needs. On the other hand, if the young athlete has undesirable motives (i.e., power, aggression), the coach should initiate a behavior modification program to change these objectives.

Structuring the Athletic Environment to Enhance Motivation

Structuring the athletic environment to fulfill the athlete's participation motives is an especially useful way to enhance motivation. Specifically, coaches can implement the following practices.

Provide Opportunities for Skill Development. One of the most frequently cited motives young athletes give for participating in sports is the improvement of their skills. Ironically, this objective is often neglected. Many coaches forget that mere participation alone does not improve skills. In fact, the old adage that practice makes perfect is incorrect. Planned, purposeful practice makes perfect (Martens, Christina, Harvey, & Sharkey, 1981). Moreover, a good knowledge of the sport does not necessarily mean a coach will be an effective instructor. Effective instruction requires that practices be planned and well organized and that all athletes, regardless of their ability, receive appropriate instruction. Equally important is the method of instruction. Smith, Smoll, Hunt, Curtis, and Coppel (1979), for example, have provided convincing evidence that a positive rather than a negative approach is most effective when coaching young athletes. Important components of a positive approach are sincerity, realistic expectations, frequent rewarding and encouraging statements, the reward of effort rather than just outcome, and having a constructive approach to mistakes.

Ensure That Practices and Games Are Fun. Coaches can unknowingly stifle the motivation of the young athlete by inhibiting fun, which can happen when children are treated like miniature adults. Considering that children's attention spans are shorter, their self-concepts more fragile, and their abilities not as fully developed as an adult's, the youth sports coach must develop realistic expectations and remember that the young athlete will make mistakes and sometimes misbehave. Patience and constructive criticism will be needed. Coaches must also remember that most young athletes have fun when they are active and participating, not when they are sitting on the bench or standing in line. The research has shown that most young athletes would rather be on a losing team and play than sit on the bench of a winning team!

Provide for the Affiliation Needs of Young Athletes. The camaraderie with the other young athletes seems to be a primary motive for participation. It is essential, then, that the youth sports coach fulfill these affiliation needs by providing time for the children to be with their friends and make new friends. For example, scheduling social events outside of practice or designating "free time" periods before practices are good ways of allowing the young athletes to make friends in a warm, friendly, social atmosphere.

Keep Practices and Games Exciting. The thrills and excitement of participation, the "natural high" of sports, are primary motives for the young athletes' involvement. Unfortunately, much of the inherent thrills and excitement of athletics may disappear over the course of the season, especially when coaches focus mainly on teaching and drilling the fundamental skills. There is no substitute for practicing fundamentals, of course, but this does not mean that practices must be boring. In fact, an effective way to prevent boredom is to organize quick and exciting drills that involve all the athletes. Similarly, incorporating change-of-pace practice activities (e.g., basketball scrimmages where no dribbling is allowed, soccer dribbling relays, water polo for swimmers) is another effective way to ensure that practices and games will remain exciting. Finally, it may also be useful to incorporate some of Bell's (1980) suggestions on teaching young athletes how to cope psychologically with the normal pain, discomfort, and boredom that accompanies the conditioning process in many sports.

Develop a Realistic View of Success.

It is incorrect to think that young athletes themselves do not value winning, especially as they grow and mature. But coaches should not view winning as the sole objective for sports participation. As this review has shown, young athletes have several reasons for participating in sport—winning is only one. When a coach focuses only on winning, therefore, it can be taken out of perspective and is often defined in only one way—beating the opponent. Thus, the youth sports coach should keep winning in perspective while not neglecting the other needs of the young athletes. Additionally, coaches should help the young athlete define winning. Winning means much more than beating the opponent; it means the young athlete should try as hard as possible to improve relative to his or her own standards or personal goals. In the heat of competition, the youth coach would do well to remember this!

Provide Opportunities for Fitness Development.

Physical fitness is not an automatic result of youth sports participation. To fulfill this participation objective, the youth sports coach must organize planned and purposeful practices specifically designed to increase fitness. Additionally, youth sports coaches can help fulfill this objective by teaching young athletes how to assess and monitor their own fitness levels.

Modifying Inappropriate Participation Motives

Although structuring the athletic environment to fulfill the athlete's needs is an important and effective way to enhance motivation, it is not always appropriate to do so. When young athletes have inappropriate motives for participation such as the need to dominate others or to win at all costs, or have an attitude of physical aggression or intimidation, it may be necessary to modify their motives for involvement. This is not easy, however. As has been noted elsewhere (Gould, 1982b), fostering psychological development in young athletes requires the coach to develop and implement strategies that will foster the development of appropriate psychological attributes in the young athlete. Moreover, psychological development takes time and will usually require a long-term concerted effort by the coach.

Several techniques or strategies that will foster psychological development in young athletes include individual and team talks, use of behavior modification principles, use of role models, and education of parents. If a coach is to effectively modify inappropriate motives, he or she must discuss the problem with the young athlete and explain why the behavior is appropriate or inappropriate (Martens, 1978). Once the athlete understands this, the coach must consistently reinforce the desirable behavior and penalize the inappropriate behavior. Key ingredients of effective behavior management include defining desirable and undesirable behaviors in measurable terms, being consistent when defining and reinforcing behaviors, and using a positive rather than a negative approach (Siedentop, 1978).

Coaches can also influence psychological change in young athletes by becoming role models themselves. For example, if a coach is attempting to teach a young athlete not to intimidate others, the coach should also demonstrate this behavior. Similarly, the coach should point to other role models such as professional athletes who display the desired behavior or attitude. Yet it is not unusual for coaches to try implementing psychological change in young athletes but find their efforts unknowingly undermined by parents and other involved adults. Consequently, coaches should not only discuss efforts to change participation motives with their athletes, but should also discuss these issues with parents as well (Martens et al., 1981).

SUMMARY

This review indicates that young athletes have multiple motives for athletic participation. Although there are substantial differences between individual athletes concerning why they participate in sports, most of the research indicates that the most important athletic objectives include improving skills, having fun, being with friends, making new friends, experiencing thrills or excitement, achieving success, and developing fitness. The research on attrition in young athletes also shows that most young athletes drop out of sport if it conflicts with work or other activities. However, a substantial minority of children have been found to drop out because of more negative reasons associated with the athletic environment, such as a lack of playing time, overemphasis on competition, boredom, lack of fun, and dislike of the coach. These findings have a number of practical coaching implications when interpreted in light of the athlete-by-situation model of motivation. Specifically, this model implies that optimal participation motivation occurs when adult leaders understand the young athlete's motives for involvement and then either structure the athletic environment to fulfill these objectives or modify the motives themselves.

Chapter 26

Leadership Research in Youth Sports

Frank L. Smoll and Ronald E. Smith
University of Washington

Highly structured athletic programs for children constitute an important part of the sport subculture in Western societies. Literally millions of youngsters have been drawn to adult-supervised athletics, and these programs have become firmly entrenched in our social and cultural milieu (Martens, 1978; Seefeldt, Gilliam, Blievernicht, & Bruce, 1978). Not only has there been tremendously rapid growth in organized youth sports, but there is no reason to anticipate a decline. Furthermore, increasing participation by young athletes has been accompanied by a greater degree of adult involvement (Berryman, 1982). Consequently, these programs are characterized by an extremely complex social system that has attracted the attention of researchers interested in studying the impact of sport participation on psychological development (see Gould, 1982a, 1984; Magill, Ash, & Smoll, 1982; Seefeldt & Gould, 1980; Smoll & Smith, 1978).

The relatively recent surge of interest in psychologically oriented youth sport research is indeed an encouraging trend, particularly since much of the research shows a reliance on psychological theories to formulate hypotheses (e.g., social learning theory and psychoanalytic theory). However, the most meaningful inquiries will likely stem from theories and research paradigms formulated in reference to the phenomenon of interest, namely sport. Future advances will thus depend not only on soundly designed empirical investigations but also on the concomitant development and testing of *sport-specific* theoretical frameworks and models that can serve as a source of testable hypotheses. Or, as Martens (1979) succinctly stated, "We clearly need to spend more time observing behavior in sport and building our own theories unique to sport. Then we can test them!" (p. 97).

This chapter presents a theoretical model for studying leadership behaviors in youth sports. First, it presents a rationale for studying leadership in youth sports settings. Next, consideration is given to the basic components of a mediational model of coach-player interactions and to some preliminary research relative to the model. In contrast to most leadership research, which has been based almost exclusively on paper-and-pencil measures, the research generated by this model emphasizes a behavioral assessment approach to measuring the coaches' behaviors in naturalistic settings. We will then review empirically derived coaching guidelines and give recommendations for implementing them. Following this we will describe additional research concerning the development and testing of a psychologically oriented training program for coaches. Finally, we will discuss a more comprehensive version of the model and cite some implications for future research.

LEADERSHIP RESEARCH
IN YOUTH SPORTS SETTINGS

Although youth sports is a social institution of major importance, considerable controversy exists about the roles that adults play in the process. However, there is general agreement that the relationship between coach and player is an important determinant of the ways in which children are ultimately affected by their participation in organized sports (Martens, 1978; Seefeldt & Gould, 1980; Smith, Smoll, Hunt, Curtis, & Coppel, 1979; Smoll, Smith, & Curtis, 1977). Coaches are not only central to the sport setting, but their influence can extend into other areas of the child's life as well. And yet, until recently there has been virtually no research on coaching behaviors, their determinants, and their impact on children.

The analysis and modification of coaching behaviors in youth sports programs has been the focus of our work. Studying coach-player interactions holds implications not only for sport psychology but also for the area of leader-group relations. In fact, sports offer an excellent setting for studying the behavior of leaders. Ilgen and Fujii (1976) emphasized the importance of field studies relating group performance and morale to leader behavior. Comparing field settings to laboratory settings, they suggested that both the greater importance of a leader's behavior to subordinates and the increased time for interactions may produce stronger relationships in the former setting. With respect to youth sports, the study of leadership behaviors has several attractive features: (a) the sport situation is sufficiently structured to permit identification of relevant situational variables, and the relationship between coach and child is typically restricted to this setting; (b) these settings elicit a wide range of leadership behaviors which can be reliably measured; and (c) the situation is an important one to children, and it evokes high levels of psychological involvement in both coaches and children. Indeed, Coddington (1972) found that children rated the possibility of failing to make the team as stressful as the possible death of a close friend. Such an important setting enhances the likelihood of identifying relations between leadership behaviors and children's reactions to them.

Because most volunteer coaches have positive and desirable motives for coaching (Martens & Gould, 1979; Smith, Smoll, & Curtis, 1978), we can assume that their limitations as coaches are due mainly to a lack of information and awareness of how they affect their players. Therefore, our efforts have focused on the development and assessment of a training program that would improve the ability of coaches to relate more effectively to their young athletes. To accomplish this, we carried out a 2-phase research project over a 7-year period. Phase I employed a large-scale study designed to relate specific coaching behaviors to players' attitudes toward their coach, teammates, themselves, and other aspects of their sport involvement. Also considered was how certain characteristics of children, such as their age and level of self-esteem, affected their responses to specific coaching practices. Phase II involved an application of the research results to derive behavioral guidelines and to develop a psychologically oriented training program for coaches. Later, the effects of the experimental training program were assessed by measuring the ways in which the program affected coaches' behaviors and the sport-related attitudes and self-esteem of the youngsters who played for them.

PRELIMINARY THEORETICAL MODEL
AND RESEARCH PARADIGM

Investigation of coach-player relationships will be most systematic if based on a conceptual model that can both accommodate existing data and guide scientific inquiry. The conceptual basis for our work is a mediational model which requires the independent measurement of both overt and player-perceived coaching behaviors. The major components of the model are schematically presented in the following simplified diagram: Coach Behaviors → Player Perception and Recall → Players' Evaluative Reactions.

A major tenet of this model is that coaching behaviors do not directly affect children's evaluative reactions (attitudes) toward the coach and other aspects of their athletic experience. Rather, it is assumed that players' attitudes are mediated by their perception and recall of the coach's behaviors. In a sense, the youngsters serve as a filter whose cognitive and affective processes mediate between the coach's behaviors and their own ultimate attitudes and reactions. That is, the effects of coaching behaviors are mediated by the meaning that players attribute to them. For instance, players may respond not only to the informational content of technical instruction but also to some message a coach unwarily communicates through the manner or timing of such instruction. So if we wish to understand how coaching behaviors affect players' reactions, we need to consider the mediating processes that occur in the player. As presented here the model implies one-way causal relationships, but it also allows for reciprocal interactions among relevant variables (Heise, 1975). For example, significant relationships may indicate not only that coaching behaviors affect team performance or morale, but also that the coach's own subsequent behaviors may be influenced by these outcomes.

PHASE I: STUDYING COACHING BEHAVIORS AND THEIR EFFECTS ON CHILDREN

The research paradigm suggested by the mediational model prompted us to measure and define the relationships between each of the model's three major components. Thus, our Phase I research measured actual coaching behaviors, player perception and recall of the behaviors, and the children's affective responses to the total situation. We also measured coaches' recall of their own behaviors. This is an important variable because it indicates the extent to which the coaches are aware of what they do.

Measurement of Coaching Behaviors and Player Attitudes

The Coaching Behavior Assessment System (CBAS) was developed to permit the direct observation and coding of coaches' behavior (Smith, Smoll, & Hunt, 1977). The CBAS comprises 12 behavioral categories that are divided into two major subclasses: reactive (elicited) and spontaneous (emitted) behaviors. As shown in Table 26-1, the reactive behaviors are responses to either desirable performance or effort, mistakes and errors, or players' misbehaviors. The spontaneous categories are subdivided into either game-relevant or irrelevant behaviors initiated by the coach.

TABLE 26-1
Response Categories of the Coaching Behavior Assessment System

---

Class I. Reactive Behaviors

Responses to desirable performance

Reinforcement	A positive, rewarding reaction, verbal or nonverbal, to a good play or good effort
Nonreinforcement	Failure to respond to a good performance

Responses to mistakes

Mistake-contingent encouragement	Encouragement given to a player following a mistake
Mistake-contingent technical instruction	Instructing or demonstrating to a player how to correct a mistake
Punishment	A negative reaction, verbal or nonverbal, following a mistake
Punitive technical instruction	Technical instruction which is given in a punitive or hostile manner following a mistake
Ignoring mistakes	Failure to respond to a player mistake

Response to misbehavior

Keeping control	Reactions intended to restore or maintain order among team members

---

Class II. Spontaneous Behaviors

Game-related

General technical instruction	Spontaneous instruction in the techniques and strategies of the sport (not following a mistake)
General encouragement	Spontaneous encouragement which does not follow a mistake
Organization	Administrative behavior which sets the stage for play by assigning duties, responsibilities, positions, etc.

Game-irrelevant

General communication	Interactions with players unrelated to the game

---

As described in greater detail elsewhere (Smith et al., 1977), the CBAS was developed on the basis of extensive naturalistic observation of coaches in a variety of team sports. Using a time-sampling procedure, observers carried portable tape recorders and essentially did a play-by-play of coaches' game and practice behaviors, including the situations in which they occurred. The behavior descriptions were transcribed and their content analyzed to develop the categories that comprise the coding system. Subsequent use of the system has proved very satisfactory in observing and coding coaching behaviors in a variety of sports. The system is sufficiently comprehensive to incorporate the vast majority of behaviors, individual differences in behavioral patterns can be discerned, and interrater reliabilities in the mid .90s can be obtained in the field (Smith et al., 1978; Smith, Zane, Smoll, & Coppel, 1983).

The Phase I research involved the study of 51 male coaches and their players in three Little League Baseball programs in the Seattle area. Each coach gave his written consent to have his behaviors coded by trained observers during an average of nearly four games. An average of 1,122 behaviors were coded for each coach during the course of the season, thus in effect revealing a behavioral profile for each coach. The children's data were collected at the end of the season in half-hour personal interviews. A total of 542 players were interviewed, representing 83% of the youngsters who played for the 51 coaches. The most important data collected during the interviews were the children's perceptions and recall of how their coach behaved and their attitudes toward him and other aspects of their sport experience. In addition, each child completed several personality measures including measures of general and athletic self-esteem. This permitted a determination of the role of personality variables in children's reactions to particular kinds of coaching behaviors as well as an assessment of postseason differences in these measures for children exposed to different kinds of coaches.

In Phase I, we thus determined what coaches were doing, what they thought they had done, what the children thought the coaches had done, and how the children felt about their experience and about themselves. These variables were analyzed as a total system, and clear-cut relationships were found between coaching behaviors and children's perceptions and attitudes. Our focus in this section is on results that bear most directly on the intervention program designed to assist coaches in creating more positive athletic experiences for youngsters. A more complete presentation of results appears elsewhere (Smith et al., 1978).

Coach Behaviors and Self-Perceptions

The distribution of behaviors within the CBAS categories (rates per 100 behaviors) indicated that nearly two-thirds of the behaviors fell within the three instructional and supportive categories (General Technical Instruction = 27.3%, General Encouragement = 21.4%, Reinforcement = 17.1%). In contrast, the frequency of punitive behaviors was relatively low in comparison with other categories (Punishment = 1.8%, Punitive Technical Instruction = 1.0%). It is interesting to note, however, that about 20% of the observed mistakes were responded to with either Punishment or Punitive Technical Instruction.

An important issue concerns the degree of accuracy with which coaches perceive their own behavior. Correlations between CBAS observed behaviors and coaches' ratings of how frequently they performed the behaviors were generally low and nonsignificant. The only significant correlation occurred for Punishment ($r = .45$). It thus appears that coaches' self-perceptions show correspondence with externally observed behaviors only for punitive behaviors. Coaches apparently have limited awareness of how frequently they engage in other forms of behavior.

Player Perceptions of Coaching Behaviors

Correlations between the mean behavioral ratings of each team and the observed CBAS behaviors of the 51 coaches revealed that players most accurately perceived punitive behaviors, reactions to mistakes, and game-irrelevant communicative behaviors of the coach. However, correlations between players' perceptions of their coaches' behaviors and the coaches' self-perceptions were low and generally nonsignificant. This indicated that there was little correspondence between the way coaches viewed themselves and how their players perceived them. Indeed, the players' perceptions tended to be more accurate in that they correlated more highly with CBAS observed behavior scores. The potential importance of increasing coaches' awareness of how they behave was thus seen as a key to changing their behaviors.

Observed Behaviors, Player Attitudes, and Self-Esteem

Relationships between observed coaching behaviors and children's attitudes indicated that coaches oriented toward technical instruction were evaluated more positively than were coaches who engaged in more General Encouragement and General Communication. Players who played for the technically instructive coaches also evaluated their teammates and the sport more positively. Furthermore, coaches scoring high on the supportive behaviors of Reinforcement and Mistake-Contingent Encouragement were evaluated more positively by their players. Finally, it is interesting to note that players evaluated their teammates and the sport more positively if they played for coaches who gave high levels of Reinforcement and support.

Also of interest were relationships between coaching behaviors and player self-esteem scores obtained after the season ended. We found that youngsters who played for coaches who gave high levels of Reinforcement and Mistake-Contingent Encouragement had higher general self-esteem scores at the end of the season than did children who played for less supportive coaches. These data provided the first evidence linking coaching behaviors to children's self-esteem, and they suggested the possibility that certain coaching behaviors may affect levels of self-esteem.

Player-Perceived Behaviors and Attitudes Toward Coaches

The correlations between the players' perceptions of their coaches' behaviors and their subsequent attitudes were generally much higher than were the observed behavior-attitude relationships. This finding is consistent with the mediational model in that players' evaluative reactions to their coaches' behaviors were indeed mediated by cognitive and perceptual processes.

Another analysis indicated that the best-liked coaches were rated as giving more frequent Reinforcement, Mistake-Contingent Encouragement, General Encouragement, and Mistake-Contingent Technical Instruction, as well as engaging in more Organization and Keeping Control behaviors. The least popular coaches were rated as more frequently engaging in Punishment and Punitive Technical Instruction following mistakes. Thus, there are substantial and meaningful relationships between player-perceived coach behaviors and attraction toward the coach.

The Role of Winning

A somewhat surprising finding was that the team's won-lost record was essentially unrelated to how well the players liked the coach and how strongly they wanted to play for the coach in the future. Furthermore, players on winning teams felt that their parents liked the coach more and that the coach liked them more than did players on losing teams. Apparently, winning made little difference to the children but they knew that it was important to the adults. It is worth noting, however, that winning assumed greater importance beyond age 12, although it continued to be a less important attitudinal determinant than coach behaviors.

GUIDELINES FOR IMPROVING COACH-PLAYER RELATIONSHIPS

The data obtained in Phase I provided some initial scientific information on coach-player relationships. From this empirical data base, we derived behavioral guidelines designed to help coaches relate more effectively to child athletes. The series of coaching do's and don'ts are based primarily on (a) a conception of success or "winning" as giving maximum effort (Smoll & Smith, 1981), and (b) a positive approach to social influence that prefers reinforcement and encouragement to punishment and criticism (Smoll & Smith, 1979).

A Winning Philosophy for Youth Sports

The conventional notion of success in sports is victory. But when winning games becomes the sole or primary goal in youth sports, children can be deprived of important opportunities to develop their skills, enjoy playing, and to grow as people. Well informed coaches recognize that success is not synonymous with winning games, nor failure with losing. Rather, the most important kind of success comes from striving to win and giving maximum effort. Coaches should realize that the only thing players have complete control over is the amount of effort they give. They have only limited control over the outcome that is achieved. Children should be taught that they are never losers if they give maximum effort in striving for excellence.

The Positive Approach to Coaching

The key distinction made within our behavioral guidelines for coaches is that of positive versus negative approaches to influencing behavior. The positive approach uses reinforcement and encouragement to strengthen desirable behaviors and motivate players to perform them. The negative approach uses various forms of punishment to eliminate undesirable behaviors. The motivating factor here is fear, and we believe that the negative approach produces stress, decreases enjoyment of athletics, and creates dislike for the coach. Our guidelines thus recommend the liberal use of reinforcement for effort as well as performance, the giving of encouragement after mistakes, and the giving of technical instruction in an encouraging and supportive fashion.

When technical instruction is given after a mistake, the guidelines recommend first complimenting the player for something done correctly, then giving the corrective instruction, focusing on the positive things that will happen in the future if the instruction is followed, rather than the negative consequences of the mistake. We discourage punitive behaviors. We recommend reinforcement as a means of establishing and strengthening encouragement and support among teammates as well as compliance with team rules. The basic principles contained in the positive approach to coaching are presented in an abridged form in Appendix A.

Increasing Self-Awareness
and Compliance With the Guidelines

One of the striking findings from our Phase I research was that coaches had very limited awareness of how frequently they behaved in various ways. Indeed, players' perceptions of their coaches' behaviors were more accurate than the self-ratings made by the coaches. Thus, to successfully implement coaching guidelines, we should try to increase coaches' awareness of what they are doing as well as their motivation to comply with the behavioral guidelines. Two behavioral change techniques are recommended in this regard, namely, behavioral feedback and self-monitoring (Smoll & Smith, 1980).

To obtain behavioral feedback, coaches can work with assistants as a team and share descriptions of each others' behaviors. They can then discuss alternate ways of dealing with difficult situations and players and prepare themselves for dealing with similar situations in the future. Other feedback procedures include getting input from the players themselves and getting feedback from a league committee.

Self-monitoring is not only an effective procedure for increasing self-awareness of behaviors and their antecedents and consequences, but it may also be an effective behavior change procedure in itself (Kazdin, 1974; Thoresen & Mahoney, 1974). Therefore, after practices and games coaches should take some time to evaluate their behaviors and actions. When going through this self-analysis, they should ask themselves what they did relative to the suggested behaviors in the guidelines. To assist in this procedure, a brief coach self-report form is presented in Table 26-2.

PHASE II: DEVELOPING AND TESTING
A COACH TRAINING PROGRAM

The research-derived coaching guidelines are the heart of a 3-hour training program which we call Coach Effectiveness Training (CET). We felt it was important not only to develop CET on the basis of sound evidence but also to measure its effects on coaches and the youngsters who play for them. In Phase II of our research project, we attempted to modify coaching behaviors and evaluate the success of the intervention program.

Thirty-one Little League Baseball coaches were randomly assigned either to an experimental (training) group or to a no-treatment control group. The experimental group coaches participated in a preseason CET program designed to help them relate more effectively to children. The intervention program was conceptualized within a cognitive-behavioral framework (cf. Bandura, 1977a). Behavioral guidelines, both verbal and written, were given to the coaches. The verbal guidelines were supplemented with demonstrations of how to behave in desirable ways. In addition to the information-modeling portion of the CET program, behavioral feedback and self-monitoring procedures were employed to increase the coaches' self-awareness and encourage them to comply with the coaching guidelines.

TABLE 26-2
A Brief Form for Self-Monitoring of Desirable Coaching Behaviors

---

Complete this form as soon as possible after a practice or game. Not only think about what you did, but also consider the kinds of situations in which the actions occurred and the kinds of players who were involved.

1. Approximately how often (give percentage) did you respond to good plays with *reinforcement*? _____

2. Approximately how often (give percentage) did you respond to mistakes/errors with each of the following communications?
   A. *Encouragement* only _____
   B. *Corrective instruction* given in an encouraging manner _____
      (Sum of A plus B should not exceed 100%.)

3. About how many times did you reinforce players for effort, complying with team rules, encouraging teammates, showing "team spirit," etc.? _____

4. How well did your team play tonight? (Check one.)

Very poorly	Not very well	Average	Quite well	Very well

5. How positive an experience *for the kids* was this practice/game?

Very negative	Somewhat negative	Neutral	Somewhat positive	Very positive

6. How positive an experience *for you* was this practice/game?

Very negative	Somewhat negative	Neutral	Somewhat positive	Very positive

7. Is there anything you might do differently if you had a chance to coach this practice/game again? (If so, briefly explain.)

The effects of the experimental CET program were measured essentially by repeating the Phase I procedures. Behavioral profiles were developed by observing experimental and control coaches during four games. At the end of the season, 325 players were interviewed to obtain player data. The experimental and control coaches were then compared on all of the behavioral and player measures.

On both behavioral measures and in players' perceptions of their coaches' behaviors, the trained coaches differed from the controls in a manner consistent with the coaching guidelines. They gave more reinforcement and encouragement and were less punitive than the controls. The behavioral differences were reflected in their players' attitudes as well, despite the fact that the average won-lost records of the two groups of coaches were quite similar. Trained coaches were liked better and were rated as better teachers of baseball skills, and players on their teams liked one another more. Furthermore, children who played for the trained coaches exhibited a significant increase in general self-esteem as compared with scores obtained a year earlier; control group children did not. Finally, we found that the greatest differences in players' attitudes toward trained as opposed to control coaches were found among children low in self-esteem. Such children apparently respond favorably to coaches who adopt the guidelines, and their feelings of self-worth increase (Smith, Smoll, & Curtis, 1979).

The above research indicates that there are specifiable relationships between coaching behaviors and children's reactions to their athletic experiences. Further, the encouraging results of the experimental training program indicate that coaches can be trained to relate more effectively to their players. We will now present an expanded model for studying leadership in youth sports.

EXPANDING THE BASIC MODEL

Despite incorporating both overt and player-perceived behaviors, the basic three-element model underlying our early research was quite limited in its scope. It needs to be elaborated. Having demonstrated significant and replicable relationships between coaching behaviors and children's attitudes, we now must specify more completely and precisely the characteristics and processes that underlie the adult leadership behaviors and mediate their effects on children. In view of this, a more comprehensive version of the model is presented in Figure 26-1. The model specifies a number of situational and individual difference variables that are expected to influence coaching behaviors, player perception and recall, and player attitudes as well as predicted empirical relationships among these three elements. Thus, our expanded theoretical model is an attempt to incorporate situational, behavioral, cognitive, and individual difference variables. A thorough discussion of the model, including supportive data, appears elsewhere (Smith & Smoll, 1982a). However, a brief overview is presented below, highlighting several of the variables and their anticipated influences and interrelationships.

In the proposed model, overt coaching behaviors are assumed to be influenced by both *individual difference* and *situational variables*. Concerning the individual leader, for example, we assume that behaviors are typically organized into patterns that reflect particular coaching goals and behavioral intentions. A goal is an anticipated positive outcome of an act or acts. A behavioral intention is a cognitive antecedent of an act

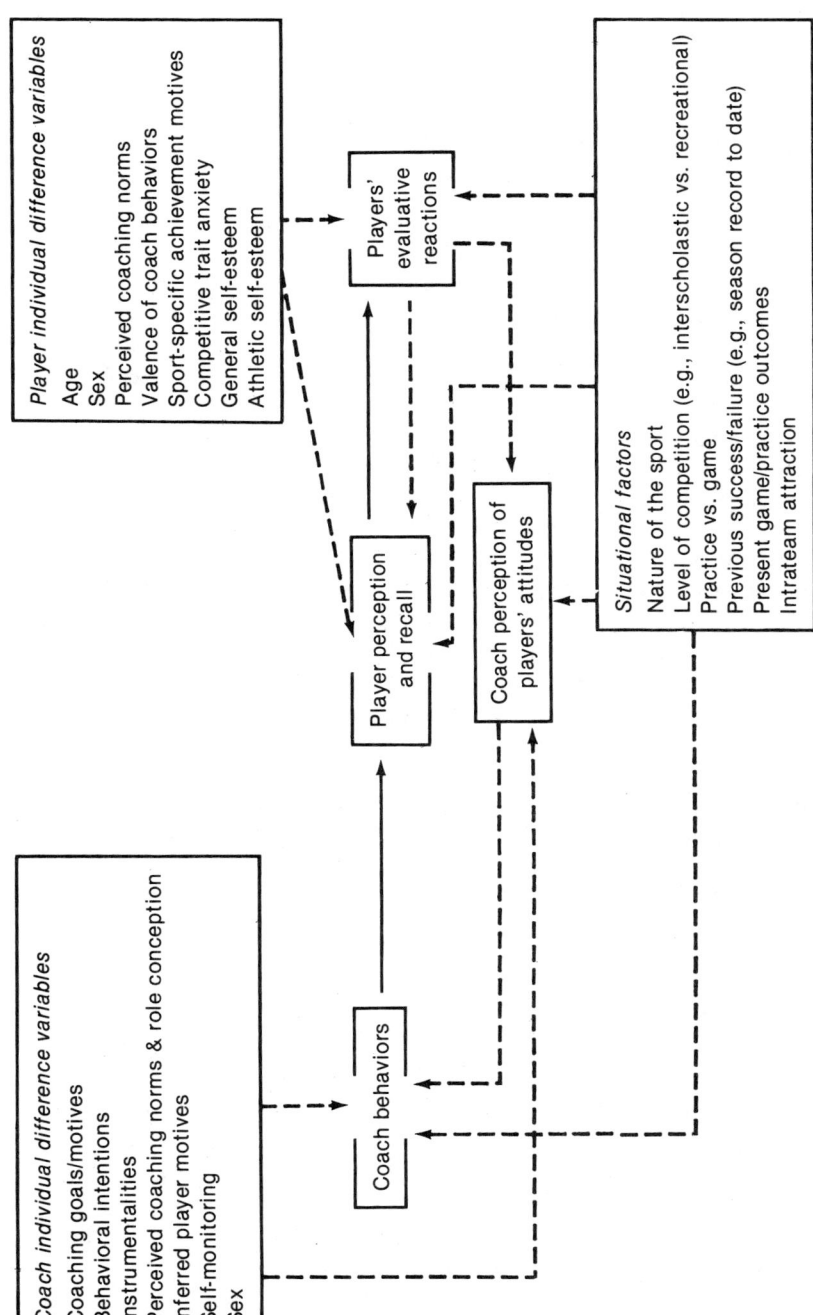

FIGURE 26-1 A model of coaching behaviors, their determinants, and their effects.

and implies a decision to behave in one way as opposed to others. The concept of behavioral intention occupies a prominent position in recent models of interpersonal behavior advanced by Fishbein and Ajzen (1975) and by Triandis (1977). These theorists cite a large body of empirical evidence which shows that under certain conditions, specific behaviors are highly predictable from behavioral intentions, and behavioral intentions in turn are predictable from a number of social, cognitive, and motivational variables. The extent and conditions under which specific coaching behaviors can be predicted from behavioral intentions should thus be an important focus of future research. Likewise, research relative to the influence of other individual difference variables should be of considerable importance.

Situational factors also influence the coach's behavior. The CBAS measures responses to three eliciting conditions: desirable player performance, mistakes, and misbehavior. But other situational conditions, both general (e.g., nature of the sport, recreational vs. competitive program) and specific (e.g., score of the game) may affect coaches' behaviors or interact with individual difference variables. Studying the effects of such factors on behavioral intentions, instrumentalities (i.e., the sum of the products of perceived likelihood of a consequence times the value of the consequence), and overt behavior is clearly an important step in the development of the proposed model.

In addition to the coach individual difference variables, the model posits a number of *player individual difference variables*, which are assumed to affect players' perceptions of coaching behaviors and their responses to them. Player attitudes about how much they like or dislike certain coaching behaviors (i.e., ratings of their valence) are among these variables. We can expect coach behaviors to have different valences for individual players. For example, some youngsters may value reinforcement more than others, and the positive or negative valence of any coaching behavior can be expected to vary as a function of other individual difference variables, experiential factors, and situational factors. Behavioral valences occupy an influential role in many theoretical conceptions of interpersonal behavior (e.g., Carson, 1969; Thibaut & Kelley, 1959; Triandis, 1977), and they are of interest as dependent variables as well as moderators of attitudinal responses to coaching behaviors. Other player individual difference variables deserve future empirical attention and, therefore, have been included in our model. For example, many personality variables could conceivably moderate relationships between coaching behaviors, player perceptions, and evaluative reactions. We have chosen to include three variables, competition anxiety, general self-esteem, and athletic self-esteem, which are of considerable importance on both theoretical and empirical grounds (Coppel, 1979; Martens, 1977; Passer, 1982; Smith et al., 1978, 1979, 1983).

It should be noted that *situational* factors undoubtedly affect children's perceptions of and reactions to coaching behaviors just as they influence the behaviors themselves. The role of situational factors affecting both coaches and players has not been explored, but a clearer specification of important situational factors is critical to the proposed model's ultimate utility.

The arrows shown in our leadership model depict hypothesized causal or moderator relationships between variables. Although it is virtually impossible to study simultaneously the effects (in some cases reciprocal) of all the hypothesized causal factors, the model provides a theoretical framework for studying direct and interactive influences. It also provides a wealth of hypotheses that are relevant not only to sport but perhaps to other leadership domains as well.

APPENDIX A

Behavioral Guidelines for Youth Sports Coaches

I. Reactions to player behaviors and game situations:
  A. Good plays
   Do: Reinforce!! Do so immediately. Let the players know that you appreciate and value their efforts. Reinforce effort as much as you do results. Look for positive things, reinforce them, and you'll see them increase. Remember, whether the kids show it or not, the positive things you say and do stick with them.
   Don't: Take their efforts for granted.
  B. Mistakes, screw-ups, boneheaded plays, and all the things the pro's seldom do
   Do: Encourage immediately after mistakes. That's when the kid needs encouragement most. Also, give *corrective instruction* on how to do it right, but always do so in an encouraging manner. Do this by emphasizing not the bad thing that just happened, but the good things that will happen if the kid follows your instruction (the "why" of it). This will motivate the player positively to correct the mistake rather than motivate him/her negatively to avoid failure and your disapproval.
   Don't: Punish when things go wrong. Punishment isn't just yelling at kids; it can be any indication of disapproval, tone of voice, or action. Kids respond much better to a positive approach. Fear of failure is reduced if you work to reduce fear of punishment.

C. Misbehaviors, lack of attention

Do: Maintain order by establishing clear expectations. Emphasize that during a game all members of the team are part of the game, even those on the bench. Use reinforcement to strengthen team participation. In other words, try to prevent misbehaviors from occurring by using the positive approach to strengthen their opposites.

Don't: Constantly nag or threaten the kids in order to prevent chaos. Don't be a drill sergeant. If a kid refuses to cooperate, quietly remove him or her from the bench for a while. Don't use physical measures (e.g., running laps). The idea here is that if you establish clear behavioral guidelines early and work to build team spirit in achieving them, you can avoid having to repeatedly *keep control*. Remember, kids want clear guidelines and expectations, but they don't want to be regimented. Try to achieve a healthy balance.

II. Getting positive things to happen:

Do: Give *instruction*. Establish your role as a teacher. Try to structure participation as a learning experience in which you're going to help the kids develop their abilities. Always give instruction in a positive fashion. Satisfy your players' desire to become the best athletes they can be. Give instruction in a clear, concise manner; if possible, demonstrate how to do it.

Do: Give *encouragement*. Encourage effort; don't demand results. Use it selectively so that it is meaningful. Be supportive without acting like a cheerleader.

Do: Concentrate on the game. Be "in the game" with the players. Set a good example for team unity.

Don't: Give either instruction or encouragement in a sarcastic or degrading manner. Make a point, then leave it. Don't let "encouragement" become irritating to the players.

(Smoll & Smith, 1979, pp. 6, 9, 14, 18)

Chapter 27

Interactions Between Gender Identity and Sport

Carole A. Oglesby
Temple University

It is all that distinguishes males from females; patterns of skills, occupations, dress, adornments, gestures, demeanor, emotional expression, erotic fantasies, and sexual behavior. (Money, 1965, p. 35)

GENDER AND SPORT

If you have observed one or one hundred occurrences of an individual being introduced to a new baby, you know what the first words spoken by the adult will be: "Is it a boy or a girl?" Knowing what to say next, what questions to ask, and what adjectives to use and avoid are all dependent upon the crucial organizing center of the situation; the gender of the baby. Those of us who remember the sixties know the anger that was generated toward boys with long hair and beads and girls in blue jeans, T-shirts, and baseball caps. "You can't tell if it is a boy or a girl" was a phrase scornfully directed toward an individual who could not be clearly identified by gender and the accompanying social role.

Psychologists and sociologists have described how each of us learns an "identity," which is composed of all the things that differentiate males from females in our culture. This identity is called a gender identity and is the "it" referred to in the quotation preceding this introduction. We must not underestimate the power of influence of gender identity. As Money describes above, gender identity influences what skills we possess, what jobs we take, what we wear, how we stand, sit, hug, and point, and how we express our emotions. It also influences, in a dramatic way, whether or not we involve ourselves in sport, the degree of intensity we exhibit, what sport or activity we identify as our own, who we choose as heroes and models, and many more considerations. To understand the patterns of involvement that human beings exhibit in sport, we must understand the interactive relations between gender identity and sport. Before we can understand, we need to clarify some deep confusion about what gender identity is and what it is not.

Gender Identity

Gender identity is sometimes inaccurately confused with biological sex. Biological sex is defined by chromosomes, gonads, internal and external genitalia, hormones, and secondary sexual characteristics (Person, 1980). Money (1965) has reported that one's gender identity can be the opposite of one's genetic sex, hormonal sex, gonadal sex, and morphology. Other concepts, distinct from but related to gender identity, are sexual behavior, reproduction, and sexual preference. Human sexual behavior has traditionally been conceptualized as intimacy shared by cross-sex peers. There is now some recognition of variations from this traditional theme and the construct of personal sexual preference has been explored. (Bell, Weinberg, & Hammersmith, 1981; Rich, 1980). Gender identity is related to, but not synonymous with, sexual preference. If these elements are not gender identity, what is an acceptable definition?

For our purposes, gender identity will refer to the following: (a) core gender identity (i.e., I am fe(male); (b) gender role identity (i.e., I am feminine/masculine); and (c) gender role behavior, the enactment of sex role expectancies (Person, 1980).

Gender identity and its achievement have been found important in facilitating psychological adjustment (Money & Erhardt, 1972; Orlofsky, 1977). Why hasn't this phenomenon drawn the systematic attention of physical education and sport psychology research? The author's contention is that, inadvertently, we have relegated these issues to the sphere of biogenetic influences. If these issues are considered at all in our research, their processes are simply controlled for, without elaboration, by the existence of separate male and female samples.

A clearer understanding of gender identity (both its traditional and contemporary forms) seems important for the contemporary student of physical education and sport psychology. This chapter will try to chart a course through this complex, confused, and emotionally charged area of inquiry. Part 1 deals with sport and the assumption of traditional gender identity; Part 2 identifies problems with traditional gender identity and sports; Part 3 identifies benefits of a contemporary trend toward the assumption of nontraditional gender identity; and Part 4 offers conclusions and recommendations for future physical educators, sport educators, and sport psychologists.

SPORT AND THE ASSUMPTION
OF TRADITIONAL GENDER IDENTITY

What are the origins of the notion that gender identity stems directly from one's sex? There are many, but we can find confirmations in any number of our own professional publications. The *Physical Fitness Research Digest* (1979), proposes the following: "It is vital to determine whether the environment is actually creating differences between the sexes that do not biologically exist or whether it is obscuring the function of existing biological sex differences by social pressures toward equalitarianism" (p. 1). The power of environmental influences on observed sex differences has been recognized for years. Further, viewing women's recent gains in performance as the obscuring of "beneficial" biological sex differences seems questionable at best. Another article in the same publication assures that

> Strength, speed and power advantages to males emerge with adolescence and the maturation of the endocrine system . . . the degree of physical differences observed in males and females may be explained by the ratio of androgens to estrogens in both sexes and thus . . . biology is the starting point for any discussion of sex differences. (President's Council on Physical Fitness and Sport, 1979, p. 2)

Exactly and precisely wrong! Biology is not the starting point of a discussion of sex differences or of gender identity. Until an equitable or approximately similar environment is created, there is little if any hope of identifying exactly what biogenetic influences or environmental influences contribute. Wittig (1976) echoes this sentiment, "Minimizing the differences in environmental variation between the sexes provides one way to explore the answer to the question concerning the environmental conditions under which particular genetic codes will be expressed" (p. 73).

Noted researchers and physicians take a stance favoring an interactionist rather than a biogenetic view of the development of gender identity. For example, Ramey (1974) states that behavioral responses are conditioned by adaptive needs and cultural strictures and that it is "the cerebral cortex, not the endocrine system that confers the almost infinite variability of human response" (p. 249). Furthermore, Money and Erhardt (1972) report that postconceptual and postnatal determinants can completely override genetic determinants of gender identity. Their extensive studies indicate that gender identity differentiation takes place primarily after birth and is largely dependent upon stimulation from and interaction with the social environment.

Gender Identity Assumption

From available evidence, the socialization of the child for appropriate gender identity begins very early. Segal (1981) recently found that parents of infants 20-37 weeks old reported perceived sex differences in infant behavior while three studies had indicated that, objectively, infants do not demonstrate sex differences in behavior. In discussing infants at this age, parents placed significantly more emphasis on their sons' masculinity than on the daughters' femininity. Also, Lott (1979) has stated that American parents' sex role ideology is extraordinarily consistent and is a "dominant feature of every major socialization experience the child is likely to have" (p. 93).

The work of Money and Erhardt (1972) summarizes the basic processes by which the child incorporates the child-rearing messages of parents regarding gender identity. They report the child learns gender identity both by identification (introjection, imitation, and modeling of same-sex parent) and complementation (analogous processes with the opposite-sex parent). Further, they create a metaphor comparing gender identity learning with bilingualism. The reader is asked to imagine bilingual children who despise and reject the language they hear at home in favor of the new language. "These children may learn to understand (the old) but never utter a word of it . . . they are ashamed of it and subject it to a heavy veto of inhibition. In the brain it is coded with a negative sign meaning unfit for use" (p. 19). Money and Erhardt propose that for boys in our society, everything female is brain-coded as negative and unfit for use. The reverse is true for girls. The negatively coded system guides what *not* to do and what to expect of the *other* sex.

For example, Rothbaum, Zigler, and Hyson (1981) postulated that parents could influence children's behavior by acting as models, collaborators, and praisers. They found that children 7 to 9 years of age were more responsive to same-sex parents acting as models or collaborators and to opposite-sex parents acting as praisers. Thus, for example, a female's involvement in sport would be enhanced if her mother models sport participation and enters into sport activities with her and her father praises such involvement. For boys, the father would be the model or coparticipant and the mother would most effectively be the praiser.

Traditional Gender Identity Definitions and Sport

The traditional gender identity definitions have been well described by researchers (Bernard, 1968; Duquin, 1978; Oglesby, 1978). Generally, these writers identify a bipolar trait system as exemplified by Ortner (1974): The male core gender identity implies that males are active, aggressive, public, cultural, rule-governed, instrumental, goal-oriented, organized, dominating, competitive, and controlled. The female core gender identity implies that females are passive, submissive, private, natural, idiosyncratic, expressive, chaotic, disorganized, subordinate, cooperative, and uncontrolled. Duquin (1978) cites support for the notion that parents, other adults, teachers, textbooks, and the media all affirm the idea that sport, vigorous physical activity, and risk-taking are appropriate behaviors for males and, in the metaphor of bilingualism, negatively coded for females.

Additional evidence to support these interpretations of traditional gender identity comes from the recent research on sexual preference from the Kinsey Institute (Bell, Weinberg, & Hammersmith, 1981). They found childhood gender nonconformity was a very strong correlate of adult sexual preference. Specifically, among males, few homosexuals (11%) reported having enjoyed "boys'" activities (i.e., boys' games, group competition, fighting) "very much." More homosexuals (46%) reported enjoying "girls'" activities (hopscotch, jacks, play house). Among women, fewer homosexuals enjoyed typical girls' activities (13%) and more reported enjoying the boys' activities of sport, fighting, and competition (71%). These data must be viewed cautiously because the sample was composed of acknowledged homosexuals and similarities between them and the total homosexual population are unknown.

Further, in the discussion of these data, there is no suggestion of a causal relationship among these activities and sexual preference. Nonetheless, the traditional place of games, sport, and competition as sexual signatures of masculinity can be seen as imposing problems for the boy who does not enjoy them and the girl who does. There is a growing body of data which suggests that the vast majority of boys and girls, those who conform to the conventions of traditional gender identity definitions, also experience difficulty due to its indirect demands for demonstrations of female inferiority and the male superiority imperative.

PROBLEMS
WITH TRADITIONAL GENDER IDENTITY

Among the propositions offered thus far is one which holds that the traditional, public perception of sport connotes an activity which is a sexual signature of masculinity. This traditional view of sport and gender identity seems to be in a state of transition. Explanations for such changes must include the demonstrable problems which the traditional view fosters. Bernard (1975) states:

> Sex role socialization in our society has been carried to such an extent as to wreck havoc on all of us. Men and women have been role-specialized out of all reasonable proportions. (p. 237)

The former social conventions, which severely limited female activity in the sphere of sport for the sake of gender identity concerns, probably constitute one of the classic cases of what Bernard calls maladaptive role specialization. Another signal of problems with traditional gender identity is the research of the last 5 years indicating that highly sex-typed individuals (i.e., high masculine males and high feminine females) do not fare so well in psychological testing. Duquin (1978) and Oglesby (1978) cite more than 10 studies revealing high feminine samples with poor adjustment, low social acceptance, and high anxiety while high masculine samples reported high anxiety, neuroticism, and low self-acceptance.

Many other areas of concern about traditional gender identity can be legitimately raised. With specific regard to sport and traditional gender identity, two such problems will be identified; one will form the remainder of this section and the second will be more fully explored in the conclusion section. One problem which might concern us is that because of the isomorphic nature of masculinity and sport as it is construed in our society, the importance of the expressive/feminine aspect of sport is never publicly acknowledged. This problem *might* concern us, but it doesn't. In fact, it is a nonconcern, a nontopic, and it is generally not seen as an issue. Because so little has been written or theorized on this matter, let us deal with it as one of the legacies of the future to be discussed in the last section.

A second problem within the traditional framework of gender identity and sport has been documented. Masculinity and femininity, as traditionally defined and displayed in sport, demand female limitation and/or inferiority and male superiority. The imperative is such that every female victory over male requires an explanation. It is not an "ordinary" event. Given the overlapping distributions of male and female populations on many performance variables, the probability of some females outperforming some males is not zero. One way to conform to the imperative, given this situation, is to separate boys from girls and men from women in competition. This has been our solution for quite awhile now, but it only cured a symptom and left the imperative in place. Is it a wild assertion to maintain that there is a traditional imperative for superiority for males and inferiority/limitation for females in sport? What data can we cite to support such an assertion?

Four studies in physical education support the existence of a masculine/superiority and feminine/inferiority imperative. For example, Rees and Andres (1980) reported that while no significant grip strength differences were found between a sample of 4- to 6-year-old boys and girls, 72% of the subjects perceived that boys would be stronger. Iso-Ahola (1979) asked fourth graders to compete against the same- and opposite-sex opponents on a motor maze in which outcomes were artificially controlled. Boys losing to girls were less likely to attribute opponent ability as the cause for the loss than were the boys who lost to boys. Bird and Williams (1980) conducted a study with 7- to 18-year-old subjects. By age 13 and continuing to 18, the male performances were attributed to effort while for females (by age 16) performance outcomes were attributed to luck. Finally Brawley, Landers, Miller, and Kearnes (1979) reported that male and female subjects both overestimated the endurance capacity of a male accomplice and underestimated the capacity of a female accomplice each performing an ambiguous task in an identical fashion. The authors felt that "an internally held expectancy for male superiority" was expressed (p. 21).

The responses noted above in sport and activity settings have also been found to exist in nonsport settings. Kohlberg (1966) and Larwood and Moely (1979) have documented a tendency among children 7- to 8 years of age to discriminate against the opposite sex. However, there are stronger taboos against femininity for boys and these may cause more resentment on their part. Maccoby and Jacklin (1974) report that during preadolescence more social pressure against inappropriate sex typing is directed at boys. Johnson (1974) suggests that anxieties about assuming masculinity and denying femininity make girls a natural target for an in-group/out-group phenomenon. Gold, Brush, and Sprotzer (1979), in studies of third, fifth, and eighth graders, found that boys made significantly more stereotyping errors about typical traits by disowning undesirable masculine traits and assigning them instead to girls. Lives apart, this is too often the course directed by the masculine/superiority and feminine/inferiority imperative. What other opportunities have emerged for us?

BENEFITS OF NONTRADITIONAL GENDER IDENTITY

One of the most influential and controversial views on gender identity was recently advanced by Bem (1975) when she postulated a new gender identity called androgyny. After some revision, Bem's model provided four possible gender orientations which are presented in Table 27-1.

The high masculine gender orientation reflected a consistent affirmation of only the traditional masculine-instrumental qualities. The high feminine gender orientation reflected a consistent affirmation of only the traditional feminine-expressive qualities. An undifferentiated gender orientation reflected low affirmations of any of the traditional sexuality

TABLE 27-1
Bem's Model of Gender Identity

	Instrumental Endorsement	Expressive Endorsement
Masculine	Hi	Lo
Feminine	Lo	Hi
Undifferentiated	Lo	Lo
Androgynous	Hi	Hi

components. The androgynous gender orientation reflected affirmations of qualities of both the instrumental and expressive.

Since Bem's initial formulation there has been quite a bit of empirical support for the notion of what Duquin (1978) has called "the androgynous advantage." The essence of this advantage is that individuals need not be limited to the expression of half of themselves and that there is a real psychological benefit in expressing one's own "cross-sex" qualities. For example, Jourard (1971) suggested that restricted self-disclosure was an aspect of the traditional male sex role and that lack of self-disclosure is unhealthy. Other research demonstrated that qualities thought to be characteristic of one sex were, in fact, bisexual. Money and Erhardt (1972) for example, state that: "Maternalism should be designated parentalism . . . the stimulus of a small infant or child is a powerful evoker of parental behavior" (p. 257). In addition, Duquin (1978) cited research indicating that cross-sex-typed individuals demonstrate greater intelligence, higher creativity, and more behavioral flexibility.

What can we conclude from this information on gender orientations? What does it mean for sport, sport participants, and the presentation of sport in socialization? We know it is important to develop a strong gender orientation. The poorest psychological scores seem to accompany the undifferentiated orientation. Further, there are strong indications that the integration of cross-sex typing into one's own orientation is beneficial as previously described.

Can we posit that contemporary sport, reflecting primarily its traditional, masculine-instrumental aspect, functions as an effective vehicle to androgyny for females? Indeed, one study by Myers and Lips (1978) found that among entrants in a national Canadian racquetball tourney, 44% of the females were androgynous while 39% were feminine sex-typed. The same study found approximately 60% of the males masculine sex-typed and only 24% androgynous in orientation. Perhaps traditional sport does not function as a vehicle for androgyny for males as it may for females. In order that sport reach its potential to offer a context for the development of humane qualities for all, it must be viewed in a nontraditional or radical way. Paradoxically, we may find the path to this radical view by looking in retrospect to "sport-for-women" which was created by physical educators of the past.

Physical educators who, for health reasons, wanted to delineate a sphere of sporting activity for women created what we shall label sport-for-women. This was sport thoroughly invested with an expressive orientation so that it would be appropriate for women (Duquin, 1978; Holland & Oglesby, 1979). This was a sporting sphere of, for, and by women. It was informed by a stereotyping consciousness in that it was believed that only women coaches, teachers, and administrators could inculcate the value orientation of feminine (now expressive) sport. This was, of course, the counterpart to the traditional public view that *generic sport* contributed to the development of the masculine orientation for males (Fisher, 1972).

One effect of the women's movement is that females have come to value cross-sex qualities, as some of the research cited has indicated. The valuing of cross-sex qualities by men has not proceeded at a similar rate. Bernard (1975) cautions that it will be tragic for society if men and women alike abandon the expressive element of culture. "In the future, the values we view as female values will be more and more needed, and it is therefore a mistake to underprize them now" (p. 5). Certainly in sport we run the risk of losing the expressive dimension altogether. As beneficial as the social changes of the past 10 years have been, the pressures to leave behind sex-segregating and stereotyping consciousness and to achieve equity for females in sport have combined to create an environment in which the inculcation of "feminine/expressive" sport values is rare for females and males. It is not for females alone to salvage, and benefit from, these important qualities. Males and females together must value and preserve the expressive orientation, in sport as in the general culture.

The initial steps to preserve the expressive orientation in sport require a clear recognition of expressiveness. After this is accomplished, we can plan and implement ways to reinforce and promote these qualities. This chapter's primary recommendation is that sport and physical education professionals should describe for themselves the expressive elements of their work, explicitly point these elements out to both proteges and peers, and reinforce their development in others. At least two viewpoints extend the description of the expressive orientation in contemporary sport.

The Integry And Sport

Sport with an expressive orientation may be viewed as an activity apart from generic sport in the same differentiated manner that sport-for-women was conceived. Some of the motivational material supporting "new games" and "cooperative games" seems to suggest these activities as things apart from, and anecdotal to, the excesses of traditional, instrumental sport.

In a somewhat similar line of thinking, a woman sport administrator may be viewed as a person apart from the "ordinary" (male) sport administrator. If athletic departments are merged along major sport/minor sport lines, the female administrator will consistently draw the minor sport/sport club assignment, a stereotyping that is unfortunate and discriminatory. Her orientation is perceived to be different from the instrumental, business sport, "winning is the only thing" orientation. She may be perceived (and perhaps is) actively opposed to that orientation. Why is she retained at all? Perhaps as a leavening agent to see that the instrumental orientation does not go too far? Or, perhaps the female sport administrator is placed in the position of academic advisor/counselor for the athletes because her orientation, again, is perceived to suit her for this role.

Institutions wishing to preserve an expressive orientation in sport may hire expressively oriented women (or men) as coaches or administrators. To assume that all women and only women are expressively oriented is stereotyping and inaccurate. To overvalue the instrumental relative to the expressive is to indirectly practice sexism. To value and search out the expressive leader is what is being recommended. Such measures are only partial and temporary, but they do serve an important purpose. They at least make it possible for children, students, or program participants to experience a reality quite apart from the excessively instrumental, compulsively competitive activity that characterizes sport in its most professionalized form. Jessie Bernard (1975), borrowing a term from economist Kenneth Boulding (1969), calls this other reality "the integry" and describes it as the "woman's world" of the traditional past. Bernard defines integry as:

> Services are performed for love or duty not monetary exchange . . . mercy tempers justice if justice is too painful . . . the weak are protected and allowance made . . . the welfare of the group is felt to be more important than self-interest and the individual more important than principle . . . no one has to achieve or earn or win in order to be cherished and protected . . . one helps others because they are members of *our* family, *our* neighborhood, *our* church, *our* city . . . such a system holds the total structure together and, without it, the total structure would fall apart. (p. 266)

Bernard suggests that while social Darwinism has been the publicly honored principle, it was the solidarity principles of the integry that held the fabric of social life together. If we believe that sport can teach us only to strive to be best, to win, and to dominate, then what or who will teach us within sport how to form a community, how to unconditionally positively regard, and how to sacrifice self-interest for a common goal? The individual sport leader who brings the integry into daily life behavior and decision-making is preserving the expressive orientation as a separate reality apart from, but connected to, sport. It must continually be emphasized that both males and females need the experiences of the integry and males and females alike can and should provide the integry setting.

The Integry In Sport

More radical than proposing the celebration of expressive activities along with "ordinary sport" is the concept of celebrating the expressive *in* sport. Many physical educators, researchers, and the general public persist in perceiving sport as an instrumental-only activity organized around aggressive behavior, compulsive competitiveness, dominance, risk-taking, and so on. In the final few pages we will demonstrate how various qualities labeled as expressive actually have a significant function in sport. The qualities can and should be taught in addition to the teaching of the instrumental qualities that currently dominate sport socialization.

Passivity.   Passivity is critical as a behavioral option for athletes and sport participants at various times in many sports. After injury, the performer must wait the appropriate amount of time to allow complete healing. Runners on certain schedules in preparing for events must not overtrain or run too many miles. Light days must be maintained. Many psychological training programs now are focusing on the development of quieting, "psych down" techniques which may be a form of passivity development. The attentiveness required of team sport participants during timeouts when a coach is speaking is yet another example of the importance of passivity and the absence of gross motor activity in traditional sport.

Submissiveness.   Each participant in the sport setting attends to the rules and conventions of the game, every game, or there is no game. Even at the conclusion of a losing, frustrating sport event, senseless aggression with the intent of injury and obtaining revenge is seldom seen and is not condoned. There are many sport researchers who believe that aggression is overly encouraged in traditional sport. Nonetheless, one still observes the great numbers of performers at the conclusion of the event submitting to the destiny of the scoreboard. Without some submissiveness to the reality of an event it is difficult to advance; we must live in the present, not the past.

Subordination.   In a similar vein, traditional sport reinforces— indeed demands—a great deal of subordination on the part of a performer. The athlete must often accept corrective feedback. He or she may be asked or required by coaches to abandon old habits and strategies in favor of new ones which may or may not seem suited to the athletes' own style of play. Performers are also expected or required to accept the role assigned to them on the team or within the team's strategy, even when this assigned role impacts negatively on their individual performance or self-perceived role.

Dependency.   In many situations, the performer must be capable of ceding personal control to a teammate or coach. The squeeze play and hit and run strategies in softball and baseball require dependency on the batter by the base runner and vice versa. Since these strategies are often employed in critical game situations, they require a significant element of trust as well as dependence.

Naturalness.   This quality is distinct from the culturally formed, ritualistic aspects of sport performance. Naturalness is an important quality for the sport performer in that it forms the basis of inventions of new techniques, equipment, and strategies. The uniqueness of the individual (e.g., the slightly shorter-than-average basketball center who uses speed to offset lack of height) is valued along with those qualities which are typical for performers in that sport or position. Naturalness also emphasizes the personal importance of one's involvement apart from concerns of nationalism, school, or organization loyalties and the like.

Improvisation.   The inverse of this quality is to be ordered or rule-bound. In sport, this would be playing only "pattern ball" or "by the book." The extremes of orderliness and improvisation are both destructive. Improvising or acting out of pattern is the basis for the brilliant strategic tactic that no one expects. It is the scrambling quarterback who freelances a play when all the patterns are run and the blocking has broken down. A game plan cannot be based on improvisation, but if the quality is not a behavioral option, the offensive effort will be predictable, sterile, and very defensible.

These qualities are often attached to the traditional feminine (now expressive) orientation in our society. We have not recognized their role or realistically encouraged their exhibition in traditional sport. In a similar vein, it may be postulated that feminine/expressive psychological qualities have an unrecognized existence and a potential beneficial role to play in the personalities of males in addition to their acknowledged importance for females. Let us leave behind the stereotypical formulations of gender identity and leave behind the stereotypical formulations of sport as an instrumental-only, and compulsively competitive, activity. It appears that these limiting stereotypes may be diminishing, if ever so slowly, in the area of sport. We can hope that our world of sport may thus provide a very positive cultural product:

> The failure of old sexual paradigms forces the search for the creation of new ones . . . but we shall need time . . . for experiment and play in which alternatives could be tried out in a spirit of light-hearted joy. (Janeway, 1980, pp. 18-19)

Sport is an important social event that can facilitate the expression of diverse *human qualities*. Shouldn't we allow these expressions their natural opportunities?

Chapter 28

Sport, Gender, and Moral Growth

Brenda Jo Bredemeier
University of California-Berkeley

Research on gender-related differences is plagued by an ironic dilemma: to study the differences is, to a certain extent, to reinforce those differences. Both the conceptualization and the study of gender-related differences are potentially destructive (Gerber, 1973; M.A. Hall, 1980) when dichotomous socialization patterns exposed through scientific inquiry affect others' views of reality. Researchers exploring gender-related differences may deplore the very differences they are highlighting as norms for human interaction, and thus perpetuate stereotypic gender role socialization. While this is an ever present danger, the author believes the risk is necessary if we are to gain insight, and eventually some control, over the patterns into which we have been cast. The intention of this chapter is to discuss gender-related differences in moral development as viewed within a sport context.

In early childhood we may have run barefoot on a damp soft cushion of grass, or enjoyed chasing balls and bubbles and butterflies. Through movement we explored and experienced ourselves and our surroundings. Among other things, we learned about ourselves as sexual beings and as moral agents. As we grew older some of our play patterns evolved into complex and socially organized activities. We learned of cultural images and values both for our gender role and as persons in

The author wishes to acknowledge the significant contributions of David Shields to the development of this chapter.

moral exchange with others. But as adults it is time to reflect on our diverse sport experiences and ask some probing questions. Differential socialization has resulted in females and males experiencing different sports, and the same sports, differently. Central to this chapter is the question of the nature and role of sport in facilitating or inhibiting the moral development of participants. Before examining this question, however, we can gain a clearer perspective of the nature of moral growth for girls and boys by briefly introducing three psychological approaches to moral development.

THE PSYCHOLOGICAL STUDY
OF MORAL GROWTH

The Psychoanalytic Approach

The earliest comprehensive understanding of moral development evolved out of Freud's psychoanalytic theory. Superego, the psychoanalytic term for morality, functions to control primitive and hedonistic impulses in keeping with internalized parental and societal values. The superego operates as a more or less rigid censor of pleasure-seeking instincts (the id) and personal thoughts and decisions (the ego).

The critical event in moral development according to Freud (1949) is the child's resolution of the Oedipal complex. As the child resolves the Oedipal complex, she or he identifies with the same-sex parent. Through this identification, the parent's superego prohibitions and ideals are internalized as the child's own, promoting conformity to familial and societal role expectations.

Psychoanalysts have theorized that there are biologically based sex differences in the superego. Males, responding to castration anxiety during their Oedipal period, are said to develop a stronger identification with their fathers than girls do with their mothers. The result is a stronger male superego. In 1925 Freud (1961) postulated that character traits which critics of every epoch have raised against women—that they show less sense of justice than men do and that their judgment is more often influenced by feelings of affection or hostility—would be amply accounted for by their less intense parental identification process.

The Social Learning Approach

More recently, social learning theorists have offered an alternative view of the development of moral behavior. Like psychoanalytic theorists, proponents of social learning theory view morality as equivalent to social norms and expectations. Moral development is seen as the process by which the child comes to adopt social regulations. The theories diverge, however, in their view of how the internalization occurs. While psycho-analytic theory highlights internal dynamic processes tied to id, ego, and superego, social learning theorists point to the role of socializing agents and situations. Such external mechanisms as operant conditioning (Aronfreed, 1968), reinforcement (Mischel & Moore, 1966), and modeling (Bandura, 1969) are seen as determinative.

A number of social learning theorists have contended that female morality is less developed than male morality. Aronfreed (1968), for example, attributed males' superior morality to (a) the higher status of the male sex role in patriarchal societies, and (b) the socialized orientation of females toward external influences and of males toward internalized self-control. Other social learning theorists have taken the opposite position, suggesting that females have stronger moral values because they are encouraged to maintain identification with their mothers while boys must shift their identification from mother to father (Sears, Maccoby, & Levin, 1957).

The Cognitive-Developmental Approach

The most recent approach to the understanding of moral development is the rejuvenation of Piaget's (1932) cognitive-developmental perspective. In contrast to the first two approaches, cognitive developmentalists do not see society as defining and dictating the moral. Rather, the child, through interacting with others, actively constructs moral meaning. Morality is equivalent to the principles used to make judgments about actions that have an impact on human welfare.

Jean Piaget (1932) was the first to study moral development from a cognitive-developmental perspective. By observing children as they played marbles and talking with them about their understanding of the rules, Piaget came to identify two broad stages in children's moral development: a heteronomous stage and an autonomous stage. At the heteronomous stage, children are constrained by adult authority and express rigid beliefs that game rules cannot be changed and must be followed. At the autonomous stage, an orientation toward cooperation with peers supersedes conformity to adult constraints, and rules are viewed as flexible means for cooperative interaction in play.

The cognitive-developmental approach makes an important distinction between the *structure* of moral reasoning and the *content* of moral thought. To illustrate, let us imagine an investigator asking an athlete whether or not she values honesty and, if so, why. The answer would reflect the specific contents of her belief system about honesty. Suppose, however, that the investigator tells a sport story in which honesty conflicts with another value, success. The interviewer then asks the athlete to choose between the competing values and explain her reasoning. With additional probing, the interviewer will uncover a patterned way of ordering and coordinating moral values. Cognitive-developmentalists have found a striking regularity in the underlying structures of moral reasoning which evolve as an individual develops.

The underlying structure that gives order to the content of moral thought is often called a stage. While particular contents of moral thought may vary considerably from one context to another, the stage of reasoning is relatively stable. Cognitive-developmentalists have posited that moral reasoning evolves through an invariant sequence of stages. Thus, learning increases both *quantitatively* and *qualitatively* through transformations in the way that material is internally organized. Each higher stage represents a more complex and adequate organization of information.

In the late 1950s Lawrence Kohlberg reexamined Piaget's work, developing an interview program of hypothetical moral dilemmas which he originally administered to 75 white adolescent males. Through this and subsequent studies, Kohlberg (1969, 1971) has posited that moral development follows an invariant six-stage sequence. The six stages are organized into three levels: the preconventional, conventional, and post-conventional levels. The levels reflect egocentric, societal, and universal or principled perspectives, as described in the following discussion.

KOHLBERG'S MORAL STAGES
AND SPORT ILLUSTRATIONS[1]

Level I—Preconventional

Stage 1: Heteronomous Morality.   In this stage right behavior means to avoid breaking rules backed by punishment, to obey for its own sake, and to avoid physical damage to persons and property. To illustrate in sport, when asked whether a pitcher should use an illegal pitch one player reasons, "No, it's wrong; it can get the pitcher expelled from the game."

Stage 2: Individualism, Instrumental Purpose, and Exchange.   In this stage right behavior means following rules only if they are in someone's immediate interest, and meeting one's own interests and

---

[1]Stage-typing is a difficult and involved process. While these illustrations are typical of the level indicated, no claim is made that the information provided is adequate for definitively stage-typing the material.

needs and letting others do the same. Right is also an equal exchange, a deal, or an agreement. A sport illustration would be two runners making a deal to each false-start twice in an attempt to tire out a third competitor.

Level II—Conventional

Stage 3: Mutual Interpersonal Expectations, Relationships, and Conformity. Right behavior in this stage is living up to the expectations of significant others in one's role as a son, sister, friend, and so forth. "Being good" is important and means having good motives and showing concern about others. It also means keeping mutual relationships such as trust, loyalty, respect, and gratitude. As a sport illustration, the coach of a football team that is far ahead in the third quarter of a game would remove his best players since that is appropriate sportspersonlike behavior.

Stage 4: Social System and Conscience. This means fulfilling the actual duties to which one has agreed. Laws are to be upheld except in extreme cases when they conflict with other fixed social duties. Right is also contributing to society, the group, or the institution. This is illustrated in sport by a boxer who refuses to throw any kidney punches, even though he is sure he could get away with it, because one ought to fight by the rules.

Level III—Post-Conventional, or Principled

Stage 5: Social Contract or Utility and Individual Rights. Here, right behavior means being aware that people hold a variety of values and opinions, and that most values and rules are relative to one's group. However, these relative rules should usually be upheld in the interest of impartiality and because they are the social contract. Some nonrelative values and rights such as *life* and *liberty*, however, must be upheld in any society regardless of majority opinion. To illustrate: When certain "legal" drugs are being used to improve athletic performance, a group of athletes attempt to change the rules so that the use of those drugs will be forbidden. The athletes reason that drug use violates the spirit of the game and is not in keeping with their rights as individuals.

Stage 6: Universal Ethical Principles. At this stage, right behavior means following self-chosen ethical principles. Particular laws or social agreements are usually valid because they rest on such principles. When laws violate these principles, one observes the principle. Principles are universal principles of justice—the equality of human rights and respect for the dignity of the individual. To illustrate in sport: In a very close gymnastics meet the leading gymnast on the losing team decides to attempt a routine he has been working on but has not yet done without safety apparatus. But the judge refuses to allow the performance, reasoning that all persons have an unforfeitable right to life and safety, and that forfeiting basic human rights cannot be justified by an appeal to lesser goods associated with athletic victory.

Moral growth, for Kohlberg, is a result of "cognitive disequilibrium." When moral conflict arises, we attempt to resolve it by using our present stage of reasoning. As we gain an ability to imaginatively take the role of others, the inadequacy of our own reasoning becomes apparent and we slowly formulate new principles to guide moral reasoning at the next level. According to Kohlberg, justice is the key to morality, and each subsequent stage of Kohlberg's model represents a more adequate understanding of the way justice can resolve moral conflicts.

Gender differences have been found by researchers using Kohlberg's model of moral development. While adult males tend to score predominantly at Stage 4, a disproportionately high number of women score at Stage 3 (Holstein, 1976). Kohlberg has attributed this female lag to inadequate societal roletaking opportunities, explaining that because women have traditionally participated less in the world of societal institutions they have not encountered stimuli that would elicit the social maintenance orientation characteristic of Stage 4.

In interpreting these findings, however, it should be noted that the characteristic value preferences of Stage 3 parallel the gender role attributes inherent in female socialization. It is ironic that when women adopt the values socially prescribed as "feminine," they are condemned as less morally mature than men! Many have argued that Kohlberg's stage definitions reflect a gender-bias in that "traditional female values," such as compassion, sympathy, and love, are given subordinate rank to such "male values" as logical consistency and detachment (Gilligan, 1977; Haan, Smith, & Block, 1968; Holstein, 1976).

Carol Gilligan (1982a) has also challenged Kohlberg's assertion that the abstract and deductive principle of justice is the sole determinant of principled moral reasoning. Based on her study of women facing an abortion decision, Gilligan has argued that while morality for men may be defined as reasoning in accordance with the principle of justice, women tend to judge themselves according to a standard of responsibility and care. Thus, situations that demand coordination between autonomy and interdependence, between the need to care for self and for others, stimulate moral growth. At a principled level, Gilligan contends, women's moral reasoning is guided by the principle of nonviolence, a principle as flexible and differentiated as Kohlberg's justice principle.

Thus women's moral weakness, depicted by low Kohlbergian stage scores, becomes inseparable from women's moral strength, characterized by an overriding concern with relationships and responsibilities. A brief explanation of the levels and transitions in Gilligan's model, and sport illustrations of these levels, follow.

GILLIGAN'S MORAL LEVELS
AND SPORT ILLUSTRATIONS

Level I—Self-Orientation

At the first level, the individual's moral concern centers primarily on his/her needs and desires. Survival and self-protection are dominant themes. For instance, a basketball coach may tell a recruiter from a competing institution that she is not interested in a particular recruit, when in reality she has been recruiting her heavily. The coach feels justified in the deception because her job security depends upon coaching success.

Transition: From Selfishness to Responsibility. During the transition to the second level, selfishness versus responsibility becomes a focal problem. The issue is one of attachment or connection to others. The person's understanding of self-interest broadens in a way that allows for an integration of responsibility and care. In a one-sided basketball game, for example, the high-scoring center begins to pass frequently to her less-experienced forward to give her an opportunity to gain experience and recognition. She does this because she feels she has been selfish in shooting so frequently.

Level II—Goodness as Self-Sacrifice

Whereas at the first level morality is seen as a matter of sanction imposed by a society of which one is more subject than citizen, at the second level moral judgment comes to rely on shared norms and expectations. Here the conventional feminine voice emerges with great clarity, defining the self and proclaiming one's worth on the basis of the ability to care for and protect others. The strength in this position lies in its capacity for caring; its limitation is the restriction it imposes on direct expression. To illustrate, in a close softball game an injured player risks further injury by returning to the game when the coach asks her to go to bat. The player doesn't want to let down her team or the coach.

Transition: From Goodness to Truth. The second transition begins with the reconsideration of the relationship between self and others as the woman begins to scrutinize the logic of self-sacrifice in the service of a morality of care. The issue of selfishness reappears. The person wonders whether responsibility should include care of the self. To make the transition to the post-conventional level, the individual must carefully distinguish between personal needs and views from those of others. The criterion for judgment thus shifts—from goodness to truth—as the morality of action comes to be assessed not on the basis of its appearance in the eyes of others, but in terms of the realities of its intention and consequence. For example, a scholarship athlete decides to stop participating in extra practices for gymnastics competition even though it has been paying off in improved performance. She has decided that her participation in gymnastics has largely been to win approval from others, and she would prefer to use the time to improve her grades.

Level III—The Morality of Nonviolence

By elevating nonviolence—the injunction against hurting—to a principle governing all moral judgment and action, one is able to assert a moral equality between self and others. Care then becomes a universal obligation and the basis for a positive assertion of responsibility. To illustrate: A swimmer in a water polo match refuses orders to deliberately aim her goal shot at the goalie's head. She reasons that all people are entitled to a life free from deliberate harm and that she is entitled to play free from the fear of possible retaliation.

SPORT AND MORAL GROWTH

Sport advocates frequently affirm that participation in sport provides opportunity for moral growth, or in common terminology—"sport builds character." Researchers investigating this contention may examine either "sportspersonlike" behaviors occurring within the realm of sport, or they may explore character changes that transcend the sport world.

Sportspersonship

The difficulty in defining sportspersonship becomes evident when one tries to assess it. After constructing an inventory to assess sportspersonship, Haskins (1960) noted it was a quality that defied exact definition! Though many researchers have tried to quantify good sportspersonship (Dawley, Troyer, & Shaw, 1951; Flory, 1958; Haskins, 1960; Kistler, 1957; Lakie, 1964; McAfee, 1955) as well as unsportspersonlike behavior (Crawford, 1957; Johnson, 1969), we do not yet have a common understanding of the construct. As Kroll (1975) has noted, most individuals reading over a sportspersonship questionnaire or inventory would conclude that a number of the keyed answers are "wrong," and even a panel of experts may not be able to agree upon a "correct" answer for each test item.

The ambiguity of sportspersonship is empirically supported by many studies. Kistler (1957) found that approximately one third of the college males surveyed in her investigation did not consider attempts to pressure officials as unsportspersonlike behavior, and that one half of the college women approved of a softball pitcher using an illegal delivery that was difficult for officials to detect.

Kroll (1975) has suggested that sportspersonship is more than just the opposite of unsportspersonship. The athlete who does not argue with the official or does not fail to shake hands with an opponent may be merely innocent of being unsportspersonlike. Kroll posits that sportspersonship differs from those rules of conduct associated with "manners" or "etiquette"; rather, it is better conceived as involving a sacrifice of success strategy in favor of a decision guided by moral criteria.

Sportspersonship research is inevitably caught in a relativistic quagmire. What one person considers to be the essence of good sportspersonship may be tangential or irrelevant to another person. Researchers invariably begin with an arbitrarily selected "bag of virtues" (Jackson, 1968), equate this bag with sportspersonship, and then seek methodologies to measure the extent to which athletes conform to that particular collection of virtues.

Since cultural stereotypes encourage the positing of different virtues for males and females, the issue is complicated further. Cultural stereotypes promote a "male" bag of virtues, including such instrumental and individualistic qualities as independence and competitiveness, in contrast to a "female" bag of virtues, containing such expressive and interpersonal qualities as sociability and cooperation.

The impact of sport on females and males, even if identical, may be evaluated differently if the investigator believes a sportswoman's bag of virtues ought to be different from that of a sportsman. Since most investigators agree that competitive sport nurtures an individualistic rather than an interpersonal orientation (Bryan, 1977), sportswomen may find themselves in a double-bind: stigmatized as "noncompetitive" if they value interpersonal harmony over individual achievement, or criticized for lacking "femininity" if they display the success-oriented "male" bag of virtues.

Character Development

The term character, which originally referred to personality structure (Freud, 1901/1960), has come to represent those culturally valued attributes deemed morally appropriate by society (Peck & Havighurst, 1960).

Intrigued by the possibility that sport and physical education are mediums through which character development can be enhanced, researchers have explored the virtues and values of female and male participants.

The classic work of McCloy (1930, 1957) illustrates efforts to assess (and thus, learn to effectively promote) character development through physical education. McCloy employed a bag of virtues approach in his research, attempting to isolate particular character traits and establish their susceptibility to the influence of physical education programs.

This bag of virtues approach characterizes the majority of studies designed to ascertain the effects of physical education and sport programs on participants' character development, and is also reflected in the work of Blanchard (1946). Operationally defining character primarily in terms of interpersonal qualities such as cooperation, self-control, and sociability, Blanchard found that over a 2-year period a sample population of 8th through 11th graders developed "desirable rather than undesirable traits" through physical activity experiences, and that "girls demonstrated a significant superiority over boys in the acquisition of wholesome character and personality traits" (p. 39). Blanchard's findings were likely confounded by her bag of virtues approach: Her conclusion that females profit more from sport experience than males do may only mean that females were better characterized by those stereotypically feminine values she chose to highlight.

Another major problem associated with the typical bag of virtues study is the determining of a cause-effect relationship: Does the sport experience result in character or personality change, or do more people who possess certain personal attributes participate in sport? In their well-known article, "Sport: If You Want to Build Character, Try Something Else," Ogilvie and Tutko (1971) contend that the qualities of character associated with athletes are probably established before they engage in sport, and that athletes who have developed these qualities to a lesser degree are not selected to continue. Of those who have examined modifications in personality characteristics due to sport involvement, few have incorporated methodologies through which causal relations could be adequately determined.

The problem of determining causality is addressed by those investigators who assess behavior before and after specified sport experiences, a process employed only intermittently and utilized most recently by Kleiber and Roberts (1981). Working within a social learning framework, they examined the impact of sport on the "prosocial" behaviors of cooperation and altruism and found that sport experience had a detrimental impact on the occurrence of prosocial behavior. Furthermore, children who were more experienced in competitive sports were significantly less altruistic than those who were less experienced, and boys were less altruistic than girls.

The investigation of sport-induced changes in participants' value orientations represents another approach to the study of character development through sport. Research grounded in the theory of professionalization demonstrates that, with age and experience, a progressive change in attitudes toward sport occurs. In a "play orientation," characteristic of those who have not yet extensively participated in sport, fairness is valued over skill and skill is more valued than success. In a "professional orientation," the value of fairness becomes increasingly subordinated to competence and winning. Professionalization of values, however, has been found to vary not only with age and sport experience but also with gender. Interestingly, males have consistently scored higher on professionalization than females at all levels of athletic involvement (Loy, 1975; Maloney & Petrie, 1974; Mantel & Vander Velden, 1974; Petrie, 1971; Sage, 1980; Webb, 1969).

Unfortunately, ambiguity underlies these value categories. Does the "professional" value hierarchy reflect a relatively high level of moral reasoning in which issues of fairness have been carefully thought through and resolved in a way that allows the elite athlete to concentrate effort on winning? Or does the relatively low emphasis on fairness reflect a moral perspective that has failed to develop because sport discourages careful attention to how one's actions affect the welfare of all concerned parties?

The meaning of the gender differences is also problematic. What are the reasons for the revealed sex differences? Reviews of literature on children's play have demonstrated significant gender-related differences in children's socialization into and through sport (Duquin, 1978, 1980; Lever, 1976; Lewko & Greendorfer, 1978). However, cross-cultural studies have revealed that these differences are by no means universal; they are closely tied to a culture's view of appropriate adult gender roles (Sutton-Smith & Roberts, 1970). In a classic series of cross-cultural studies, Roberts and Sutton-Smith (1962) linked game involvement patterns for girls and boys with cultural orientations in child training and found that most societies emphasize the values of obedience and responsibility for girls and of achievement for boys. The literature clearly shows that gender differences in the values of sport participants are rooted in divergent socialization patterns.

The influence of sport, however, may not only buttress socialization processes, it may buck them as well. The professionalization literature also indicates that the interaction of gender and athletic involvement yields a configuration of value orientations that sometimes runs counter to cultural stereotypes. Bredemeier (1980) investigated the expressive and instrumental value preferences of sport participants both in relation to sport and everyday life. She found that while males at all levels of sport involvement preferred instrumental values for both sport and everyday life, females' preferences varied depending upon level of involvement: Professional female athletes preferred instrumental over expressive values both in sport and everyday life; intercollegiate female competitors expressed a mixed orientation, valuing instrumentality in sport and expressivity in life; female recreational participants affirmed an expressive value orientation in both sport and everyday life.

The movement toward an instrumental value orientation by women participating at higher levels of sport runs counter to general socialization patterns, demonstrating that sport may indeed have a powerful influence on value preferences. Yet the professionalization literature does not adequately address the issue of moral development through sport because (a) there is no direct way to infer development in moral maturity from the available information about changes in value preferences, and (b) the cause-effect debate remains unresolved.

SPORT AS A FACILITATOR OF MORAL GROWTH FOR FEMALES AND MALES

Though it is evident that the literature is plagued with both theoretical and empirical weaknesses, the meaningfulness and the validity of the contention that sport promotes moral growth is being questioned. In 1982 the American Academy of Physical Educators identified moral development as one of the three most critical social issues facing contemporary physical educators, and published a position statement (Park, 1983) calling for a theoretical and practical response.

Bredemeier and Shields (1983) have initiated a research program which is grounded in Haan's (1978) structural developmental model of interactional morality and is designed to explore the relations between sport involvement and moral development for females and males. Current research by Bredemeier and Shields (1983) and Bredemeier (1983) has revealed that reasoning about moral issues in sport is significantly higher for nonathletes than for athletes, and for female athletes than for male athletes. Also, reasoning about moral issues in everyday life is significantly higher for athletes than is reasoning about moral issues in sport. In response to the Academy's call for a practical response, Haan's model has been implemented to provide concrete intervention strategies designed to enhance moral growth through physical education and sport.

Most questions about the moral adequacy of contemporary sport have arisen out of concerns about the dissonance between the reality of a harsh competitive sport ethic and the vision of sport as an opportunity for females and males to expand human and humane potentialities. To the extent that competition is allowed to dominate interpersonal relationships in sport, sport's potential for facilitating moral development is diminished. Kleiber and Roberts (1981) have advocated a restructuring of the sport experience that may mitigate negative competitive effects. The objectives in their proposed revision are to foster interdependence, encourage cooperation, and emphasize responsibility for the sport process among competitors.

These aims are congruent with the perspective of Oglesby (Holland & Oglesby, 1979; Oglesby, 1978) who views sport as an inherently ambiguous contest in which the noble or the base in human personality and spirit may be displayed, and in which expressivity and instrumentality may be experienced. Oglesby (Holland & Oglesby, 1979) contends that the instrumental model of competitive sport that men have developed is inadequate, and she asserts that "a claiming and valuing of the expressive is absolutely necessary if sport is to be salvaged as a developmental cultural product" (p. 86).

Felshin (1974) contended that it was women who would liberate sport participants from the bonds of the "Lombardian Ethic." She predicted that the dialectic of women and sport would yield new configurations of personal and social understandings of sport. However, the synthesis of the expressivity arising out of feminine experience and the instrumentality of a social institution historically dominated by males has not occurred as Felshin envisioned.

Women have not effected significant change in the structure and practices of sport because they have not been jointly involved with men in constructing sport experiences. The integration of women's and men's sport realms has been prompted by such discordant occurrences as the passage of Title IX and the incorporation of women's intercollegiate athletics by the NCAA. Integration, however, seldom means mutual exchange; more often the values and perspectives of the minority are modified or lost as they become absorbed by the majority.

Although for many the hope has been that women would transform the value orientation of contemporary sport, it may be that sport will have a particularly detrimental impact on the moral development of its female participants. If Gilligan is accurate, female moral development is promoted through such processes as personalizing the "other," creating bonds of intimacy, developing an ethic of responsibility and care, and searching for means to avoid harm. Yet, traditional male sport has discouraged these processes. Male morality, if Kohlberg's theory can be used to portray it, is more detached, formal, and rule-oriented; thus one is led to hypothesize that sport experiences may not be so disadvantageous for male participants. These gender differences, however, may be more apparent than real. Haan (1977, 1978) would maintain that Kohlberg's stages, particularly the higher stages, may actually reflect a tendency to distort moral information by inappropriately over-intellectualizing. Gilligan (1982b) has found that males reaching midlife begin to discover the value of intimacy, relationships, and care.

Rather than reflect the true nature of male moral development, Kohlberg's stages may reflect a tendency of educated adolescent white males to personally disassociate themselves from the intricacies of interpersonal moral conflict through appeal to abstract moral principles. Competitive sport, then, may encourage in males the tendency to personally detach oneself from moral conflict and to reason only abstractly about moral rights and duties. Thus, contemporary sport in its current structure may be detrimental to the moral development of both women and men.

How can sport experiences come to facilitate moral growth? Gilligan and Haan agree that moral development evolves from engaging in situations in which real moral decisions and choices must be made. Careful attention to the needs and interests of all parties must be weighed and coordinated. Concern for the well-being of all must be integrated with a thorough knowledge of the other gained through dialogue and bonds of intimacy. Experiences must be created in which moral judgment is tied to moral action, with participants viewing themselves as moral agents, aware of alternative choices of action and cognizant of the probable consequences of those choices (McIntosh, 1979; Park, 1980). The manifestation of moral development through sport is contingent upon the provision of opportunities for these experiences.

In conclusion, it is important to remember that sport is devoid of inherent social meaning. As a social institution and as a personal activity, sport transmits a variety of values and meanings to women and men. If sport is to provide moral education it must be restructured on both a societal and a personal level. This reconstruction may be best guided by a true integration of the principles of justice and nonviolence, so that together females and males may recreate sport experiences in which moral reasoning and action is oriented toward fairness and care for self and others in the pursuit of excellence.

PART VIII

EXERCISE AND PSYCHOLOGICAL WELL-BEING

Most of the text thus far has generally emphasized how psychological factors such as personality, anxiety, and motivation can affect an individual's intensity, persistence, and performance in sport. However, the previous section on socialization demonstrated that participation in competitive sport can also affect an individual's self-esteem, moral development, and attitudes. On a larger scale, some recent innovative research has suggested that participation in regular physical exercise can have a positive effect on psychological well-being and mental health. The following example demonstrates this phenomenon.

You begin work at about 8 a.m., meet deadlines and fight hassles all day, and then maneuver through heavy traffic to get home. You immediately change into your running outfit and go out for your 5-mile run. As you get into your run, you can feel the stress of the day dissipating from your body and you start to feel more relaxed and at ease. You finish your run a little winded yet refreshed, energized, and ready for the evening's activities.

A regular pattern of physical activity is rapidly gaining popularity as North Americans become more aware of both the physiological and psychological benefits of regular physical activity. The physiological benefits of aerobic exercise (i.e., running, cycling, swimming) have long been known. They include increased blood flow to the heart, lowered resting heart rate, increased capacity of the lungs to deliver large quantities of oxygenated blood to all parts of the body, lowered blood pressure, and lowered blood lactate levels.

It is certainly not a new idea that the mind and body function in unison, but only recently have researchers and practitioners systematically begun to study the potential *psychological* benefits of exercise. As John F. Kennedy once stated, "The Greeks knew that intelligence and skill can only function at the peak of their capacity when the body is healthy and strong — that hearty spirits and tough minds usually inhabit sound bodies." Similarly, in a classic study, overweight executives were put on a jogging program to lose weight and regain a level of fitness. At the conclusion of the program, however, results indicated that the most important effects of the program were not physiological but psychological, with the executives displaying positive changes in self-esteem and other personality traits.

Motivation and Exercise Adherence

Despite the potential benefits of habitual physical activity from the standpoint of physiological adaptation and psychological wellness, maintaining one's exercise participation is a major problem. Statistics from various adult fitness programs indicate that approximately 50% of the people who begin a health-related exercise program quit within the first 6 months. On the other hand, estimates of the National Running and Fitness Association show that membership increased by 50% between 1980-1981 (from 20 to 30 million). This is a startling paradox; more and more people are getting into exercise but half of them are dropping out after only 6 months. A possible explanation is that the commercial sector has been marketing the concept of exercise very heavily in North America. In addition, many physicians, dieticians, exercise physiologists, and psychologists have been talking and writing about the positive effects of exercise on physical and mental health. Yet although people have been exhorted to exercise, they have not been schooled sufficiently on how to stick with it. In many respects this parallels attempts at quitting smoking, at dieting, and at reducing alcohol or drug dependency. That is, starting a program is much easier than sticking with it. In fact, research has shown that all of the above treatments including exercise have similar adherence rates: There is a rapid and substantial decrease in the percentage of participants during the initial 3 to 6 months, followed by a leveling off to a stable plateau over the next 12 to 15 months. This suggests that common factors may influence adherence or therapeutic compliance in general.

In the first chapter, Rod Dishman thoroughly reviews the relatively recent but burgeoning literature on exercise adherence. Dishman argues that the best way to view adherence behavior is to take an interactionalist point of view, which considers both personal and environmental influences. Along these lines, the situational factors found to be most important for enhancing adherence include injury avoidance, convenience of exercise setting, employment status, attitude and support of spouse, and the number of people in one's exercise group. The most important personal factors include attitudes toward health, extraversion/introversion, self-motivation, degree of commitment, and physiological fitness. Although these are reviewed independently, Dishman states that it is the interaction of a person's biological and psychological makeup and his/her particular situation that allow for the best prediction of adherence behavior. He then offers several strategies for changing behavior to maximize one's motivation for staying with an exercise program.

Psychological Well-Being and Exercise

If an individual is motivated enough to stay in an exercise program and exercise regularly, then he or she may benefit psychologically in a number of ways. This is particularly true if the activities are aerobic and can be sustained for at least 30 minutes. For example, many runners have reported experiencing a kind of altered state of consciousness during their run which has been popularized as the "runner's high"—a euphoric sensation in which the runner feels a heightened sense of well-being, enhanced appreciation of nature, and a loss of self-consciousness. Runners describe these sensations as elation, gracefulness, exhilaration, rapture, and spirituality. Since these are such positive feelings, individuals seek out this kind of activity on a regular basis. So it's not surprising that some active people feel deprived when they can no longer exercise and get their "high"! In fact, what starts out for many people as a positive addiction can potentially turn into a negative addiction. It is both psychologically and physiologically healthy to incorporate a daily regimen of exercise into our lifestyle, but if we become controlled by exercise to the point that we shun work, school, or family responsibilities, exercise can actually be harmful. Furthermore, research has demonstrated that some people experience withdrawal symptoms (similar to withdrawing from drugs or alcohol) after 24 to 36 hours without exercise. This can be particularly distressing if one becomes injured and is unable to exercise for a long time.

In the second chapter, Michael Sachs discusses the components of the runner's high and addresses the issue of positive and negative addiction. Besides the fact that one feels better after exercise, Sachs provides evidence of a relationship between exercise and improvement in such psychological parameters as self-confidence, feelings of control, imaginativeness, and self-sufficiency. The chapter concludes with some guidelines not only for improving adherence to exercise programs, but also for structuring programs to achieve a positive addiction (in Sachs' terms, "healthy habits").

Another focus of research in terms of the psychological effects of exercise has been the effects of aerobic activity on reducing stress and depression. For example, it has been estimated that 10 million Americans suffer from anxiety neurosis and 10 to 30% of patients seen by general practitioners are afflicted with this disorder. It has also been estimated that 30 to 70% of all patients examined by general practitioners and internists have conditions that originated in unrelieved stress. Furthermore, valium, a tranquilizing agent, it taken by approximately 15% of the American population. Such statistics point to the overwhelming need for people to learn to cope with stress or reduce it in their lives. The statistics on depression are equally as alarming: Approximately 15 million Americans are beset each year with symptoms of depression and up to 10% of them will score in the depressed range of standard depression questionnaires at any given time.

Until recently, anxiety disorders and depression have been treated almost exclusively with drugs or therapy. However, as Gary Buffone notes in his chapter, there is new evidence that aerobic exercise can serve as an adjunct or alternative to the treatment of nonpsychotic depression and anxiety disorders. For example, running could provide a natural, practical, inexpensive, and time-efficient adjunct to the traditional therapies. This is an exciting possibility and researchers have been actively investigating this area in recent years. Buffone notes that although there are still some conflicts in the literature, it does appear that aerobic exercise is related to reductions in anxiety and depression. Only time and good empirical research will answer all the questions in this area, of course, but aerobic exercise appears to offer great potential for coping with the increase in stress and anxiety experienced in contemporary society.

Peak Experiences in Sport

Sport or physical activity has another way of affecting the performer psychologically, more specifically through what has come to be known as a peak experience. Although hard to define, peak experiences are usually described as those moments of highest happiness and fulfillment which are accompanied by loss of fears, inhibitions, and insecurities. Peak experiences are relatively rare in sport but they do serve as a reminder of the great intrinsic satisfaction that sport participation can provide. Athletes generally report the experience as temporary, unique, and beyond one's control, but when it does happen it stands apart from the normal happenings and experiences.

In the final chapter, Kenneth Ravizza provides an overview of the phenomenon of peak experience in sport. He relates peak experiences to the concept of "flow" developed by Csikszentmihalyi, since they appear to contain many of the same common elements. These experiences are characterized by a merging of the player's actions and awareness, centering of attention, loss of personal ego, control of personal action and the external environment, and demands for action and clear feedback. After describing and giving examples of the elements of peak experiences, Ravizza discusses the difficulty in studying this state of consciousness and suggests how we may more effectively explore the psychological components that accompany optimal performance. Ravizza's chapter best describes the extremely positive psychological experiences that one can gain through sport. While not all participants will experience the runner's high or the peak experience, it is important to remember that sport and physical activities can be presented and experienced in a manner that has the capacity for considerable enjoyment. Sport is an environment that we create!

Chapter 29

Motivation
and Exercise Adherence

Rod K. Dishman
University of California-Davis

Most of the chapters in this book are devoted exclusively to sport. The focus is on factors that influence an athlete's behavior and chances for success in competition. This reflects society's interest in athletic excellence and the fact that the bulk of study and practice in the field of sport psychology has been predominantly performance-related (Dishman, 1982b). This chapter, and those that follow, Chapters 30 and 31 by Sachs and Buffone, will instead focus on health-related aspects of sport and exercise. Research now supports long-held beliefs about potential health benefits of recreational and medically supervised sport and exercise (Dishman, in press b). The proper type and amount of physical activity can help reduce symptoms of tension, anxiety, and moderate depression; it can also diminish some of the risk for coronary heart disease and low back disorder. These health benefits associated with sport and exercise are as important to understand as are performance benefits. Estimates reveal that each year 30 million American adults suffer from cardiovascular disease, 75 million have some form of low back pain or disability, and 25 million experience some type of mood disturbance. Vigorous physical activity can be a preventive medicine for these health disorders that are so prevalent.

Approximately half of the people who begin a health-related exercise program, however, will quit within the first 6 months (Dishman, 1982a; Martin & Dubbert, 1982; Oldridge, 1982). Ensuring that those who might benefit from physical exertion do in fact exercise has thus become a primary challenge for both physical and health educators and behavioral medicine clinicians (Dishman, in press a). This is especially true concerning the medical treatment of coronary heart disease (Pollock & Schmidt, 1979), obesity (Stunkard, 1980), and psychiatric depression (Greist, Klein, Eischens, Faris, Gurman, & Morgan, 1979).

THE PROBLEM OF EXERCISE ADHERENCE

The problem of staying with an exercise program (i.e., exercise adherence) assumes increasing significance for the professional working in physical education today. In times of economic hardship, physical education has usually been forced to justify its existence as a curriculum in public education. The health and exercise relationship is an excellent argument in its favor, yet the question of exercise adherence actually precedes this argument. In other words, are skills and knowledge being taught that will encourage exercise to become an effective health-promoting component of an adult lifestyle? Unfortunately, there is no research evidence on the effectiveness of public education in promoting exercise. But attempts to educate people in a short period of time about the importance of exercise have yielded disappointing results (Reid & Morgan, 1979). The complexity of exercise behavior is further reinforced by the current exercise patterns found in the United States. The National Running and Fitness Association estimates that participant membership increased 50% between 1980 and 1981 (from 20 million to 30 million). Figures released by the National Center for Health Statistics and by Harris polls indicate that 50-60 million adult Americans are now exercising. However, the same reports reveal that two-thirds of adults do not actually exercise on a regular basis; they do not exercise enough to benefit.

Observations of human habits can shed some light on these paradoxical exercise statistics. The accelerated marketing of exercise in the United States has resulted in a mass persuasion campaign to sell leisure exercise to the public. This has largely been encouraged by the profitable return on an investment that exercise can yield (e.g., the sale of exercise accessories such as shoes, warm-up suits, rackets, balls, etc.). The figures just cited suggest that heavy media advertising has done more than merely influence consumer attitudes about exercise; it has also prompted increased involvement, at least in getting started. But staying with an exercise program once begun is a different behavioral issue. Exercise can perhaps be compared in many respects to attempts at dieting, quitting smoking, reducing alcohol intake, or other "New Year resolutions." That is, people attempt to consciously change what has for them become a habit unconducive to their health or well-being. People start, but they don't finish. Why?

A CONCEPTUAL MODEL
FOR VIEWING EXERCISE ADHERENCE

A conceptual framework is presented in Figure 29-1 to illustrate that exercise determinants can be either psychological, biological, or situational in origin. These groupings are not independent of each other, however. Several examples will illustrate the existence of a complex interaction between them so that the decision to exercise (or not to) is probably a product of abstract conceptual beliefs (thoughts) and concrete sensory perceptions (feelings) that a person brings to or experiences during exer-

Factors influencing the decision
to stay with
an exercise program

| The exerciser | 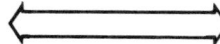 | Situational factors |

Biological

Traits
  Body composition
  Aerobic fitness
Health status (CHD)
  Asymptomatic vs. diseased
  Multiple heart attacks

Psychological

Traits
  Self-motivation
  Other "personality" factors
  (extraversion, attitudes/beliefs,
  coronary-prone behavior)
Sensory states
  Symptomatic pain
  Perceived exertion

Lifestyle-related

Support from "significant
  others"
Vocational status
Recreational activity patterns
Smoking

Exercise setting

Accessibility or convenience
Small group vs. alone
Moderate intensity
  (e.g., < 85% Max HR)

Behavior change strategies

Contracts
Behavioral contingencies
Social reinforcement
Benefit/cost evaluation
Self-monitoring
Stimulus-cueing
*Sensory distraction
Goal setting
  Tailoring to the exerciser
  Daily flexibility
  Perceived choice of activity
  Distal vs. proximal (i.e., long-
  term vs. immediate)

FIGURE 29-1 Behavioral influences in health-related exercise.

cise. These likely interact with situational factors in the exercise setting, some of which may be readily changed. Others are largely environmental characteristics or personal traits that are difficult to alter. Although most behavioral influences will be discussed as if they influence everyone in the same way, it is important to remember that each individual is unique. That is, a certain factor may not influence the average person but may be a very important consideration for a specific individual. Also, what might be a critical influence in the early stages of an exercise program may become less important later on. The reverse is also true: A factor unimportant early in a program can become very significant.

Relevance for Athletic Conditioning?   A problem similar to health-related exercise concerns athletic conditioning in competitive sport. Biological fitness for performance is as important an ingredient for athletic success as are psychological and physical skills, but only a handful of studies on training motivation exist (Donahue, Gillis, & King, 1980). Although the actual motivating agents are likely to be different or unique for a given sport, the conceptual framework used in this chapter to describe health-related training may help account for some aspects of physical training for athletic competition (e.g., the role of self-motivation in endurance sport, Dishman, 1982c; see Chapter 7 by Kirschenbaum & Wittrock).

SITUATIONAL INFLUENCES

It is already known that several characteristics of the setting in which exercise occurs exert reliable influences on a person's ability to stay with a program (Dishman, 1982a). For example, in one study (Pollock, Gettman, Milesis, Bah, Durstine, & Johnson, 1977), 17% of the subjects who dropped out of a 20-week running program did so because of injury resulting from the intense activity. In this case, it is obvious that other potential motivating factors would be subordinated by a physical impairment. However, other setting influences may be so straightforward that the scope of their impact is overlooked. First of all, most exercise clinicians agree that a small group setting is better than exercising alone or in a large group. This suggests that social relationships can develop during an exercise program to reinforce behavior for many people. Having a regular partner can be effective because many people are more likely to keep a commitment to another person than to themselves.

Secondly, several studies conducted in Europe and North America have agreed that the exercise setting should be accessible or convenient to the exerciser. For Finnish business executives (Teraslinna, Partanen, Koskela, Partanen, & Oja, 1969), Canadian heart patients (Andrew,

Oldridge, Parker, Cunningham, Rechnitzer, Jones et al., 1981), and American university professors (Hanson, 1977), who chose either not to become involved or to discontinue their involvement, the exercise location was less convenient than it was for those who decided to become or remain involved. These findings indicate that we may be more influenced than we realize by the geography we create for ourselves or which is due to life decisions initially unrelated to exercise. Where a person lives and works is likely to exert a substantial force on exercise patterns that is seldom consciously acknowledged.

Other studies suggest that a similar influence can originate from aspects of a person's overall lifestyle — factors impinging on a person as a result of his or her daily routine. For example, a consistent finding in exercise rehabilitation programs for Canadians who have suffered a heart attack is that those who work at blue collar jobs and do not pursue recreational physical activity during their leisure time are likely to quit the program (Oldridge, 1979). Smokers are also more inclined to drop out (Massie & Shephard, 1971; Nye & Poulsen, 1974). In addition, one study (Oldridge, Wicks, Hanley, Sutton, & Jones, 1978) has indicated that the incidence of dropout is increased among persons believed to be prone to developing coronary heart disease because their general behavior patterns are characterized by hard-driving intensity, time-urgency, abrupt rapid-paced verbal and behavioral expression of thought, and by a heightened emotional response to stress. These people perhaps lack the patience to wait for fitness changes to occur, or they may set other achievement goals that conflict with exercise.

Viewed in unison, these findings suggest that decisions to exercise may largely be influenced by external factors that surround us, factors that may frequently be the result of previous lifestyle decisions originally not tied to exercise. In many cases the influence may go undetected. It is ironic that many of the lifestyle components that seem to be related to an increased likelihood of quitting exercise are also believed to be factors that exaggerate the risk of developing coronary heart disease. Thus, from the standpoint of health, people who may need to exercise the most appear most likely to quit!

Surprisingly, other aspects of a person's exercise history that would seemingly encourage adherence appear to be unrelated to exercise behavior in organized programs and to one's activity outside a formal exercise setting. For example, the exercise patterns of former high school and college athletes, regardless of sport or the degree of athletic success, do not differ from those of former nonathletes (Dishman, 1981b; Morgan, 1981a). In fact, one study done in the 1950s showed that nonathletes actually became more active than their athletic counterparts when they reached middle age. Although this seems to run counter to what we might expect, it is likely that the influences we experience in our immediate day-to-day living eventually can erode previous exercise habits or feelings we hold about exercise. A consistent finding (Dishman, 1982a) to illustrate this has been that a spouse's attitude toward a participant's involvement is a greater influence on the participant's behavior than is his or her own attitude!

Behavior Change Strategies

It is clear that some of the factors regarded as situational in origin are not easily changed. For example, socioeconomic status and attitudes of a spouse or close friend are probably not quickly altered. Also, attempts to modify lifestyle components such as smoking and the coronary-prone behavior pattern represent complex dilemmas, and the best modification approaches are not well defined. (Leventhal & Cleary, 1980; Suinn, 1982). However, when certain situational factors thought to relate strongly to exercise behavior have been changed, exercise patterns have also changed in a significant way. These interventions often take advantage of existing lifestyle and situational influences (see Dishman, 1982a; Martin & Dubbert, 1982).

Several studies conducted with clinical exercise programs have used *behavioral contracting* and *lotteries* to enhance member participation. For example, a participant might be required to sign an initial agreement publicly committing him/herself to staying with the program for a specified period of time. The amount of exercise required of a person might be determined by a random drawing. Some programs require that money be deposited, which will be returned if the program is successfully completed. Others involve a *behavioral contingency* in which the attainment of a valued goal (e.g., new clothes or preferred recreational activity) is based upon first exercising a prescribed amount. Exercise can also be made dependent upon other established habits that already have a high rate of occurrence (the Premack principle).

Because failure to reach the objectives a person establishes at the beginning of a program has been associated with quitting (Danielson & Wanzel, 1978), various types of *goal-setting techniques* have also been used. In one approach, called *self-monitoring*, participants are required to keep records of their completion of specific aspects of their exercise behavior (Oldridge & Jones, 1983). This might involve objective indicators such as mileage in a running program; resistance, sets, and repetitions in a weight training program; time spent exercising or the monitoring of heart rate during the activity, and so forth. These may be chosen by the exerciser or by the program staff. Although the latter approach has the advantage of providing goals based on professional knowledge which may offer the potential for more efficient fitness gains (if the goals are followed), some research (Martin, 1983) has shown that flexible daily exercise goals selected by the individual promote adherence to exercise more than do fixed or rigid goals provided by an exercise leader. Moreover, a study conducted in a health spa setting showed that attendance was better when participants believed they had chosen the types of exercise to be used when in reality the decision was out of their hands (Thompson & Wankel, 1980). Short-term goals such as, "I will run 15 minutes today" have surprisingly been shown to be less effective than long-term training goals such as, "I will exercise for 6 weeks" (Martin, 1983).

Another approach, *stimulus-cueing*, has been used as an aid to the goal-setting approach (Keefe & Blumenthal, 1980). This involves the identification and use of objects, ideas, or other behaviors associated with exercise to create an environment, or a behavioral ritual that will remind one to exercise (e.g., placing exercise clothes at the foot of the bed each night). Situational cues can make it difficult to ignore an earlier commitment to exercise. An analogous situation develops naturally when a person becomes motivated by the same exercise in the same place at the same time. This seems to occur in a way similar to associational learning or classical conditioning of behavior.

Change the Setting

Another effective approach involves direct *manipulation of the setting* in which exercise occurs in order to capitalize on some of the situational factors that, according to exercise clinicians, correspond with better adherence. One strategy is simply for exercise leaders to increase the amount of one-to-one encouragement and verbal reinforcement to individuals during the actual exercise (Martin, 1983). In these instances, the program staff are active participants in the exercise. This has proven superior to encouragement directed at the entire exercise group at the end of each session. The use of social reinforcement as an aid to exercise behavior has also assumed a very different form. For cardiac patients who do not have to be closely monitored during exercise, simply moving them from the group environment so that they could exercise at home has improved adherence. The effectiveness of this approach can largely be attributed to factors in the home environment such as a supportive spouse and a convenient location.

What is it That Really Works?

A problem with much of the experimental research that has tried to influence exercise by changing its setting or by manipulating the exerciser is that the studies have not been able to prove that any subsequent change in behavior actually resulted from the intervention approach taken. In many cases, simply altering the exercise in any way might be motivating to the exerciser (the Hawthorne effect). Or if individuals believe a technique will be effective, this belief may influence their behavior (participant expectation). Sometimes the relationship with the exercise clinician (therapist effects) will motivate an exerciser regardless of the approaches actually used to implement the program.

It is difficult to design research studies that can conclusively show that specific aspects of a behavior change strategy produced the results. More often, it is likely that a generalized result stems from some other aspect of the setting, from exerciser beliefs, or the way in which the change was introduced. This is an important consideration when evaluating the effectiveness of most of the change studies done in exercise programs. Some studies have indicated that reinforcement from others (fellow exercisers or exercise leaders) may actually be the single most important influence. But whether one approach is better than another has not been determined. As a result, there is probably a great deal of error involved in selecting what to change in order to facilitate exercise and how to go about it. Different people respond to different methods. However, one simple approach shown to directly and consistently enhance exercise behavior has included a rational decision-making procedure in which the person evaluates the costs and benefits he/she anticipates from participating in physical activity (Wankel & Thompson, 1977). How long this effect can last or how often it will work for a person is not known.

CHARACTERISTICS OF THE EXERCISER THAT MAY INTERACT WITH SITUATIONAL INFLUENCES

Conceptual Factors

Attempts to predict exercise behavior by measuring psychological traits (enduring or stable characteristics) have adopted three basic approaches. The first has studied *attitudes* toward exercise. Results indicate that although attitudes can predict a person's initial involvement and the type of exercise selected, the fact that a person views exercise as a positive experience or is attracted to physical activities does not ensure he or she will stay with an exercise program. A second approach has examined the relationship between the *beliefs* that a person holds about the health consequences of exercise and actual adherence to an exercise program. Health beliefs have not predicted whether the typical person will carry out an exercise program (Dishman, 1982a). However, they have been positively related to the amount of exercise completed among participants who remain in a running/jogging program for 5 to 12 months. They have also been related to exercise behavior among people who represent extremes of the general population. That is, exercise behavior differs between individuals who strongly believe there is a relationship between exercise and health and those who strongly discount such a relationship. Belief in the health benefits of exercise can also lead heart attack patients to comply with an exercise prescription (Andrew et al., 1981).

Because a person's attitudes about exercise have not helped predict long-term behavior, a third approach has focused on *personality* variables that are believed to enhance adaptability to some of the behavioral demands that exercise settings typically impose. Two of the most notable are extraversion and self-motivation. As noted earlier, small group exercise settings are generally best at promoting adherence, and several studies have shown that reinforcements such as encouragement or social approval are strong influences on behavior. It is not surprising, therefore, that at least two studies (Blumenthal, Williams, Wallace, Williams, & Needles, 1982; Massie & Shephard, 1971) have found that individuals who are characterized as extraverts are more likely to remain in a program than are introverts. That the adherence of extraverts apparently increases in a group setting is consistent with their tendency to be reinforced by the social atmosphere typical of group exercise. Such a match between the person and the setting makes adherence easier. On the other hand, a home-based or individualized exercise program might be more appropriate for the person with introverted tendencies.

Self-Motivation. Beyond the person's compatibility with the social aspects of an exercise program, it is likely that some people are better able to adapt to exercise demands because they are simply more self-motivated to exercise. They may be better able to reinforce themselves for their own behavior and are perhaps less sensitive to, or less dependent on, situational influence. Self-motivation basically means a person is reinforced more by his/her ideas or goals than by those of others. Temporary feelings or a behavioral setting's immediate external influence do not override a person's own goals in deciding to behave a certain way. Self-motivated people seem better able than others to stick to a behavioral decision or to finish what they start. This explanation for exercise adherence has been confirmed in several different types of settings. People who score high on a paper-and-pencil test of self-motivation (Dishman & Ickes, 1981) have consistently been observed to stay with exercise for a longer period of time than those who score low. (Dishman, 1983; Dishman, Ickes, & Morgan, 1980; Gale, Eckhoff, Mogel, & Rodnik, in press; Martin, 1983; Snyder, Franklin, Foss, & Rubenfire, 1982; Stone, 1983; Wankel & Graham, 1982). This has occurred in programs designed for athletic conditioning, adult fitness, preventive medicine, cardiac patients, commercial spas, corporate fitness, and community-based programs.

Results have usually been similar for men and women (Dishman, 1982a). *Dropouts* do not always score low on self-motivation (Gale et al., in press; Robinson & Carron, 1982; Wankel & Yardley, 1983; Ward & Morgan, in press), but adding biological traits can boost up to 80-90% accuracy the ability of self-motivation to predict who will *adhere* (Dishman, 1982c; Ward & Morgan, in press).

Self-motivation is considered to be a generalized trait which describes behavior patterns that are similar even though aspects of the behavioral setting differ. It does not specifically tap exercise behavior. For most behaviors, tests which ask questions that are specifically phrased according to the behavior being studied are better predictors of subsequent behavior. Concerning exercise adherence, however, specific factors such as attitudes and beliefs about exercise have not predicted with enough accuracy to be of practical use, but the generalized self-motivation variable has. This adds some credence to the proposal that a certain amount of behavioral similarity exists across various health-care settings despite differences in the particular target behavior.

Viewed collectively, these studies imply that self-motivated individuals are better suited to overcome situational barriers in the exercise setting such as an inconvenient time or place, an unsupportive spouse, inappropriate goals, or insufficient social interaction. This is also consistent with results from behavior change studies that have used contract procedures to promote exercise. Adherence rates are substantially higher among both healthy and symptomatic (e.g., coronary heart disease) participants who agree to commit themselves to the program in a behavioral contract (Oldridge & Jones, 1983). Because one of the characteristics of highly self-motivated persons is the ability to commit themselves to the pursuit of a goal (Dishman, 1983; Dishman & Ickes, 1981), the effectiveness of behavioral interventions may depend on one's level of self-motivation (Wankel & Graham, 1982) or other personality factors (e.g., need for structure imposed by others or need for freedom of choice, Tu & Rothstein, 1979).

Most people who drop out of adult exercise programs do so within the first 3 to 6 months. For many of those who remain after this initial period, exercise is more likely to become an enduring habit. This suggests two important considerations. First, people who remain may have psychological and biological skills that neutralize situational barriers to exercise. Both biological and behavioral changes are usually greatest during the first few weeks of a program, and these may simply be too abrupt for the low-motivated individual to endure. Also, after fitness gains plateau, self-motivation may help offset fewer rewards from tangible advances in performance health. Second, if this is so, those who are dropout prone should be identified at the onset of a program so that the situation or program can be modified to support them through what seems to be a critical period of adjustment.

When it is not feasible to administer the entire self-motivation test (40 items), a shorter 7-item version (Falls, Baylor, & Dishman, 1980) has yielded similar results (Snyder, Franklin, Foss, & Rubenfire, 1982; Stone, 1983). In fact, simply asking individuals if they plan to stay with the program may also indicate a rough estimate of who in fact will eventually remain (Oldridge & Jones, 1983). Thus, although self-estimates of previous exercise do not predict eventual adherence (Dishman, 1981b), projected estimates of anticipated exercise behavior may (Riddle, 1980).

Sensory Factors

Another approach based on psychological assessments has focused on states (temporary or transient thoughts and feelings) rather than traits. These have included both disease symptoms that are perceptible and the sensations that normally accompany physical work. Patients in preventive medicine programs who report angina (chest pain which often accompanies heart disease) during exercise stress, for example, are more likely to stay with an exercise program. Because cardiac patients who comply with exercise programs are also more likely to believe exercise will benefit their health, the presence of sensory events such as angina probably serves both to reinforce their knowledge that they have the disease and to motivate them to try to offset their health deficiency.

"Normal" Exercise Sensations. Among healthy exercisers, estimates show 85% report that they feel better as a result of their activity. Although there is no direct evidence that these feeling states promote adherence to exercise (Blumenthal et al., 1982; Ward & Morgan, in press), it is clear that what a person thinks (feels) he or she is doing can be as critical as what is actually done (Morgan, 1981b). This is apparently true for exercise adherence; studies based on the clinical impressions of program staff have shown that exercisers who perceive excessive stress during exercise tend to drop out even when the actual physical stress is equally difficult for all participants (Ingjer & Dahl, 1979). Other indirect support for the role of sensory factors comes from a behavior change study in which adherence was better for subjects who dissociated (i.e., turned their attention away) from exercise sensations than it was for those who associated (i.e., focused on bodily sensations) and mentally instructed themselves on exercise technique during the activity (Martin, 1983). Of course, there is increased risk for injury if sensations of excessive stress are ignored (Morgan, 1981b).

Sensations and Exercise Goals. The above findings have implications for the way exercise goals are set for participants. Needed are standardized physiological guidelines (e.g., American College of Sports

Medicine) which specify that the frequency, duration, relative physiological intensity, and type of exercise should be similar for everyone if similar fitness increases are to be assured. However, these standards are typically modified for the person with a fitness or health handicap in order to avoid excessive stress. What has been largely ignored, however, is that certain people may also have behavioral handicaps due to their psychological characteristics. Therefore, it is simply naive to expect that the same exercise plan can work for everyone when the goal is to facilitate adherence. Thus, just as flexible daily goals, choice of activity, or social support may help psychologically tailor exercise to the person who lacks self-motivation, a modified behavior prescription that considers the perceptual or subjective cost, as well as the objective or actual metabolic strain of exercise, may also enhance adherence. This may be particularly true for the individual less equipped for exercise because of biological traits such as obesity, poor health, or a low working capacity (Gutmann, Squires, Pollock, Foster, & Anholm, 1981).

Biologic Factors

As illustrated for many of the situational influences on exercise, a person's behavior may not reflect only conscious thoughts or feelings. It can be markedly influenced by events that are not psychological in nature. It is likely that both an individual's *willingness* and *ability* to stay with an exercise program are also dependent upon biological factors. These may interact not only with motivational factors or beliefs about the outcomes of exercise, but they may also largely determine how physically demanding the exercise will actually be and how demanding it will feel to the exerciser.

A study done at the University of Wisconsin examined biologic influences on exercise participation in a prevention/rehabilitation program for coronary heart disease (CHD) (Dishman, 1981a). Recorded over a 5-year period was the behavior of more than 360 persons, some diagnosed as healthy, some as having multiple risk factors that might lead to CHD, and some as having confirmed CHD. Results demonstrated a relationship between exercise attendance and the presence of disease. Healthy people tended to drop out during the first month of involvement, whereas those diagnosed as having CHD were likely to remain for at least a year. Knowledge of low cardiovascular fitness was also associated with a longer length of stay, and this is consistent with the idea that belief in the health benefits of exercise is an effective motivator of exercise behavior only when there is evidence of a health deficiency or disability (Andrew et al., 1981; Dishman, 1982a).

However, a point of diminishing returns may occur in diseased patients if no evidence of health benefits is seen after a period of involvement, or if the patients do not perceive the activity as effective in promoting health. These points are reinforced by the tendency for cardiac rehabilitation patients to drop out if they have experienced recurrent heart attacks, and by the increased dropout rates observed when recreational activities are substituted for more vigorous exercise believed by patients to be necessary for promoting health (Oldridge, 1982). The role of biological health is emphasized further by the converse finding among healthy individuals who are neutral in their attitudes and beliefs about exercise. When given a choice, these individuals tend to select low intensity, low frequency exercise (Sidney & Shephard, 1976), and this has been shown to promote adherence (Ballantyne, Clark, Dyker, Gillis, Hawthorne, Henry et al., 1978).

A biologic impact on exercise behavior has also been seen by Scandinavian researchers (Ingjer & Dahl, 1979), who found that among participants in a 16-week running program, those who dropped out by the 9th week had experienced less fitness gains than their counterparts who were still active. This difference could not be attributed to differences in training volume because all began at the same fitness level, and all worked at the same frequency and duration at an intensity that was adjusted according to each person's fitness. However, when measured by a biopsy of muscle tissue from the leg, those who dropped out had, from the beginning, comparatively less of the type of muscle fibers known to facilitate aerobic work. This biologic trait could very likely have influenced both their ability to reach training goals and their perception of effort during the exercise.

SUMMARY

The association between regular exercise and health is perhaps outweighed only by our lack of understanding about the factors that determine whether or not people exercise. This chapter has discussed factors that current research indicates are the most important behavioral influences. Characteristics of the person who attempts an exercise program and situational factors that the person experiences are believed to interact with each other and to be equally important motivational elements.

Situational factors may be aspects of the exercise or its setting, or they may describe various components of a person's lifestyle outside of exercise, that is, other habits which either facilitate or compete with exercise. It appears the average person will have a better chance of staying with an exercise program that is conveniently located and easily accessible. Also, exercise in a small group is generally preferred to a large group or to exercising alone. This seems particularly true for extraverted individuals who are reinforced by social interaction. The importance of social reinforcement is also evidenced by the impact of a spouse's attitude toward exercise and the motivating effect that encouragement by others has in general. High intensity exercise should be avoided to reduce the risk of injury. For low-motivated people especially, the activity should permit the exerciser to stay within a zone of comfort; the adage, "no pain, no gain" does not apply to health-related exercise. Depending on a person's health status, sensory factors may also be important behavioral influences. Beliefs about the health benefits of exercise appear to take precedence only when a person is aware that he or she has a health deficiency. Moreover, if evidence indicates that no benefits are occurring, an unhealthy individual may be more likely to quit exercising.

However, there are important exceptions to these general rules. Some individuals have an inherent behavioral advantage whereas others appear unduly handicapped. Self-motivated individuals, who appear less sensitive to situational influences, are able to reinforce themselves so that inconvenience, lack of social support, the type of exercise, competing lifestyle behaviors, failure to quickly reach a training goal, and other common barriers to exercise have less impact. This psychological tolerance for the behavioral demands of exercise seems to be enhanced if a person is also more fit for its biological demands. Being lean, light of body weight in relation to height, and capable of high levels of aerobic activity seem most critical. On the other hand, the undermotivated, overweight individual who smokes and is not involved in other recreational activity during leisure time is quite likely to stop a program once it is started. Ironically, then, the person who might benefit the most from exercise is the one most inclined to quit. Although it is not clear how readily these characteristics can be altered to facilitate exercise behavior, they may help identify the exerciser who is likely to drop out. This will allow the program staff to design a more individualized program that may facilitate adherence.

The behavior change techniques outlined in this chapter can then serve as guidelines that promote adherence in both group and individual exercise. It should be noted that encouragement or approval from some-one the person values may be a basic component of most strategies originating outside of him/herself. Attempts at behavior change that emanate more from the exerciser than from the program staff emphasize the importance of setting appropriate goals, and this procedure highlights the necessity of planning the exercise setting and its activity to match the participant's willingness and ability to exercise. It may be more effective to fit the program to the exerciser than to fit the exerciser to the program. The person who has always found it difficult to commit him/herself to a behavioral goal will benefit from flexible daily goals in which he/she perceives some freedom of choice in the activity. However, the activity should be such that individualized goals can be approached in a reasonable period of time (e.g., 6 weeks). This requires knowledge of how and at what rate biological adaptations occur with exercise, as well as knowledge of the special demands and changes that accompany exercise for individuals with atypical health or fitness characteristics.

Knowledge of the basic principles from psychology and exercise physiology are simply a must if a person is to predictably increase his or her chances for staying with an exercise program. Moreover, a person without professional training (which ideally would lead to some form of recognized certification such as those endorsed by the American College of Sports Medicine) in both the physiological and psychological basis of exercise adaptations, and who is not trained in fundamental behavior change techniques, does not possess even the minimal skills for prescribing or supervising exercise in a health care setting.

Of course, an ultimate goal for those who advocate exercise adherence is self-regulation of behavior by the person, not continual reliance on an exercise professional. This is important because the Centers for Disease Control now estimate that 50% of the deaths from the 10 leading causes of death in the United States are linked to lifestyle behaviors, one of which is insufficient exercise (Hamburg, 1983). Exercise can be medicine for many people. Perhaps continued study can explain, and reverse, why more than two-thirds of American adults do not exercise enough to benefit. Exercise adherence clearly plays an essential role in behavioral health.

Chapter 30

Psychological Well-Being and Vigorous Physical Activity

Michael L. Sachs
University of Maryland

An important and exciting area in the field of sport psychology is that of psychological well-being and vigorous physical activity. The finding that vigorous physical activity is often associated with feelings of well-being has profound implications for coaches, physical educators, psychologists, and the participants themselves.

Earlier chapters (e.g., Chapter 5 by Silva) have noted the benefits of a multioperational approach to sport psychology research. This approach, advocated for physical education research by Morgan (1973a), highlights the importance of considering both psychological and biological factors in examining behavior. In particular, when focusing on behavior in sport, one finds obvious psychological and physiological relationships because physical activity is indeed a *physical* activity. It is important to keep in mind, therefore, that much of the discussion here and in other chapters in this volume should be considered within an integrated context.

The emphasis in this chapter is on vigorous physical activity—activity at a moderate to intense level (70-80% of maximum heart rate) engaged in long enough to allow for aerobic benefits (usually at least 15-20 minutes). The activities most often considered in examining the relationship of exercise to psychological well-being are those rhythmic, aerobic activities such as running, walking, cycling, swimming, and cross-country skiing. While other activities such as basketball, tennis, and racquetball may have some impact on psychological states, they are considered less optimal than the aerobic activities. The aerobic activities provide continuous, rhythmic movement that more readily permits the individual to experience the physiological and psychological benefits associated with exercise. Furthermore, although the emphasis is on vigorous physical activity in general, much of the research that is discussed deals with running, which is the activity most frequently studied.

Why is exercise potentially beneficial in enhancing psychological well-being? Greist, Klein, Eischens, Faris, Gurman, and Morgan (1978) have identified a number of factors that may help explain why vigorous physical activity (particularly running) is associated with the reduction of depression. These factors include mastery, patience, capacity for change, generalization, distraction, positive habit or "addiction," symptom relief, consciousness alteration, and biochemical changes that accompany aerobic activity. These factors (singly or in combination) most likely account for the enhanced psychological well-being we see resulting from vigorous physical activity.

While it remains for future research to definitively answer the question of why exercise enhances psychological well-being, for now we can suggest that the reason lies in a complex interplay of success experiences achieved through exercise, the distraction or consciousness alteration possibilities inherent in participating in vigorous physical activity, and physiological/biochemical changes that occur as a result of acute and long-term participation (note the multioperational explanation). At the moment it may be less important to know why exercise works than to note that it does work. Researchers and practitioners have demonstrated clearly that exercise can be related to enhanced psychological well-being.

The "Feel Better Phenomenon"

Psychological well-being may incorporate a number of different factors. However, it can also be examined more narrowly, in terms of the well-being a person feels during and after exercise. Morgan (1973b) has noted the "feel better phenomenon," which is a response that participants in vigorous physical activity consistently report after exercise. While this phenomenon is frequently noted in the literature (Brunner, 1969; Burgess, 1976; Harris, 1978; Morgan, Roberts, Brand, & Feinerman, 1970; Morgan, Roberts, & Feinerman, 1971; Roth, 1974), it is not always supported by reductions in test scores, such as scores on Zung's Self-Rating Depression Scale (e.g., Morgan et al., 1970).

While the feel better phenomenon appears to be pervasive in the literature on exercise, and appears to be significant in promoting participation in physical activity, other aspects of exercise psychology are important to consider as well. These include addiction to exercise, the runner's high, personality changes, exercise as therapy, and physiological/biochemical changes that accompany running.

ADDICTION TO EXERCISE

One must first consider the importance of addiction to exercise in promoting psychological well-being. Addiction to exercise is dependence, of a psychological and/or physiological nature, upon a regular regimen of exercise, characterized by withdrawal symptoms after 24-36 hours without exercise (Sachs, 1981). Note that this definition incorporates both psychological and physiological factors. A regular regimen of exercise may encompass any physical activity, although addiction is usually referred to in relation to running. The withdrawal symptoms most commonly noted include anxiety, tension, guilt, irritability, nervousness, muscle twitching, and a bloated feeling (Sachs, 1981; Sachs & Pargman, 1979, 1984). These withdrawal symptoms are seen as critical in determining the existence and degree of addiction to running.

The 24- to 36-hour time period refers to that time when the individual expects to exercise but for some reason (family, work commitments, injury, etc.) finds that he/she cannot. We would not expect withdrawal symptoms on a day when the individual had planned to rest (most sound exercise programs build in one or two days per week of rest), but would expect such symptoms on days when exercise had been planned but participation was not possible.

The concept of a positive addiction to physical activity, and running in particular, was popularized by Glasser (1976) in his book, *Positive Addiction*. During the same time period, Kostrubala (1976) also noted the positively addicting aspects of running in his book, *The Joy of Running*. Running, or exercise, as a positive addiction is seen as increasing the individual's psychological and physical strength. It is an activity that enhances the individual's state of well-being and functioning.

It is appropriate to note here some of the many suggested positive psychological benefits that vigorous physical activity can offer. These include reduced levels of tension and anxiety, and improvements in such psychological factors as self-confidence, feelings of control, imaginativeness, and self-sufficiency (Buffone, 1980; Dienstbier, 1984; Dienstbier, Crabbe, Johnson, Thorland, Jorgensen, Sadar, & LaVelle, 1981; Harris, 1981a, 1981b; Kostrubala, 1976; Morgan, 1981a; Pargman, 1980; Sachs & Buffone, 1984; Sacks & Sachs, 1981; Spino, 1976). Exercise as a positive addiction means that some or all of these psychological benefits may occur as the individual continues to participate in vigorous physical activity. It is particularly important to note that a positive addiction to exercise means that the individual views exercise as an important aspect of his/her existence, yet one that blends well with responsibilities of work, home, family, and friends, and complements these aspects of the person's life.

In positive addiction, the *person controls* his/her involvement in exercise. However, as Morgan (1979b, 1979d) has noted, for some individuals *exercise controls them*. For them exercise has become a negative addiction, controlling their lives and eliminating other choices in life. Their lives must be structured around the need to exercise regularly, and they may even experience additional withdrawal symptoms such as fatigue, listlessness, and decreased ability to concentrate. In addition, they may miss scheduled appointments because of the need to run. These individuals need to learn effective coping strategies and perhaps should seek the help of a therapist to decrease their dependence upon exercise and shift their involvement away from a negative addiction and toward a positive addiction (Sachs & Pargman, 1984).

Strictly speaking, it is best not to use the term addiction when discussing a positive relationship of the individual to exercise. Addiction implies *controlling* an individual's existence to the extent that it can hurt his or her functioning. While this is clearly the case in negative addiction to exercise, this is not the case in positive "addiction." Peele (1981) has suggested using a term such as "healthy habits" to characterize activities, such as exercise, which enhance people's sense of themselves and their feeling of being in control of their health and well-being. Whether one uses the term healthy habits or retains the more common and popular term, addiction, it is clear that exercise in general can enhance the quality of life for individuals. It is interesting to note that exercise behavior has a bipolar dimension, with nonadherence at one extreme (i.e., the individual participates rarely, if at all, in physical activity) and addiction at the other (see Chapter 29 by Dishman for an elaboration on this area).

THE RUNNER'S HIGH

The runner's high is an experience directly related to the psychological well-being that may be derived from vigorous physical activity. It is described by at least 27 different adjectives or phrases in the literature, including terms such as euphoria, strength, speed, power, gracefulness, spirituality, sudden realization of one's potential, glimpse of perfection, moving without effort, and spin out (Sachs, 1980). The runner's high has been defined by Sachs (1980) as a euphoric sensation experienced during running, usually unexpected, in which the runner feels a *heightened sense of well-being*, enhanced appreciation of nature, and transcendence of barriers of time and space.

The terms used above in defining the runner's high will bring to mind the material in Ravizza's chapter on the peak experience. The runner's high concept has its roots in the same soil as does the peak experience since both are considered altered states of consciousness (Ludwig, 1966; Marsh, 1977). Chapter 32 by Ravizza presents many of the factors that could be discussed here, so only those characteristics peculiar to the runner's high will be noted here. As Ravizza indicates, the peak experience may occur with any sport or physical activity. The runner's high, however, is more similar to the type of flow experience that Csikszentmihalyi (1975) discusses, since it requires a more rhythmic, long-lasting activity that is not interrupted by stops and starts and strategy decisions as in sports such as basketball and football. There are reports of similar "flow" or "runner's high" type experiences in swimming, for example, but for the most part running is the activity discussed.

Some studies investigating the runner's high have indicated that only about 9 to 10% of all runners experience the runner's high (Sachs, 1978a; Weinberg, 1980), whereas other studies have suggested that about 78% of all runners experience this phenomenon (Lilliefors, 1978). Sachs' (1980) research on this phenomenon found that 77% of the runners had experienced the runner's high at least a few times. Furthermore, several respondents indicated that they experienced the high during nearly 30% of their regular runs. The considerable difference between findings of 9-10% and 77-78% of runners experiencing the runner's high suggests that there is much more to learn about the characteristics, intensity, and frequency of this phenomenon. Although there are occasional descriptions of the runner's high experience which are analagous to characterizations of peak experiences (Black, 1979; Sime, personal communication, August 1979; female runner, personal communication, October 1980), for most runners the high appears to basically reflect an enhanced sense of well-being and a distinct sense of affect such as increased strength, power, and gracefulness (Sachs, 1980, 1984).

The runner's high may be pictured as a phenomenon that cannot be predicted, that is facilitated by cool, calm weather with low humidity and few distractions, and that requires a relatively long distance (6 or more miles, at least 30 minutes of running) at a comfortable pace (although there must be no concern with pace or time) (Sachs, 1980). However, notable individual differences are expressed by runners, and for each runner a slightly different set of conditions may be necessary to facilitate the experience of the runner's high. For most runners, the runner's high is a very positive state of affairs, a general feeling of well-being that encompasses descriptions of "floating, effortless running" and feelings of relaxation, pleasant sensations, and drifting (Sachs, 1980). A few runners experience the "super high," or the peak experience as described in the Ravizza chapter. The super high has been described as when you're "real-

ly into a flow, all systems are go, you're running fast but feeling effortless, there's no strain, you're almost part of the environment" (Sachs,
1980, p. 121). This super state is rarely reached but is reported to be
unusually euphoric when experienced. Whether experienced as a runner's
high or a super high, this is a very positive and fulfilling aspect of running for those fortunate enough to have experienced it.

PERSONALITY CHANGES

The psychological well-being that comes from vigorous physical activity
is reflected as well in personality changes suggested in the literature. The
concept of personality and sport has been comprehensively discussed in
earlier chapters in Section II. However, a few notes concerning the
special relationship of personality and vigorous physical activity are appropriate here. Basically, findings in this area have suggested that
physical activity may modify state variables such as anxiety and depression (see Chapter 31 by Buffone), but not trait variables such as introver-
sion and extraversion (Morgan, 1973b). There is evidence, however, that
in addition to reducing levels of anxiety and depression, exercise can improve such psychological parameters as self-confidence, feelings of control, imaginativeness, and self-sufficiency (Buffone, 1980; Dienstbier,
1984; Dienstbier et al., 1981; Harris, 1981a, 1981b; Kostrubala, 1976;
Morgan, 1981a; Pargman, 1980; Sachs & Buffone, 1984; Sacks & Sachs,
1981; Spino, 1976). Other changes in personality have been cited in the
exercise psychology literature, but the factors cited above are those most
frequently noted as susceptible to modification through vigorous
exercise.

Dienstbier and his colleagues at the University of Nebraska
(Dienstbier, 1984; Dienstbier et al., 1981) have conducted research that
may prove to have significant implications for our thinking in this area.
In keeping with a multioperational orientation, they note that the
physiological systems involved in aerobic exercise and in the experience
of emotional states are frequently the same. Running may therefore be
expected to have an impact on short-term emotional functioning and
temperament. Dienstbier (1984) goes on to note that:

> Running may stimulate the development of the capacity of the sympathetic nervous
> system and associated glandular responses; in turn, this increased physiological
> capacity may be the major cause for indications of reduced emotional tension in
> both state and trait studies, as well as the major cause of reduced anxiety. (p. 269)

While Morgan (1973b) may be correct in stating that physical activity may not *generally* modify trait variables, a growing body of
literature strongly suggests that *some* trait variables may indeed be

modified by regular, vigorous physical activity (Dienstbier, 1984). Certainly, the evidence is consistent that a number of state variables, anxiety and depression in particular, may be modified by regular vigorous physical activity. Hopefully future research will clarify the question of how physical activity and personality traits may interact.

EXERCISE THERAPY

Having established to the satisfaction of most researchers and practitioners that psychological well-being may be derived from vigorous physical activity, it has been suggested that exercise might be used therapeutically. Exercise therapy, the term currently in use, is the prescription of exercise as a mode of therapy—as the sole psychotherapeutic tool or as an adjunct to other modes of therapy. The exercise most often used in therapy is running. The use of running in therapy has ranged from specific clinical applications, including agoraphobia (Orwin, 1973), a situational phobia (Orwin, 1974), and elevator phobia (Muller & Armstrong, 1975), to general treatment of depression and anxiety and enhancement of psychological characteristics (Berger, 1984a; Buffone, 1980; Folkins & Sime, 1981; Greist, Klein, Eischens, Faris et al., 1978; Morgan, 1981a; Sachs & Buffone, 1984; Sacks & Sachs, 1981).

It is important to note that the current focus on running in therapy does not exclude other forms of exercise. The clinician who uses exercise in therapy will quickly realize that running is not for everyone, and that other physical activities may well have the desired effect in therapy. One component of the use of physical activity that is of particular interest for us is that, for a physical activity to be most effective in therapy, it appears that this activity should be vigorous. Furthermore, it should involve the individual for a period of time without interruption and should require reduced cognitive focus and decision making.

The concept of exercise as therapy has been with us for a long time. The holistic approach dates back to the ancient Greeks with their ideal of *mens sana in corpore sano*—"a healthy mind in a healthy body." Exercise has been demonstrated to be an effective tool in promoting psychological well-being. The following chapter by Buffone examines more completely the use of physical activity as a therapeutic adjunct.

PHYSIOLOGICAL-BIOCHEMICAL CHANGES

In considering the multioperational approach noted earlier, we must realize that the psychological changes discussed here are accompanied by numerous physiological-biochemical changes as a result of exercise. A number of basic physiological benefits of regular, vigorous physical activity include improved cardiovascular fitness, reduced body weight and percent body fat, improved muscle tone, and increased energy (Pollock, Wilmore, & Fox, 1978; Sharkey, 1979). These changes, in conjunction with the psychological benefits of exercise, are conducive to creating the positive effects often associated with exercise.

The relationship of psychological well-being and vigorous physical activity may be highlighted in neurochemical research on opiate-like peptides known as the endorphins (Durden-Smith, 1978; Riggs, 1981; Sachs, 1984; Snyder, 1977a, 1977b, 1980; Villet, 1978). The endorphins have been implicated as being significant in experiencing the runner's high and in the development of addiction to exercise (Mandell, 1979; Pargman & Baker, 1980; Riggs, 1981; Sachs, 1984; Sachs & Pargman, 1984).

The endorphins are naturally occurring substances that have been termed the brain's own opiates. They are particularly important in regulating emotion and perceiving pain. Glasser has suggested that the endorphins might be the missing link in his search for "the addictive factor in positive addiction" (1978, p. 2).

Appenzeller and his colleagues, for example, have conducted a number of studies linking running and the endorphins (Appenzeller, 1980, 1981a, 1981b; Appenzeller & Schade, 1979; Appenzeller, Standefer, Appenzeller, & Atkinson, 1980). They note,

> Endurance running produces a marked increase in β-endorphin. Whether this increase persists after physical activity and is responsible for the "runner's high," the behavorial alterations of endurance-trained individuals, improved libido, heightened pain threshold, absence of depression, and other anecdotal effects of endurance training remains conjectural. (Appenzeller et al., 1980, p. 419)

The important point made in the above quote is that the relationship of the endorphins to the runner's high (as well as to other aspects of the running experience) remain unanswered. With respect to the runner's high, for example, why don't all runners experience this phenomenon? Does the mechanism of the endorphins somehow work differently for these runners? The integrated approach comes into focus here in that research on the endorphins has been primarily concerned with endorphins taken from the bloodstream. These peripheral measurements raise the question of what effects endorphins at the central level (i.e., the brain) have on the exercise experience. Clearly, there is much left to discover in this area, and future studies may show that the endorphins play a significant role in promoting psychological well-being as a function of participation in vigorous physical activity.

CONCLUSION

The literature reviewed here has indicated a consistent relationship between psychological well-being and vigorous physical activity. Given the establishment of this relationship, what practical implications can be derived? How can coaches, teachers, and others in health-related fields structure their environments to make people more aware of the potential benefits?

The first, and perhaps most important, point to make concerns *adherence.* Certainly, the positive psychological and physiological effects of exercise cannot be obtained if the individual does not participate on a regular basis (Dishman, 1981b; Dishman & Gettman, 1980). We should note, however, the critical nature of structuring the exercise setting in such a way that work-out goals are attained, the risk of injury is reduced, social contacts (especially initially) are frequent and reinforcing, and the exercise is tailored to the individual's needs and interests (Buffone, Sachs, & Dowd, 1984).

The second point relates to goal setting, an area significant to adherence as well. Structuring the exercise situation so that the individual is involved in developing reasonable, attainable, short-term (as well as long-term) goals will enhance the quality of the individual's participation by providing for frequent success.

A third point relating to adherence is the quality and quantity of social relationships. Specifically, in the initial stages, social relationships can be significant in reinforcing an individual's participation in an activity and increasing the likelihood of adherence. A positive environment, with reinforcement derived from others, enhances the psychological benefits that may be obtained from the activity.

Fourth, the nature of the exercise environment is important in deriving positive experiences from participation. Exercising regularly in hot, humid conditions, in a stressful situation, creates an unpleasant environment. Indeed, to experience the runner's high one generally needs cool, calm conditions. Structuring the exercise environment (to the degree possible) so that climatic conditions are favorable to vigorous physical activity, with as few distractions as possible (i.e., not running in midtown Manhattan in New York City at noon), and occasionally varying the scenery will most likely produce beneficial effects. Furthermore, structuring exercise sessions in pleasant surroundings, such as a local park or forest, can add the beauty of nature to the positive feelings derived from the exercise.

Finally, a coach, teacher, or other health professional can highlight the positive physiological and psychological benefits that the individual can potentially derive from the exercise experience. This approach may make these benefits more salient and meaningful to the individual. Pointing out in particular any favorable climatic and environmental conditions, the pleasure of "working up a good sweat," and certain existential or centering experiences (which enhance the relevance and meaning of the exercise experience for each person; e.g., Hendricks & Carlson, 1982; Spino, 1976, 1977), may all enhance the exercise experience. The practitioner who is aware of the positive psychological and physiological benefits of the exercise experience can highlight them for the participant, and can thus play a significant role in enhancing one's exercise and health experience.

Chapter 31

Exercise
as a Therapeutic Adjunct

Gary W. Buffone
Psychologist, Jacksonville, FL

Although considerable attention has been directed toward cognitive and behavioral approaches in counseling and psychotherapy (e.g. Bandura, 1969; Beck, 1976; Craighead, Kazdin, & Mahoney, 1976; Foreyt & Rathjen, 1978) the use of physical interventions in the therapeutic process was a neglected area of inquiry until the late 1970s (Dickerson, 1978; Driscoll, 1976; Greist, Klein, Eischens, & Faris, 1978). A major purpose of this chapter will be to review the studies that have examined the use of physical exercise in psychotherapy, and to examine the implications of this research for the physical and mental health practitioner.

Researchers in the fields of psychosomatic and behavioral medicine have begun to experimentally establish the fact that the mind can affect the body (Pelletier, 1977). This is illustrated by the prevalence of such psychosomatic disorders as migraine headaches, peptic ulcers, hypertension, bronchial asthma, and sexual impotence. It is also becoming evident that the body, appropriately utilized, can affect the mind in constructive ways (Folkins & Sime, 1981). Although a number of studies demonstrate the positive psychological effects of exercise on physical health (Bonanno & Lies, 1974; Buccola & Stone, 1975; Cooper, 1968), only recently has systematic research concerned the psychological changes associated with exercise.

Exercise engaged in solely for physical benefits has been shown to have a positive effect on the psychological state of individuals in a number of diverse settings. For example, physically strenuous exercise is effective in improving the psychological functioning of individuals experiencing a wide range of problems (Folkins & Sime, 1981; Sacks & Sachs, 1981). Specifically, there seems to be clinical agreement that a number of physical and psychological changes occur when an individual exercises at 75 to 80% of his or her maximum cardiac output for 30 minutes 4 or 5 times a week (Berger, 1984b). Research suggests that these changes include improved mood, self-esteem, and work performance as well as increased cardiovascular endurance and improvements in muscle tone, digestion, fat loss, and blood volume (Folkins & Sime, 1981; Pollock, Wilmore, & Fox, 1978). Thus, it would seem appropriate for the counselor to employ an exercise treatment as an adjunct, considering the wide range of psychological problems that appear amenable to an exercise approach.

Aerobic Activity and Psychological Well-Being

Considering that physical exercise facilitates various psychological changes, how much exercise is necessary in order to produce a significant effect? The types of physical exercise that appear to offer the greatest physiological, as well as psychological, effect are those classified as aerobic (Cooper, 1968). This exercise prescription is discussed in greater detail by Sachs in the previous chapter. Research has suggested that the prescribed exercise must be strenuous in order to produce significant psychological change (Morgan, Roberts, & Feinerman, 1971; Sime, 1977). Aerobic (with oxygen) exercises are distinguished from anaerobic (without oxygen) activities in that aerobic exercise produces lasting cardiovascular changes if engaged in consistently over an extended period of time. Aerobic activities include running, bicycling, swimming, brisk walking, and cross-country skiing.

Since most of the research on aerobic exercise programs has reported significant psychological changes, the question is which of these exercises is most compatible for inclusion in a psychotherapeutic regimen? Of the aerobic activities mentioned, running has received much attention in both the professional and popular literature (Fixx, 1977; Glover & Shephard, 1977). Running provides a natural, practical, inexpensive, and time-efficient adjunct to traditional psychotherapies. One study on the use of running for treating depression found that running was four times more cost-effective than more traditional, verbal oriented psychotherapies (Greist, Klein, Eischens, & Faris, 1978). This is important, considering the spiraling cost of health care and the present trend toward cost-effectiveness in counseling. Additionally, running therapies provide additional health benefits such as increased respiratory efficiency and cardiovascular endurance, as well as improvement in muscle tone, digestion, blood volume, and fat loss (Pollock, Wilmore, & Fox, 1978).

The use of running as therapy can also encourage a more positive, health-promoting approach which can be or is learned by the client. Harper (1978) has provided a set of simple guidelines to use in developing a running program for clients. Finally, running can be assigned as a self-regulatory task for the client to use in a self-management program. Although only running is discussed here, the counselor or professional should consider various aerobic exercises when designing an exercise program that the client can enjoy and maintain.

Even though a somatic or exercise therapy appears considerably promising for treating a number of emotional disorders, it is certainly not a panacea for the psychic ills of modern humanity. In spite of what exercise evangelists preach, there are certainly contraindications associated with such a treatment. For example, it is clear that an aerobic exercise therapy should not be prescribed for people with physical complications such as gross obesity (40% over ideal weight), severe heart disease, enlarged heart, and high blood pressure that cannot be controlled by medication, or for individuals who have recently had a heart attack (Lance, 1977). Running may also be contraindicated for individuals who are severely depressed, have a tenuous contact with reality, or are suicidally inclined (Kostrubala, 1976).

Running and the Reduction of Anxiety and Depression

As research into the use of running and exercise continues, we are beginning to determine which emotional problems respond best to such an approach. Specifically, running has been extensively cited as an effective way to reduce anxiety and depression although the results of these studies have been somewhat equivocal. Morgan and his colleagues (Morgan, 1981a; Morgan et al., 1971) have conducted a number of studies in this area but have not consistently reported reductions in anxiety as a result of physical activity. However, Morgan (1973b) has reported consistent reductions in *state* anxiety with acute physical exercise. This finding has been supported by others (Seeman, 1978) who noted a significant decrease in state anxiety following vigorous exercise. This decrease appeared transitory, however, as anxiety levels returned to the control level by the fifth hour after exercise. No studies to date have conclusively reported significant reductions in *trait* anxiety as a result of physical exercise.

The reduction of depression through exercise is perhaps as well studied as that of anxiety. Greist, Klein, Eischens, and Faris (1978) in a well controlled study found that running was at least as effective as time-limited or time-unlimited psychotherapy in alleviating the symptoms of moderate depression. Other researchers (Blue, 1979; Brown, Ramirez, &

Taub, 1978; Kavanaugh, Shephard, & Tuck, 1973) have supported these findings and suggested that aerobic running can relieve moderate depression. Buffone (1980) has also suggested that although exercise may play an important role in this improvement, nonspecific factors (i.e., therapist's personality, social interaction) may also heavily influence favorable outcomes found in this research. Berger (1984b) and Buffone (1984a, b) provide excellent and comprehensive reviews of the impact of running on anxiety and depression. Berger also presents an interesting discussion of the effects of exercise on self-esteem and general well-being.

IMPORTANT CONSIDERATIONS IN EMPLOYING EXERCISE AS THERAPY

Obviously, a precise diagnosis of the psychological problem and an individually tailored exercise prescription are vitally important in enhancing well-being. The client may not respond to an exercise prescription and thus the counselor must watch for signs of discontent so that an alternative treatment may be employed. It seems likely that running as treatment would be most effective if used in conjunction with verbal or cognitive forms of therapy. This is consistent with Lazarus' (1976) suggestion that a multimodal therapeutic approach is more effective than the use of a single intervention.

Another thing to consider is the potential misuse of exercise therapy by unqualified individuals. There are several criteria that a therapist should consider before dispensing exercise prescriptions. For example, Kostrubala (1976) has suggested that the counselor (therapist) be trained in mental health and show an ability and interest in running. Additionally, a running therapist should be able to dispense advice about athletic training equipment, breathing, posture, and other aspects of the running experience. Thus, some formal training in physical education, sports medicine, or other related health field may be invaluable to the counselor.

For their part, most coaches and physical educators are not trained in mental health although they would be capable of managing the training aspects of running therapy. Of course, coaches should be aware of the psychological benefits and potential dangers of serious exercise participation.

Although these qualifications for counselors are perhaps overly stringent, it seems important that the counselor be deeply committed to exercise in order to model appropriate behaviors and provide guidance and information to clients as necessary. Furthermore, incorrect training information and supervision could result in a disabling injury, which would discourage the client from further participation in strenuous physical activities. Injury prevention is vital because a running or exercise therapy program cannot be effective unless the client can continue the exercise.

Maintaining the exercise program, once established in therapy, is a third important consideration for the practitioner. Here the counselor fulfills a vital role by consistently reinforcing physical participation, modeling appropriate behaviors, establishing external rewards in the client's environment, and teaching the client self-control techniques (such as charting, self-reinforcement) so that he/she will continue the exercise program after completing therapy. Several models and approaches for encouraging exercise adherence have been suggested (Buffone, Sachs, & Dowd, 1984; Dishman, 1979; Dishman & Gettman, 1980; also see the Dishman chapter in this text) that discuss the general factors which appear to affect adherence.

Exercise behaviors in particular seem to have an advantage of becoming "addictive" if engaged in consistently over an extended period of time (see Chapter 30 by Sachs). Solomon and Bumpus (1978), who suggest the running-meditation response as an adjunct in therapy, note:

> We emphasize running three to five days a week simply because regularity leads to addiction, a key factor in the success of this method. The more frequently the patient runs, the more he will experience the pleasurable and desirable efforts of running and, consequently, the more quickly he will become addicted. Addiction usually occurs in two to four months. Once the patient is "hooked," he will feel a compulsion to run. If he does not, he will experience withdrawal symptoms, such as anxiety, not feeling well or insomnia. (p. 585)

Other researchers have noted the addictive qualities of regular physical exercise (Glasser, 1976; Sachs, 1981; Sachs & Pargman, 1979). This addiction could conceivably be an alternative to the negative addictions such as alcohol, drugs, smoking, and overeating, which often resist traditional counseling methods. In this way, running, once established as a lifetime habit, could carry treatment effects beyond therapy; it could be used by the client as a preventive medicine in warding off daily stresses for life. Yet it is also important for the clinician to be sensitive to symptoms of a negative addiction (Morgan, 1979b), which may require professional attention (see Chapter 30 by Sachs).

Implications for Exercise Counselors

Current research in the areas of counseling, psychology, and medicine is just beginning to indicate that physical exercise can have a positive effect on mental health. Physically strenuous or aerobic exercises have proven valuable in reducing moderate levels of anxiety and depression, building confidence, reducing body fat, enhancing habit control, increasing body awareness and image, alleviating phobias, increasing productivity, and improving sleep (Folkins & Sime, 1981). Physical exercise programs also offer considerable promise in certain preventive health programs in the expanding field of behavioral medicine. For example, evidence from recent studies suggests that exercise plays a major role in reducing the risks of coronary attacks and arterial disease, obesity, hypertension, and the risks associated with elevated blood lipids, cigarette smoking, and "Type A" personality characteristics (Bonanno & Lies, 1974; Buccola & Stone, 1975; Cooper, 1968). Other areas of application that have yet to be developed (Buffone, 1984a) could include application to developmentally disabled, elderly, adolescent, and other populations.

It seems evident that aerobic activities maintained over a period of time can produce positive results when applied to a number of problems commonly encountered by counselors. For this reason, a physical exercise approach involving one or more forms of aerobic activity deserves further consideration as a valuable adjunct to therapies already in use. At this point the question is not whether changes occur, but why? In the running treatment of depression, for example, there are numerous explanations. Greist, Klein, Eischens, and Faris (1978) give the following explanation for the therapeutic effects of running:

> This approach to the treatment of depression can be conceptualized as graded skill training or practice with built in reinforcement. By regularly filling time with comfortable, rhythmical movement of large muscle groups, the positive reinforcements of physical adaptation . . . and psychological benefits follow. (p. 280)

Additional hypotheses that may help explain the beneficial effects of running relate to mastery, capacity for change, distraction, positive habit, consciousness alteration, patience, and biochemical changes. The various theories that attempt to explain these changes are too numerous to examine thoroughly in this chapter (see Berger, 1984b for a review).

Several questions concerning the use of running as therapy still remain. Exactly what factors during aerobic exercise are actually responsible for producing the psychological changes? Can these factors be isolated and refined to yield even better therapeutic results? Which traditional therapeutic procedures presently in use are most compatibly combined with exercise prescriptions? Which clinical problems seem most amenable to an exercise approach? Finally, what other contraindications would preclude the use of this technique? Questions like these still remain to be answered by future research. In general, studies of the psychological effects of physical exercise have been poorly designed. These and related methodological issues are examined in Silva and Shultz's (1984) excellent discussion of the current state of research in the psychology and therapeutics of running.

Preliminary research evidence does strongly suggest, however, that aerobic exercise can have a positive impact on an individual's psychological state. As present research continues to answer these questions, we will become more aware of the intricacies of the body-mind relationship. This will provide counselors with yet another tool in the quest to help individuals improve the quality of their lives.

Chapter 32

Qualities of the Peak Experience in Sport

Kenneth Ravizza
California State University-Fullerton

The traditional emphasis on improved sport performance has focused upon the physical components of sport. The psychological aspects typically have consisted of various game strategies designed to manipulate the opposition. In some sports such as football, highly complex strategies or play-calling systems have rapidly become the preferred route to success. Efforts have focused upon extensive physical conditioning, mastery of fundamentals and strategies, and pep talks which are somehow intended to help players achieve optimal performance. Some of these techniques have been strikingly successful, and the late Vince Lombardi stands out as the most renowned practitioner of this approach. In contrast, only limited attempts have been made to enhance the participant's psychological preparation for significant contests. Today we are in a stage of transition in which coaches are more receptive to psychological preparatory methods that complement the basic physical training because they have begun to recognize the importance of these methods in obtaining optimal performance.

Consequently, coaches and sport scientists around the world have become increasingly interested in the psychological aspects of sport. Extensive research has focused on a wide range of topics such as personality profiles of athletes (Morgan, 1980a), the arousal performance relationship (Landers, 1980; Martens & Landers, 1970), team cohesion (Bird, 1977a; Carron, 1982), and coping strategies (Nideffer & Deckner, 1979; Orlick, 1980; Suinn, 1972a).

This chapter focuses on one aspect of the psychological experience that characterizes an athlete's most fulfilling psychoemotional moments while participating in sport. This naturally occurring state of altered consciousness will be referred to as the peak experience. These rare moments, when the participant is performing optimally and experiencing heightened levels of awareness, offer great significance in advancing our understanding of the nature of optimal sport performance.

This chapter will introduce the reader to the phenomenon of the peak experience in sport by examining the major qualities of the peak experience, followed by a discussion of the problems and limitations in studying peak experiences. It will also present the ramifications for educators, coaches, athletes, and psychologists.

THE PHENOMENON
OF THE PEAK EXPERIENCE IN SPORT

Humanistic Psychological Tradition

Cultures throughout the world have designated labels for ultimate life experiences that stand out from the usual ebb and flow of daily existence. Scientists, philosophers, and theologians have explored these phenomena in an effort to advance society's understanding of the human condition. Maslow (1968) introduced the peak experience concept to explain those moments when an individual experiences feelings of total unity, inner strength, and wholeness of being. Maslow was a prime force in the development of humanistic psychology, a school of thought that places considerable emphasis on the healthy aspects of the individual's personality. Maslow's theory assumes that each individual has a unique inner nature which is good or neutral, rather than bad. The focus of the humanistic perspective is grounded in the belief that in developing one's capabilities to the fullest, the person's inner nature is able to overcome habit and cultural pressure in choosing the life direction most fulfilling for him or her. This enhances the inherent quest for reaching one's full potential.

Maslow (1968) suggested the term *peak experience* to describe "those moments of highest happiness and fulfillment," which are accompanied by loss of fears, inhibitions, and insecurities. He described this experience as an ecstatic, nonvoluntary moment of total integration and internal peace.

PEAK EXPERIENCES IN SPORT

Consideration of the athlete's aesthetic experience while participating in sport has emerged only in the last two decades. Sport philosophers

(Arnold, 1979; Metheny, 1968; Slusher, 1967; Weiss, 1969) have speculated that the potential psychological impact of the sport experience lies
in the athlete's pursuit of a personal excellence. Ravizza (1975, 1977) and
C. Thomas (1977) have systematically explored the athlete's feelings related to sport participation. These investigations of meaningful moments
in sport focused upon the athlete's greatest experience while participating
in sport.

A related investigation of peak experience can be found in the work
of Csikszentmihalyi (1977), which explored the "flow" experience in the
context of play activities. This study focused on the intrinsically rewarding aspect of play in a wide variety of situations, including formal sport
activities, to determine whether various play activities have common
reward elements. The author hypothesized that by learning what makes
leisure activities enjoyable or have flow, it would be possible to decrease
dependence on extrinsic rewards in other areas of life. According to
Csikszentmihalyi (1977), this "flow experience" is composed of a merging
of the player's actions and awareness, centering of higher attention, loss
of personal ego, control of personal action and the external environment, demands for action and clear feedback, and an intrinsic reward
system. The flow experience has great similarity to the peak experience
except that, characteristically, flow is more voluntary in nature.

Murphy's (1978) examination of sport activities specifically resulted in the description of 12 features that contributed to an altered state
of consciousness in sport. Murphy (1977) further compared extraordinary psychic events reported by athletes to mystical phenomena.

The remainder of this section will discuss sport peak experiences
that this author has studied in order to familiarize the reader with
specific qualities of the peak experience (Ravizza, 1975). These investigations have made it clear that although athletes discuss a wide range of
feelings that make up their individualized peak experience, the qualities
reported fall into one of the three major categories: focused awareness,
complete control of self and the environment, and transcendence of self.

In order to experience focused awareness, the athlete must develop
sufficient concentration to exclude external variables (e.g., crowd) that
may negatively affect performance. Control of self and the environment
denotes a dimension in which the athlete experiences an internal power
over his or her own movements and the obstacles that the game or contest presents. Finally, transcendence of self captures the concept that the
athlete is being directed by the power of the merged self and the movement experience.

Qualities of the Peak Experience in Sport

The peak experience in sport is a rare personal moment that remains
etched in the athlete's consciousness. It serves as a reminder of the great

intrinsic satisfaction that sport participation can provide. Peak experiences during an athlete's career are relatively rare but their intensity acts as a standard, or qualitative reference point, for subjectively evaluating future performance.

The nature of the peak experience characteristically includes three common traits which are not subject to specific intervention techniques. Athletes always report the experience as temporary, nonvoluntary, and unique. Thus, the experience never produces a lasting enhanced mental state and no known available method can pinpoint its occurrence. Yet, when the peak experience does happen it stands apart from the usual game experience or practice routine.

As a precondition to a peak experience the athlete must achieve a mastery of the basic skills. This prerequisite is met when the athlete need no longer think about technical elements of skill execution. It is important to point out that circumstances or the sport environment need not be extraordinary in order for a peak experience to occur. The uniqueness lies in the way that one experiences the phenomenon. For example, a championship victory or a national record are not necessarily unique experiences. It is the quality of uniqueness that makes the participant regard the experiences as a personal treasure, greater than any trophy. The following section should expand our understanding of the components that commonly comprise the peak experience.

Focused Awareness

Every athletic contest has potential distractions that inhibit optimal performance by distracting the athlete's attention from the appropriate focal point. During the peak experience, the athlete's concentration is so immersed in the activity that the mental focus automatically adjusts to the task-relevant cues. The height of this focused awareness is manifested by complete absorption in the movement task and frequently includes altered perceptions about time, space, and the quality of the experience. A lacrosse player captured the essence of this focused awareness when she said, "It was a world within a world . . . focused right there. I was not aware of the external. My concentration was so great I didn't think of anything else" (Ravizza, 1977, p. 38).

Centered Present Focus.   During the peak experience, all consciousness is channeled into the present moment. Control is exercised over movement while the athlete fully lives the experience. Mental energy is not wasted dwelling on past or future actions over which there is no control. Centered focus is an internal physical and mental preparation made that initially produces a balanced perspective. A woman gymnast reports, "Right before I start, I totally block out various distractions. It's as if things are melting away . . . I think of the routine as a whole and it is just there and I am doing it" (Ravizza, 1982, p. 10). Thus, a relationship between the athlete and the movement task is created. For example, the high jumper prepares internally by stretching and adjusting his/her body position. After this ritual is completed the focus of attention shifts entirely to the bar, clearing all past thoughts and future distractions. At this point the athlete is centered on the high jump, ready to execute the movement.

Narrow Focus of Attention. In the midst of the peak experience the most exclusive kind of visual perceiving, listening, or feeling exists. Attention focuses appropriately upon the object of perception. The athlete observes from a nonjudging, nonclassifying perspective that heightens the viewing of the object in its entirety. This experience permits the athlete to shift instantly in response to movement cues. A football player discusses his experience of a narrow focus as follows: "This is one time I concentrated my whole being on one thing . . . I am just hitting him [the ball carrier] and nothing else" (Ravizza, 1977, p. 38).

Complete Absorption. In contrast to routine activities, the sport environment creates an environment that augments the individual's ability to be totally involved in the task at hand. In the peak experience context the competitor who concentrates intensely is surrounded by a state of silence where external concerns do not intrude. The focus is on execution of the appropriate movement task. The conduct of the crowd or previous playing errors are physical or mental distractions that are not part of the athlete's consciousness. A gymnast experiences complete absorption in the following manner: "It is just me and the routine; there is a complete silence. I forget time and just totally get into it . . . It is strange because it is just me and the beam. I am so into it that I do not notice anything else" (Ravizza, 1982, p. 9). Closely linked with this quality of intense concentration are different types of altered perceptions, the occurrence of which varies widely among athletes. There are at least three areas in which discernible variations from the usual movement perceptions are experienced: (a) the quality of the experience, (b) time disorientation, and (c) spatial alteration.

The quality of the athlete's perceived experience is heightened in that there is a quicker and clearer focus on movement cues. The athlete experiences a sense of awe and wonder with the quality of the experience. The perception may be so rich as to include temporal and spatial changes. Time disorientation is manifested in one of two ways. For example, an entire event or segment of it might seem to slip by in the briefest of moments. On the other hand, a few seconds in time may be perceived as endless slow motion. Spatial alteration occurs in the perception of equipment, the field, and/or opposing players. Thus, the baseball player may perceive the ball as moving in slow motion and seeming larger than usual. The gymnast may perceive the width of the balance beam as wider than its objective measurements. In contrast, when an athlete is under extreme stress and lacks control of the situation, objects appear faster or sometimes smaller than usual. An extreme example of this occurs when an athlete becomes so tense that he/she hardly perceives anything (tunnel vision).

Complete Control of Self and the Environment

To reach specific goals in competitive situations, the athlete's dual concern is to learn to master the self and work to control the situation. The intensity of the peak experience pushes the athlete to new levels of performance in the pursuit of these goals. There is a fusion between the perfect nature of the movement and the willingness to dispense with the usual caution of not making an error. The athlete is in charge of the situation. A football player's report of his feelings of control demonstrates the individual's ultimate exercise of psychological power: "Things were under control; my body could do anything . . . it was almost like my body was not there. Everything out there could in no way affect me. I could do anything I wanted" (Ravizza, 1975, p. 402). This sense of control acts as a guide for the athlete as though each movement is choreographed in advance.

Perfection.   Athletes describe the peak experience as euphoric, memorable, and worthwhile, an event complete in itself and independent from all external circumstances. The experience of a perfect moment leads the athlete to an understanding of intrinsic satisfaction and therefore becomes a self-validating moment. A downhill skier captured this feeling of perfection with the following statement: "I felt like I was radiating in every direction, not with pressure but with joy. I felt a tremendous amount of heat. I was totally filled up with joy like a helium balloon, and it was fantastic" (Ravizza, 1975, p. 399). Comment or congratulations from a coach, another player, or spectators becomes unnecessary because the perfect quality of the experience is irrefutable and frequently transcends the final, even losing, score.

Loss of Fear.   Physical injury and emotional fear in sport are learned from past injuries, prior mistakes in performance, and critical comments from significant others. Furthermore, many athletes are trained to be too critical of their performance. Athletes often approach competition with an orientation toward the fear of making mistakes. In contrast, during peak experiences one strives for excellence, undaunted by past mistakes and the dangers inherent in the sport. There is no doubt that more frequent injuries and mental errors will happen to the athlete whose primary motivation is to avoid mistakes. Persistent fear of failure reduces the athlete's ability to achieve total concentration because a part of his or her consciousness is distracted in evaluating ongoing performance. An athlete cannot be totally absorbed in the task while at the same time trying to avoid mistakes.

Transcendence of Self

Athletes who are totally involved in the present, centered on the task, and feeling at the height of their power may experience harmony or oneness with the movement. Such an experience can be called transcendence of self. Athletes simply do the appropriate task without consciously thinking about it. To reach this level of intensity the athlete must surrender the usual thinking-evaluating self to the experience. The initial motivation is provided by going all out. Total involvement sets the conditions for the peak experience. The athlete has no further control over whether a feeling of harmony will be reached.

Harmony and Oneness. Harmony and oneness represent a mental state in which the athlete's total self is integrated physically and mentally in the experience. The objects of perception (implements of the game) are experienced as an intricate part of the self. There is no distinction between the individual and the experience; instead, the two flow together in a unified whole. No longer are muscles fighting muscles, no longer is the athlete fighting the environment; now there is a blending of all levels between one's self, the movement, and/or the team. An Olympic cyclist describes his feelings of integration as follows: "I am at one with everything. There is no distinction between myself, the bicycle, track, speed or anything. There is a oneness with everything" (Ravizza, 1975, p. 402).

Noncritical and Effortless. In order for harmony to occur, the athlete must be able to execute the basic skills automatically. If one consciously criticizes ongoing performance then part of the self is not totally immersed in the activity. Rather, it is involved in giving performance commands. As the athlete learns to surrender the self to the experience, he or she becomes increasingly aware of moving toward harmony. The intense enjoyment and intrinsic satisfaction often involved with the transcendence experience demands that the athlete let the feelings occur without stopping to dwell on or evaluate them.

The athlete has to surrender him/herself to the experience. It is as if the athlete could continue moving forever, no longer having to exert himself/herself consciously. A butterfly swimmer captures the blending of self and the experience that occurs with the following comment: "I couldn't feel any pain, which is really weird, for me . . . take away the pain and it is effortless . . . my whole body was doing it with ease" (Ravizza, 1975, p. 403). In team sports, the feeling of harmony may be experienced when each of the individuals involved blend together to form a synergy that is greater than any individual effort. Each individual feels the team "clicking," and there is a concentration and rhythm that wasn't there before.

A skier's comments summarize the three major categories that comprise a peak experience:

> Everything was so perfect, everything was so right, that it couldn't be any other way. The closest thing I can say about it was that there seemed to be tracks in the snow that my skis were made to fit in . . . It was no longer me and the hill, but it was both of us. It was just right. I belonged there. (Ravizza, 1975, p. 399)

CONSIDERATIONS IN EXAMINING PEAK EXPERIENCES IN SPORT

Having examined the basic features of the peak experience in the previous section, the reader might find it helpful to pause and consider the nature of the investigations used to study this type of psychological phenomenon. To date, researchers investigating peak experience have relied primarily on a two-step research strategy, the first step involving detailed athlete interviews which described this psychological phenomenon. In the second step, the researcher rigorously analyzed the content of the interviews and attempted to extract its major characteristics.

The one potential weakness of this technique is that it relies on the athlete's accurate recall and description of the phenomenon as well as the researcher's skill and integrity in objectively ascertaining the major features of the phenomenon under study. This type of phenomenological technique for studying psychological experience works best when used as a preliminary research technique, followed by behavioristic measures such as standardized psychological inventories. An investigation using more traditional methods to evaluate altered states of consciousness is under way at present, but no conclusions have yet been published (Adair, 1982).

To the coach, athlete, and researcher, the phenomenon of peak experience often appears at first glance to be unrelated to everyday practice and performance. Consequently, many people in sport have considered the peak experience as a rare and irrelevant, although interesting, phenomenon. The focus of the author's present research is that the peak experience may constitute a distant point on a continuum of normal sport experience. Thus, a detailed analysis of its characteristics may provide important clues to the nature of intervening points along the same continuum.

The peak experience is a valuable glimpse into a higher state of consciousness that many athletes have not yet experienced or described. At present, the significance of the peak experience in sport lies in the experience itself and also in the investigation of whether greater personal fulfillment in sport increases the likelihood of improved performance levels.

A second methodological consideration that may retard research in this area is that such a highly subjective, complex, psychological phenomenon requires much of the researcher's time, effort, and care. When dealing with relatively unfamiliar aspects of consciousness, the investigator will need a great deal of patience because he or she needs to create an interviewing environment that encourages spontaneity while balancing the need to keep the interview focused.

THE USE OF PEAK EXPERIENCE TO IMPROVE OPTIMAL LEVELS OF PERFORMANCE

One way in which modern researchers have conceptualized the whole notion of optimal performance is to characterize performance as an inverted-U function (Landers, 1980; Martens & Landers, 1970). Peak experience may enhance performance because it lends insight into the nature of the athlete's consciousness while he/she is performing at an optimal level. It then becomes a matter of duplicating selected aspects of these experiences, thereby setting up the psychological foundation necessary for consistent and optimal levels of performance. For example, one aspect of the peak experience is focused awareness of what is occurring at the moment. Athletes can become more sensitive to this heightened awareness by employing relaxation, breathing, and centering techniques. Specialists (Nideffer & Deckner, 1979; Orlick, 1980; Railo & Unestahl, 1979; Ravizza & Rotella, 1982; Suinn, 1972a) currently working with athletes have employed these techniques effectively in developing focused awareness and control over self and the environment in order to set the conditions for optimal performance. Whether or not a transcendental experience will occur from this is beyond our knowledge or control at the present time.

Obviously, exploration of psychological as well as physical performance requires an increased rapport between the coach and players, and between the athletes themselves. Ultimately such open-ended rapport can be useful both on and off the field. For example, when athletes share their pregame anxiety with the coach and their teammates, some of their tension will be relieved because they are no longer nourishing the illusion of being in control. They no longer need to waste energy in pretending all is well.

Finally, the peak experience is an intrinsic experience that is self-validating. It is vital for the athlete to have some internal feelings of value rather than to rely only on the evaluation of significant others, coaches, or teammates. The peak experience teaches the athlete an awareness of his/her own significance independent of what others have to say. Athletes gradually realize more of their inner beauty as they recognize the wealth of potential that they possess. Reflection upon the peak experience contributes to an awareness of the "ultimate athlete" (Leonard, 1975) within, thereby adding to the athlete's self-confidence.

SUMMARY

Like any altered state of consciousness, the peak experience is a difficult phenomenon to study. Yet it has tremendous potential significance for the achievement of optimal performance in sport. We cannot guarantee peak experiences, but their occurrence gives intrinsic satisfaction and acts as a valuable reference point in the achievement of performance goals. Athletes need to develop a fuller awareness of their sport experiences in order to gain control over the self and the sport environment. As coaches and researchers, we can help the athlete develop along a path that permits each to attain his or her fullest capabilities.

References

ADAIR, J. (1982). *Construction and validation of an instrument designed to assess states of consciousness during movement activity*. Unpublished doctoral dissertation, Temple University.

ADLER, A. (1929). *The practice and theory of individual psychology*. New York: Harcourt, Brace & World.

ALBRECHT, D. (1979). Zursportartspezifischen aggression in Wettkampfspeil. *Sportwissenshaft*, 9:78-91.

ALDERMAN, R.B. (1974). *Psychological behavior in sport*. Toronto: Saunders.

ALDERMAN, R.B. (1978). Strategies for motivating young athletes. In W.F. Straub (Ed.), *Sport psychology: An analysis of athlete behavior*. Ithaca, NY: Mouvement.

ALDERMAN, R.B. (1980). Sport psychology: Past, present, and future dilemmas. In P. Klavora & K. Wipper (Eds.), *Psychological and sociological factors in sport*. Toronto: University of Toronto.

ALDERMAN, R.B., & Wood, N.L. (1976). An analysis of incentive motivation in young Canadian athletes. *Canadian Journal of Applied Sport Sciences*, 1:169-176.

ALLISON, M.G., & Ayllon, T. (1980). Behavioral coaching in the development of skills in football, gymnastics, and tennis. *Journal of Applied Behavior Analysis*, 13:297-314.

ALLPORT, F.H. (1924). *Social psychology*. Boston: Houghton Mifflin.

ALLPORT, G.W. (1937). *Personality: A psychological interpretation*. New York: Henry Holt.

ALLPORT, G. (1968). The historical background of modern social psychology. In G. Lindzey & E. Aronson (Eds.), *The handbook of social psychology*. Reading, MA: Addison-Wesley.

ALTMAIER, E.M., Leary, M.R., Ross, S.L., & Thornbrough, M. (1982). Matching stress inoculation's treatment components to clients' anxiety model. *Journal of Counseling Psychology*, 29:331-336.

ANDERSON, A.B. (1975). Combined effects of interpersonal attraction and goal-path clarity on the cohesiveness of task oriented groups. *Journal of Personality and Social Psychology*, 31:68-75.

ANDERSON, W.G. (1899). Studies in the effects of physical training. *American Physical Education Review*, 4:265-278.

ANDREW, G.M., Oldridge, N.B., Parker, J.O., Cunningham, D.A., Rechnitzer, P.A., Jones, N.L., Buck, C., Kavanagh, T., Shephard, R.J., Sutton, J.R., & McDonald, W. (1981). Reasons for dropout from exercise programs in post coronary patients. *Medicine and Science in Sports and Exercise*, 13:165-168.

ANDREWS, R. (1974). A Spearman rank order correlation for 18 N.H.L. teams. *National Hockey League Guide*.

APPENZELLER, O. (1980, July). Report from Otto Appenzeller, M.D., *The AMJA Newsletter*, 31.

APPENZELLER, O. (1981a). Does running affect mood? (In Reader's Forum) *Runner's World*, 16:13.

APPENZELLER, O. (1981b). What makes us run? *New England Journal of Medicine*, 305:578-580.

APPENZELLER, O., & Schade, D.R. (1979). Neurology of endurance training: III. Sympathetic activity during a marathon run. *Neurology*, 29:542.

APPENZELLER, O., Standefer, J., Appenzeller, J., & Atkinson, R. (1980). Neurology of endurance training: V. Endorphins. *Neurology*, 30:418-419.

ARDREY, R. (1962). *African genesis*. New York: Atheneum.

ARMS, R., Russell, G., & Sandilands, M. (1979). Effects of the hostility of spectators on viewing aggressive sports. *Social Psychology Quarterly*, 42:275-279.

ARNOLD, G.E., & Straub, W.F. (1972). Personality and group cohesiveness as determinants of success among interscholastic basketball teams. *Proceedings: Fourth Canadian Symposium on Psychomotor Learning and Sport Psychology*. Ottawa: Health and Welfare Canada.

ARNOLD, M.B. (1960). *Emotion and personality*. New York: Columbia University Press.

ARNOLD, P. (1979). *Meaning in movement, sport and physical education*. London: Heinemann.

ARONFREED, J. (1968). *Conduct and conscience: The socialization of internalized control over behavior*. New York: Academic.

ATKINSON, J.W. (1957). Motivational determinants of risk-taking behaviors. *Psychological Review*, 64:359-372.

ATKINSON, J.W. (1964). *An introduction to motivation*. Princeton, NJ: Van Nostrand.

ATKINSON, J.W., & Feather, N.T. (1966). *A theory of achievement motivation*. New York: Wiley.

AUSTIN, W.R., & Worchel, S. (1979). *The social psychology of intergroup relations*. Monterey, CA: Brooks/Cole.

BAHRKE, M.S. (1979). Exercise, meditation and anxiety reduction: A review. *American Corrective Therapy Journal*, 33:41-44.

BAHRKE, M.S., & Morgan, W.P. (1978). Anxiety reduction following exercise and meditation. *Cognitive Therapy and Research*, 2:323-333.

BALL, D.W. (1975). A note on methods in the sociological study of sport. In D.W. Ball & J.W. Loy (Eds.), *Sport and the social order: Contributions to the sociology of sport*. Reading, MA: Addison-Wesley.

BALL, J.R., & Carron, A.V. (1976). The influence of team cohesion and participation motivation upon performance success in intercollegiate ice hockey. *Canadian Journal of Applied Sport Sciences*, 1:271-275.

BALLANTYNE, D., Clark, A., Dyker, G.S., Gills, C.R., Hawthorne, V.M., Henry, D.A., Hole, D.S., Murdoch, R.M., Semple, T., & Stewart, G.M. (1978, July). Prescribing exercise for the healthy: Assessment of compliance and effects on plasma lipids and lipoproteins. *Health Bulletin*, 36:169-176.

BANDURA, A. (1962). Social learning through imitation. In M.R. Jones (Ed.), *Nebraska symposium on motivation*. Lincoln: University of Nebraska Press.

BANDURA, A. (1965). Influence of models' reinforcement contingencies on the acquisition of imitative responses. *Journal of Personality and Social Psychology*, 1:589-595.

BANDURA, A. (1969). *Principles of behavior modification*. New York: Holt, Rinehart & Winston.

BANDURA, A. (1973). *Aggression: A social learning analysis*. Englewood Cliffs, NJ: Prentice-Hall.

BANDURA, A. (1977a). *Social learning theory*. New York: Prentice-Hall.

BANDURA, A. (1977b). Self-efficacy: Toward a unifying theory of behavioral change. *Psychological Review*, 84:191-215.

BANDURA, A. (1978). The self-system in reciprocal determinism. *American Psychologist*, 33:334-348.

BANDURA, A. (1982). Self-efficacy mechanism in human agency. *American Psychologist*, 37:122-147.

BANDURA, A., Adams, N.E., Hardy, A.B., & Howells, G.N. (1980). Tests of the generality of self-efficacy theory. *Cognitive Therapy and Research*, 4:39-66.

BANDURA, A., & Huston, A. (1961). Identification of a process of incidental learning. *Journal of Abnormal and Social Psychology*, 63:311-318.

BANDURA, A., Ross, D. & Ross, S. (1961). Transmission of aggression through imitation of aggressive models. *Journal of Abnormal and Social Psychology*, 63:575-582.

BANDURA, A., & Schunk, D. (1981). Cultivating competence, self-efficacy, and intrinsic interest through proximal self-motivation. *Journal of Personality and Social Psychology*, 41:586-598.

BARON, R.A. (1970). Attraction toward the model and model's competence as determinants of adult imitative behavior. *Journal of Personality and Social Psychology*, 14:345-351.

BARON, R.A., Byrne, D., & Kantowitz, B. (1980). *Psychology: Understanding behavior* (2nd. ed.). New York: Holt, Rinehart & Winston.

BARON, R., Moore, D., & Sanders, G.S. (1978). Distraction as a source of drive in social facilitation research. *Journal of Personality and Social Psychology*, 36:816-824.

BARRETT, C. (1969). Systematic desensitization therapy versus implosive therapy. *Journal of Abnormal Psychology*, 74:587-592.

BARROW, J.C. (1977). The variables of leadership: A review and conceptual framework. *Academy of Management Review*, 2:231-251.

BASLER, M.L., Fisher, A.C., & Mumford, N.L. (1976). Arousal and anxiety correlates of gymnastic performance. *Research Quarterly*, 47:586-589.

BASS, R.M. (1980). Team productivity and individual member competencies. *Small Group Behavior*, 11:431-504.

BAUM, M. (1970). Extinction of avoidance responding through response prevention (flooding). *Psychological Bulletin*, 74:276-284.

BECK, A.T. (1976). *Cognitive therapy and the emotional disorders*. New York: International Universities Press.

BECK, R.C. (1978). *Motivation: Theory and principles*. Englewood Cliffs, NJ: Prentice-Hall.

BEISSER, A. (1967). *The madness in sports*. New York: Appleton-Century-Crofts.

BELL, A.P., Weinberg, M.S., & Hammersmith, S.K. (1981). *Sexual preference: Its development in men and women*. Bloomington: Indiana University Press.

BELL, K. (1976). Relaxation training for competitive swimming. *Swimming Technique*, 13(2):41-43.

BELL, K. (1980). *The nuts and bolts of psychology for swimmers*. Austin, TX: Keith F. Bell, PhD.

BELL, K. (1981). Where are the limits? *Swimmers*, 4:27.

BEM, D.J., & Funder, D.C. (1978). Predicting more of the people more of the time: Assessing the personality of situations. *Psychological Review*, 85:485-501.

BEM, S. (1975). Sex role adaptability: One consequence of psychological androgyny. *Journal of Personality and Social Psychology*, 31:634-643.

BENNETT, B. (1978, April). Psych-up or psych-out. *International Gymnast*, pp. 65-67.

BENNETT, B.K., & Stothart, C.M. (1980). The effects of a relaxation-based cognitive technique on sport performances. In P. Klavora & K. Wipper (Eds.), *Psychological and sociological factors and sport*. Toronto: University Press.

BENSON, H. (1975). *The relaxation response*. New York: Morrow.

BERGER, B.G. (1984a). Running away from anxiety and depression: A female as well as male race. In M.L. Sachs & G.W. Buffone (Eds.), *Running as therapy: An integrated approach*. Lincoln: University of Nebraska Press.

BERGER, B.G. (1984b). Running away from anxiety and depression: Special considerations for the female client. In M.L. Sachs & G.W. Buffone (Eds.), *Running as therapy: An integrated approach*. Lincoln: University of Nebraska Press.

BERGER, S.M. (1962). Conditioning through vicarious instigation. *Psychological Review*, 69:450-466.

BERKOWITZ, L. (1954). Group standards, cohesiveness, and productivity. *Human Relations*, 7:509-519.

BERKOWITZ, L. (1956). Group norms among bomber crews: Patterns of perceived crew attitudes, "active" crew attitudes, and crew liking related to air crew effectiveness in Far Eastern combat. *Sociometry*, 19, 141-153.

BERKOWITZ, L. (1965). *Advances in experimental social psychology* (Vol.2). New York: Academic.

BERKOWITZ, L. (1970). Experimental investigations of hostility catharsis. *Journal of Consulting and Clinical Psychology*, 35:1-7.

BERNARD, J. (1968). *The sex game*. London: Leslie Frewin Press.

BERNARD, J. (1975). *Women, wives, mothers: Values and options*. Chicago: Aldine.

BERNSTEIN, F. (1973, March 16). *The New Yorker*, pp. 87-88.

BERRIDGE, H. (1935). An experiment in the psychology of competition. *Research Quarterly*, (Suppl.) 6:37-42.

BERRYMAN, J.W. (1982). The rise of highly organized sports for preadolescent boys. In R.A. Magill, M.J. Ash, & F.L. Smoll (Eds.), *Children in sport: A contemporary anthology* (2nd ed.). Champaign, IL: Human Kinetics.

BILLING, J.E. (1975). A taxonomy of sport forms. *National College Physical Education Association for Men Proceedings*, pp. 34-39.

BIRCH, D., & Veroff, J. (1966). *Motivation: A study of action*. Belmont, CA: Brooks/Cole.

BIRCH, J.S. (1980). *The relationship between aggression and performance outcome in professional ice hockey*. Unpublished master's thesis, University of Waterloo.

BIRD, A.M. (1977a). Team structure and success as related to cohesiveness and leadership. *Journal of Social Psychology*, 103:217-223.

BIRD, A.M. (1977b). Development of a model for predicting team performance. *Research Quarterly*, 48:24-32.

BIRD, A.M., & Williams, I.M. (1980). A developmental-attributional analysis of sex-role stereotypes for sport performance. *Developmental Psychology*, 16:312-322.

BISHOP, D.W., & Witt, P.A. (1970). Source of behavioral variance during leisure time. *Journal of Personality and Social Psychology*, 16:352-360.

BLACK, J. (1979). The brain according to Mandell. *The Runner*, 1:78-80, 82, 84, 87.

BLANCHARD, B. (1946). A comparative analysis of secondary-school boys' and girls' character and personality traits in physical education classes. *Research Quarterly*, 17:33-39.

BLOCK, J. (1978). *The Q-sort method in personality assessment and psychiatric research*. Palo Alto, CA: Consulting Psychologists Press. (Originally publ. 1961.)

BLUE, F.R. (1979). Aerobic running as a treatment for moderate depression. *Perceptual and Motor Skills*, 48:228.

BLUMENTHAL, J.A., Williams, R.S., Wallace, A.G., Williams, R.B., & Needles, T.L. (1982). Physiological and psychological variables predict compliance to prescribed exercise therapy in patients recovering from myocardial infarction. *Psychosomatic Medicine*, 44:519-527.

BOHM, D. (1981). On self deception in the individual, in groups, and in society as a whole. In H. Kellerman (Ed.), *Group cohesion: Theoretical and clinical perspectives*. New York: Grune & Stratton.

BONANNO, J.A., & Lies, J.E. (1974). Effects of physical training on coronary risk factors. *American Journal of Cardiology*, 33:760-764.

BORDEN, R.J. (1975). Witnessed aggression: Influence of an observer's sex and values on aggressive responding. *Journal of Personality and Social Psychology*, 31:567-573.

BORDEN, R.J. (1980). Audience influence. In P.B. Paulus (Ed.), *Psychology of group influence*. Hillsdale, NJ: Erlbaum.

BORKOVEC, T.D. (1976). Physiological and cognitive processes in the regulation of anxiety. In G.E. Schwartz & D. Shapiro (Eds.), *Consciousness and self-regulation: Advances in research*. New York: Plenum.

BOTTERILL, C. (1978). Psychology of coaching. *Coaching Review*, 1:46-55.

BOTTERILL, C. (1979). Goal setting with athletes. *Sports Science Periodical on Research and Technology in Sport*, BU-1:1-8.

BOTTERILL, C. (1980). Psychology of coaching. In R. Suinn (Ed.), *Psychology in sports: Methods and applications*. Minneapolis: Burgess.

BOULDING, K. (1969). The grants economy. *Michigan Academician*, 1 (winter):3-11.

BOULOUGOURIS, J.C., & Bassiakos, L. (1973). Case histories and shorter communications: Prolonged flooding in cases with obsessive-compulsive neurosis. *Behaviour Research and Therapy*, 11:227-231.

BOULOUGOURIS, J.C., & Marks, I.M. (1969). Implosion (flooding): A new treatment for phobias. *British Medical Journal*, 2:721-723.

BOULOUGOURIS, J.C., Marks, I.M., & Marset, P. (1971). Superiority of flooding (implosion) to desensitization for reducing pathological fear. *Behaviour Research and Therapy*, 9:7-16.

BOYCE, T.W., Jensen, E.W., Cassell, J.C., Collier, A.M., Smith, A.H., & Raimey, C.T. (1977). Influence of life events and family routines on childhood respiratory tract illness. *Pediatrics*, 60:609-615.

BRADLEY, G.W. (1978). Self-serving biases in the attribution process: A reexamination of the fact or fiction question. *Journal of Personality and Social Psychology*, 36:56-71.

BRAMEL, D. (1969). Interpersonal attraction, hostility, and perception. In J. Mills (Ed.), *Experimental social psychology*. New York: Macmillan.

BRAMWELL, S.T., Masuda, M., Wagner, N.N., & Holmes, T.H. (1975). Psychosocial factors in athletic injuries. *Journal of Human Stress*, 1:16-20.

BRAWLEY, L.R. (1980). *Children's causal attributions in a competitive sport: A motivational interpretation*. Unpublished doctoral dissertation, Pennsylvania State University.

BRAWLEY, L., Landers, D., Miller, L., & Kearnes, K. (1979). Sex bias in evaluating motor performance. *Journal of Sport Psychology*, 1:15-24.

BREDEMEIER, B.J. (1980). *The assessment of expressive and instrumental power value orientations in sport and in everyday life*. Paper presented at International Women and Sport Conference, Rome.

BREDEMEIER, B.J. (1983). *Athletic aggression: A moral concern*. In J. Goldstein (Ed.), Sports violence. New York: Springer-Verlag.

BREDEMEIER, B.J., & Shields, D.L. (1983). Body and balance: Developing moral structures through physical education. University of Oregon: Microform Publications.

BRICKMAN, P. (1977). Crime and punishment in sports and society. *Journal of Social Issues*, 33:140-164.

BRODEN, M., Hall, R.V., & Mitts, B. (1971). The effect of self-recording on the classroom behavior of two eighth-grade students. *Journal of Applied Behavior Analysis*, 4:191-199.

BROWN, B.R., & Garland, H. (1971). The effects of incompetency, audience acquaintanceship, and anticipated evaluative feedback on face-saving behavior. *Journal of Experimental Social Psychology*, 7:490-502.

BROWN, J.M. (1982). *Attitude towards violence and self reports of participation in contact sports*. Unpublished manuscript, Lafayette College.

BROWN, J.M., & Davies, N. (1978). Attitude towards violence among college athletes. *Journal of Sport Behavior*, 1:61-70.

BROWN, R.S., Ramirez, D.E., & Taub, J.M. (1978). The prescription of exercise for depression. *The Physician and Sportsmedicine*, 1:34-45.

BRUNER, J.S. (1957). Going beyond the information given. In J.A. Bruner, E. Brunswick, L. Festinger, F. Heider, K.F. Muenzinger, C.E. Osgood, & D. Rapaport (Eds.), *Contemporary approaches to cognition*. Cambridge: Harvard University Press.

BRUNNER, B.C. (1969). Personality and motivating factors influencing adult participation in vigorous physical activity. *Research Quarterly*, 40:464-469.

BRYAN, J.H. (1977). Prosocial behavior. In H.L. Ham (Ed.), *Psychological processes in early education*. New York: Academic.

BUCCOLA, V.A., & Stone, W.J. (1975). Effects of jogging and cycling programs on physiological and personality variables in aged men. *Research Quarterly*, 46:134-139.

BUDGE, S. (1981). Group cohesiveness reexamined. *Group*, 5:10-18.

BUFFONE, G.W. (1980). *Psychological changes associated with cognitive-behavioral therapy and an aerobic running program in the treatment of depression*. Unpublished doctoral dissertation, Florida State University.

BUFFONE, G.W. (1984a). Future directions: The potential of exercise as therapy. In M.L. Sachs & G.W. Buffone (Eds.), *Running as therapy: An integrated approach*. Lincoln: University of Nebraska Press.

BUFFONE, G.W. (1984b). Running and depression. In M.L. Sachs & G.W. Buffone (Eds.), *Running as therapy: An integrated approach*. Lincoln: University of Nebraska Press.

BUFFONE, G.W., Sachs, M.L., & Dowd, E.T. (1984). Cognitive-behavioral strategies for facilitating maintenance of exercise behavior. In M.L. Sachs & G.W. Buffone (Eds.), *Running as therapy: An integrated approach*. Lincoln: University of Nebraska Press.

BUKOWSKI, W.M., & Moore, D. (1980). Winners' and losers' attributions for success and failure in a series of athletic events. *Journal of Sport Psychology*, 2:195-210.

BURGESS, S.S. (1976). *Stimulus-seeking, extraversion, and neuroticism in regular, occasional, and non-exercisers*. Unpublished master's thesis, Florida State University.

BURTON, A.L. (1977). *Sources of hostility variance in sport situations*. Unpublished master's thesis, Ithaca College.

BUSS, A.H. (1961). *The psychology of aggression*. New York: Wiley.

BUSS, A.H. (1971). Aggression pays. In J.L. Singer (Ed.), *The control of aggression and violence*. New York: Academic.

BUTT, D.S. (1980). Some potentials of sport psychology: A reply to Alderman. In P. Klavora & K. Wipper (Eds.), *Psychological and sociological factors in sport*. Toronto: University of Toronto.

CALABRIA, P. (1980, Jan.26). New York's ornery fans. *The Sporting News*, 189(4):45.

CARRON, A.V. (1968). Motor performance under stress. *Research Quarterly*, 39:463-469.

CARRON, A.V. (1975). Personality and athletics: A review. In B.S. Rushall (Ed.), *The status of psychomotor learning and sport psychology research*. Dartmouth, N.S.: Sport Science Associates.

CARRON, A.V. (1980). *Social psychology of sport*. Ithaca, NY: Mouvement.

CARRON, A.V. (1982). Cohesiveness in sport groups: Interpretations and considerations. *Journal of Sport Psychology*, 4:123-138.

CARRON, A.V., & Ball, J.R. (1977). Cause-effect characteristics of cohesiveness and participation motivation in intercollegiate hockey. *International Review of Sport Sociology*, 12:49-60.

CARRON, A.V., & Bennett, B. (1976). The effects of initial habit strength differences upon performance in a coaction situation. *Journal of Motor Behavior*, 8:297-304.

CARRON, A.V., Brawley, L.R., & Widmeyer, W.N. (1982). *Cohesion, performance, and satisfaction in tennis dyads*. Paper presented at NASPSPA Conference, College Park, MD.

CARRON, A.V., & Chelladurai, P. (1978). Psychological factors and athletic success: An analysis of coach-athlete interpersonal behavior. *Canadian Journal of Applied Sport Sciences*, 3:43-50.

CARRON, A.V., & Chelladurai, P. (1981a). The dynamics of group cohesion in sport. *Journal of Sport Psychology*, 3:123-139.

CARRON, A.V., & Chelladurai, P. (1981b). Cohesiveness as a factor in sport performance. *International Review of Sport Sociology*, 16:21-41.

CARRON, A.V., & Chelladurai, P. (1982). *Cohesiveness, coach-athlete compatibility, participation orientation, and their relationship to relative performance and satisfaction.* Paper presented at NASPSPA Conference, College Park, MD.

CARSON, R.C. (1969). *Interaction concepts of personality.* Chicago: Aldine.

CARTWRIGHT, D. (1951). Achieving change in people: Some applications of group dynamic theory. *Human Relations*, 4:381-392.

CARTWRIGHT, D. (1968). The nature of group cohesiveness. In D. Cartwright & A. Zander (Eds.), *Group dynamics: Research and theory* (3rd ed.). New York: Harper & Row.

CARTWRIGHT, D., & Zander, A. (Eds.) (1968). *Group dynamics: Research and theory* (3rd ed.). New York: Harper & Row.

CARVER, C.S., Blaney, P.H., & Scheier, M.F. (1979a). Focus of attention, chronic expectancy, and responses to a feared stimulus. *Journal of Personality and Social Psychology*, 37:1186-1195.

CARVER, C.S., Blaney, P.H., & Scheier, M.F. (1979b). Reassertion and giving up: The interactive role of self-directed attention and outcome expectancy. *Journal of Personality and Social Psychology*, 37:1859-1871.

CARVER, C.S., & Scheier, M.F. (1981). *Attention and self-regulation: A control theory approach to human behavior.* New York: Springer-Verlag.

CARVER, C.S., & Scheier, M.F. (1982). Control theory: A useful conceptual framework for personality-social, clinical, and health psychology. *Psychological Bulletin*, 92:111-135.

CASE, R.W. (1980). *An examination of the leadership behaviors of selected successful basketball coaches at four competitive levels.* Unpublished doctoral dissertation, The Ohio State University.

CHELLADURAI, P. (1978). *A contingency model of leadership in athletics.* Unpublished doctoral dissertation, University of Waterloo.

CHELLADURAI, P. (1981). The coach as motivator and chameleon of leadership styles. *Sports Science Periodical on Research and Technology in Sport.* Ottawa: Coaching Association of Canada.

CHELLADURAI, P. (1984). Discrepancy between preferences and perceptions of leadership behavior and satisfaction of athletes in varying sports. *Journal of Sport Psychology* 6:27-41.

CHELLADURAI, P., & Arnott, M. (1983). *Decision styles in coaching: Preferences of basketball players.* Unpublished manuscript, University of Western Ontario.

CHELLADURAI, P., & Carron, A.V. (1978). *Leadership.* Ottawa: CAHPER (Monograph).

CHELLADURAI, P., & Carron, A.V. (1982). *Individual and task differences and preferred leadership.* Paper presented at NASPSPA Conference, College Park, MD.

CHELLADURAI, P., & Carron, A.V. (1983). Athletic maturity and preferred leadership. *Journal of Sport Psychology*, 5:371-380.

CHELLADURAI, P., & Haggerty, T.R. (1978). A normative model of decision styles in coaching. *Athletic Administration*, 13:6-9.

CHELLADURAI, P., & Saleh, S.D. (1978). Preferred leadership in sports. *Canadian Journal of Applied Sport Sciences*, 3:85-92.

CHELLADURAI, P., & Saleh, S.D. (1980). Dimensions of leader behavior in sports: Development of a leadership scale. *Journal of Sport Psychology*, 2:34-45.

COACHING Association of Canada. (1981). *National Coaching Certification Program, Level III Coaching Theory*. Ottawa: Author.

CODDINGTON, R.D. (1972). The significance of life events as etiologic factors in the diseases of children II: A study of a normal population. *Journal of Psychosomatic Research*, 16:204-213.

CODDINGTON, R.D., & Troxell, J.R. (1980). The effect of emotional factors on football injury rates: A pilot study. *Journal of Human Stress*, 6(4):2-5.

COHEN, J.L. (1980). Social facilitation: Audience versus evaluation apprehension. *Motivation and Emotion*, 4:21-34.

COHEN, J.L., & Davis, J.H. (1973). Effects of audience status, evaluation, and the time of action on hidden-word problems. *Journal of Personality and Social Psychology*, 27:74-85.

COLEMAN, J.S. (1961, Nov.). Athletics in high school. *Annals of the American Academy of Political and Social Science*, pp. 338-343.

COLLETTI, G., & Brownell, K.D. (1982). The physical and emotional benefits of social support: Application to obesity, smoking, and alcoholism. In M. Hersen, R.M. Eisler, & P.M. Miller (Eds.), *Progress in behavior modification* (Vol.13). New York: Academic.

COMREY, A.L. (1953). Group performance in a manual dexterity task. *Journal of Applied Psychology*, 37:207-210.

COMREY, A.L., & Deskin, G. (1954a). Further results on group manual dexterity in men. *Journal of Applied Psychology*, 38:116-118.

COMREY, A.L., & Deskin, G. (1954b). Group manual dexterity in women. *Journal of Applied Psychology*, 38:178-180.

COMREY, A.L., & Staats, C.K. (1955). Group performance in a cognitive task. *Journal of Applied Psychology*, 39:354-356.

CONDRY, J. (1977). Enemies of exploration: Self-initiated versus other-initiated learning. *Journal of Personality and Social Psychology*, 35:459-477.

COOPER, K.G. (1968). *Aerobics*. New York: Bantam Books.

COOPERSMITH, S. (1967). *The antecedents of self-esteem*. San Francisco: Freeman.

COPPEL, D.B. (1979). *Children's reactions to recreational versus competitive emphases in youth sport programs*. Paper presented at Western Psychological Association meeting, San Diego.

CORBIN, C.B. (1967). Effects of mental practice on skill development after controlled practice. *Research Quarterly*, 38:534-538.

CORBIN, C.B. (1972). Mental practice. In W.P. Morgan (Ed.), *Ergogenic aids and muscular performance*. New York: Academic.

CORBIN, C.B., & Nix, C. (1979). Sex-typing of physical activities and success predictions of children before and after cross-sex competition. *Journal of Sport Psychology*, 1:43-52.

CORY, A. (1968). *Effects of success and failure on projected aggression during an individual competitive sport*. Unpublished master's thesis, University of Maryland.

COTTRELL, N.B. (1968). Performance in the presence of other human beings: Mere presence audience and affiliation effects. In E.C. Simmel, R.A. Hoppe, & G.A. Milton (Eds.), *Social facilitation and imitative behavior*. Boston: Allyn & Bacon.

COTTRELL, N.B. (1972). Social facilitation. In C.G. McClintock (Ed.), *Experimental social psychology*. New York: Holt, Rinehart & Winston.

COTTRELL, N.B., Wack, D.L., Sekerak, G.J., & Rittle, R.H. (1968). Social facilitation of dominant responses by the presence of an audience and the mere presence of others. *Journal of Personality and Social Psychology*, 9:245-250.

CRABBE, J.M. (1971). *Social facilitation effects on children during early stages of motor learning*. Unpublished doctoral dissertation, University of Iowa.

CRAIGHEAD, W.E., Kazdin, A.E., & Mahoney, M.J. (1976). *Behavior modification: Principles, issues and applications*. Boston: Houghton-Mifflin.

CRATTY, B.J. (1964). *Movement behavior and motor learning*. Philadelphia: Lea & Febiger.

CRATTY, B.J. (1967). *Psychology and physical activity*. Englewood Cliffs, NJ: Prentice-Hall.

CRATTY, B.J. (1973). *Psychology in contemporary sport*. Englewood Cliffs, NJ: Prentice-Hall.

CRATTY, B.J., (1981). *Social psychology in athletics*. Englewood Cliffs, NJ: Prentice-Hall.

CRAWFORD, M.M. (1957). *Critical incidents in intercollegiate athletics and derived standards for professional ethics*. Unpublished EdD dissertation, University of Texas.

CREEL, J. (1980). Objectives for winning. *Athletic Journal*, 60:42, 64.

CRIDDLE, W.D. (1971). The physical presence of other individuals as a factor in social facilitation. *Psychonomic Science*, 22:229-230.

CROWNE, D., & Marlowe, D. (1964). *The approval motive*. New York: Wiley.

CSIKSZENTMIHALYI, M. (1975). *Beyond boredom and anxiety*. San Francisco: Jossey-Bass.

CSIKSZENTMIHALYI, M. (1977). Play and intrinsic rewards. *Journal of Humanistic Psychology*, 15:41-63.

CULLEN, J.B., & Cullen, F.T. (1975). The structural and contextual conditions of group norm violation: Some implications from the game of ice hockey. *International Review of Sport Sociology*, 10:69-78.

CUMMINS, R.A. (1914). A study of the effect of basketball practice on motor reaction attention and suggestibility. *Psychological Review*, 21:356-369.

CZARNECKI, L.R. (1977). *Sources of anxiety variance in sport situations*. Unpublished master's thesis, Ithaca College.

DANIELS, F.S., & Landers, D.M. (1981). Biofeedback and shooting performance: A test of disregulation and systems theory. *Journal of Sport Psychology*, 3:271-282.

DANIELSON, R.R. (1978). Contingency model of leadership effectiveness: An empirical investigation of its application in sport. In F. Landry & W.A.R. Orban (Eds.), *Motor learning, sport psychology, pedagogy, and didactics of physical activity, Book 7*. Miami, FL: Symposia Specialists.

DANIELSON, R.R., & Wanzel, R.S. (1978). Exercise objectives of fitness program dropouts. In D.M. Landers & R.W. Christina (Eds.), *Psychology of motor behavior and sport — 1977*. Champaign, IL: Human Kinetics.

DANISH, S.J., & Hale, B.D. (1981). Toward an understanding of the practice of sport psychology. *Journal of Sport Psychology*, 3:90-99.

DASHIELL, J.F. (1935). Experimental studies of the influence of social situations on the behavior of individual human adults. In C. Murchison (Ed.), *A handbook of social psychology*. Worcester, MA: Clark University Press.

DAVIDSON, R.J., & Schwartz, G.E. (1976). The psychobiology of relaxation and related stress states. In D.I. Mostofsky (Ed.), *Behavior control and modification of physiological activity*. Englewood Cliffs, NJ: Prentice-Hall.

DAVIS, E.C., & Lawther, J.D. (1941). *Successful teaching in physical education*. New York: Prentice-Hall.

DAVIS, J.H., & Restle, F. (1963). The analysis of problems and prediction of group problem solving. *Journal of Abnormal and Social Psychology*, 66:103-116.

DAVIS, K. (1963). Case for participative management. *Business Horizons*, Graduate School of Business, Indiana University.

DAVISON, G.C., & Valins, S. (1969). Maintenance of self-attributed and drug-attributed behavior change. *Journal of Personality and Social Psychology*, 11:25-33.

DAWLEY, D.J., Troyer, M.E., & Shaw, J.H. (1951). Relationship between observed behavior in elementary school physical education and test responses. *Research Quarterly*, 22:71-76.

deCHARMS, R. (1968). *Personal causation*. New York: Academic.

deCHARMS, R. (1976). *Enhancing motivation: Change in the classroom*. New York: Irvington.

DECI, E.L. (1971). Effects of externally mediated rewards on intrinsic motivation. *Journal of Personality and Social Psychology*, 18:105-115.

DECI, E.L. (1972a). The effects of contingent and noncontingent rewards and controls on intrinsic motivation. *Organizational Behavior and Human Performance*, 8:217-229.

DECI, E.L. (1972b). Intrinsic motivation, extrinsic reinforcement, and inequity. *Journal of Personality and Social Psychology*, 22:113-120.

DECI, E.L. (1975). *Intrinsic motivation*. New York: Plenum.

DECI, E.L., Betley, G., Kahle, J., & Abrams, L. (1977). *When trying to win: Competition, rewards, sex and intrinsic motivation*. Unpublished manuscript, University of Rochester.

DECI, E.L., Casio, W.F., & Krusell, J. (1975). Cognitive evaluation theory and some comments on the Calder-Staw critique. *Journal of Personality and Social Psychology*, 31:81-85.

DESHAIES, P., Pargman, D. & Thiffault, C. (1979). A psychobiological profile of individual performance in junior hockey players. In G.C. Roberts & K.M. Newell (Eds.), *Psychology of motor behavior and sport—1978*. Champaign, IL: Human Kinetics.

DEUTSCH, M., & Krauss, R.M. (1962). Studies of interpersonal bargaining. *Journal of Conflict Resolution*, 6:52-76.

DEVEREUX, E.C. (1976). Backyard versus Little League baseball: The impoverishment of children's games. In D.M. Landers (Ed.), *Social problems in athletics*. Urbana: University of Illinois Press.

deVRIES, H.A. (1968). Immediate and long term effects of exercise upon resting muscle potential. *Journal of Sports Medicine and Physical Fitness*, 8:1-11.

deVRIES, H.A., & Adams, G.M. (1972). Electromyographic comparison of single doses of exercise and meprobomate as to effects on muscular relaxation. *American Journal of Physical Medicine*, 51:130-141.

DICKERSON, D.D. (1978). *Mind/body unity: An interactional study of the psychological effects of physiological change*. Unpublished doctoral dissertation, California School of Professional Psychology.

DIENER, E., & Wallbom, M. (1976). Effects of self-awareness on antinormative behavior. *Journal of Research in Personality*, 10:107-111.

DIENSTBIER, R.A. (1984). The impact of exercise on personality. In M.L. Sachs & G.W. Buffone (Eds.), *Running as therapy: An integrated approach.* Lincoln: University of Nebraska Press.

DIENSTBIER, R.A., Crabbe, J., Johnson, G.O., Thorland, W., Jorgensen, J.A., Sadar, M.M., & LaVelle, D.C. (1981). Exercise and stress tolerance. In M.H. Sacks & M.L. Sachs (Eds.), Psychology of running. Champaign, IL: Human Kinetics.

DISHMAN, R.K. (1979). Biological and behavioral influences on exercise adherence. *Medicine and Science in Sports*, 11:80.

DISHMAN, R.K. (1981a). Biologic influences on exercise adherence. *Research Quarterly for Exercise and Sport*, 52:143-159.

DISHMAN, R.K. (1982b). Contemporary sport psychology. In R.L. Terjung (Ed.), *Exercise and Sport Science Reviews*, 10:120-159.

DISHMAN, R.K. (1982c). Psychobiologic predictors of exercise behavior. In J.T. Partington, T. Orlick, & J.H. Salmela (Eds.), *Sport in perspective*. Ottawa: Coaching Association of Canada.

DISHMAN, R.K. (1983). Predicting exercise compliance using psychometric and behavioral measures of commitment. *Medicine and Science in Sports and Exercise* (abstract), 15(2):118.

DISHMAN, R.K. (in press a). Exercise adherence and dependence. In W.P. Morgan & S.E. Goldston (Eds.), *Coping with mental stress: The potential and limits of exercise intervention.* Rockville, MD: National Institute of Mental Health.

DISHMAN, R.K. (in press b). Exercise and sport psychology in behavioral medicine. *Medical Clinics of North America.*

DISHMAN, R.K., & Gettman, L.R. (1980). Psychobiologic influences on exercise adherence. *Journal of Sport Psychology*, 2:295-310.

DISHMAN, R.K., & Ickes, W. (1981). Self-motivation and adherence to therapeutic exercise. *Journal of Behavioral Medicine*, 4:421-438.

DISHMAN, R.K., Ickes, W., & Morgan, W.P. (1980). Self-motivation and adherence to habitual physical activity. *Journal of Applied Social Psychology*, 10:115-132.

DOLLARD, J., Doob, J., Miller, N., Mowrer, O., & Sears, R. (1939). *Frustration and aggression*, New Haven: Yale University Press.

DISHMAN, R.K., Ickes, W., & Morgan, W.P. (1980). Self-motivation and adherence to habitual physical activity. *Journal of Applied Social Psychology*, 10:115-132.

DOLLARD, J., Doob, J., Miller, N., Mowrer, A., & Sears, R. (1939). *Frustration and aggression*, New Haven: Yale University Press.

DONAHUE, J.A., Gillis, J.H., & King, K. (1980). Behavior modification in sport and physical education. *Journal of Sport Psychology*, 2:311-328.

DONNELLY, P., Carron, A.V., & Chelladurai, P. (1978). *Group cohesion and sport.* Ottawa: CAHPER Sociology of Sport Monograph Series.

DRISCOLL, R. (1976). Anxiety reduction using physical exertion and positive images. *Psychological Record*, 26:87-94.

DUDA, J.L. (1981). *A cross-cultural analysis of achievement motivation in sport and the classroom.* Unpublished doctoral dissertation, University of Illinois.

DUFFY, E. (1962). *Activation and behavior.* New York: Wiley.

DUQUIN, M. (1978). The androgynous advantage. In C.A. Oglesby (Ed.), *Women and sport: From myth to reality.* Philadelphia: Lea & Febiger.

DUQUIN, M. (1980). *A review of psycho-social sex differences affecting the learning and development of motor skills.* Paper presented at National NASPSPA Convention, Boulder, CO.

DURDEN-SMITH, J. (1978). A chemical cure for madness. *Quest,* 2:31-36, 38.

DUSEK, J.B. (1980). The development of test anxiety in children. In I.G. Sarason (Ed.), *Test anxiety: Theory, research, and applications.* Hillsdale, NJ: Erlbaum.

DUVAL, S., & Friedan, G. (1979). *Objective self-awareness, task complexity, and performance.* Unpublished manuscript, University of Southern California.

DUVAL, S., & Wicklund, R.A. (1972). *A theory of objective self-awareness.* New York: Academic.

DWECK, C.G. (1975). The role of expectations and attributions in the alleviation of learned helplessness. *Journal of Personality and Social Psychology,* 31:674-685.

EASTERBROOK, J.A. (1959). The effect of emotion on cue utilization and the organization of behavior. *Psychological Review,* 66:183-201.

EASTWOOD, J.M. (1974). The effects of viewing a film of professional hockey on aggression. *Medicine and Science in Sports,* 6:158-163.

EIFERMAN, R.R. (1971). Social play in childhood. In R. Herron & B. Sutton-Smith (Eds.), *Child's play.* New York: Wiley.

ELIG, T.W., & Frieze, I.H. (1979). Measuring causal attributions for success and failure. *Journal of Personality and Social Psychology,* 37:621-634.

ELLIOTT, R. (1964). Physiological activity and performance: A comparison of kindergarten children with young adults. *Psychological Monographs,* 78 (10, Whole No.587).

ELLIS, A. (1962). *Reason and emotion in psychotherapy.* New York: Lyle Stuart.

ELLIS, A., & Grieger, R. (1977). *Handbook of rational emotive therapy.* New York: Springer.

EMERSON, R. (1966). Mount Everest: A case study of communication feedback and sustained goal striving. *Sociometry,* 29:213-227.

ENDLER, N.S., & Hunt, J.M. (1966). Sources of behavioral variance as measured by the S-R Inventory of Anxiousness. *Psychological Bulletin,* 65:338-346.

ENDLER, N.S., & Hunt, J.M. (1968). Inventories of hostility and comparisons of the proportions of variance from persons, responses, and situations for hostility and anxiousness. *Journal of Personality and Social Psychology,* 9:309-315.

ENDLER, N.S., Hunt, J.M., & Rosenstein, A.J. (1962). An S-R inventory of anxiousness. *Psychological Monographs,* 76 (17, Whole No.536).

ENDLER, N.S., & Magnusson, D. (Eds.). (1976). *Interactional psychology and personality.* Washington: Hemisphere.

ENDLER, N.S., & Okada, M. (1975). A multidimensional measure of trait anxiety: The S-R inventory of general trait anxiousness. *Journal of Consulting and Clinical Psychology,* 43:319-329.

ENOCH, J.R., & McLemore, S.D. (1967). On the meaning of group cohesion. *Southwestern Social Science Quarterly,* 48:174-182.

EPSTEIN, M.L. (1980). The relationship of mental imagery and mental rehearsal to performance of a motor task. *Journal of Sport Psychology,* 2:211-220.

ERLE, F.J. (1981). *Leadership in competitive and recreational sport.* Unpublished master's thesis, University of Western Ontario.

ERON, L.B., Walder, L.O., & Lefkowitz, M.M. (1971). *Learning of aggression in children*. Boston: Little, Brown & Co.

EWING, M.E. (1981). *Achievement orientations and sport behavior of males and females*. Doctoral dissertation, University of Illinois.

FALBO, T., & Beck, R.C. (1979). Naive psychology and the attributional model of achievement. *Journal of Personality*, 47:185-195.

FALLS, H., Baylor, A., & Dishman, R.K. (1980). *Essentials of fitness*. Philadelphia: Saunders.

FALLS, J., & Surface, W. (1976, Dec.26). War in the grandstand. *Parade Magazine*, pp. 7-11.

FAULKNER, R.R. (1974). Making violence by doing work: Selves, situations and the world of professional hockey. *Sociology of Work and Occupations*, 1:288-312.

FEATHER, N.T. (1966). Effects of prior success and failure on expectations of success and subsequent performance. *Journal of Personality and Social Psychology*, 3:287-298.

FEATHER, N.T., & Saville, M.R. (1967). Effects of amount of prior success and failure on expectations of success and subsequent task performance. *Journal of Personality and Social Psychology*, 5:226-232.

FELSHIN, J. (1974). The triple option . . . For women in sport. *Quest*, 21:36-40.

FELTZ, D.L. (1981). Graduate sport psychology: Looking back and to the future. *The Sport Psychologist*, 2(6).

FELTZ, D.L., Gould, D., Horn, T.S., & Perlichkoff, L. (1982). *Perceived competence among youth sport participants and dropouts*. Paper presented at NASPSPA Conference, College Park, MD.

FELTZ, D.L., & Landers, D.M. (1983). The effects of mental practice on motor skill learning and performance: A meta-analysis. *Journal of Sport Psychology*, 5:25-57.

FENICHEL, O. (1954). *Collected papers of Otto Fenichel* (1st ed.). New York: Norton.

FENZ, W.D., & Epstein, S. (1967). Gradients of physiological arousal of experienced and novice parachutists as a function of an approaching jump. *Psychosomatic Medicine*, 29:33-51.

FENZ, W.D., & Jones, G.B. (1972). Individual differences in physiological arousal and performance in sport parachutists. *Psychosomatic Medicine*, 34:1-8.

FESHBACH, S. (1955). The drive-reducing function of fantasy behavior. *Journal of Abnormal and Social Psychology*, 50:3-11.

FESHBACH, S., & Singer, R. (1971). *Television and aggression*. Philadelphia: Jossey-Bass.

FESTINGER, L. (1950). Informal social communication. *Psychological Review*, 57:271-282.

FESTINGER, L., Schachter, S., & Back, K. (1950). *Social pressures in informal groups*. New York: Harper.

FIEDLER, F.E. (1967). *A theory of leadership effectiveness*. New York: McGraw-Hill.

FISHBEIN, M., & Ajzen, I. (1973). Attribution of responsibility: A theoretical note. *Journal of Experimental and Social Psychology*, 9:148-153.

FISHBEIN, M., & Ajzen, I. (1975). *Belief, attitude, intention and behavior: An introduction to theory and research*. Reading, MA: Addison-Wesley.

FISHER, A.C. (1972). Sport as an agent of masculine orientation. *The Physical Educator*, 29:120.

FISHER, A.C. (1976). *Psychology of sport: Issues and insights.* Palo Alto, CA: Mayfield.

FISHER, A.C. (1977). Sport personality assessment: Fact, fiction and methodological re-examination. In R.E. Stadulis (Ed.), *Research and practice in physical education.* Champaign, IL: Human Kinetics.

FISHER, A.C. (1979). Multidimensional scaling of sport personality data: An individual differences approach. *Journal of Sport Psychology,* 1:76-86.

FISHER, A.C., Borowicz, S.K., & Morris, H.H. (1978). Behavioral rigidity across sport situations. In D.M. Landers & R.W. Christina (Eds.), *Psychology of motor behavior and sport—1977.* Champaign, IL: Human Kinetics.

FISHER, A.C., Horsfall, J.S., & Morris, H.H. (1977). Sport personality assessment: A methodological re-examination. *International Journal of Sport Psychology,* 8:92-102.

FISHER, A.C., & Zwart, E.F. (1982). Psychological analysis of athletes' anxiety responses. *Journal of Sport Psychology,* 4:139-158.

FITZ, G.W. (1895). A local reaction. *Psychological Review,* 2:37-42.

FIXX, J.G. (1977). *The complete book of running.* New York: Random House.

FLOOD, M., & Endler, N.S. (1980). The interaction model of anxiety: An empirical test in an athletic competition situation. *Journal of Research in Personality,* 14:329-339.

FLORY, C. (1958). *Sportsmanship attitudes of college students toward situations in competitive athletics.* Unpublished EdD dissertation, University of Texas.

FOA, U.G., Mitchell, T.R., & Fiedler, F.E. (1971). Differentiation matching. *Behavioral Science,* 16:130-142.

FOLKINS, C.H., & Sime, W.E. (1981). Physical fitness training and mental health. *American Psychologist,* 36:373-389.

FOOT, H.C., & Lee, T.R. (1970). Social feedback in the learning of a motor skill. *British Journal of Social and Clinical Psychology,* 9:309-319.

FOREYT, J.P., & Rathjen, D.P. (1978). *Cognitive behavior therapy.* New York: Plenum.

FORGAS, J.P., Brennan, G., Howe, S., Kane, J.F., & Sweet, S. (1980). Audience effects on squash players' performance. *Journal of Social Psychology,* 11:41-47.

FORSYTH, D.R. (1980). The functions of attributions. *Social Psychology Quarterly,* 43:184-189.

FRALEIGH, W. (1979). *Definition of a good sport contest.* Unpublished manuscript, SUNY at Brockport.

FREUD, S. (1900). *The interpretation of dreams.* In standard edition, Vols. 4 & 5, London: Hogarth Press, 1953. (First German ed. 1900)

FREUD, S. (1901). *The psychopathology of everyday life.* In standard edition, Vol. 6, London: Hogarth Press, 1960. (First German ed. 1901)

FREUD, S. (1917). *Introductory lectures on psycho-analysis.* In standard edition, Vols.15 & 16, London: Hogarth Press, 1963. (First German ed. 1917)

FREUD, S. (1925). Some psychical consequences of the anatomical distinction between the sexes. In J. Strachey (Ed.), *The standard edition of the complete psychological works of Sigmund Freud* (Vol. 19). London: Hogarth Press, 1961. (Originally publ. 1925)

FREUD, S. (1949). *Outline of psychoanalysis.* New York: Norton.

FRY, D.A.P., McClements, J.D., & Sefton, J.M. (1981). *A report on participation in the Saskatoon Hockey Association.* Saskatoon, Canada: SASK Sport.

FRY, L.W., Kerr, S., & Lee, C. (1983). *An extension and test of path goal leadership theory, using athletic teams as research samples.* Paper presented at Academy of Management annual meeting, Dallas.

GAINTER, G. (1976). *Athletes' and coaches' expectations of coaches.* Unpublished doctoral dissertation, Arizona State University.

GALE, J.B., Eckhoff, W.T., Mogel, S.F., & Rodnick, J.E. (in press). Factors related to adherence to an exercise program for healthy adults. *Medicine and Science in Sports and Exercise.*

GANZER, V.J. (1968). The effects of audience presence and test anxiety on learning and retention in a serial learning situation. *Journal of Personality and Social Psychology,* 8:194-199.

GEEN, R.G. (1980). The effects of being observed on performance. In P.B. Paulus (Ed.), *Psychology of group influence.* Hillsdale, NJ: Erlbaum.

GEEN, R.G., & Gange, J.G. (1977). Drive theory of social facilitation: Twelve years of theory and research. *Psychological Bulletin,* 84:1267-1288.

GENOV, F. (1970). The nature of mobilization readiness of the sportsman and the influence of different factors upon its formation. In G.S. Kenyon (Ed.), *Contemporary psychology of sport.* Chicago: Athletic Institute.

GERBER, E. (1973). *The unimportance of sex role identification of why all roses are roses.* 49th Annual Conference of the Western Society for Physical Education for College Women, Salem, OR.

GIBBARD, G.S., Hartman, J.J., & Mann, R.D. (Eds.) (1974). *Analysis of groups.* San Francisco: Jossey-Bass.

GILBERT, M. (1977). *An empirical evaluation of Fiedler's contingency model of leadership.* Unpublished doctoral dissertation, Universite du Quebec a Trois-Rivieres.

GILL, D.L. (1977). Cohesiveness and performance in sport groups. In R.S. Hutton (Ed.), *Exercise and Sport Science Reviews,* 5:131-155.

GILL, D.L. (1979). The prediction of group motor performance from individual member abilities. *Journal of Motor Behavior,* 11:113-122.

GILL, D.L., & Gross, J.B. (1979). The influence of group success-failure on selected interpersonal variables. In G.C. Roberts & K.M. Newell (Eds.), *Psychology of motor behavior and sport — 1978.* Champaign, IL: Human Kinetics.

GILL, D.L., Gross, J.B., & Huddleston, S. (1981). Participation motivation in youth sports. In G.C. Roberts & D.M. Landers (Eds.), *Psychology of motor behavior and sport — 1980.* Champaign, IL: Human Kinetics.

GILL, D.L., & Martens, R. (1977). The role of task type and success-failure in group competition. *International Journal of Sport Psychology,* 8:160-177.

GILLIGAN, C. (1977). In a different voice: Women's conceptions of self and morality. *Harvard Educational Review,* 47:481-517.

GILLIGAN, C. (1982a). *In a different voice: Psychological theory and women's development.* Cambridge: Harvard University Press.

GILLIGAN, C. (1982b). Why should a woman be more like a man? *Psychology Today,* 16:68-77.

GIRODO, M. (1974). Yoga meditation and flooding in the treatment of anxiety neurosis. *Journal of Behavior Therapy and Experimental Psychiatry,* 5:157-160.

GLASS, G.V. (1977). Integrating findings: The meta-analysis of research. *Review of Research in Education,* 5:351-379.

GLASSER, W. (1976). *Positive addiction*. New York: Harper & Row.

GLASSER, W. (1978, March). The positive addiction experiment. *Starting Line*, 2:2.

GLEITMAN, H. (1981). *Psychology*. New York: Norton.

GLOVER, B., & Shephard, J. (1977). *The runner's handbook*. New York: Penguin Books.

GOLD, A.R., Brush, L.E., & Sprotzer, E.R. (1979). *The importance of a neutral category in research in sex stereotypes*. Paper presented at Society for Research in Child Development, San Francisco.

GOLDFRIED, M.R. (1971). Systematic desensitization as training in self-control. *Journal of Consulting and Clinical Psychology*, 37:228-234.

GOLDFRIED, M.R., & Davison, G.C. (1976). *Clinical behavior therapy*. New York: Holt, Rinehart & Winston.

GOLDFRIED, M.R., & Goldfried, A.P. (1980). Cognitive change methods. In F. Kanfer & A. Goldstein (Eds.), *Helping people change* (2nd ed.). Elmsford, NY: Pergamon.

GOLDFRIED, M.R., Linehan, M.M., & Smith, J.L. (1978). The reduction of test anxiety through rational restructuring. *Journal of Consulting and Clinical Psychology*, 46:32-39.

GOLDSTEIN, J., & Arms, R. (1971). Effects of observing athletic contests on hostility. *Sociometry*, 54:83-91.

GORE, W.V., & Taylor, D.A. (1973). The nature of the audience as it affects social inhibition. *Representative Research in Social Psychology*, 4:18-27.

GORNEY, R. (1972). *The human agenda*. New York: Simon & Schuster.

GOSSET, D.M., & Widmeyer, W.N. (1981). Improving cohesion's prediction of performance outcome in sports. *Psychology of motor behavior and sport — 1981: Abstracts*. Monterey, CA: NASPSPA.

GOTTMAN, J.M., & McFall, R.M. (1972). Self-monitoring effects in a program for potential high school dropouts: A time series analysis. *Journal of Consulting and Clinical Psychology*, 39:273-281.

GOULD, D. (1976). *The history of American sport psychology*. Unpublished manuscript, University of Illinois.

GOULD, D. (1980). *Motivating young athletes*. East Lansing, MI: Youth Sports Institute.

GOULD, D. (1982a). Sport psychology in the 1980's: Status, direction and challenge in youth sports research. *Journal of Sport Psychology*, 4:203-218.

GOULD, D. (1982b). Fostering psychological development in young athletes: A reaction. In T. Orlick, J.T. Partington, & J.H. Salmela (Eds.), *Mental training for coaches and athletes*. Ottawa: Coaching Association of Canada.

GOULD, D. (1984). Psychosocial development and children's sports. In J.R. Thomas (Ed.), *Motor development during preschool and elementary years*. Minneapolis: Burgess.

GOULD, D., Feltz, D., Horn, T., & Weiss, M. (1982). Reasons for discontinuing involvement in competitive youth swimming. *Journal of Sport Behavior*, 5:155-165.

GOULD, D., Feltz, D.L., Weiss, M., & Petlichkoff, L. (1982). Participation motives in competitive youth swimmers. In T. Orlick, J.T. Partington, & J.H. Salmela (Eds.), *Mental training for coaches and athletes*. Ottawa: Coaching Association of Canada.

GOULD, D., Horn, T., & Spreemann, J. (1983a). Perceived anxiety of elite junior wrestlers. *Journal of Sport Psychology*, 5:58-71.

GOULD, D., Horn, T., & Spreemann, J. (1983b). Sources of stress in junior elite wrestlers. *Journal of Sport Psychology*, 5:159-171.

GOULD, D., Weinberg, R.S., & Jackson, A. (1980). Effect of mental preparation strategies on a muscular endurance task. *Journal of Sport Psychology*, 2:329-339.

GOULD, D., Weiss, M., & Weinberg, R.S. (1981). Psychological characteristics of successful and nonsuccessful Big Ten wrestlers. *Journal of Sport Psychology*, 3:69-81.

GOWAN, G.R., Botterill, C.B., & Blimkie, C.J.R. (1979). Bridging the gap between sport science and sport practice. In P. Klavora & J.V. Daniel (Eds.), *Coach, athlete, and the sport psychologist*. Toronto: University of Toronto.

GRAND, R., & Carron, A.V. (1982). *The relationship of task and social cohesion to role clarity, role acceptance and role performance*. Unpublished manuscript, University of Western Ontario.

GRAVEL, R., Lemieux, G., & Ladouceur, R. (1980). Effectiveness of a cognitive behavioral treatment package for cross-country ski racers. *Cognitive Therapy and Research*, 4:83-89.

GREENE, D., & Lepper, M.R. (1974). Effects of extrinsic rewards on children's subsequent intrinsic interest. *Child Development*, 45:1141-1145.

GREIST, J.H., Klein, M.H., Eischens, R.R., & Faris, J.T. (1978). Running out of depression. *The Physician and Sportsmedicine*, 6:49-56.

GREIST, J.H., Klein, M.H., Eischens, R.R., Faris, J., Gurman, A.S., & Morgan, W.P. (1978). Running through your mind. *Journal of Psychosomatic Research*, 22:259-294.

GREIST, J.H., Klein, M.H., Eischens, R.R., Faris, J., Gurman, A.S., & Morgan, W.P. (1979). Running as treatment for depression. *Comprehensive Psychiatry*, 20:41-54.

GRIFFIN, L.E. (1978). *Why children participate in youth sports*. Paper presented at AAHPER Conference, Kansas City, MO.

GRIFFIN, M.R. (1972). An analysis of state and trait anxiety experienced in sports competition at different age levels. *Foil* (spring), pp.58-64.

GRIFFITH, C.R. (1926). *Psychology of coaching*. New York: Scribners.

GRIFFITH, C.R. (1928). *Psychology of athletics*. New York: Scribners.

GRIFFITHS, T.J., Steel, D.H., & Vaccaro, P. (1982). Anxiety of scuba divers: A multidimensional approach. *Perceptual and Motor Skills*, 55:611-614.

GROSS, J.B. (1982). *Effects of knowledge of results upon individual performance on a motor task under alone and group situations*. Unpublished doctoral dissertation, University of Iowa.

GROSS, N., & Martin, W. (1952). On group cohesiveness. *American Journal of Sociology*, 57:533-546.

GRUSH, J.E. (1978). Audiences can inhibit or facilitate competitive behavior. *Personality and Social Psychology Bulletin*, 4:119-122.

GUTIN, B. (1973). Exercise induced activation and human performance: A review. *Research Quarterly*, 44:256-268.

GUTMANN, M., Squires, R., Pollock, M., Foster, C., & Anholm, J. (1981). Perceived exertion-heartrate relationship during exercise testing and training in cardiac patients. *Journal of Cardiac Rehabilitation*, 1:52-59.

HAAN, N. (1977). *Coping and defending: Processes of self-environment organization*. San Francisco: Academic.

HAAN, N. (1978). Two moralities in action contexts: Relationship to thought, ego regulation, and development. *Journal of Personality and Social Psychology*, 36:286-305.

HAAN, N., Smith, B., & Block, J. (1968). Moral reasoning of young adults: Political-social behavior, family background and personality correlates. *Journal of Personality and Social Psychology*, 10:183-201.

HAAS, J. & Roberts, G.C. (1975). Effect of evaluative others upon learning and performance of a complex motor task. *Journal of Motor Behavior*, 7:81-90.

HACKER, C.M., & Williams, J.M. (1981). Cohesion, satisfaction, and performance in intercollegiate field hockey. *Psychology of motor behavior and sport—1981: Abstracts*. Monterey, CA: NASPSPA.

HALL, E.G., & Erffmeyer, E.S. (1983). The effect of visuo-motor behavior rehearsal with videotaped modeling on free throw accuracy of intercollegiate female basketball players. *Journal of Sport Psychology*, 5:343-346.

HALL, G.S. (1908). *Physical education in colleges: Report of the National Education Association*. Chicago: University of Chicago Press.

HALL, M.A. (1980). *Sport, sex roles and sex identity*. Paper presented at North American Society for the Sociology of Sport, Denver.

HALL, S.M. (1980). Self-management and therapeutic maintenance: Theory and research. In P. Karoly & J.J. Steffen (Eds.), *Improving the long-term effects of psychotherapy: Models of durable outcome*. New York: Gardner.

HALLIWELL, W. (1978). Intrinsic motivation in sport. In W.F. Straub (Ed.), *Sport psychology: An analysis of athlete behavior*. Ithaca, NY: Mouvement.

HALLIWELL, W. (1979). Strategies for enhancing motivation in sport. In P. Klavora & J. Daniel (Eds.), *Coach, athlete and the sport psychologist*. Toronto: University of Toronto.

HAMBURG, D.A. (1983). Frontiers of research in neurobiology. *Science*, 222. (Editorial)

HANSON, D.L. (1967). Cardiac response to participation in Little League baseball competition as determined by telemetry. *Research Quarterly*, 38:384-388.

HANSON, M.G. (1977). *Coronary heart disease, exercise and motivation in middle aged males*. (Doctoral dissertation, University of Wisconsin, Madison, 1976) DAI, 37, 2755B.

HARDMAN, K. (1968). *The personality differences between top class game players and players of lesser ability*. Unpublished master's thesis, University of Manchester.

HARDMAN, K. (1973). A dual approach to the study of personality and performance in sport. In H.T.A. Whiting, K. Hardman, L. Hendry, & M. Jones (Eds.), *Personality and performance in physical education and sport*. London: Kimpton.

HARKINS, S.G., Latane, B., & Williams, K.D. (1980). Social loafing: Allocational effort or taking it easy? *Journal of Experimental Social Psychology*, 16:457-465.

HARMON, J.M., & Johnson, W.R. (1952). The emotional reactions of college athletes. *Research Quarterly*, 23:391-397.

HARPER, F.D. (1978). Outcomes of jogging: Implications for counseling. *Personnel and Guidance Journal*, 57:74-78.

HARRIS, D.V. (1977). A short history of the North American Society for the Psychology of Sport and Physical Activity. In K. Fiege (Ed.), *The development of sport psychology*. Kiel: Bisp.

HARRIS, D.V. (1978, Jan.). The happy addict. *womenSports*, 5:53.

HARRIS, M.B. (1981a). Runners' perceptions of the benefits of running. *Perceptual and Motor Skills*, 52:153-154.

HARRIS, M.B. (1981b). Women runners' views of running. *Perceptual and Motor Skills*, 53:395-402.

HARTER, S. (1978). Effectance motivation reconsidered: Toward a developmental model. *Human Development*, 21:34-64.

HARTMAN, J.J. (1981). Group cohesion and the regulation of self-esteem. In H. Kellerman (Ed.), *Group cohesion: Theoretical and clinical perspectives*. New York: Grune & Stratton.

HASKINS, M.J. (1960). Problem solving test of sportsmanship. *Research Quarterly*, 31:601-606.

HASSETT, J. (1978). *A primer of psychophysiology*. San Francisco: Freeman.

HAYTHORN, W.W. (1968). The composition of groups: A review of the literature. *Acta Psychologica*, 28:97-128.

HEIBY, E.M. (1982). A self-reinforcement questionnaire. *Behaviour Research and Therapy*, 20:397-401.

HEIDE, F.J., & Borkovec, T.D. (1983). Relaxation-induced anxiety: Paradoxical anxiety enhancement due to relaxation training. *Journal of Consulting and Clinical Psychology*, 51:171-182.

HEIDER, F. (1958). *The psychology of interpersonal relations*. New York: Wiley.

HEISE, D.R. (1975). *Causal analysis*. New York: Wiley.

HENDRICKS, C.G., Thoresen, C.E., & Hubbard, D.R. (1974). *Effects of behavioral self-observation on elementary teachers and students*. Stanford Center for Research and Development, Memorandum No.121.

HENDRICKS, G., & Carlson, J. (1981). *The centered athlete: A conditioning program for your mind*. Englewood Cliffs, NJ: Prentice-Hall.

HENDRY, L.B. (1974). Human factors in sports systems: Suggested models for analyzing athlete-coach interaction. *Human Factors*, 16:528-544.

HENNIS, G.M., & Ulrich, C. (1958). Study of psychic stress in freshman college women. *Research Quarterly*, 29:172-179.

HERMANS, H.J.M., ter Laak, J.J.F., & Maes, P.C.J.M. (1972). Achievement motivation and fear of failure in family and school. *Developmental Psychology*, 6:520-528.

HERSEY, P., & Blanchard, K.H. (1969, May). Lifecycle theory of leadership. *Training and Development Journal*, pp. 26-34.

HERSEY, P., & Blanchard, K.H. (1977). *Management of organizational behavior* (3rd ed.). Englewood Cliffs, NJ: Prentice-Hall.

HESLIN, R. (1964). Predicting group task effectiveness from member characteristics. *Psychological Bulletin*, 62:248-256.

HIGHLEN, P.S., & Bennett, B.B. (1979). Psychological characteristics of successful and nonsuccessful elite wrestlers: An exploratory study. *Journal of Sport Psychology*, 1:123-137.

HIGHLEN, P.S., & Bennett, B.B. (1983). Elite divers and wrestlers: A comparison between open and closed-skill athletes. *Journal of Sport Psychology*, 5:390-409.

HILL, K.T. (1972). Anxiety in the evaluative context. In W. Hartup (Ed.), *The young child* (Vol. 2). Washington: National Association for the Education of Young Children.

HILL, K.T., & Sarason, S.B. (1966). The relation of test anxiety and defensiveness to test and school performance over the elementary school years: A further longitudinal study. *Monographs of the Society for Research in Child Development*, 31 (2, Serial No.104).

HOGUE, M. (1980). Awards and rewards. *Coaching: Women's Athletics*, 6:18-19, 24.

HOLLAND, J., & Oglesby, C. (1979). Women in sport: The synthesis begins. *Annals of the American Academy of Political and Social Science*, 445:80-90.

HOLSTEIN, C. (1976). Development of moral judgment: A longitudinal study of males and females. *Child Development*, 47:51-61.

HORNE, T.E. (1982). *Compatibility in coach-athlete relationships*. Unpublished master's thesis, University of Western Ontario.

HORNEY, K. (1924). On the genesis of the castration complex in women. *International Journal of Psychoanalysis*, 5:50-65.

HOUSE, R.J. (1971). A path-goal theory of leader effectiveness. *Administrative Science Quarterly*, 16:321-338.

HOUSE, R.J., & Dessler, G. (1974). The path-goal theory of leadership: Some post hoc and a priori tests. In J.G. Hunt & L.L. Larson (Eds.), *Contingency approaches to leadership*. Carbondale: Southern Illinois University Press.

HOWELL, M.L. (1953). Influence of emotional tension on speed of reaction and movement. *Research Quarterly*, 24:22-32.

HRYCAIKO, D.W. (1978). The effects of competition and social reinforcement upon perceptual motor performance. *Journal of Motor Behavior*, 10:159-168.

HULL, C.L. (1943). *Principles of behavior*. New York: Appleton-Century-Crofts.

HUNT, P.J., & Hillery, J.M. (1973). Social facilitation in a coaching situation: An examination of the effects over learning trials. *Journal of Experimental Social Psychology*, 9:563-571.

HUSMAN, B.F. (1954). *An analysis of aggression in boxers, wrestlers, and cross-country runners as measured by the Rosenzweig P-F Study, selected TAT pictures and a sentence completion test*. Unpublished doctoral dissertation, University of Maryland.

HUSMAN, B.F. (1955). Aggression in boxers and wrestlers as measured by projective techniques. *Research Quarterly*, 26:421-425.

HUSMAN, B. (1970). Psychological and psychosomatic problems of athletes. *Maryland State Medical Journal*, 19:71-77.

ILGEN, D.R., & Fujii, D.S. (1976). An investigation of the validity of leader behavior descriptions obtained from subordinates. *Journal of Applied Psychology*, 61:642-651.

INCIONG, P. (1974). *Leadership style and team success*. Unpublished doctoral dissertation, University of Utah.

INGHAM, A.G., Levinger, G., Graves, J., & Peckham, V. (1974). The Ringelmann effect: Studies of group size and group performance. *Journal of Experimental Social Psychology*, 10:371-384.

INGJER, F., & Dahl, H.A. (1979). Dropouts from an endurance training program. *Scandinavian Journal of Sports Sciences*, 1:20-22.

ISO-AHOLA, S.E. (1977a). Effects of team outcome on children's self-perceptions in Little League baseball. *Scandinavian Journal of Psychology*, 19:38-42.

ISO-AHOLA, S.E. (1977b). Immediate attributional effects of success and failure in the field: Testing some laboratory hypotheses. *European Journal of Social Psychology*, 7:275-296.

ISO-AHOLA, S.E. (1979). Sex role stereotypes and causal attributions for success and failure in motor performance. *Research Quarterly*, 50:630-640.

ISO-AHOLA, S.E., & Roberts, G.C. (1977). Causal attributions following success and failure at an achievement motor task. *Research Quarterly*, 48:543-549.

JACKSON, C.O. (1933). An experimental study of the effect of fear on muscular coordination. *Research Quarterly*, 4:71-79.

JACKSON, P. (1968). *Life in the classroom*. New York: Holt, Rinehart & Winston.

JACOBS, A., & Sachs, L.B. (1971). *The psychology of private events*. New York: Academic.

JACOBSON, E. (1930). Electrical measurements of neuromuscular states during mental activities. I. Imagination of movement involving skeletal muscles. *American Journal of Physiology*, 91:547-608.

JACOBSON, E. (1938). *Progressive relaxation*. Chicago: University of Chicago Press.

JAMIESON, D., & Wendelboe, L.R. (1981). Mental training: A case study on competitive swimmers. *Coaching Review*, 4:42-46.

JANEWAY, E. (1980). Who is Sylvia? On the loss of sexual paradigms. In C.R. Stimpson & E.S. Person (Eds.), *Women, sex, and sexuality*. Chicago: University of Chicago Press.

JOHNSON, K. (1974). Development of human values through sport: A sociological perspective. *Proceedings of National AAHPER Conference at Springfield College*. Washington: AAHPER.

JOHNSON, M.L. (1969). Construction of sportsmanship attitude scales. *Research Quarterly*, 40:312-316.

JOHNSON, R. (1972). *Aggression in man and animals*. Philadelphia: Saunders.

JOHNSON, W.R. (1949). A study of emotion revealed in two types of athletic sports contests. *Research Quarterly*, 20:72-79.

JOHNSON, W.R. (1960). *Science and medicine of exercise and sports*. New York: Harper & Row.

JOHNSON, W.R., & Hutton, D.H. (1955). Effects of a combative sport upon personality dynamics as measured by a projective test. *Research Quarterly*, 26:49-53.

JOHNSON, W.R., Hutton, D.H., & Johnson, G.B. (1954). Personality traits of some champion athletes as measured by two projective tests: The Rorschach and H-T-P. *Research Quarterly*, 25:484-485.

JOHNSTON, S., Cunningham, J.D., Passer, M.W., & Kanouse, D.E. (1974). Effects of social influence on attributions for success and failure. *Personality and Social Psychology Bulletin*, 1:100-102.

JOHNSTON-O'CONNOR, E.J., & Kirschenbaum, D.S. (in press). Something succeeds like success: Positive self-monitoring in golf. *Cognitive Therapy and Research*.

JONES, M.B. (1974). Regressing group on individual effectiveness. *Organizational Behavior and Human Performance*, 11:426-451.

JONES, R.G. (1968). *A factored measure of Ellis' irrational belief systems with personality and maladjustment correlated*. Wichita, KS: Test Systems Inc.

JOURARD, S. (1971). *The transparent self*. New York: Van Nostrand.

JUNG, C.G. (1926). *The structure and dynamics of the psyche*. In Collected works (Vol. 8). Princeton: Princeton Univeristy Press. (First German ed. 1926).

KANDEL, H.J., Ayllon, T., & Rosenbaum, M.S. (1977). Flooding or systematic exposure in the treatment of extreme social withdrawal in children. *Journal of Behavior Therapy and Experimental Psychiatry*, 8:75-81.

KANE, J. (1966). Personality description of soccer ability. *Research in Physical Education*, 1:54-64.

KANFER, F.H. (1971). The maintenance of behavior by self-generated stimuli and reinforcement. In A. Jacobs & L.B. Sachs (Eds.), *The psychology of private events*. New York: Academic.

KANFER, F.H., & Karoly, P. (1972). Self-control: A behavioristic excursion into the lion's den. *Behavior Therapy*, 3:398-416.

KAROLY, P. (1977). Behavioral self-management in children: Concepts, methods, issues, and directions. In M. Hersen, R.M. Eisler, & P.M. Miller (Eds.), *Progress in behavior modification* (Vol. 5). New York: Academic.

KAROLY, P., & Kanfer, F.H. (1982). *Self-management and behavior change: From theory to practice.* New York: Pergamon.

KATZ, R.L. (1955, Jan/Feb). Skills of an effective administrator. *Harvard Business Review*, pp. 33-42.

KAVANAUGH, T., Shephard, R.J., & Tuck, J.A. (1973). Depression after myocardial infarction. *Canadian Medical Association Journal*, 113:23-27.

KAZDIN, A.E. (1974). Self-monitoring and behavior change. In M.J. Mahoney & C.E. Thoresen (Eds.), *Self-control: Power to the person.* Monterey, CA: Brooks/Cole.

KAZDIN, A.E., & Wilcoxon, L.A. (1976). Systematic desensitization and nonspecific treatment effects: A methodological evaluation. *Psychological Bulletin*, 83:729-758.

KEEFE, F.K., & Blumenthal, J.A. (1980). The life fitness program: A behavioral approach to making exercise a habit. *Journal of Behavior Therapy and Experimental Psychiatry*, 11:31, 34.

KEEFE, J. (1981). Violence in sports is on the rise. *American Bar Association Journal*, 67:17-26.

KELLERMAN, H. (Ed.) (1981). *Group cohesion: Theoretical and clinical perspectives.* New York: Grune & Stratton.

KELLEY, H.H., & Michela, J.L. (1980). Attribution theory and research. In M.R. Rosenzweig & L.W. Porter (Eds.), *Annual review of psychology* (Vol. 31). Palo Alto: Annual Reviews Inc.

KELLOR, F.A. (1898). A psychological basis for physical culture. *Education*, 19:100-104.

KERLINGER, F.N. (1973). *Foundations of behavioral research* (2nd ed.). New York: Holt, Rinehart & Winston.

KIMBLE, G.A., & Perlmuter, L.C. (1970). The problem of volition. *Psychological Review*, 77:361-384.

KINGSMORE, J. (1968). *The effect of professional wrestling and professional basketball contests upon the aggressive tendencies of male spectators.* Unpublished doctoral dissertation. University of Maryland.

KIRSCHENBAUM, D.S. (1976). *When self-regulation fails: Tests of some preliminary hypotheses.* (Doctoral dissertation, University of Cincinnati, 1975.) DAI, 36, 9-B, 4692.

KIRSCHENBAUM, D.S., & Bale, R.M. (1980). Cognitive-behavioral skills in golf: Brain power golf. In R.M. Suinn (Ed.), *Psychology in sports: Methods and applications.* Minneapolis: Burgess.

KIRSCHENBAUM, D.S., & Karoly, P. (1977). When self-regulation fails: Tests of some preliminary hypotheses. *Journal of Consulting and Clinical Psychology*, 45:1116-1125.

KIRSCHENBAUM, D.S., Ordman, A.M., Tomarken, A.J., & Holtzbauer, R. (1982). Effects of differential self-monitoring and level of mastery on sports performance: Brain power bowling. *Cognitive Therapy and Research*, 6:335-342.

KIRSCHENBAUM, D.S., & Smith, R.J. (1983). Sequencing effects in simulated coach feedback: Continuous criticism, or praise, can debilitate performance. *Journal of Sport Psychology*, 5:332-342.

KIRSCHENBAUM, D.S., & Tomarken, A.J. (1982). On facing the generalization problem: The study of self-regulatory failure. In P.C. Kendall (Ed.), *Advances in cognitive-behavioral research and therapy* (Vol. 1). New York: Academic.

KIRSCHENBAUM, D.S., Tomarken, A.J., & Humphrey, L.L. (in press). Affect and adult self-regulation. *Journal of Personality and Social Psychology.*

KIRSCHENBAUM, D.S., Wittrock, D.A., Smith, R.J., & Monson, W. (1984). Criticism inoculation training: Concept in search of strategy. *Journal of Sport Psychology*, 6:77-93.

KISTLER, J.W. (1957). Attitude expressed about behavior demonstrated in certain specific situations occurring in sports. *Annual Proceedings of College Physical Education Association*, 60:55-58.

KLAVORA, P. (1978). An attempt to derive inverted-U curves based on the relationship between anxiety and athletic performance. In D.M. Landers & R.W. Christina (Eds.), *Psychology of motor behavior and sport—1977.* Champaign, IL: Human Kinetics.

KLAVORA, P., & Daniel, J.V. (Eds.). (1979). *Coach, athlete and the sport psychologist.* Toronto: University of Toronto.

KLEIBER, D.A., & Hemmer, S. (1981). Sex differences in the relationship of locus of control and recreational sport participation. *Sex Roles*, 7:801-810.

KLEIBER, D.A., & Roberts, G.C. (1981). The effects of sport experience in the development of social character: An exploratory investigation. *Journal of Sport Psychology*, 3:114-122.

KLEIN, M. (1950). *The psychoanalysis of children.* London: Hogarth Press.

KLEIN, M., & Christiansen, G. (1969). Group composition, group structure and group effectiveness of basketball teams. In J.W. Loy & G.S. Kenyon (Eds.), *Sport, culture and society.* New York: Macmillan.

KOHFELD, D.L., & Weitzel, W. (1969). Some relations between personality factors and social facilitation. *Journal of Experimental Research in Personality*, 3:287-292.

KOHLBERG, L. (1966). A cognitive developmental analysis of children's sex role concepts and attitudes. In E.C. Maccoby (Ed.), *The development of sex differences.* Stanford: Stanford University Press.

KOHLBERG, L. (1969). Stage and sequence: The cognitive developmental approach to socialization. In D.A. Goslin (Ed.), *Handbook of socialization theory and research.* New York: Rand-McNally.

KOHLBERG, L. (1971). From is to ought: How to commit the naturalistic fallacy and get away with it in the study of moral development. In T. Mischel (Ed.), *Cognitive development and epistemology.* New York: Academic.

KORMAN, A.K. (1974). *The psychology of motivation.* Englewood Cliffs, NJ: Prentice-Hall.

KOSTRUBALA, T. (1976). *The joy of running.* Philadelphia: Lippincott.

KRAWITZ, G., Rimm, D.C., & Zimmerman, J. (1978). *Flooding versus an equally credible placebo in treatment of acrophobia.* Unpublished master's thesis, Old Dominion University.

KROHNE, H.W. (1980). Parental child-rearing behavior and the development of anxiety and coping strategies in children. In I.G. Sarason & C.D. Spielberger (Eds.), *Stress and anxiety* (Vol. 7). Washington: Hemisphere.

KROLL, W. (1970). Current strategies and problems in personality assessment of athletes. In L.E. Smith (Ed.), *Psychology of motor learning.* Chicago: Athletic Institute.

KROLL, W. (1975). *Psychology of sportsmanship.* Paper presented at AAHPER Convention, Atlantic City.

KROLL, W. (1979). The stress of high performance athletics. In P. Klavora & J.V. Daniel (Eds.), *Coach, athlete, and the sport psychologist.* Toronto: University of Toronto.

KROLL, W., & Lewis, G. (1970). America's first sport psychologist. *Quest*, 13:1-4.

KRUGLANSKI, A.W. (1980). Lay epistemologic process and contents: Another look at attribution theory. *Psychological Review*, 87:70-87.

KRUGLANSKI, A.W., & Jaffe, Y. (in press). Lay epistemology: A theory for cognitive therapy. In L.Y. Abramson (Ed.), *An attributional perspective in clinical psychology*.

KUBIE, L.S. (1952). Problems and techniques of psychoanalytic validation and progress. In E. Pumpian-Mindlin (Ed.), *Psychoanalysis as science*. Stanford, CA: Stanford University Press.

KUHL, J. (1981). Motivational and functional helplessness: The moderating effect of state versus action orientation. *Journal of Personality and Social Psychology*, 40:155-170.

KUHN, T.S. (1970). *The structure of scientific revolutions* (2nd ed.). Chicago: University of Chicago Press.

KUKLA, A. (1978). An attribution theory of choice. In L. Berkowitz (Ed.), *Advances in experimental social psychology* (Vol. 11). New York: Academic.

KUSHNIR, T. (1978). The importance of familiarization with the history of experimental social psychology—A tribute to J.F. Dashiell. *European Journal of Social Psychology*, 8:407-411.

LACEY, J.I. (1959). Psychophysiological approaches to the evaluation of psychotherapeutic process and outcome. In E.A. Rubenstein & M.B. Parloff (Eds.), *Research in psychotherapy*. Washington: American Psychological Association.

LACEY, J.I. (1967). Somatic response patterning and stress: Some revisions of activation theory. In M.H. Appley & R. Trumbell (Eds.), *Psychological stress: Issues in research*. New York: Appleton-Century-Crofts.

LAIRD, D.A. (1923). Changes in motor control under the influence of razzing. *Journal of Experimental Psychology*, 6:236-246.

LAKIE, W.L. (1964). Expressed attitudes of various groups of athletes toward athletic competition. *Research Quarterly*, 35:497-503.

LANCE, K. (1977). *Running for health and beauty: A complete guide for women*. New York: Bobs-Merrill.

LANDERS, D.M. (1974). Taxonomic considerations in measuring group performance and the analysis of selected group motor performance tasks. In M.G. Wade & R. Martens (Eds.), *Psychology of motor behavior and sport—1973*. Champaign, IL: Human Kinetics.

LANDERS, D.M. (1975a). Social facilitation and human performance—A review of contemporary and past research. In D.M. Landers (Ed.), *Psychology of sport and motor behavior II*, University Park: Pennsylvania State University.

LANDERS, D.M. (1975b). Observational learning of a motor skill: Temporal spacing of demonstrations and audience presence. *Journal of Motor Behavior*, 7:281-287.

LANDERS, D.M. (1978). Motivation and performance: The role of arousal and attentional factors. In W.F. Straub (Ed.), *Sport psychology: An analysis of athlete behavior*. Ithaca, NY: Mouvement.

LANDERS, D.M. (1980). The arousal-performance relationship revisited. *Research Quarterly for Exercise and Sport*, 51:77-90.

LANDERS, D.M. (1982). Arousal, attention, and skilled performance: Further considerations. *Quest*, 33:271-283.

LANDERS, D.M., Bauer, R.S., & Feltz, D.L. (1978). Social facilitation during the initial stage of motor learning: A re-examination of Martens' audience study. *Journal of Motor Behavior*, 10:325-337.

LANDERS, D.M., Christina, R.W., Hatfield, B.D., Daniels, F.S., & Doyle, L.A. (1980). Moving competitive shooting into the scientist's lab. *American Rifleman*, 128(4):36-37, 76-77.

LANDERS, D.M., Christina, R.W., Hatfield, B.D., Daniels, F.S., Wilkinson, M.O., Doyle, L.A., & Feltz, D.L. (1981). A comparison of elite and subelite competitive shooters on selected physical, psychological and psychophysiological tests. In G.C. Roberts & D.M. Landers (Eds.), *Psychology of motor behavior and sport—1980*. Champaign, IL: Human Kinetics.

LANDERS, D.M., & Crum, T. (1971). The effects of team success and formal structure on interpersonal relations and cohesiveness on baseball teams. *International Journal of Sport Psychology*, 2:88-96.

LANDERS, D.M., Furst, D.M., & Daniels, F.S. (1981). *Anxiety/attention and ability level in open and closed shooting activities*. Paper presented at annual meeting of NASPSPA, Asilomar, CA.

LANDERS, D.M., & Lueschen, G. (1974). Team performance outcome and the cohesiveness of competitive coaching groups. *International Review of Sport Sociology*, 9:57-71.

LANDERS, D.M., & McCullagh, P.D. (1976). Social facilitation of motor performance. *Exercise and Sport Science Reviews*, 4:125-162.

LANG, P.J. (1971). The application of psychophysiological methods to the study of psychotherapy and behavior modification. In A.E. Bergin & S.L. Garfield (Eds.), *Handbook of psychotherapy and behavior change*. New York: Wiley.

LARWOOD, L., & Moely, B. (1979). Sex role and developmental evaluations in a just world. *Sex Roles*, 5:19-29.

LATANE, B., Harkins, S.G., & Williams, K.D. (1980). *Many hands make light the work: Social loafing as a social disease*. Unpublished manuscript, The Ohio State University.

LATANE, B., Williams, K.D., & Harkins, S.G. (1979). Many hands make light the work: The causes and consequences of social loafing. *Journal of Personality and Social Psychology*, 37:823-832.

LATHAM, G., & Yukl, G. (1975). A review of research on the application of goal setting in organizations. *Academy of Management Journal*, 18:824-845.

LAU, R.R., & Russell, D. (1980). Attributions in the sport pages. *Journal of Personality and Social Psychology*, 39:29-38.

LAZARUS, A.A. (1971). *Behavior therapy and beyond*. New York: McGraw-Hill.

LAZARUS, A.A. (1976). *Multimodal behavior therapy*. New York: Springer.

LAZARUS, R.S. (1966). *Psychological stress and the coping process*. New York: McGraw-Hill.

LAZARUS, R.S., & Averill, J.R. (1972). Emotion and cognition: With special reference to anxiety. In C.D. Spielberger (Ed.), *Anxiety: Current trends in theory and research* (Vol. 2). New York: Academic.

LEFCOURT, H.M. (1976). *Locus of control: Current trends in theory and research*. Hillsdale, NJ: Erlbaum.

LEFEBVRE, L.M., & Passer, M.W. (1974). The effects of game location and importance on aggression in team sport. *International Journal of Sport Psychology*, 5:102-110.

LEFKOWITZ, M.M., Walder, L.O., Eron, L.D., & Heusman, L. (1973). Preference for televised contact sports as related to sex differences in aggression. *Developmental Psychology*, 9:417-420.

LEHRER, P.M., Schoicket, S., Carrington, P., & Woolfolk, R.L. (1981). Physiological and cognitive responses to stressful stimuli in subjects practicing progressive relaxation and clinically standardized meditation. *Behaviour Research and Therapy*, 18:293-304.

LEHRER, P.M., & Woolfolk, R.L. (1982). Self-report assessment of anxiety: Somatic, cognitive, and behavioral modalities. *Behavioral Assessment*, 4:167-177.

LENK, H. (1969). Top performance despite internal conflict: An antithesis to a functionalistic proposition. In J.W. Loy & G.S. Kenyon (Eds.), *Sport, culture and society*. London: Macmillan.

LENK, H. (Ed.) (1977). *Team dynamics*. Champaign, IL: Stipes.

LEONARD, F.E., & Afflect, G.B. (1947). *A guide to the history of physical education*. Philadelphia: Lea & Febiger.

LEONARD, G. (1975). *The ultimate athlete*. New York: Viking.

LEPPER, M.R., & Greene, D. (1975). Turning play into work: Effects of adult surveillance and extrinsic rewards on children's intrinsic motivation. *Journal of Personality and Social Psychology*, 31:479-486.

LEPPER, M.R., Greene, D., & Nisbett, R.E. (1973). Undermining children's intrinsic interest with extrinsic rewards: A test of the overjustification hypothesis. *Journal of Personality and Social Psychology*, 28:129-137.

LEVENTHAL, H. (1980). Toward a comprehensive theory of emotion. In L. Berkowitz (Ed.), *Advances in experimental social psychology* (Vol. 13). New York: Academic.

LEVENTHAL, H., & Cleary, P.D. (1980). The smoking problem: A review of the research and theory in behavioral risk modification. *Psychological Bulletin*, 88:370-405.

LEVENTHAL, H., Nerenz, D., & Strauss, A. (1980). Self-regulation and the mechanisms for symptom appraisal. In D. Mechanic (Ed.), *Psychological epidemiology*. New York: Neale Watson.

LEVER, J. (1976). Sex differences in the games children play. *Social Problems*, 23:478-487.

LEWIN, K. (1948). *Resolving social conflicts*. New York: Harper.

LEWIN, K. (1951). The nature of field theory. In M.H. Marx (Ed.), *Psychological theory*. New York: Macmillan.

LEWKO, J.H., & Greendorfer, S.L. (1978). Family influences and sex differences in children's socialization into sport: A review. In D.M. Landers & R.W. Christina (Eds.), *Psychology of motor behavior and sport — 1977*. Champaign, IL: Human Kinetics.

LIKERT, R. (1961). *New patterns of management*. New York: McGraw-Hill.

LILLIEFORS, F. (1978). *The running mind*. Mountain View, CA: World Publications.

LOCKE, E.A., Cartledge, N., & Knerr, C.S. (1970). Studies of the relationship between satisfaction, goal setting and performance. *Organizational Behavior and Human Performance*, 5:135-158.

LOCKE, E.A., Saari, L.M., Shaw, K.N., & Latham, G.P. (1981). Goal setting and task performance: 1969-1980. *Psychological Bulletin*, 90:125-152.

LOMBARDO, J.P., & Catalono, J.F. (1975). The effect of failure and the nature of the audience on performance of a complex motor task. *Journal of Motor Behavior*, 7:29-35.

LORENZ, C. (1966). *On aggression*. New York: Harcourt, Brace & World.

LORGE, I., & Solomon, H. (1955). Two models of group behavior in the solution of eureka-type problems. *Psychometrika*, 20:139-148.

LOTT, B. (1979). Sex-role ideology and children's drawings: Does the Jack-o-lantern smile or scare? *Sex Roles*, 5:93-97. ·

LOWE, R., & McGrath, J.E. (1971). Stress, arousal, and performance: Some findings calling for a new theory. *Project Report AF 1161-1167*, AFOSR.

LOWRY, C. (1972). *Leadership functions, sources of power and sources of group attraction involved in women's intercollegiate team sport groups.* Unpublished doctoral dissertation, Texas Woman's University.

LOY, J.W. (1974). A brief history of the North American Society for the Psychology of Sport and Physical Activity. In M.G. Wade & R. Martens (Eds.), *Psychology of motor behavior and sport — 1973.* Champaign, IL: Human Kinetics.

LOY, J.W. (1975). *The professionalization of attitudes toward play as a function of selected social identities and level of sport participation.* Paper presented at international seminar on Play in Physical Education and Sport, Tel Aviv.

LOY, J.W., McPherson, B.D., & Kenyon, G. (1978). *Sport and social systems.* Reading, MA: Addison-Wesley.

LUDWIG, A.M. (1966). Altered states of consciousness. *Archives of General Psychiatry*, 15:225-234.

MACCOBY, E., & Jacklin, C. (1974). *The psychology of sex differences.* Stanford, CA: Stanford University Press.

MAEHR, M.L. (1974). Toward a framework for the cross-cultural study of achievement motivation: McClelland reconsidered and redirected. In M.G. Wade & R. Martens (Eds.), *Psychology of motor behavior and sport — 1973.* Champaign, IL: Human Kinetics.

MAEHR, M.L. (1983). On doing well in science: Why Johnny no longer excels: Why Sarah never did. In S. Paris, G. Olson, & H. Stevenson (Eds.), *Learning and motivation in the classroom.* Hillsdale, NJ: Erlbaum.

MAEHR, M.L., & Nicholls, J.G. (1980). Culture and achievement motivation: A second look. In N. Warren (Ed.), *Studies in cross-cultural psychology.* New York: Academic.

MAGILL, R.A., & Ash, M.J. (1979). Academic, psycho-social, and motor charcteristics of participants and nonparticipants in children's sport. *Research Quarterly*, 50:230-240.

MAGILL, R.A., Ash, M.J., & Smoll, F.L. (Eds.) (1982). *Children in sport: A contemporary anthology* (2nd ed.). Champaign, IL: Human Kinetics.

MAGNUSSON, D., & Endler, N.S. (Eds.) (1977). *Personality at the crossroads: Current issues in interactional psychology.* Hillsdale, NJ: Erlbaum.

MAHONEY, M.J. (1974). *Cognition and behavior modification.* Cambridge, MA: Ballinger.

MAHONEY, M.J. (1979). Cognitive skills and athletic performance. In P.C. Kendall & S.D. Hollon (Eds.), *Cognitive-behavioral interventions: Theory, research, and procedures.* New York: Academic.

MAHONEY, M.J., & Avener, M. (1977). Psychology of the elite athlete: An exploratory study. *Cognitive Therapy and Research*, 1:135-141.

MAHONEY, M.J., & Thoresen, C.E. (1974). *Self-control: Power to the person.* Monterey, CA: Brooks/Cole.

MALONEY, T.L., & Petrie, B.M. (1974). Professionalization of attitudes toward play among Canadian school pupils as a function of sex, grade and athletic participation. *Journal of Leisure Research*, 4:184-195.

MANDELL, A.J. (1979). The second second wind. *Psychiatric Annals*, 9:57, 61-62, 66-69.

MANDLER, G., Mandler, J.M., & Uviller, E.T. (1958). Autonomic feedback: The perception of autonomic activity. *Journal of Abnormal and Social Psychology*, 56:367-373.

MANLEY, M.J, & Rosemier, R.A. (1972). Developmental trends in general and test anxiety among junior and senior high school students. *Journal of Genetic Psychology*, 120:219-226.

MANN, L. (1974). On being a sore loser: How fans react to their team's failure. *Australian Journal of Psychology*, 26:37-47.

MANTEL, R.C., & Vander Velden, L. (1974). The relationship between the professionalization of attitude toward play of preadolescent boys and participation in organized sport. In G.H. Sage (Ed.), *Sport and American society* (2nd ed.). Reading, MA: Addison-Wesley.

MARSH, C. (1977). A framework for describing subjective states of consciousness. In N.E. Zinberg (Ed.), *Alternate states of consciousness*. New York: The Free Press.

MARTENIUK, R. (1976). *Information processing and motor skill*. New York: Holt, Rinehart & Winston.

MARTENS, R. (1969). Effect of an audience on learning and performance of a complex motor skill. *Journal of Personality and Social Psychology*, 12:252-260.

MARTENS, R. (1971). Anxiety and motor behavior: A review. *Journal of Motor Behavior*, 3:151-179.

MARTENS, R. (1974a). Arousal and motor performance. *Exercise and Sport Sciences Reviews*, 2:155-188.

MARTENS, R. (1974b). *Psychological kinesiology: An undisciplined subdiscipline*. Paper presented at NASPSPA annual meeting, Anaheim, CA.

MARTENS, R. (1975a). *Social psychology and physical activity*. New York: Harper & Row.

MARTENS, R. (1975b). The paradigmatic crisis in American sport personology. *Sportwissenschaft*, 5:9-24.

MARTENS, R. (1977). *Sport competition anxiety test*. Champaign, IL: Human Kinetics.

MARTENS, R. (1978). *Joy and sadness in children's sports*. Champaign, IL: Human Kinetics.

MARTENS, R. (1979). About smocks and jocks. *Journal of Sport Psychology*, 1:94-99.

MARTENS, R. (1980a). From smocks to jocks: A new adventure for sport psychologists. In P. Klavora & K. Wipper (Eds.), *Psychological and sociological factors in sport*. Toronto: University of Toronto.

MARTENS, R. (1980b). The uniqueness of the young athlete: Psychological considerations. *American Journal of Sports Medicine*, 8:382-385.

MARTENS, R. (1981). American coaching effectiveness program. *Sportsline*, 3(4):2-3.

MARTENS, R., Burton, D., Rivkin, F., & Simon, J. (1980). Reliability and validity of the competitive state anxiety inventory (CSAI). In C.H. Nadeau, W.R. Halliwell, K.M. Newell, & G.C. Roberts (Eds.), *Psychology of motor behavior and sport — 1979*. Champaign, IL: Human Kinetics.

MARTENS, R., Burton, D., Vealey, R., Smith, D., & Bump, L. (1982). *Cognitive and somatic dimensions of competitive anxiety*. Presented at NASPSPA annual conference, University of Maryland.

MARTENS, R., Burwitz, L., & Zuckerman, J. (1976). Modeling effects of motor performance. *Research Quarterly*, 47:277-291.

MARTENS, R., Christina, R.W., Harvey, J.S. Jr., & Sharkey, B.J. (1981). *Coaching young athletes.* Champaign, IL: Human Kinetics.

MARTENS, R., & Gill, D.L. (1976). State anxiety among successful competitors who differ in competitive trait anxiety. *Research Quarterly,* 47:698-708.

MARTENS, R., & Gould, D. (1979). Why do adults volunteer to coach children's sports? In G.C. Roberts & K.M. Newell (Eds.), *Psychology of motor behavior and sport—1978.* Champaign, IL: Human Kinetics.

MARTENS, R., Landers, D.M. (1969). Coaction effects on a muscular endurance task. *Research Quarterly,* 40:733-737.

MARTENS, R., & Landers, D.M. (1970). Motor performance under stress: A test of the inverted-U hypothesis. *Journal of Personality and Social Psychology,* 16:29-37.

MARTENS, R., & Landers, D.M. (1972). Evaluation potential as a determinant of coaction effects. *Journal of Experimental Social Psychology,* 8:347-359.

MARTENS, R., Landers, D.M., & Loy, J. (1972). *Sport cohesiveness questionnaire.* Washington: AAHPER.

MARTENS, R., & Peterson, J.A. (1971). Group cohesiveness as a determinant of success and member satisfaction in team performance. *International Review of Sport Sociology,* 6:49-61.

MARTENS, R., Rivkin, F., & Burton, D. (1980). Who predicts anxiety better: Coaches or athletes? In C.H. Nadeau, W.R. Halliwell, K.M. Newell, & G.C. Roberts (Eds.), *Psychology of motor behavior and sport—1979.* Champaign, IL: Human Kinetics.

MARTENS, R., & Simon, J.A. (1976). Comparison of three predictors of state anxiety in competitive situations. *Research Quarterly,* 47:381-387.

MARTIN, G.L., & Hrycaiko, D.C. (Eds.) (1984). *Behavior modification and coaching: Principles, procedures, and research.* Springfield, IL: Thomas.

MARTIN, J. (1983). *The behavioral management of exercise and fitness.* Submitted for publication.

MARTIN, J.E., & Dubbert, P.M. (1982). Exercise applications and promotion in behavioral medicine: Current status and future directions. *Journal of Consulting and Clinical Psychology,* 50:1004-1017.

MARTIN, L. (1976). Effects of competition upon the aggressive responses of college basketball players and wrestlers. *Research Quarterly,* 47:388-393.

MASLOW, A. (1968). *Toward a psychology of being* (2nd ed.). New York: Van Nostrand Reinhold.

MASSIE, J.F., & Shephard, R.J. (1971). Physiological and psychological effects of training—A comparison of individual and gymnasium programs, with a characterization of the exercise "dropout." *Medicine and Science in Sports,* 3:110-117.

MASTERS, J.C., & Santrock, J.W. (1976). Studies in the self-regulation of behavior: Effects of contingent cognitive and affective events. *Developmental Psychology,* 12:334-348.

MAY, R (1972). *Power and innocence.* New York: Norton.

McAFEE, R. (1955). Sportsmanship attitude of 6th, 7th and 8th grade boys. *Research Quarterly,* 26:120.

McCARTHY, J.F., & Kelly, B.R. (1978a). Aggression, performance variables, and anger self-report in ice hockey players. *Journal of Psychology,* 99:97-101.

McCARTHY, J.F., & Kelly, B.R. (1978b). Aggressive behavior and its effect on performance over time in ice hockey athletes: An archival study. *International Journal of Sport Psychology,* 9:90-96.

McCLELLAND, D.C. (1951). *Personality*. New York: Dryden.

McCLELLAND, D.C., & Burnham, D.H. (1976). Power is the great motivator. *Harvard Business Review*, 54:100-110.

McCLEMENTS, J.D., & Botterill, C.B. (1979). Goal-setting in shaping of future performance of athletes. In P. Klavora & J. Daniel (Eds.), *Coach, athlete, and the sport psychologist*. Toronto: University of Toronto.

McCLEMENTS, J.D., & Botterill, C.B. (1980). Goal-setting and performance. In R. Suinn (Ed.), *Psychology in sports: Methods and applications*. Minneapolis: Burgess.

McCLEMENTS, J.D., & Botterill, C.B. (1981, April). Planning for commitment. *Sports Science Periodical on Research and Technology in Sport*, 8.

McCLOY, C. (1930). Character building through physical education. *Research Quarterly*, 1:41-61.

McCLOY, C. (1957). General factors or components of character as related to physical education. *Research Quarterly*, 28:269.

McCUTCHEON, B.A., & Adams, H.E. (1975). The physiological basis of implosive therapy. *Behaviour Research and Therapy*, 13:93-100.

McGRATH, J.E. (1962). The influence of positive interpersonal relations on adjustment and effectiveness in rifle teams. *Journal of Abnormal and Social Psychology*, 65:365-375.

McGRATH, J.E., & Altman, I. (1966). *Small group research: A synthesis and critique of the field*. New York: Holt, Rinehart & Winston.

McINTOSH, P. (1979). *Fair play: Ethics in sport and physical education*. London: Heinemann.

McMURTRY, W.P. (1974). *Investigation and inquiry into violence in amateur hockey*. Ministry of Community and Social Services. Public Inquires Act of 1971, Province of Ontario, Toronto, Canada.

McPHERSON, B.D. (1975). Past, present, and future perspectives for research in sport sociology. *International Review of Sport Sociology*, 10:55-71.

McPHERSON, B.D., & Taylor, A.W. (1980). Physical activity scientists: Their present and future role. In F.J. Hayden (Ed.), *Body and mind in the 90's*. Hamilton, Ontario: School of P.E. McMaster University.

MEICHENBAUM, D.H. (1977). *Cognitive-behavior modification: An integrative approach*. New York: Plenum.

MELNICK, M.J., & Chemers, M.M. (1974). Effects of group social structure on the success of basketball teams. *Research Quarterly*, 45:1-8.

MENDOZA, D., & Wickman, H. (1978). "Inner" darts: Effects of mental practice on performance of dart throwing. *Perceptual and Motor Skills*, 47:1195-1199.

MENNINGER, K., Moyman, M, & Pruyser, P. (1963). *The vital balance*. New York: Viking.

METHENY, E. (1968). *Movement and meaning*. New York: McGraw-Hill.

MEYERS, A.W., Schleser, R. (1980). A cognitive behavioral intervention for improving basketball performance. *Journal of Sport Psychology*, 2:69-73.

MEYERS, A.W., Schleser, R., Cooke, C.J., & Cuviller, C. (1979). Cognitive contributions to the development of gymnastic skills. *Cognitive Therapy and Research*, 3:75-85.

MIFFLIN, L. (1974, Dec. 13). Hockey violence brushed off by NHL Prexy Ziegler. *Chicago Daily News*, p. 72.

MIHEVIC, P.M. (1981). Anxiety, depression, and exercise. *Quest*, 33:140-153.

MIKALACHKI, A. (1969). *Group cohesion reconsidered*. London, Canada: University of Western Ontario School of Business Administration.

MILGRAM, S. (1963). Behavioral study of obedience. *Journal of Abnormal and Social Psychology*, 67:371-378.

MILGRAM, S. (1964). Group pressure and action against a person. *Journal of Abnormal and Social Psychology*, 69:137-143.

MILGRAM, S. (1965). Some conditions of obedience and disobedience to authority. *Human Relations*, 18:57-76.

MILES, W.R. (1928). Studies in physical exertion: I. A multiple chronograph for measuring groups of men. *American Physical Education Review*, 33:379-387.

MILES, W.R. (1931). Studies in physical exertion: II. Individual and group reaction time in football charging. *Research Quarterly*, 2(3):5-13.

MILES, W.R., & Graves, B.C. (1931). Studies in physical exertion: III. Effect of signal variation in football charging. *Research Quarterly*, 2(3):14-31.

MILLER, C. (1979). Aggression in everyday life. *The American Journal of Psychoanalysis*, 39(2):99-112.

MILLER, D.T. (1976). Ego-involvement and attributions for success and failure. *Journal of Personality and Social Psychology*, 34:901-906.

MILLER, D.T., & Ross, M. (1975). Self-serving bias in the attributions of causality: Fact or fiction? *Psychological Bulletin*, 82:213-225.

MILLER, N. (1941). The frustration-aggression hypothesis. *Psychological Review*, 48:337-342.

MILLS, T.M. (1964). *Group transformation: An analysis of a learning group*. Englewood Cliffs, NJ: Prentice-Hall.

MINEKA, S. (1979). The role of fear in theories of avoidance learning, flooding, and extinction. *Psychological Bulletin*, 86:985-1010.

MISCHEL, W. (1968). *Personality and assessment*. New York: Wiley.

MISCHEL, W. (1971). *Introduction to personality*. New York: Holt, Rinehart & Winston.

MISCHEL, W. (1973). Toward a cognitive social learning reconceptualization of personality. *Psychological Review*, 80:252-283.

MISCHEL, W. (1977). On the future of personality measurement. *American Psychologist*, 32:246-254.

MISCHEL, W., & Moore, B. (1966). Effects of attention to symbolically presented rewards upon self-control. *Journal of Personality and Social Psychology*, 3:390-396.

MISCHEL, W., & Peake, P.K. (1982). Beyond deja vu in the search for cross-situational consistency. *Psychological Review*, 89:730-755.

MISSIURO, W. (1964). The development of reflex activity in children. In E. Jokl & E. Simon (Eds.), *International research in sport and physical education*. Springfield, IL: Thomas.

MOMENT, D., & Zaleznik, A. (1965). *The dynamics of interpersonal behavior*. New York: Wiley.

MONEY, J. (1965). *Sex research: New developments*. New York: Holt, Rinehart & Winston.

MONEY, J., & Erhardt, A. (1972). *Man and woman/boy and girl*. Baltimore: Johns Hopkins University Press.

MORGAN, W.P. (1970). *Contemporary readings in sport psychology*. Springfield, IL: Thomas.

MORGAN, W.P. (1972). Sport psychology. In R.N. Singer (Ed.), *The psychomotor domain: Movement behaviors*. Philadelphia: Lea & Febiger.

MORGAN, W.P. (1973a). Efficacy of psychobiologic inquiry in the exercise and sport sciences. *Quest*, 20:39-47.

MORGAN, W.P. (1973b). Influence of acute physical activity on state anxiety. *National College of Physical Education Association for Men Proceedings*, pp. 113-121.

MORGAN, W.P. (1979a). Anxiety reduction following acute exercise. *Psychiatric Annals*, 9:141-147.

MORGAN, W.P. (1979b). Negative addiction in runners. *The Physician and Sportsmedicine*, 7:56-63, 67-70.

MORGAN, W.P. (1979c). Prediction of performance in athletics. In P. Klavora & J.V. Daniel (Eds.), *Coach, athlete, and the sport psychologist*. Toronto: University of Toronto.

MORGAN, W.P. (1979d). Running into addiction. *The Runner*, 1:72-74, 76.

MORGAN, W.P. (1980a). Sport personology. The credulous-skeptical argument in perspective. In W.F. Straub (Ed.), *Sport psychology: An analysis of athlete behavior* (2nd ed.). Ithaca, NY: Mouvement.

MORGAN, W.P. (1980b). The trait psychology controversy. *Research Quarterly for Exercise and Sport*, 51:50-76.

MORGAN, W.P. (1981a). Psychological benefits of physical activity. In F.J. Nagle & H.J. Montoye (Eds.), *Exercise in health and disease*. Springfield, IL: Thomas.

MORGAN, W.P. (1981b). Psychophysiological self-awareness during vigorous physical activity. *Research Quarterly for Exercise and Sport*, 52:385-427.

MORGAN, W.P., Hirota, K., Balke, B., & Weitz, G.A. (1976). Hypnotic perturbation of perceived exertion: Ventilatory consequences. *American Journal of Clinical Hypnosis*, 18:182-190.

MORGAN, W.P., Horstman, D.H., Cymerman, A., & Stokes, J. (1983). Facilitation of physical performance by means of a cognitive strategy. *Cognitive Therapy and Research*, 7:251-264.

MORGAN, W.P., Raven, P.B., Drinkwater, B.L., & Horvath, S.M. (1973). Perceptual and metabolic responsivity to standard bicycle ergometry following various hypnotic suggestions. *International Journal of Clinical and Experimental Hypnosis*, 21:86-101.

MORGAN, W.P., Roberts, J.A., Brand, F.R., & Feinerman, A.D. (1970). Psychological effect of chronic physical activity. *Medicine and Science in Sports*, 2:213-217.

MORGAN, W.P., Roberts, J.A., & Feinerman, A.D. (1971). Psychologic effect of acute physical activity. *Archives of Physical Medicine and Rehabilitation*, 52:422-425.

MORGANSTERN, K.P. (1973). Implosive therapy and flooding procedures: A critical review. *Psychological Bulletin*, 79:318-334.

MORRIS, D. (1967). *The naked ape*. New York: McGraw-Hill.

MOSHER, D.L. (1965). The interaction of fear and guilt in inhibiting unacceptable behavior. *Journal of Consulting Psychology*, 29:161-167.

MOWDAY, R.T. (1978). The exercise of upward influence. *Administrative Science Quarterly*, 23:137-156.

MULLER, B., & Armstrong, H.E. (1975). A further note on the "running treatment" for anxiety. *Psychotherapy: Theory, Research, and Practice*, 12:385-387.

MURPHY, H.H. (1916). Distribution of practice periods in learning. *Journal of Educational Psychology*, 7:150-162.

MURPHY, M. (1977). Sport as yoga. *Journal of Humanistic Psychology*, 17:21-33.

MURPHY, M., & White, R. (1978). *The psychic side of sports*. Reading, MA: Addison-Wesley.

MURRAY, D.G., & Johnson, C.L. (1975). Improving athletic teams: A social psychological approach. In D. Landers (Ed.), *Psychology of sport and motor behavior II*. University Park: Pennsylvania State University.

MYERS, A.M., & Lips, H.M. (1978). Participation in competitive amateur sports as a function of psychological androgyny. *Sex Roles*, 4:571-579.

NAGLE, F.J., Morgan, W.P., Hellickson, R.O., Serfass, R.C., & Alexander, J.F. (1975). Spotting success traits in Olympic contenders. *The Physician and Sportsmedicine*, 3:31-34.

NAPIER, H.S. (1968). Individual vs. group learning on three different tasks. *Journal of Psychology*, 69:249-257.

NELSON, L.R., & Furst, M.L. (1972). An objective study of the effects of expectation on competitive performance. *Journal of Psychology*, 81:69-72.

NESS, R.G., & Patton, R.W. (1979). The effects of beliefs on maximum weight-lifting performance. *Cognitive Therapy and Research*, 3:205-211.

NESVIG, D. (1980). Use of groups to improve athletic performance. In R.M. Suinn (Ed.), *Psychology in sports: Methods and applications*. Minneapolis: Burgess.

NEWMAN, A., Dickstein, R., & Gargan, M. (1978). Developmental effects in social facilitation and in being a model. *Journal of Psychology*, 99:143-150.

NICHOLLS, J.G. (1978). The development of the concepts of effort and ability, perception of own attainment, and the understanding that difficult tasks require more ability. *Child Development*, 49:800-814.

NICHOLLS, J.G. (1979). Quality and equality in intellectual development: The role of motivation in education. *American Psychologist*, 34:1071-1084.

NICHOLLS, J.G. (1980). *Striving to demonstrate and develop ability: A theory of achievement motivation*. Paper presented at a symposium, University of Bielefeld, West Germany.

NICHOLLS, J.G., & Miller, A.T. (in press). Development and its discontents: The differentiation of the concept of ability. In J.G. Nicholls (Ed.), *The development of achievement motivation*. Greenwich, CT: JAI Press.

NICKLAUS, J. (1974). *Golf my way*. New York: Simon & Schuster.

NIDEFFER, R.M. (1976a). *The inner athlete: Mind plus muscle for winning*. New York: Crowell.

NIDEFFER, R.M. (1976b). Test of attentional and interpersonal style. *Journal of Personality and Social Psychology*, 34:394-404.

NIDEFFER, R.M. (1979). *Predicting human behavior: A theory and test of attentional and interpersonal style* (Manual). San Diego: Enhanced Performance Associates.

NIDEFFER, R.M. (1981). *The ethics and practice of applied sport psychology*. Ithaca, NY: Mouvement.

NIDEFFER, R.M., & Deckner, C.M. (1979). A case study of improved athletic performance following the use of relaxation procedures. *Perceptual and Motor Skills*, 30:821-822.

NIDEFFER, R.M., & Sharpe, R.C. (1978). *A.C.T.: Attention control training*. New York: Wyden Books.

NIXON, H.L. (1977). "Cohesiveness" and team success: A theoretical reformulation. *Review of Sport and Leisure*, 2:36-57.

NOBLE, C.E., Fuchs, J.E., Robel, D.P., & Chambers, R.W. (1958). Individual vs. social performance on two perceptual-motor tasks. *Perceptual and Motor Skills*, 8:131-134.

NOBLE, S.G. (1922). The acquisition of skill in the throwing of basketball goals. *School and Society*, 16:640-644.

NOEL, R.C. (1980). The effect of visuo-motor behavior rehearsal on tennis performance. *Journal of Sport Psychology*, 2:221-226.

NOVACO, R.W. (1975). *Anger control: The development and evaluation of an experimental treatment*. Lexington, MA: Heath.

NYE, G.R., & Poulsen, W.T. (1974). An activity programme for coronary patients: A review of morbidity, mortality, and adherence after five years. *New Zealand Medical Journal*, 79:1010-1020.

NYE, S.L. (1979). *Self-instructional stress management training. A comparison of the effects of induced affect and covert modeling in a cognitive restructuring treatment program for test anxiety*. Unpublished doctoral dissertation, University of Washington.

OBERMEIER, G.E., Landers, D.M., & Ester, M.A. (1977). Social facilitation of speed events: The coaction effect in racing dogs and trackmen. In R.W. Christina & D.M. Landers (Eds.), *Psychology of motor behavior and sport — 1976* (Vol. 2). Champaign, IL: Human Kinetics.

OGILVIE, B.C., & Tutko, T.A. (1965). The psychological profile of champions. In F. Antonelli (Ed.), *Proceedings of First International Congress of Sport Psychology*, Rome.

OGILVIE, B.C., & Tutko, T.A. (1966). *Problem athletes and how to handle them*. London: Pelham Books.

OGILVIE, B.C., & Tutko, T.A. (1970). Self perceptions as compared with measured personality of selected male physical educators. In G.S. Kenyon (Ed.), *Contemporary psychology of sport*. Chicago: The Athetic Institute.

OGILVIE, B.C., & Tutko, T.A. (1971). Sport: If you want to build character, try something else. *Psychology Today*, 5:60-63.

OGILVIE, B.C., & Tutko, T.A. (1972). Motivation and psychometric approach in coaching. In J.E. Kane (Ed.), *Psychological aspects of physical education and sport*. London: Routledge & Kegan Paul.

OGLESBY, C.A. (1978). *Women and sport: From myth to reality*. Philadelphia: Lea & Febiger.

OLDRIDGE, N.B. (1979). Compliance of post-myocardial infarction patients to exercise programs. *Medicine and Science in Sports*, 11:373-375.

OLDRIDGE, N.B. (1982). Compliance and exercise in primary and secondary prevention of coronary heart disease: A review. *Preventive Medicine*, 11:56-70.

OLDRIDGE, N.B., & Jones, N. (1983). Improving patient compliance in cardiac exercise rehabilitation: Effects of written agreement and self-monitoring. *Journal of Cardiac Rehabilitation*, 3:257-262.

OLDRIDGE, N.B., Wicks, J.R., Hanley, R., Sutton, J., & Jones, N. (1978). Noncompliance in an exercise rehabilitation program for men who have suffered a myocardial infarction. *Canadian Medical Association Journal*, 118:361-375.

O'NEAL, F.W. (1936). A behavior frequency rating scale for the measurement of character personality in high school physical education classes for boys. *Research Quarterly*, 7:67-76.

ORLICK, T.D. (1973, Jan/Feb). Children's sports — A revolution is coming. *Canadian Association for Health, Physical Education and Recreation Journal*, pp. 12-14.

ORLICK, T.D. (1974, Nov/Dec). The athletic dropout — A high price of inefficiency. *CAHPER Journal*, pp. 21-27.

ORLICK, T.D. (1980). *In pursuit of excellence*. Champaign, IL: Human Kinetics.

ORLICK, T.D., & Botterill, C. (1975). *Every kid can win*. Chicago: Nelson-Hall.

ORLOFSKY, J.L. (1977). Sex-role orientation, identity formation, and self-esteem in college men and women. *Sex Roles*, 3:561-576.

ORTNER, S. (1974). Is female to male as nature is to culture? In M. Rosaldo & L. Lamphere (Eds.), *Women, culture and society*. Stanford, CA: Stanford University Press.

ORWIN, A. (1973). "The running treatment": A preliminary communication on a new use for an old treatment (physical activity) in the agoraphobic syndrome. *British Journal of Psychiatry*, 122:275-279.

ORWIN, A. (1974). Treatment of a situational phobia—A case for running. *British Journal of Psychiatry*, 125:95-98.

OUCHI, W. (1981). *Theory Z: How American business can meet the Japanese challenge.* Reading, MA: Addison-Wesley.

OXENDINE, J.B. (1967). *Psychology and motor learning.* New York: Appleton-Century-Crofts.

OXENDINE, J.B. (1970). Emotional arousal and motor performance. *Quest*, 13:23-32.

PAPANEK, J. (1977, Oct. 31). The enforcers. *Sports Illustrated*, pp. 43-49.

PARGMAN, D. (1980). The way of the runner: An examination of motives for running. In R.M. Suinn (Ed.), *Psychology in sports: Methods and applications*. Minneapolis: Burgess.

PARGMAN, D., & Baker, M.C. (1980). Running high: Enkephalin indicted. *Journal of Drug Issues*, 10:341-349.

PARK, R.J. (1980). Citius, altius, fortius. *The Academy papers*. Reston, VA: American Academy of Physical Education, No.14.

PARK, R.J. (1983, Jan.). Three major issues: The Academy takes a stand. *Journal of Physical Education, Recreation and Dance*, pp. 52-53.

PARKE, R.D., Ewall, W., & Slaby, R.G. (1972). Hostile and helpful verbalizations as regulators of nonverbal aggression. *Journal of Personality and Social Psychology*, 23:243-248.

PASSER, M.W. (1981). Children in sport: Participation motives and psychological stress. *Quest*, 33:231-244.

PASSER, M.W. (1982). Psychological stress in youth sports. In R.A. Magill, M.J. Ash, & F.L. Smoll (Eds.), *Children in sport: A contemporary anthology* (2nd ed.). Champaign, IL: Human Kinetics.

PASSER, M.W. (1983). Fear of failure, fear of evaluation, perceived competence, and self-esteem in competitive-trait-anxious children. *Journal of Sport Psychology*, 5:172-188.

PASSER, M.W., & Scanlan, T.K. (1980). *A sociometric analysis of popularity and leadership status among players on youth soccer teams.* Paper presented at NASPSPA annual meeting, Boulder, CO.

PATRICK, G.T.W. (1903). The psychology of football. *American Journal of Psychology*, 14:104-117.

PAULUS, P.B., & Cornelius, W.L. (1974). An analysis of gymnastic performance under conditions of practice and spectator observation. *Research Quarterly*, 45:56-63.

PAULUS, P.B., Judd, B.B., & Bernstein, I.H. (1977). Social facilitation and sports. In R.W. Christina & D.M. Landers (Eds.), *Psychology of motor behavior and sport—1976* (Vol. 2). Champaign, IL: Human Kinetics.

PAULUS, P.B., & Murdoch, P. (1971). Anticipated evaluation and audience presence in the enhancement of dominant responses. *Journal of Experimental Social Psychology*, 7:280-291.

PAULUS, P.B., Shannon, J.C., Wilson, D.L., & Boone, T.D. (1972). The effect of spectator presence on gymnastic performance in a field situation. *Psychonomic Science*, 29:88-90.

PECK, R.F., & Havighurst, R.J. (1960). *The psychology of character development*. New York: Wiley.

PEELE, S. (1981). *How much is too much: Healthy habits or destructive addictions*. NY: Prentice-Hall.

PELLETIER, K.R. (1977). *Mind as healer, mind as slayer: A holistic approach to preventing stress disorders*. New York: Dell. ✓

PENNEBAKER, J.W. (1982). *The psychology of physical symptoms*. New York: Springer-Verlag. ✓

PERSON, E.S. (1980). Sexuality as the mainstay of identity: Psychoanalytic perspectives. In C.R. Stimpson & E.S. Person (Eds.), *Women, sex and sexuality*. Chicago: University of Chicago Press.

PETLICHKOFF, L.M. (1982). *Motives interscholastic athletes have for participation and reasons for discontinued involvement in school sponsored sport*. Unpublished master's thesis, Michigan State University.

PETRIE, B.M. (1971). Achievement orientation in adolescent attitudes toward play. *International Review of Sport Sociology*, 6:89-99.

PHARES, E.J. (1976). *Locus of control in personality*. Morristown, NJ: General Learning Press.

PHARES, E.J., & Lamiell, J.T. (1977). Personality. *Annual Review of Psychology*, 28:114-140.

PHILLIPS, B.N., Pitcher, G.D., Worsham, M.E., & Miller, S.C. (1980). Test anxiety and the school environment. In I.G. Sarason (Ed.), *Test anxiety: Theory, research, and applications*. Hillsdale, NJ: Erlbaum.

PHILLIPS, J.B., & Endler, N.S. (1982). Academic examinations and anxiety: The interaction model empirically tested. *Journal of Research in Personality*, 16:303-318.

PIAGET, J. (1932). *The moral judgment of the child*. New York: Harcourt & Brace.

PIERCE, W.J. (1980). *Psychological perspective of youth sport participants and nonparticipants*. Unpublished doctoral dissertation, Virginia Polytechnic Institute & State University.

PILZ, G. (1979). Attitudes toward different forms of aggressive and violent behavior in competitive sports: Two empirical studies. *Journal of Sport Behavior*, 2:3-26.

PILZ, G., & LeFebvre, L. (1981). Aggression in sport. In: *Leisure in crisis time*. Brussels: Foundation Van Cle.

PLUTCHIK, R. (1981). Group cohesion in a psychoevolutionary context. In H. Kellerman (Ed.), *Group cohesion: Theoretical and clinical perspectives*. New York: Grune & Stratton.

POLLAK, J.M. (1979). Obsessive-compulsive personality: A review. *Psychological Bulletin*, 86:225-241.

POLLOCK, M.L., Gettman, L.R., Milesis, C.A., Bah, M., Durstine, L., & Johnson, M. (1977). Effects of frequency and duration of training on attrition and incidence of injury. *Medicine and Science in Sports*, 9:31-36.

POLLOCK, M.L., & Schmidt, D.H. (Eds.) (1979). *Heart disease and rehabilitation*. Boston: Houghton Mifflin.

POLLOCK, M.L., Wilmore, J.H., & Fox, S.M. (1978). *Health and fitness through physical activity*. New York: Wiley.

POOLEY, J.C. (1981). *Drop-outs from sport: A case study of boys' age-group soccer.* Paper presented at AAHPERD Conference, Boston.

PORTER, L.W., & Lawler, E.E. (1968). *Managerial attitudes and performance.* Homewood, IL: Richard D. Irwin.

PRESIDENT's Council on Physical Fitness and Sport. (1979). *Physical Fitness Research Digest*, 9, Washington, DC.

RACHMAN, S., & de Silva, P. (1978). Abnormal and normal obsessions. *Behaviour Research and Therapy*, 16:233-248.

RAGSDALE, C.E. (1930). *The psychology of motor learning.* Ann Arbor: Edward Bros.

RAILO, W., & Unestahl, L. (1979). The Scandinavian practice of sport psychology. In P. Klavora & J. Daniel (Eds.), *Coach, athlete, and the sport psychologist.* Toronto: University of Toronto.

RAMEY, E. (1974). Sex hormones and executive ability. In R. Kundsin (Ed.), *Women and success in American society: The anatomy of achievement.* New York: Morrow & Co.

RAVIZZA, K. (1975). A subjective study of the athlete's greatest moment in sport. *Proceedings of the 7th Canadian Psychomotor Learning and Sport Psychology Symposium*, pp. 399-404.

RAVIZZA, K. (1977). Peak experiences in sport. *Journal of Humanistic Psychology*, 17:35-40.

RAVIZZA, K. (1982). Concentration: Its relationship to gymnastics and Hatha yoga. *International Gymnast Technical Supplement*, 2(4):8-11.

RAVIZZA, K., & Rotella, R. (1982). Cognitive somatic behavioral intervention in gymnastics. In L. Zaichkowsky & W. Sime (Eds.), *Stress management in sport.* Reston, VA: AAHPERD.

RAYNOR, J.O. (1970). Relationship between achievement-related motives, future orientation, and academic performance. *Journal of Personality and Social Psychology*, 15:28-33.

REDMOND, G. (1980). Sport history in academe: 1930 to the present. *Proceedings of 1980 North American Society for Sport History Convention.* Banff.

REES, C.R., & Andres, F.F. (1980). Strength differences: Real and imagined. *Journal of Physical Education and Research*, 2:61.

REID, E.L., & Morgan, R.W. (1979). Exercise prescription: A clinical trial. *American Journal of Public Health*, 69:591-595.

REJESKI, W.J., & Brawley, L.R. (1983). Attribution theory in sport: Current status and new perspectives. *Journal of Sport Psychology*, 5:77-99.

REJESKI, W.J., & Lowe, C.A. (1980). The role of ability and effort in attributions for sport achievement. *Journal of Personality*, 48:223-244.

RESCORLA, R.A., & Solomon, R.L. (1967). Two-process learning theory: Relationships between Pavlovian conditioning and instrumental learning. *Psychological Review*, 74:151-182.

RICH, A. (1980, summer). Compulsory heterosexuality and lesbian existence. *Signs*, pp. 631-658.

RICHARDSON, A. (1967a). Mental practice: A review and discussion. Part I. *Research Quarterly*, 38:95-107.

RICHARDSON, A. (1967b). Mental practice: A review and discussion. Part II. *Research Quarterly*, 38:263-273.

RICHARDSON, B.E. Jr. (1936). A behavior frequency rating scale for measurement of character and personality in physical education. *Research Quarterly*, 7:57-66.

RIDDLE, P.K. (1980). Attitudes, beliefs, behavioral intentions, and behavior of women and men toward regular jogging. *Research Quarterly for Exercise and Sport*, 51:663-674.

RIGGS, C.E. Jr. (1981). Endorphins, neurotransmitters and/or neuromodulators and exercise. In M.H. Sacks & M.L. Sachs (Eds.), *Psychology of running*. Champaign, IL: Human Kinetics.

RIMM, D.C., & Masters, J.C. (1979). *Behavior therapy: Techniques and empirical findings* (2nd. ed.). New York: Academic.

ROBERTS, G.C. (1972). Effect of achievement motivation and social environment on performance of a motor task. *Journal of Motor Behavior*, 4:37-46.

ROBERTS, G.C. (1975). Win-loss causal attributions of Little League players. *Movement*, 7:315-322.

ROBERTS, G.C. (1978). Children's assignment of responsibility for winning and losing. In F.L. Smoll & R.E. Smith (Eds.), *Psychological perspectives of youth sports*. Washington: Hemisphere.

ROBERTS, G.C. (1980). Children in competition: A theoretical perspective and recommendations for practice. *Motor Skills: Theory Into Practice*, 4:37-50.

ROBERTS, G.C. (1982). Achievement motivation in sport. In R. Terjung (Ed.), *Exercise and sport science reviews* (Vol. 10). Philadelphia: Franklin Institute Press.

ROBERTS, G.C. (in press). Achievement motivation in children's sport. In J. Nicholls (Ed.), *The development of achievement motivation*. Greenwich, CT: JAI Press.

ROBERTS, G.C., Duda, J.L., & Devinatz, V. (1982). *"Gone with the win": Losers can be winners too*. Paper presented at NASPSPA Conference, College Park, MD.

ROBERTS, G.C., Kleiber, D.A., & Duda, J.L. (1981). An analysis of motivation in children's sport: The role of perceived competence in participation. *Journal of Sport Psychology*, 3:206-216.

ROBERTS, G.C., & Pascuzzi, D. (1979). Causal attributions in sport: Some theoretical implications. *Journal of Sport Psychology*, 1:203-211.

ROBERTS, J. (1972). *The effects of degree of involvement upon the level of aggression of spectators before and after a university basketball game*. Unpublished master's thesis, University of Maryland.

ROBERTS, J., & Sutton-Smith, B. (1962). Child training and game involvement. *Ethnology*, 11:166-185.

ROBERTSON, I. (1981). *Children's perceived satisfactions and stresses in sport*. Paper presented at the Australian Conference on Health, Physical Education and Recreation.

ROBINSON, T., & Carron, A. (1982). Personal and situational factors associated with dropping out versus maintaining participation in competitive sport. *Journal of Sport Psychology*, 4:364-378.

ROHSENOW, D.J., & Smith, R.E. (1982). Irrational beliefs as predictors of negative affective states. *Motivation and Emotion*, 6:299-314.

ROSEN, B., & d'Andrade, R.C.T. (1959). The psychosocial origins of achievement motivation. *Sociometry*, 22:185-218.

ROSENBAUM, M. (1980). A schedule for assessing self-control behaviors: Preliminary findings. *Behavior Therapy*, 11:109-121.

ROSS, M. (1981). Self-centered biases in attributions of responsibility: Antecedents and consequences. In E.T. Higgins, C.P. Herman, & M.P. Zanna (Eds.), *Social cognition: The Ontario symposium*. Hillsdale, NJ: Erlbaum.

ROSS, M., & Fletcher, G. (in press). Social and cultural factors in cognition. In G. Lindzey & E. Aronson (Eds.), *Handbook of social psychology.* Reading, MA: Addison-Wesley (2nd ed. 1968).

ROTH, W.T. (1974). Some motivational aspects of exercise. *Journal of Sports Medicine and Physical Fitness,* 14:40-47.

ROTHBAUM, F., Zigler, E., & Hyson, M.C. (1981). Modeling, praise and collaborating: Effects of adult behavior on children of the same sex and opposite sex. *Journal of Experimental Child Psychology,* 31:403-423.

ROTTER, J. (1954). *Social learning and clinical psychology.* Englewood Cliffs, NJ: Prentice-Hall.

ROTTER, J.B. (1966). Generalized expectancies for internal versus external control of reinforcement. *Psychological Monographs,* 80 (1, Whole No.609).

ROTTER, J.B., Chance, J.E., & Phares, E.J. (1972). *Applications of a social learning theory of personality.* New York: Holt, Rinehart & Winston.

ROZENSKY, R.H., & Bellack, A.S. (1976). Individual differences in self-reinforcement style and performance in self and therapist-controlled weight reduction programs. *Behaviour Research and Therapy,* 14:357-364.

RUDER, M.K., & Gill, D.L. (1981). *Immediate effects of win-loss on perceptions of cohesiveness in intramural and intercollegiate volleyball teams.* Paper presented at NASPSPA Conference, Monterey, CA.

RUSHALL, B. (1979). *Psyching in sports.* London: Pelham Books.

RUSSELL, D. (1982). The causal dimension scale: A measure of individuals' perceived causes. *Journal of Personality and Social Psychology,* 42:1137-1145.

RUSSELL, G.W. (1974). Machiavellanism, locus of control, aggression, performance and precautionary behavior in ice hockey. *Human Relations,* 9:825-837.

RUSSELL, G.W. (1979). Hero selection by Canadian ice hockey players: Skill or aggression. *Canadian Journal of Applied Sport Sciences,* 4:309-313.

RYAN, E.D. (1961). Motor performance under stress as a function of the amount of practice. *Perceptual and Motor Skills,* 13:103-106.

RYAN, E.D. (1970). The cathartic effect of vigorous motor activity on aggressive behavior. *Research Quarterly,* 41:542-551.

RYAN, E.D. (1979). *Athletic scholarships and intrinsic motivation.* Paper presented at NASPSPA Conference, Trois-Rivieres, P.Q.

RYAN, E.D. (1981). The emergence of psychological research as related to performance in physical activity. In G.A. Brooks (Ed.), *Perspectives on the academic discipline of physical education.* Champaign, IL: Human Kinetics.

RYAN, E.D., & Simons, J. (1982). Efficacy of mental imagery in enhancing mental rehearsal of motor skills. *Journal of Sport Psychology,* 4:41-51.

SACHS, M.L. (1978a). *Selected psychological considerations in running.* Invited presentation, Running Clinic, Tallahassee, FL.

SACHS, M.L. (1978b). An analysis of aggression in female softball players. *Review of Sport and Leisure,* 3:85-97.

SACHS, M.L. (1980). *On the trail of the runner's high — A descriptive and experimental investigation of characteristics of an elusive phenomenon.* Unpublished doctoral dissertation, Florida State University.

SACHS, M.L. (1981). Running addiction. In M.H. Sacks & M.L. Sachs (Eds.), *The psychology of running.* Champaign, IL: Human Kinetics.

SACHS, M.L. (1984). The runner's high. In M.L. Sachs, & G.W. Buffone (Eds.), *Running as therapy: An integrated approach.* Lincoln: University of Nebraska Press.

SACHS, M.L., & Buffone, G.W. (Eds.) (1984). *Running as therapy: An integrated approach.* Lincoln: University of Nebraska Press.

SACHS, M.L., & Pargman, D. (1979). Running addiction: A depth interview examination. *Journal of Sport Behavior*, 2:143-155.

SACHS, M.L., & Pargman, D. (1984). Running addiction. In M.L. Sachs & G.W. Buffone (Eds.), *Running as therapy: An integrated approach.* Lincoln: University of Nebraska Press.

SACKS, M.H., & Sachs, M.L. (Eds.) (1981). *Psychology of running.* Champaign, IL: Human Kinetics.

SAGE, G.H. (Ed.) (1974). *Sport and American society.* Reading, MA: Addison-Wesley.

SAGE, G.H. (1975). An occupational analysis of the college coach. In D.W. Ball & J.W. Loy (Eds.), *Sport and the social order: Contributions to the sociology of sport.* Reading, MA: Addison-Wesley.

SAGE, G.H. (1980). Orientations toward sport of male and female intercollegiate athletes. *Journal of Sport Psychology*, 2:355-362.

SALMELA, J.H. (1981). *The world sport psychology sourcebook.* Ithaca, NY: Mouvement.

SANDERS, G.S. (1981). Driven by distraction—An integrative review of social facilitation theory and research. *Journal of Experimental Social Psychology*, 40:1102-1117.

SANDERS, G.S. & Baron, R.S. (1975). The motivating effects of distraction on task performance. *Journal of Personality and Social Psychology*, 32:956-963.

SAPP, M., & Haubenstricker, J. (1978). *Motivation for joining and reasons for not continuing in youth sports programs in Michigan.* Paper presented at AAHPER Conference, Kansas City, MO.

SARASON, S.B., Davidson, K.S., Lighthall, F.F., Waite, R.R., & Ruebush, B.K. (1960). *Anxiety in elementary school children.* New York: Wiley.

SARASON, I.G. (1980). Life stress, self-preoccupation, and social supports. In I.G. Sarason & C.D. Spielberger (Eds.), *Stress and anxiety* (Vol. 7). Washington: Hemisphere.

SASFY, J., & Okun, M. (1974). Form of evaluation and audience expertness as joint determinants of audience effects. *Journal of Experimental Social Psychology*, 10:461-467.

SCANLAN, T.K. (1975). *The effect of competition trait anxiety and success-failure on the perception of threat in a competitive situation.* Unpublished doctoral dissertation, University of Illinois.

SCANLAN, T.K. (1977). The effects of success-failure on the perception of threat in a competitive situation. *Research Quarterly*, 48:144-153.

SCANLAN, T.K. (1978a). Social evaluation: A key developmental element in the competition process. In R.A. Magill, M.J. Ash, & F.L. Smoll (Eds.), *Children in sport: A contemporary anthology.* Champaign, IL: Human Kinetics.

SCANLAN, T.K. (1978b). Antecedents of competitiveness. In R.A. Magill, M.J. Ash, & F.L. Smoll (Eds.), *Children in sport: A contemporary anthology.* Champaign, IL: Human Kinetics.

SCANLAN, T.K. (1982, March). Motivation and stress in competitive youth sports. *Journal of Physical Education, Recreation, and Dance*, pp. 27-28, 36.

SCANLAN, T.K., & Lewthwaite, R. (1982). *Competitive stress in young wrestlers: Intrapersonal, situational, and significant other influences.* Paper presented at NASPSPA annual meeting, College Park, MD.

SCANLAN, T.K., & Passer, M.W. (1978a). Anxiety-inducing factors in competitive youth sport. In F.L. Smoll & R.E. Smith (Eds.), *Psychological perspectives in youth sports*. Washington: Hemisphere.

SCANLAN, T.K., & Passer, M.W. (1978b). Factors related to competitive stress among male youth sport participants. *Medicine and Science in Sports*, 10:103-108.

SCANLAN, T.K., & Passer, M.W. (1979a). Sources of competitive stress in young female athletes. *Journal of Sport Psychology*, 1:151-159.

SCANLAN, T.K., & Passer, M.W. (1979b). Factors influencing the competitive performance expectancies of young female athletes. *Journal of Sport Psychology*, 1:212-220.

SCANLAN, T.K., & Passer, M.W. (1980). Self-serving biases in the competitive sport setting: An attributional dilemma. *Journal of Sport Psychology*, 2:124-136.

SCANLAN, T.K., & Passer, M.W. (1981a). Competitive stress and the youth sport experience. *Physical Educator*, 38:144-151.

SCANLAN, T.K., & Passer, M.W. (1981b). Determinants of competitive expectancies of young male athletes. *Journal of Personality*, 49:60-70.

SCHACHTER, S. (1951). Deviation, rejection and communication. *Journal of Abnormal and Social Psychology*, 46:190-207.

SCHACHTER, S., Ellertson, N., McBride, D., & Gregory, D. (1951). An experimental study of cohesiveness and productivity. *Human Relations*, 4:229-238.

SCHAEFER, S. (1977). *The motivation process*. Cambridge, MA: Winthrop.

SCHEIN, E.H. (1980). *Organizational psychology* (3rd ed.). Englewood Cliffs, NJ: Prentice-Hall.

SCHLENKER, B.R. (1976). *Egocentric perceptions in cooperative groups: A conceptualization and research review* (NR 170-797). Office of Naval Research (Code 452), Arlington, VA: Organizational Effectiveness Research Programs.

SCHLENKER, B.R., & Miller, R.S. (1977). Egocentrism in groups: Self-serving biases or logical information processing? *Journal of Personality and Social Psychology*, 35:755-764.

SCHNORE, M.M. (1959). Individual patterns of physiological activity as a function of task differences and degree of arousal. *Journal of Experimental Psychology*, 58:117-128.

SCHWARTZ, G.E., Davidson, R.J., & Goleman, D.J. (1978). Patterning of cognitive and somatic processes in the self-regulation of anxiety: Effects of meditation versus exercise. *Psychosomatic Medicine*, 40:321-328.

SCOTT, J.P. (1975). *Aggression*. Chicago: University of Chicago Press.

SCOTT, W.E., & Cherrington, D.J. (1974). Effects of competitive, cooperative, and individualistic reinforcement contingencies. *Journal of Personality and Social Psychology*, 30:748-758.

SCRIPTURE, E.W. (1899). Cross-education. *Popular Science Monthly*, 56:589-596.

SEARS, R., Maccoby, E., & Levin, H. (1957). *Patterns of child rearing*. Evanston, IL: Row, Peterson.

SEASHORE, S.E. (1954). *Group cohesiveness in the industrial work group*. Ann Arbor: University of Michigan.

SEEFELDT, V., Blievernicht, D., Bruce, R., & Gilliam, T. (1978). *Joint legislative study on youth sport programs, Phase II: Agency-sponsored sports*, State of Michigan.

SEEFELDT, V., Gilliam, T., Blievernicht, D., & Bruce, R. (1978). Scope of youth sports programs in the state of Michigan. In F.L. Smoll & R.E. Smith (Eds.), *Psychological perspectives in youth sports*. Washington: Hemisphere.

SEEFELDT, V., & Gould, D. (1980). *Physical and psychological effects of athletic competition on children and youth.* Washington: ERIC Clearinghouse on Teacher Education.

SEEMAN, J.C. (1978). *Changes in state anxiety following vigorous exercise.* Unpublished master's thesis, University of Arizona.

SEGAL, J. (1981). Age of infants and parental sex-role perceptions. *Journal of Psychology*, 107:267-272.

SEIDNER, M.L., & Kirschenbaum, D.S. (1980). Behavioral contracts: Effects of pretreatment information and intention statements. *Behavior Therapy*, 11:689-698.

SELIGMAN, M.E.P. (1975). *Helplessness.* San Francisco: Freeman.

SELZNICK, P. (1959). The sociology of law. In R.K. Merton, L. Broom, & L.S. Cottrell (Eds.), *Sociology today.* New York: Basic Books.

SHAFFER, T.E. (1980). The uniqueness of the young athlete: Introductory remarks. *American Journal of Sports Medicine*, 8:370-371.

SHARKEY, B.J. (1979). *Physiology of fitness.* Champaign, IL: Human Kinetics.

SHAVER, K.G. (1975). *An introduction to attribution processes.* Cambridge, MA: Winthrop.

SHAW, M.E. (1976). *Group dynamics: The psychology of small group behavior* (2nd ed.). New York: McGraw-Hill.

SHELTON, T.O., & Mahoney, M.J. (1978). The content and effect of "psyching-up" strategies in weight lifters. *Cognitive Therapy and Research*, 2:275-284.

SHELTON, T.O., & Mahoney, M.J. (1980). *Mental practice with varsity basketball players: Parameters of influence.* Paper presented at convention of Association for the Advancement of Behavior Therapy.

SHERIF, C.W. (1972). Females in the competitive process. In D. Harris (Ed.), *Proceedings of women in sport: A national research conference.* University Park: Pennsylvania State University.

SHERIF, M. (1970). Group conflict and cooperation. In P.B. Smith (Ed.), *Group processes.* New York: Penguin Books.

SHERIF, M., & Sherif, C. (1969). *Social psychology.* New York: Harper & Row.

SIDNEY, K.H., & Shephard, R.J. (1976). Attitude toward health and physical activity in the elderly: Effects of a physical training program. *Medicine and Science in Sports*, 8:246-252.

SIEDENTOP, D. (1978). The management of practice behavior. In W.F. Straub (Ed.), *Sport psychology: An analysis of athlete behavior.* Ithaca, NY: Mouvement.

SILVA, J.M. (1978). Understanding aggressive behavior and its effects upon athletic performance. In W.F. Straub (Ed.), *Sport psychology: An analysis of athlete behavior.* Ithaca, NY: Mouvement.

SILVA, J.M. (1979a). Behavioral and situational factors affecting concentration and skill performance. *Journal of Sport Psychology*, 1:221-227.

SILVA, J.M. (1979b). Changes in the affective state of guilt as a function of exhibiting proactive assertion or hostile aggression. In G.C. Roberts & K.M. Newell (Eds.), *Psychology of motor behavior and sport — 1978.* Champaign, IL: Human Kinetics.

SILVA, J.M. (1980). Assertive and aggressive behavior in sport: A definitional clarification. In C.H. Nadeau, W.R. Halliwell, K.M. Newell, & G.C. Roberts (Eds.), *Psychology of motor behavior and sport — 1979.* Champaign, IL: Human Kinetics.

SILVA, J.M. (1981). Normative compliance and rule-violating behavior in sport. *International Journal of Sport Psychology*, 12:10-18.

SILVA, J.M. (1982a). *The current status of applied sport psychology: A national survey.* Paper presented at AAHPERD Convention, Houston.

SILVA, J.M. (1982b). Competitive sport environments: Performance enhancement through cognitive intervention. *Behavior Modification*, 6:443-463.

SILVA, J.M. (1983). The perceived legitimacy of rule violating behavior in sport. *Journal of Sport Psychology*, 5:438-448.

SILVA, J.M., & Shultz, B.B. (1984). Research in the psychology and therapeutics of running: A methodological and interpretive review. In M.L. Sachs & G.W. Buffone (Eds.), *Running as therapy: An integrated approach.* Lincoln: University of Nebraska Press.

SILVA, J.M., Shultz, B.B., Haslam, R.W., Martin, T.P., & Murray, D.F. (1983). *Discriminating characteristics of contestants at the United States Olympic wrestling trials.* Manuscript submitted for publication.

SILVA, J.M., Shultz, B.B., Haslam, R.W., & Murray, D. (1981). A psychophysiological assessment of elite wrestlers. *Research Quarterly for Exercise and Sport*, 52:348-358.

SIME, W.E. (1977). A comparison of exercise and meditation in reducing physiological response to stress. *Medicine and Science in Sports*, 9:55.

SIMON, J.A., & Martens, R. (1977). SCAT as a predictor of A-states in varying competitive situations. In R.W. Christina & D.M. Landers (Eds.), *Psychology of motor behavior and sport — 1976* (Vol. 2). Champaign, IL: Human Kinetics.

SIMON, J.A., & Martens, R. (1979). Children's anxiety in sport and nonsport evaluative activities. *Journal of Sport Psychology*, 1:160-169.

SINGER, R.N. (1965). Effect of spectators on athletes and non-athletes performing a gross motor task. *Research Quarterly*, 36:473-482.

SINGER, R.N. (1967). *Motor learning and human performance.* New York: Macmillan.

SINGER, R.N. (1969). Personality differences between and within baseball and tennis players. *Research Quarterly*, 40:582-588.

SINGER, R.N. (1972). *Coaching, athletics, and psychology.* New York: McGraw-Hill.

SINGER, R.N., Harris, D., Kroll, W., Martens, R., & Sechrest, L. (1977). Psychological testing of athletes. *Journal of Physical Education and Recreation*, 48:30-32.

SIPES, R.G. (1973, Feb). War, sports and aggression: An empirical test of two rival theories. *American Anthropologist*, pp. 64-86.

SKUBIC, E. (1956). Studies of Little and Middle League baseball. *Research Quarterly*, 26:97-110.

SLUSHER, H. (1967). *Man, sport and existence.* Philadelphia: Lea & Febiger.

SMITH, M.D. (1975). The legitimation of violence: Hockey players' perceptions of their reference groups' sanctions for assault. *Canadian Review of Sociology and Anthropology*, 12:72-80.

SMITH, M.D. (1978). From professional to youth hockey violence: The role of the mass media. In M. Garnmon & A. Beyer (Eds.), *Violence in Canada.* Toronto: Methuen.

SMITH, M.D. (1979). Social determinants of violence in ice hockey: A review. *Canadian Journal of Applied Sport Sciences*, 4:76-82.

SMITH, M.D. (1980). Hockey violence: Interring some myths. In W.F. Straub (Ed.), *Sport psychology: An analysis of athlete behavior.* Ithaca, NY: Mouvement.

SMITH, R.E. (1980a). A cognitive-affective approach to stress management training for athletes. In C.H. Nadeau, W.R. Halliwell, K.M. Newell, & G.C. Roberts (Eds.), *Psychology of motor behavior and sport — 1979.* Champaign, IL: Human Kinetics.

SMITH, R.E. (1980b). Development of an integrated coping response through cognitive-affective stress management training. In I.G. Sarason & C.D. Spielberger (Eds.), *Stress and anxiety* (Vol. 7). Washington: Hemisphere.

SMITH, R.E., & Ascough, J.C. (1984). Induced affect in stress management training. In S. Burchfield (Ed.), *Stress: Psychological and physiological interaction.* Washington: Hemisphere.

SMITH, R.E., & Nye, S.L. (1973). A comparison of implosive therapy and systematic desensitization in the treatment of test anxiety. *Journal of Consulting and Clinical Psychology*, 41:37-42.

SMITH, R.E., & Sharpe, T.M. (1970). Treatment of school phobia with implosive therapy. *Journal of Consulting and Clinical Psychology*, 35:239-243.

SMITH, R.E., & Smoll, F.L. (1982a). *Leadership behaviors in youth sports: A theoretical model and research paradigm.* Unpublished manuscript.

SMITH, R.E., & Smoll, F.L. (1982b). Psychological stress: A conceptual model and some intervention strategies in youth sports. In R.A. Magill, M.J. Ash, & F.L. Smoll (Eds.), *Children in sport: A contemporary anthology* (2nd ed.). Champaign, IL: Human Kinetics.

SMITH, R.E., Smoll, F.L., & Curtis, B. (1978). Coaching behaviors in Little League baseball. In F.L. Smoll & R.E. Smith (Eds.), *Psychological perspectives in youth sports.* Washington: Hemisphere.

SMITH, R.E., Smoll, F.L., & Curtis, B. (1979). Coach effectiveness training: A cognitive-behavioral approach to enhancing relationship skills in youth sport coaches. *Journal of Sport Psychology*, 1:59-75.

SMITH, R.E., Smoll, F.L., & Hunt, E. (1977). A system for the behavioral assessment of athletic coaches. *Research Quarterly*, 48:401-407.

SMITH, R.E., Smoll, F.L., Hunt, E., Curtis, B., & Coppel, D.B. (1979). Psychology and the bad news bears. In G.C. Roberts & K.M. Newell (Eds.), *Psychology of motor behavior and sport—1978.* Champaign, IL: Human Kinetics.

SMITH, R.E., Zane, N.W.S., Smoll, F.L., & Coppel, D.B. (1983). Behavioral assessment in youth sports: Coaching behaviors and children's attitudes. *Medicine and Science in Sports and Exercise*, 15:208-214.

SMOLEV, B. (1976). The relationship between sport and aggression. *The humanistic and mental health aspects of sport, exercise, and recreation.* Chicago: American Medical Association.

SMOLL, F.L., & Smith, R.E. (Eds.) (1978). *Psychological perspectives in youth sports.* Washington: Hemisphere.

SMOLL, F.L., & Smith, R.E. (1979). *Improving relationship skills in youth sport coaches.* East Lansing: Michigan Institute for the Study of Youth Sports.

SMOLL, F.L., & Smith, R.E. (1980). Psychologically oriented coach training programs: Design, implementation, and assessment. In C.H. Nadeau, W.R. Halliwell, K.M. Newell, & G.C. Roberts (Eds.), *Psychology of motor behavior and sport—1979.* Champaign, IL: Human Kinetics.

SMOLL, F.L., & Smith R.E. (1981). Developing a healthy philosophy of winning in youth sports. In V. Seefeldt, F.L. Smoll, R.E. Smith, & D. Gould (Eds.), *A winning philosophy for youth sports programs.* East Lansing: Michigan Institute for the Study of Youth Sports.

SMOLL, F.L., Smith, R.E., & Curtis, B. (1977). Coaching roles and relationships. In J.R. Thomas (Ed.), *Youth sports guide for parents and coaches.* Washington: AAHPER.

SNYDER, E., & Spreitzer, E. (1973). Family influences and involvement in sport. *Research Quarterly*, 44:249-255.

SNYDER, G., Franklin, B., Foss, M., & Rubenfire, M. (1982). Characteristics of compliers and non-compliers to cardiac exercise therapy programs. *Medicine and Science in Sports and Exercise*, 14:179.

SNYDER, S.H. (1977a). The brain's own opiates. *Chemical & Engineering News*, 55:26-35.

SNYDER, S.H. (1977b). Opiate receptors and internal opiates. *Scientific American*, 236:44-56.

SNYDER, S.H. (1980). *Biological aspects of mental disorder*. New York: Oxford University Press.

SOCCER referee dead. (1978, Nov.26). *Rochester Democrat & Chronicle*, p. 5.

SOLOMON, E.G., & Bumpus, A.K. (1978). The running meditation response: An adjunct to psychotherapy. *American Journal of Psychotherapy*, 32:583-592.

SOLVENKO, R., & Knight, J.A. (1967). *Motivations in play, games, and sports*. Springfield, IL: Thomas.

SONSTROEM, R.J., & Bernardo P.B. (1982). Intraindividual pregame state anxiety and basketball performance: A re-examination of the inverted-U curve. *Journal of Sport Psychology*, 4:235-245.

SPENCE, J.T. (1971). What can you say about a twenty-year-old theory that won't die? *Journal of Motor Behavior*, 3:193-203.

SPENCE, J.T., & Spence, K.W. (1966). The motivational components of manifest anxiety: Drive and drive stimuli. In C.D. Spielberger (Ed.), *Anxiety and behavior*. New York: Academic.

SPENCE, K.W. (1956). *Behavior theory and conditioning*. New Haven: Yale University Press.

SPENCE, K.W. (1964). Anxiety (drive) level and performance in eyelid conditioning. *Psychological Bulletin*, 61:129-139.

SPENCE, K.W., Farber, I.E., & McFann, H.H. (1956). The relation of anxiety (drive) level to performance in competitional and non-competitional paired associates learning. *Journal of Experimental Psychology*, 52:296-305.

SPIELBERGER, C.D. (Ed.) (1966). *Anxiety and behavior*. New York: Academic.

SPIELBERGER, C.D. (Ed.) (1972). *Anxiety: Current trends in theory and research* (Vol. 1), New York: Academic.

SPIELBERGER, C.D. (1973). *Preliminary test manual for the state-trait anxiety inventory for children*. Palo Alto, CA: Consulting Psychologists Press.

SPIELBERGER, C.D., Gorsuch, R.L., & Lushene, R.E. (1970). *Manual for the state-trait anxiety inventory (self-evaluation questionnaire)*. Palo Alto, CA: Consulting Psychologists Press.

SPINELLI, P.R., & Barrios, B.A. (1980). Psyching the college athlete: A comprehensive sports psychology training package. In R.M. Suinn (Ed.), *Psychology in sports: Methods and applications*. Minneapolis: Burgess.

SPINK, K.S. (1980). *The role of ego-involvement, objective outcome, and perceived performance in the determination of causal attributions*. Unpublished doctoral dissertation, University of Illinois.

SPINK, K.S., & Roberts, G.C. (1980). Ambiguity of outcome and causal attributions. *Journal of Sport Psychology*, 2:237-244.

SPINO, M. (1976). *Beyond jogging: The inner spaces of running*. New York: Berkeley.

SPINO, M. (1977). *Running home*. New York: Berkeley.

STAATS, A.W. (1967). An outline of an integrated learning theory of attitude formation and function. In M. Fishbein (Ed.), *Readings in attitude theory and measurement*. New York: Wiley.

STAMPFL, T.G., & Levis, D.J. (1967). Essentials of implosive therapy: A learning theory-based psychodynamic behavioral therapy. *Journal of Abnormal Psychology*, 72:496-503.

STARCH, D. (1911). *Experiments in educational psychology*. New York: Macmillan.

STATE of Michigan (1978). *Joint legislative study on youth sport programs, Phase II. Agency-sponsored sports*. East Lansing: Author.

STAUB, E. (1968). Duration of stimulus-exposure as determinant of the efficacy of flooding procedures in the elimination of fear. *Behaviour Research and Therapy*, 6:131-132.

STEINER, I.D. (1972). *Group process and productivity*. New York: Academic.

STOGDILL, R.M. (1959). *Individual behavior and group achievement*. New York: Oxford University Press.

STOGDILL, R.M. (1972). Group productivity, drive, and cohesiveness. *Organizational Behavioral and Human Performance*, 8:26-43.

STOKES, T.F., & Baer, D.M. (1977). An implicit technology of generalization. *Journal of Applied Behavior Analysis*, 10:349-368.

STONE, A. (1950). Catharsis theory on aggression. *Social Relations Laboratory Bulletin*. Harvard University, 2:9-13.

STONE, W.J. (1983, Aug/Sept). Predicting who will drop out. *Corporate Fitness & Recreation*, pp. 31-35.

STRAUB, W.F. (Ed.) (1978). *Sport psychology: An analysis of athlete behavior*. Ithaca, NY: Mouvement.

STUNKARD, A.J. (1980). *Obesity*. Philadelphia: Saunders.

SUINN, R.M. (1972a). Removing emotional obstacles to learning and performance by visuomotor behavioral rehearsal. *Behavior Therapy*, 3:308-310.

SUINN, R.M. (1972b). Behavior rehearsal training for ski races: Brief report. *Behavior Therapy*, 3:210-212.

SUINN, R.M. (1976, July). Body thinking: Psychology for Olympic champs. *Psychology Today*, pp. 38-43.

SUINN, R.M. (1977). Behavioral methods at the winter Olympic Games. *Behavior Therapy*, 8:283-284.

SUINN, R.M. (Ed.) (1980). *Psychology in sports: Methods and applications*. Minneapolis: Burgess.

SUINN, R.M. (1982). Intervention with Type A behaviors. *Journal of Consulting and Clinical Psychology*, 5:933-949.

SUINN, R., & Richardson, F. (1971). Anxiety management training: A nonspecific behavior therapy program for anxiety control. *Behavior Therapy*, 2:498-510.

SUTTON-SMITH, B., & Roberts, J. (1970). The cross-cultural and psychological study of games. In G. Luschen (Ed.), *The cross-cultural analysis of sport and games*. Champaign, IL: Stipes.

SWARTZ, D., & Wayne, R. (1979). How to mentally prepare for better performances. *Runner's World*, 14:90-91, 93, 96.

TATUM, J. (1980). *They call me assassin*. New York: Avon.

TAYLOR, A.W. (1976). Human performance and sport: New perspectives for research in exercise physiology. *Canadian Journal of Applied Sport Sciences*, 1:109-113.

TAYLOR, D.M., & Doria, J.R. (1981). Self-serving and group-serving bias in attribution. *Journal of Social Psychology*, 113:201-211.

TAYLOR, J.A. (1951). The relationship of anxiety to the conditioned eyelid response. *Journal of Experimental Psychology*, 41:81-92.

TAYLOR, J.A. (1953). A personality scale of manifest anxiety. *Journal of Abnormal and Social Psychology*, 48:285-290.

TAYLOR, S.E., & Fiske, S.T. (1981). Getting inside the head: Methodologies for process analysis in attribution and social cognition. In J. Harvey, W. Ickes, & R. Kidd (Eds.), *New directions in attribution research* (Vol. 3). Hillsdale, NJ: Erlbaum.

TEDESCHI, J.T., Gaes, G.G., & Rivera, A.N. (1977). Aggression and the use of coercive power. *Journal of Social Issues*, 33:101-125.

TEDESCHI, J.T., Smith, R., & Brown, R. (1974). A reinterpretation of research on aggression. *Psychological Bulletin*, 81:540-562.

TERASLINNA, P., Partanen, T., Koskela, A., Partanen, K., & Oja, P. (1969). Characteristics affecting willingness of executives to participate in an activity program aimed at coronary heart disease prevention. *Journal of Sports Medicine and Physical Fitness*, 9:224-229.

TETLOCK, P.E., & Levi, A. (1982). Attribution bias: On the inconclusiveness of the cognition-motivation debate. *Journal of Experimental Social Psychology*, 18:68-88.

THIBAUT, J.W., & Kelley, H.H. (1959). *The social psychology of groups*. New York: Wiley.

THIRER, J. (1981). The psychological perspective: Analysis of violence in sport. *Journal of Sport and Social Issues*, 5:37-43.

THIRER, J., & Rampey, M.S. (1979). Effect of abusive spectators' behavior on performance of home and visiting intercollegiate basketball teams. *Perceptual and Motor Skills*, 48:1047-1053.

THOMAS, C. (1977). Beautiful, just beautiful. In D. Allen & B. Fahey (Eds.), *Being human in sport*. Philadelphia: Lea & Febiger.

THOMAS, J.R. (Ed.) (1977). *Youth sports guide for coaches and parents*. Washington: AAHPER.

THOMPSON, C.E., & Wankel, L.M. (1980). The effects of perceived activity choice upon frequency of exercise behavior. *Journal of Applied Social Psychology*, 10:436-444.

THORESEN, C.E., & Mahoney, M.J. (1974). *Behavioral self-control*. New York: Holt, Rinehart & Winston.

TINTO, V. (1975). Dropouts from higher education: A theoretical synthesis of recent research. *Review of Educational Research*, 45:89-125.

TITLEY, R.W. (1976). The loneliness of a long-distance kicker. *The Athletic Journal*, 57:74-80.

TOLMAN, E.C. (1934). Theories of learning. In F.A. Moss (Ed.), *Comparative psychology*. Englewood Cliffs, NJ: Prentice-Hall.

TOLMAN, E. (1949). There is more than one kind of learning. *Psychological Review*, 56:144-155.

TOMARKEN, A.J., & Kirschenbaum, D.S. (1982). Self-regulatory failure: Accentuate the positive. *Journal of Personality and Social Psychology*, 43:584-597.

TRIANDIS, H.C. (1977). *Interpersonal behavior*. Monterey, CA: Brooks/Cole.

TRIPLETT, N. (1897). The dynamogenic factors in pacemaking and competition. *American Journal of Psychology*, 9:507-553.

TU, J., & Rothstein, A. (1979). Improvement of jogging performance through application of personality specific motivational techniques. *Research Quarterly for Exercise and Sport*, 50:97-103.

TUCKMAN, B. (1965). Developmental sequence in small groups. *Psychological Bulletin*, 63:384-399.

TURNER, E. (1968). *The effect of viewing college football, basketball, and wrestling on the elicited aggressive responses of male spectators*. Unpublished doctoral dissertation, University of Maryland.

ULRICH, C. (1957). Measurement of stress evidenced by college women in situations involving competition. *Research Quarterly*, 28:160-172.

ULRICH, C., & Burke, R.K. (1957). Effect of motivational stress upon physical performance. *Research Quarterly*, 28:403-412.

UNDERWOOD, G.L., & Whitwood, J.R. (1980). Aggression in sport—A study of an English first division soccer team. *FIEP Bulletin*, 50:31-39.

VANDER VELDEN, H. (1972). *Relationships among member, team and situational variables and basketball team success: A social-psychological enquiry*. Unpublished doctoral dissertation, University of Wisconsin.

VANDEWEGHE, E. (1979). *Growing with sport: A parent's guide to the child athlete*. Englewood Cliffs, NJ: Prentice-Hall.

VANEK, M., & Cratty, B.J. (1970). *Psychology and the superior athlete*. London: Collier-Macmillan.

VAN SCHOYCK, S.R., & Grasha, A.F. (1981). Attentional style variations and athletic ability: The advantages of a sport-specific test. *Journal of Sport Psychology*, 3:149-165.

VAZ, E. (1972). The culture of young hockey players: Some initial observations. In A.W. Taylor (Ed.), *Training: Scientific basis and application*. Springfield, IL: Thomas.

VAZ, E.W. (1979). Institutionalized rule violation and control in organized minor league hockey. *Canadian Journal of Applied Sport Sciences*, 4:83-90.

VEROFF, J. (1969). Social comparison and the development of achievement motivation. In C.P. Smith (Ed.), *Achievement-related motives in children*. New York: Russell Sage Foundation.

VILLET, B. (1978). Opiates of the mind. *The Atlantic*, 241:82-89.

VITELLI, R., & Frisch, G.R. (1982). Relationships between trait anxiety and leisure-time activities: A comparison of the unidimensional and multidimensional models of anxiety. *Perceptual and Motor Skills*, 54:371-376.

VOLKAMER, M. (1971). Zuraggresivitat in Konkurrenzorientierten Sozialen Systemen (Investigations into the aggressiveness in competitive social systems). *Sportwissenschaft*, 1:33-64.

VOS STRACHE, C. (1979). Players' perceptions of leadership qualities for coaches. *Research Quarterly*, 50:679-686.

WACHTEL, P.L. (1967). Conceptions of broad and narrow attention. *Psychological Bulletin*, 68:417-429.

WADE, T.C. (1974). Relative effects on performance and motivation of self-monitoring correct and incorrect responses. *Journal of Experimental Psychology*, 77:245-248.

WALTERS, R.H., & Brown, M. (1963). Studies of reinforcement of aggression. III. Transfer of responses to an interpersonal situation. *Child Development*, 34:563-571.

WANKEL, L.M. (1969). *The interaction of competition and ability levels in the performance and learning of a motor task.* Unpublished master's thesis, University of Alberta.

WANKEL, L.M. (1972). Competition in motor performance: An experimental analysis of motivational components. *Journal of Experimental Social Psychology*, 8:427-437.

WANKEL, L.M. (1973). An examination of illegal aggression in intercollegiate hockey. *Proceedings of the Fourth Canadian Psychomotor Learning and Sports Psychology Symposium*, University of Waterloo.

WANKEL, L.M. (1975a). Social facilitation: A review of theory and research pertaining to motor behavior. In B.S. Rushall (Ed.), *The status of psychomotor learning and sport psychology research*. Dartmouth, N.S.: Sport Science Associates.

WANKEL, L.M. (1975b). A new energy source for sport psychology research: Toward a conversion from D.C. (drive conceptualizations) to A.C. (attributional cognitions). In D.M. Landers (Ed.), *Psychology of sport and motor behavior II*. University Park: Pennsylvania State University.

WANKEL, L.M. (1975c). The effects of social reinforcement and audience presence upon the motor performance of boys with different levels of initial ability. *Journal of Motor Behavior*, 7:207-216.

WANKEL, L.M. (1980). Social facilitation of motor performance: Perspective and prospective. In C.H. Nadeau, W.R. Halliwell, K.M. Newell, & G.C. Roberts (Eds.), *Psychology of motor behavior and sport—1979*. Champaign, IL: Human Kinetics.

WANKEL, L.M., & Graham, J. (1982). *The effects of a decision balance-sheet intervention upon exercise adherence of high and low self-motivated females.* Manuscript submitted for publication.

WANKEL, L.M., & Pabich, P. (1982). The minor sport experience: Factors contributing to or detracting from enjoyment. In T. Orlick, J.T. Partington, & J.H. Salmela (Eds.), *Mental training for coaches and athletes*. Ottawa: Coaching Association of Canada.

WANKEL, L.M., & Thompson, C. (1977). Motivating people to be physically active: Self-persuasion vs. balanced decision-making. *Journal of Applied Social Psychology*, 7:332-340.

WANKEL, L.M., & Yardley, J.K. (1983). *An investigation of the effectiveness of a structural social support program for increasing exercise adherence of high and low self-motivated adults.* Manuscript submitted for publication.

WARD, A, & Morgan, W.P. (in press). Adherence patterns of healthy men and women enrolled in an adult exercise program. *Journal of Cardiac Rehabilitation*.

WEARY, G. (1980). Examination of affect and egotism as mediators of bias in causal attributions. *Journal of Personality and Social Psychology*, 38:348-357.

WEBB, H. (1969). Professionalization of attitudes toward play among adolescents. In G.S. Kenyon (Ed.), *Aspects of contemporary sport sociology*. Chicago: The Athletic Institute.

WEGNER, N., & Zeaman, D. (1956). Team and individual performance on a motor learning task. *Journal of General Psychology*, 55:127-142.

WEINBERG, R.S. (1979). Intrinsic motivation in a competitive setting. *Medicine and Science in Sport*, 11:146-149.

WEINBERG, R.S., & Genuchi, M. (1980). Relationship between competitive trait anxiety, state anxiety, and golf performance: A field study. *Journal of Sport Psychology*, 2:148-154.

WEINBERG, R.S., Gould, D., & Jackson, A. (1979). Expectations and performance: An empirical test of Bandura's self-efficacy theory. *Journal of Sport Psychology*, 1:320-331.

WEINBERG, R.S., Gould D., & Jackson, A. (1980). Cognition and motor performance: Effect of psyching-up strategies on three motor tasks. *Cognitive Therapy and Research*, 4:239-245.

WEINBERG, R.S., Gould, D., Yukelson, D., & Jackson, A. (1981). The effect of pre-existing and manipulated self-efficacy on a competitive muscular endurance task. *Journal of Sport Psychology*, 3:345-354.

WEINBERG, R.S., & Jackson, A. (1979). Competition of extrinsic rewards: Effect of intrinsic motivation and attribution. *Research Quarterly*, 50:494-502.

WEINBERG, R.S., & Ragan, J. (1979). Effects of competition, success/failure and sex on intrinsic motivation. *Research Quarterly*, 50:503-510.

WEINBERG, R.S., Seabourne, T.G., & Jackson, A. (1981). Effects of visuo-motor behavior rehearsal, relaxation, and imagery on karate performance. *Journal of Sport Psychology*, 3:228-238.

WEINBERG, W.T. (1980). Relationship of commitment to running scale to runners' performances and attitudes. In *Abstracts: Research papers 1980 AAHPERD convention.* Washington: AAHPERD

WEINER, B. (1972). *Theories of motivation: From mechanism to cognition.* Chicago: Markham.

WEINER, B. (1974). *Achievement motivation and attribution theory.* Morristown, NJ: General Learning Press.

WEINER, B. (1979). A theory of motivation for some classroom experiences. *Journal of Educational Psychology*, 71:3-25.

WEINER, B., Nierenberg, R., & Goldstein, M. (1976). Social learning (locus of control) versus attributional (causal stability) interpretations of expectancy of success. *Journal of Personality*, 44:52-68.

WEINER, B., Russell, D., & Lerman, D. (1979). The cognition-emotion process in achievement related contexts. *Journal of Personality and Social Psychology*, 37:1211-1220.

WEISS, P. (1969). *Sport: A philosophic inquiry.* Carbondale: Southern Illinois University Press.

WEISS, R.F., & Miller, F.G. (1971). The drive theory of social facilitation. *Psychological Review*, 78:44-57.

WEISS, W. (1968). Effects of mass media on communication. In G. Lindzey & E. Aronson (Eds.), *Handbook of social psychology* (Vol. 5), (2nd ed.). Reading, MA: Addison-Wesley.

WHITE, R.W. (1959). Motivation reconsidered: The concept of competence. *Psychological Review*, 66:297-333.

WHITING, H.T.A. (1974). Sports psychology in perspective. In J.D. Brooke (Ed.), *British proceedings of sport psychology.* Salford, England: University of Salford.

WHITING, H.T.A., & Hendry, L. (1969). A study of international table tennis players. In H.T.A. Whiting (Ed.), *Acquiring ball skill.* Philadelphia: Lea & Febiger.

WICKLUND, R.A. (1980). Group contact and self-focused attention. In P.B. Paulus (Ed.), *Psychology of group influence.* Hillsdale, NJ: Erlbaum.

WIDMEYER, W.N. (1976). *When cohesion predicts performance outcome in sport.* Unpublished doctoral dissertation, University of Illinois.

WIDMEYER, W.N., & Birch, J.S. (1979). The relationship between aggression and performance outcome in ice hockey. *Canadian Journal of Applied Sport Sciences*, 4:91-94.

WIDMEYER, W.N., & Birch, J.S. (1981). *Aggression in professional ice hockey: A strategy for success or a reaction to failure?* Paper presented at NASPSPA Conference, Monterey, CA.

WIDMEYER, W.N., & Martens, R. (1978). When cohesion predicts performance outcome in sport. *Research Quarterly*, 49:372-380.

WIEST, W.M., Porter, L.W., & Ghiselli, E.E. (1961). Relationships between individual proficiency and team performance and efficiency. *Journal of Applied Psychology*, 45:435-440.

WILLIAMS, K., Harkins, S., & Latane, B. (1981). Identifiability and social loafing: Two cheering experiments. *Journal of Personality and Social Psychology*, 40:303-311.

WILLIAMS, L.R.T. (1978a). Prediction of high level rowing ability. *Journal of Sports Medicine*, 18:11-17.

WILLIAMS, L.R.T. (1978b). Transcendental meditation and mirror tracing. *Perceptual and Motor Skills*, 46:371-378.

WILSON, V.E., Berger, B.G., & Bird, E.I. (1981). Effects of running and of an exercise class. *Perceptual and Motor Skills*, 53:472-474.

WITTIG, M.A. (1976). Sex differences in intellectual functioning: How much of a difference do genes make? *Sex Roles*, 2:63-74.

WOLPE, J. (1958). *Psychotherapy by reciprocal inhibition.* Stanford, CA: Stanford University Press.

WOLPE, J. (1978). Cognition and causation in human behavior and its therapy. *American Psychologist*, 33:437-446.

WOODEN, J. (1972). *They call me coach.* Waco, TX: Word Books.

WOOLFOLK, R.L., Lehrer, P.M., McCann, B.S., & Rooney, A.J. (1982). Effects of progressive relaxation and meditation on cognitive and somatic manifestations of daily stress. *Behaviour Research and Therapy*, 20:461-467.

WRIGHT, J., & Mischel, W. (1982). Influence of affect on cognitive social learning person variables. *Journal of Personality and Social Psychology*, 43:901-914.

YERKES, R.M., & Dodson, J.D. (1980). The relation of strength of stimulus to rapidity of habit formation. *Journal of Comparative and Neurological Psychology*, 18:459-482.

YULE, W., Sacks, B., & Hersov, L. (1974). Successful flooding treatment of a noise phobia in an eleven-year-old. *Journal of Behavior Therapy and Experimental Psychiatry*, 5:209-211.

ZAJONC, R.B. (1962). The effects of feedback and probability of group success on individual and group performance. *Human Relations*, 15:149-161.

ZAJONC, R.B. (1965). Social facilitation. *Science*, 149:269-274.

ZAJONC, R.B. (1980a). Compresence. In P.B. Paulus (Ed.), *Psychology of group influence.* Hillsdale, NJ: Erlbaum.

ZAJONC, R.B. (1980b). Feeling and thinking: Preferences need no inferences. *American Psychologist*, 35:151-175.

ZAJONC, R.B., & Nieuwenhuyse, B. (1964). Relationship between word frequency and recognition: Perceptual response or bias? *Journal of Experimental Psychology*, 67:276-285.

ZANDER, A. (1971). *Motives and goals in groups.* New York: Academic.

ZANDER, A. (1974). Productivity and group success: Team spirit vs. the individual achiever. *Psychology Today*, 8:64-68.

ZANDER, A. (1975). Motivation and performance of sports groups. In D.M. Landers (Ed.), *Psychology of sport and motor behavior II.* University Park: Pennsylvania State University Press.

ZANDER, A. (1978). Motivation and performance of sports groups. In W.F. Straub (Ed.), *Sport psychology: An analysis of athlete behavior.* Ithaca, NY: Mouvement.

ZANDER, A., & Meadow, H. (1965). Strength of group and desire for attainable group aspirations. *Journal of Personality*, 33:122-139.

ZANDER, A., & Wolfe, D. (1964). Administrative rewards and coordination among committee members. *Administrative Science Quarterly*, 9:50-69.

ZEMORE, R. (1975). Systematic desensitization as a method of teaching a general anxiety-reducing skill. *Journal of Consulting and Clinical Psychology*, 43:157-161.

ZILLMAN, D. (1978). *Hostility and aggression.* Hillsdale, NJ: Erlbaum.

ZILLMAN, D., Johnson, R.C., & Day, K. (1974). Provoked and unprovoked aggressiveness in athletes. *Journal of Research in Personality*, 8:139-152.

ZILLMAN, D., Katcher, A., & Milavsky, B. (1972). Excitation transfer from physical exercise to subsequent aggressive behavior. *Journal of Experimental Social Psychology*, 8:247-259.

ZIMMERMAN, B.J. (1970). The relationship between teacher class behavior and student school anxiety. *Psychology in the Schools*, 7:89-93.

ZUCKERMAN, M. (1979). Attribution of success and failure revisited, or: The motivational bias is alive and well in attribution theory. *Journal of Personality*, 47:245-287.

Author Index

Subject Index

Ability, 222-226, 228
  and ego-involvement, 226
  perceived ability, 223-224, 227
  perception of, 227
  and task involvement, 227

Achievement motivation, 173-174, 306, 325
  and goals, 217-219, 221, 226-227
  competitive ability, 218-223, 226-227
  social approval, 220-222
  sport mastery, 220-221, 223, 226-228
  and group success, 325-326
  and approach motive, 325
  subjective meaning of, 217-218

Adherence
  addiction to exercise, 436-438, 442
    negative, 438
    positive, 437-438, 442
  biological factors, 431
  and exercise, 421-434
    conceptual model, 422
    influences of, 423-434
  self-motivation, 428-429, 433

Affect
  and emotion, 56, 82, 86
  negative, 75, 130, 136-137

Aggression
  and assertive behavior, 248-251, 273
  attitude toward violence, 264-265
  and catharsis, 252, 257-258
  circular effects, 253-254, 257-258
  and concentration, 272-273, 285-287
  definition of, 244, 247-248, 261-263, 266, 274
  expectancies, 255-256

  and guilt, 256-257, 263-265
  and hero selection, 270
  intent to injure, 248-250
  intimidation, 262, 264, 277
  labeling, 247, 261, 263
  legitimizing of, 242, 254-272, 278
  misrepresenting consequences of, 263
  and natural inhibitions, 252
  origins of, 251
  and performance, 245, 274-286, 309
  and personality, 74
  and projective techniques, 258-259
  reduction of, 272-273, 285-286
  and reinforcement, 255-258, 263, 268-272
  and ritual, 252
  and rules
    constitutive, 248-249, 258, 265-266
    normative, 244, 258, 265-266
    violations of, 262, 265-268, 285
  and social environment, 250, 256
  and socialization, 242-243, 256, 264-268
  as species preservation, 252
  spectating and, 258-259
  theories of, 242-244, 251-257, 278
  types of
    extropunitive, 247
    hostile, 244, 248, 272
    instrumental, 244, 248, 272
    intropunitive, 247-248
  and youth sport, 276
  (see also Assertion)

Altered state of consciousness, 454, 459, 461
  altered perceptions, 456
  (see also Peak experience)